BERNARD SHAW

COMPLETE PLAYS WITH PREFACES

VOLUME II

SHAW IN 1916 WHEN HE WAS WRITING ABOUT THE WAR. PHOTOGRAPH BY BENNINGTON

BERNARD SHAW

COMPLETE PLAYS WITH PREFACES

Volume II

DODD, MEAD & COMPANY
NEW YORK
1962

LIBRARY OF CONGRESS CATALOG CARD NUMBER: 62-13608

PRINTED IN THE UNITED STATES OF AMERICA

CONTENTS

BACK TO METHUSELAH

(A METABIOLOGICAL PENTATEUCH)
A PLAY CYCLE IN FIVE PARTS

Written during 1918 to 1920

First Performed New York 1922

CONTENTS TO PREFACE

CONTENTS TO PREFACE

PREFACE
THE INFIDEL HALF CENTURY
THE DAWN OF DARWINISM

ONE day early in the eighteen hundred and sixties, I, being then a small boy, was with my nurse, buying something in the shop of a petty newsagent, bookseller, and stationer in Camden Street, Dublin, when there entered an elderly man, weighty and solemn, who advanced to the counter, and said pompously, "Have you the works of the celebrated Buffoon?"

My own works were at that time unwritten, or it is possible that the shop assistant might have misunderstood me so far as to produce a copy of Man and Superman. As it was, she knew quite well what he wanted; for this was before the Education Act of 1870 had produced shop assistants who know how to read and know nothing else. The celebrated Buffoon was not a humorist, but the famous naturalist Buffon. Every literate child at that time knew Buffon's Natural History as well as Esop's Fables. And no living child had heard the name that has since obliterated Buffon's in the popular consciousness: the name of Darwin.

Ten years elapsed. The celebrated Buffoon was forgotten; I had doubled my years and my length; and I had discarded the religion of my forefathers. One day the richest and consequently most dogmatic of my uncles came into a restaurant where I was dining, and found himself, much against his will, in conversation with the most questionable of his nephews. By way of making myself agreeable, I spoke of modern thought and Darwin. He said, "Oh, thats the fellow who wants to make out that we all have tails like monkeys." I tried to explain that what Darwin had insisted on in this connection was that some monkeys have no tails. But my uncle was as impervious to what Darwin really said as any Neo-Darwinian nowadays. He died impenitent, and did not mention me in his will.

Twenty years elapsed. If my uncle had been alive, he would have known all about Darwin, and known it all wrong.

In spite of the efforts of Grant Allen to set him right, he would have accepted Darwin as the discoverer of Evolution, of Heredity, and of modification of species by Selection. For the pre-Darwinian age had come to be regarded as a Dark Age in which men still believed that the book of Genesis was a standard scientific treatise, and that the only additions to it were Galileo's demonstration of Leonardo da Vinci's simple remark that the earth is a moon of the sun, Newton's theory of gravitation, Sir Humphry Davy's invention of the safety-lamp, the discovery of electricity, the application of steam to industrial purposes, and the penny post. It was just the same in other subjects. Thus Nietzsche, by the two or three who had come across his writings, was supposed to have been the first man to whom it occurred that mere morality and legality and urbanity lead nowhere, as if Bunyan had never written Badman. Schopenhauer was credited with inventing the distinction between the Covenant of Grace and the Covenant of Works which troubled Cromwell on his deathbed. People talked as if there had been no dramatic or descriptive music before Wagner; no impressionist painting before Whistler; whilst as to myself, I was finding that the surest way to produce an effect of daring innovation and originality was to revive the ancient attraction of long rhetorical speeches; to stick closely to the methods of Molière; and to lift characters bodily out of the pages of Charles Dickens.

THE ADVENT OF THE NEO-DARWINIANS

This particular sort of ignorance does not always or often matter. But in Darwin's case it did matter. If Darwin had really led the world at one bound from the book of Genesis to Heredity, to Modification of Species by Selection, and to Evolution, he would have been a philosopher and a prophet as well as an eminent professional naturalist, with geology as a hobby. The delusion that he had actually achieved this feat did no harm at first, because if people's views are sound, about evolution or anything else, it does not make two straws difference whether they call the revealer of their views Tom or Dick. But later on such apparently negligible errors have awkward consequences. Darwin was given an imposing reputation as not only an Evolutionist, but as *the* Evolutionist, with the immense majority who never read his books. The few who never read any others were led by them to concentrate exclusively on Circumstantial Selection as the explanation of all the transformations and adaptations which were the evidence for Evolution. And they presently found themselves so cut off by this specialization from the majority who knew Darwin only by his spurious reputation, that they were obliged to distinguish themselves, not as Darwinians, but as Neo-Darwinians.

Before ten more years had elapsed, the Neo-Darwinians were practically running current Science. It was 1906; I was fifty; I had published my own view of evolution in a play called Man and Superman; and I found that most people were unable to understand how I could be an Evolutionist and not a Neo-Darwinian, or why I habitually derided Neo-Darwinism as a ghastly idiocy, and would fall on its professors slaughterously in public discussions. It was in the hope of making me clear the matter up that the Fabian Society, which was then organizing a series of lectures on Prophets of the Nineteenth Century, asked me to deliver a lecture on the prophet Darwin. I did so; and scraps of that lecture, which was never published, variegate these pages.

POLITICAL INADEQUACY OF THE HUMAN ANIMAL

Ten more years elapsed. Neo-Darwinism in politics had produced a European catastrophe of a magnitude so appalling, and a scope so unpredictable, that as I write these lines in 1920, it is still far from certain whether our civilization will survive it. The circumstances of this catastrophe, the boyish cinema-fed romanticism which made it possible to impose it on the people as a crusade, and especially the ignorance and errors of the victors of Western Europe when its violent phase had passed and the time for reconstruction arrived, confirmed a doubt which had grown steadily in my mind during my forty years public work as a Socialist: namely, whether the human animal, as he exists at present, is capable of solving the social problems raised by his own aggregation, or, as he calls it, his civilization.

COWARDICE OF THE IRRELIGIOUS

Another observation I had made was that good-natured unambitious men are cowards when they have no religion. They are dominated and exploited not only by greedy and often half-witted and half-alive weaklings who will do anything for cigars, champagne, motor cars, and the more childish and selfish uses of money, but by able and sound administrators who can do nothing else with them than dominate and exploit them. Government and exploitation become synonymous under such circumstances; and the world is finally ruled by the childish, the brigands, and the blackguards. Those who refuse to stand in with them are persecuted and occasionally executed when they give any trouble to the exploiters. They fall into poverty when they lack lucrative specific talents. At the present moment one half of Europe, having knocked the other half down, is trying to kick it to death, and may succeed: a procedure which is, logically, sound Neo-Darwinism. And the good-natured majority are looking on in helpless horror, or allowing themselves to be persuaded by the newspapers of their exploiters that the kicking is not only a sound commercial investment, but an act of divine justice of which they are the ardent instruments.

But if Man is really incapable of organizing a big civilization, and cannot organize even a village or a tribe any too well, what is the use of giving him a religion? A religion may make him hunger and thirst for righteousness; but will it endow him with the practical capacity to satisfy that appetite? Good intentions do not carry with them a grain of political science, which is a very complicated one. The most devoted and indefatigable, the most able and disinterested students of this science in England, as far as I know, are my friends Sidney and Beatrice Webb. It has taken them forty years of preliminary work, in the course of which they have published several treatises comparable to Adam Smith's Wealth of Nations, to formulate a political constitution adequate to existing needs. If this is the measure of what can be done in a lifetime by extraordinary ability, keen natural aptitude, exceptional opportunities, and freedom from the preoccupations of bread-winning, what are we to expect from the parliament man to whom political science is as remote and distasteful as the differential calculus, and to whom such an elementary but vital point as the law of economic rent is a *pons asinorum* never to be approached, much less crossed? Or from the common voter who is mostly so hard at work all day earning a living that he cannot keep awake for five minutes over a book?

IS THERE ANY HOPE IN EDUCATION?

The usual answer is that we must educate our masters: that is, ourselves. We must teach citizenship and political science at school. But must we? There is no must about it, the hard fact being that we must *not* teach political science or citizenship at school. The schoolmaster who attempted it would soon find himself penniless in the streets without pupils, if not in the dock pleading to a pompously worded indictment for sedition against the exploiters. Our schools teach the morality of feudalism corrupted by commercialism, and hold up the military conqueror, the robber baron, and the profiteer, as models of the illustrious and the successful. In vain do the prophets who see through this imposture preach and teach a better gospel: the individuals whom they convert are doomed to pass away in a few years; and the new generations are dragged back in the schools to the morality of the fifteenth century, and think themselves Liberal when they are defending the ideas of Henry VII, and gentlemanly when they are opposing to them the ideas of Richard III. Thus the educated man is a greater nuisance than the uneducated one: indeed it is the inefficiency and sham of the educational side of our schools (to which, except under compulsion, children would not be sent by their parents at all if they did not act as prisons in which the immature are kept from worrying the mature) that save us from being dashed on the rocks of false doctrine instead of drifting down the midstream of mere ignorance. There is no way out through the schoolmaster.

HOMEOPATHIC EDUCATION

In truth, mankind cannot be saved from without, by schoolmasters or any other sort of masters: it can only be lamed and enslaved by them. It is said that if you wash a cat it will never again wash itself. This may or may not be true: what is certain is that if you teach a man anything he will never learn it; and if you cure him of a disease he will be unable to cure himself the next time it attacks him. Therefore, if you want to see a cat clean, you throw a bucket of mud over it, when it will immediately take extraordinary pains to lick the mud off, and finally be cleaner than it was before. In the same way doctors who are up-to-date (say .00005 per cent of all the registered practitioners, and 20 per cent of the unregistered ones), when they want to rid you of a disease or a symptom, inoculate you with that disease or give you a drug that produces that symptom, in order to provoke you to resist it as the mud provokes the cat to wash itself.

Now an acute person will ask me why, if this be so, our false education does not provoke our scholars to find out the truth. My answer is that it sometimes does. Voltaire was a pupil of the Jesuits; Samuel Butler was the pupil of a hopelessly conventional and erroneous country parson. But then Voltaire was Voltaire, and Butler was Butler: that is, their minds were so abnormally strong that they could throw off the doses of poison that paralyse ordinary minds. When the doctors inoculate you and the homeopathists dose you, they give you an infinitesimally attenuated dose. If they gave you the virus at full strength it would overcome your resistance and produce its direct effect. The doses of false doctrine given at public schools and universities are so big that they overwhelm the resistance that a tiny dose would provoke. The normal student is corrupted beyond redemption, and will drive the genius who resists out of the country if he can. Byron and Shelley had to fly to Italy, whilst Castlereagh and Eldon ruled the roost at home. Rousseau was hunted from frontier to frontier; Karl Marx starved in exile in a Soho lodging; Ruskin's articles were refused by the magazines (he was too rich to be otherwise persecuted); whilst mindless forgotten nonentities governed the land; sent men to the prison or the gallows for blasphemy and sedition (meaning the truth about Church and State); and sedulously stored up the social disease and corruption which explode from time to time in gigantic boils that have to be lanced by a million bayonets. This is the result of allopathic education. Homeopathic education has not yet been officially tried, and would obviously be a delicate matter if it were. A body of schoolmasters inciting their pupils to infinitesimal peccadilloes with the object of provoking them to exclaim, "Get thee behind me, Satan," or telling them white lies about history for the sake of being contradicted, insulted, and refuted, would certainly do less harm than our present educational allopaths do; but then nobody will advocate homeopathic education. Allopathy has produced the poisonous illusion that it enlightens instead of darkening. The suggestion may, however, explain why, whilst most people's minds succumb to inculcation and environment, a few react vigorously: honest and decent people coming from thievish slums, and sceptics and realists from country parsonages.

THE DIABOLICAL EFFICIENCY OF TECHNICAL EDUCATION

But meanwhile—and here comes the horror of it—our technical instruction is honest and efficient. The public schoolboy who is carefully blinded, duped, and corrupted as to the nature of a society based on profiteering, and is taught to honor parasitic idleness and luxury, learns to shoot and ride and keep fit with all the assistance and guidance that can be procured for him by the most anxiously sincere desire that he may do these things well, and if possible superlatively well. In the army he learns to fly; to drop bombs; to use machine-guns to the utmost of his capacity. The discovery of high explosives is rewarded and dignified: instruction in the manufacture of the weapons, battleships, submarines, and land batteries by which they are applied destructively, is quite genuine: the instructors know their business, and really mean the learners to succeed. The result is that powers of destruction that could hardly without uneasiness be entrusted to infinite wisdom and infinite benevolence are placed in the hands of romantic schoolboy patriots who, however generous by nature, are by education ignoramuses, dupes, snobs, and sportsmen to whom fighting is a religion and killing an accomplishment; whilst political power, useless under such circumstances except to militarist imperialists in chronic terror of invasion and subjugation, pompous tufthunting fools, commercial adventurers to whom the organization by the nation of its own industrial services would mean checkmate, financial parasites on the money market, and stupid people who cling to the *status quo* merely because they are used to it, is obtained by heredity, by simple purchase, by keeping newspapers and pretending that they are organs of public opinion, by the wiles of seductive women, and by prostituting ambitious talent to the service of the profiteers, who call the tune because, having secured all the spare plunder, they alone can afford to pay the piper. Neither the rulers nor the ruled understand high politics. They do not even know that there is such a branch of knowledge as political science; but between them they can coerce and enslave with the deadliest efficiency, even to the wiping out of civilization, because their education as slayers has been honestly and thoroughly carried out. Essentially the rulers are all defectives; and there is nothing worse than government by defectives who wield irresistible powers of physical coercion. The commonplace sound people submit, and compel the rest to submit, because they have been taught to do so as an article of religion and a point of honor. Those in whom natural enlightenment has reacted against artificial education submit because they are compelled; but they would resist, and finally resist effectively, if they were not cowards. And they are cowards because they have neither an officially accredited and established religion nor a generally recognized point of honor, and are all at sixes and sevens with their various private speculations, sending their children perforce to the schools where they will be corrupted for want of any other schools. The rulers are equally intimidated by the immense extension and cheapening of the means of slaughter and destruction. The British Government is more afraid of Ireland now that submarines, bombs, and poison gas are cheap and easily made than it was of the German Empire before the war; consequently the old British caution which maintained a balance of power through command of the sea is intensified into a terror that sees security in nothing short of absolute military mastery of the entire globe: that is, in an impossibility that will yet seem possible in detail to soldiers and to parochial and insular patriotic civilians.

FLIMSINESS OF CIVILIZATION

This situation has occurred so often before, always with the same result of a collapse of civilization (Professor Flinders Petrie has let out the secret of previous collapses), that the rich are instinctively crying "Let us eat and drink; for tomorrow we die," and the poor, "How long, O Lord, how long?" But the pitiless reply still is that God helps those who help themselves. This does not mean that if Man cannot find the remedy no remedy will be found. The power that produced Man when the monkey was not up to the mark, can produce a higher creature than Man if Man does not come up to the mark. What it means is that if Man is to be saved, Man must save himself. There seems no compelling reason why he should be saved. He is by no means an ideal creature. At his present best many of his ways are so unpleasant that they are unmentionable in polite society, and so painful that he is compelled to pretend that pain is often a good. Nature holds no brief for the human experiment: it must stand or fall by its results. If Man will not serve,

Nature will try another experiment.

What hope is there then of human improvement? According to the Neo-Darwinists, to the Mechanists, no hope whatever, because improvement can come only through some senseless accident which must, on the statistical average of accidents, be presently wiped out by some other equally senseless accident.

CREATIVE EVOLUTION

But this dismal creed does not discourage those who believe that the impulse that produces evolution is creative. They have observed the simple fact that the will to do anything can and does, at a certain pitch of intensity set up by conviction of its necessity, create and organize new tissue to do it with. To them therefore mankind is by no means played out yet. If the weight lifter, under the trivial stimulus of an athletic competition, can "put up a muscle," it seems reasonable to believe that an equally earnest and convinced philosopher could "put by a brain." Both are directions of vitality to a certain end. Evolution shews us this direction of vitality doing all sorts of things: providing the centipede with a hundred legs, and ridding the fish of any legs at all; building lungs and arms for the land and gills and fins for the sea; enabling the mammal to gestate its young inside its body, and the fowl to incubate hers outside it; offering us, we may say, our choice of any sort of bodily contrivance to maintain our activity and increase our resources.

VOLUNTARY LONGEVITY

Among other matters apparently changeable at will is the duration of individual life. Weismann, a very clever and suggestive biologist who was unhappily reduced to idiocy by Neo-Darwinism, pointed out that death is not an eternal condition of life, but an expedient introduced to provide for continual renewal without overcrowding. Now Circumstantial Selection does not account for natural death: it accounts only for the survival of species in which the individuals have sense enough to decay and die on purpose. But the individuals do not seem to have calculated very reasonably: nobody can explain why a parrot should live ten times as long as a dog, and a turtle be almost immortal. In the case of man, the operation has overshot its mark: men do not live long enough: they are, for all the purposes of high civilization, mere children when they die; and our Prime Ministers, though rated as mature, divide their time between the golf course and the Treasury Bench in parliament. Presumably, however, the same power that made this mistake can remedy it. If on opportunist grounds Man now fixes the term of his life at three score and ten years, he can equally fix it at three hundred, or three thousand, or even at the genuine Circumstantial Selection limit, which would be until a sooner-or-later-inevitable fatal accident makes an end of the individual. All that is necessary to make him extend his present span is that tremendous catastrophes such as the late war shall convince him of the necessity of at least outliving his taste for golf and cigars if the race is to be saved. This is not fantastic speculation: it is deductive biology, if there is such a science as biology. Here, then, is a stone that we have left unturned, and that may be worth turning. To make the suggestion more entertaining than it would be to most people in the form of a biological treatise, I have written Back to Methuselah as a contribution to the modern Bible.

Many people, however, can read treatises and cannot read Bibles. Darwin could not read Shakespear. Some who can read both, like to learn the history of their ideas. Some are so entangled in the current confusion of Creative Evolution with Circumstantial Selection by their historical ignorance that they are puzzled by any distinction between the two. For all their sakes I must give here a little history of the conflict between the view of Evolution taken by the Darwinians (though not altogether by Darwin himself) and called Natural Selection, and that which is emerging, under the title of Creative Evolution, as the genuinely scientific religion for which all wise men are now anxiously looking.

THE EARLY EVOLUTIONISTS

The idea of Evolution, or Transformation as it is now

sometimes called, was not first conceived by Charles Darwin, nor by Alfred Russel Wallace, who observed the operation of Circumstantial Selection simultaneously with Charles. The celebrated Buffoon was a better Evolutionist than either of them; and two thousand years before Buffon was born, the Greek philosopher Empedocles opined that all forms of life are transformations of four elements, Fire, Air, Earth, and Water, effected by the two innate forces of attraction and repulsion, or love and hate. As lately as 1860 I myself was taught as a child that everything was made out of these four elements. Both the Empedocleans and the Evolutionists were opposed to those who believed in the separate creation of all forms of life as described in the book of Genesis. This "conflict between religion and science," as the phrase went then, did not perplex my infant mind in the least: I knew perfectly well, without knowing that I knew it, that the validity of a story is not the same as the occurrence of a fact. But as I grew up I found that I had to choose between Evolution and Genesis. If you believed that dogs and cats and snakes and birds and beetles and oysters and whales and men and women were all separately designed and made and named in Eden garden at the beginning of things, and have since survived simply by reproducing their kind, then you were not an Evolutionist. If you believed, on the contrary, that all the different species are modifications, variations, and elaborations of one primal stock, or even of a few primal stocks, then you were an Evolutionist. But you were not necessarily a Darwinian; for you might have been a modern Evolutionist twenty years before Charles Darwin was born, and a whole lifetime before he published his Origin of Species. For that matter, when Aristotle grouped animals with backbones as blood relations, he began the sort of classification which, when extended by Darwin to monkeys and men, so shocked my uncle.

Genesis had held the field until the time (1707–1778) of Linnæus the famous botanist. In the meantime the microscope had been invented. It revealed a new world of hitherto invisible creatures called Infusorians, as common water was found to be an infusion of them. In the eighteenth century naturalists were very keen on the Infusorian Amœbas, and were much struck by the way in which the members of this old family behaved and developed. But it was still possible for Linnæus to begin a treatise by saying "There are just so many species as there were forms created in the beginning," though there were hundreds of commonplace Scotch gardeners, pigeon fanciers, and stock breeders then living who knew better. Linnæus himself knew better before he died. In the last edition of his System of Nature, he began to wonder whether the transmutation of species by variation might not be possible. Then came the great poet who jumped over the facts to the conclusion. Goethe said that all the shapes of creation were cousins; that there must be some common stock from which all the species had sprung; that it was the environment of air that had produced the eagle, of water the seal, and of earth the mole. He could not say how this happened; but he divined that it did happen. Erasmus Darwin, the grandfather of Charles, carried the environment theory much further, pointing out instance after instance of modifications made in species apparently to adapt it to circumstances and environment: for instance, that the brilliant colours of the leopard, which make it so conspicuous in Regent's Park, conceal it in a tropical jungle. Finally he wrote, as his declaration of faith, "The world has been evolved, not created: it has arisen little by little from a small beginning, and has increased through the activity of the elemental forces embodied in itself, and so has rather grown than come into being at an almighty word. What a sublime idea of the infinite might of the great Architect, the Cause of all causes, the Father of all fathers, the Ens Entium! For if we would compare the Infinite, it would surely require a greater Infinite to cause the causes of effects than to produce the effects themselves." In this, published in the year 1794, you have nineteenth-century Evolution precisely defined. And Erasmus Darwin was by no means its only apostle. It was in the air then. A German biologist named Treviranus, whose book was published in 1802, wrote, "In every living being there exists a capacity for endless diversity of form. Each possesses the power of adapting its organization to the variations of the external world; and it is this power, called into activity by cosmic changes, which has enabled the simple zoophytes of the primitive world to climb to higher and higher stages of organization, and has brought endless variety into nature." There you have your evolution of Man from the amœba all complete whilst Nelson was still alive on the seas. And in 1809, before the battle of Waterloo, a French soldier named Lamarck, who had beaten his musket into a microscope and turned zoologist, declared that species were an illusion produced by the shortness of our individual lives, and that they were constantly changing and melting into one another and into new forms as surely as the hand of a clock is continually moving, though it moves so slowly that it looks stationary to us. We have since come to think that its industry is less continuous: that the clock stops for a long time, and then is suddenly "put on" by a mysterious finger. But never mind that just at present.

THE ADVENT OF THE NEO-LAMARCKIANS

I call your specia attention to Lamarck, because later on there were Neo-Lamarckians as well as Neo-Darwinians. I was a Neo-Lamarckian. Lamarck passed on from the conception of Evolution as a general law to Charles Darwin's department of it, which was the method of Evolution. Lamarck, whilst making many ingenious suggestions as to the reaction of external causes on life and habit, such as changes of climate, food supply, geological upheavals and so forth, really held as his fundamental proposition that living organisms changed because they wanted to. As he stated it, the great factor in Evolution is use and disuse. If you have no eyes, and want to see, and keep trying to see, you will finally get eyes. If, like a mole or a subterranean fish, you have eyes and dont want to see, you will lose your eyes. If you like eating the tender tops of trees enough to make you concentrate all your energies on the stretching of your neck, you will finally get a long neck, like the giraffe. This seems absurd to inconsiderate people at the first blush; but it is within the personal experience of all of us that it is just by this process that a child tumbling about the floor becomes a boy walking erect; and that a man sprawling on the road with a bruised chin, or supine on the ice with a bashed occiput, becomes a bicyclist and a skater. The process is not continuous, as it would be if mere practice had anything to do with it; for though you may improve at each bicycling lesson *during* the lesson, when you begin your next lesson you do not begin at the point at which you left off: you relapse apparently to the beginning. Finally, you succeed quite suddenly, and do not relapse again. More miraculous still, you at once exercise the new power unconsciously. Although you are adapting your front wheel to your balance so elaborately and actively that the accidental locking of your handle bars for a second will throw you off; though five minutes before you could not do it at all, yet now you do it as unconsciously as you grow your finger nails. You have a new faculty, and must have created some new bodily tissue as its organ. And you have done it solely by willing. For here there can be no question of Circumstantial Selection, or the survival of the fittest. The man who is learning how to ride a bicycle has no advantage over the non-cyclist in the struggle for existence: quite the contrary. He has acquired a new habit, an automatic unconscious habit, solely because he wanted to, and kept trying until it was added unto him.

HOW ACQUIREMENTS ARE INHERITED

But when your son tries to skate or bicycle in his turn, he does not pick up the accomplishment where you left it, any more than he is born six feet high with a beard and a tall hat. The set-back that occurred between your lessons occurs again. The race learns exactly as the individual learns. Your son relapses, not to the very beginning, but to a point which no mortal method of measurement can distinguish from the beginning. Now this is odd; for certain other habits of yours, equally acquired (to the Evolutionist, of course, all habits are acquired), equally unconscious, equally automatic, are transmitted without any perceptible relapse. For instance, the very first act of your son when he enters the world as a separate individual is to yell with indignation: that yell which Shakespear thought the most tragic and piteous of all sounds. In the act of yelling he begins to breathe: another habit, and not even a necessary one, as the object of breathing can be achieved in other ways, as by deep sea fishes. He circulates his blood by pumping it with his heart. He demands a meal, and proceeds at once to perform the most elaborate chemical operations on the food he swallows. He manufactures teeth; discards them; and replaces them with fresh ones. Compared to these habitual feats, walking, standing upright, and bicycling are the merest trifles; yet it is only by going through the wanting, trying process that he can stand, walk, or cycle, whereas in the other and far more difficult and complex habits he not only does not consciously want nor consciously try, but actually consciously objects very strongly. Take that early habit of cutting the teeth: would he do that if he could help it? Take that later habit of decaying and eliminating himself by death—equally an acquired habit, remember—how he abhors it! Yet the habit has become so rooted, so automatic, that he must do it in spite of himself, even to his own destruction.

We have here a routine which, given time enough for it to operate, will finally produce the most elaborate forms of organized life on Lamarckian lines without the intervention of Circumstantial Selection at all. If you can turn a pedestrian into a cyclist, and a cyclist into a pianist or violinist, without the intervention of Circumstantial Selection, you can turn an amœba into a man, or a man into a superman, without it. All of which is rank heresy to the Neo-Darwinian, who imagines that if you stop Circumstantial Selection, you not only stop development but inaugurate a rapid and disastrous degeneration.

Let us fix the Lamarckian evolutionary process well in our minds. You are alive; and you want to be more alive. You want an extension of consciousness and of power. You want, consequently, additional organs, or additional uses of your existing organs: that is, additional habits. You get them because you want them badly enough to keep trying for them until they come. Nobody knows how: nobody knows why: all we know is that the thing actually takes place. We relapse miserably from effort to effort until the old organ is modified or the new one created, when suddenly the impossible becomes possible and the habit is formed. The moment we form it we want to get rid of the consciousness of it so as to economize our consciousness for fresh conquests of life; as all consciousness means preoccupation and obstruction. If we had to think about breathing or digesting or circulating our blood we should have no attention to spare for anything else, as we find to our cost when anything goes wrong with these operations. We want to be unconscious of them just as we wanted to acquire them; and we finally win what we want. But we win unconsciousness of our habits at the cost of losing our control of them; and we also build one habit and its corresponding functional modification of our organs on another, and so become dependent on our old habits. Consequently we have to persist in them even when they hurt us. We cannot stop breathing to avoid an attack of asthma, or to escape drowning. We can lose a habit and discard an organ when we no longer need them, just as we acquired them; but this process is slow and broken by relapses; and relics of the organ and the habit long survive its utility. And if other and still indispensable habits and modifications have been built on the ones we wish to discard, we must provide a new foundation for them before we demolish the old one. This is also a slow process and a very curious one.

THE MIRACLE OF CONDENSED RECAPITULATION

The relapses between the efforts to acquire a habit are important because, as we have seen, they recur not only from effort to effort in the case of the individual, but from generation to generation in the case of the race. This relapsing from generation to generation is an invariable characteristic of the evolutionary process. For instance, Raphael, though descended from eight uninterrupted generations of painters, had to learn to paint apparently as if no Sanzio had ever handled a brush before. But he had also to learn to breathe, and digest, and circulate his blood. Although his father and mother were fully grown adults when he was conceived, he was not conceived or even born fully grown: he had to go back and begin as a speck of protoplasm, and to struggle through an embryonic lifetime, during part of which he was indistinguishable from an embryonic dog, and had neither a skull nor a backbone. When he at last acquired these articles, he was for some time doubtful whether he was a bird or a fish. He had to compress untold centuries of development into nine months before he was human enough to break loose as an independent being. And even then he was still so incomplete that his parents might well have exclaimed "Good Heavens! have you learnt nothing from our experience that you come into the world in this ridiculously elementary state? Why cant you talk and walk and paint and behave decently?" To that question Baby Raphael had no answer. All he could have said was that this is how evolution or transformation happens. The time may come when the same force that compressed the development of millions of years into nine months may pack many more millions into even a shorter space; so that Raphaels may be born painters as they are now born breathers and blood circulators. But they will still begin as specks of protoplasm, and acquire the faculty of painting in their mother's womb at quite a late stage of their embryonic life. They must recapitulate the history of mankind in their own persons, however briefly they may condense it.

Nothing was so astonishing and significant in the discoveries of the embryologists, nor anything so absurdly little appreciated, as this recapitulation, as it is now called: this power of hurrying up into months a process which was once so long and tedious that the mere contemplation of it is unendurable by men whose span of life is three-score-and-ten. It widened human possibilities to the extent of enabling us to hope that the most prolonged and difficult operations of our minds may yet become instantaneous, or, as we call it, instinctive. It also directed our attention to examples of this packing up of centuries into seconds which were staring us in the face in all directions. As I write these lines the newspapers are occupied by the exploits of a child of eight, who has just defeated twenty adult chess players in twenty games played simultaneously, and has been able afterwards to reconstruct all the twenty games without any apparent effort of memory. Most people, including myself, play chess (when they play it at all) from hand to mouth, and can hardly recall the last move but one, or foresee the next but two. Also, when I have to make an arithmetical calculation, I have to do it step by step with pencil and paper, slowly, reluctantly, and with so little confidence in the result that I dare not act on it without "proving" the sum by a further calculation involving more ciphering. But there are men who can neither read, write, nor cipher, to whom the answer to such sums as I can do is instantly obvious without any conscious calculation at all; and the result is infallible. Yet some of these natural arithmeticians have but a small vocabulary; are at a loss when they have to find words for any but the simplest everyday occasions; and cannot for the life of them describe mechanical operations which they perform daily in the course of their trade; whereas to me the whole vocabulary of English literature, from Shakespear to the latest edition of the Encyclopædia Britannica, is so completely and instantaneously at my call that I have never had to consult even a thesaurus except once or twice when for some reason I wanted a third or fourth synonym. Again, though I have tried and failed to draw recognizable portraits of persons I have seen every day for years, Mr Bernard Partridge, having seen a man once, will, without more strain than is involved in eating a sandwich, draw him to the life. The keyboard of a piano is a device I have never been able to master; yet Mr Cyril Scott uses it exactly as I use my own fingers; and to Sir Edward Elgar an orchestral score is as instantaneously intelligible at sight as a page of Shakespear is to me. One man cannot, after trying for years, finger the flute fluently. Another will take up a flute with a newly invented arrangement of keys on it, and play it at once with hardly a mistake. We find people to whom writing is so difficult that they prefer to sign their name with a mark, and beside them men who master systems of shorthand and improvise new systems of their own as easily as they learnt the alphabet. These contrasts are to be seen on all hands, and have nothing to do with variations in general intelligence, nor even in the specialized intelligence proper to the faculty in question: for example, no composer or dramatic poet has ever pretended to be able to perform all the parts he writes for the singers, actors, and players who are his executants. One might as well expect Napoleon to be a fencer, or the Astronomer Royal to know how many beans make five any better than his bookkeeper. Even exceptional command of language does not imply the possession of ideas to express: Mezzofanti, the master of fifty-eight languages, had less to say in them than Shakespear with his little Latin and less Greek; and public life is the paradise of voluble windbags.

All these examples, which might be multiplied by millions, are cases in which a long, laborious, conscious, detailed process of acquirement has been condensed into an instinctive and unconscious inborn one. Factors which formerly had to be considered one by one in succession are integrated into what seems a single simple factor. Chains of hardly soluble problems have coalesced in one problem which solves itself the moment it is raised. What is more, they have been pushed back (or forward, if you like) from post-natal to prenatal ones. The child in the womb may take some time over them; but it is a miraculously shortened time.

The time phenomena involved are curious, and suggest that we are either wrong about our history or else that we enormously exaggerate the periods required for the prenatal acquirement of habits. In the nineteenth century we talked very glibly about geological periods, and flung millions of eons about in the most lordly manner in our reaction against Archbishop Ussher's chronology. We had a craze for big figures, and positively liked to believe that the progress made by the child in the womb in a month was represented in prehistoric time by ages and ages. We insisted that Evolution advanced more slowly than any snail ever crawled, and that Nature does not proceed by leaps and bounds. This was all very well as long as we were dealing with such acquired habits as breathing or digestion. It was possible to believe that dozens of epochs had gone to the slow building up of these habits. But when we have to consider the case of a man born not only as an accomplished metabolist, but with such an aptitude for shorthand and keyboard manipulation that he is a stenographer or pianist at least five sixths ready-made as soon as he can control his hands intelligently, we are forced to suspect either that keyboards and shorthand are older inventions than we suppose, or else that acquirements can be assimilated and stored as congenital qualifications in a shorter time than we think; so that, as between Lyell and Archbishop Ussher, the laugh may not be with Lyell quite so uproariously as it seemed fifty years ago.

HEREDITY AN OLD STORY

It is evident that the evolutionary process is a hereditary one, or, to put it less drily, that human life is continuous and immortal. The Evolutionists took heredity for granted. So did everybody. The human mind has been soaked in heredity as long back as we can trace its thought. Hereditary peers, hereditary monarchs, hereditary castes and trades and classes were the best known of social institutions, and in some cases of public nuisances. Pedigree men counted pedigree dogs and pedigree horses among their most cher-shed possessions. Far from being unconscious of heredity, or sceptical, men were insanely credulous about it: they not only believed in the transmission of qualities and habits from generation to generation, but expected the son to begin mentally where the father left off.

This belief in heredity led naturally to the practice of Intentional Selection. Good blood and breeding were eagerly sought after in human marriage. In dealing with plants and animals, selection with a view to the production of new varieties and the improvement and modification of species had been practised ever since men began to cultivate them. My pre-Darwinian uncle knew as well as Darwin that the race-horse and the dray-horse are not separate creations from the Garden of Eden, but adaptations by deliberate human selection of the medieval war-horse to modern racing and industrial haulage. He knew that there are nearly two hundred different sorts of dogs, all capable of breeding with one another and of producing cross varieties unknown to Adam. He knew that the same thing is true of pigeons. He knew that gardeners had spent their lives trying to breed black tulips and green carnations and unheard-of orchids, and had actually produced flowers just as strange to Eve. His quarrel with the Evolutionists was not a quarrel with the evidence for Evolution: he had accepted enough of it to prove Evolution ten times over before he ever heard of it. What he repudiated was cousinship with the ape, and the implied suspicion of a rudimentary tail, because it was offensive to his sense of his own dignity, and because he thought that apes were ridiculous, and tails diabolical when associated with the erect posture. Also he believed that Evolution was a heresy which involved the destruction of Christianity, of which, as a member of the Irish Church (the pseudo-Protestant one), he conceived himself a pillar. But this was only his ignorance; for a man may deny his descent from an ape and be eligible as a churchwarden without being any the less a convinced Evolutionist.

DISCOVERY ANTICIPATED BY DIVINATION

What is more, the religious folk can claim to be among the pioneers of Evolutionism. Weismann, Neo-Darwinist though he was, devoted a long passage in his History of Evolution to the Nature Philosophy of Lorenz Oken, published in 1809. Oken defined natural science as "the science of the everlasting transmutations of the Holy Ghost in the world." His religion had started him on the right track, and not only led him to think out a whole scheme of Evolution in abstract terms, but guided his aim in a significantly good scientific shot which brought him within the scope of Weismann. He not only defined the original substance from which all forms of life have developed as protoplasm, or, as he called it, primitive slime (*Urschleim*), but actually declared that this slime took the form of vesicles out of which the universe was built. Here was the modern cell morphology guessed by a religious thinker long before the microscope and the scalpel forced it on the vision of mere laboratory workers who could not think and had no religion. They worked hard to discover the vital secrets of the glands by opening up dogs and cutting out the glands, or tying up their ducts, or severing their nerves, thereby learning, negatively, that the governors of our vital forces do not hold their incessant conversations through the nerves, and, positively, how miserably a horribly injured dog can die, leaving us to infer that we shall probably perish likewise if we grudge our guineas to Harley Street. Lorenz Oken *thought* very hard to find out what was happening to the Holy Ghost, and thereby made a contribution of extraordinary importance to our understanding of uninjured creatures. The man who was scientific enough to see that the Holy Ghost is a scientific fact got easily in front of the blockheads who could only sin against it. Hence my uncle was turning his back on very respectable company when he derided Evolution, and would probably have recanted and apologized at once had anybody pointed out to him what a solecism he was committing.

The metaphysical side of Evolution was thus no novelty when Darwin arrived. Had Oken never lived, there would still have been millions of persons trained from their childhood to believe that we are continually urged upwards by a forced called the Will of God. In 1819 Schopenhauer published his treatise on The World as Will, which is the metaphysical complement to Lamarck's natural history, as it demonstrates that the driving force behind Evolution is a will-to-live, and to live, as Christ said long before, more abundantly. And the earlier philosophers, from Plato to Leibnitz, had kept the human mind open for the thought of the universe as one idea behind all its physically apprehensible transformations.

CORRECTED DATES FOR THE DISCOVERY OF EVOLUTION

All this, remember, is the state of things in the pre-Darwin period, which so many of us still think of as a pre-evolutionary period. Evolutionism was the rage before Queen Victoria came to the throne. To fix this chronology, let me repeat the story told by Weismann of the July revolution in Paris in 1830, when the French got rid of Charles the Tenth. Goethe was then still living; and a French friend of his called on him and found him wildly excited. "What do you think of the great event?" said Goethe. "The volcano is in eruption; and all is in flames. There can no longer be discussion with closed doors." The Frenchman replied that no doubt it was a terrible business; but what could they expect with such a ministry and such a king? "Stuff!" said Goethe: "I am not thinking of these people at all, but of the open rupture in the French Academy between Cuvier and St Hilaire. It is of the utmost importance to science." The rupture Goethe meant was about Evolution, Cuvier contending that there were four species, and St Hilaire that there was only one.

From 1830, when Darwin was an apparently unpromising lad of twenty-one, until 1859, when he turned the world upside down by his Origin of Species, there was a slump in

Evolutionism. The first generation of its enthusiasts was ageing and dying out; and their successors were being taught from the Book of Genesis, just as Edward VI was (and Edward VII too, for that matter). Nobody who knew the theory was adding anything to it. This slump not only heightened the impression of entire novelty when Darwin brought the subject to the front again: it probably prevented him from realizing how much had been done before, even by his own grandfather, to whom he was accused of being unjust. Besides, he was not really carrying on the family business. He was an entirely original worker; and he was on a new tack, as we shall see presently. And he would not in any case have thought much, as a practical naturalist, of the more or less mystical intellectual speculations of the Deists of 1790–1830. Scientific workers were very tired of Deism just then. They had given up the riddle of the Great First Cause as insoluble, and were calling themselves, accordingly, Agnostics. They had turned from the inscrutable question of Why things existed, to the spade work of discovering What was really occurring in the world and How it really occurred.

With all his attention bent in this new direction, Darwin soon noticed that a good deal was occurring in an entirely unmystical and even unmeaning way of which the older speculative Deist-Evolutionists had taken little or no account. Nowadays, when we are turning in weary disgust and disillusion from Neo-Darwinism and Mechanism to Vitalism and Creative Evolution, it is difficult to imagine how this new departure of Darwin's could possibly have appealed to his contemporaries as exciting, agreeable, above all as hopeful. Let me therefore try to bring back something of the atmosphere of that time by describing a scene, very characteristic of its superstitions, in which I took what was then considered an unspeakably shocking part.

DEFYING THE LIGHTNING: A FRUSTRATED EXPERIMENT

One evening in 1878 or thereabouts, I, being then in my

earliest twenties, was at a bachelor party of young men of the professional class in the house of a doctor in the Kensingtonian quarter of London. They fell to talking about religious revivals; and an anecdote was related of a man who, having incautiously scoffed at the mission of Messrs Moody and Sankey, a then famous firm of American evangelists, was subsequently carried home on a shutter, slain by divine vengeance as a blasphemer. A timid minority, without quite venturing to question the truth of the incident—for they naturally did not care to run the risk of going home on shutters themselves—nevertheless shewed a certain disposition to cavil at those who exulted in it; and something approaching to an argument began. At last it was alleged by the most evangelical of the disputants that Charles Bradlaugh, the most formidable atheist on the Secularist platform, had taken out his watch publicly and challenged the Almighty to strike him dead in five minutes if he really existed and disapproved of atheism. The leader of the cavillers, with great heat, repudiated this as a gross calumny, declaring that Bradlaugh had repeatedly and indignantly contradicted it, and implying that the atheist champion was far too pious a man to commit such a blasphemy. This exquisite confusion of ideas roused my sense of comedy. It was clear to me that the challenge attributed to Charles Bradlaugh was a scientific experiment of a quite simple, straightforward, and proper kind to ascertain whether the expression of atheistic opinions really did involve any personal risk. It was certainly the method taught in the Bible, Elijah having confuted the prophets of Baal in precisely that way, with every circumstance of bitter mockery of their god when he failed to send down fire from heaven. Accordingly I said that if the question at issue were whether the penalty of questioning the theology of Messrs Moody and Sankey was to be struck dead on the spot by an incensed deity, nothing could effect a more convincing settlement of it than the very obvious experiment attributed to Mr Bradlaugh, and that consequently if he had not tried it, he ought to have tried it. The omission, I added, was one which could easily be remedied there and then, as I happened to share Mr Bradlaugh's views as to the absurdity of the belief in these violent interferences with the order of nature by a short-tempered and thin-skinned supernatural deity. Therefore —and at that point I took out my watch.

The effect was electrical. Neither sceptics nor devotees were prepared to abide the result of the experiment. In vain did I urge the pious to trust in the accuracy of their deity's aim with a thunderbolt, and the justice of his discrimination between the innocent and the guilty. In vain did I appeal to the sceptics to accept the logical outcome of their scepticism: it soon appeared that when thunderbolts were in question there were no sceptics. Our host, seeing that his guests would vanish precipitately if the impious challenge were uttered, leaving him alone with a solitary infidel under sentence of extermination in five minutes, interposed and forbade the experiment, pleading at the same time for a change of subject. I of course complied, but could not refrain from remarking that though the dreadful words had not been uttered, yet, as the thought had been formulated in my mind, it was very doubtful whether the consequences could be averted by sealing my lips. However, the rest appeared to feel that the game would be played according to the rules, and that it mattered very little what I thought so long as I said nothing. Only the leader of the evangelical party, I thought, was a little preoccupied until five minutes had elapsed and the weather was still calm.

IN QUEST OF THE FIRST CAUSE

Another reminiscence. In those days we thought in terms of time and space, of cause and effect, as we still do; but we do not now demand from a religion that it shall explain the universe completely in terms of cause and effect, and present the world to us as a manufactured article and as the private property of its Manufacturer. We did then. We were invited to pity the delusion of certain heathens who held that the world is supported by an elephant who is supported by a tortoise. Mahomet decided that the mountains are great weights to keep the world from being blown away into space. But we refuted these orientals by asking triumphantly what the tortoise stands on? Freethinkers asked which came first: the owl or the egg. Nobody thought of saying that the ultimate problem of existence, being clearly insoluble and even unthinkable on causation lines, could not be a causation problem. To pious people this would have been flat atheism, because they assumed that God must be a Cause, and sometimes called him The Great First Cause, or, in still choicer language, The Primal Cause. To the Rationalists it would have been a renunciation of reason. Here and there a man would confess that he stood as with a dim lantern in a dense fog, and could see but a little way in any direction into infinity. But he did not really believe that infinity was infinite or that the eternal was also sempiternal: he assumed that all things, known and unknown, were caused.

Hence it was that I found myself one day towards the end of the eighteen-seventies in a cell in the old Brompton Oratory arguing with Father Addis, who had been called by one of his flock to attempt my conversion to Roman Catholicism. The universe exists, said the father: somebody must have made it. If that somebody exists, said I, somebody must have made him. I grant that for the sake of argument, said the Oratorian. I grant you a maker of God. I grant you a maker of the maker of God. I grant you as long a line of makers as you please; but an infinity of makers is unthinkable and extravagant: it is no harder to believe in number one than in number fifty thousand or fifty million; so why not accept number one and stop there, since no attempt to get behind him will remove your logical difficulty? By your leave, said I, it is as easy for me to believe that the universe made itself as that a maker of the universe made himself: in fact much easier; for the universe visibly exists and makes itself as it goes along, whereas a maker for it is a hypothesis. Of course we could get no further on these lines. He rose and said that we were like two men working a saw, he pushing it forward and I pushing it back, and cutting nothing; but when we had dropped the subject and were walking through the refectory, he returned to it for a moment to say that he should go mad if he lost his belief. I, glorying in the robust callousness of youth and the comedic spirit, felt quite comfortable and said so; though I was touched, too, by his evident sincerity.

These two anecdotes are superficially trivial and even comic; but there is an abyss of horror beneath them. They reveal a condition so utterly irreligious that religion means nothing but belief in a nursery bogey, and its inadequacy is demonstrated by a toy logical dilemma, neither the bogey nor the dilemma having anything to do with religion, or being serious enough to impose on or confuse any properly educated child over the age of six. One hardly knows which is the more appalling: the abjectness of the credulity or the flippancy of the scepticism. The result was inevitable. All who were strongminded enough not to be terrified by the bogey were left stranded in empty contemptuous negation, and argued, when they argued at all, as I argued with Father Addis. But their position was not intellectually comfortable. A member of parliament expressed their discomfort when, objecting to the admission of Charles Bradlaugh into parliament, he said "Hang it all, a man should believe in something or somebody." It was easy to throw the bogey into the dust-bin; but none the less the world, our corner of the universe, did not look like a pure accident: it presented evidences of design in every direction. There was mind and purpose behind it. As the anti-Bradlaugh member would have put it, there must be somebody behind the something: no atheist could get over that.

PALEY'S WATCH

Paley had put the argument in an apparently unanswerable form. If you found a watch, full of mechanism exquisitely adapted to produce a series of operations all leading to the fulfilment of one central purpose of measuring for mankind the march of the day and night, could you believe that it was not the work of a cunning artificer who had designed and contrived it all to that end? And here was a far more wonderful thing than a watch, a man with all his organs ingeniously contrived, cords and levers, girders and kingposts, circulating systems of pipes and valves, dialysing membranes, chemical retorts, carburettors, ventilators, inlets and outlets, telephone transmitters in his ears, light recorders and lenses in his eyes: was it conceivable that this was the work of chance? that no artificer had wrought here? that there was no purpose in this, no design, no guiding intelligence? The thing was incredible. In vain did Helmholtz declare that "the eye has every possible defect that can be found in an optical instrument, and even some peculiar to itself," and that "if an optician tried to sell me an instrument which had all these defects I should think myself quite justified in blaming his carelessness in the strongest terms, and sending him back his instrument." To discredit the optician's skill was not to get rid of the optician. The eye might not be so cleverly made as Paley thought; but it was made somehow, by somebody.

And then my argument with Father Addis began all over again. It was easy enough to say that every man makes his own eyes: indeed the embryologists had actually caught him doing it. But what about the very evident purpose that prompted him to do it? Why did he want to see, if not to extend his consciousness and his knowledge and his power? That purpose was at work everywhere, and must be something bigger than the individual eye-making man. Only the stupidest muckrakers could fail to see this, and even to know it as part of their own consciousness. Yet to admit it seemed to involve letting the bogey come back, so inextricably had we managed to mix up belief in the bogey's existence with belief in the existence of design in the universe.

THE IRRESISTIBLE CRY OF ORDER, ORDER!

Our scornful young scientific and philosophic lions of today must not blame the Church of England for this confusion of thought. In 1562 the Church, in convocation in London "for the avoiding of diversities of opinions and for the establishment of consent touching true religion," proclaimed in their first utterance, and as an Article of Religion, that God is "without body, parts, or passions," or, as we say, an *Élan Vital* or Life Force. Unfortunately neither parents, parsons, nor pedagogues could be induced to adopt that article. St John might say that "God is spirit" as pointedly as he pleased; our Soverign Lady Elizabeth might ratify the Article again and again; serious divines might feel as deeply as they could that a God with body, parts, and passions could be nothing but an anthropomorphic idol: no matter: people at large could not conceive a God who was not anthropomorphic: they stood by the Old Testament legends of a God whose parts had been seen by one of the patriarchs, and finally set up as against the Church a God who, far from being without body, parts, or passions, was composed of nothing else, and of very evil passions too. They imposed this idol in practice on the Church itself, in spite of the First Article, and thereby homeopathically produced the atheist, whose denial of God was simply a denial of the idol and a demonstration against an unbearable and most unchristian idolatry. The idol was, as Shelley had been expelled from Oxford for pointing out, an almighty fiend, with a petty character and unlimited power, spiteful, cruel, jealous, vindictive, and physically violent. The most villainous schoolmasters, the most tyrannical parents, fell far short in their attempts to imitate it. But it was not its social vices that brought it low. What made it scientifically intolerable was that it was ready at a moment's notice to upset the whole order of the universe on the most trumpery provocation, whether by stopping the sun in the valley of Ajalon or sending an atheist home dead on a shutter (the shutter was indispensable because it marked the utter unpreparedness of the atheist, who, unable to save himself by a deathbed repentance, was subsequently roasted through all eternity in blazing brimstone). It was this disorderliness, this refusal to obey its own laws of nature, that created a scientific need for its destruction. Science could stand a cruel and unjust god; for nature was full of suffering and injustice. But a disorderly god was impossible. In the Middle Ages a compromise had been made by which two different orders of truth, religious and scientific, had been recognized, in order that a schoolman might say that two and two make four without being burnt for heresy. But the nineteenth century, steeped in a meddling, presumptuous, reading-and-writing, socially and politically powerful ignorance inconceivable by Thomas Aquinas or even Roger Bacon, was incapable of so convenient an arrangement; and science was strangled by bigoted ignoramuses claiming infallibility for their interpretation of the Bible, which was regarded, not as a literature nor even as a book, but partly as an oracle which answered and settled all questions, and partly as a talisman to be carried by soldiers in their breast pockets or placed under the pillows of persons who were afraid of ghosts. The tract shops exhibited in their windows bullet-dinted testaments, mothers' gifts to their soldier sons whose lives had been saved by it; for the muzzle-loaders of those days could not drive a projectile through so many pages.

THE MOMENT AND THE MAN

This superstition of a continual capricious disorder in nature, of a lawgiver who was also a lawbreaker, made atheists in all directions among clever and lightminded people. But atheism did not account for Paley's watch. Atheism accounted for nothing; and it was the business of science to account for everything that was plainly accountable. Science had no use for mere negation: what was desired by it above all things just then was a demonstration that the evidences of design could be explained without resort to the hypothesis of a personal designer. If only some genius, whilst admitting Paley's facts, could knock the brains out of Paley by the discovery of a method whereby watches could happen without watchmakers, that genius was assured of such a welcome from the thought of his day as no natural philosopher had ever enjoyed before.

The time being thus ripe, the genius appeared; and his name was Charles Darwin. And now, what did Darwin really discover?

Here, I am afraid, I shall require once more the assistance of the giraffe, or, as he was called in the days of the celebrated Buffoon, the camelopard (by children, cammyleopard). I do not remember how this animal imposed himself illustratively on the Evolution controversy; but there was no getting away from him then; and I am old-fashioned enough to be unable to get away from him now. How did he come by his long neck? Lamarck would have said, by wanting to get at the tender leaves high up on the tree, and trying until he succeeded in wishing the necessary length of neck into existence. Another answer was also possible: namely, that some prehistoric stockbreeder, wishing to produce a natural curiosity, selected the longest-necked animals he could find, and bred from them until at last an animal with an abnormally long neck was evolved by intentional selection, just as the race-horse or the fantail pigeon has been evolved. Both these explanations, you will observe, involve consciousness, will, design, purpose, either on the part of the animal itself or on the part of a superior intelligence controlling its destiny. Darwin pointed out—and this and no more was Darwin's famous discovery—that a third explanation, involving neither will nor purpose nor design either in the animal or anyone else, was on the cards. If your neck is too short to reach your food, you die. That may be the simple explanation of the fact that all the surviving animals that feed on foliage have necks or trunks long enough to reach it. So bang goes your belief that the necks must have been designed to reach the food. But Lamarck did not believe that the necks were so designed in the beginning: he believed that the long necks were evolved by wanting and trying. Not necessarily, said Darwin. Consider the effect on the giraffes of the natural multiplication of their numbers, as insisted on by Malthus. Suppose the average height of the foliage-eating animals is four feet, and that they increase in numbers until a time comes when all the trees are eaten away to within four feet of the ground. Then the animals who happen to be an inch or two short of the average will die of starvation. All the animals who happen to be an inch or so above the average will be better fed and stronger than the others. They will secure the strongest and tallest mates; and their progeny will survive whilst the average ones and the sub-average ones will die out. This process, by which the species gains, say, an inch in reach, will repeat itself until the giraffe's neck is so long that he can always find food enough within his reach, at which point, of course, the selective process stops and the length of the giraffe's neck stops with it. Otherwise, he would grow until he could browse off the trees in the moon. And this, mark you, without the intervention of any stock-breeder, human or divine, and without will, purpose, design, or even consciousness beyond the blind will to satisfy hunger. It is true that this blind will, being in effect a will to live, gives away the whole case; but still, as compared to the open-eyed intelligent wanting and trying of Lamarck, the Darwinian process may be described as a chapter of accidents. As such, it seems simple, because you do not at first realize all that it involves. But when its whole significance dawns on you, your heart sinks into a heap of sand within you. There is a hideous fatalism about it, a ghastly and damnable reduction of beauty and intelligence, of strength and purpose, of honor and aspiration, to such casually picturesque changes as an avalanche may make in a mountain landscape, or a railway accident in a human figure. To call this Natural Selection is a blasphemy, possible to many for whom Nature is nothing but a casual aggregation of inert and dead matter, but eternally impossible to the spirits and souls of the righteous. If it be no blasphemy, but a truth of science, then the stars of heaven, the showers and dew, the winter and summer, the fire and heat, the mountains and hills, may no longer be called to exalt the Lord with us by praise: their work is to modify all things by blindly starving and murdering everything that is not lucky enough to survive in the universal struggle for hogwash.

THE BRINK OF THE BOTTOMLESS PIT

Thus did the neck of the giraffe reach out across the whole heavens and make men believe that what they saw there was a gloaming of the gods. For if this sort of selection could turn an antelope into a giraffe, it could conceivably turn a pond full of amœbas into the French Academy. Though Lamarck's way, the way of life, will, aspiration, and achievement, remained still possible, this newly shewn way of hunger, death, stupidity, delusion, chance, and bare survival was also possible: was indeed most certainly the way in which many apparently intelligently designed transformations had actually come to pass. Had I not preluded with the apparently idle story of my revival of the controversial methods of Elijah, I should be asked how it was that the explorer who opened up this gulf of despair, far from being stoned or crucified as the destroyer of the honor of the race and the purpose of the world, was hailed as Deliverer, Savior, Prophet, Redeemer, Enlightener, Rescuer, Hope Giver, and Epoch Maker; whilst poor Lamarck was swept aside as a crude and exploded guesser hardly worthy to be named as his erroneous forerunner. In the light of my anecdote, the explanation is obvious. The first thing the gulf did was to swallow up Paley, and the Disorderly Designer, and Shelley's Almighty Fiend, and all the rest of the pseudo-religious rubbish that had blocked every upward and onward path since the hopes of men had turned to Science as their true Savior. It seemed such a convenient grave that nobody at first noticed that it was nothing less than the bottomless pit, now become a very real terror. For though Darwin left a path round it for his soul, his followers presently dug it right across the whole width of the way. Yet for the moment, there was nothing but wild rejoicing: a sort of scientific mafficking. We had been so oppressed by the notion that everything that happened in the world was the arbitrary personal act of an arbitrary personal god of dangerously jealous and cruel personal character, so that even the relief of the pains of childbed and the operating table by chloroform was objected to as an interference with his arrangements which he would probably resent, that we just jumped at Darwin. When Napoleon was asked what would happen when he died, he said that Europe would express its intense relief with a great "Ouf!" Well, when Darwin killed the god who objected to chloroform, everybody who had ever thought about it said "Ouf!" Paley was buried fathoms deep with his watch, now fully accounted for without any divine artificer at all. We were so glad to be rid of both that we never gave a thought to the consequences. When a prisoner sees the door of his dungeon open, he dashes for it without stopping to think where he shall get his dinner outside. The moment we found that we could do without Shelley's almighty fiend intellectually, he went into the gulf that seemed only a dustbin with a suddenness that made our own lives one of the most astonishing periods in history. If I had told that uncle of mine that within thirty years from the date of our conversation I should be exposing myself to suspicions of the grossest superstition by questioning the sufficiency of Darwin; maintaining the reality of the Holy Ghost; and declaring that the phenomenon of the Word becoming Flesh was occurring daily, he would have regarded me as the most extravagant madman our family had ever produced. Yet it was so. In 1906 I might have vituperated Jehovah more heartily than ever Shelley did without eliciting a protest in any circle of thinkers, or shocking any public audience accustomed to modern discussion; but when I described Darwin as "an intelligent and industrious pigeon fancier," that blasphemous levity, as it seemed, was received with horror and indignation. The tide has now turned; and every puny whipster may say what he likes about Darwin; but anyone who wants to know what it was to be a Lamarckian during the last quarter of the nineteenth century has only to read Mr Festing Jones's memoir of

Samuel Butler to learn how completely even a man of genius could isolate himself by antagonizing Darwin on the one hand and the Church on the other.

WHY DARWIN CONVERTED THE CROWD

I am well aware that in describing the effect of Darwin's discovery on naturalists and on persons capable of serious reflection on the nature and attributes of God, I am leaving the vast mass of the British public out of account. I have pointed out elsewhere that the British nation does not consist of atheists and Plymouth Brothers; and I am not now going to pretend that it ever consisted of Darwinians and Lamarckians. The average citizen is irreligious and unscientific: you talk to him about cricket and golf, market prices and party politics, not about evolution and relativity, transubstantiation and predestination. Nothing will knock into his head the fateful distinction between Evolution as promulgated by Erasmus Darwin, and Circumstantial (so-called Natural) Selection as revealed by his grandson. Yet the doctrine of Charles reached him, though the doctrine of Erasmus had passed over his head. Why did not Erasmus Darwin popularize the word Evolution as effectively as Charles?

The reason was, I think, that Circumstantial Selection is easier to understand, more visible and concrete, than Lamarckian evolution. Evolution as a philosophy and physiology of the will is a mystical process, which can be apprehended only by a trained, apt, and comprehensive thinker. Though the phenomena of use and disuse, of wanting and trying, of the manufacture of weight lifters and wrestlers from men of ordinary strength, are familiar enough as facts, they are extremely puzzling as subjects of thought, and lead you into metaphysics the moment you try to account for them. But pigeon fanciers, dog fanciers, gardeners, stock breeders, or stud grooms, can understand Circumstantial Selection, because it is their business to produce transformation by imposing on flowers and animals a Selection From Without. All that Darwin had to say to them was that the mere chapter of accidents is always doing on a huge scale what they themselves are doing on a very small scale. There is hardly a laborer attached to an English country house who has not taken a litter of kittens or puppies to the bucket, and drowned all of them except the one he thinks the most promising. Such a man has nothing to learn about the survival of the fittest except that it acts in more ways than he has yet noticed; for he knows quite well, as you will find if you are not too proud to talk to him, that this sort of selection occurs naturally (in Darwin's sense) too: that, for instance, a hard winter will kill off a weakly child as the bucket kills off a weakly puppy. Then there is the farm laborer. Shakespear's Touchstone, a court-bred fool, was shocked to find in the shepherd a natural philosopher, and opined that he would be damned for the part he took in the sexual selection of sheep. As to the production of new species by the selection of variations, that is no news to your gardener. Now if you are familiar with these three processes: the survival of the fittest, sexual selection, and variation leading to new kinds, there is nothing to puzzle you in Darwinism.

That was the secret of Darwin's popularity. He never puzzled anybody. If very few of us have read The Origin of Species from end to end, it is not because it overtaxes our mind, but because we take in the whole case and are prepared to accept it long before we have come to the end of the innumerable instances and illustrations of which the book mainly consists. Darwin becomes tedious in the manner of a man who insists on continuing to prove his innocence after he has been acquitted. You assure him that there is not a stain on his character, and beg him to leave the court; but he will not be content with enough evidence: he will have you listen to all the evidence that exists in the world. Darwin's industry was enormous. His patience, his perseverance, his conscientiousness reached the human limit. But he never got deeper beneath or higher above his facts than an ordinary man could follow him. He was not conscious of having raised a stupendous issue, because, though it arose instantly, it was not his business. He was conscious of having discovered a process of transformation and modification which accounted for a great deal of natural history. But he did not put it forward as accounting for the whole of natural history. He included it under the heading of Evolution, though it was only pseudo-evolution at best; but he revealed it as *a* method of evolution, not as *the* method of evolution. He did not pretend that it excluded other methods, or that it was the chief method. Though he demonstrated that many transformations which had been taken as functional adaptations (the current phrase for Lamarckian evolution) either certainly were or conceivably might be due to Circumstantial Selection, he was careful not to claim that he had superseded Lamarck or disproved Functional Adaptation. In short, he was not a Darwinian, but an honest naturalist working away at his job with so little preoccupation with theological speculation that he never quarrelled with the theistic Unitarianism into which he was born, and remained to the end the engagingly simple and socially easy-going soul he had been in his boyhood, when his elders doubted whether he would ever be of much use in the world.

HOW WE RUSHED DOWN A STEEP PLACE

Not so the rest of us intellectuals. We all began going to the devil with the utmost cheerfulness. Everyone who had a mind to change, changed it. Only Samuel Butler, on whom Darwin had acted homeopathically, reacted against him furiously; ran up the Lamarckian flag to the top-gallant peak; declared with penetrating accuracy that Darwin had "banished mind from the universe"; and even attacked Darwin's personal character, unable to bear the fact that the author of so abhorrent a doctrine was an amiable and upright man. Nobody would listen to him. He was so completely submerged by the flowing tide of Darwinism that when Darwin wanted to clear up the misunderstanding on which Butler was basing his personal attacks, Darwin's friends, very foolishly and snobbishly, persuaded him that Butler was too ill-conditioned and negligible to be answered.

That they could not recognize in Butler a man of genius mattered little: what did matter was that they could not understand the provocation under which he was raging. They actually regarded the banishment of mind from the universe as a glorious enlightenment and emancipation for which he was ignorantly ungrateful. Even now, when Butler's eminence is unchallenged, and his biographer, Mr Festing Jones, is enjoying a vogue like that of Boswell or Lockhart, his memoirs shew him rather as a shocking example of the bad controversial manners of our country parsonages than as a prophet who tried to head us back when we were gaily dancing to our damnation across the rainbow bridge which Darwinism had thrown over the gulf which separates life and hope from death and despair. We were intellectually intoxicated with the idea that the world could make itself without design, purpose, skill, or intelligence: in short, without life. We completely overlooked the difference between the modification of species by adaptation to their environment and the appearance of new species: we just threw in the word "variations" or the word "sports" (fancy a man of science talking of an unknown factor as a sport instead of as *x*!) and left them to "accumulate" and account for the difference between a cockatoo and a hippopotamus. Such phrases set us free to revel in demonstrating to the Vitalists and Bible worshippers that if we once admit the existence of any kind of force, however unintelligent, and stretch out the past to unlimited time for such force to operate accidentally in, that force may conceivably, by the action of Circumstantial Selection, produce a world in which every function has an organ perfectly adapted to perform it, and therefore presents every appearance of having been designed, like Paley's watch, by a conscious and intelligent artificer for the purpose. We took a perverse pleasure in arguing, without the least suspicion that we were reducing ourselves to absurdity, that all the books in the British Museum library might have been written word for word as they stand on the shelves if no human being had ever been conscious, just as the trees stand in the forest doing wonderful things without consciousness.

And the Darwinians went far beyond denying consciousness to trees. Weismann insisted that the chick breaks out of its eggshell automatically; that the butterfly, springing into the air to avoid the pounce of the lizard, "does not wish to avoid death; knows nothing about death," what has happened being simply that a flight instinct evolved by Circumstantial Selection reacts promptly to a visual impression produced by the lizard's movement. His proof is that the butterfly immediately settles again on the flower, and repeats the performance every time the lizard springs, thus shewing that it learns nothing from experience, and—Weismann concludes—is not conscious of what it does.

It should hardly have escaped so curious an observer that when the cat jumps up on the dinner table, and you put it down, it instantly jumps up again, and finally establishes its right to a place on the cloth by convincing you that if you put it down a hundred times it will jump up a hundred and one times; so that if you desire its company at dinner you can have it only on its own terms. If Weismann really thought that cats act thus without any consciousness or any purpose, immediate or ulterior, he must have known very little about cats. But a thoroughgoing Weismannite, if any such still survive from those mad days, would contend that I am not at present necessarily conscious of what I am doing; that my writing of these lines, and your reading of them, are effects of Circumstantial Selection; that I need know no more about Darwinism than a butterfly knows of a lizard's appetite; and that the proof that I actually **am** doing it unconsciously is that as I have spent forty years in writing in this fashion without, as far as I can see, producing any visible effect on public opinion, I must be incapable of learning from experience, and am therefore a mere automaton. And the Weismannite demonstration of this would of course be an equally unconscious effect of Circumstantial Selection.

DARWINISM NOT FINALLY REFUTABLE

Do not too hastily say that this is inconceivable. To Circumstantial Selection all mechanical and chemical reactions are possible, provided you accept the geologists' estimates of the great age of the earth, and therefore allow time enough for the circumstances to operate. It is true that mere survival of the fittest in the struggle for existence plus sexual selection fail as hopelessly to account for Darwin's own life work as for my conquest of the bicycle; but who can prove that there are not other soulless factors, unnoticed or undiscovered, which only require imagination enough to fit them to the evolution of an automatic Jesus or Shakespear? When a man tells you that you are a product of Circumstantial Selection solely, you cannot finally disprove it. You can only tell him out of the depths of your inner conviction that he is a fool and a liar. But as this, though British, is uncivil, it is wiser to offer him the counter-assurance that you are the product of Lamarckian evolution, formerly called Functional Adaptation and now Creative Evolution, and challenge him to disprove *that*, which he can no more do than you can disprove Circumstantial Selection, both forces being conceivably able to produce anything if you only give them rope enough. You may also defy him to act for a single hour on the assumption that he may safely cross Oxford Street in a state of unconsciousness, trusting to his dodging reflexes to react automatically and promptly enough to the visual impression produced by a motor bus, and the audile impression produced by its hooter. But if you allow yourself to defy him to explain any particular action of yours by Circumstantial Selection, he should always be able to find some explanation that will fit the case if only he is ingenious enough and goes far enough to find it. Darwin found several such explanations in his controversies. Anybody who really wants to believe that the universe has been produced by Circumstantial Selection co-operating with a force as inhuman as we conceive magnetism to be can find a logical excuse for his belief if he tries hard enough.

The stultification and damnation which ensued are illustrated by a comparison of the ease and certainty with which Butler's mind moved to humane and inspiring conclusions with the grotesque stupidities and cruelties of the idle and silly controversy which arose among the Darwinians as to whether acquired habits can be transmitted from parents to offspring. Consider, for example, how Weismann set to work on that subject. An Evolutionist with a live mind would first have dropped the popular expression "acquired habits," because to an Evolutionist there are no other habits and can be no others, a man being only an amœba with acquirements. He would then have considered carefully the process by which he himself had acquired his habits. He would have assumed that the habits with which he was born must have been acquired by a similar process. He would have known what a habit is: that is, an action voluntarily attempted until it has become more or less automatic and involuntary; and it would never have occurred to him that injuries or accidents coming from external sources against the will of the victim could possibly establish a habit: that, for instance, a family could acquire a habit of being killed in railway accidents.

And yet Weismann began to investigate the point by behaving like the butcher's wife in the old catch. He got a colony of mice, and cut off their tails. Then he waited to see whether their children would be born without tails. They were not, as Butler could have told him beforehand. He then cut off the children's tails, and waited to see whether the grandchildren would be born with at least rather short tails. They were not, as I could have told him beforehand. So with the patience and industry on which men of science pride themselves, he cut off the grandchildren's tails too, and waited, full of hope, for the birth of curtailed great-grandchildren. But their tails were quite up to the mark, as any fool could have told him beforehand. Weismann then gravely drew the inference that acquired habits cannot be transmitted. And yet Weismann was not a born imbecile. He was an exceptionally clever and studious man, not without roots of imagination and philosophy in him which Darwinism killed as weeds. How was it that he did not see that he was not experimenting with habits or characteristics at all? How had he overlooked the glaring fact that his experiment had been tried for many generations in China on the feet of Chinese women without producing the smallest tendency on their part to be born with abnormally small feet? He must have known about the bound feet even if he knew nothing of the mutilations, the clipped ears and docked tails, practised by dog fanciers and horse breeders on many generations of the unfortunate animals they deal in. Such amazing blindness and stupidity on the part of a man who was naturally neither blind nor stupid is a telling illustration of what Darwin unintentionally did to the minds of his disciples by turning their attention so exclusively towards the part played in Evolution by accident and violence operating with entire callousness to suffering and sentiment.

A vital conception of Evolution would have taught Weismann that biological problems are not to be solved by assaults on mice. The scientific form of his experiment would have been something like this. First, he should have procured a colony of mice highly susceptible to hypnotic suggestion. He should then have hypnotized them into an urgent conviction that the fate of the musque world depended on the disappearance of its tail, just as some ancient and forgotten experimenter seems to have convinced the cats of the Isle of Man. Having thus made the mice desire to lose their tails with a life-or-death intensity, he would very soon have seen a few mice born with little or no tail. These would be recognized by the other mice as superior beings, and privileged in the division of food and in sexual selection. Ultimately the tailed mice would be put to death as monsters by their fellows, and the miracle of the tailless mouse completely achieved.

The objection to this experiment is not that it seems too

funny to be taken seriously, and is not cruel enough to overawe the mob, but simply that it is impossible because the human experimenter cannot get at the mouse's mind. And that is what is wrong with all the barren cruelties of the laboratories. Darwin's followers did not think of this. Their only idea of investigation was to imitate "Nature" by perpetrating violent and senseless cruelties, and watch the effect of them with a paralyzing fatalism which forbade the smallest effort to use their minds instead of their knives and eyes, and established an abominable tradition that the man who hesitates to be as cruel as Circumstantial Selection itself is a traitor to science. For Weismann's experiment upon the mice was a mere joke compared to the atrocities committed by other Darwinians in their attempts to prove that mutilations could not be transmitted. No doubt the worst of these experiments were not really experiments at all, but cruelties committed by cruel men who were attracted to the laboratory by the fact that it was a secret refuge left by law and public superstition for the amateur of passionate torture. But there is no reason to suspect Weismann of Sadism. Cutting off the tails of several generations of mice is not voluptuous enough to tempt a scientific Nero. It was a mere piece of one-eyedness; and it was Darwin who put out Weismann's humane and sensible eye. He blinded many another eye and paralyzed many another will also. Ever since he set up Circumstantial Selection as the creator and ruler of the universe, the scientific world has been the very citadel of stupidity and cruelty. Fearful as the tribal god of the Hebrews was, nobody ever shuddered as they passed even his meanest and narrowest Little Bethel or his proudest war-consecrating cathedral as we shudder now when we pass a physiological laboratory. If we dreaded and mistrusted the priest, we could at least keep him out of the house; but what of the modern Darwinist surgeon whom we dread and mistrust ten times more, but into whose hands we must all give ourselves from time to time? Miserably as religion had been debased, it did at least still proclaim that our relation to one another was that of a fellowship in which we were all equal and members one of another before the judgment-seat of our common father. Darwinism proclaimed that our true relation is that of competitors and combatants in a struggle for mere survival, and that every act of pity or loyalty to the old fellowship is a vain and mischievous attempt to lessen the severity of the struggle and preserve inferior varieties from the efforts of Nature to weed them out. Even in Socialist Societies which existed solely to substitute the law of fellowship for the law of competition, and the method of providence and wisdom for the method of rushing violently down a steep place into the sea, I found myself regarded as a blasphemer and an ignorant sentimentalist because whenever the Neo-Darwinian doctrine was preached there I made no attempt to conceal my intellectual contempt for its blind coarseness and shallow logic, or my natural abhorrence of its sickening inhumanity.

THE GREATEST OF THESE IS SELF-CONTROL

As there is no place in Darwinism for free will, or any other sort of will, the Neo-Darwinists held that there is no such thing as self-control. Yet self-control is just the one quality of survival value which Circumstantial Selection must invariably and inevitably develop in the long run. Uncontrolled qualities may be selected for survival and development for certain periods and under certain circumstances. For instance, since it is the ungovernable gluttons who strive the hardest to get food and drink, their efforts would develop their strength and cunning in a period of such scarcity that the utmost they could do would not enable them to over-eat themselves. But a change of circumstances involving a plentiful supply of food would destroy them. We see this very thing happening often enough in the case of the healthy and vigorous poor man who becomes a millionaire by one of the accidents of our competitive commerce, and immediately proceeds to dig his grave with his teeth. But the self-controlled man survives all such changes of circumstance, because he adapts himself to them, and eats neither as much as he can hold nor as little as he can scrape along on, but as much as is good for him. What *is* self-control? It is nothing but a highly developed vital sense, dominating and regulating the mere appetites. To overlook the very existence of this supreme sense; to miss the obvious inference that it is the quality that distinguishes the fittest to survive; to omit, in short, the highest moral claim of Evolutionary Selection: all this, which the Neo-Darwinians did in the name of Natural Selection, shewed the most pitiable want of mastery of their own subject, the dullest lack of observation of the forces upon which Natural Selection works.

A SAMPLE OF LAMARCKO-SHAVIAN INVECTIVE

The Vitalist philosophers made no such mistakes. Nietzsche, for example, thinking out the great central truth of the Will to Power instead of cutting off mouse-tails, had no difficulty in concluding that the final objective of this Will was power over self, and that the seekers after power over others and material possessions were on a false scent.

The stultification naturally became much worse as the first Darwinians died out. The prestige of these pioneers, who had the older evolutionary culture to build on, and were in fact no more Darwinian in the modern sense than Darwin himself, ceased to dazzle us when Huxley and Tyndall and Spencer and Darwin passed away, and we were left with the smaller people who began with Darwin and took in nothing else. Accordingly, I find that in the year 1906 I indulged my temper by hurling invectives at the Neo-Darwinians in the following terms.

"I really do not wish to be abusive; but when I think of these poor little dullards, with their precarious hold of just that corner of evolution that a blackbeetle can understand —with their retinue of twopenny-halfpenny Torquemadas wallowing in the infamies of the vivisector's laboratory, and solemnly offering us as epoch-making discoveries their demonstrations that dogs get weaker and die if you give them no food; that intense pain makes mice sweat; and that if you cut off a dog's leg the three-legged dog will have a four-legged puppy, I ask myself what spell has fallen on intelligent and humane men that they allow themselves to be imposed on by this rabble of dolts, blackguards, impostors, quacks, liars, and, worst of all, credulous conscientious fools. Better a thousand times Moses and Spurgeon [a then famous preacher] back again. After all, you cannot understand Moses without imagination nor Spurgeon without metaphysics; but you can be a thorough-going Neo-Darwinian without imagination, metaphysics, poetry, conscience, or decency. For 'Natural Selection' has no moral significance: it deals with that part of evolution which has no purpose, no intelligence, and might more appropriately be called accidental selection, or better still, Unnatural Selection, since nothing is more unnatural than an accident. If it could be proved that the whole universe had been produced by such Selection, only fools and rascals could bear to live."

THE HUMANITARIANS AND THE PROBLEM OF EVIL

Yet the humanitarians were as delighted as anybody with Darwinism at first. They had been perplexed by the Problem of Evil and the Cruelty of Nature. They were Shelleyists, but not atheists. Those who believed in God were at a terrible disadvantage with the atheist. They could not deny the existence of natural facts so cruel that to attribute them to the will of God is to make God a demon. Belief in God was impossible to any thoughtful person without belief in the Devil as well. The painted Devil, with his horns, his barbed tail, and his abode of burning brimstone, was an incredible bogey; but the evil attributed to him was real enough; and the atheists argued that the author of evil, if he exists, must be strong enough to overcome God, else God is morally responsible for everything he permits the Devil to do. Neither conclusion delivered us from the horror of attributing the cruelty of nature to the workings of an evil will, or could reconcile it with our impulses towards justice, mercy, and a higher life.

A complete deliverance was offered by the discovery of Circumstantial Selection: that is to say, of a method by which horrors having every appearance of being elaborately planned by some intelligent contriver are only accidents without any moral significance at all. Suppose a watcher from the stars saw a frightful accident produced by two crowded trains at full speed crashing into one another! How could he conceive that a catastrophe brought about by such elaborate machinery, such ingenious preparation, such skilled direction, such vigilant industry, was quite unintentional? Would he not conclude that the signal-men were devils?

Well, Circumstantial Selection is largely a theory of collisions: that is, a theory of the innocence of much apparently designed devilry. In this way Darwin brought intense relief as well as an enlarged knowledge of facts to the humanitarians. He destroyed the omnipotence of God for them; but he also exonerated God from a hideous charge of cruelty. Granted that the comfort was shallow, and that deeper reflection was bound to shew that worse than all conceivable devil-deities is a blind, deaf, dumb, heartless, senseless mob of forces that strike as a tree does when it is blown down by the wind, or as the tree itself is struck by lightning. That did not occur to the humanitarians at the moment: people do not reflect deeply when they are in the first happiness of escape from an intolerably oppressive situation. Like Bunyan's pilgrim they could not see the wicket gate, nor the Slough of Despond, nor the castle of Giant Despair; but they saw the shining light at the end of the path, and so started gaily towards it as Evolutionists.

And they were right; for the problem of evil yields very easily to Creative Evolution. If the driving power behind Evolution is omnipotent only in the sense that there seems no limit to its final achievement; and if it must meanwhile struggle with matter and circumstance by the method of trial and error, then the world must be full of its unsuccessful experiments. Christ may meet a tiger, or a High Priest arm-in-arm with a Roman Governor, and be the unfittest to survive under the circumstances. Mozart may have a genius that prevails against Emperors and Archbishops, and a lung that succumbs to some obscure and noxious property of foul air. If all our calamities are either accidents or sincerely repented mistakes, there is no malice in the Cruelty of Nature and no Problem of Evil in the Victorian sense at all. The theology of the women who told us that they became atheists when they sat by the cradles of their children and saw them strangled by the hand of God is succeeded by the theology of Blanco Posnet, with his "It was early days when He made the croup, I guess. It was the best He could think of then; but when it turned out wrong on His hands He made you and me to fight the croup for Him."

HOW ONE TOUCH OF DARWIN MAKES THE WHOLE WORLD KIN

Another humanitarian interest in Darwinism was that Darwin popularized Evolution generally, as well as making his own special contribution to it. Now the general conception of Evolution provides the humanitarian with a scientific basis, because it establishes the fundamental equality of all living things. It makes the killing of an animal murder in exactly the same sense as the killing of a man is murder. It is sometimes necessary to kill men as it is always necessary to kill tigers; but the old theoretic distinction between the two acts has been obliterated by Evolution. When I was a child and was told that our dog and our parrot, with whom I was on intimate terms, were not creatures like myself, but were brutal whilst I was reasonable, I not only did not believe it, but quite consciously and intellectually formed the opinion that the distinction was false; so that afterwards, when Darwin's views were first unfolded to me, I promptly said that I had found out all that for myself before I was ten years old; and I am far from sure that my youthful arrogance was not justified; for this sense of the kinship of all forms of life is all that is needed to make Evolution not only a conceivable theory, but an inspiring one. St Anthony was ripe for the Evolution theory when he preached to the fishes, and St Francis when he called the birds his little brothers. Our vanity, and our snobbish conception of Godhead as being, like earthly kingship, a supreme class distinction instead of the rock on which Equality is built, had led us to insist on God offering us special terms by placing us apart from and above all the rest of his creatures. Evolution took that conceit out of us; and now, though we may kill a flea without the smallest remorse, we at all events know that we are killing our cousin. No doubt it shocks the flea when the creature that an almighty Celestial Flea created expressly for the food of fleas, destroys the jumping lord of creation with his sharp and enormous thumbnail; but no flea will ever be so foolish as to preach that in slaying fleas Man is applying a method of Natural Selection which will finally evolve a flea so swift that no man can catch him, and so hardy of constitution that Insect Powder will have no more effect on him than strychnine on an elephant.

WHY DARWIN PLEASED THE SOCIALISTS

The Humanitarians were not alone among the agitators in their welcome to Darwin. He had the luck to please everybody who had an axe to grind. The Militarists were as enthusiastic as the Humanitarians, the Socialists as the Capitalists. The Socialists were specially encouraged by Darwin's insistence on the influence of environment. Perhaps the strongest moral bulwark of Capitalism is the belief in the efficacy of individual righteousness. Robert Owen made desperate efforts to convince England that her criminals, her drunkards, her ignorant and stupid masses, were the victims of circumstance: that if we would only establish his new moral world we should find that the masses born into an educated and moralized community would be themselves educated and moralized. The stock reply to this is to be found in Lewes's Life of Goethe. Lewes scorned the notion that circumstances govern character. He pointed to the variety of character in the governing rich class to prove the contrary. Similarity of circumstance can hardly be carried to a more desolating dead level than in the case of the individuals who are born and bred in English country houses, and sent first to Eton or Harrow, and then to Cxford or Cambridge, to have their minds and habits formed. Such a routine would destroy individuality if anything could. Yet individuals come out from it as different as Pitt from Fox, as Lord Russell from Lord Curzon, as Mr Winston Churchill from Lord Robert Cecil. This acceptance of the congenital character of the individual as the determining factor in his destiny had been reinforced by the Lamarckian view of Evolution. If the giraffe can develop his neck by wanting and trying, a man can develop his character in the same way. The old saying, "Where there is a will, there is a way," condenses Lamarck's theory of functional adaptation into a proverb. This felt bracingly moral to strong minds, and reassuringly pious to feeble ones. There was no more effective retort to the Socialist than to tell him to reform himself before he pretends to reform society. If you were rich, how pleasant it was to feel that you owed your riches to the superiority of your own character! The industrial revolution had turned numbers of greedy dullards into monstrously rich men. Nothing could be more humiliating and threatening to them than the view that the falling of a shower of gold into their pockets was as pure an accident as the falling of a shower of hail on their umbrellas, and happened alike to the just and unjust. Nothing could be more flattering and fortifying to them than the assumption that they were rich because they were virtuous.

Now Darwinism made a clean sweep of all such self-righteousness. It more than justified Robert Owen by discovering in the environment of an organism an influence on it more potent than Owen had ever claimed. It implied that street arabs are produced by slums and not by original sin: that prostitutes are produced by starvation wages and not by feminine concupiscence. It threw the authority of science on the side of the Socialist who said that he who would reform himself must first reform society. It suggested that if we want healthy and wealthy citizens we must have healthy and wealthy towns; and that these can exist only in healthy and wealthy countries. It could be led to the conclusion that the type of character which remains indifferent to the welfare of its neighbors as long as its own personal appetite is satisfied is the disastrous type, and the type which is deeply concerned about its environment the only possible type for a permanently prosperous community. It shewed that the surprising changes which Robert Owen had produced in factory children by a change in their circumstances which does not seem any too generous to us nowadays, were as nothing to the changes—changes not only of habits but of species, not only of species but of orders—which might conceivably be the work of environment acting on individuals without any character or intellectual consciousness whatever. No wonder the Socialists received Darwin with open arms.

DARWIN AND KARL MARX

Besides, the Socialists had an evolutionary prophet of their own, who had discredited Manchester as Darwin discredited the Garden of Eden. Karl Marx had proclaimed in his Communist Manifesto of 1848 (now enjoying Scriptural authority in Russia) that civilization is an organism evolving irresistibly by circumstantial selection; and he published the first volume of his Das Kapital in 1867. The revolt against anthropomorphic idolatry, which was, as we have seen, the secret of Darwin's success, had been accompanied by a revolt against the conventional respectability which covered not only the brigandage and piracy of the feudal barons, but the hypocrisy, inhumanity, snobbery, and greed of the bourgeoisie, who were utterly corrupted by an essentially diabolical identification of success in life with big profits. The moment Marx shewed that the relation of the bourgeoisie to society was grossly immoral and disastrous, and that the whited wall of starched shirt fronts concealed and defended the most infamous of all tyrannies and the basest of all robberies, he became an inspired prophet in the mind of every generous soul whom his book reached. He had said and proved what they wanted to have proved; and they would hear nothing against him. Now Marx was by no means infallible: his economics, half borrowed, and half home-made by a literary amateur, were not, when strictly followed up, even favorable to Socialism. His theory of civilization had been promulgated already in Buckle's History of Civilization, a book as epoch-making in the minds of its readers as Das Kapital. There was nothing about Socialism in the widely read first volume of Das Kapital: every reference it made to workers and capitalists shewed that Marx had never breathed industrial air, and had dug his case out of bluebooks in the British Museum. Compared to Darwin, he seemed to have no power of observation: there was not a fact in Das Kapital that had not been taken out of a book, nor a discussion that had not been opened by somebody else's pamphlet. No matter: he exposed the bourgeoisie and made an end of its moral prestige. That was enough: like Darwin he had for the moment the World Will by the ear. Marx had, too, what Darwin had not: implacability and a fine Jewish literary gift, with terrible powers of hatred, invective, irony, and all the bitter qualities bred, first in the oppression of a rather pampered young genius (Marx was the spoilt child of a well-to-do family) by a social system utterly uncongenial to him, and later on by exile and poverty. Thus Marx and Darwin between them toppled over two closely related idols, and became the prophets of two new creeds.

WHY DARWIN PLEASED THE PROFITEERS ALSO

But how, at this rate, did Darwin succeed with the capitalists too? It is not easy to make the best of both worlds when one of the worlds is preaching a Class War, and the other vigorously practising it. The explanation is that Darwinism was so closely related to Capitalism that Marx regarded it as an economic product rather than as a biological theory. Darwin got his main postulate, the pressure of population on the available means of subsistence, from the treatise of Malthus on Population, just as he got his other postulate of a practically unlimited time for that pressure to operate from the geologist Lyell, who made an end of Archbishop Ussher's Biblical estimate of the age of the earth as 4004 B.C. plus A.D. The treatises of the Ricardian economists on the Law of Diminishing Return, which was only the Manchester School's version of the giraffe and the trees, were all very fiercely discussed when Darwin was a young man. In fact the discovery in the eighteenth century by the French Physiocrats of the economic effects of Commercial Selection in soils and sites, and by Malthus of a competition for subsistence which he attributed to pressure of population on available subsistence, had already brought political science into that unbreathable atmosphere of fatalism which is the characteristic blight of Darwinism. Long before Darwin published a line, the Ricardo-Malthusian economists were preaching the fatalistic Wages Fund doctrine, and assuring the workers that Trade Unionism is a vain defiance of the inexorable laws of political economy, just as the Neo-Darwinians were presently assuring us that Temperance Legislation is a vain defiance of Natural Selection, and that the true way to deal with drunkenness is to flood the country with cheap gin and let the fittest survive. Cobdenism is, after all, nothing but the abandonment of trade to Circumstantial Selection.

It is hardly possible to exaggerate the importance of this preparation for Darwinism by a vast political and clerical propaganda of its moral atmosphere. Never in history, as far as we know, had there been such a determined, richly subsidized, politically organized attempt to persuade the human race that all progress, all prosperity, all salvation, individual and social, depend on an unrestrained conflict for food and money, on the suppression and elimination of the weak by the strong, on Free Trade, Free Contract, Free Competition, Natural Liberty, Laisser-faire: in short, on "doing the other fellow down" with impunity, all interference by a guiding government, all organization except police organization to protect legalized fraud against fisticuffs, all attempt to introduce human purpose and design and forethought into the industrial welter being "contrary to the laws of political economy." Even the proletariat sympathized, though to them Capitalist liberty meant only wage slavery without the legal safeguards of chattel slavery. People were tired of governments and kings and priests and providences, and wanted to find out how Nature would arrange matters if she were let alone. And they found it out to their cost in the days when Lancashire used up nine generations of wage slaves in one generation of their masters. But their masters, becoming richer and richer, were very well satisfied; and Bastiat proved convincingly that Nature had arranged Economic Harmonies which would settle social questions far better than theocracies or aristocracies or mobocracies, the real *deus ex machina* being unrestrained plutocracy.

THE POETRY AND PURITY OF MATERIALISM

Thus the stars in their courses fought for Darwin. Every faction drew a moral from him; every catholic hater of faction founded a hope on him; every blackguard felt justified by him; and every saint felt encouraged by him. The notion that any harm could come of so splendid an enlightenment seemed as silly as the notion that the atheists would steal all our spoons. The physicists went further than the Darwinians. Tyndall declared that he saw in Matter the promise and potency of all forms of life, and with his Irish graphic lucidity made a picture of a world of magnetic atoms, each atom with a positive and a negative pole, arranging itself by attraction and repulsion in orderly crystalline structure. Such a picture is dangerously fascinating to thinkers oppressed by the bloody disorders of the living world. Craving for purer subjects of thought, they find in the contemplation of crystals and magnets a happiness more dramatic and less childish than the happiness found by the mathematicians in abstract numbers, because they see in the crystals beauty and movement without the corrupting appetites of fleshly vitality. In such Materialism as that of Lucretius and Tyndall there is a nobility which produces poetry: John Davidson found his highest inspiration in it. Even its pessimism as it faces the cooling of the sun and the return of the ice-caps does not degrade the pessimist: for example, the Quincy Adamses, with their insistence on modern democratic degradation as an inevitable result of solar shrinkage, are not dehumanized as the vivisectionists are. Perhaps nobody is at heart fool enough to believe that life is at the mercy of temperature: Dante was not troubled by the objection that Brunetto could not have lived in the fire nor Ugolino in the ice.

But the physicists found their intellectual vision of the world incommunicable to those who were not born with it. It came to the public simply as Materialism; and Materialism lost its peculiar purity and dignity when it entered into the Darwinian reaction against Bible fetichism. Between the two of them religion was knocked to pieces; and where there had been a god, a cause, a faith that the universe was ordered however inexplicable by us its order might be, and therefore a sense of moral responsibility as part of that order, there was now an utter void. Chaos had come again. The first effect was exhilarating: we had the runaway child's sense of freedom before it gets hungry and lonely and frightened. In this phase we did not desire our God back again. We printed the verses in which William Blake, the most religious of our great poets, called the anthropomorphic idol Old Nobodaddy, and gibed at him in terms which the printer had to leave us to guess from his blank spaces. We had heard the parson droning that God is not mocked; and it was great fun to mock Him to our hearts' content and not be a penny the worse. It did not occur to us that Old Nobodaddy, instead of being a ridiculous fiction, might be only an impostor, and that the exposure of this Koepenik Captain of the heavens, far from proving that there was no real captain, rather proved the contrary: that, in short, Nobodaddy could not have impersonated anybody if there had not been Somebodaddy to impersonate. We did not see the significance of the fact that on the last occasion on which God had been "expelled with a pitchfork," men so different as Voltaire and Robespierre had said, the one that if God did not exist it would be necessary to invent him, and the other that after an honest attempt to dispense with a Supreme Being in practical politics, some such hypothesis had been found quite indispensable, and could not be replaced by a mere Goddess of Reason. If these two opinions were quoted at all, they were quoted as jokes at the expense of Nobodaddy. We were quite sure for the moment that whatever lingering superstition might have daunted these men of the eighteenth century, we Darwinians could do without God, and had made a good riddance of him.

THE VICEROYS OF THE KING OF KINGS

Now in politics it is much easier to do without God than to do without his viceroys and vicars and lieutenants; and we begin to miss the lieutenants long before we begin to miss their principal. Roman Catholics do what their confessors advise without troubling God; and Royalists are content to worship the King and ask the policeman. But God's trustiest lieutenants often lack official credentials. They may be professed atheists who are also men of honor and high public spirit. The old belief that it matters dreadfully to God whether a man thinks himself an atheist or not, and that the extent to which it matters can be stated with exactness as one single damn, was an error: for the divinity is in the honor and public spirit, not in the mouthed *credo* or *non credo*. The consequences of this error became grave when the fitness of a man for public trust was tested, not by his honor and public spirit, but by asking him whether he believed in Nobodaddy or not. If he said yes, he was held fit to be a Prime Minister, though, as our ablest Churchman has said, the real implication was that he was either a fool, a bigot, or a liar. Darwin destroyed this test; but when it was only thoughtlessly dropped, there was no test at all; and the door to public trust was open to the man who had no sense of God because he had no sense of anything beyond his own business interests and personal appetites and ambitions. As a result, the people who did not feel in the least inconvenienced by being no longer governed by Nobodaddy soon found themselves very acutely inconvenienced by being governed by fools and commercial adventurers. They had forgotten not only God but Goldsmith, who had warned them that "honor sinks where commerce long prevails."

The lieutenants of God are not always persons: some of them are legal and parliamentary fictions. One of them is Public Opinion. The pre-Darwinian statesman and publicists were not restrained directly by God; but they restrained themselves by setting up an image of a Public Opinion which would not tolerate any attempt to tamper with British liberties. Their favorite way of putting it was that any Government which proposed such and such an infringement of such and such a British liberty would be hurled from office in a week. This was not true: there was no such public opinion, no limit to what the British people would put up with in the abstract, and no hardship short of immediate and sudden starvation that it would not and did not put up with in the concrete. But this very helplessness of the people had forced their rulers to pretend that they were not helpless, and that the certainty of a sturdy and unconquerable popular resistance forbade any trifling with Magna Carta or the Petition of Rights or the authority of parliament. Now the reality behind this fiction was the divine sense that liberty is a need vital to human growth. Accordingly, though it was difficult enough to effect a political reform, yet, once parliament had passed it, its wildest opponent had no hope that the Government would cancel it, or shelve it, or be bought off from executing it. From Walpole to Campbell-

Bannerman there was no Prime Minister to whom such renagueing or trafficking would ever have occurred, though there were plenty who employed corruption unsparingly to procure the votes of members of parliament for their policy.

POLITICAL OPPORTUNISM IN EXCELSIS

The moment Nobodaddy was slain by Darwin, Public Opinion, as divine deputy, lost its sanctity. Politicians no longer told themselves that the British public would never suffer this or that: they allowed themselves to know that for their own personal purposes, which are limited to their ten or twenty years on the front benches in parliament, the British Public can be humbugged and coerced into believing and suffering everything that it pays to impose on them, and that any false excuse for an unpopular step will serve if it can be kept in countenance for a fortnight: that is, until the terms of the excuse are forgotten. The people, untaught or mistaught, are so ignorant and incapable politically that this in itself would not greatly matter; for a statesman who told them the truth would not be understood, and would in effect mislead them more completely than if he dealt with them according to their blindness instead of to his own wisdom. But though there is no difference in this respect between the best demagogue and the worst, both of them having to present their cases equally in terms of melodrama, there is all the difference in the world between the statesman who is humbugging the people into allowing him to do the will of God, in whatever disguise it may come to him, and one who is humbugging them into furthering his personal ambition and the commercial interests of the plutocrats who own the newspapers and support him on reciprocal terms. And there is almost as great a difference between the statesman who does this naïvely and automatically, or even does it telling himself that he is ambitious and selfish and unscrupulous, and the one who does it on principle, believing that if everyone takes the line of least material resistance the result will be the survival of the fittest in a perfectly harmonious universe. Once produce an atmosphere of fatalism on principle, and it matters little what the opinions or superstitions of the individual statesmen concerned may be. A Kaiser who is a devout reader of sermons, a Prime Minister who is an emotional singer of hymns, and a General who is a bigoted Roman Catholic may be the executants of the policy; but the policy itself will be one of unprincipled opportunism; and all the Governments will be like the tramp who walks always with the wind and ends as a pauper, or the stone that rolls down the hill and ends as an avalanche: their way is the way to destruction.

THE BETRAYAL OF WESTERN CIVILIZATION

Within sixty years from the publication of Darwin's Origin of Species political opportunism had brought parliaments into contempt; created a popular demand for direct action by the organized industries ("Syndicalism"); and wrecked the centre of Europe in a paroxysm of that chronic terror of one another, that cowardice of the irreligious, which, masked in the bravado of militarist patriotism, had ridden the Powers like a nightmare since the Franco-Prussian war of 1870-71. The sturdy old cosmopolitan Liberalism vanished almost unnoticed. At the present moment all the new ordinances for the government of our Crown Colonies contain, as a matter of course, prohibitions of all criticism, spoken or written, of their ruling officials, which would have scandalized George III and elicited Liberal pamphlets from Catherine II. Statesmen are afraid of the suburbs, of the newspapers, of the profiteers, of the diplomatists, of the militarists, of the country houses, of the trade unions, of everything ephemeral on earth except the revolutions they are provoking; and they would be afraid of these if they were not too ignorant of society and history to appreciate the risk, and to know that a revolution always seems hopeless and impossible the day before it breaks out, and indeed never does break out until it seems hopeless and impossible; for rulers who think it possible take care to insure the risk by ruling reasonably. This brings about a condition fatal to all political stability: namely, that you never know where to have the politicians. If the fear of God was in them it might be possible to come to some general understanding as to what God disapproves of; and Europe might pull together on that basis. But the present panic, in which Prime Ministers drift from election to election, either fighting or running away from everybody who shakes a fist at them, makes a European civilization impossible. Such peace and prosperity as we enjoyed before the war depended on the loyalty of the Western States to their own civilization. That loyalty could find practical expression only in an alliance of the highly civilized Western Powers against the primitive tyrannies of the East. Britain, Germany, France, and the United States of America could have imposed peace on the world, and nursed modern civilization in Russia, Turkey, and the Balkans. Every meaner consideration should have given way to this need for the solidarity of the higher civilization. What actually happened was that France and England, through their clerks the diplomatists, made an alliance with Russia to defend themselves against Germany; Germany made an alliance with Turkey to defend herself against the three; and the two unnatural and suicidal combinations fell on one another in a war that came nearer to being a war of extermination than any wars since those of Timur the Tartar; whilst the United States held aloof as long as they could, and the other States either did the same or joined in the fray through compulsion, bribery, or their judgment as to which side their bread was buttered. And at the present moment, though the main fighting has ceased through the surrender of Germany on terms which the victors have never dreamt of observing, the extermination by blockade and famine, which was what forced Germany to surrender, still continues, although it is certain that if the vanquished starve the victors will starve too, and Europe will liquidate its affairs by going, not into bankruptcy, but into chaos.

Now all this, it will be noticed, was fundamentally nothing

but an idiotic attempt on the part of each belligerent State to secure for itself the advantage of the survival of the fittest through Circumstantial Selection. If the Western Powers had selected their allies in the Lamarckian manner intelligently, purposely, and vitally, *ad majorem Dei gloriam*, as what Nietzsche called good Europeans, there would have been a League of Nations and no war. But because the selection relied on was purely circumstantial opportunist selection, so that the alliances were mere marriages of convenience, they have turned out, not merely as badly as might have been expected, but far worse than the blackest pessimist had ever imagined possible.

CIRCUMSTANTIAL SELECTION IN FINANCE

How it will all end we do not yet know. When wolves combine to kill a horse, the death of the horse only sets them fighting one another for the choicest morsels. Men are no better than wolves if they have no better principles: accordingly, we find that the Armistice and the Treaty have not extricated us from the war. A handful of Serbian regicides flung us into it as a sporting navvy throws a bull pup at a cat; but the Supreme Council, with all its victorious legions and all its prestige, cannot get us out of it, though we are heartily sick and tired of the whole business, and know now very well that it should never have been allowed to happen. But we are helpless before a slate scrawled with figures of National Debts. As there is no money to pay them because it was all spent on the war (wars have to be paid for on the nail) the sensible thing to do is to wipe the slate and let the wrangling States distribute what they can spare, on the sound communist principle of from each according to his ability, to each according to his need. But no: we have no principles left, not even commercial ones; for what sane commercialist would decree that France must not pay for her failure to defend her own soil; that Germany must pay for her success in carrying the war into the enemy's country; and that as Germany has not the money to pay, and under our commercial system can make it only by becoming once more a commercial competitor of England and France, which neither of them will allow, she must borrow the money from England, or America, or even from France: an arrangement by which the victorious creditors will pay one another, and wait to get their money back until Germany is either strong enough to refuse to pay or ruined beyond the possibility of paying? Meanwhile Russia, reduced to a scrap of fish and a pint of cabbage soup a day, has fallen into the hands of rulers who perceive that Materialist Communism is at all events more effective than Materialist Nihilism, and are attempting to move in an intelligent and ordered manner, practising a very strenuous Intentional Selection of workers as fitter to survive than idlers; whilst the Western Powers are drifting and colliding and running on the rocks, in the hope that if they continue to do their worst they will get Naturally Selected for survival without the trouble of thinking about it.

THE HOMEOPATHIC REACTION AGAINST DARWINISM

When, like the Russians, our Nihilists have it urgently borne in on them, by the brute force of rising wages that never overtake rising prices, that they are being Naturally Selected for destruction, they will perhaps remember that "Dont Care came to a bad end," and begin to look round for a religion. And the whole purpose of this book is to shew them where to look. For, throughout all the godless welter of the infidel half-century, Darwinism has been acting not only directly but homeopathically, its poison rallying our vital forces not only to resist it and cast it out, but to achieve a new Reformation and put a credible and healthy religion in its place. Samuel Butler was the pioneer of the reaction as far as the casting out was concerned; but the issue was confused by the physiologists, who were divided on the question into Mechanists and Vitalists. The Mechanists said that life is nothing but physical and chemical action; that they have demonstrated this in many cases of so-called vital phenomena; and that there is no reason to doubt that with improved methods they will presently be able to demonstrate it in all of them. The Vitalists said that a dead body and a live one are physically and chemically identical, and that the difference can be accounted for only by the existence of a Vital Force. This seems simple; but the Anti-Mechanists objected to be called Vitalists (obviously the right name for them) on two contradictory grounds. First, that vitality is scientifically inadmissible, because it cannot be isolated and experimented with in the laboratory. Second, that force, being by definition anything that can alter the speed or direction of matter in motion (briefly, that can overcome inertia), is essentially a mechanistic conception. Here we had the New Vitalist only half extricated from the Old Mechanist, objecting to be called either, and unable to give a clear lead in the new direction. And there was a deeper antagonism. The Old Vitalists, in postulating a Vital Force, were setting up a comparatively mechanical conception as against the divine idea of the life breathed into the clay nostrils of Adam, whereby he became a living soul. The New Vitalists, filled by their laboratory researches with a sense of the miraculousness of life that went far beyond the comparatively uninformed imaginations of the authors of the Book of Genesis, regarded the Old Vitalists as Mechanists who had tried to fill up the gulf between life and death with an empty phrase denoting an imaginary physical force.

These professional faction fights are ephemeral, and need not trouble us here. The Old Vitalist, who was essentially a Materialist, has evolved into the New Vitalist, who is, as every genuine scientist must be, finally a metaphysician. And as the New Vitalist turns from the disputes of his youth to the future of his science, he will cease to boggle at the name Vitalist, or at the inevitable, ancient, popular, and quite correct use of the term Force to denote metaphysical as well as physical overcomers of inertia.

Since the discovery of Evolution as the method of the Life Force, the religion of metaphysical Vitalism has been gaining the definiteness and concreteness needed to make it assimilable by the educated critical man. But it has always been with us. The popular religions, disgraced by their Opportunist cardinals and bishops, have been kept in credit by canonized saints whose secret was their conception of themselves as the instruments and vehicles of divine power and aspiration: a conception which at moments becomes an actual experience of ecstatic possession by that power. And above and below all have been millions of humble and obscure persons, sometimes totally illiterate, sometimes unconscious of having any religion at all, sometimes believing in their simplicity that the gods and temples and priests of their district stood for their instinctive righteousness, who have kept sweet the tradition that good people follow a light that shines within and above and ahead of them, that bad people care only for themselves, and that the good are saved and blessed and the bad damned and miserable. Protestantism was a movement towards the pursuit of a light called an inner light because every man must see it with his own eyes and not take any priest's word for it or any Church's account of it. In short, there is no question of a new religion, but rather of redistilling the eternal spirit of religion and thus extricating it from the sludgy residue of temporalities and legends that are making belief impossible, though they are the stock-in-trade of all the Churches and all the Schools.

RELIGION AND ROMANCE

It is the adulteration of religion by the romance of miracles and paradises and torture chambers that makes it reel at the impact of every advance in science, instead of being clarified by it. If you take an English village lad, and teach him that religion means believing that the stories of Noah's Ark and the Garden of Eden are literally true on the authority of God himself, and if that boy becomes an artisan and goes into the town among the sceptical city proletariat, then, when the jibes of his mates set him thinking, and he sees that these stories cannot be literally true, and learns that no candid prelate now pretends to believe them, he does not make any fine distinctions: he declares at once that religion is a fraud, and parsons and teachers hypocrites and liars. He becomes indifferent to religion if he has little conscience, and indignantly hostile to it if he has a good deal.

The same revolt against wantonly false teaching is happening daily in the professional classes whose recreation is reading and whose intellectual sport is controversy. They banish the Bible from their houses, and sometimes put into the hands of their unfortunate children Ethical and Rationalist tracts of the deadliest dullness, compelling these wretched infants to sit out the discourses of Secularist lecturers (I have delivered some of them myself), who bore them at a length now forbidden by custom in the established pulpit. Our minds have reacted so violently towards provable logical theorems and demonstrable mechanical or chemical facts that we have become incapable of metaphysical truth, and try to cast out incredible and silly lies by credible and clever ones, calling in Satan to cast out Satan, and getting more into his clutches than ever in the process. Thus the world is kept sane less by the saints than by the vast mass of the indifferent, who neither act nor react in the matter. Butler's preaching of the gospel of Laodicea was a piece of common sense founded on his observation of this.

But indifference will not guide nations through civilization to the establishment of the perfect city of God. An indifferent statesman is a contradiction in terms; and a statesman who is indifferent on principle, a Laisser-faire or Muddle-Through doctrinaire, plays the deuce with us in the long run. Our statesmen must get a religion by hook or crook; and as we are committed to Adult Suffrage it must be a religion capable of vulgarization. The thought first put into words by the Mills when they said "There is no God; but this is a family secret," and long held unspoken by aristocratic statesmen and diplomatists, will not serve now; for the revival of civilization after the war cannot be effected by artificial breathing: the driving force of an undeluded popular consent is indispensable, and will be impossible until the statesman can appeal to the vital instincts of the people in terms of a common religion. The success of the Hang the Kaiser cry at the last General Election shews us very terrifyingly how a common irreligion can be used by myopic demagogy; and common irreligion will destroy civilization unless it is countered by common religion.

THE DANGER OF REACTION

And here arises the danger that when we realize this we shall do just what we did half a century ago, and what Pliable did in The Pilgrim's Progress when Christian landed him in the Slough of Despond: that is, run back in terror to our old superstitions. We jumped out of the frying-pan into the fire; and we are just as likely to jump back again, now that we feel hotter than ever. History records very little in the way of mental activity on the part of the mass of mankind except a series of stampedes from affirmative errors into negative ones and back again. It must therefore be said very precisely and clearly that the bankruptcy of Darwinism does not mean that Nobodaddy was Somebodaddy *with* "body, parts, and passions" after all; that the world was made in the year 4004 B.C.; that damnation means an eternity of blazing brimstone; that the Immaculate Conception means that sex is sinful and that Christ was parthenogenetically brought forth by a virgin descended in like manner from a line of virgins right back to Eve; that the Trinity is an anthropomorphic monster with three heads which are yet only one head; that in Rome the bread and wine on the altar become flesh and blood, and in England, in a still more mystical manner, they do and they do not; that the Bible is an infallible scientific manual, an accurate historical chronicle, and a complete guide to conduct; that we may lie and cheat and murder and then wash ourselves innocent in the blood of the lamb on Sunday at the cost of a *credo* and a penny in the plate, and so on and so forth. Civilization cannot be saved by people not only crude enough to believe these things, but irreligious enough to believe that such belief constitutes a religion. The education of children cannot safely be left in their hands. If dwindling sects like the

Church of England, the Church of Rome, the Greek Church, and the rest, persist in trying to cramp the human mind within the limits of these grotesque perversions of natural truths and poetic metaphors, then they must be ruthlessly banished from the schools until they either perish in general contempt or discover the soul that is hidden in every dogma. The real Class War will be a war of intellectual classes; and its conquest will be the souls of the children.

A TOUCHSTONE FOR DOGMA

The test of a dogma is its universality. As long as the Church of England preaches a single doctrine that the Brahman, the Buddhist, the Mussulman, the Parsee, and all the other sectarians who are British subjects cannot accept, it has no legitimate place in the counsels of the British Commonwealth, and will remain what it is at present, a corrupter of youth, a danger to the State, and an obstruction to the fellowship of the Holy Ghost. This has never been more strongly felt than at present, after a war in which the Church failed grossly in the courage of its profession, and sold its lilies for the laurels of the soldiers of the Victoria Cross. All the cocks in Christendom have been crowing shame on it ever since; and it will not be spared for the sake of the two or three faithful who were found even among the bishops. Let the Church take it on authority, even my authority (as a professional legend maker) if it cannot see the truth by its own light: no dogma can be a legend. A legend can pass an ethnical frontier as a legend, but not as a truth; whilst the only frontier to the currency of a sound dogma as such is the frontier of capacity for understanding it.

This does not mean that we should throw away legend and parable and drama: they are the natural vehicles of dogma; but woe to the Churches and rulers who substitute the legend for the dogma, the parable for the history, the drama for the religion! Better by far declare the throne of God empty than set a liar and a fool on it. What are called wars of religion are always wars to destroy religion by affirming the historical truth or material substantiality of some legend, and killing those who refuse to accept it as historical or substantial. But who has ever refused to accept a good legend with delight *as* a legend? The legends, the parables, the dramas, are among the choicest treasures of mankind. No one is ever tired of stories of miracles. In vain did Mahomet repudiate the miracles ascribed to him: in vain did Christ furiously scold those who asked him to give them an exhibition as a conjuror: in vain did the saints declare that God chose them not for their powers but for their weaknesses; that the humble might be exalted, and the proud rebuked. People will have their miracles, their stories, their heroes and heroines and saints and martyrs and divinities to exercise their gifts of affection, admiration, wonder, and worship, and their Judases and devils to enable them to be angry and yet feel that they do well to be angry. Every one of these legends is the common heritage of the human race; and there is only one inexorable condition attached to their healthy enjoyment, which is that no one shall believe them literally. The reading of stories and delighting in them made Don Quixote a gentleman: the believing them literally made him a madman who slew lambs instead of feeding them. In England today good books of Eastern religious legends are read eagerly; and Protestants and Atheists read Roman Catholic legends of the Saints with pleasure. But such fare is shirked by Indians and Roman Catholics. Freethinkers read the Bible: indeed they seem to be its only readers now except the reluctant parsons at the church lecterns, who communicate their discomfort to the congregation by gargling the words in their throats in an unnatural manner that is as repulsive as it is unintelligible. And this is because the imposition of the legends as literal truth at once changes them from parables into falsehoods. The feeling against the Bible has become so strong at last that educated people not only refuse to outrage their intellectual consciences by reading the legend of Noah's Ark, with its funny beginning about the animals and its exquisite end about the birds: they will not read even the chronicles of King David, which may very well be true, and are certainly more candid than the official biographies of our contemporary monarchs.

WHAT TO DO WITH THE LEGENDS

What we should do, then, is to pool our legends and make a delightful stock of religious folk-lore on an honest basis for all mankind. With our minds freed from pretence and falsehood we could enter into the heritage of all the faiths. China would share her sages with Spain, and Spain her saints with China. The Ulster man who now gives his son an unmerciful thrashing if the boy is so tactless as to ask how the evening and the morning could be the first day before the sun was created, or to betray an innocent calf-love for the Virgin Mary, would buy him a bookful of legends of the creation and of mothers of God from all parts of the world, and be very glad to find his laddie as interested in such things as in marbles or Police and Robbers. That would be better than beating all good feeling towards religion out of the child, and blackening his mind by teaching him that the worshippers of the holy virgins, whether of the Parthenon or St Peter's, are fire-doomed heathens and idolaters. All the sweetness of religion is conveyed to the world by the hands of story-tellers and image-makers. Without their fictions the truths of religion would for the multitude be neither intelligible nor even apprehensible; and the prophets would prophesy and the teachers teach in vain. And nothing stands between the people and the fictions except the silly falsehood that the fictions are literal truths, and that there is nothing in religion but fiction.

A LESSON FROM SCIENCE TO THE CHURCHES

Let the Churches ask themselves why there is no revolt against the dogmas of mathematics though there is one against the dogmas of religion. It is not that the mathematical dogmas are more comprehensible. The law of inverse squares is as incomprehensible to the common man as the Athanasian creed. It is not that science is free from legends, witchcraft, miracles, biographic boostings of quacks as heroes and saints, and of barren scoundrels as explorers and discoverers. On the contrary, the iconography and hagiology of Scientism are as copious as they are mostly squalid. But no student of science has yet been taught that specific gravity consists in the belief that Archimedes jumped out of his bath and ran naked through the streets of Syracuse shouting Eureka, Eureka, or that the law of inverse squares must be discarded if anyone can prove that Newton was never in an orchard in his life. When some unusually conscientious or enterprising bacteriologist reads the pamphlets of Jenner, and discovers that they might have been written by an ignorant but curious and observant nurserymaid, and could not possibly have been written by any person with a scientifically trained mind, he does not feel that the whole edifice of science has collapsed and crumbled, and that there is no such thing as smallpox. It may come to that yet; for hygiene, as it forces its way into our schools, is being taught as falsely as religion is taught there; but in mathematics and physics the faith is still kept pure, and you may take the law and leave the legends without suspicion of heresy. Accordingly, the tower of the mathematician stands unshaken whilst the temple of the priest rocks to its foundation.

THE RELIGIOUS ART OF THE TWENTIETH CENTURY

Creative Evolution is already a religion, and is indeed now unmistakably the religion of the twentieth century, newly arisen from the ashes of pseudo-Christianity, of mere scepticism, and of the soulless affirmations and blind negations of the Mechanists and Neo-Darwinians. But it cannot become a popular religion until it has its legends, its parables, its miracles. And when I say popular I do not mean apprehensible by villagers only. I mean apprehensible by Cabinet Ministers as well. It is unreasonable to look to the professional politician and administrator for light and leading in religion. He is neither a philosopher nor a prophet: if he were, he would be philosophizing and prophesying, and not neglecting both for the drudgery of practical government. Socrates and Coleridge did not remain soldiers, nor could John Stuart Mill remain the representative of Westminster in the House of Commons even when he was willing. The Westminster electors admired Mill for telling them that much of the difficulty of dealing with them arose from their being inveterate liars. But they would not vote a second time for the man who was not afraid to break the crust of mendacity on which they were all dancing; for it seemed to them that there was a volcanic abyss beneath, not having his philosophic conviction that the truth is the solidest standing ground in the end. Your front bench man will always be an exploiter of the popular religion or irreligion. Not being an expert, he must take it as he finds it; and before he can take it, he must have been told stories about it in his childhood and had before him all his life an elaborate iconography of it produced by writers, painters, sculptors, temple architects, and artists of all the higher sorts. Even if, as sometimes happens, he is a bit of an amateur in metaphysics as well as a professional politician, he must still govern according to the popular iconography, and not according to his own personal interpretations if these happen to be heterodox.

It will be seen then that the revival of religion on a scientific basis does not mean the death of art, but a glorious rebirth of it. Indeed art has never been great when it was not providing an iconography for a live religion. And it has never been quite contemptible except when imitating the iconography after the religion had become a superstition. Italian painting from Giotto to Carpaccio is all religious painting; and it moves us deeply and has real greatness. Compare with it the attempts of our painters a century ago to achieve the effects of the old masters by imitation when they should have been illustrating a faith of their own. Contemplate, if you can bear it, the dull daubs of Hilton and Haydon, who knew so much more about drawing and scumbling and glazing and perspective and anatomy and "marvellous foreshortening" than Giotto, the latchet of whose shoe they were nevertheless not worthy to unloose. Compare Mozart's Magic Flute, Beethoven's Ninth Symphony, Wagner's Ring, all of them reachings-forward to the new Vitalist art, with the dreary pseudo-sacred oratorios and cantatas which were produced for no better reason than that Handel had formerly made splendid thunder in that way, and with the stale confectionery, mostly too would-be pious to be even cheerfully toothsome, of Spohr and Mendelssohn, Stainer and Parry, which spread indigestion at our musical festivals until I publicly told Parry the bludgeoning truth about his Job and woke him to conviction of sin. Compare Flaxman and Thorwaldsen and Gibson with Phidias and Praxiteles, Stevens with Michael Angelo, Bouguereau's Virgin with Cimabue's, or the best operatic Christs of Scheffer and Müller with the worst Christs that the worst painters could paint before the end of the fifteenth century, and you must feel that until we have a great religious movement we cannot hope for a great artistic one. The disillusioned Raphael could paint a mother and child, but not a queen of Heaven as much less skilful men had done in the days of his great-grandfather; yet he could reach forward to the twentieth century and paint a Transfiguration of the Son of Man as they could not. Also, please note, he could decorate a house of pleasure for a cardinal very beautifully with voluptuous pictures of Cupid and Psyche; for this simple sort of Vitalism is always with us, and, like portrait painting, keeps the artist supplied with subject matter in the intervals between the ages of faith; so that your sceptical Rembrandts and Velasquezs are at least not compelled to paint shop fronts for want of anything else to paint in which they can really believe.

THE ARTIST-PROPHETS

And there are always certain rare but intensely interesting anticipations. Michael Angelo could not very well believe in Julius II or Leo X, or in much that they believed in; but he could paint the Superman three hundred years before Nietzsche wrote Also Sprach Zarathustra and Strauss set it to music. Michael Angelo won the primacy among all modern painters and sculptors solely by his power of shewing us superhuman persons. On the strength of his decoration and color alone he would hardly have survived his own death twenty years; and even his design would have had only an academic interest; but as a painter of prophets and sibyls he is greatest among the very greatest in his craft, because we aspire to a world of prophets and sibyls. Beethoven never heard of radio-activity nor of electrons dancing in vortices of inconceivable energy; but pray can anyone explain the last movement of his Hammerklavier Sonata, Opus 106, otherwise than as a musical picture of these whirling electrons? His contemporaries said he was mad, partly perhaps because the movement was so hard to play; but we, who can make a pianola play it to us over and over until it is as familiar as Pop Goes the Weasel, know that it is sane and methodical. As such, it must represent something; and as all Beethoven's serious compositions represent some process within himself, some nerve storm or soul storm, and the storm here is clearly one of physical movement, I should much like to know what other storm than the atomic storm could have driven him to this oddest of all those many expressions of cyclonic energy which have given him the same distinction among musicians that Michael Angelo has among draughtsmen.

In Beethoven's day the business of art was held to be "the sublime and beautiful." In our day it has fallen to be the imitative and voluptuous. In both periods the word passionate has been freely employed; but in the eighteenth century passion meant irresistible impulse of the loftiest kind: for example, a passion for astronomy or for truth. For us it has come to mean concupiscence and nothing else. One might say to the art of Europe what Antony said to the corpse of Cæsar: "Are all thy conquests, glories, triumphs, spoils, shrunk to this little measure?" But in fact it is the mind of Europe that has shrunk, being, as we have seen, wholly preoccupied with a busy spring-cleaning to get rid of its superstitions before readjusting itself to the new conception of Evolution.

EVOLUTION IN THE THEATRE

On the stage (and here I come at last to my own particular function in the matter), Comedy, as a destructive, derisory, critical, negative art, kept the theatre open when sublime tragedy perished. From Molière to Oscar Wilde we had a line of comedic playwrights who, if they had nothing fundamentally positive to say, were at least in revolt against falsehood and imposture, and were not only, as they claimed, "chastening morals by ridicule," but, in Johnson's phrase, clearing our minds of cant, and thereby shewing an uneasiness in the presence of error which is the surest symptom of intellectual vitality. Meanwhile the name of Tragedy was assumed by plays in which everyone was killed in the last act, just as, in spite of Molière, plays in which everyone was married in the last act called themselves comedies. Now neither tragedies nor comedies can be produced according to a prescription which gives only the last moments of the last act. Shakespear did not make Hamlet out of its final butchery, nor Twelfth Night out of its final matrimony. And he could not become the conscious iconographer of a religion because he had no conscious religion. He had therefore to exercise his extraordinary natural gifts in the very entertaining art of mimicry, giving us the famous "delineation of character" which makes his plays, like the novels of Scott, Dumas, and Dickens, so delightful. Also, he developed that curious and questionable art of building us a refuge from despair by disguising the cruelties of Nature as jokes. But with all his gifts, the fact remains that he never found the inspiration to write an original play. He furbished up old plays, and adapted popular stories, and chapters of history from Holinshed's Chronicle and Plutarch's biographies, to the stage. All this he did (or did not; for there are minus quantities in the algebra of art) with a recklessness which shewed that his trade lay far from his conscience. It is true that he never takes his characters from the borrowed story, because it was less trouble and more fun to him to create them afresh; but none the less he heaps the murders and villainies of the borrowed story on his own essentially gentle creations without scruple, no matter how incongruous they may be. And all the time his vital need for a philosophy drives him to seek one by the quaint professional method of introducing philosophers as characters into his plays, and even of making his heroes philosophers; but when they come on the stage they have no philosophy to expound: they are only pessimists and railers; and their occasional would-be philosophic speeches, such as The Seven Ages of Man and The Soliloquy on Suicide, shew how deeply in the dark Shakespear was as to what philosophy means. He forced himself in among the greatest of playwrights without having once entered that region in which Michael Angelo, Beethoven, Goethe, and the antique Athenian stage poets are great. He would really not be great at all if it were not that he had religion enough to be aware that his religionless condition was one of despair. His towering King Lear would be only a melodrama were it not for its express admission that if there is nothing more to be said of the universe than Hamlet has to say, then "as flies to wanton boys are we to the gods: they kill us for their sport."

Ever since Shakespear, playwrights have been struggling with the same lack of religion; and many of them were forced to become mere panders and sensation-mongers because, though they had higher ambitions, they could find no better subject matter. From Congreve to Sheridan they were so sterile in spite of their wit that they did not achieve between them the output of Molière's single lifetime; and they were all (not without reason) ashamed of their profession, and preferred to be regarded as mere men of fashion with a rakish hobby. Goldsmith's was the only saved soul in that pandemonium.

The leaders among my own contemporaries (now veterans) snatched at minor social problems rather than write entirely without any wider purpose than to win money and fame. One of them expressed to me his envy of the ancient Greek playwrights because the Athenians asked them, not for some "new and original" disguise of the half-dozen threadbare plots of the modern theatre, but for the deepest lesson they could draw from the familiar and sacred legends of their country. "Let us all," he said, "write an Electra, an Antigone, an Agamemnon, and shew what we can do with it." But he did not write any of them, because these legends are no longer religious: Aphrodite and Artemis and Poseidon are deader than their statues. Another, with a commanding position and every trick of British farce and Parisian drama at his fingers' ends, finally could not write without a sermon to preach, and yet could not find texts more fundamental than the hypocrisies of sham Puritanism, or the matrimonial speculation which makes our young actresses as careful of their reputations as of their complexions. A third, too tender-hearted to break our spirits with the realities of a bitter experience, coaxed a wistful pathos and a dainty fun out of the fairy cloudland that lay between him and the empty heavens. The giants of the theatre of our time, Ibsen and Strindberg, had no greater comfort for the world than we: indeed much less; for they refused us even the Shakespearian-Dickensian consolation of laughter at mischief, accurately called comic relief. Our emancipated young successors scorn us, very properly. But they will be able to do no better whilst the drama remains pre-Evolutionist. Let them consider the great exception of Goethe. He, no richer than Shakespear, Ibsen, or Strindberg in specific talent as a playwright, is in the empyrean whilst they are gnashing their teeth in impotent fury in the mud, or at best finding an acid enjoyment in the irony of their predicament. Goethe is Olympian: the other giants are infernal in everything but their veracity and their repudiation of the irreligion of their time: that is, they are bitter and hopeless. It is not a question of mere dates. Goethe was an Evolutionist in 1830: many playwrights, even young ones, are still untouched by Creative Evolution in 1920. Ibsen was Darwinized to the extent of exploiting heredity on the stage much as the ancient Athenian playwrights exploited the Eumenides; but there is no trace in his plays of any faith in or knowledge of Creative Evolution as a modern scientific fact. True, the poetic aspiration is plain enough in his Emperor or Galilean; but it is one of Ibsen's distinctions that nothing was valid for him but science; and he left that vision of the future which his Roman seer calls "the third Empire" behind him as a Utopian dream when he settled down to his serious grapple with realities in those plays of modern life with which he overcame Europe, and broke the dusty windows of every dry-rotten theatre in it from Moscow to Manchester.

MY OWN PART IN THE MATTER

In my own activities as a playwright I found this state of things intolerable. The fashionable theatre prescribed one serious subject: clandestine adultery: the dullest of all subjects for a serious author, whatever it may be for audiences who read the police intelligence and skip the reviews and leading articles. I tried slum-landlordism, doctrinaire Free Love (pseudo-Ibsenism), prostitution, militarism, marriage, history, current politics, natural Christianity, national and individual character, paradoxes of conventional society, husband-hunting, questions of conscience, professional delusions and impostures, all worked into a series of comedies of manners in the classic fashion, which was then very much out of fashion, the mechanical tricks of Parisian "construction" being *de rigueur* in the theatre. But this, though it occupied me and established me professionally, did not constitute me an iconographer of the religion of my time, and thus fulfil my natural function as an artist. I was quite conscious of this; for I had always known that civilization needs a religion as a matter of life or death; and as the conception of Creative Evolution developed I saw that we were at last within reach of a faith which complied with the first condition of all the religions that have ever taken hold of humanity: namely, that it must be, first and fundamentally, a science of metabiology. This was a crucial point with me; for I had seen Bible fetichism, after standing up to all the rationalistic batteries of Hume, Voltaire, and the rest, collapse before the onslaught of much less gifted Evolutionists, solely because they discredited it as a biological document; so that from that moment it lost its hold, and left literate Christendom faithless. My own Irish eighteenth-centuryism made it impossible for me to believe anything until I could conceive it as a scientific hypothesis, even though the abominations, quackeries, impostures, venalities, credulities, and delusions of the camp followers of science, and the brazen lies and priestly pretensions of the pseudo-scientific cure-mongers, all sedulously inculcated by modern "secondary education," were so monstrous that I was sometimes forced to make a verbal distinction between science and knowledge lest I should mislead my readers. But I never forgot that without knowledge even wisdom is more dangerous than mere opportunist ignorance, and that somebody must take the Garden of Eden in hand and weed it properly.

Accordingly, in 1901, I took the legend of Don Juan in its Mozartian form and made it a dramatic parable of Creative Evolution. But being then at the height of my invention and comedic talent, I decorated it too brilliantly and lavishly. I surrounded it with a comedy of which it formed only one act, and that act was so completely episodical (it was a dream which did not affect the action of the piece) that the comedy could be detached and played by itself: indeed it could hardly be played at full length owing to the enormous length of the entire work, though that feat has been performed a few times in Scotland by Mr Esmé Percy, who led one of the forlorn hopes of the advanced drama at that time. Also I supplied the published work with an imposing framework consisting of a preface, an appendix called The Revolutionist's Handbook, and a final display of aphoristic fireworks. The effect was so vertiginous, apparently, that nobody noticed the new religion in the centre of the intellectual whirlpool. Now I protest I did not cut these cerebral capers in mere inconsiderate exuberance. I did it because the worst convention of the criticism of the theatre current at that time was that intellectual seriousness is out of place on the stage; that the theatre is a place of shallow amusement; that people go there to be soothed after enormous intellectual strain of a day in the city: in short, that a playwright is a person whose business it is to make unwholesome confectionery out of cheap emotions. My answer to this was to put all intellectual goods in the shop window under the sign of Man and Superman. That part of my design succeeded. By good luck and acting, the comedy triumphed on the stage; and the book was a good deal discussed. Since then the sweet-shop view of the theatre has been out of countenance; and its critical exponents have been driven to take an intellectual pose which, though often more trying than their old intellectually nihilistic vulgarity, at least concedes the dignity of the theatre, not to mention the usefulness of those who live by criticizing it. And the younger playwrights are not only taking their art seriously, but being taken seriously themselves. The critic who ought to be a newsboy is now comparatively rare.

I now find myself inspired to make a second legend of Creative Evolution without distractions and embellishments. My sands are running out; the exuberance of 1901 has aged into the garrulity of 1920; and the war has been a stern intimation that the matter is not one to be trifled with. I abandon the legend of Don Juan with its erotic associations, and go back to the legend of the Garden of Eden. I exploit the eternal interest of the philosopher's stone which enables men to live for ever. I am not, I hope, under more illusion than is humanly inevitable as to the crudity of this my beginning of a Bible for Creative Evolution. I am doing the best I can at my age. My powers are waning; but so much the better for those who found me unbearably brilliant when I was in my prime. It is my hope that a hundred apter and more elegant parables by younger hands will soon leave mine as far behind as the religious pictures of the fifteenth century left behind the first attempts of the early Christians at iconography. In that hope I withdraw and ring up the curtain.

POSTSCRIPT AFTER TWENTYFIVE YEARS

ONE of the many summits in the mountain range of human selfconceit is the introduction by an author of his book as a World Classic. He cannot with any decency do it himself. And when he is invited to do so by a publisher whose prestige has been won in serious literature, his gratified compliance must be in the vein of apology and explanation rather than a fanfare of brazen exultation.

Therefore, though I am not addicted to what I have called "the modest cough of the minor poet" I will try to be as apologetic as my nature permits. I have never claimed a greater respect for playmaking than for the commoner crafts; and as every joiner is (or used to be) not only allowed but challenged to produce a masterpiece, I feel no shame in hawking my masterpiece without a cry of stinking fish.

Besides, I do not regard my part in the production of my books and plays as much greater than that of an amanuensis or an organ-blower. An author is an instrument in the grip of Creative Evolution, and may find himself starting a movement to which in his own little person he is intensely opposed. When I am writing a play I never invent a plot: I let the play write itself and shape itself, which it always does even when up to the last moment I do not foresee the way out. Sometimes I do not see what the play was driving at until quite a long time after I have finished it; and even then I may be wrong about it just as any critical third party may.

Take for examples the masterpieces of Dante, of Michael Angelo, and of John Bunyan. The three are beyond all question world classics notwithstanding the legendary fictions and childish superstitions which adapted them to the mental habits of their time, and still make them intelligible and interesting as stories, but which also aberrate them again and again into flat absurdity. Dante would have placed Mahomet in paradise had he realized that his Divine Comedy, with its ridiculous hell, its Sunday school purgatory, and its Feminist heaven, was driving at the same world Catholicism as the Koran. When Michael Angelo painted in the Sistine Chapel the series of Bible illustrations which culminated in the gigantic fable of the Last Judgement, he did not know that the series would be "continued in our next" by Nietzsche in his Thus Spake Zoroaster, the twain being driven more or less in spite of themselves to shew, Michael Angelo physically, Nietzsche mentally, not what mankind is but what it might become. Bunyan, when he was writing The Pilgrim's Progress, knew very well that he was being moved not by personal lust to become a Great Writer, but by "grace abounding to the meanest of sinners." Yet, if when his Holy War was sinking into the quicksand of sectarian nonsense in which it ends, he had been shewn a copy of Peer Gynt as an account of what his pilgrim would come to, or congratulated on having in The Life and Death of Mr Badman developed to a point not reached by Ibsen until three hundred years later, he would have been considerably scandalized.

I shall not go on to suggest that Goldsmith's Deserted Village should be used as a preface to Henry George's Progress and Poverty, and Keats's Isabella to Marx's Capital; but as a playwright I must not pass over my predecessor Shakespear. If he could be consulted as to the inclusion of one of his plays in the present series he would probably choose his Hamlet because in writing it he definitely threw over his breadwinning trade of producing potboilers which he frankly called As You Like It, Much Ado About Nothing, and What You Will. After a few almost Ibsenish essays in As You Dont Like It, he took up an old play about the ghost of a murdered king who haunted his son crying for revenge, with comic relief provided by the son pretending to be that popular curiosity and laughing-stock, a village idiot. Shakespear, transfiguring this into a tragedy on the ancient Athenian level, could not have been quite unconscious of the evolutionary stride he was taking. But he did not see his way clearly enough to save the tons of ink and paper and years of "man's time" that have been wasted, and are still being wasted, on innumerable volumes of nonsense about the meaning of Hamlet, though it is now as clear as daylight. Hamlet as a prehistoric Dane is morally bound to kill his uncle, politically as rightful heir to the usurped throne, and filially as "the son of a dear father murdered" and a mother seduced by an incestuous adulterer. He has no doubt as to his duty in the matter. If he can convince himself that the ghost who has told him all this is really his father's spirit and not a lying devil tempting him to perdition, then, he says, "I know my course."

But when fully convinced he finds to his bewilderment that he cannot kill his uncle deliberately. In a sudden flash of rage he can and does stab at him through the arras, only to find that he has killed poor old Polonius by mistake. In a later transport, when the unlucky uncle poisons not only Hamlet's mother but his own accomplice and Hamlet himself, Hamlet actually does at last kill his enemy on the spur of the moment; but this is no solution of his problem: it cuts the Gordian knot instead of untying it, and makes the egg stand on end only by breaking it. In the soliloquy beginning "Oh what a rogue and peasant slave am I" Shakespear described this moral bewilderment as a fact (he must have learnt it from his own personal development); but he did not explain it, though the explanation was staring him in the face as it stares in mine. What happened to Hamlet was what had happened fifteen hundred years before to Jesus. Born into the vindictive morality of Moses he has evolved into the Christian perception of the futility and wickedness of revenge and punishment, founded on the simple fact that two blacks do not make a white. But he is not philosopher enough to comprehend this as well as apprehend it. When he finds he cannot kill in cold blood he can only ask "Am I a coward?" When he cannot nerve himself to recover his throne he can account for it only by saying "I lack ambition." Had Shakespear plumbed his play to the bottom he would hardly have allowed Hamlet to send Rosencrantz and Guildenstern to their death by a forged death warrant without a moment's scruple.

Two and a half centuries later the same thing occurs to the author of another world classic, Charles Montagu Doughty, who, compared to Shakespear, can be catalogued only as a bigoted simpleton when, undeveloped at the age of 32, he travelled in Arabia. To him the Arabs were dangerous and damned heathens, corrupted by a false religion invented by an impostor named Mahomet who had forged a spurious Bible called the Koran. To defend himself against them he armed himself with a loaded revolver and carried it wherever he went.

The protection seemed very necessary; for the Bedouins were so like himself (or he like them) that they regarded him as a damned infidel; and the fanatically pious among them considered it their religious duty to kill and despoil the Nazarene. Again and again his bags were rifled and the knife was at his throat. Yet with the revolver in his hand and his assailants at his mercy he did not discharge it. Like Hamlet he could not bring himself to judge and kill. Like Shakespear he could not see why: he could only record the simple fact. Yet his travel diary, published long after with the now famous title Arabia Deserta, is a world classic.

This logicless sequel puzzles the student of literature who is trying to find out what qualifies a book to rank as a classic. Doughty, when he began his two years roaming through the Arabian deserts, was what we call an educated English gentleman who had gone through a professional training in medicine. Yet he writes like a child of ten for the most part; and his diary, with scraps of memoranda stuck in anyhow in no order except the order of date, is in no sense a considered work of art. His interests are those of an amateur explorer only; and the comments on Bedouin life, character, and religion, which make his book so readable, change from day to day, from place to place, from meal to meal. On one page all the Bedouins he has known are "a merry crew of squalid wretches, iniquitous, fallacious, and fanatical." Two pages later the Beni Salim are "of gentle and honest manners; and I was never better entertained in nomad menzils." Many of his entertainers were more civilized, tolerant, and sceptical than he. His style is certainly unique; but it suggests the simplicity of a man who had never read a book in his life except the Bible, which he often quotes, less with any artistic appreciation than to shew that its descriptions tally with the facts of eastern life and thought as he found them.

There must have been something majestic or gigantic about the man that made him classic in himself. He was already a poet, for twice in his travel diary he explodes into half a page of prophetic rhapsody; and when he came home he spent the rest of his life in writing immense prophetic epics in blank verse of a Himalayan magnificence and natural eminence that would have made Milton gasp. Small wonder that when the knife was at his throat it got no farther; and when he arrived at the next oasis penniless and in rags, the rulers there clothed him and made those who had robbed him give him back their booty and repay him his stolen money to the last farthing. Englishmen who met him have described him to me as "a mountain of a man"; and extant portraits bear them out as far as portraits can.

It is clear then that in him as in Hamlet-Shakespear a step in evolution had occurred and taken all the vulgar fight out of him without taking any of the courage. And this brings me Back to Methuselah, and to the right of my "metabiological pentateuch" to be included in a list of world classics. Like Shakespear I had to write potboilers until I was rich enough to satisfy my evolutionary appetite (or, as they say, give way to my inspiration) by writing what came to me without the least regard to the possibility of lucrative publication or performance. Like Shakespear again, I was a born dramatist, which means a born artist-biologist struggling to take biology a step forward on its way to positive science from its present metaphysical stage in which the crude facts of life and death, growth and decay, evolution and reversion, consciousness and unconsciousness, selfpreservation and selfsacrifice, defy the methods of investigation we employ in our research laboratories, and have to be made apprehensible by fictions, pictures, and symphonies in which they are instinctively arranged in a manner which gives a mysterious pleasure to some of the readers, spectators, and listeners, and provokes others to passionate denial and persecution. When I am not potboiling for myself or others I am being driven by my evolutionary appetite to write these fictions. Even when I have the box office in view I am not free to choose the most lucrative sort of fiction. Evolution keeps creeping in. I write such shameless potboilers as Pygmalion, Fanny's First Play, and You Never Can Tell, to oblige theatre managers or aspiring players; but at least I do not write detective stories to oblige publishers. I am clever enough at the tricks of my trade to be able to combine some worldly potboiling with my transcendental metabiology, but only up to an impassable boundary. If I could not do this, and had either to prosper as a stockbroker or starve as a metabiologist I should starve, as Mozart and Beethoven very nearly did when they composed symphonies instead of sentimental drawingroom ballads.

In writing Back to Methuselah I threw over all economic considerations, and faced the apparent impossibility of a performance during my lifetime. When a professional manager of whom I had never heard (though his name, by the way, was Barry Jackson, and he was already famous in the Midlands) approached me with a view to a performance, I asked him whether he had no regard for his wife and family. He replied that he was not married, and that he kept a theatre out of his private means as other similarly endowed plutocrats kept racehorses or steam yachts. In short, he was doing it to gratify his evolutionary appetite and could afford the cost. So I gave him my blessing and a performing licence; and he went ahead and produced the Methuselah cycle at his Birmingham Repertory Theatre, where he had made theatrical history by many notable experiments and revivals while London was barely marking time. When I asked him what he had lost by the Methuselah adventure he said with every appearance of satisfaction, "Only £2500." Later on, when he repeated it in London and I repeated my question, he answered exultantly "I have not lost: I have made twenty pounds." The twenty pounds did not give him a dock laborer's wages for his trouble; but it left him none the poorer, and my conscience all the lighter.

Clearly then, Back to Methuselah was not a commercial job: it came straight from the Life Force operating as an *élan vital* through myself and Barry Jackson. What, then, are world classics?

Well, they all try to solve, or at least to formulate, the riddles of creation. In them the Life Force is struggling towards its goal of godhead by incarnating itself in creatures with knowledge and power enough to control nature and circumstances. A classic author has to consider how far he dare go; for though he is writing for the enlightenment of mankind he may not be willing to venture as far as martyrdom for its sake. Descartes burnt one of his books to escape being burnt for having written it. Galileo had to deny what he believed to escape the same fate. The priests forced these alternatives on them not because they did not agree with them, but because they had to govern the people, and the people could be governed only by fictions and miracles, not by the latest steps in science. If the people will not obey their rulers unless they see the blood of St Januarius liquefy, then the priests must work that miracle for them or let them run wild. As long as civilization seems to stand or fall with the belief that God stopped the movement of the sun in its orbit to oblige Joshua as casually as the driver of a tramcar stops his vehicle to pick up a passenger, popes and emperors must take care that no physicist is allowed to tell the mob that it is the earth that moves round the sun and not the sun round the earth, even when they are entirely convinced that the physicist is right. When I was a municipal councillor I had to connive at bogus miracles, pretending that tubs of soap and water were as magical as the cauldron of Macbeth's witches, because my constituents believed in magic, not in soap and sunshine. It is useless to parrot the old saying that the blood of the martyrs is the seed of the Church, and expect scientific heretics to die to advertize their heresies rather than recant to save their lives. Descartes, when he burnt his book, knew that its truths would inevitably be rediscovered and become familiar, and that this would only be retarded by his being burnt for publishing them.

As for me I can write safely on the assumption that Galileo and Descartes knew much more about physics than Moses. But I am not therefore free to publish anything I like. Plays of mine have been banned for many years on grounds injuriously defamatory to myself; and at least one of my books is on the index in Eire, apparently because the heroine does not wear petticoats. The disciples of Pavlov would burn me if they had Torquemada's power. But State intolerance is founded, not now on crude fanaticism, but on the fear that if the people discover that the miracles they believe in are either fables or frauds, and that the scriptures they accept as Divine revelations are questionable in any sentence, they will empty the baby out with the bath water, and defy all religion and all morality. And in fact many of them have done so as far as such defiance is practicable, which is not very far, as disbelief in the Bible story of the ten commandments is no defence against being imprisoned for theft or hanged for murder.

Now it is hardly possible for men engaged daily in the starkly realistic practice of government, which is full of surprises for simpletons, to share the credulities of the crowd. They soon become arch heretics themselves; and as such they persecute heresy only as long as they believe that, as Ibsen put it, society is held together by chain stitched seams which will ravel out if a single stitch is cut. But they find out that this does not in fact happen. When experience taught them that Voltaire could laugh at Habbakuk and call on them to crush the Church as an infamy without immediately bringing down French civilization about their ears they inferred that their own scepticisms could be tolerated safely, and allowed the laws against them to fall into desuetude, without, however, daring to repeal them. It is fairly safe for me personally to fill my books and plays with heresies and even be accepted as a world classic on the strength of them; but it is none the less within quite recent historical memory that the vogue of Voltaire and his fellow-heretic Rousseau was followed by the French Revolution, and that Rousseau's "Get rid of your miracles and the whole world will fall at the feet of Christ" has ended in whole States falling at the feet of Pavlov and Hitler.

The moral of this is that heretical teaching must be made irresistibly attractive by fine art if the heretics are not to starve or burn. I have to make my heresies pleasing as plays to extract the necessary shillings from those to whom they are also intensely irritating. Back to Methuselah, having begun its stage career by extracting £2500 from the pocket of Sir Barry Jackson, presently enabled him to extract a surplus of £20 from the pockets of his audiences.

Now the artistic attractions of the Methuselah cycle must operate in the theatre without explanation; but its heresies can be discussed on paper in prefaces or postscripts. First among them is the evanescence of God Almighty, and His replacement by a creative force striving by trial and error towards a goal of allknowingness and almighty power over nature. But this aspiring fallibility is either indignantly rejected or personified and deified in an imaginary Supreme Being in the sky if not on earth.

Hence our gods, saviors, prophets, saints, heroes, and the like. It is through such conceits that we are governed and governable; yet only by debunking them can we evolve towards the goal. Most of us dont want to evolve. When God becomes too remote, too awful, and too cruel to be bearable, and we have to invent something more human, and call it Messiah or Christ, or Zoroaster or Buddha, we immediately destroy its humanity by insisting on its superhuman sinless perfection and unerring knowledge and wisdom; so that it becomes as incredible as God was unbearable.

Our villagers, contemplating the mischief and horror of the Four Years war in 1917, said "Well, I suppose there must be a God; but what *is* He thinking of to let all this go on?" Now to admit that God can err, or that He is powerless in any particular, is to deprive Him of the attributes that qualify Him as God; but it is a very healthy admission for the strongminded. It increases our sense of responsibility for social welfare, and is radiant with boundless hopes of human betterment. Our will to live depends on hope; for we die of despair, or, as I have called it in the Methuselah cycle, discouragement. What damns Darwinian Natural Selection as a creed is that it takes hope out of evolution, and substitutes a paralysing fatalism which is utterly discouraging. As Butler put it, it "banishes Mind from the universe." The generation that felt nothing but exultant relief when it was delivered from the tyranny of an Almighty Busybody by a soulless Determinism has nearly passed away, leaving a vacuum which Nature abhors.

Readers of my preface will remember that it was a remark by Weismann that set me on the track of Methuselah. He suggested that death is a result of Natural Selection, not "natural" in the ordinary sense, lifetimes varying in duration from the immortality of the eternally splitting amœba to the brief span of the drosophila fly. Immortality is natural, death only an artifice to make it bearable as a burden and get rid of its garments of flesh as they wear out. The legend of Methuselah is neither incredible nor unscientific. Life has lengthened considerably since I was born; and there is no reason why it should not lengthen ten times as much after my death.

This possibility came to me when history and experience had convinced me that the social problems raised by millionfold national populations are far beyond the political capacity attainable in three score and ten years of life by slowgrowing mankind. On all hands as I write the cry is that our statesmen are too old, and that Leagues of Youth must be formed everywhere to save civilization from them. But despairing ancient pioneers tell me that the young are worse than the old; and the truth seems to be that our statesmen are not old enough for their jobs. Life is too short for the experience and development needed to change romantic schoolboys and golfing sportsmen, or even prematurely forced Quakers, into wise senators. In the nineteenth century we reacted from an effete feudalism into a Cobden-Croce world in which the love of money is the root of all good, and freedom of contract and thought man's choicest treasure ("heartbreaking nonsense" Carlyle called it), and are now reacting into either a Marxist world in which the millennium will be guaranteed by a new Catholicism in which the proletarians of all lands are to unite, or an idolatry of imaginary Carlylean heroes and bogus Nietzschean superman; but we have no sages old enough and wise enough to make a synthesis of these reactions, and to develop the magnetic awe-inspiring force which must replace the policeman's baton as the instrument of authority. Though I am very far from being as clever and well informed as people think, I am not below the average in political capacity; yet in my 89th year I am no more fit to rule millions of men than a boy of 12. Physically I am failing: my senses, my locomotive powers, my memory, are decaying at a rate which threatens to make a Struldbrug of me if I persist in living; yet my mind still feels capable of growth; for my curiosity is keener than ever. My soul goes marching on; and if the Life Force would give me a body as durable as my mind, and I knew better how to feed and lodge and dress and behave, I might begin a political career as a junior civil servant and evolve into a capable Cabinet minister in another hundred years or so.

The Agnostics and Atheists and Determinist Diehards who have thrown over the creeds whipped into them in their childhood are surprised and alarmed to see Creative Evolution reviving much that they have discarded as superstitious. For example, the Creative Evolutionist believes firmly in Providence and in what used to be called the will of God. But he also insists strongly on the first of the 39 Articles of the Church of England, which, in a blinding flash of inspiration (it unfortunately did not last long enough to prevent its contradiction in the following articles) affirms that God has neither body, parts, nor passions, and is therefore not a Person but an incorporeal Purpose, unable to do anything directly, but mysteriously able to create corporeal organs and agents to accomplish that purpose, which, as far as we can see, is the attainment of infinite wisdom and infinite power. Instead of dwelling morbidly on the quite unedifying and not too interesting inference that in the beginning the earth was a wisp of blazing gas torn off from the sun, the votary of Creative Evolution goes back to the old and very pregnant lesson that in the beginning was the Thought; and the Thought was with God; and the Thought *was* God, the Thought being what the Greeks meant by "the Word". He believes in the thought made flesh as the first step in the main process of Creative Evolution. He believes in a new Jerusalem, and resolves, like Blake, that he will not cease from mental fight nor shall his sword sleep in his hand till he has built that paradise in England's green and pleasant land.

We are only just discovering that there is such a thing as wishful thinking; but the Creative Evolutionist knows that all thinking is wishful, and that we cannot think until our wishes or fears or cupidities or curiosities create what we call attention. I have known this since my childhood, when somebody shewed me that if I held up my two forefingers in a line from my eyes, I could see two of the nearest when I looked at the farthest, or vice versa, because I had on my two retinas two separate images of everything in sight except the thing I wanted to see. Yet I was conscious of them only when I co-ordinated them. Later on, when I threw over my childish belief in the infallibility of the Bible on discovering that much of it is obsolete or wicked, what struck me most was that the obsolescences and wickednesses had never been hidden from me: they had been staring me in the face all the time. I had simply not thought about them. There must have been an evolutionary growth in my mind which directed my attention to them. Attention is the first symptom of thought. John the Evangelist would have worded it so, had he been born a Victorian.

Civilization is at present an imposture: we are a crowd of savages on whom a code of makeshift regulations is forced by penalties for breaking them. They are never explained to us. When I was sent to school I was confronted by a new set of rules and made aware that if I broke them I should be punished. As no other reason for obeying them was given to me I concluded naturally that I could break them without the slightest loss of selfrespect, and indeed with some pride in my independence and cleverness, as long as I was not found out. My hero in fiction was the rebel, not the goodygoody citizen, whom I despised. This attitude became a habit which I have never been able to shake off quite completely. Yet it would have been easy without overstraining my childish powers of comprehension to make me understand that people cannot live together, and be fed, clothed, lodged, and protected from robbery and murder, unless they agree to do certain things at the same moments in the same order, and meanwhile abstain from doing certain other things however tempting: in short, that social behavior is expected behavior, and that to behave unexpectedly, to be original as we call it, though without this eccentricity there can be no improvement, is to assume a dangerous responsibility. A child must begin as a Conservative, and learn later that though it must tolerate change it must do so very critically. That is to say it must be an intelligent and voluntary Conservative and not merely a dunderhead with a stock of dictated habits. When I associated with other boys in secret gangs it was to do mischief for the fun of it, to wreck and steal and circumvent law and order, to emulate Dick Turpin and Jack Sheppard, and generally to defy the commandments and do whatever our teachers and the police told us we must not do. If we had had even the simplest lessons in citizenship we should, like the Boy Scouts and Girl Guides of a later time, have conspired to do good instead of evil. No doubt we should also have played at the cruelties of the criminal law; for children, who like exercising authority as their elders do, will, if not carefully policed, do diabolical things to one-another in imitation of the vindictive side of law and parental authority. To remedy this we must reform the law and re-educate the parents.

All this faces us with the dilemma that civilization means stabilization; and creative evolution means change. As the two must operate together we must carefully define their spheres, and co-ordinate them instead of quarrelling and persecuting as we do at present. We must not stay as we are, doing always what was done last time, or we shall stick in the mud. Yet neither must we undertake a new world as catastrophic Utopians, and wreck our civilization in our hurry to mend it. Professional science must cease to mean the nonsense of Weismann and the atrocities of Pavlov, in which life is a purposeless series of accidents and reflexes, and logic only a thoughtless association of ideas. Still less must it mean mere erudition in the scriptures of the saints, prophets, and metaphysicians from Augustin and Aquinas to Butler and Bergson and Shaw. It must renounce magic and yet accept miracle; for as biology is still in the metaphysical stage (all its new knowledge of chromosomes and hormones only substitutes millions of miracles for the single mystery formerly called the soul or the breadth of life); and as physics, in spite of its miraculous electrons and its abolition of matter, is nearer to the positive stage, the metaphysicians and artist-philosophers must cooperate with the astronomers and physiologists in separate but friendly and at the edges overlapping departments of social service. Both are trying to see a little farther into the dark; and whether the electronic microscope or the philosopher's brain has pierced it farthest is not worth quarrelling about; for the darkness beyond still forces us to tolerate both microscopic revelation and metaphysical speculation with all its guesses and hypotheses and dramatizations of how far thought can reach. We must have a hypothesis as a frame of reference before we can reason; and Creative Evolution, though the best we can devize so far, is basically as hypothetical and provisional as any of the creeds.

The history of modern thought now teaches us that when we are forced to give up the creeds by their childishness and their conflicts with science we must either embrace Creative Evolution or fall into the bottomless pit of an utterly discouraging pessimism. This happened in dateless antiquity to Ecclesiastes the preacher, and in our own era to Shakespear and Swift. "George Eliot" (Marian Evans) who, incredible as it now seems, was during my boyhood ranked in literature as England's greatest mind, was broken by the fatalism that ensued when she discarded God. In her most famous novel Middlemarch, which I read in my teens and almost venerated, there is not a ray of hope: the characters have no more volition than billiard balls: they are moved only by circumstances and heredity. "As flies to wanton boys are we to the gods: they kill us for their sport" was Shakespear's anticipation of George Eliot. Had Swift seen men as creatures evolving towards godhead he would not have been discouraged into the absurdity of describing them as irredeemable Yahoos enslaved by a government of horses ruling them by sheer moral superiority. Even Ibsen, though his characters, like Shakespear's, reek with volition, perpetrated a tragedy called Ghosts, in which an omnipotent god is discarded for an inevitable syphilis. One of the masters of comedy among my playwright colleagues drowned himself because he thought he was going his father's way like Oswald Alving. Even a mind so keen and powerful as that of Dr Inge has been troubled by the notion that Life cannot survive extremes of temperature, nor reach inconceivable heights long after the cooling of the sun makes a good riddance of Yahoo mankind. (The sun, by the way, is getting hotter by the latest guesses.) Discouragement does in fact mean death; and it is better to cling to the hoariest of the savage old creator-idols, however diabolically vindictive than to abondon all hope in a world of "angry apes", and perish in despair like Shakespear's Timon. Goethe rescued us from this horror with his "Eternal Feminine that draws us forward and upward" which was the first modern manifesto of the mysterious force in creative evolution.

That is what made Faust a world classic. If it does not do the same for this attempt of mine, throw the book into the fire; for Back to Methuselah is a world classic or it is nothing.

Ayot Saint Lawrence
1944

A Glimpse of the Domesticity of Franklyn Barnabas was originally intended to be Act II of Part II in Back to Methuselah. It was withheld by Shaw from performance or publication with the play in 1921 and later published in Short Stories, Scraps and Shavings in 1932. It was first performed in New York in 1960.

A GLIMPSE OF THE DOMESTICITY OF FRANKLYN BARNABAS

IF you have read Back to Methuselah you will remember Franklyn Barnabas, the ex-clergyman who, with his gruff brother Conrad, the biologist, had come to the conclusion that the duration of human life must be extended to three hundred years, not in the least as all the stupid people thought because people would profit by a longer experience, but because it was not worth their while to make any serious attempt to better the world or their own condition when they had only thirty or forty years of full maturity to enjoy before they doddered away into decay and death. The brothers Barnabas were in fact the first discoverers of the staringly obvious truth that it is our expectation of life, and not our experience of it, that determines our conduct and character. Consequently the very vulgar proposition that you cannot change human nature, and therefore cannot make the revolutionary political and economic changes which are now known to be necessary to save our civilization from perishing like all previous recorded ones, is valid only on the assumption that you cannot change the duration of human life. If you can change that, then you can change political conduct through the whole range which lies between the plague-stricken city's policy of "Let us eat and drink; for tomorrow we die" and the longsighted and profound policies of the earthly paradises of More, Morris, Wells, and all the other Utopians.

It was with this thesis of the Barnabases that I was concerned when I wrote Back to Methuselah; and though I got interested enough in Franklyn personally to go a little way into his domestic history, I had to discard my researches as both irrelevant and certain to sidetrack my main theme and confuse my biological drama with a domestic comedy.

Also I had amused myself by bringing Franklyn Barnabas into contact with a notable social philosopher of our day for the mere fun of caricaturing him. But this proved a hopeless enterprise; for, like all really great humorists, he had himself exploited his own possibilities so thoroughly in that direction that I could produce nothing but a manifestly inferior copy of a gorgeous original. Still, even a bad caricature may have some value when the original has dissolved into its elements for remanufacture by the Life Force. As we cannot now have a photograph of Shakespear, much less a portrait by a master, we cling to the inhuman caricature by Droeshout as at least a corrective to the commonplace little bust of a commonplace little gent in the shrine in Stratford church; and so I think it possible that my thumbnail sketch, inadequate and libellous as it is, may give a hint or two to some future great biographer as to what the original of Immenso Champernoon was like in the first half of his career, when, in defiance of the very order of nature, he began without a figure as a convivial immensity with vine leaves in his hair, deriding his own aspect, and in middle life slimmed into a Catholic saint, thereby justifying my reminder to those who took him too lightly of old, that Thomas Aquinas began as a comically fat man and ended as The Divine Doctor.

Until the other day I believed that my studies of the Barnabas home out Hampstead way, with my Champernoon caricature, had perished in the waste-paper basket which has swallowed many discarded pages of my works. But they have just turned up in the course of a hunt for matter wherewith to complete a collected edition of my works; and, being much at a loss for padding for this particular volume of scraps of fiction, I looked through them and thought they might prove not only readable, but perhaps useful to married ladies with interesting husbands who attract husband stealers. Such ladies, if they are at all bearable, have all the trumps in their hands, and need never be beaten if they understand the game and play it with the requisite audacity and contempt for the danger.

Here, then, are a few scraps of the scenes which took place in the suburban villa in which the brothers Barnabas made their famous attempt to persuade our political leaders in the first years after the war to discard their obsolete party programs and raise the slogan of Back to Methuselah.

Conrad Barnabas the biologist is in the library waiting for his brother Franklyn. Franklyn comes in presently looking worried and irritated. The conversation proceeds as follows.

CONRAD. Anything wrong?

FRANKLYN. As usual.

CONRAD. Clara broken out again?

FRANKLYN. She left the house on Saturday, saying that she would live with me no longer. My worthy brother-in-law wants to see me about her.

CONRAD. What! Immenso Champernoon! Dont say he's coming here.

FRANKLYN. He is.

CONRAD. Oh, Lord!

FRANKLYN. Perhaps if you start a discussion with him he may forget to talk about Clara. I really cannot stand any more of it. I have been a very good husband to her for twenty years, as husbands go; and now I sometimes regret that we did not separate at our first quarrel.

CONRAD. Well, Clara has been a fairly good wife to you, as wives go. She keeps the house very well.

FRANKLYN. A well-kept house is an excellent thing as far as it goes. But it is not an indispensable condition of life to me. Constitutionally I am an untidy irregular man. We all are, we Barnabases. You are.

CONRAD. But I knew better than to marry. You knew what you were doing, you know.

FRANKLYN. I dont think anyone knows quite what he is doing when he marries.

CONRAD. Widowers do. And they marry.

FRANKLYN. It suits them, perhaps. Besides, a married man forms married habits and becomes dependent on marriage, just as a sailor becomes dependent on the sea. But there are limits. I know a sailor who was torpedoed nine times, and yet went to sea again. But the tenth time finished him: he took a job in the docks. Well, Clara has torpedoed me nine times. If she is going to do it again she may find it once too often.

CONRAD. I cannot make out what you have to quarrel about. Whats wrong with her, or you?

FRANKLYN. If you want to know whats wrong with me, you must ask her. What is wrong with her is that she is a bluestocking.

CONRAD. Oh, come! Thats rather out of date, isnt it? I dont believe the women students at Cambridge know the meaning of the word. You dont object at this time of day to a woman cultivating her mind and being educated?

FRANKLYN. Not at all. Nobody ever does: among our set of people at any rate. A bluestocking is not an educated woman or a woman with a cultivated mind.

CONRAD. What else?

FRANKLYN. A bluestocking is a woman who has a mania for intellectual subjects without having a ray of intellect.

CONRAD. Oho! Thats not a bluestocking: it's a university professor. When a man is mentally incapable of abstract thought he takes to metaphysics; and they make him a professor. When he is incapable of conceiving quantity in the abstract he takes to mathematics; and they make him a professor. When he is incapable of distinguishing between a clockwork mouse and a real one he takes to biology; and they make him a professor. And so on. The fact is, these chaps are clockwork mice themselves. By tutoring them and coaching them and stuffing them with textbooks you wind them up, and they go. You feel safe with them because you always know how far they will go and how they will go. But Clara is not like that. She hasnt been wound up. She is not a fool.

FRANKLYN. Isnt she?

CONRAD. Well, not that sort of fool. These people have no minds at all: Clara has a very restless mind, not to say a fidgety one. What has she been worrying about now?

FRANKLYN. Indian religions. Theosophy. Yoga. Reincarnation. Karma. Anything from the East.

CONRAD. Damn the East! Are we never to look at home for our religion?

FRANKLYN. Amen. She calls Creative Evolution Western Materialism, cockney blasphemy, and all the rest of it. Says she wont live in the house with it.

CONRAD. But a woman doesnt leave her home for a thing like that. Whats the row, really?

FRANKLYN. Oh, what is the row always, in married life? It's not Creative Evolution, it's because I discuss Creative Evolution with Mrs Etteen and refuse to discuss it with Clara. How can I discuss it with a woman who tells me I dont understand it, and that the truth about it is all in the Vedantas or the Upanishads or the last number of the Theosophical Journal or some other nigger scripture?

CONRAD. Mrs Etteen? Who is she?

FRANKLYN. Oh—er—a lady.

CONRAD. Thank God I'm not married, and can discuss Creative Evolution with anyone I like.

FRANKLYN. And now I shall have to sit here and keep my temper while Immenso gasses about domestic virtue.

CONRAD. Why need you keep your temper? I tell you frankly, I intend to lose mine.

FRANKLYN. It wont make the smallest difference to Immenso.

THE PARLOR MAID [*announcing*] Mr Champernoon. [*She withdraws*].

Immenso Champernoon is a man of colossal mould, with the head of a cherub on the body of a Falstaff, which he carries with ease and not without grace. At forty or thereabouts his hair is still brown and curly. He is friendly, a little shy, and jokes frequently enough to be almost always either still enjoying the last or already anticipating the next. He is careless of his dress and person, in marked contrast to Franklyn, who, though untidy as to his papers, looks comparatively valeted and manicured.

FRANKLYN. Conrad's here, Imm. You dont mind, do you?

CONRAD [*striving not to let Immenso's large and genial aspect disarm him*] I can go.

IMMENSO. Not at all. Delighted to see you, doctor. [*He sits down on the sofa, which groans beneath the burden*].

FRANKLYN. Well, what is the latest? Has Clara made up her mind to a separation, or has she discovered a new religion, or have you a treaty of good behavior in your pocket which I am to sign?

IMMENSO. I really forget what she said.

CONRAD. You forget!

IMMENSO. The way I look at it is this. A man is not a balloon.

CONRAD. Some men are damned like one.

IMMENSO [*grinning genially*] Like all men of science you are the dupe of appearances. For instance, *I* am superficially like a balloon. I fancy that was in your mind when you introduced the subject of balloons.

CONRAD. It is just possible. But it was you who introduced the subject.

IMMENSO. Let me suggest an experiment. Procure a balloon; and place it on the lawn. Place me at the same time on the roof. Detach us both simultaneously from the lawn and from the roof. The balloon will immediately shoot up into the heavens and be lost. *I* will, on the contrary, descend to earth with destructive force, and probably make a considerable dent in it. In other words, you will not know where to find the balloon; and you will know where to find me. That is the essential difference.

FRANKLYN. Yes, yes; but what has it to do with Clara?

IMMENSO. This. The earth is my home. If my home were in the skies I could not be a married man. You conceive me at the altar trying to get married, with the bride, the bridesmaids, the best man, the pew opener, and the parson all holding me down. But they would have to let go sooner or later. And then up I would shoot. My head would strike the stars. My coat would be whitened in the milky way. And my wife would be that most pitiful of all widows, a grass widow. The natural occupation of the grass widow is to make hay whilst the sun shines. But my widow could not, because my bulk would obscure the sun. I should be a perpetual eclipse—

FRANKLYN. My dear Imm: I shall be delighted to hear your views on balloons, on grass, and on eclipses when we have nothing else to talk about. I have no doubt they will be extremely entertaining. But just at present I want to know what Clara intends to do, or intends me to do.

IMMENSO. But dont you see that that is just what I am coming to?

CONRAD. I'm damned if *I* do.

IMMENSO. If you ask me—

CONRAD. I dont. It would be much shorter to ask a policeman.

IMMENSO. You could not ask a better man. A policeman would tell you at once that the whole police system, like all other eternally stable systems, depends, not on the wandering policeman but on the fixed point policeman. Not on the rolling stone policeman, a human avalanche who gathers no moss, but on the monumental policeman whom you always know where to find.

FRANKLYN. Again I ask you, Imm, what message have you brought to me from Clara?

IMMENSO. Again I tell you, Frank, I bring to you the message of gravitation which saves me from the fate of the balloon, and of the fixed point policeman on whom Conrad depends for his knowledge of the way to Putney. That is important, because if you cant find the way to Putney you cant find the way to paradise.

FRANKLYN. Yes. You were about to say that Clara told you to tell me—?

IMMENSO. As a matter of detail she told me not to tell you. But what she said was that you could never live alone, because, as she put it, you are no anchorite.

FRANKLYN. Did you defend me from the monstrously false accusation which that implies?

IMMENSO. I pointed out that she was your anchor, and

that if a man's anchor belied its own nature and swam away from him, it could hardly blame him for drifting.

FRANKLYN. And what did she say to that?

IMMENSO. She said there was no use talking to me. She said I was making puns of her distress.

FRANKLYN. And was that all?

IMMENSO. No. You may have noticed that when a woman says there is no use talking to a man, he can very seldom get a word in edgeways for the following half hour.

CONRAD. If she shut you up, she is a woman in a thousand.

IMMENSO. That is an almost perfect example of a modern scientific definition. It has the air of exactitude which arithmetic alone can give. Yet as, from the moment the population exceeds nine hundred and ninety-nine, every woman is a woman in a thousand, it means absolutely nothing whatever.

FRANKLYN. We make you a present of modern science, Imm: nobody here worships it any more than you do—[*Conrad is about to protest*]—no, Con: you sit quiet and say nothing. I shall sit quiet and say nothing. When Imm is tired of playing with his own mind, he will perhaps have a human impulse, and relieve my anxiety to learn what Clara intends to do.

IMMENSO [*coloring at the implied reproach*] I am not inconsiderate, I hope. Certainly not intentionally so. But what Clara intends to do is her affair. What you intend to do is your affair. My only comment is that probably neither of you will do it. On the other hand I am deeply concerned, as a Christian, and may I say as a friend—if a brother-in-law may presume so far—with what you both ought to do.

FRANKLYN. And what is that?

IMMENSO. Anchor yourself to the hearthstone. Make that your fixed point. There must be fixed points in life or we shall become a community of balloons. Even for balloons there must be fixed gas works, a necessity quaintly met by the House of Commons. There must be irrevocable contracts. What is the first question we ask a man? His name.

What is the second? His address. A man without a name is nobody. A man without an address is a vagabond. A man with two addresses is a libertine. A man with two solicitors and two bankers is a rogue. What is a marriage? Two persons with one name, one address. Not a changeable name, but one rooted in history, buried in parish registers to undergo a glorious resurrection in every generation; not a changeable address, but one hearthstone rooted in the solid earth of the motherland as a rock of ages, one certainty among all the uncertainties, one star among all the planets and meteors, one unshakable and unchangeable thing that is and was and ever shall be. You must have a root; and this matter of the root is also the root of the matter.

FRANKLYN. Marriage is not one of the certainties. Are there any certainties? Everything passes away; everything gets broken; we get tired of everything. Including marriages.

IMMENSO. No. Nothing can pass unless it passes something. A bus passes Piccadilly Circus; but Piccadilly Circus remains. I get tired of Clara; but I remain. So does Clara, by the way. And though everything gets broken you cannot break the thinnest glass goblet without striking it against a fixed object. You cannot break it by striking it against a butterfly. Has Con here ever considered, as a curious point in entomology, that you cannot break a butterfly at all? Foolish people say you can break it on a wheel; but it has never been done. Whistler survived his stodgiest enemies.

CONRAD. We have now got from the hearthstone to the butterfly as the emblem of constancy.

IMMENSO. You are a bachelor, Con: it has been your dreadful fate to sip every flower and change every hour until Polly your passion requited. Has she ever done so? No: she eludes you in every form except that of the Polyglot Bible, in which you find the words SUPER HANC PETRAM: Upon this rock will I build my Church. What is that rock? The hearthstone. Come back to the hearthstone, Frank.

FRANKLYN. Like a bad penny.

IMMENSO. Not at all. A bad penny is nailed to the

counter. Now it is the chief glory and peculiar quality of the hearthstone that you cannot nail anything to it. Also that though you can stand by it you cannot fall by it without getting your head under the grate. You can stand by it; sit by it: you can even, when Clara is indiscreetly curious, lie by it; but you cannot be nailed to it nor fall by it nor inconvenience yourself in any way by it.

FRANKLYN. What are we to do with this fellow, Con?

CONRAD. It's a pathological case. Theres a disease called echolalia. It sets stupid people gabbling rhymes: that is, words that echo each other. Imm here, being a clever chap, gabbles ideas that echo. He's by way of being a pundit, and is really only a punster.

IMMENSO. Be it so. You may say the same of Plato, of Shakespear. At all events, I keep to the point, which is the home.

FRANKLYN. Clara is the point.

IMMENSO. She is the point inasmuch as you have a tendency to stray from her. But the definition of a point is position without magnitude. Now Clara has both position and magnitude; and you will find that the more you attempt to destroy her position, the more oppressive her magnitude will become.

FRANKLYN. Imm: I know your trick of never arguing, but simply talking every idea out of my head except your own ideas. But it's no use your preaching the virtues of an imaginary world of irrevocable contracts to me. We are struggling out of a tyranny of sacred traditions, immutable laws, and irrevocable contracts into a freedom in which we may prove all things and hold fast to that which is good. If I find married life with Clara intolerable, I shall chuck it and chuck her; and thats all about it.

IMMENSO: Many men begin by chucking the woman they love. The saying that "each man slays the thing he loves" would be more true if it ran that "each man chucks the thing he loves"; but he usually chucks it under the chin. In any other sense you will find it difficult to chuck Clara.

CONRAD. Tell me this. Suppose Frank and Clara, instead of having at the outside twenty-five years more to live, had two hundred and fifty! Suppose that having brought up one family to the point at which that family naturally breaks up and the young people depart and make new families of their own, they were left to sit and stare at one another for two centuries, or to begin over again with another family, would you still admit no time limit to their contract? Does it occur to you that under such circumstances it might become unreasonable, or be considered indecent, or even declared illegal, for marriages to last for three centuries?

IMMENSO [*reflectively*] I see. You mean that when a tie has endured for, say fifty years, it becomes so intimate, so sacred, that it establishes, in effect, a relation far closer than the relation of consanguinity, and should be placed on the list of degrees within which marriage is forbidden; that the two may become one flesh so completely that even as brother and sister they would be more remote from one another, and that consequently marriage between them would become unthinkable through its very perfection. That is an idea which commands my respect. When they made you a man of science, Con, they killed a poet, more's the pity!

CONRAD. I never meant any such infernal nonsense. I meant that only fools stick in the same groove for ever, and that the law of change is a biological law.

IMMENSO. Well, if you come to that, I must remind you—though without prejudice to my eternal and unchangeable derision, loathing, contempt, and utter disbelief in biology and all other ologies whatever except perhaps the doxology—that it is a biological law that Frank and Clara shall have only one life and can bring up only one family, and that they must make the best of it.

CONRAD. I deny that it is a biological law. It is nothing but a bad habit. We can live as long as we like. Do you know what people really die of?

IMMENSO. Of reasonableness. They do not want to live for ever.

CONRAD. Of laziness, and want of conviction, and failure to make their lives worth living. That is why. That is sound scientific biology for you. I believe that we are on the brink of a generation that will live longer. Or else we are on the brink of destruction.

IMMENSO. The slain poet has his revenge. He rises from the dead as a scientific madman.

CONRAD. Gasbag!

IMMENSO. Oh, that this too too solid flesh would melt, thaw, and resolve itself into a gas! Call me a Jack Pudding, Con. That will not smell of the laboratory; but it will hit me in the stomach.

FRANKLYN. I am sorry to again make a digression. What does Clara want me to do? She sends me word that it is her firm intention never to cross my threshold again, and that I must see you about it. I have seen you; and I am as wise as I was before. There is no use asking you whether she gave you any message for me, as you will immediately proceed to deliver the message of the universe. Did she give you a letter?

IMMENSO [*producing a key*] She gave me this. She thinks it is her latchkey; but as a matter of fact I tried to open the door with it, and found it would not work; so I had to ring for admission in the usual course. But she undoubtedly believed that it was the key of this house when she gave it me. It is symbolically the key of your house. Actually, now that I look at it, I believe it is the key of mine. She has been staying with us for a few days. So if you will allow me I will keep it [*he replaces it in his pocket*].

FRANKLYN. Then she is in earnest about never crossing the threshold?

Mrs Franklyn Barnabas (Clara) flounces in through the window. She is a very active lady of fifty or thereabouts, rather under than over, and is richly but hastily and untidily dressed.

CLARA. I must apologize for entering unannounced by this way instead of through the front door as a stranger should. But Frank can hardly expect me to make a parade of our unhappy differences before the servants.

FRANKLYN. I never suggested for a moment that you should.

CLARA. And Imm took the wrong key: you know how incorrigibly careless he is. Give it back to me.

IMMENSO. Two wrongs will not make a right. I had better keep it.

CLARA. I see Con has come here to talk about me. I wish you would mind your own business, Con.

CONRAD. Damn your silly business! I came here to talk about something serious.

CLARA [*smiling*] Dont be naughty, Con. But it serves me right for spoiling you. And the first thing I see when I come into the place is Savvy playing tennis with that young rector. I call it hypocrisy. She does not believe in the Thirty-nine Articles. What right has she to lead that young man on? One would think that she had seen enough of the tragedy of a marriage between two people of different religious beliefs in this house.

FRANKLYN. I quite agree.

CLARA [*flushing*] Do you indeed? Then I think thats a very nasty thing of you to say. You are always worse when you have been talking to Con behind my back. And Imm has been making mischief, I suppose, as usual.

IMMENSO [*bounding from his chair*] *I* make mischief! ! !

CONRAD [*rising angrily*] How can Frank help talking about you to me when you make his life a hell?

FRANKLYN [*who has also risen*] You take offence at your own words. I am long past caring whether you find my remarks nasty or not.

CLARA. Have you all had tea?

This simple question deflates the three men hopelessly.

CONRAD. Tcha! [*he sits down angrily*].

FRANKLYN [*sitting down limply*] Have you had tea, Imm? I forgot to ask you.

IMMENSO [*sitting down ponderously*] I am banting. I have given up afternoon tea.

CLARA [*snatching her hat off carelessly and throwing it aside*]

Who has been here while I have been away? [*She sits*]. What have you been doing? How much was the garden account on Saturday? I saw grapes at six and sixpence a pound not a patch on ours. Did you go through cook's books?

FRANKLYN. I know nothing whatever about it. Campbell will tell you about the garden. I told him not to bother me. I gave cook a cheque for what she asked, and sent her book to my solicitor to check.

CLARA. To your solicitor!

FRANKLYN. You have complained so much about the trouble of housekeeping that I have made up my mind to try another plan.

CLARA [*rising*] Well, did you ever! I shall talk to cook about letting you be so ridiculous: what right had she to ask you for a cheque? it is my house and my business. [*Making for the garden door*] Where is Campbell? [*She goes out*].

FRANKLYN [*slowly*] Why do the servants stay?

CONRAD. Why do you stay?

IMMENSO [*rising*] That raises the question, why do *I* stay? My work, it would appear, is done.

CONRAD. Running away, eh?

IMMENSO. Most moral victories have that appearance.

FRANKLYN. Well, off with you. You have the brother's privilege. You can run away from Clara.

Clara returns, in a much better humour.

CLARA. Imm: are you staying to dinner?

IMMENSO. It has not been suggested.

FRANKLYN. I took it as a matter of course, Imm, if you care to.

CLARA. Youd better. [*Immenso resumes his seat*]. Frank: only fancy! cook's become a Theosophist.

FRANKLYN. Indeed? Did she get that in before you complained about the cheque she got from me?

CLARA [*coaxing*] But dear Frank, what was she to do? She needed the money to keep the house going. You must not blame her.

FRANKLYN. I do not blame her.

CLARA. Well, then, what are you talking about? Come, darling: dont be cross. Dont worry about the house. Cook was very glad to see me back; and no wonder: she must have had a dreadful time of it. Dont make me feel that I am more welcome in the kitchen than I am here. Arnt you going to kiss me?

FRANKLYN. Yes, yes. [*He kisses her*] There, dear, there. You are perfectly welcome.

CLARA. Con looks very cheap. Shall I get you some ammoniated quinine, Con? You look just as you did when you were sickening for the influenza last year twelvemonths.

CONRAD. I am quite well.

CLARA. You always say that. It is really very hard that I cant go away for a week without everybody getting ill.

CONRAD. I tell you I am not ill.

CLARA. Well, if youre not, I must say you are not very cordial in your manner. You know how glad I always am to see you here. I think you might shew that you are glad to see me.

CONRAD. Do you want me to kiss you?

CLARA. You may if you like. Nobody can say that I bear malice. [*She advances her cheek in his direction*].

CONRAD [*desperate*] Oh, very well. [*He gets up and kisses her*].

CLARA. Thats better. Now you have quite a color. [*He is, in fact, blushing slightly*].

Savvy, Franklyn's daughter, looks in. She is rather pleasant as a modern bright young thing; but she jars on her father by her dowdiness and rowdiness. She fears neither God nor man.

SAVVY. Mamma: Campbell's here.

CLARA. What does he want?

SAVVY. Nothing. You said you wanted him. About the grapes.

CLARA [*springing up*] Oh yes, of course. They were six and sixpence at Covent Garden. You dont mind my running away for a moment, do you: I promise to come back in a jiffy. [*She hurries out*].

SAVVY. Has she given in? Or have you?

CONRAD. Stalemate, Savvy.

SAVVY. Does that mean that she is coming back?

FRANKLYN. Yes, dear. Yes.

SAVVY. I'm rather glad, you know. The house was getting into a bit of a mess. [*She goes out*].

IMMENSO. I think you have summed up the situation correctly in one word, Con.

CONRAD. Have I? What word?

IMMENSO. Stalemate. That is exactly what is wrong with Frank.

FRANKLYN. What do you mean?

IMMENSO. My meaning is obvious. You are Clara's mate; and in the course of a too monotonous domestic routine you have become stale.

FRANKLYN. And Clara? Do you find her any fresher?

IMMENSO. Clara, with an instinct that amounts to genius, has recognized the situation. Finding herself stale, she takes herself off and then comes back and woos you afresh. What we have just witnessed here is a renewal of the honeymoon.

CONRAD. Tcha!

IMMENSO. Clara went away a stale mate, and returned a bride. Why dont you do the same, Frank? Why do you stick here in a groove, like a tram car? An Englishman's house is his castle; and when I am a frequent visitor it may be called the Elephant and Castle. But what is the Elephant and Castle? It is not a place at which tram cars stay: it is a point of continual departure and continual return. It is an ark which sends out doves every minute, and to which the doves return when the waters have abated. I shall write a book describing the adventures of a husband who leaves his wife every month only to return and woo her afresh, thus making himself a perpetual bridegroom, his wife a perpetual bride, and his life a perpetual honeymoon. Thus we reconcile the law of change and the irrevocable contract. Thus John Bull in his daily round of work, John Doin' as you may call him, becomes also Don Juan—

FRANKLYN. For heaven's sake, Imm, if you must make puns, make good ones, I—

Clara returns, looking serious.

CLARA. Frank: whats to be done? Campbell is thinking of turning Roman Catholic. He wants my advice about it.

FRANKLYN. What about the grapes?

CLARA. Do you think the grapes more important than tne man's soul? I shall certainly not encourage him. And dont you encourage him either, Imm. You are always defending the Church of Rome; and I live in daily fear of your joining it just for an intellectual lark.

IMMENSO. I suggest to you Clara, that Campbell's case is not a simple case of the grapes, but of the fox and the grapes. Now THE fox par excellence was George Fox the Quaker. A Roman Catholic fox is therefore an absurdity. Campbell should turn Quaker.

CLARA. I never know whether you are serious or not, Imm; and neither does anyone else; but Campbell would not join the Society of Friends: he is too cantankerous. I am greatly concerned about Campbell. He has the Keltic imagination: he is the most dreadful liar. And he has a Scottish philosophic subtlety that is almost Eastern. I advised him to read some Indian poetry. I will lend him the poems of Stupendranath Begorr.

IMMENSO. Stupendranath told me a curious thing about his uncle. He lost all his property by gambling in stocks, and had to live by getting married at the rate of two hundred a year.

CLARA. No man has a right to get married on two hundred a year. His wife must be a slave.

IMMENSO. I dont mean two hundred pounds a year: I mean two hundred marriages a year. Under our tolerant rule polygamy is unlimited in India. This gentleman conferred his high caste on the daughters of Indian snobs by marrying them. They made him handsome presents on each occasion; and these presents furnished him with a large income.

CLARA. But how could he support thousands of wives?

IMMENSO. He did not take them away with him. He left them on their parents' hands.

CLARA. And you approve of this! You advocate it! You support it!

IMMENSO. Not for a moment. I simply mention it.

CLARA. Then why do you mention it? It ought not to be mentioned. You would not mention it if you had not some sympathy with it.

CONRAD. If it is good enough for the British Empire it is good enough for you. You support the British Empire, dont you?

CLARA. Of course I support the British Empire. I am a Briton, I am proud to say. I believe we have a sacred mission to spread British ideas, British feelings, and British institutions over the whole world, because they are the best, the wholesomest, the cleanest, the freest. I would not have anyone in my house who questioned that for a moment. But if your silly story were true, it would mean that Stupendranath's vicious uncle, a black man, a gambler, and a bigamist, were imposing his abominable habits and customs on the British Government. I will write to the Secretary of State for India and have this man prosecuted.

FRANKLYN. My dear: you have been entertaining in our house for fully quarter of a century scores of people who spend their lives in trying to improve British institutions of one kind or another into something more reasonable. If they had been conventional patriots you would have called them dull and refused to invite them. What is the use of saying that you would not have such people in your house?

CLARA. Tell me this. Have I ever once—once during that quarter of a century, as you pompously call it to cover up the weakness of your argument—have I ever once invited or entertained Stupendranath's uncle or any of his shameless wives?

FRANKLYN. I did not say you had.

CLARA. Then what are you talking about?

FRANKLYN. I dont know. Ask Imm: he started this unfortunate subject.

IMMENSO. I cant help feeling that the future of British ideas depends on totally unreasonable people like Clara.

CLARA. Unreasonable! Pray why—

IMMENSO [*forcibly*] No, Clara: you may put down a husband because his domestic peace and comfort for the next week depends on his submission. But you cannot put down a brother. I can trample on you with impunity, because I can walk out afterwards to a comfortable home as long as I am careful to allow my own wife to trample on me. I say you are an utterly unreasonable woman; and I do not care a dump whether you like it or not. As it happens I am now defending you; and—

CLARA. You are a great fat fool, Imm; and I am perfectly capable of defending myself.

IMMENSO. The Roman conqueror had a slave to whisper to him "Remember that thou art mortal." The frankness of the British family relation provides me with a sister to remind me that I am a great fat fool. Why is England still England? Because there are so many people like Clara in it. She believes in her ideas, in her culture, in her morals, and backs them against the universe.

CONRAD. Does that give her any right to shove them down other people's throats with a bayonet?

IMMENSO. Yes: I should say it does. If the German shoves his ideas down our throats with music, and the French with wit, and the Italians with rhetorical paintings and romance, why should not we, being more handy with the bayonet than with any of these things, not carry on our propaganda with cold steel? By doing so we stake our lives and all our possessions on our ideas. Is not that more heroic than merely staking them on the success of an opera, an epigram, or a picture? What are we in India for, if not to lock up Stupendranath's uncle as a bigamist? When we put down the burning of widows and sent the car of Juggernaut to the jobmaster's scrap heap, we did India the only sort of service that could justify our interference with her. When we consented to tolerate Stupendranath's uncle we were hauling down the flag, and surrendering to the oriental. I grant you we have no right to govern India, because the Indians can govern themselves at least as well as we govern ourselves, which is not saying much. But we have a sacred right to persecute India. We have no right in the East except the right of the Crusader. The Catholic Englishman imposing British justice, British religion, and British institutions on the Hindoo is God's apostle. A Liberal Englishman undertaking to regulate oriental polygamy and idolatry is an officious meddler, an apostate, and, as Clara puts it, a fat fool.

CLARA. Nonsense! Why shouldnt the poor people have their own religions and their own institutions? I am sure they are just as respectable as ours. The Salvation Army killed Aunt Martha by playing under her window when she had worn her nerves to rags with neuralgia and morphia. And you justify such a thing!

FRANKLYN. Serve you right, Imm, for trying to take her part. You had better accept Clara as a true Briton and leave it at that. Why persist in expressing her views when you know very well that she hasn't got any?

CLARA. Dont be rude, Frank. It just comes to this, that when you men say things, they are views; but when I say a thing, you just say anything that comes handy for the sake of contradicting and shewing off your superior male intellects. What I say is that the Salvation Army is noisy. You say that it is as quiet as a church mouse; and you call that a view. It may be a view; but it's a lie; and you ought to be ashamed of pretending to believe it. I say that our institutions are a disgrace, right down from the silly humbugs in Parliament to the borough council dustmen who never come when they are wanted and have to be cleaned up after for half a day when they do come. I say we are the most stupid, prejudiced, illiterate, drinking, betting, immoral, lazy, idle, unpunctual, good-for-nothing people on the face of the earth, as you would know if you had to keep the house and deal with them instead of sitting here airing your views. And I say that the Indians, and the Chinese, and the Japanese, and the Burmese are people with souls, and have the most wonderful ancient books of wisdom, and make far better brass work and pottery than Tottenham Court Road can. These may not be views; but they are facts. Imm there thinks he is ever so much wiser than Confucius or Lao-Tse; but when I read Lao-Tse and then try to read Imm's stuff afterwards it bores me to tears.

IMMENSO. Lao-Tse, being only a sage, cannot draw tears. For that, you need sage and onions.

CLARA. What a silly joke! You great baby.

Savvy looks in again.

SAVVY. Mrs Etteen's motor has just stopped at the gate. Look out. [*She vanishes*].

CLARA. I believe that woman has been here every day since I left.

FRANKLYN [*indignantly*] I have not seen Mrs Etteen for six weeks past. As you object to my seeing her; and I do not care two straws whether I see her or not, you can tell her that I am out, or busy, or anything you please: I will hide myself somewhere until she goes. [*He makes for the door*].

CLARA. No, Frank, you must stay. What—[*he goes out*]. Now that is a beastly thing of Frank to do. He will tell her next time he sees her that I drove him away.

CONRAD. Well, so you did.

CLARA. I did nothing of the sort. I asked him to stay. He makes himself ridiculous over her; and then people say that *I* make him ridiculous—that I am a jealous wife and all sorts of things. You shall just see how jealous I am.

The parlor maid enters, followed by a slender lady, beautifully dressed, with an expression of delicate patience that almost suggests suffering. Her eyes, violet in color, have a softness and depth that make her romantically attractive. Age inscrutable, but certainly under fifty and possibly under forty.

THE PARLOR MAID. Mrs Etteen. [*She withdraws*].

MRS ETTEEN [*approaching Clara and speaking with a deprecating shyness that gives a curious penetration to the audacity of what she says*] I am so disappointed to find you here.

CLARA. Pray why?

MRS ETTEEN. That silly Mrs Topham told me that you had deserted your husband; and as I have adored him for years, I just rushed to offer myself as an unworthy substitute.

CLARA. Well, I'm sure! Theres nothing like being candid, is there? Have you had tea?

MRS ETTEEN. Yes, thank you. Is this your famous brother, Mr Immenso Champernoon?

Immenso, who has been sitting as if mesmerized, too shy to look at anyone, starts convulsively to his feet and presents himself for inspection with his hands hanging limply at his sides and his eyes directed to the carpet.

CLARA. Yes: thats Immenso. He's no use to you: he's happily married. Imm: this is Mrs Etteen.

IMMENSO [*murmuring thunderously*] Ahooroo. Eh plea. [*He is understood to have said "How do you do? Very pleased." They shake hands*].

CLARA. Doctor Conrad Barnabas, Franklyn's brother. Unmarried. Fair game; so he wont interest you.

MRS ETTEEN. You are very naughty, Clara. How do you do, Doctor? I have read your book [*shaking hands*].

CONRAD. How do you do?

CLARA. I can be quite as candid as you, Rosie darling. Sure youve had tea?

MRS ETTEEN. Quite. [*She sits down next Immenso and turns her eyes full on him*]. Mr Champernoon: you are the wisest man in England when you are not talking glorious nonsense. Can you explain something to me?

IMMENSO [*trying to recover his assurance in the dangerous warmth of the violet eyes*] Explanation is not a difficult art. I should say that any fool can explain anything. Whether he can leave you any the wiser is another matter.

MRS ETTEEN. Would you believe that I have been married

three times?

IMMENSO. Does that need an explanation? Have you not such a thing in your house as a mirror?

MRS ETTEEN. Oh! Gallant! You make me blush.

CLARA. You be careful, Imm. You are only mortal, like that Roman conqueror you were talking about.

MRS ETTEEN. I should be very proud to make a conquest of you, Mr Champernoon; and, as it happens, what I am going to ask you is why I cannot.

IMMENSO [*rising rather heavily and moving to a distant seat*] Will you think me very boorish if I beg you to begin our acquaintance at the beginning and not at the end?

CLARA. Nothing doing, Rosie.

MRS ETTEEN. I know. But isnt it queer? I am not an ugly woman. I am not a very unamiable woman. I dont think I am an exceptionally stupid woman. I do think I am rather a fascinating woman: at least I always secure the attention of men. I have even infatuated more than one. And the upshot of it all is that I have had three husbands, and have been unable to keep one of them, though I have taken the greatest trouble to charm and please them. And here is Clara, who never cares what she does or says, who buys her clothes anywhere and flings them on anyhow, who bullies us and quarrels with us and rides roughshod over all our poor little susceptibilities, and yet keeps her wonderful husband without an effort, though we all want to take him from her.

CLARA. Whats the matter with my clothes? I dont get them anywhere: I get them from Valentino's, where you get yours; and I pay what I am asked. What more can I do? You dont expect me to spend my life bothering about my appearance, do you? I am not a professional husband stealer.

MRS ETTEEN. You dont need to steal husbands, dear. Youve got the best one in the market for nothing. But we poor pretty things dress and dress, and paint and paint, and dye and dye, and charm and charm, and all in vain. They wont stay with us even if we catch them once in a while. That is what I want you to explain to me, Mr Champernoon.

It is so unjust.

IMMENSO [*tackling the subject ponderously and seriously*] I take it that a married life, to be permanent, must be part of nature's daily food. Now nature's daily food is not excessively agreeable. A man cannot live on Bath buns.

MRS ETTEEN. An elephant can.

IMMENSO. A very palpable hit, Mrs Etteen. I had, in fact, compared myself to an elephant just before you came in. And curiously enough, I live very largely on buns. But they are plain currant buns. An attempt to live on Bath buns would result in a surfeit of sweetness. If I call Clara a currant bun—

CLARA. I shall call you a sausage roll; so there!

IMMENSO. My sister, who has no illusions about me, will call me a sausage roll. But you, Mrs Etteen, will draw the moral that by laying yourself out to be exquisitely sweet, you may be making it impossible for a plain man to endure your charm for longer than a very brief honeymoon.

MRS ETTEEN. But why does the same thing not apply to very charming men? Franklyn Barnabas is the most charming man I know; but Clara does not get tired of him. What is your answer to that?

IMMENSO. My answer is that perhaps she does get tired of him.

CLARA. Now you hold your tongue, Imm. That was not why I went away.

MRS ETTEEN. Oh! You did go away then?

CLARA. Now that Imm has been inconsiderate enough to let it out, you had better be told that Frank and I separated because he and his brother here have set up a new religion which I simply decline to entertain, and which I hope I have heard the last of.

MRS ETTEEN [*sadly*] The separation did not last very long, did it?

CLARA. Nearly a week. Do you call that nothing?

MRS ETTEEN. You see, he came back.

CLARA. He came back! What do you mean? *I* came back.

You dont suppose he left me.

MRS ETTEEN. I hoped it. But why dont you get tired of him if what your brother says is true? Surely Franklyn is a Bath bun, if ever there was one.

IMMENSO. I should describe him rather as a Bath Oliver. A Bath Oliver has no sweetness; but it has a certain Cromwellian cleanness and plainness. Hence, no doubt, the name Oliver.

MRS ETTEEN. That is rather funny. But it leaves me lonely, and Clara triumphant. Doctor Conrad: has science nothing to say?

CONRAD. Yes. Science tells you that the trouble is that Frank is not an amoeba.

MRS ETTEEN. What is an amoeba?

CONRAD. Our common ancestor. An early form of life which you will find in the nearest ditch.

MRS ETTEEN. And where does Franklyn come in?

CONRAD. The amoeba can split himself into two amoebas, and the two can split themselves into four and so on. Well, Frank cannot split himself up into a dozen Franks so that there shall be a Frank for every woman who wants him. Theres only one of him; and Clara's got it. Hadnt you better make up your mind to that?

MRS ETTEEN. But Franklyn can split himself up. There is a place in America called Salt Lake City, where the Mormons live. All the best men there were amoebas. They divided themselves among a dozen or twenty women. Why should not Franklyn divide himself between Clara and me? Why should she have this treasure of a man all to herself?

CLARA. Youd better ask him. If he decides to give you a share you can have the lot.

MRS ETTEEN. Greedy!

CLARA. All or nothing for me, thank you.

MRS ETTEEN. You see what a wonderful man he is. She never gets tired of him.

CLARA. Yes I do. I get tired of him, and of the house, and of the children, and of Conrad, and of Imm; and so would you if you took on my job. But they belong here and I belong here; and you dont, darling; and thats what makes all the difference.

IMMENSO. I think that settles it, Mrs Etteen.

MRS ETTEEN. *I* dont. I have an absolute inner conviction that I belong to Franklyn and that Franklyn belongs to me. We must have been married to one another in a former existence. I feel that Clara is only accepting a fact, as all sensible women do. I began by accepting facts myself. But I now believe that the progress of the world depends on the people who refuse to accept facts and insist on the satisfaction of their instincts.

CLARA. It depends a good deal on the sort of instincts you have, doesnt it?

MRS ETTEEN. Oh, if you satisfy the lower instincts and starve the higher, experience pulls you up very short indeed. Besides, Clara, you dont mean that my admiration for Franklyn is a low instinct. You cannot blame me for sharing your own taste.

CLARA. Admire as much as you please. Women make me ill the way they slobber over Frank; and he never looks really contemptible except when he is encouraging them and purring and making sheep's eyes at them. But I suppose he is there to be admired, like my diamond cross. Mothers have the trouble of keeping children clean and fed and well-behaved for old maids and old bachelors to pet and admire; and I suppose wives must be content to keep husbands presentable for unattached females to flirt with. But there are limits.

MRS ETTEEN. If you will let me feed him and do all the troublesome part I will let you come and admire him as often as you like.

CLARA. Rosie: you have the devil's own cheek.

MRS ETTEEN. I! I am the greatest coward alive.

CLARA. But take care. You think that the risk you run is only to be thrown out of the house as you deserve. But that isnt the risk you run at all. You can stay to dinner if you like:

Imm is dining with us, and Conrad, and the rector. You can just trot over the house and look for Franklyn if you want to: he is somewhere about, waiting til you have gone. But some day, if you dont take care, you will be taken at your word. For two pins I would just throw over all this marriage business and leave you in possession. It is no sinecure for me, nor for any woman.

MRS ETTEEN [*rising, and not trying to conceal that she is wounded*] If he is waiting for me to go, I had better go. [*She goes to the door. It opens in her face; and Franklyn enters*].

FRANKLYN [*with a courteous air of delighted surprise*] What! You here, Mrs Etteen! How do you do?

MRS ETTEEN. Didnt you know? [*She turns and looks at Clara*].

CLARA. I had to tell her you were waiting for her to go, Frank. If Rosie wont be a lady and tell lies enough to make herself agreeable, she must not complain if the truth hits her harder than she bargains for. People with soft corns shouldnt stand on other people's toes.

Mrs Etteen, greatly distressed, snatches out her handkerchief.

CLARA. Sit down, Rosie; and dont be a fool: you can stay to dinner.

MRS ETTEEN [*struggling inarticulately with her tears*] I am so sorry—[*she cannot go on*].

CLARA. Frank: take her round the garden and talk to her. It is you that have upset her.

MRS ETTEEN. Oh no.

FRANKLYN. Come.

MRS ETTEEN [*taking his arm*] I am so ashamed—so sorry —[*She goes out into the garden on Franklyn's arm*].

CONRAD. You got the best of that, Clara.

CLARA. I should think so, indeed. I always get the best of it. She used to frighten me and fluster me. Thats the worst of the way women are brought up: we are trained never to tell the truth or to face the truth: all we know is how to play cat's cradle with one another; and of course the consequence is that the moment we are faced by anyone who just throws the truth in our faces, we get rattled and make fools of ourselves. Rosie played that game on me and nearly drove me mad. I dont know what I should have done if Frank hadnt taken me in hand and shewed me the trick of it. Then I played it on her. I can play her head off at it. When she tries to terrify me by putting a few of her cards on the table: I put the whole pack on the table, both hers and mine; and as I have the ace of trumps I win every time. She came here as a thief to steal Frank from me. Now she comes as a beggar; and I throw her a scrap of him occasionally. She is having her scrap now, in the garden, poor wretch!

CONRAD. Yes: that is what women are: dogs fighting one another for the best bones. And what are we men? The bones you fight for. You dont catch me getting married.

CLARA. Oh indeed! You are glad enough to come here and be taken care of and pet the children without any expense or responsibility, all the same. You cuckoo! [*She flings the epithet in his face and sweeps scornfully out of the room*].

CONRAD [*rising*] Damn her impudence! I will never enter this house again.

IMMENSO. That will not solve the problem. The bachelor solution is no solution. The bachelor is either a hermit or a cuckoo. Go and get married, Con. Better be a husband than a domestic parasite.

CONRAD. I shall go out of this house, anyhow. Good evening.

IMMENSO. I doubt if she will let you. However, you can try. Good evening.

CONRAD. I will jolly soon see whether she can stop me [*he leaves the room*].

Immenso takes a paper and begins to read, putting his feet up, and making himself quite comfortable on the sofa.

CLARA'S VOICE. Where are you going, Con?

CONRAD'S VOICE. I am going out of this house, never to darken your doors again: thats where I'm going.

CLARA'S VOICE. You are going to do nothing of the sort,

because I have locked up all your things in your room.

THE TWO VOICES SIMULTANEOUSLY.

I tell you I am going. Give me the key of my room instantly. Do you suppose I am going to stay in a house where I am told to my face that I am a sponge, a parasite, a-a-a-a cuckoo? I'm damned if I'll stand it. You can keep your house and your children and your unfortunate devil of a husband. I tell you I wont. What pleasure is it to you to have me if you grudge every morsel I eat and drink, and are jealous every time I talk to Savvy? Youre as jealous as—

Now dont be ridiculous, Con: you know very well you brought it on yourself by saying that Rosie and I were two dogs fighting for a bone. If you go, what am I to say to Frank and Savvy? Am I to tell them the nasty things you said about them? And there is roast chicken being done expressly for you; and I have not the least intention of allowing you to waste it. So be good, and remember that we dine at half-past seven, and that half-past seven means half-past seven and not eight as it usually—

The voices fade out of hearing. Immenso, who at the first sound of them has looked up from his paper to listen, smiles broadly; crosses his shins; and settles himself to read until the rector comes to dinner.

We may as well skip the dinner, as the presence of the rector puts a stop to domestic bickering without adding to the brilliancy of the general conversation. Readers of Back to Methuselah will remember the Reverend William Haslam as a very young man who had been shoved into a Church living, as he expressed it, by his father, who was a friend of the patron and a schoolfellow of the bishop. Being at this stage of his career a complete unbeliever, with only two passions, one for lawn tennis and the other for Savvy Barnabas, and being afflicted with perfect clearness of mind as to his unworthiness as a parson (being a hollow fraud, he calls it) he is not very interesting even in ordinary Hampstead society. In the presence of intellects like those of Champernoon and the Barnabases he is a mere cipher in a continuous collar. Nobody, himself least of all, has the faintest suspicion that he alone of all that gifted company is destined to survive three hundred years and be three times an archbishop.

For the present, then, it makes no difference to the dinner party when he slips away from it at the earliest possible moment with Savvy, and takes refuge in the library, where we may now have a look at them as they sit on the sofa, each with an arm round the other's ribs.

HASLAM. Look here, darling: hadnt you better tell your father that we're going to be married?

SAVVY. He wont care.

HASLAM. But he ought to know, you know.

SAVVY. Well, you can tell him if you like. I am not going to intrude my affairs on him when he doesnt even pretend to take any interest in them. I dont mind telling Nunky.

HASLAM. When is it to be? He may as well know the worst at once.

SAVVY. As soon as you like. Now that both Nunky and Papa have gone raving mad on this stunt of theirs about living for ever, life here is becoming unbearable. They expect a dress to last ten years because they expect me to last three hundred. Promise me that when we are married, I shall never hear the words Creative Evolution again.

HASLAM. I promise. I cant keep Adam and Eve out of the lessons in church; but I can keep Creative Evolution out of them. Oh, by the way! I am afraid you will have to come to church. Do you mind very much?

SAVVY. Not a bit. I had to do it in college, you know. Thatll be all right, Bill.

HASLAM. I always rip through pretty fast; and I never preach more than seven minutes: old Lady Mumford makes such an awful row if I do.

SAVVY. Does that matter?

HASLAM. I should think it does. Her big subscription just barely makes the two ends meet in the church accounts. Consequently in our parish Lady Mumford is to all intents and purposes the Church of England.

Franklyn and Conrad come in.

HASLAM [*to Franklyn*] By the way, sir, I think you ought to know. Would you mind if Savvy and I were to get married?

CONRAD. Hallo!

HASLAM. Yes: I know it sounds rather sudden. But theres no immediate hurry. Any time will do.

SAVVY. No it wont.

HASLAM. I dont mean our marriage, darling.

FRANKLYN. You mean only my consent, is that it?

HASLAM. Well, I suppose that is what it comes to. Ha! ha! Priceless!

FRANKLYN. Well, Savvy: you know your own business best.

CONRAD. There is no gainsaying the urge of Creative Evolution.

SAVVY [*desperately*] Oh, Nunky, do drop it for a moment. [*To Haslam*] Lets get married tomorrow. You can perform the ceremony yourself, cant you?

HASLAM. I think I shall ask the blooming bishop. It would be awful cheek; but I think he'd like it.

Clara, Mrs Etteen, and Immenso come in.

CLARA. Franklyn: go and play billiards. You will not digest your dinner if you sit there talking to Conrad.

FRANKLYN. Oh, goodness gracious, may I not have indigestion and intelligent conversation if I prefer it to running round a billiard table after my health?

CLARA. You will be very disagreeable if you get indigestion. And Con wants to smoke. Off with you.

FRANKLYN. Oh, very well. [*He goes out sulkily*].

CONRAD. Anything for a quiet life. [*He goes out taking his pipe out of his pocket as he goes*].

CLARA. Savvy: take Rosie and Imm to the drawing

room; and let us have some music. Imm hasnt heard Rosie play; and the sooner he gets it over, the better.

MRS ETTEEN [*moving towards the door*] Do you really want any music, Mr Champernoon?

IMMENSO [*going with her*] In moods of battle and victory I want the bagpipes, Mrs Etteen. My wife imitates them on the black keys of the piano. I do the drum, with a dinner gong. [*They go out*].

SAVVY. Come along, Bill.

Haslam rises with alacrity.

CLARA. No: Bill will stay and talk to me. You clear out.

Savvy, surprised, looks at Haslam, whose countenance has fallen; then goes out slowly.

CLARA. Sit down.

Haslam sits down.

CLARA [*sitting down also*] Am I, too, privileged to call you Bill, Mr Haslam?

HASLAM. Certainly, if you like.

CLARA. You mustnt suppose because Mr Barnabas is blind, I am. What are your intentions, young man?

HASLAM [*his eyes twinkling*] I have just declared them to Mr Barnabas.

CLARA. What!!!

HASLAM [*enjoying his retort immensely*] Priceless!

CLARA. I see nothing priceless about it. I think it was great impudence of you to speak to Mr Barnabas before Savvy had said a word to me. What did Franklyn say?

HASLAM. You came in before he had time to say anything. But it seemed to go down all right.

CLARA. A nice father! Didnt he ask you a single question?

HASLAM. You didnt give him a chance.

CLARA. What means have you?

HASLAM. The stipend is £180; and the rectory lets for £300 a year furnished.

CLARA. Genteel poverty. And nothing to look forward to. They wont make you an archbishop.

HASLAM. I should think not. Ha! ha! Priceless!

CLARA. Very well. All I have to say is that if she is fool enough to marry you *I* cant stop her. So dont hope to get out of it that way. You have let yourself in for it; and now you must make the best of it.

HASLAM. It is rather awful. That is, of course, when it isnt delightful.

CLARA. What about your own people?

HASLAM. Oh, they expect me to make an ass of myself. I am the fool of the family. They look to my brother to marry money.

CLARA. Well, you seem to have a fairly sensible family: thats one comfort. I wish I could say as much for us. You know, dont you, that Con is as mad as a hatter, and that Franklyn is going soft in the same way? They think theyre going to live for three hundred years. I dont know what is to become of us. I have to keep up appearances; but—[*she almost breaks down*].

HASLAM [*much concerned*] Oh, dont take it that way, Mrs Barnabas. I had no idea you were worrying about it. I am really awfully sorry.

CLARA. Did you suppose I was a fool? Or did you think I believed all that stuff about Creative Evolution, or whatever they call it?

HASLAM. It's only a fad. I assure you men get the wildest fads without going a bit dotty. Jolly good thing for them, too. If they dont take to a fad they take to drink or to gambling on the stock exchange, or to the classics or something horribly tiresome.

CLARA [*a little consoled*] You really think that, Bill?

HASLAM. Quite sure of it. My brother's mad on golf. My mother's mad on gardening. Theyre not intellectual, you know. Mr Barnabas and the doctor have to go mad on something intellectual. This three hundred years stunt is a priceless refuge for them.

CLARA. Well, you comfort me. I need it badly, God knows. Thank you. For myself, I had far rather have a comforting son-in-law than one with lots of money. Savvy'd spend it all anyhow, if you had a million. The way she runs through boots! And theyre forty-five shillings a pair now.

HASLAM. It's awfully good of you to take to me like this, Mrs Barnabas.

CLARA. There are not so many people in the world that one can take to. [*Looking at him critically*] After all, you may come to be an archbishop yet. Old Archbishop Chettle, who was my father's tutor at Durham, was just as ridiculous as you are.

HASLAM. People dont mind it so much when they come to know me.

CLARA. I am a little ridiculous myself, you know. I cannot suffer fools gladly. You dont seem to mind. Can you put up with me as a mother-in-law? I wont come too often.

HASLAM. You will suit me down to the ground. Fancy your turning out so pricelessly jolly as this!

CLARA [*pleased*] Very well. Now run off to the drawing room, and ask Rosie to play.

HASLAM. I'd a jolly sight rather hear Savvy play.

CLARA. Savvy doesnt want to play. Rosie is dying for an excuse to play Saint Nepomuk's Eve because it always fetches Franklyn from the billiard room to listen to her. Imm will never think of asking her to play: he will only talk her head off. Be kind to her, and ask her for something by Hugo Wolf.

HASLAM. Rather a lark it would be, wouldnt it, if Uncle Imm were to cut Mr Barnabas out with Mrs Etteen?

CLARA. Imm has no ear for music. She cant do it with the piano anyhow.

A hollow chord of G flat and D flat is heard droning from the drawing room piano. Then The Campbells are Coming is played on the black keys.

A drum obbligato begins on the dinner gong, played at first with childish enjoyment, and proceeding, in a rapid crescendo, to ecstasy.

HASLAM. She is doing it with the piano! Priceless!

CLARA [*indignantly*] Well!

SAVVY [*rushing in*] Mother: do come and stop Uncle Imm. If he starts dancing he will shake the house down. Oh, listen to them. [*She puts her fingers in her ears*].

CLARA [*rushing out*] Stop, stop! Imm! Rosie! Stop that horrible noise.

SAVVY [*shutting the door with a slam*] Did you ever hear anything like it? Uncle Imm is the greatest baby.

The noise suddenly stops with the sound of the dinner gong being torn from Imm's grasp and flung down on the carpet, presumably by Clara. The piano takes the hint and stops too.

SAVVY. What did mother want with you?

HASLAM. To ask me my intentions. Priceless!

SAVVY. Did she make a row?

HASLAM. Not a bit. She was awfully nice about it. She's a stunning good sort.

SAVVY. Bill!!

HASLAM. She is, really. I had no idea. We shall get on first rate.

SAVVY. Then I cry off. She has got round you.

HASLAM. Why? Arnt you glad?

SAVVY. Glad! When I am marrying you to get rid of her! Bill: the match is off. If she has got round you I might just as well stay at home. How does she get round people? Why am I the only person she doesnt think it worth her while to get round?

HASLAM. She didnt get round me: she went straight at me; and over I went. What could I do? I was prepared to hold my end up if she started fighting. But she fell on my neck. It wasnt my fault.

SAVVY. It's too disgusting. All men are the same: theyre no good when it comes to tackling a woman who can see nobody's point of view except her own.

HASLAM. She seems to like me in a sort of way.

SAVVY. She always wanted a son. All women do who like men: the women who want girls only want live dolls. I was a disappointment because I was a girl. And now she comes and grabs you from me, as she grabs everything.

HASLAM. I feel just the same about my father, you know. How mother ever stuck it out with him I cant imagine.

SAVVY. You neednt boast about your mother: look at my father! See how he has stuck it out.

HASLAM. Parents are a ghastly fraud, if you ask me. But theyre necessary, I suppose.

SAVVY. Bill: youre very aggravating. I want to quarrel; and you wont. You have no sand in you.

HASLAM. Whats the good of quarrelling? If I felt like that I should jolly well punch your head and have done with it.

SAVVY [*throwing her arms violently round him and punctuating her epithets with savage kisses*] Pig. Fool. Idiot. Sillybilly.

HASLAM. Darling.

The dinner gong is heard bumping against something outside. They spring apart. Immenso enters in the character of a Highland chieftain carrying the gong like a target, and a hockey stick like a claymore. He has heightened the illusion by draping his shoulder with a travelling rug. He marches about, humming The Campbells. Mrs Etteen follows, half annoyed, half amused, and sits down on the sofa.

SAVVY [*still excited, to Immenso*] Sillybilly, sillybilly, sillybilly! Fat boy of Peckham! [*She snatches a ruler from the writing table. Immenso disposes himself immediately for combat. She makes a feint which he utterly fails to parry, and stabs him with the ruler. He falls ponderously and cautiously*]. Slain! slain! Mrs Etteen will receive your last breath. Come, Bill. [*She runs out*].

HASLAM. Priceless! [*He runs out after her*].

IMMENSO [*rising with difficulty*] "Unwounded from the dreadful close; but breathless all, Fitzjames arose."

MRS ETTEEN. Mr Champernoon: would you mind growing up for a moment, and condescending to treat me as an adult person?

IMMENSO. If you insist on our keeping up that dreary affectation I am bound to obey you. [*He throws down the hockey stick, the rug, and finally the gong*]. Farewell, ye real things. How good it is to hear your solid thump on the floor! The human boy sleeps with you there. The literary gasbag floats gently to your feet, madam. [*He sits down on the chair furthest away from her*].

MRS ETTEEN. But you have not floated to my feet. You have floated to the opposite end of the room.

IMMENSO. I need space if I am to treat you as a public meeting. I understand that you prefer that to Fitzjames.

MRS ETTEEN. There is a mystic region between the public meeting and the playground in which you have not been seen yet. It is the region in which men and women meet when they are alone together.

IMMENSO [*troubled and grave*] I had better say at once frankly, Mrs Etteen, that in that region I must put up a notice inscribed Nothing Doing. I am married; and I take marriage honorably and seriously. I am not putting this forward as a criticism of your attitude towards it. I only suggest that our attitudes are incompatible. Therefore will you allow me to continue to regard you as a public meeting.

MRS ETTEEN. By all means, if you can.

A pause. Mrs Etteen bears the silence calmly. Immenso is embarrassed by it.

IMMENSO [*at last*] The difficulty is that there is nothing before the meeting.

MRS ETTEEN. Just so. Come, Mr Champernoon! cant you get over this ridiculous shyness, and behave as Nature intended men and women to behave when they are alone together? Come and quarrel with me, or make love to me, or do something human. Search your soul for something to say to me that will not leave me cold and desolate.

IMMENSO. After searching my soul most carefully, absolutely the only remark that occurs to me is that we have been having wonderfully fine weather for the last fortnight. That is the commonplace but tragic truth.

MRS ETTEEN. That is the only thing you can find words for. But there is something between us that you cannot find words for: even you, who are so great a master of words.

IMMENSO. What, for example?

MRS ETTEEN. Say, a sense of deadly peril.

IMMENSO [*slowly*] Mrs Etteen: there are certain things I cannot say to a lady. One of them is that I feel perfectly safe with her.

MRS ETTEEN. So much the better! Can you really talk to me exactly as you would talk to the baker?

IMMENSO. I cannot say that. The baker is an organic part of society. Without the baker I should perish or live on snails. I am not convinced that beautiful ladies—shall I call them love ladies?—are an organic part of society. Without them I should not perish. I should flourish.

MRS ETTEEN. Without love ladies there would be no love children. Have you noticed that love children, like love ladies, are very beautiful?

IMMENSO. The statistics of illegitimate children—

MRS ETTEEN [*quickly*] I did not say illegitimate children, Mr Champernoon: I said love children. There are more love children born in wedlock than out of it: at least I hope so. But there are very few born at all, either in or out of wedlock.

IMMENSO. I have known some very beautiful persons of the sort you mean. I may be prejudiced against them because I, alas! am not an entrancingly beautiful person; but some of them were infernal rascals.

MRS ETTEEN. Spendthrifts and libertines and so forth, eh?

IMMENSO. I am myself a bit of a spendthrift as far as my means allow. No: I should call them thieves, if people who order goods they cannot pay for are thieves. I should call them rascals, because people who borrow money heartlessly from poorer people than themselves on the security of false promises to pay are in my opinion rascals. And libertines, certainly, of both sexes.

MRS ETTEEN. And yet charming people, all the same. Centres of exquisite happiness. Living fountains of love.

IMMENSO. That is why I hate them. They bring these

precious things into contempt. They are living blasphemies.

MRS ETTEEN. And so you have to put up with plain dowdy people, and have children as ugly as yourself. What sort of world is it where the ugly practical people, the people who can deal with money and material things, and be thoroughly mean about them, succeed, and the beautiful people who live in noble dreams and continually strive to realize them, are ruined and despised? Do you suppose they like borrowing from poor people, who are the only ones simple enough to lend, or that they enjoy being dunned by tradesmen? Is it their fault that when they offer love, they are told that unless they steal it they must pay for it with all their worldly goods, with their liberty, with nearly the whole of their lives? Is that right? You are a clever man: you are a professional moralist. Is there nothing wrong in it? Give me an honest answer. Dont preach at me; but tell me as man to woman. Do you not feel sometimes that it is all wrong?

IMMENSO. As a professional moralist I can make out a case against it. I can make out a case for it just as easily. Cases do not impress me. They never impress people who have the knack of making them. It's no use giving tracts to a missionary.

MRS ETTEEN. Yes: I was wrong to argue about it. The moment one argues one goes wrong at once. It is deeper than argument. You may say what you like; but can you feel that the beautiful people are all wrong and that the ugly people are all right? Would you think them beautiful and ugly if you really believed that?

IMMENSO. I have noticed that there are subjective and objective people; and—

MRS ETTEEN. Beautiful subjective people and ugly objective people?

IMMENSO [*uneasy under her greater conviction*] Beauty is a matter of taste, after all. One man's meat is another man's poison. Lots of people do not think my wife beautiful. They are nitwits; but they have a right to their opinion.

MRS ETTEEN [*with dignity*] Mr Champernoon: is it possible that you think I am discussing the question of sex with you?

IMMENSO [*taken aback*] Well—er— Well, good heavens! what else are we discussing?

MRS ETTEEN. *I* am discussing beauty, which is not a matter of taste at all, but a matter of fact as to which no difference of opinion is possible among cultivated people. Can you produce a single person of any culture who thinks the Venus of Milo or the Hermes of Praxiteles ugly? Can you produce a single person who thinks—

IMMENSO. Who thinks me beautiful? Not one.

MRS ETTEEN. I have seen worse, Mr Champernoon. [*He bows*]. You are very like Balzac, of whom Rodin made one of the greatest statues in the world. But dont you see that this sex attraction, though it is so useful for keeping the world peopled, has nothing to do with beauty: that it blinds us to ugliness instead of opening our eyes to beauty. It is what enables us to endure a world full of ugly sights and sounds and people. You can do without the Venus of Milo because the young lady at the refreshment bar can make you forget her. I dont want to talk about such attractions: they are only the bait in the trap of marriage: they vanish when they have served their turn. But have you never known really beautiful people, beautiful as girls, beautiful as matrons, beautiful as grandmothers, or men to match them? Do you not want a world of such beautiful people, instead of what the gentleman in Mr. Granville-Barker's play calls "this farmyard world of sex"? Will you dare to tell me that the world was no worse when the lords of creation were monkeys than it is now that they are men, ugly as most of them are? Do you really want us all to become like ants and bees because ants and bees are industrious and goody goody?

IMMENSO. As I am myself a species of human bumble bee, I cannot give you an unprejudiced opinion.

MRS ETTEEN. No: you shall not ride off on a quip, Mr Champernoon. Stand to your guns. You thought I was going to entice you into a flirtation: you see now that I am trying to convert you to a religion of beauty.

IMMENSO. I am not sure that I do not think you all the more dangerous. You might pervert me intellectually; but on the other ground I am invincible. I cannot flirt. I am not what is called a lady's man, Mrs Etteen.

MRS ETTEEN. You cannot flirt! Mr Champernoon: you are the most incorrigible flirt in England, and the very worst sort of flirt too. You flirt with religions, with traditions, with politics, with everything that is most sacred and important. You flirt with the Church, with the Middle Ages, with the marriage question, with the Jewish question, even with the hideous cult of gluttony and drunkenness. Every one of your discussions of these questions is like a flirtation with a worthless woman: you pay her the most ingenious and delightful compliments, driving all your legitimate loves mad with distress and jealousy; but you are not a bit in earnest: behind all your sincere admiration of her priceless pearls and her pretty paint you loathe the creature's flesh and blood. You are all flirts, you intellectuals. If you flirted with housemaids and dairymaids, or with chorus girls, I could forgive you; but to flirt with ghastly old hags because they were the mistresses of kings and of all the oppressors of the earth is despicable and silly.

IMMENSO [*reddening*] I deny that innuendo. I was in a Liberal set, a Protestant set, an atheist set, a Puritan set. I had everything to lose by defending the Church and the Middle Ages, by denouncing Puritanism, by affirming the existence of God.

MRS ETTEEN. Then you had not even the excuse of wanting money or a knighthood. You flirted with these old, wicked, outworn things from pure devilment, because you were a born coquette.

IMMENSO. I do not admit that these institutions are wicked or outworn. I admit that they are old, which proves at least that they were not jerry built.

MRS ETTEEN. Cruelty is old. Slavery is old. Greed, ambition, plague, pestilence and famine are old. They are not jerry built either. Are they any the better for that? I am not so clever as you, Mr Champernoon; but I can see that if we did not indulge you by stepping softly about the room because we want to admire your wonderful houses of cards, they would come down at the first resolute footfall. As often as not it is your own foot that comes down when some abominable oppression stings you into earnestness; and—

IMMENSO. And who can expect any house to stand that earthshaking shock?

MRS ETTEEN. A jibe at your size has got you out of many a controversial difficulty.

IMMENSO. I protest I have exploited it only in the interests of good humor. I laugh at it with the wrong side of my mouth. [*He sits down beside her*]. But I still defend the past. My roots are in the past: so are yours.

MRS ETTEEN. My roots are in the past: my hopes are in the future.

IMMENSO. The past is as much a part of eternity as the future. Beware of ingratitude to the past. What is gratitude? The cynic says, a sense of favors to come. Many people would say that we cannot be grateful to the past because we have nothing to expect from it. But if we had no memory of favors from the past we could have no faith in favors from the future. Why do I uphold the Church: I, who know as much of the crimes of the Churches as you do? Not for what the Church did for men, but for what men did for the Church. It brought us no gifts; but it drew forth gifts from us. And that is just as it should be. I love the Church because Michelangelo painted its churches. You complain of it because the churches did not paint Michelangelo. Well, suppose they h a d painted him! Suppose they had tarred and feathered him! Would you not place the painting of Michelangelo, with the burning of John Huss or Giordano Bruno or Joan of Arc, among the crimes of the Churches?

MRS ETTEEN. That is a very pretty little juggle with words, and very funny. But when you are talking of Michel-

cl

angelo you are talking of a man so great that he was literally a demigod. When you talk of the Church, you are talking of a pack of common men calling themselves clergymen and priests, and trying to persuade us that they are demigods by wearing ugly black clothes. Michelangelo did not paint for them: he painted for me, and for people like you and me. We are the spectators for whom he painted: we are the Church which drew out his gifts. It was for us that Bach and Beethoven composed, that Phidias and Rodin made statues, that the poets sang and the philosophers became seers. It is you who are faithless and disloyal in giving the allegiance we owe to them to corrupt gangs of little lawyers and politicians and priests and adventurers organized as States and Churches and dressed up like actors to seem the thing they are not. They pretend to see events with glass eyes, and to hear the music of the spheres with ass's ears. [*She pauses. Immenso is staring before him like a man in a trance.*] Are you listening? [*He does not answer*]. I know. You are thinking how you can work all this into an article.

IMMENSO [*waking up suddenly*] Damn it, I am. [*He salutes*]. *Touché!*

MRS ETTEEN. *Plait-il?*

IMMENSO. That is what a fencer says to his adversary when he acknowledges a hit. Yes: you got in that time. But why should I not make it into an article? It is my trade.

MRS ETTEEN. Couldnt you make it into an action of some sort. Couldnt you kill somebody, for instance, as all the people who are in earnest do?

IMMENSO. I am prepared to kill. You may think it boasting; but, like Hamlet, I do not hold my life at a pin's fee when my fate cries out. As I am not going to kill anybody—shall I say as we are not going to kill anybody?—I suppose our fate does not cry out.

MRS ETTEEN. Oh yes: I am as great a coward, as futile a creature as you: dont think I dont know it. Shall I tell you why that is?

IMMENSO. You evidently will, whether I say yes or no.

MRS ETTEEN. It is because we have not really finished with the sensualities, the crudities, the vulgarities and superstitions that are holding us back. We have not had time to exhaust them, to survive them, to be forced to provide for a spiritual future on earth when they are all dead in us, just as we are forced to provide for bread in our present old age. We do not live long enough—

IMMENSO [*starting*] What! Are you on this Back-to-Methuselah tack too? Has all this been the craze of my brothers-in-law at second hand?

MRS ETTEEN. Oh, very manly man that you are, it does not occur to you that Franklyn Barnabas may have had this from me. Did he ever speak of it before he met me?

IMMENSO. Now that you mention it, no. But it began with Conrad; and you certainly did not work in his laboratory.

MRS ETTEEN. Conrad never saw the scope of his idea any more than Weismann, from whom he got it. He saw how it affected science: he knew that he had to die when he was just beginning to discover what science really is, and had just found out that the experience of people who die at seventy is only a string of the mistakes of immaturity. He had the skeleton of the great faith; but it was Franklyn who put the flesh on it. And it was I, the woman, who made that flesh for him out of my own. That is my relation to Franklyn. That is what Clara would call the intrigue between us.

IMMENSO [*gravely*] She should call it the tragedy of the man who does not trust his wife. He should tell Clara.

MRS ETTEEN. He tells her everything she can understand. If he tries to tell her more it is thrown back in his face like a blow. She is jealous of me; and with good reason.

IMMENSO. But why should he not explain to her the nature of his interest in you, or rather of your common interest in the great faith, as you call it? It is perfectly innocent.

MRS ETTEEN. Will you go home and tell your wife that you find me a very interesting person, and that though you began by keeping at the other end of the room, you have been sitting almost in my lap for the last five minutes?

IMMENSO [*springs up with an inarticulate exclamation. Then, with Johnsonian courtesy*] I beg your pardon, Mrs Etteen. [*He is about to sit down again further from her, but corrects himself, and sits scrupulously as close to her as before*].

MRS ETTEEN. Have I won your interest fairly or have I not? Have I played a single low trick, or practised a single woman's wile?

IMMENSO. You are not a single woman, Mrs—

MRS ETTEEN. Tut! tut! tut! no puns, no jokes, no evasion. Was it fair play or foul play?

IMMENSO. You have landed a very large fish, Mrs Etteen. But you fished fairly. I wish to announce in all honor that I adore you [*he kisses her hand*]. I say it in all honor; and I mean it. And yet I know I shall not tell my wife. Will that be honorable?

MRS ETTEEN. You make too much fuss about it. Do you suppose that there is not among our literary geniuses some writer whose best books she sometimes devours with just a tiny little more relish than your second best? But she does not tell you so. Is that dishonorable, or is it simply kindness—loving-kindness, as the Bible says.

IMMENSO. I hope so.

MRS ETTEEN. Every good wife should commit a few infidelities to keep her husband in countenance. The extent to which married people strain their relations by pretending that there is only one man or woman in the world for them is so tragic that we have to laugh at it to save ourselves from crying. But we shant be so foolish when we all live three hundred years.

How this conversation ended I cannot tell; for I never followed up the adventure of Immenso Champernoon with Mrs Etteen, and dont believe it came to anything.

"LINK" FOR BACK TO METHUSELAH

THIS "link" was written for a B.B.C. radio broadcast of Back to Methuselah, presented on 2nd January 1935.

The "link" is meant to join Part I of Back to Methuselah to the ghostly finale of Part V.

ANNOUNCER. We must now ask the listener to make a colossal jump from the beginning of recorded time to the utmost horizon of the future. Not that the author has left the gap unfilled. He has shown us in three intervening plays first, how Adam's choice of a thousand years for a reasonable lifetime became shortened by war, by disease, by unwholesome living of all sorts, until it shrank to our present span of seventy years, which our Insurance Companies will tell you is considerably in excess of the real average duration of human life to-day.

It is at this point that the author gives us a play of modern political life to convince you that seventy years is far too short a time to qualify for the work of governing the world wisely. Two brothers, a sociologist and a biologist, decide that a lifetime of three hundred years is necessary if civilisation is to be saved.

Then in another play he moves just far enough into the future to show you certain people mysteriously growing older and older without showing any signs of age and being compelled to conceal their extraordinary and incredible condition by staging imaginary deaths—mostly sham drownings—and reappearing under false names and false ages: also how the strange people at last find out each other's existence and get together to form a colony of long livers, who attain the age of three hundred years.

The next play makes a further and much longer leap into the future, showing us these long livers in sole possession of the British Isles, acquiring in their later years such an intensification of their psychic powers that they are consulted as oracles by short livers like ourselves from all the rest of the world in search of advice, which the poor creatures are unable to understand or follow. The very presence of a long liver discourages and even kills the short livers unless elaborate precautions are taken.

All this development of the great Methuselah theme brings us to the last play—the final limit of our famous author's imagination—where thirty thousand years hence we find a world in which the short livers have long been discouraged out of existence and all have returned to Adam's first state of immortality and have acquired powers and knowledge which, compared with ours, may be described as omnipotence and omniscience. We are shown one day's life under these conditions; but when the night falls, the spirit of the beginning stirs again in the forest and the voices from the Garden of Eden are heard calling out of the darkness. Listen. . . .

From the typescript in the Hanley Collection, University of Texas.

PART I IN THE BEGINNING

ACT I

THE Garden of Eden. Afternoon. An immense serpent is sleeping with her head buried in a thick bed of Johns-wort, and her body coiled in apparently endless rings through the branches of a tree, which is already well grown; for the days of creation have been longer than our reckoning. She is not yet visible to anyone unaware of her presence, as her colors of green and brown make a perfect camouflage. Near her head a low rock shews above the Johnswort.

The rock and tree are on the border of a glade in which lies a dead fawn all awry, its neck being broken. Adam, crouching with one hand on the rock, is staring in consternation at the dead body. He has not noticed the serpent on his left hand. He turns his face to his right and calls excitedly.

ADAM. Eve! Eve!

EVE'S VOICE. What is it, Adam?

ADAM. Come here. Quick. Something has happened.

EVE [*running in*] What? Where? [*Adam points to the fawn*]. Oh! [*She goes to it; and he is emboldened to go with her*]. What is the matter with its eyes?

ADAM. It is not only its eyes. Look. [*He kicks it*].

EVE. Oh dont! Why doesnt it wake?

ADAM. I dont know. It is not asleep.

EVE. Not asleep?

ADAM. Try.

EVE [*trying to shake it and roll it over*] It is stiff and cold.

ADAM. Nothing will wake it.

EVE. It has a queer smell. Pah! [*She dusts her hands, and draws away from it*]. Did you find it like that?

ADAM. No. It was playing about; and it tripped and went head over heels. It never stirred again. Its neck is wrong [*he stoops to lift the neck and shew her*].

EVE. Dont touch it. Come away from it.

They both retreat, and contemplate it from a few steps' distance with growing repulsion.

EVE. Adam.

ADAM. Yes?

EVE. Suppose you were to trip and fall, would you go like that?

ADAM. Ugh! [*He shudders and sits down on the rock*].

EVE [*throwing herself on the ground beside him, and grasping his knee*] You must be careful. Promise me you will be careful.

ADAM. What is the good of being careful? We have to live here for ever. Think of what for ever means! Sooner or later I shall trip and fall. It may be tomorrow; it may be after as many days as there are leaves in the garden and grains of sand by the river. No matter: some day I shall forget and stumble.

EVE. I too.

ADAM [*horrified*] Oh no, no. I should be alone. Alone for ever. You must never put yourself in danger of stumbling. You must not move about. You must sit still. I will take care of you and bring you what you want.

EVE [*turning away from him with a shrug, and hugging her ankles*] I should soon get tired of that. Besides, if it happened to you, *I* should be alone. I could not sit still then. And at last it would happen to me too.

ADAM. And then?

EVE. Then we should be no more. There would be only the things on all fours, and the birds, and the snakes.

ADAM. That must not be.

EVE. Yes: that must not be. But it might be.

ADAM. No. I tell you it must not be. I know that it must not be.

EVE. We both know it. How do we know it?

ADAM. There is a voice in the garden that tells me things.

EVE. The garden is full of voices sometimes. They put all sorts of thoughts into my head.

ADAM. To me there is only one voice. It is very low; but it is so near that it is like a whisper from within myself. There is no mistaking it for any voice of the birds or beasts, or for your voice.

EVE. It is strange that I should hear voices from all sides and you only from within. But I have some thoughts that come from within me and not from the voices. The thought that we must not cease to be comes from within.

ADAM [*despairingly*] But we shall cease to be. We shall fall like the fawn and be broken. [*Rising and moving about in his agitation*] I cannot bear this knowledge. I will not have it. It must not be, I tell you. Yet I do not know how to prevent it.

EVE. That is just what I feel; but it is very strange that you should say so: there is no pleasing you. You change your mind so often.

ADAM [*scolding her*] Why do you say that? How have I changed my mind?

EVE. You say we must not cease to exist. But you used to complain of having to exist always and for ever. You sometimes sit for hours brooding and silent, hating me in your heart. When I ask you what I have done to you, you say you are not thinking of me, but of the horror of having to be here for ever. But I know very well that what you mean is the horror of having to be here with me for ever.

ADAM. Oh! That is what you think, is it? Well, you are wrong. [*He sits down again, sulkily*]. It is the horror of having to be with myself for ever. I like you; but I do not like myself. I want to be different; to be better; to begin again and again; to shed myself as a snake sheds its skin. I am tired of myself. And yet I must endure myself, not for a day or for many days, but for ever. That is a dreadful thought. That is what makes me sit brooding and silent and hateful. Do you never think of that?

EVE. No: I do not think about myself: what is the use? I am what I am: nothing can alter that. I think about you.

ADAM. You should not. You are always spying on me. I can never be alone. You always want to know what I have been doing. It is a burden. You should try to have an existence of your own, instead of occupying yourself with my existence.

EVE. I have to think about you. You are lazy: you are dirty: you neglect yourself: you are always dreaming: you would eat bad food and become disgusting if I did not watch you and occupy myself with you. And now some day, in spite of all my care, you will fall on your head and become dead.

ADAM. Dead? What word is that?

EVE [*pointing to the fawn*] Like that. I call it dead.

ADAM [*rising and approaching it slowly*] There is something uncanny about it.

EVE [*joining him*] Oh! It is changing into little white worms.

ADAM. Throw it into the river. It is unbearable.

EVE. I dare not touch it.

ADAM. Then I must, though I loathe it. It is poisoning the air. [*He gathers its hooves in his hand and carries it away in the direction from which Eve came, holding it as far from him as possible*].

Eve looks after them for a moment; then, with a shiver of disgust, sits down on the rock, brooding. The body of the serpent becomes visible, glowing with wonderful new colors. She rears her head slowly from the bed of Johnswort, and speaks into Eve's ear in a strange seductively musical whisper.

THE SERPENT. Eve.

EVE [*startled*] Who is that?

THE SERPENT. It is I. I have come to shew you my beautiful new hood. See [*she spreads a magnificent amethystine hood*]!

EVE [*admiring it*] Oh! But who taught you to speak?

THE SERPENT. You and Adam. I have crept through the grass, and hidden, and listened to you.

EVE. That was wonderfully clever of you.

THE SERPENT. I am the most subtle of all the creatures of the field.

EVE. Your hood is most lovely. [*She strokes it and pets the serpent*]. Pretty thing! Do you love your godmother Eve?

THE SERPENT. I adore her. [*She licks Eve's neck with her double tongue*].

EVE [*petting her*] Eve's wonderful darling snake. Eve will never be lonely now that her snake can talk to her.

THE SNAKE. I can talk of many things. I am very wise. It was I who whispered the word to you that you did not know. Dead. Death. Die.

EVE [*shuddering*] Why do you remind me of it? I forgot it when I saw your beautiful hood. You must not remind me of unhappy things.

THE SERPENT. Death is not an unhappy thing when you have learnt how to conquer it.

EVE. How can I conquer it?

THE SERPENT. By another thing, called birth.

EVE. What? [*Trying to pronounce it*] B-birth?

THE SERPENT. Yes, birth.

EVE. What is birth?

THE SERPENT. The serpent never dies. Some day you shall see me come out of this beautiful skin, a new snake with a new and lovelier skin. That is birth.

EVE. I have seen that. It is wonderful.

THE SERPENT. If I can do that, what can I not do? I tell you I am very subtle. When you and Adam talk, I hear you say "Why?" Always "Why?" You see things; and you say "Why?" But I dream things that never were; and I say "Why not?" I made the word dead to describe my old skin that I cast when I am renewed. I call that renewal being born.

EVE. Born is a beautiful word.

THE SERPENT. Why not be born again and again as I am, new and beautiful every time?

EVE. I! It does not happen: that is why.

THE SERPENT. That is how; but it is not why. Why not?

EVE. But I should not like it. It would be nice to be new again; but my old skin would lie on the ground looking just like me; and Adam would see it shrivel up and—

THE SERPENT. No. He need not. There is a second birth.

EVE. A second birth?

THE SERPENT. Listen. I will tell you a great secret. I am

very subtle; and I have thought and thought and thought. And I am very wilful, and must have what I want; and I have willed and willed and willed. And I have eaten strange things: stones and apples that you are afraid to eat.

EVE. You dared!

THE SERPENT. I dared everything. And at last I found a way of gathering together a part of the life in my body—

EVE. What is the life?

THE SERPENT. That which makes the difference between the dead fawn and the live one.

EVE. What a beautiful word! And what a wonderful thing! Life is the loveliest of all the new words.

THE SERPENT. Yes: it was by meditating on Life that I gained the power to do miracles.

EVE. Miracles? Another new word.

THE SERPENT. A miracle is an impossible thing that is nevertheless possible. Something that never could happen, and yet does happen.

EVE. Tell me some miracle that you have done.

THE SERPENT. I gathered a part of the life in my body, and shut it into a tiny white case made of the stones I had eaten.

EVE. And what good was that?

THE SERPENT. I shewed the little case to the sun, and left it in its warmth. And it burst; and a little snake came out; and it became bigger and bigger from day to day until it was as big as I. That was the second birth.

EVE. Oh! That is too wonderful. It stirs inside me. It hurts.

THE SERPENT. It nearly tore me asunder. Yet I am alive, and can burst my skin and renew myself as before. Soon there will be as many snakes in Eden as there are scales on my body. Then death will not matter: this snake and that snake will die; but the snakes will live.

EVE. But the rest of us will die sooner or later, like the fawn. And then there will be nothing but snakes, snakes, snakes everywhere.

THE SERPENT. That must not be. I worship you, Eve. I must have something to worship. Something quite different to myself, like you. There must be something greater than the snake.

EVE. Yes: it must not be. Adam must not perish. You are very subtle: tell me what to do.

THE SERPENT. Think. Will. Eat the dust. Lick the white stone: bite the apple you dread. The sun will give life.

EVE. I do not trust the sun. I will give life myself. I will tear another Adam from my body if I tear my body to pieces in the act.

THE SERPENT. Do. Dare it. Everything is possible: everything. Listen. I am old. I am the old serpent, older than Adam, older than Eve. I remember Lilith, who came before Adam and Eve. I was her darling as I am yours. She was alone: there was no man with her. She saw death as you saw it when the fawn fell; and she knew then that she must find out how to renew herself and cast the skin like me. She had a mighty will: she strove and strove and willed and willed for more moons than there are leaves on all the trees of the garden. Her pangs were terrible: her groans drove sleep from Eden. She said it must never be again: that the burden of renewing life was past bearing: that it was too much for one. And when she cast the skin, lo! there was not one new Lilith but two: one like herself, the other like Adam. You were the one: Adam was the other.

EVE. But why did she divide into two, and make us different?

THE SERPENT. I tell you the labor is too much for one. Two must share it.

EVE. Do you mean that Adam must share it with me? He will not. He cannot bear pain, nor take trouble with his body.

THE SERPENT. He need not. There will be no pain for him. He will implore you to let him do his share. He will be in your power through his desire.

EVE. Then I will do it. But how? How did Lilith work

this miracle?

THE SERPENT. She imagined it.

EVE. What is imagined?

THE SERPENT. She told it to me as a marvellous story of something that never happened to a Lilith that never was. She did not know then that imagination is the beginning of creation. You imagine what you desire; you will what you imagine; and at last you create what you will.

EVE. How can I create out of nothing?

THE SERPENT. Everything must have been created out of nothing. Look at that thick roll of hard flesh on your strong arm! That was not always there: you could not climb a tree when I first saw you. But you willed and tried and willed and tried; and your will created out of nothing the roll on your arm until you had your desire, and could draw yourself up with one hand and seat yourself on the bough that was above your head.

EVE. That was practice.

THE SERPENT. Things wear out by practice: they do not grow by it. Your hair streams in the wind as if it were trying to stretch itself further and further. But it does not grow longer for all its practice in streaming, because you have not willed it so. When Lilith told me what she had imagined in our silent language (for there were no words then) I bade her desire it and will it; and then, to our great wonder, the thing she had desired and willed created itself in her under the urging of her will. Then I too willed to renew myself as two instead of one; and after many days the miracle happened, and I burst from my skin with another snake interlaced with me; and now there are two imaginations, two desires, two wills to create with.

EVE. To desire, to imagine, to will, to create. That is too long a story. Find me one word for it all: you, who are so clever at words.

THE SERPENT. In one word, to conceive. That is the word that means both the beginning in imagination and the end in creation.

EVE. Find me a word for the story Lilith imagined and told you in your silent language: the story that was too wonderful to be true, and yet came true.

THE SERPENT. A poem.

EVE. Find me another word for what Lilith was to me.

THE SERPENT. She was your mother.

EVE. And Adam's mother?

THE SERPENT. Yes.

EVE [*about to rise*] I will go and tell Adam to conceive.

THE SERPENT [*laughs*]!!!

EVE [*jarred and startled*] What a hateful noise! What is the matter with you? No one has ever uttered such a sound before.

THE SERPENT. Adam cannot conceive.

EVE. Why?

THE SERPENT. Lilith did not imagine him so. He can imagine: he can will: he can desire: he can gather his life together for a great spring towards creation: he can create all things except one; and that one is his own kind.

EVE. Why did Lilith keep this from him?

THE SERPENT. Because if he could do that he could do without Eve.

EVE. That is true. It is I who must conceive.

THE SERPENT. Yes. By that he is tied to you.

EVE. And I to him!

THE SERPENT. Yes, until you create another Adam.

EVE. I had not thought of that. You are very subtle. But if I create another Eve he may turn to her and do without me. I will not create any Eves, only Adams.

THE SERPENT. They cannot renew themselves without Eves. Sooner or later you will die like the fawn; and the new Adams will be unable to create without new Eves. You can imagine such an end; but you cannot desire it, therefore cannot will it, therefore cannot create Adams only.

EVE. If I am to die like the fawn, why should not the rest die too? What do I care?

THE SERPENT. Life must not cease. That comes before

everything. It is silly to say you do not care. You do care. It is that care that will prompt your imagination; inflame your desires; make your will irresistible; and create out of nothing.

EVE [*thoughtfully*] There can be no such thing as nothing. The garden is full, not empty.

THE SERPENT. I had not thought of that. That is a great thought. Yes: there is no such thing as nothing, only things we cannot see. The chameleon eats the air.

EVE. I have another thought: I must tell it to Adam. [*Calling*] Adam! Adam! Coo-ee!

ADAM'S VOICE. Coo-ee!

EVE. This will please him, and cure his fits of melancholy.

THE SERPENT. Do not tell him yet. I have not told you the great secret.

EVE. What more is there to tell? It is I who have to do the miracle.

THE SERPENT. No: he, too, must desire and will. But he must give his desire and his will to you.

EVE. How?

THE SERPENT. That is the great secret. Hush! he is coming.

ADAM [*returning*] Is there another voice in the garden besides our voices and the Voice? I heard a new voice.

EVE [*rising and running to him*] Only think, Adam! Our snake has learnt to speak by listening to us.

ADAM [*delighted*] Is it so? [*He goes past her to the stone, and fondles the serpent*].

THE SERPENT [*responding affectionately*] It is so, dear Adam.

EVE. But I have more wonderful news than that. Adam: we need not live for ever.

ADAM [*dropping the snake's head in his excitement*] What! Eve: do not play with me about this. If only there may be an end some day, and yet no end! If only I can be relieved of the horror of having to endure myself for ever! If only the care of this terrible garden may pass on to some other gardener! If only the sentinel set by the Voice can be relieved! If only the rest and sleep that enable me to bear it from day to day could grow after many days into an eternal rest, an eternal sleep, then I could face my days, however long they may last. Only, there must be some end, some end: I am not strong enough to bear eternity.

THE SERPENT. You need not live to see another summer; and yet there shall be no end.

ADAM. That cannot be.

THE SERPENT. It can be.

EVE. It shall be.

THE SERPENT. It is. Kill me; and you will find another snake in the garden to-morrow. You will find more snakes than there are fingers on your hands.

EVE. I will make other Adams, other Eves.

ADAM. I tell you you must not make up stories about this. It cannot happen.

THE SERPENT. I can remember when you were yourself a thing that could not happen. Yet you are.

ADAM [*struck*] That must be true. [*He sits down on the stone*].

THE SERPENT. I will tell Eve the secret; and she will tell it to you.

ADAM. The secret! [*He turns quickly towards the serpent, and in doing so puts his foot on something sharp*]. Oh!

EVE. What is it?

ADAM [*rubbing his foot*] A thistle. And there, next to it, a briar. And nettles, too! I am tired of pulling these things up to keep the garden pleasant for us for ever.

THE SERPENT. They do not grow very fast. They will not overrun the whole garden for a long time: not until you have laid down your burden and gone to sleep for ever. Why should you trouble yourself? Let the new Adams clear a place for themselves.

ADAM. That is very true. You must tell us your secret. You see, Eve, what a splendid thing it is not to have to live for ever.

EVE [*throwing herself down discontentedly and plucking at the grass*] That is so like a man. The moment you find we need not last for ever, you talk as if we were going to end today. You must clear away some of those horrid things, or we shall be scratched and stung whenever we forget to look where we are stepping.

ADAM. Oh yes, some of them, of course. But only some. I will clear them away tomorrow.

THE SERPENT [*laughs*]! ! !

ADAM. That is a funny noise to make. I like it.

EVE. I do not. Why do you make it again?

THE SERPENT. Adam has invented something new. He has invented tomorrow. You will invent things every day now that the burden of immortality is lifted from you.

EVE. Immortality? What is that?

THE SERPENT. My new word for having to live for ever.

EVE. The serpent has made a beautiful word for being. Living.

ADAM. Make me a beautiful word for doing things tomorrow; for that surely is a great and blessed invention.

THE SERPENT. Procrastination.

EVE. That is a sweet word. I wish I had a serpent's tongue.

THE SERPENT. That may come too. Everything is possible.

ADAM [*springing up in sudden terror*] Oh!

EVE. What is the matter now?

ADAM. My rest! My escape from life!

THE SERPENT. Death. That is the word.

ADAM. There is a terrible danger in this procrastination.

EVE. What danger?

ADAM. If I put off death until tomorrow, I shall never die. There is no such day as tomorrow, and never can be.

THE SERPENT. I am very subtle; but Man is deeper in his thought than I am. The woman knows that there is no such thing as nothing: the man knows that there is no such day as tomorrow. I do well to worship them.

ADAM. If I am to overtake death, I must appoint a real

day, not a tomorrow. When shall I die?

EVE. You may die when I have made another Adam. Not before. But then, as soon as you like. [*She rises, and passing behind him, strolls off carelessly to the tree and leans against it, stroking a ring of the snake*].

ADAM. There need be no hurry even then.

EVE. I see you will put if off until tomorrow.

ADAM. And you? Will you die the moment you have made a new Eve?

EVE. Why should I? Are you eager to be rid of me? Only just now you wanted me to sit still and never move lest I should stumble and die like the fawn. Now you no longer care.

ADAM. It does not matter so much now.

EVE [*angrily to the snake*] This death that you have brought into the garden is an evil thing. He wants me to die.

THE SERPENT [*to Adam*] Do you want her to die?

ADAM. No. It is I who am to die. Eve must not die before me. I should be lonely.

EVE. You could get one of the new Eves.

ADAM. That is true. But they might not be quite the same. They could not: I feel sure of that. They would not have the same memories. They would be—I want a word for them.

THE SERPENT. Strangers.

ADAM. Yes: that is a good hard word. Strangers.

EVE. When there are new Adams and new Eves we shall live in a garden of strangers. We shall need each other. [*She comes quickly behind him and turns up his face to her*]. Do not forget that, Adam. Never forget it.

ADAM. Why should I forget it? It is I who have thought of it.

EVE. I, too, have thought of something. The fawn stumbled and fell and died. But you could come softly up behind me and [*she suddenly pounces on his shoulders and throws him forward on his face*] throw me down so that I should die. I should not dare to sleep if there were no reason why you should not make me die.

ADAM [*scrambling up in horror*] Make you die!!! What a frightful thought!

THE SERPENT. Kill, kill, kill, kill. That is the word.

EVE. The new Adams and Eves might kill us. I shall not make them. [*She sits on the rock and pulls him down beside her, clasping him to her with her right arm*].

THE SERPENT. You must. For if you do not there will be an end.

ADAM. No: they will not kill us: they will feel as I do. There is something against it. The Voice in the garden will tell them that they must not kill, as it tells me.

THE SERPENT. The voice in the garden is your own voice.

ADAM. It is; and it is not. It is something greater than me: I am only a part of it.

EVE. The Voice does not tell me not to kill you. Yet I do not want you to die before me. No voice is needed to make me feel that.

ADAM [*throwing his arm round her shoulder with an expression of anguish*] Oh no: that is plain without any voice. There is something that holds us together, something that has no word—

THE SERPENT. Love. Love. Love.

ADAM. That is too short a word for so long a thing.

THE SERPENT [*laughs*]!!!

EVE [*turning impatiently to the snake*] That heart-biting sound again! Do not do it. Why do you do it?

THE SERPENT. Love may be too long a word for so short a thing soon. But when it is short it will be very sweet.

ADAM [*ruminating*] You puzzle me. My old trouble was heavy; but it was simple. These wonders that you promise to do may tangle up my being before they bring me the gift of death. I was troubled with the burden of eternal being; but I was not confused in my mind. If I did not know that I loved Eve, at least I did not know that she might cease to love me, and come to love some other Adam and desire my death. Can you find a name for that knowledge?

THE SERPENT. Jealousy. Jealousy. Jealousy.

ADAM. A hideous word.

EVE [*shaking him*] Adam: you must not brood. You think too much.

ADAM [*angrily*] How can I help brooding when the future has become uncertain? Anything is better than uncertainty. Life has become uncertain. Love is uncertain. Have you a word for this new misery?

THE SERPENT. Fear. Fear. Fear.

ADAM. Have you a remedy for it?

THE SERPENT. Yes. Hope. Hope. Hope.

ADAM. What is hope?

THE SERPENT. As long as you do not know the future you do not know that it will not be happier than the past. That is hope.

ADAM. It does not console me. Fear is stronger in me than hope. I must have certainty. [*He rises threateningly*]. Give it to me; or I will kill you when next I catch you asleep.

EVE [*throwing her arms round the serpent*] My beautiful snake. Oh no. How can you even think such a horror?

ADAM. Fear will drive me to anything. The serpent gave me fear. Let it now give me certainty or go in fear of me.

THE SERPENT. Bind the future by your will. Make a vow.

ADAM. What is a vow?

THE SERPENT. Choose a day for your death; and resolve to die on that day. Then death is no longer uncertain but certain. Let Eve vow to love you until your death. Then love will be no longer uncertain.

ADAM. Yes: that is splendid: that will bind the future.

EVE [*displeased, turning away from the serpent*] But it will destroy hope.

ADAM [*angrily*] Be silent, woman. Hope is wicked. Happiness is wicked. Certainty is blessed.

THE SERPENT. What is wicked? You have invented a word.

ADAM. Whatever I fear to do is wicked. Listen to me, Eve; and you, snake, listen too, that your memory may hold my vow. I will live a thousand sets of the four seasons—

THE SERPENT. Years. Years.

ADAM. I will live a thousand years; and then I will endure no more: I will die and take my rest. And I will love Eve all that time and no other woman.

EVE. And if Adam keeps his vow I will love no other man until he dies.

THE SERPENT. You have both invented marriage. And what he will be to you and not to any other woman is husband; and what you will be to him and not to any other man is wife.

ADAM [*instinctively moving his hand towards her*] Husband and wife.

EVE [*slipping her hand into his*] Wife and husband.

THE SERPENT [*laughs*]!!!

EVE [*snatching herself loose from Adam*] Do not make that odious noise, I tell you.

ADAM. Do not listen to her: the noise is good: it lightens my heart. You are a jolly snake. But you have not made a vow yet. What vow do you make?

THE SERPENT. I make no vows. I take my chance.

ADAM. Chance? What does that mean?

THE SERPENT. It means that I fear certainty as you fear uncertainty. It means that nothing is certain but uncertainty. If I bind the future I bind my will. If I bind my will I strangle creation.

EVE. Creation must not be strangled. I tell you I will create, though I tear myself to pieces in the act.

ADAM. Be silent, both of you. I will bind the future. I will be delivered from fear. [*To Eve*] We have made our vows; and if you must create, you shall create within the bounds of those vows. You shall not listen to that snake any more. Come [*he seizes her by the hair to drag her away*].

EVE. Let me go, you fool. It has not yet told me the secret.

ADAM [*releasing her*] That is true. What is a fool?

EVE. I do not know: the word came to me. It is what you are when you forget and brood and are filled with fear. Let us listen to the snake.

ADAM. No: I am afraid of it. I feel as if the ground were giving way under my feet when it speaks. Do you stay and listen to it.

THE SERPENT [*laughs*]!!!

ADAM [*brightening*] That noise takes away fear. Funny. The snake and the woman are going to whisper secrets. [*He chuckles and goes away slowly, laughing his first laugh*].

EVE. Now the secret. The secret. [*She sits on the rock and throws her arms round the serpent, who begins whispering to her*].

Eve's face lights up with intense interest, which increases until an expression of overwhelming repugnance takes its place. She buries her face in her hands.

ACT II

A *FEW centuries later. Morning. An oasis in Mesopotamia. Close at hand the end of a log house abuts on a kitchen garden. Adam is digging in the middle of the garden. On his right, Eve sits on a stool in the shadow of a tree by the doorway, spinning flax. Her wheel, which she turns by hand, is a large disc of heavy wood, practically a fly-wheel. At the opposite side of the garden is a thorn brake with a passage through it barred by a hurdle.*

The two are scantily and carelessly dressed in rough linen and leaves. They have lost their youth and grace; and Adam has an unkempt beard and jaggedly cut hair; but they are strong and in the prime of life. Adam looks worried, like a farmer. Eve, better humored (having given up worrying), sits and spins and thinks.

A MAN'S VOICE. Hallo, mother!

EVE [*looking across the garden towards the hurdle*] Here is Cain.

ADAM [*uttering a grunt of disgust*]!!! [*He goes on digging without raising his head*].

Cain kicks the hurdle out of his way, and strides into the garden. In pose, voice, and dress he is insistently warlike. He is equipped with huge spear and broad brass-bound leather shield; his casque is a tiger's head with bull's horns; he wears a scarlet cloak with gold brooch over a lion's skin with the claws dangling; his feet are in sandals with brass ornaments; his shins are in brass greaves; and his bristling military moustache glistens with oil. To his parents he has the self-assertive, not-quite-at-ease manner of a revolted son who knows that he is not forgiven nor approved of.

CAIN [*to Adam*] Still digging? Always dig, dig, dig. Sticking in the old furrow. No progress! no advanced ideas! no adventures! What should I be if I had stuck to the digging you taught me?

ADAM. What are you now, with your shield and spear, and your brother's blood crying from the ground against you?

CAIN. I am the first murderer: you are only the first man.

Anybody could be the first man: it is as easy as to be the first cabbage. To be the first murderer one must be a man of spirit.

ADAM. Begone. Leave us in peace. The world is wide enough to keep us apart.

EVE. Why do you want to drive him away? He is mine. I made him out of my own body. I want to see my work sometimes.

ADAM. You made Abel also. He killed Abel. Can you bear to look at him after that?

CAIN. Whose fault was it that I killed Abel? Who invented killing? Did *I*? No: he invented it himself. I followed your teaching. I dug and dug and dug. I cleared away the thistles and briars. I ate the fruits of the earth. I lived in the sweat of my brow, as you do. I was a fool. But Abel was a discoverer, a man of ideas, of spirit: a true Progressive. He was the discoverer of blood. He was the inventor of killing. He found out that the fire of the sun could be brought down by a dewdrop. He invented the altar to keep the fire alive. He changed the beasts he killed into meat by the fire on the altar. He kept himself alive by eating meat. His meal cost him a day's glorious health-giving sport and an hour's amusing play with the fire. You learnt nothing from him: you drudged and drudged and drudged, and dug and dug and dug, and made me do the same. I envied his happiness, his freedom. I despised myself for not doing as he did instead of what you did. He became so happy that he shared his meal with the Voice that had whispered all his inventions to him. He said that the Voice was the voice of the fire that cooked his food, and that the fire that could cook could also eat. It was true: I saw the fire consume the food on his altar. Then I, too, made an altar, and offered my food on it, my grains, my roots, my fruit. Useless: nothing happened. He laughed at me; and then came my great idea: why not kill him as he killed the beasts? I struck; and he died, just as they did. Then I gave up your old silly drudging ways, and lived as he had lived, by the chase, by the killing, and by the fire. Am I not better than you? stronger, happier, freer?

ADAM. You are not stronger: you are shorter in the wind: you cannot endure. You have made the beasts afraid of us; and the snake has invented poison to protect herself against you. I fear you myself. If you take a step towards your mother with that spear of yours I will strike you with my spade as you struck Abel.

EVE. He will not strike me. He loves me.

ADAM. He loved his brother. But he killed him.

CAIN. I do not want to kill women. I do not want to kill my mother. And for her sake I will not kill you, though I could send this spear through you without coming within reach of your spade. But for her, I could not resist the sport of trying to kill you, in spite of my fear that you would kill me. I have striven with a boar and with a lion as to which of us should kill the other. I have striven with a man: spear to spear and shield to shield. It is terrible; but there is no joy like it. I call it fighting. He who has never fought has never lived. That is what has brought me to my mother today.

ADAM. What have you to do with one another now? She is the creator, you the destroyer.

CAIN. How can I destroy unless she creates? I want her to create more and more men: aye, and more and more women, that they may in turn create more men. I have imagined a glorious poem of many men, of more men than there are leaves on a thousand trees. I will divide them into two great hosts. One of them I will lead; and the other will be led by the man I fear most and desire to fight and kill most. And each host shall try to kill the other host. Think of that! all those multitudes of men fighting, fighting, killing, killing! The four rivers running with blood! The shouts of triumph! the howls of rage! the curses of despair! the shrieks of torment! That will be life indeed: life lived to the very marrow: burning, overwhelming life. Every man who has not seen it, heard it, felt it, risked it, will feel a humbled fool in the presence of the man who has.

EVE. And I! I am to be a mere convenience to make men

for you to kill!

ADAM. Or to kill you, you fool.

CAIN. Mother: the making of men is your right, your risk, your agony, your glory, your triumph. You make my father here your mere convenience, as you call it, for that. He has to dig for you, sweat for you, plod for you, like the ox who helps him to tear up the ground or the ass who carries his burdens for him. No woman shall make me live my father's life. I will hunt: I will fight and strive to the very bursting of my sinews. When I have slain the boar at the risk of my life, I will throw it to my woman to cook, and give her a morsel of it for her pains. She shall have no other food; and that will make her my slave. And the man that slays me shall have her for his booty. Man shall be the master of Woman, not her baby and her drudge.

Adam throws down his spade, and stands looking darkly at Eve.

EVE. Are you tempted, Adam? Does this seem a better thing to you than love between us?

CAIN. What does he know of love? Only when he has fought, when he has faced terror and death, when he has striven to the spending of the last rally of his strength, can he know what it is to rest in love in the arms of a woman. Ask that woman whom you made, who is also my wife, whether she would have me as I was in the days when I followed the ways of Adam, and was a digger and a drudge?

EVE [*angrily throwing down her distaff*] What! You dare come here boasting about that good-for-nothing Lua, the worst of daughters and the worst of wives! You her master! You are more her slave than Adam's ox or your own sheep-dog. Forsooth, when you have slain the boar at the risk of your life, you will throw her a morsel of it for her pains! Ha! Poor wretch: do you think I do not know her, and know you, better than that? Do you risk your life when you trap the ermine and the sable and the blue fox to hang on her lazy shoulders and make her look more like an animal than a woman? When you have to snare the little tender birds because it is too much trouble for her to chew honest food, how much of a great warrior do you feel then? You slay the tiger at the risk of your life; but who gets the striped skin you have run that risk for? She takes it to lie on, and flings you the carrion flesh you cannot eat. You fight because you think that your fighting makes her admire and desire you. Fool: she makes you fight because you bring her the ornaments and the treasures of those you have slain, and because she is courted and propitiated with power and gold by the people who fear you. You say that *I* make a mere convenience of Adam: I who spin and keep the house, and bear and rear children, and am a woman and not a pet animal to please men and prey on them! What are you, you poor slave of a painted face and a bundle of skunk's fur? You were a man-child when I bore you. Lua was a woman-child when I bore her. What have you made of yourselves?

CAIN [*letting his spear fall into the crook of his shield arm, and twirling his moustache*] There is something higher than man. There is hero and superman.

EVE. Superman! You are no superman: you are Anti-Man: you are to other men what the stoat is to the rabbit; and she is to you what the leech is to the stoat. You despise your father; but when he dies the world will be the richer because he lived. When you die, men will say, "He was a great warrior; but it would have been better for the world if he had never been born." And of Lua they will say nothing; but when they think of her they will spit.

CAIN. She is a better sort of woman to live with than you. If Lua nagged at me as you are nagging, and as you nag at Adam, I would beat her black and blue from head to foot. I have done it too, slave as you say I am.

EVE. Yes, because she looked at another man. And then you grovelled at her feet, and cried, and begged her to forgive you, and were ten times more her slave than ever; and she, when she had finished screaming and the pain went off a little, she forgave you, did she not?

CAIN. She loved me more than ever. That is the true

nature of woman.

EVE [*now pitying him maternally*] Love! You call that love! You call that the nature of woman! My boy: this is neither man nor woman nor love nor life. You have no real strength in your bones nor sap in your flesh.

CAIN. Ha! [*he seizes his spear and swings it muscularly*].

EVE. Yes: you have to twirl a stick to feel your strength: you cannot taste life without making it bitter and boiling hot: you cannot love Lua until her face is painted, nor feel the natural warmth of her flesh until you have stuck a squirrel's fur on it. You can feel nothing but a torment, and believe nothing but a lie. You will not raise your head to look at all the miracles of life that surround you; but you will run ten miles to see a fight or a death.

ADAM. Enough said. Let the boy alone.

CAIN. Boy! Ha! ha!

EVE [*to Adam*] You think, perhaps, that his way of life may be better than yours after all. You are still tempted. Well, will you pamper me as he pampers his woman? Will you kill tigers and bears until I have a heap of their skins to lounge on? Shall I paint my face and let my arms waste into pretty softness, and eat partridges and doves, and the flesh of kids whose milk you will steal for me?

ADAM. You are hard enough to bear with as you are. Stay as you are; and I will stay as I am.

CAIN. You neither of you know anything about life. You are simple country folk. You are the nurses and valets of the oxen and dogs and asses you have tamed to work for you. I can raise you out of that. I have a plan. Why not tame men and women to work for us? Why not bring them up from childhood never to know any other lot, so that they may believe that we are gods, and that they are here only to make life glorious for us?

ADAM [*impressed*] That is a great thought, certainly.

EVE [*contemptuously*] Great thought!

ADAM. Well, as the serpent used to say, why not?

EVE. Because I would not have such wretches in my

house. Because I hate creatures with two heads, or with withered limbs, or that are distorted and perverted and unnatural. I have told Cain already that he is not a man and that Lua is not a woman: they are monsters. And now you want to make still more unnatural monsters, so that you may be utterly lazy and worthless, and that your tamed human animals may find work a blasting curse. A fine dream, truly! [*To Cain*] Your father is a fool skin deep; but you are a fool to your very marrow; and your baggage of a wife is worse.

ADAM. Why am I a fool? How am I a greater fool than you?

EVE. You said there would be no killing because the Voice would tell our children that they must not kill. Why did it not tell Cain that?

CAIN. It did; but I am not a child to be afraid of a Voice. The Voice thought I was nothing but my brother's keeper. It found that I was myself, and that it was for Abel to be himself also, and look to himself. He was not my keeper any more than I was his: why did he not kill me? There was no more to prevent him than there was to prevent me: it was man to man; and I won. I was the first conqueror.

ADAM. What did the Voice say to you when you thought all that?

CAIN. Why, it gave me right. It said that my deed was as a mark on me, a burnt-in mark such as Abel put on his sheep, that no man should slay me. And here I stand unslain, whilst the cowards who have never slain, the men who are content to be their brothers' keepers instead of their masters, are despised and rejected, and slain like rabbits. He who bears the brand of Cain shall rule the earth. When he falls, he shall be avenged sevenfold: the Voice has said it; so beware how you plot against me, you and all the rest.

ADAM. Cease your boasting and bullying, and tell the truth. Does not the Voice tell you that as no man dare slay you for murdering your brother, you ought to slay yourself?

CAIN. No.

ADAM. Then there is no such thing as divine justice, unless you are lying.

CAIN. I am not lying: I dare all truths. There is divine justice. For the Voice tells me that I must offer myself to every man to be killed if he can kill me. Without danger I cannot be great. That is how I pay for Abel's blood. Danger and fear follow my steps everywhere. Without them courage would have no sense. And it is courage, courage, courage, that raises the blood of life to crimson splendor.

ADAM [*picking up his spade and preparing to dig again*] Take yourself off then. This splendid life of yours does not last for a thousand years; and I must last for a thousand years. When you fighters do not get killed in fighting one another or fighting the beasts, you die from mere evil in yourselves. Your flesh ceases to grow like man's flesh: it grows like a fungus on a tree. Instead of breathing, you sneeze, or cough up your insides, and wither and perish. Your bowels become rotten; your hair falls from you; your teeth blacken and drop out; and you die before your time, not because you will, but because you must. I will dig, and live.

CAIN. And pray, what use is this thousand years of life to you, you old vegetable? Do you dig any better because you have been digging for hundreds of years? I have not lived as long as you; but I know all there is to be known of the craft of digging. By quitting it I have set myself free to learn nobler crafts of which you know nothing. I know the craft of fighting and of hunting: in a word, the craft of killing. What certainty have you of your thousand years? I could kill both of you; and you could no more defend yourselves than a couple of sheep. I spare you; but others may kill you. Why not live bravely, and die early and make room for others? Why, I—I! that know many more crafts than either of you, am tired of myself when I am not fighting or hunting. Sooner than face a thousand years of it I should kill myself, as the Voice sometimes tempts me to do already.

ADAM. Liar: you denied just now that it called on you to pay for Abel's life with your own.

CAIN. The Voice does not speak to me as it does to you. I

am a man: you are only a grown-up child. One does not speak to a child as to a man. And a man does not listen and tremble in silence. He replies: he makes the Voice respect him: in the end he dictates what the Voice shall say.

ADAM. May your tongue be accurst for such blasphemy!

EVE. Keep a guard on your own tongue; and do not curse my son. It was Lilith who did wrong when she shared the labor of creation so unequally between man and wife. If you, Cain, had had the trouble of making Abel, or had had to make another man to replace him when he was gone, you would not have killed him: you would have risked your own life to save his. That is why all this empty talk of yours, which tempted Adam just now when he threw down his spade and listened to you for a while, went by me like foul wind that has passed over a dead body. That is why there is enmity between Woman the creator and Man the destroyer. I know you: I am your mother. You are idle: you are selfish. It is long and hard and painful to create life: it is short and easy to steal the life others have made. When you dug, you made the earth live and bring forth as I live and bring forth. It was for that that Lilith set you free from the travail of women, not for theft and murder.

CAIN. The Devil thank her for it! I can make better use of my time than to play the husband to the clay beneath my feet.

ADAM. Devil? What new word is that?

CAIN. Hearken to me, old fool. I have never in my soul listened willingly when you have told me of the Voice that whispers to you. There must be two Voices: one that gulls and despises you, and another that trusts and respects me. I call yours the Devil. Mine I call the Voice of God.

ADAM. Mine is the Voice of Life: yours the Voice of Death.

CAIN. Be it so. For it whispers to me that death is not really death: that it is the gate of another life: a life infinitely splendid and intense: a life of the soul alone: a life without clods or spades, hunger or fatigue—

EVE. Selfish and idle, Cain. I know.

CAIN. Selfish, yes: a life in which no man is his brother's keeper, because his brother can keep himself. But am I idle? In rejecting your drudgery, have I not embraced evils and agonies of which you know nothing? The arrow is lighter in the hand than the spade; but the energy that drives it through the breast of a fighter is as fire to water compared with the strength that drives the spade into the harmless dirty clay. My strength is as the strength of ten because my heart is pure.

ADAM. What is that word? What is pure?

CAIN. Turned from the clay. Turned upward to the sun, to the clear clean heavens.

ADAM. The heavens are empty, child. The earth is fruitful. The earth feeds us. It gives us the strength by which we made you and all mankind. Cut off from the clay which you despise, you would perish miserably.

CAIN. I revolt against the clay. I revolt against the food. You say it gives us strength: does it not also turn into filth and smite us with diseases? I revolt against these births that you and mother are so proud of. They drag us down to the level of the beasts. If that is to be the last thing as it has been the first, let mankind perish. If I am to eat like a bear, if Lua is to bring forth cubs like a bear, then I had rather be a bear than a man; for the bear is not ashamed: he knows no better. If you are content, like the bear, I am not. Stay with the woman who gives you children: I will go to the woman who gives me dreams. Grope in the ground for your food: I will bring it from the skies with my arrows, or strike it down as it roams the earth in the pride of its life. If I must have food or die, I will at least have it at as far a remove from the earth as I can. The ox shall make it something nobler than grass before it comes to me. And as the man is nobler than the ox, I shall some day let my enemy eat the ox; and then I will slay and eat him.

ADAM. Monster! You hear this, Eve?

EVE. So that is what comes of turning your face to the

clean clear heavens! Man-eating! Child-eating! For that is what it would come to, just as it came to lambs and kids when Abel began with sheep and goats. You are a poor silly creature after all. Do you think I never have these thoughts: I! who have the labor of the child-bearing: I! who have the drudgery of preparing the food? I thought for a moment that perhaps this strong brave son of mine, who could imagine something better, and could desire what he imagined, might also be able to will what he desired until he created it. And all that comes of it is that he wants to be a bear and eat children. Even a bear would not eat a man if it could get honey instead.

CAIN. I do not want to be a bear. I do not want to eat children. I do not know what I want, except that I want to be something higher and nobler than this stupid old digger whom Lilith made to help you to bring me into the world, and whom you despise now that he has served your turn.

ADAM [*in sullen rage*] I have half a mind to shew you that my spade can split your undutiful head open, in spite of your spear.

CAIN. Undutiful! Ha! ha! [*Flourishing his spear*] Try it, old everybody's father. Try a taste of fighting.

EVE. Peace, peace, you two fools. Sit down and be quiet; and listen to me. [*Adam, with a weary shrug, throws down his spade. Cain, with a laughing one, throws down his shield and spear. Both sit on the ground*]. I hardly know which of you satisfies me least, you with your dirty digging, or he with his dirty killing. I cannot think it was for either of these cheap ways of life that Lilith set you free. [*To Adam*] You dig roots and coax grains out of the earth: why do you not draw down a divine sustenance from the skies? He steals and kills for his food; and makes up idle poems of life after death; and dresses up his terror-ridden life with fine words and his disease-ridden body with fine clothes, so that men may glorify and honor him instead of cursing him as murderer and thief. All you men, except only Adam, are my sons, or my sons' sons, or my sons' sons' sons: you all come to see me: you all shew off before me: all your little wisdoms and accomplishments are trotted out before mother Eve. The diggers come: the fighters and killers come: they are both very dull; for they either complain to me of the last harvest, or boast to me of the last fight; and one harvest is just like another, and the last fight only a repetition of the first. Oh, I have heard it all a thousand times. They tell me too of their last-born: the clever thing the darling child said yesterday, and how much more wonderful or witty or quaint it is than any child that ever was born before. And I have to pretend to be surprised, delighted, interested; though the last child is like the first, and has said and done nothing that did not delight Adam and me when you and Abel said it. For you were the first children in the world, and filled us with such wonder and delight as no couple can ever again feel while the world lasts. When I can bear no more, I go to our old garden, that is now a mass of nettles and thistles, in the hope of finding the serpent to talk to. But you have made the serpent our enemy: she has left the garden, or is dead: I never see her now. So I have to come back and listen to Adam saying the same thing for the ten-thousandth time, or to receive a visit from the last great-great-grandson who has grown up and wants to impress me with his importance. Oh, it is dreary, dreary! And there is yet nearly seven hundred years of it to endure.

CAIN. Poor mother! You see, life is too long. One tires of everything. There is nothing new under the sun.

ADAM [*to Eve, grumpily*] Why do you live on, if you can find nothing better to do than complain?

EVE. Because there is still hope.

CAIN. Of what?

EVE. Of the coming true of your dreams and mine. Of newly created things. Of better things. My sons and my sons' sons are not all diggers and fighters. Some of them will neither dig nor fight: they are more useless than either of you: they are weaklings and cowards: they are vain; yet they are dirty and will not take the trouble to cut their hair.

They borrow and never pay; but one gives them what they want, because they tell beautiful lies in beautiful words. They can remember their dreams. They can dream without sleeping. They have not will enough to create instead of dreaming; but the serpent said that every dream could be willed into creation by those strong enough to believe in it. There are others who cut reeds of different lengths and blow through them, making lovely patterns of sound in the air; and some of them can weave the patterns together, sounding three reeds at the same time, and raising my soul to things for which I have no words. And others make little mammoths out of clay, or make faces appear on flat stones, and ask me to create women for them with such faces. I have watched those faces and willed; and then I have made a woman-child that has grown up quite like them. And others think of numbers without having to count on their fingers, and watch the sky at night, and give names to the stars, and can foretell when the sun will be covered with a black saucepan lid. And there is Tubal, who made this wheel for me which has saved me so much labor. And there is Enoch, who walks on the hills, and hears the Voice continually, and has given up his will to do the will of the Voice, and has some of the Voice's greatness. When they come, there is always some new wonder, or some new hope: something to live for. They never want to die, because they are always learning and always creating either things or wisdom, or at least dreaming of them. And then you, Cain, come to me with your stupid fighting and destroying, and your foolish boasting; and you want me to tell you that it is all splendid, and that you are heroic, and that nothing but death or the dread of death makes life worth living. Away with you, naughty child; and do you, Adam, go on with your work and not waste your time listening to him.

CAIN. I am not, perhaps, very clever; but—

EVE [*interrupting him*] Perhaps not; but do not begin to boast of that. It is no credit to you.

CAIN. For all that, mother, I have an instinct which tells

me that death plays its part in life. Tell me this: who invented death?

Adam springs to his feet. Eve drops her distaff. Both shew the greatest consternation.

CAIN. What is the matter with you both?

ADAM. Boy: you have asked us a terrible question.

EVE. You invented murder. Let that be enough for you.

CAIN. Murder is not death. You know what I mean. Those whom I slay would die if I spared them. If I am not slain, yet I shall die. Who put this upon me? I say, who invented death?

ADAM. Be reasonable, boy. Could you bear to live for ever? You think you could, because you know that you will never have to make your thought good. But I have known what it is to sit and brood under the terror of eternity, of immortality. Think of it, man: to have no escape! to be Adam, Adam, Adam through more days than there are grains of sand by the two rivers, and then be as far from the end as ever! I, who have so much in me that I hate and long to cast off! Be thankful to your parents, who enabled you to hand on your burden to new and better men, and won for you an eternal rest; for it was we who invented death.

CAIN [*rising*] You did well: I, too, do not want to live for ever. But if you invented death, why do you blame me, who am a minister of death?

ADAM. I do not blame you. Go in peace. Leave me to my digging, and your mother to her spinning.

CAIN. Well, I will leave you to it, though I have shewn you a better way. [*He picks up his shield and spear*]. I will go back to my brave warrior friends and their splendid women. [*He strides to the thorn brake*]. When Adam delved and Eve span, where was then the gentleman? [*He goes away roaring with laughter, which ceases as he cries from the distance*] Good-bye, mother.

ADAM [*grumbling*] He might have put the hurdle back, lazy hound! [*He replaces the hurdle across the passage*].

EVE. Through him and his like, death is gaining on life.

Already most of our grandchildren die before they have sense enough to know how to live.

ADAM. No matter. [*He spits on his hands, and takes up the spade again*]. Life is still long enough to learn to dig, short as they are making it.

EVE [*musing*] Yes, to dig. And to fight. But is it long enough for the other things, the great things? Will they live long enough to eat manna?

ADAM. What is manna?

EVE. Food drawn down from heaven, made out of the air, not dug dirtily from the earth. Will they learn all the ways of all the stars in their little time? It took Enoch two hundred years to learn to interpret the will of the Voice. When he was a mere child of eighty, his babyish attempts to understand the Voice were more dangerous than the wrath of Cain. If they shorten their lives, they will dig and fight and kill and die; and their baby Enochs will tell them that it is the will of the Voice that they should dig and fight and kill and die for ever.

ADAM. If they are lazy and have a will towards death I cannot help it. I will live my thousand years: if they will not, let them die and be damned.

EVE. Damned? What is that?

ADAM. The state of them that love death more than life. Go on with your spinning; and do not sit there idle while I am straining my muscles for you.

EVE [*slowly taking up her distaff*] If you were not a fool you would find something better for both of us to live by than this spinning and digging.

ADAM. Go on with your work, I tell you; or you shall go without bread.

EVE. Man need not always live by bread alone. There is something else. We do not yet know what it is; but some day we shall find out; and then we will live on that alone; and there shall be no more digging nor spinning, nor fighting nor killing.

She spins resignedly; he digs impatiently.

PART II THE GOSPEL OF THE BROTHERS BARNABAS

THE GOSPEL OF THE BROTHERS BARNABAS

IN the first years after the war an impressive-looking gentleman of 50 is seated writing in a well-furnished spacious study. He is dressed in black. His coat is a frock-coat; his tie is white; and his waistcoat, though it is not quite a clergyman's waistcoat, and his collar, though it buttons in front instead of behind, combine with the prosperity indicated by his surroundings, and his air of personal distinction, to suggest the clerical dignitary. Still, he is clearly neither dean nor bishop; he is rather too starkly intellectual for a popular Free Church enthusiast; and he is not care-worn enough to be a great headmaster.

The study windows, which have broad comfortable window seats, overlook Hampstead Heath towards London. Consequently, it being a fine afternoon in spring, the room is sunny. As you face these windows, you have on your right the fireplace, with a few logs smouldering in it, and a couple of comfortable library chairs on the hearthrug; beyond it and beside it the door; before you the writing-table, at which the clerical gentleman sits a little to your left facing the door with his right profile presented to you; on your left a settee; and on your right a couple of Chippendale chairs. There is also an upholstered square stool in the middle of the room, against the writing-table. The walls are covered with bookshelves above and lockers beneath.

The door opens; and another gentleman, shorter than the clerical one, within a year or two of the same age, dressed in a well-worn tweed lounge suit, with a short beard and much less style in his bearing and carriage, looks in.

THE CLERICAL GENTLEMAN [*familiar and by no means cordial*] Hallo! I didnt expect you until the five o'clock train.

THE TWEEDED GENTLEMAN [*coming in very slowly*] I have something on my mind. I thought I'd come early.

THE CLERICAL GENTLEMAN [*throwing down his pen*] What is on your mind?

THE TWEEDED GENTLEMAN [*sitting down on the stool, heavily preoccupied with his thought*] I have made up my mind at last about the time. I make it three hundred years.

THE CLERICAL GENTLEMAN [*sitting up energetically*] Now that is extraordinary. Most extraordinary. The very last words I wrote when you interrupted me were "at least three centuries." [*He snatches up his manuscript, and points to it*]. Here it is: [*reading*] "the term of human life must be extended to at least three centuries."

THE TWEEDED GENTLEMAN. How did you arrive at it?

A parlor maid opens the door, ushering in a young clergyman.

THE PARLOR MAID. Mr Haslam. [*She withdraws*].

The visitor is so very unwelcome that his host forgets to rise; and the two brothers stare at the intruder, quite unable to conceal their dismay. Haslam, who has nothing clerical about him except his collar, and wears a snuff-colored suit, smiles with a frank schoolboyishness that makes it impossible to be unkind to him, and explodes into obviously unpremeditated speech.

HASLAM. I'm afraid I'm an awful nuisance. I'm the rector; and I suppose one ought to call on people.

THE TWEEDED GENTLEMAN [*in ghostly tones*] We're not Church people, you know.

HASLAM. Oh, I dont mind that, if you dont. The Church people here are mostly as dull as ditch-water. I've heard such a lot about you; and there are so jolly few people to talk to. I thought you perhaps wouldnt mind. Do you mind? for of course I'll go like a shot if I'm in the way.

THE CLERICAL GENTLEMAN [*rising, disarmed*] Sit down, Mr—er?

HASLAM. Haslam.

THE CLERICAL GENTLEMAN. Mr Haslam.

THE TWEEDED GENTLEMAN [*rising and offering him the stool*] Sit down. [*He retreats towards the Chippendale chairs*].

HASLAM [*sitting down on the stool*] Thanks awfully.

THE CLERICAL GENTLEMAN [*resuming his seat*] This is my brother Conrad, Professor of Biology at Jarrowfields University: Dr Conrad Barnabas. My name is Franklyn. Franklyn Barnabas. I was in the Church myself for some years.

HASLAM [*sympathizing*] Yes: one cant help it. If theres a

living in the family, or one's Governor knows a patron, one gets shoved into the Church by one's parents.

CONRAD [*sitting down on the furthest Chippendale with a snort of amusement*] Mp!

FRANKLYN. One gets shoved out of it, sometimes, by one's conscience.

HASLAM. Oh yes; but where is a chap like me to go? I'm afraid I'm not intellectual enough to split straws when theres a job in front of me, and nothing better for me to do. I daresay the Church was a bit thick for you; but it's good enough for me. It will last my time, anyhow [*he laughs good-humoredly*].

FRANKLYN [*with renewed energy*] There again! You see, Con. It will last his time. Life is too short for men to take it seriously.

HASLAM. Thats a way of looking at it, certainly.

FRANKLYN. I was not shoved into the Church, Mr Haslam; I felt it to be my vocation to walk with God, like Enoch. After twenty years of it I realized that I was walking with my own ignorance and self-conceit, and that I was not within a hundred and fifty years of the experience and wisdom I was pretending to.

HASLAM. Now I come to think of it, old Methuselah must have had to think twice before he took on anything for life. If I thought I was going to live nine hundred and sixty years, I dont think I should stay in the Church.

FRANKLYN. If men lived even a third of that time, the Church would be very different from the thing it is.

CONRAD. If I could count on nine hundred and sixty years I could make myself a real biologist, instead of what I am now: a child trying to walk. Are you sure you might not become a good clergyman if you had a few centuries to do it in?

HASLAM. Oh, theres nothing much the matter with me: it's quite easy to be a decent parson. It's the Church that chokes me off. I couldnt stick it for nine hundred years. I should chuck it. You know, sometimes, when the bishop, who is the most priceless of fossils, lets off something more than usually out-of-date, the bird starts in my garden.

FRANKLYN. The bird?

HASLAM. Oh yes. Theres a bird there that keeps on singing "Stick it or chuck it: stick it or chuck it"—just like that—for an hour on end in the spring. I wish my father had found some other shop for me.

The parlor maid comes back.

THE PARLOR MAID. Any letters for the post, sir?

FRANKLYN. These. [*He proffers a basket of letters. She comes to the table and takes them*].

HASLAM [*to the maid*] Have you told Mr Barnabas yet?

THE PARLOR MAID [*flinching a little*] No, sir.

FRANKLYN. Told me what?

HASLAM. She is going to leave you?

FRANKLYN. Indeed? I'm sorry. Is it our fault, Mr Haslam?

HASLAM. Not a bit. She is jolly well off here.

THE PARLOR MAID [*reddening*] I have never denied it, sir: I couldnt ask for a better place. But I have only one life to live; and I maynt get a second chance. Excuse me, sir; but the letters must go to catch the post. [*She goes out with the letters*].

The two brothers look inquiringly at Haslam.

HASLAM. Silly girl! Going to marry a village woodman and live in a hovel with him and a lot of kids tumbling over one another, just because the fellow has poetic-looking eyes and a moustache.

CONRAD [*demurring*] She said it was because she had only one life.

HASLAM. Same thing, poor girl! The fellow persuaded her to chuck it; and when she marries him she'll have to stick it. Rotten state of things, I call it.

CONRAD. You see, she hasnt time to find out what life really means. She has to die before she knows.

HASLAM [*agreeably*] Thats it.

FRANKLYN. She hasnt time to form a well-instructed

conscience.

HASLAM [*still more cheerfully*] Quite.

FRANKLYN. It goes deeper. She hasnt time to form a genuine conscience at all. Some romantic points of honor and a few conventions. A world without conscience: that is the horror of our condition.

HASLAM [*beaming*] Simply fatuous. [*Rising*] Well, I suppose I'd better be going. It's most awfully good of you to put up with my calling.

CONRAD [*in his former low ghostly tone*] You neednt go, you know, if you are really interested.

HASLAM [*fed up*] Well, I'm afraid I ought to—I really must get back—I have something to do in the—

FRANKLYN [*smiling benignly and rising to proffer his hand*] Goodbye.

CONRAD [*gruffly, giving him up as a bad job*] Goodbye.

HASLAM. Goodbye. Sorry—er—

As the rector moves to shake hands with Franklyn, feeling that he is making a frightful mess of his departure, a vigorous sunburnt young lady with hazel hair cut to the level of her neck, like an Italian youth in a Gozzoli picture, comes in impetuously. She seems to have nothing on but her short skirt, her blouse, her stockings, and a pair of Norwegian shoes: in short, she is a Simple-Lifer.

THE SIMPLE-LIFER [*swooping on Conrad and kissing him*] Hallo, Nunk. Youre before your time.

CONRAD. Behave yourself. Theres a visitor.

She turns quickly and sees the rector. She instinctively switches at her Gozzoli fringe with her fingers, but gives it up as hopeless.

FRANKLYN. Mr Haslam, our new rector. [*To Haslam*] My daughter Cynthia.

CONRAD. Usually called Savvy, short for Savage.

SAVVY. I usually call Mr Haslam Bill, short for William. [*She strolls to the hearthrug, and surveys them calmly from that commanding position*].

FRANKLYN. You know him?

SAVVY. Rather. Sit down, Bill.

FRANKLYN. Mr Haslam is going, Savvy. He has an engagement.

SAVVY. I know. I'm the engagement.

CONRAD. In that case, would you mind taking him into the garden while I talk to your father?

SAVVY [*to Haslam*] Tennis?

HASLAM. Rather!

SAVVY. Come on. [*She dances out. He runs out boyishly after her*].

FRANKLYN [*leaving his table and beginning to walk up and down the room discontentedly*] Savvy's manners jar on me. They would have horrified her grandmother.

CONRAD [*obstinately*] They are happier manners than Mother's manners.

FRANKLYN. Yes: they are franker, wholesomer, better in a hundred ways. And yet I squirm at them. I cannot get it out of my head that Mother was a well-mannered woman, and that Savvy has no manners at all.

CONRAD. There wasnt any pleasure in Mother's fine manners. That makes a biological difference.

FRANKLYN. But there was beauty in Mother's manners, grace in them, style in them: above all, decision in them. Savvy is such a cub.

CONRAD. So she ought to be, at her age.

FRANKLYN. There it comes again! Her age! her age!

CONRAD. You want her to be fully grown at eighteen. You want to force her into a stuck-up, artificial, premature self-possession before she has any self to possess. You just let her alone: she is right enough for her years.

FRANKLYN. I have let her alone; and look at the result! Like all the other young people who have been let alone, she becomes a Socialist. That is, she becomes hopelessly demoralized.

CONRAD. Well, arnt you a Socialist?

FRANKLYN. Yes; but that is not the same thing. You and I were brought up in the old bourgeois morality. We were taught bourgeois manners and bourgeois points of honor. Bourgeois manners may be snobbish manners: there may be no pleasure in them, as you say; but they are better than no manners. Many bourgeois points of honor may be false; but at least they exist. The women know what to expect and what is expected of them. Savvy doesnt. She is a Bolshevist and nothing else. She has to improvize her manners and her conduct as she goes along. It's often charming, no doubt; but sometimes she puts her foot in it frightfully; and then I feel that she is blaming me for not teaching her better.

CONRAD. Well, you have something better to teach her now, at all events.

FRANKLYN. Yes; but it is too late. She doesnt trust me now. She doesnt talk about such things to me. She doesnt read anything I write. She never comes to hear me lecture. I am out of it as far as Savvy is concerned. [*He resumes his seat at the writing-table*].

CONRAD. I must have a talk to her.

FRANKLYN. Perhaps she will listen to you. You are not her father.

CONRAD. I sent her my last book. I can break the ice by asking her what she made of it.

FRANKLYN. When she heard you were coming, she asked me whether all the leaves were cut, in case it fell into your hands. She hasnt read a word of it.

CONRAD [*rising indignantly*] What!

FRANKLYN [*inexorably*] Not a word of it.

CONRAD [*beaten*] Well, I suppose it's only natural. Biology is a dry subject for a girl; and I am a pretty dry old codger. [*He sits down again resignedly*].

FRANKLYN. Brother: if that is so; if biology as you have worked at it, and religion as I have worked at it, are dry subjects like the old stuff they taught under these names, and we two are dry old codgers, like the old preachers and professors, then the Gospel of the Brothers Barnabas is a delusion. Unless this withered thing religion, and this dry thing science, have come alive in our hands, alive and intensely interesting, we may just as well go out and dig the garden until it is time to dig our graves. [*The parlor maid returns. Franklyn is impatient at the interruption*]. Well? what is it now?

THE PARLOR MAID. Mr Joyce Burge on the telephone, sir. He wants to speak to you.

FRANKLYN [*astonished*] Mr Joyce Burge!

THE PARLOR MAID. Yes, sir.

FRANKLYN [*to Conrad*] What on earth does this mean? I havnt heard from him nor exchanged a word with him for years. I resigned the chairmanship of the Liberal Association and shook the dust of party politics from my feet before he was Prime Minister in the Coalition. Of course, he dropped me like a hot potato.

CONRAD. Well, now that the Coalition has chucked him out, and he is only one of the half-dozen leaders of the Opposition, perhaps he wants to pick you up again.

THE PARLOR MAID [*warningly*] He is holding the line, sir.

FRANKLYN. Yes: all right [*he hurries out*].

The parlor maid goes to the hearthrug to make up the fire. Conrad rises and strolls to the middle of the room, where he stops and looks quizzically down at her.

CONRAD. So you have only one life to live, eh?

THE PARLOR MAID [*dropping on her knees in consternation*] I meant no offence, sir.

CONRAD. You didnt give any. But you know you could live a devil of a long life if you really wanted to.

THE PARLOR MAID [*sitting down on her heels*] Oh, dont say that, sir. It's so unsettling.

CONRAD. Why? Have you been thinking about it?

THE PARLOR MAID. It would never have come into my head if you hadnt put it there, sir. Me and cook had a look at your book.

CONRAD. What!

You and cook
Had a look
At my book!

And my niece wouldnt open it! The prophet is without honor in his own family. Well, what do you think of living for several hundred years? Are you going to have a try for it?

THE PARLOR MAID. Well, of course youre not in earnest, sir. But it does set one thinking, especially when one is going to be married.

CONRAD. What has that to do with it? He may live as long as you, you know.

THE PARLOR MAID. Thats just it, sir. You see, he must take me for better for worse, til death do us part. Do you think he would be so ready to do that, sir, if he thought it might be for several hundred years?

CONRAD. Thats true. And what about yourself?

THE PARLOR MAID. Oh, I tell you straight out, sir, I'd never promise to live with the same man as long as that. I wouldnt put up with my own children as long as that. Why, cook figured it out, sir, that when you were only 200, you might marry your own great-great-great-great-great-great-grandson and not even know who he was.

CONRAD. Well, why not? For all you know, the man you are going to marry may be your great-great-great-great-great-great-grandmother's great-great-great-great-great-great-grandson.

THE PARLOR MAID. But do you think it would ever be thought respectable, sir?

CONRAD. My good girl, all biological necessities have to be made respectable whether we like it or not; so you neednt worry yourself about that.

Franklyn returns and crosses the room to his chair, but does not sit down. The parlor maid goes out.

CONRAD. Well, what does Joyce Burge want?

FRANKLYN. Oh, a silly misunderstanding. I have promised to address a meeting in Middlesborough; and some fool has put it into the papers that I am "coming to Middlesborough," without any explanation. Of course, now that we are on the eve of a general election, political people think I am coming there to contest the parliamentary seat. Burge knows that I have a following, and thinks I could get into the House of Commons and head a group there. So he insists on coming to see me. He is staying with some people at Dollis Hill, and can be here in five or ten minutes, he says.

CONRAD. But didnt you tell him that it's a false alarm?

FRANKLYN. Of course I did; but he wont believe me.

CONRAD. Called you a liar, in fact?

FRANKLYN. No: I wish he had: any sort of plain speaking is better than the nauseous sham goodfellowship our democratic public men get up for shop use. He pretends to believe me, and assures me his visit is quite disinterested; but why should he come if he has no axe to grind? These chaps never believe anything they say themselves; and naturally they cannot believe anything anyone else says.

CONRAD [*rising*] Well, I shall clear out. It was hard enough to stand the party politicians before the war; but now that they have managed to half kill Europe between them, I cant be civil to them, and I dont see why I should be.

FRANKLYN. Wait a bit. We have to find out how the world will take our new gospel. [*Conrad sits down again*]. Party politicians are still unfortunately an important part of the world. Suppose we try it on Joyce Burge.

CONRAD. How can you? You can tell things only to people who can listen. Joyce Burge has talked so much that he has lost the power of listening. He doesnt listen even in the House of Commons.

Savvy rushes in breathless, followed by Haslam, who remains timidly just inside the door.

SAVVY [*running to Franklyn*] I say! Who do you think has just driven up in a big car?

FRANKLYN. Mr Joyce Burge, perhaps.

SAVVY [*disappointed*] Oh, they know, Bill. Why didnt you tell us he was coming? I have nothing on.

HASLAM. I'd better go, hadnt I?

CONRAD. You just wait here, both of you. When you start yawning, Joyce Burge will take the hint, perhaps.

SAVVY [*to Franklyn*] May we?

FRANKLYN. Yes, if you promise to behave yourself.

SAVVY [*making a wry face*] That will be a treat, wont it?

THE PARLOR MAID [*entering and announcing*] Mr Joyce Burge. [*Haslam hastily moves to the fireplace; and the parlor maid goes out and shuts the door when the visitor has passed in*].

FRANKLYN [*hurrying past Savvy to his guest with the false cordiality he has just been denouncing*] Oh! Here you are. Delighted to see you. [*He shakes Burge's hand, and introduces Savvy*] My daughter.

SAVVY [*not daring to approach*] Very kind of you to come.

Joyce Burge stands fast and says nothing; but he screws up his cheeks into a smile at each introduction, and makes his eyes shine in a very winning manner. He is a well-fed man turned fifty, with broad forehead, and grey hair which, his neck being short, falls almost to his collar.

FRANKLYN. Mr Haslam, our rector.

Burge conveys an impression of shining like a church window; and Haslam seizes the nearest library chair on the hearth, and swings it round for Burge between the stool and Conrad. He then retires to the window seat at the other side of the room, and is joined by Savvy. They sit there, side by side, hunched up with their elbows on their knees and their chins on their hands, providing Burge with a sort of Strangers' Gallery during the ensuing sitting.

FRANKLYN. I forget whether you know my brother Conrad. He is a biologist.

BURGE [*suddenly bursting into energetic action and shaking hands heartily with Conrad*] By reputation only, but very well, of course. How I wish I could have devoted myself to biology! I have always been interested in rocks and strata and volcanoes and so forth: they throw such a light on the age of the earth. [*With conviction*] There is nothing like biology. "The cloud-capped towers, the solemn binnacles, the gorgeous temples, the great globe itself: yea, all that it inherit shall dissolve, and, like this influential pageant faded, leave not a rack behind." Thats biology, you know: good sound biology. [*He sits down. So do the others, Franklyn on the stool, and Conrad on his Chippendale*]. Well, my dear Barnabas, what do you think of the situation? Dont you think the time has come for us to make a move?

FRANKLYN. The time has always come to make a move.

BURGE. How true! But what is the move to be? You are a man of enormous influence. We know that. Weve always known it. We have to consult you whether we like it or not. We—

FRANKLYN [*interrupting firmly*] I never meddle in party politics now.

SAVVY. It's no use saying you have no influence, daddy. Heaps of people swear by you.

BURGE [*shining at her*] Of course they do. Come! let me prove to you what we think of you. Shall we find you a first-rate constituency to contest at the next election? One that wont cost you a penny. A metropolitan seat. What do you say to the Strand?

FRANKLYN. My dear Burge, I am not a child. Why do you go on wasting your party funds on the Strand? You know you cannot win it.

BURGE. We cannot win it; but you—

FRANKLYN. Oh, please!

SAVVY. The Strand's no use, Mr Burge. I once canvassed for a Socialist there. Cheese it.

BURGE. Cheese it!

HASLAM [*spluttering with suppressed laughter*] Priceless!

SAVVY. Well, I suppose I shouldnt say cheese it to a Right Honorable. But the Strand, you know! Do come off it.

FRANKLYN. You must excuse my daughter's shocking manners, Burge; but I agree with her that popular democratic statesmen soon come to believe that everyone they speak to is an ignorant dupe and a born fool into the bargain.

BURGE [*laughing genially*] You old aristocrat, you! But believe me, the instinct of the people is sound—

CONRAD [*cutting in sharply*] Then why are you in the Opposition instead of in the Government?

BURGE [*shewing signs of temper under this heckling*] I deny that I am in the Opposition morally. The Government does not represent the country. I was chucked out of the Coalition by a Tory conspiracy. The people want me back. I dont want to go back.

FRANKLYN [*gently remonstrant*] My dear Burge: of course you do.

BURGE [*turning on him*] Not a bit of it. I want to cultivate my garden. I am not interested in politics: I am interested in roses. I havnt a scrap of ambition. I went into politics because my wife shoved me into them, bless her! But I want to serve my country. What else am I for? I want to save my country from the Tories. They dont represent the people. The man they have made Prime Minister has never represented the people; and you know it. Lord Dunreen is the bitterest old Tory left alive. What has he to offer to the people?

FRANKLYN [*cutting in before Burge can proceed—as he evidently intends—to answer his own question*] I will tell you. He has ascertainable beliefs and principles to offer. The people know where they are with Lord Dunreen. They know what he thinks right and what he thinks wrong. With your followers they never know where they are. With you they never know where they are.

BURGE [*amazed*] With me!

FRANKLYN. Well, where are you? What are you?

BURGE. Barnabas: you must be mad. You ask me what I am?

FRANKLYN. I do.

BURGE. I am, if I mistake not, Joyce Burge, pretty well known throughout Europe, and indeed throughout the world, as the man who—unworthily perhaps, but not quite unsuccessfully—held the helm when the ship of State weathered the mightiest hurricane that has ever burst with earth-shaking violence on the land of our fathers.

FRANKLYN. I know that. I know who you are. And the earth-shaking part of it to me is that though you were placed in that enormously responsible position, neither I nor anyone else knows what your beliefs are, or even whether you have either beliefs or principles. What we did know was that your Government was formed largely of men who regarded you as a robber of henroosts, and whom you regarded as enemies of the people.

BURGE [*adroitly, as he thinks*] I agree with you. I agree with you absolutely. I dont believe in coalition governments.

FRANKLYN. Precisely. Yet you formed two.

BURGE. Why? Because we were at war. That is what you fellows never would realize. The Hun was at the gate. Our country, our lives, the honor of our wives and mothers and daughters, the tender flesh of our innocent babes, were at stake. Was that a time to argue about principles?

FRANKLYN. I should say it was the time of all others to confirm the resolution of our own men and gain the confidence and support of public opinion throughout the world by a declaration of principle. Do you think the Hun would ever have come to the gate if he had known that it would be shut in his face on principle? Did he not hold his own against you until America boldly affirmed the democratic principle and came to our rescue? Why did you let America snatch that honor from England?

BURGE. Barnabas: America was carried away by words, and had to eat them at the Peace Conference. Beware of eloquence: it is the bane of popular speakers like you.

FRANKLYN } [*exclaiming* } Well!!
SAVVY } *all* } I like that!
HASLAM } *together*] } Priceless!

BURGE [*continuing remorselessly*] Come down to facts. It wasnt principle that won the war: it was the British fleet and the blockade. America found the talk: I found the shells. You cannot win wars by principles; but you can win elections by them. There I am with you. You want the next election to be fought on principles: that is what it comes to, doesnt it?

FRANKLYN. I dont want it to be fought at all? An election

is a moral horror, as bad as a battle except for the blood: a mud bath for every soul concerned in it. You know very well that it will not be fought on principle.

BURGE. On the contrary it will be fought on nothing else. I believe a program is a mistake. I agree with you that principle is what we want.

FRANKLYN. Principle without program, eh?

BURGE. Exactly. There it is in three words.

FRANKLYN. Why not in one word? Platitudes. That is what principle without program means.

BURGE [*puzzled but patient, trying to get at Franklyn's drift in order to ascertain his price*] I have not made myself clear. Listen. I am agreeing with you. I am on your side. I am accepting your proposal. There isnt going to be any more coalition. This time there wont be a Tory in the Cabinet. Every candidate will have to pledge himself to Free Trade, slightly modified by consideration for our Overseas Dominions; to Disestablishment; to Reform of the House of Lords; to a revised scheme of Taxation of Land Values; and to doing something or other to keep the Irish quiet. Does that satisfy you?

FRANKLYN. It does not even interest me. Suppose your friends d o commit themselves to all this! What does it prove about them except that they are hopelessly out of date even in party politics? that they have learnt nothing and forgotten nothing since 1885? What is it to me that they hate the Church and hate the landed gentry; that they are jealous of the nobility, and have shipping shares instead of manufacturing businesses in the Midlands? I can find you hundreds of the most sordid rascals, or the most densely stupid reactionaries, with all these qualifications.

BURGE. Personal abuse proves nothing. Do you suppose the Tories are all angels because they are all members of the Church of England?

FRANKLYN. No; but they stand together as members of the Church of England, whereas your people, in attacking the Church, are all over the shop. The supporters of the

Church are of one mind about religion: its enemies are of a dozen minds. The Churchmen are a phalanx: your people are a mob in which atheists are jostled by Plymouth Brethren, and Positivists by Pillars of Fire. You have with you all the crudest unbelievers and all the crudest fanatics.

BURGE. We stand, as Cromwell did, for liberty of conscience, if that is what you mean.

FRANKLYN. How can you talk such rubbish over the graves of your conscientious objectors? All law limits liberty of conscience: if a man's conscience allows him to steal your watch or to shirk military service, how much liberty do you allow it? Liberty of conscience is not my point.

BURGE [*testily*] I wish you would come to your point. Half the time you are saying that you must have principles; and when I offer you principles you say they wont work.

FRANKLYN. You have not offered me any principles. Your party shibboleths are not principles. If you get into power again you will find yourself at the head of a rabble of Socialists and anti-Socialists, of Jingo Imperialists and Little Englanders, of cast-iron Materialists and ecstatic Quakers, of Christian Scientists and Compulsory Inoculationists, of Syndicalists and Bureaucrats: in short, of men differing fiercely and irreconcilably on every principle that goes to the root of human society and destiny; and the impossibility of keeping such a team together will force you to sell the pass again to the solid Conservative Opposition.

BURGE [*rising in wrath*] Sell the pass again! You accuse me of having sold the pass!

FRANKLYN. When the terrible impact of real warfare swept your parliamentary sham warfare into the dustbin, you had to go behind the backs of your followers and make a secret agreement with the leaders of the Opposition to keep you in power on condition that you dropped all legislation of which they did not approve. And you could not even hold them to their bargain; for they presently betrayed the secret and forced the coalition on you.

BURGE. I solemnly declare that this is a false and monstrous accusation.

FRANKLYN. Do you deny that the thing occurred? Were the uncontradicted reports false? Were the published letters forgeries?

BURGE. Certainly not. But *I* did not do it. I was not Prime Minister then. It was that old dotard, that played-out old humbug Lubin. He was Prime Minister then, not I.

FRANKLYN. Do you mean to say you did not know?

BURGE [*sitting down again with a shrug*] Oh, I had to be told. But what could I do? If we had refused we might have had to go out of office.

FRANKLYN. Precisely.

BURGE. Well, could we desert the country at such a crisis? The Hun was at the gate. Everyone has to make sacrifices for the sake of the country at such moments. We had to rise above party; and I am proud to say we never gave party a second thought. We stuck to—

CONRAD. Office?

BURGE [*turning on him*] Yes, sir, to office: that is, to responsibility, to danger, to heart-sickening toil, to abuse and misunderstanding, to a martyrdom that made us envy the very soldiers in the trenches. If you had had to live for months on aspirin and bromide of potassium to get a wink of sleep, you wouldnt talk about office as if it were a catch.

FRANKLYN. Still, you admit that under our parliamentary system Lubin could not have helped himself?

BURGE. On that subject my lips are closed. Nothing will induce me to say one word against the old man. I never have; and I never will. Lubin is old: he has never been a real statesman: he is as lazy as a cat on a hearthrug: you cant get him to attend to anything: he is good for nothing but getting up and making speeches with a peroration that goes down with the back benches. But I say nothing against him. I gather that you do not think much of me as a statesman; but at all events I can get things done. I can hustle: even you will admit that. But Lubin! Oh my stars, Lubin!! If you only knew—

The parlor maid opens the door and announces a visitor.

THE PARLOR MAID. Mr Lubin.

BURGE [*bounding from his chair*] Lubin! Is this a conspiracy?

They all rise in amazement, staring at the door. Lubin enters: a man at the end of his sixties, a Yorkshireman with the last traces of Scandinavian flax still in his white hair, undistinguished in stature, unassuming in his manner, and taking his simple dignity for granted, but wonderfully comfortable and quite self-assured in contrast to the intellectual restlessness of Franklyn and the mesmeric self-assertiveness of Burge. His presence suddenly brings out the fact that they are unhappy men, ill at ease, square pegs in round holes, whilst he flourishes like a primrose.

The parlor maid withdraws.

LUBIN [*coming to Franklyn*] How do you do, Mr Barnabas? [*He speaks very comfortably and kindly, much as if he were the host, and Franklyn an embarrassed but welcome guest*]. I had the pleasure of meeting you once at the Mansion House. I think it was to celebrate the conclusion of the hundred years peace with America.

FRANKLYN [*shaking hands*] It was long before that: a meeting about Venezeula, when we were on the point of going to war with America.

LUBIN [*not at all put out*] Yes: you are quite right. I knew it was something about America. [*He pats Franklyn's hand*]. And how have you been all this time? Well, eh?

FRANKLYN [*smiling to soften the sarcasm*] A few vicissitudes of health naturally in so long a time.

LUBIN. Just so. Just so. [*Looking round at Savvy*] The young lady is—?

FRANKLYN. My daughter, Savvy.

Savvy comes from the window between her father and Lubin.

LUBIN [*taking her hand affectionately in both his*] And why has she never come to see us?

BURGE. I dont know whether you have noticed, Lubin,

that I am present.

Savvy takes advantage of this diversion to slip away to the settee, where she is stealthily joined by Haslam, who sits down on her left.

LUBIN [*seating himself in Burge's chair with ineffable comfortableness*] My dear Burge: if you imagine that it is possible to be within ten miles of your energetic presence without being acutely aware of it, you do yourself the greatest injustice. How are you? And how are your good newspaper friends? [*Burge makes an explosive movement; but Lubin goes on calmly and sweetly*] And what are you doing here with my old friend Barnabas, if I may ask?

BURGE [*sitting down in Conrad's chair, leaving him standing uneasily in the corner*] Well, just what you are doing, if you want to know. I am trying to enlist Mr Barnabas's valuable support for my party.

LUBIN. Your party, eh? The newspaper party?

BURGE. The Liberal Party. The party of which I have the honor to be leader.

LUBIN. Have you now? Thats very interesting; for I thought *I* was the leader of the Liberal Party. However, it is very kind of you to take it off my hands, if the party will let you.

BURGE. Do you suggest that I have not the support and confidence of the party?

LUBIN. I dont suggest anything, my dear Burge. Mr Barnabas will tell you that we all think very highly of you. The country owes you a great deal. During the war, you did very creditably over the munitions; and if you were not quite so successful with the peace, nobody doubted that you meant well.

BURGE. Very kind of you, Lubin. Let me remark that you cannot lead a progressive party without getting a move on.

LUBIN. You mean y o u cannot. I did it for ten years without the least difficulty. And very comfortable, prosperous, pleasant years they were.

BURGE. Yes; but what did they end in?

LUBIN. In you, Burge. You dont complain of that, do you?

BURGE [*fiercely*] In plague, pestilence, and famine; battle, murder, and sudden death.

LUBIN [*with an appreciative chuckle*] The Nonconformist can quote the prayer-book for his own purposes, I see. How you enjoyed yourself over that business, Burge! Do you remember the Knock-Out Blow?

BURGE. It came off: dont forget that. Do you remember fighting to the last drop of your blood?

LUBIN [*unruffled, to Franklyn*] By the way, I remember your brother Conrad—a wonderful brain and a dear good fellow—explaining to me that I couldnt fight to the last drop of my blood, because I should be dead long before I came to it. Most interesting, and quite true. He was introduced to me at a meeting where the suffragettes kept disturbing me. They had to be carried out kicking and making a horrid disturbance.

CONRAD. No: it was later, at a meeting to support the Franchise Bill which gave them the vote.

LUBIN [*discovering Conrad's presence for the first time*] Youre right: it was. I knew it had something to do with women. My memory never deceives me. Thank you. Will you introduce me to this gentleman, Barnabas?

CONRAD [*not at all affably*] I am the Conrad in question. [*He sits down in dudgeon on the vacant Chippendale*].

LUBIN. Are you? [*Looking at him pleasantly*] Yes: of course you are. I never forget a face. But [*with an arch turn of his eyes to Savvy*] your pretty niece engaged all my powers of vision.

BURGE. I wish youd be serious, Lubin. God knows we have passed through times terrible enough to make any man serious.

LUBIN. I do not think I need to be reminded of that. In peace time I used to keep myself fresh for my work by banishing all wordly considerations from my mind on Sundays, but war has no respect for the Sabbath; and there have been

Sundays within the last few years on which I have had to play as many as sixty-six games of bridge to keep my mind off the news from the front.

BURGE [*scandalized*] Sixty-six games of bridge on Sunday!!!

LUBIN. You probably sang sixty-six hymns. But as I cannot boast either your admirable voice or your spiritual fervor, I had to fall back on bridge.

FRANKLYN. If I may go back to the subject of your visit, it seems to me that you may both be completely superseded by the Labor Party.

BURGE. But I am in the truest sense myself a Labor leader. I—[*he stops, as Lubin has risen with a half-suppressed yawn, and is already talking calmly, but without a pretence of interest*].

LUBIN. The Labor Party! Oh no, Mr Barnabas. No, no, no, no, no. [*He moves in Savvy's direction*]. There will be no trouble about that. Of course we must give them a few seats: more, I quite admit, than we should have dreamt of leaving to them before the war; but—[*by this time he has reached the sofa where Savvy and Haslam are seated. He sits down between them; takes her hand; and drops the subject of Labor*]. Well, my dear young lady? What is the latest news? Whats going on? Have you seen Shoddy's new play? Tell me all about it, and all about the latest books, and all about everything.

SAVVY. You have not met Mr Haslam. Our Rector.

LUBIN [*who has quite overlooked Haslam*] Never heard of him. Is he any good?

SAVVY. I was introducing him. This is Mr Haslam.

HASLAM. How d'ye do?

LUBIN. I beg your pardon, Mr Haslam. Delighted to meet you. [*To Savvy*] Well, now, how many books have you written?

SAVVY [*rather overwhelmed but attracted*] None. I dont write.

LUBIN. You dont say so! Well, what do you do? Music?

Shirt-dancing?

SAVVY. I dont do anything.

LUBIN. Thank God! You and I were born for one another. Who is your favorite poet, Sally?

SAVVY. Savvy.

LUBIN. Savvy! I never heard of him. Tell me all about him. Keep me up to date.

SAVVY. It's not a poet. *I* am Savvy, not Sally.

LUBIN. Savvy! Thats a funny name, and very pretty. Savvy. It sounds Chinese. What does it mean?

CONRAD. Short for Savage.

LUBIN [*patting her hand*] La belle Sauvage.

HASLAM [*rising and surrendering Savvy to Lubin by crossing to the fireplace*] I suppose the Church is out of it as far as progressive politics are concerned.

BURGE. Nonsense! That notion about the Church being unprogressive is one of those shibboleths that our party must drop. The Church is all right essentially. Get rid of the establishment; get rid of the bishops; get rid of the candlesticks; get rid of the 39 articles; and the Church of England is just as good as any other Church; and I dont care who hears me say so.

LUBIN. It doesnt matter a bit who hears you say so, my dear Burge. [*To Savvy*] Who did you say your favorite poet was?

SAVVY. I dont make pets of poets. Who's yours?

LUBIN. Horace.

SAVVY. Horace who?

LUBIN. Quintus Horatius Flaccus: the noblest Roman of them all, my dear.

SAVVY. Oh, if he is dead, that explains it. I have a theory that all the dead people we feel especially interested in must have been ourselves. You must be Horace's reincarnation.

LUBIN [*delighted*] That is the very most charming and penetrating and intelligent thing that has ever been said to me. Barnabas: will you exchange daughters with me? I can give you your choice of two.

FRANKLYN. Man proposes. Savvy disposes.

LUBIN. What does Savvy say?

BURGE. Lubin: I came here to talk politics.

LUBIN. Yes: you have only one subject, Burge. I came here to talk to Savvy. Take Burge into the next room, Barnabas; and let him rip.

BURGE [*half-angry, half-indulgent*] No; but really, Lubin, we are at a crisis—

LUBIN. My dear Burge, life is a disease; and the only difference between one man and another is the stage of the disease at which he lives. You are always at the crisis: I am always in the convalescent stage. I enjoy convalescence. It is the part that makes the illness worth while.

SAVVY [*half-rising*] Perhaps I'd better run away. I am distracting you.

LUBIN [*making her sit down again*] Not at all, my dear. You are only distracting Burge. Jolly good thing for him to be distracted by a pretty girl. Just what he needs.

BURGE. I sometimes envy you, Lubin. The great movement of mankind, the giant sweep of the ages, passes you by and leaves you standing.

LUBIN. It leaves me sitting, and quite comfortable, thank you. Go on sweeping. When you are tired of it, come back; and you will find England where it was, and me in my accustomed place, with Miss Savvy telling me all sorts of interesting things.

SAVVY [*who has been growing more and more restless*] Dont let him shut you up, Mr Burge. You know, Mr Lubin, I am frightfully interested in the Labor movement, and in Theosophy, and in reconstruction after the war, and all sorts of things. I daresay the flappers in your smart set are tremendously flattered when you sit beside them and are nice to them as you are being nice to me; but I am not smart; and I am no use as a flapper. I am dowdy and serious. I want you to be serious. If you refuse, I shall go and sit beside Mr Burge, and ask him to hold my hand.

LUBIN. He wouldnt know how to do it, my dear. Burge

has a reputation as a profligate—

BURGE [*starting*] Lubin: this is monstrous. I—

LUBIN [*continuing*]—but he is really a model of domesticity. His name is coupled with all the most celebrated beauties; but for him there is only one woman; and that is not you, my dear, but his very charming wife.

BURGE. You are destroying my character in the act of pretending to save it. Have the goodness to confine yourself to your own character and your own wife. Both of them need all your attention.

LUBIN. I have the privilege of my age and of my transparent innocence. I have not to struggle with your volcanic energy.

BURGE [*with an immense sense of power*] No, by George!

FRANKLYN. I think I shall speak both for my brother and myself, and possibly also for my daughter, if I say that since the object of your visit and Mr Joyce Burge's is to some extent political, we should hear with great interest something about your political aims, Mr Lubin.

LUBIN [*assenting with complete good humor, and becoming attentive, clear, and businesslike in his tone*] By all means, Mr Barnabas. What we have to consider first, I take it, is what prospect there is of our finding you beside us in the House after the next election.

FRANKLYN. When I speak of politics, Mr Lubin, I am not thinking of elections, or available seats, or party funds, or the registers, or even, I am sorry to have to add, of parliament as it exists at present. I had much rather you talked about bridge than about electioneering: it is the more interesting game of the two.

BURGE. He wants to discuss principles, Lubin.

LUBIN [*very cool and clear*] I understand Mr Barnabas quite well. But elections are unsettled things: principles are settled things.

CONRAD [*impatiently*] Great Heavens!—

LUBIN [*interrupting him with quiet authority*] One moment, Dr Barnabas. The main principles on which modern civilized society is founded are pretty well understood among educated people. That is what our dangerously half-educated masses and their pet demagogues—if Burge will excuse that expression—

BURGE. Dont mind me. Go on. I shall have something to say presently.

LUBIN. —that is what our dangerously half-educated people do not realize. Take all this fuss about the Labor Party, with its imaginary new principles and new politics. The Labor members will find that the immutable laws of political economy take no more notice of their ambitions and aspirations than the law of gravitation. I speak, if I may say so, with knowledge; for I have made a special study of the Labor question.

FRANKLYN [*with interest and some surprise*] Indeed?

LUBIN. Yes. It occurred quite at the beginning of my career. I was asked to deliver an address to the students at the Working Men's College; and I was strongly advised to comply, as Gladstone and Morley and others were doing that sort of thing at the moment. It was rather a troublesome job, because I had not gone into political economy at the time. As you know, at the university I was a classical scholar; and my profession was the Law. But I looked up the text-books, and got up the case most carefully. I found that the correct view is that all this Trade Unionism and Socialism and so forth is founded on the ignorant delusion that wages and the production and distribution of wealth can be controlled by legislation or by any human action whatever. They obey fixed scientific laws, which have been ascertained and settled finally by the highest economic authorities. Naturally I do not at this distance of time remember the exact process of reasoning; but I can get up the case again at any time in a couple of days; and you may rely on me absolutely, should the occasion arise, to deal with all these ignorant and unpractical people in a conclusive and convincing way, except, of course, as far as it may be advisable to indulge and flatter them a little so as to let them down without creating ill feeling in the working-class electorate. In short, I can get that lecture up again almost at a moment's notice.

SAVVY. But, Mr Lubin, I have had a university education too; and all this about wages and distribution being fixed by immutable laws of political economy is obsolete rot.

FRANKLYN [*shocked*] Oh, my dear! That is not polite.

LUBIN. No, no, no. Dont scold her. She mustnt be scolded. [*To Savvy*] I understand. You are a disciple of Karl Marx.

SAVVY. No, no. Karl Marx's economics are all rot.

LUBIN [*at last a little taken aback*] Dear me!

SAVVY. You must excuse me, Mr Lubin; but it's like hearing a man talk about the Garden of Eden.

CONRAD. Why shouldnt he talk about the Garden of Eden? It was a first attempt at biology anyhow.

LUBIN [*recovering his self-possession*] I am sound on the Garden of Eden. I have heard of Darwin.

SAVVY. But Darwin is all rot.

LUBIN. What! Already!

SAVVY. It's no good your smiling at me like a Cheshire cat, Mr Lubin; and I am not going to sit here mumchance like an old-fashioned goody goody wife while you men monopolize the conversation and pay out the very ghastliest exploded drivel as the latest thing in politics. I am not giving you my own ideas, Mr Lubin, but just the regular orthodox science of today. Only the most awful old fossils think that Socialism is bad economics and that Darwin invented Evolution. Ask Papa. Ask Uncle. Ask the first person you meet in the street. [*She rises and crosses to Haslam*]. Give me a cigaret, Bill, will you?

HASLAM. Priceless. [*He complies*].

FRANKLYN. Savvy has not lived long enough to have any manners, Mr Lubin; but that is where you stand with the younger generation. Dont smoke, dear.

Savvy, with a shrug of rather mutinous resignation, throws the cigaret into the fire. Haslam, on the point of lighting one for himself, changes his mind.

LUBIN [*shrewd and serious*] Mr Barnabas: I confess I am surprised; and I will not pretend that I am convinced. But I am open to conviction. I may be wrong.

BURGE [*in a burst of irony*] Oh no. Impossible! Impossible!

LUBIN. Yes, Mr Barnabas, though I do not possess Burge's genius for being always wrong, I have been in that position once or twice. I could not conceal from you, even if I wished to, that my time has been so completely filled by my professional work as a lawyer, and later on by my duties as leader of the House of Commons in the days when Prime Ministers were also leaders—

BURGE [*stung*] Not to mention bridge and smart society.

LUBIN. —not to mention the continual and trying effort to make Burge behave himself, that I have not been able to keep my academic reading up to date. I have kept my classics brushed up out of sheer love for them; but my economics and my science, such as they were, may possibly be a little rusty. Yet I think I may say that if you and your brother will be so good as to put me on the track of the necessary documents, I will undertake to put the case to the House or to the country to your entire satisfaction. You see, as long as you can shew these troublesome half-educated people who want to turn the world upside down that they are talking nonsense, it really does not matter very much whether you do it in terms of what Miss Barnabas calls obsolete rot or in terms of what her granddaughter will probably call unmitigated tosh. I have no objection whatever to denounce Karl Marx. Anything I can say against Darwin will please a large body of sincerely pious voters. If it will be easier to carry on the business of the country on the understanding that the present state of things is to be called Socialism, I have no objection in the world to call it Socialism. There is the precedent of the Emperor Constantine, who saved the society of his own day by agreeing to call his Imperialism Christianity. Mind: I must not go ahead of the electorate. You must not call a voter a Socialist until—

FRANKLYN. Until he is a Socialist. Agreed.

LUBIN. Oh, not at all. You need not wait for that. You must not call him a Socialist until he wishes to be called a Socialist: that is all. Surely you would not say that I must not address my constituents as gentlemen until they are gentlemen. I address them as gentlemen because they wish to be so addressed. [*He rises from the sofa and goes to Franklyn, placing a reassuring hand on his shoulder*]. Do not be afraid of Socialism, Mr Barnabas. You need not tremble for your property or your position or your dignity. England will remain what England is, no matter what new political names may come into vogue. I do not intend to resist the transition to Socialism. You may depend on me to guide it, to lead it, to give suitable expression to its aspirations, and to steer it clear of Utopian absurdities. I can honestly ask for your support on the most advanced Socialist grounds no less than on the soundest Liberal ones.

BURGE. In short, Lubin, youre incorrigible. You dont believe anything is going to change. The millions are still to toil—the people—my people—for I am a man of the people—

LUBIN [*interrupting him contemptuously*] Dont be ridiculous, Burge. You are a country solicitor, further removed from the people, more foreign to them, more jealous of letting them up to your level, than any duke or any archbishop.

BURGE [*hotly*] I deny it. You think I have never been poor. You think I have never cleaned my own boots. You think my fingers have never come out through the soles when I was cleaning them. You think—

LUBIN. I think you fall into the very common mistake of supposing that it is poverty that makes the proletarian and money that makes the gentleman. You are quite wrong. You never belonged to the people: you belonged to the impecunious. Impecuniosity and broken boots are the lot of the unsuccessful middle class, and the commonplaces of the early struggles of the professional and younger son class. I defy you to find a farm laborer in England with broken boots. Call a mechanic one of the poor, and he'll punch your head. When you talk to your constituents about the toiling millions, they dont consider that you are referring to them. They are all third cousins of somebody with a title or a park. I am a Yorkshireman, my friend, I know England; and you dont. If you did you would know—

BURGE. What do you know that I dont know?

LUBIN. I know that we are taking up too much of Mr Barnabas's time. [*Franklyn rises*]. May I take it, my dear Barnabas, that I may count on your support if we succeed in forcing an election before the new register is in full working order?

BURGE [*rising also*] May the party count on your support? I say nothing about myself. Can the party depend on you? Is there any question of yours that I have left unanswered?

CONRAD. We havnt asked you any, you know.

BURGE. May I take that as a mark of confidence?

CONRAD. If I were a laborer in your constituency, I should ask you a biological question?

LUBIN. No you wouldnt, my dear Doctor. Laborers never ask questions.

BURGE. Ask it now. I have never flinched from being heckled. Out with it. Is it about the land?

CONRAD. No.

BURGE. Is it about the Church?

CONRAD. No.

BURGE. Is it about the House of Lords?

CONRAD. No.

BURGE. Is it about Proportional Representation?

CONRAD. No.

BURGE. Is it about Free Trade?

CONRAD. No.

BURGE. Is it about the priest in the school?

CONRAD. No.

BURGE. Is it about Ireland?

CONRAD. No.

BURGE. Is it about Germany?

CONRAD. No.

BURGE. Well, is it about Republicanism? Come! I wont flinch. Is it about the Monarchy?

CONRAD. No.

BURGE. Well, what the devil is it about, then?

CONRAD. You understand that I am asking the question in the character of a laborer who earned thirteen shillings a week before the war and earns thirty now, when he can get it?

BURGE. Yes: I understand that. I am ready for you. Out with it.

CONRAD. And whom you propose to represent in parliament?

BURGE. Yes, yes, yes. Come on.

CONRAD. The question is this. Would you allow your son to marry my daughter, or your daughter to marry my son?

BURGE [*taken aback*] Oh, come! Thats not a political question.

CONRAD. Then, as a biologist, I dont take the slightest interest in your politics; and I shall not walk across the street to vote for you or anyone else at the election. Good evening.

LUBIN. Serve you right, Burge! Dr Barnabas: you have my assurance that my daughter shall marry the man of her choice, whether he be lord or laborer. May *I* count on your support?

BURGE [*hurling the epithet at him*] Humbug!

SAVVY. Stop. [*They all stop short in the movement of leave-taking to look at her*]. Daddy: are you going to let them off like this? How are they to know anything if nobody ever tells them? If you dont, I will.

CONRAD. You cant. You didnt read my book; and you know nothing about it. You just hold your tongue.

SAVVY. I just wont, Nunk. I shall have a vote when I am thirty; and I ought to have it now. Why are these two ridiculous people to be allowed to come in and walk over us as if the world existed only to play their silly parliamentary game?

FRANKLYN [*severely*] Savvy: you really must not be uncivil to our guests.

SAVVY. I'm sorry. But Mr Lubin didnt stand on much ceremony with me, did he? And Mr Burge hasnt addressed a single word to me. I'm not going to stand it. You and Nunk have a much better program than either of them. It's the only one we are going to vote for; and they ought to be told about it for the credit of the family and the good of their own souls. You just tip them a chapter from the gospel of the brothers Barnabas, Daddy.

Lubin and Burge turn inquiringly to Franklyn, suspecting a move to form a new party.

FRANKLYN. It is quite true, Mr Lubin, that I and my brother have a little program of our own which—

CONRAD [*interrupting*] It's not a little program: it's an almighty big one. It's not our own: it's the program of the whole of civilization.

BURGE. Then why split the party before you have put it to us? For God's sake let us have no more splits. I am here to learn. I am here to gather your opinions and represent them. I invite you to put your views before me. I offer myself to be heckled. You have asked me only an absurd nonpolitical question.

FRANKLYN. Candidly, I fear our program will be thrown away on you. It would not interest you.

BURGE [*with challenging audacity*] Try. Lubin can go if he likes; but I am still open to new ideas, if only I can find them.

FRANKLYN [*to Lubin*] Are you prepared to listen, Mr Lubin; or shall I thank you for your very kind and welcome visit, and say good evening?

LUBIN [*sitting down resignedly on the settee, but involuntarily making a movement which looks like the stifling of a yawn*] With pleasure, Mr Barnabas. Of course you know that before I can adopt any new plank in the party platform, it will have to reach me through the National Liberal Federation, which you can approach through your local Liberal and Radical Association.

FRANKLYN. I could recall to you several instances of the addition to your party program of measures of which no local branch of your Federation had ever dreamt. But I understand that you are not really interested. I will spare you, and drop the subject.

LUBIN [*waking up a little*] You quite misunderstand me. Please do not take it in that way. I only—

BURGE [*talking him down*] Never mind the Federation: *I* will answer for the Federation. Go on, Barnabas: go on. Never mind Lubin [*he sits down in the chair from which Lubin first displaced him*].

FRANKLYN. Our program is only that the term of human life shall be extended to three hundred years.

LUBIN [*softly*] Eh?

BURGE [*explosively*] What!

SAVVY. Our election cry is "Back to Methuselah!"

HASLAM. Priceless!

Lubin and Burge look at one another.

CONRAD. No. We are not mad.

SAVVY. Theyre not joking either. They mean it.

LUBIN [*cautiously*] Assuming that, in some sense which I am for the moment unable to fathom, you are in earnest, Mr Barnabas, may I ask what this has to do with politics?

FRANKLYN. The connection is very evident. You are now, Mr Lubin, within immediate reach of your seventieth year. Mr Joyce Burge is your junior by about eleven years. You will go down to posterity as one of a European group of immature statesmen and monarchs who, doing the very best for your respective countries of which you were capable, succeeded in all-but-wrecking the civilization of Europe, and did, in effect, wipe out of existence many millions of its inhabitants.

BURGE. Less than a million.

FRANKLYN. That was our loss alone.

BURGE. Oh, if you count foreigners—!

HASLAM. God counts foreigners, you know.

SAVVY [*with intense satisfaction*] Well said, Bill.

FRANKLYN. I am not blaming you. Your task was beyond human capacity. What with our huge armaments, our terrible engines of destruction, our systems of coercion manned by an irresistible police, you were called on to control powers so gigantic that one shudders at the thought of their being entrusted even to an infinitely experienced and benevolent God, much less to mortal men whose whole life does not last a hundred years.

BURGE. We won the war: dont forget that.

FRANKLYN. No: the soldiers and sailors won it, and left you to finish it. And you were so utterly incompetent that the multitudes of children slain by hunger in the first years of peace made us all wish we were at war again.

CONRAD. It's no use arguing about it. It is now absolutely certain that the political and social problems raised by our civilization cannot be solved by mere human mushrooms who decay and die when they are just beginning to have a glimmer of the wisdom and knowledge needed for their own government.

LUBIN. Quite an interesting idea, Doctor. Extravagant. Fantastic. But quite interesting. When I was young I used to feel my human limitations very acutely.

BURGE. God knows I have often felt that I could not go on if it had not been for the sense that I was only an instrument in the hands of a Power above us.

CONRAD. I'm glad you both agree with us, and with one another.

LUBIN. I have not gone so far as that, I think. After all, we have had many very able political leaders even within your recollection and mine.

FRANKLYN. Have you read the recent biographies—Dilke's, for instance—which revealed the truth about them?

LUBIN. I did not discover any new truth revealed in these books, Mr Barnabas.

FRANKLYN. What! Not the truth that England was

governed all that time by a little woman who knew her own mind?

SAVVY. Hear, hear!

LUBIN. That often happens. Which woman do you mean?

FRANKLYN. Queen Victoria, to whom your Prime Ministers stood in the relation of naughty children whose heads she knocked together when their tempers and quarrels became intolerable. Within thirteen years of her death Europe became a hell.

BURGE. Quite true. That was because she was piously brought up, and regarded herself as an instrument. If a statesman remembers that he is only an instrument, and feels quite sure that he is rightly interpreting the divine purpose, he will come out all right, you know.

FRANKLYN. The Kaiser felt like that. Did he come out all right?

BURGE. Well, let us be fair, even to the Kaiser. Let us be fair.

FRANKLYN. Were you fair to him when you won an election on the program of hanging him?

BURGE. Stuff! I am the last man alive to hang anybody; but the people wouldnt listen to reason. Besides, I knew the Dutch wouldnt give him up.

SAVVY. Oh, dont start arguing about poor old Bill. Stick to our point. Let these two gentlemen settle the question for themselves. Mr Burge: do you think Mr Lubin is fit to govern England?

BURGE. No. Frankly, I dont.

LUBIN [*remonstrant*] Really!

CONRAD. Why?

BURGE. Because he has no conscience: thats why.

LUBIN [*shocked and amazed*] Oh!

FRANKLYN. Mr Lubin: do you consider Joyce Burge qualified to govern England?

LUBIN [*with dignified emotion, wounded, but without bitterness*] Excuse me, Mr Barnabas; but before I answer that question I want to say this. Burge: we have had differences of opinion; and your newspaper friends have said hard things of me. But we worked together for years; and I hope I have done nothing to justify you in the amazing accusation you have just brought against me. Do you realize that you said that I have no conscience?

BURGE. Lubin: I am very accessible to an appeal to my emotions; and you are very cunning in making such appeals. I will meet you to this extent. I dont mean that you are a bad man. I dont mean that I dislike you, in spite of your continual attempts to discourage and depress me. But you have a mind like a looking-glass. You are very clear and smooth and lucid as to what is standing in front of you. But you have no foresight and no hindsight. You have no vision and no memory. You have no continuity; and a man without continuity can have neither conscience nor honor from one day to another. The result is that you have always been a damned bad minister; and you have sometimes been a damned bad friend. Now you can answer Barnabas's question and take it out of me to your heart's content. He asked you was I fit to govern England.

LUBIN [*recovering himself*] After what has just passed I sincerely wish I could honestly say yes, Burge. But it seems to me that you have condemned yourself out of your own mouth. You represent something which has had far too much influence and popularity in this country since Joseph Chamberlain set the fashion; and that is mere energy without intellect and without knowledge. Your mind is not a trained mind: it has not been stored with the best information, nor cultivated by intercourse with educated minds at any of our great seats of learning. As I happen to have enjoyed that advantage, it follows that you do not understand my mind. Candidly, I think that disqualifies you. The peace found out your weaknesses.

BURGE. Oh! What did it find out in you?

LUBIN. You and your newspaper confederates took the peace out of my hands. The peace did not find me out because it did not find me in.

FRANKLYN. Come! Confess, both of you! You were only flies on the wheel. The war went England's way; but the peace went its own way, and not England's way nor any of the ways you had so glibly appointed for it. Your peace treaty was a scrap of paper before the ink dried on it. The statesmen of Europe were incapable of governing Europe. What they needed was a couple of hundred years training and experience: what they had actually had was a few years at the bar or in a counting-house or on the grouse moors and golf courses. And now we are waiting, with monster cannons trained on every city and seaport, and huge aeroplanes ready to spring into the air and drop bombs every one of which will obliterate a whole street, and poison gases that will strike multitudes dead with a breath, until one of you gentlemen rises in his helplessness to tell us, who are as helpless as himself, that we are at war again.

CONRAD. Aha! What consolation will it be for us then that you two are able to tell off one another's defects so cleverly in your afternoon chat?

BURGE [*angrily*] If you come to that, what consolation will it be that you two can sit there and tell both of us off? you, who have had no responsibility! you, who havnt lifted a finger, as far as I know, to help us through this awful crisis which has left me ten years older than my proper age! Can you tell me a single thing you did to help us during the whole infernal business?

CONRAD. We're not blaming you: you hadnt lived long enough. No more had we. Cant you see that three-score-and-ten, though it may be long enough for a very crude sort of village life, isnt long enough for a complicated civilization like ours? Flinders Petrie has counted nine attempts at civilization made by people exactly like us; and every one of them failed just as ours is failing. They failed because the citizens and statesmen died of old age or over-eating before they had grown out of schoolboy games and savage sports and cigars and champagne. The signs of the end are always the same: Democracy, Socialism, and Votes for Women. We shall go to smash within the lifetime of men now living unless we recognize that we must live longer.

LUBIN. I am glad you agree with me that Socialism and Votes for Women are signs of decay.

FRANKLYN. Not at all: they are only the difficulties that overtax your capacity. If you cannot organize Socialism you cannot organize civilized life; and you will relapse into barbarism accordingly.

SAVVY. Hear, hear!

BURGE. A useful point. We cannot put back the clock.

HASLAM. *I* can. Ive often done it.

LUBIN. Tut tut! My dear Burge: what are you dreaming of? Mr Barnabas: I am a very patient man. But will you tell me what earthly use or interest there is in a conclusion that cannot be realized? I grant you that if we could live three hundred years we should all be, perhaps wiser, certainly older. You will grant me in return, I hope, that if the sky fell we should all catch larks.

FRANKLYN. Your turn now, Conrad. Go ahead.

CONRAD. I dont think it's any good. I dont think they want to live longer than usual.

LUBIN. Although I am a mere child of 69, I am old enough to have lost the habit of crying for the moon.

BURGE. Have you discovered the elixir of life or have you not? If not, I agree with Lubin that you are wasting our time.

CONRAD. Is your time of any value?

BURGE [*unable to believe his ears*] My time of any value! What do you mean?

LUBIN [*smiling comfortably*] From your high scientific point of view, I daresay, none whatever, Professor. In any case I think a little perfectly idle discussion would do Burge good. After all, we might as well hear about the elixir of life as read novels, or whatever Burge does when he is not playing golf on Walton Heath. What is your elixir, Dr Barnabas? Lemons? Sour milk? Or what is the latest?

BURGE. We were just beginning to talk seriously; and now you snatch at the chance of talking rot. [*He rises*]. Good evening. [*He turns to the door*].

CONRAD [*rudely*] Die as soon as you like. Good evening.

BURGE [*hesitating*] Look here. I took sour milk twice a day until Metchnikoff died. He thought it would keep him alive for ever; and he died of it.

CONRAD. You might as well have taken sour beer.

BURGE. You believe in lemons?

CONRAD. I wouldnt eat a lemon for ten pounds.

BURGE [*sitting down again*] What do you recommend?

CONRAD [*rising with a gesture of despair*] Whats the use of going on, Frank? Because I am a doctor, and because they think I have a bottle to give them that will make them live for ever, they are listening to me for the first time with their mouths open and their eyes shut. Thats their notion of science.

SAVVY. Steady, Nunk! Hold the fort.

CONRAD [*growls and sits down*]!!!

LUBIN. You volunteered the consultation, Doctor. I may tell you that, far from sharing the credulity as to science which is now the fashion, I am prepared to demonstrate that during the last fifty years, though the Church has often been wrong, and even the Liberal Party has not been infallible, the men of science have always been wrong.

CONRAD. Yes: the fellows you call men of science. The people who make money by it, and their medical hangers-on. But has anybody been right?

LUBIN. The poets and story tellers, especially the classical poets and story tellers, have been, in the main, right. I will ask you not to repeat this as my opinion outside; for the vote of the medical profession and its worshippers is not to be trifled with.

FRANKLYN. You are quite right: the poem is our real clue to biological science. The most scientific document we possess at present is, as your grandmother would have told you quite truly, the story of the Garden of Eden.

BURGE [*pricking up his ears*] Whats that? If you can establish that, Barnabas, I am prepared to hear you out with my very best attention. I am listening. Go on.

FRANKLYN. Well, you remember, dont you, that in the Garden of Eden Adam and Eve were not created mortal, and that natural death, as we call it, was not a part of life, but a later and quite separate invention?

BURGE. Now you mention it, thats true. Death came afterwards.

LUBIN. What about accidental death? that was always possible.

FRANKLYN. Precisely. Adam and Eve were hung up between two frightful possibilities. One was the extinction of mankind by their accidental death. The other was the prospect of living for ever. They could bear neither. They decided that they would just take a short turn of a thousand years, and meanwhile hand on their work to a new pair. Consequently, they had to invent natural birth and natural death, which are, after all, only modes of perpetuating life without putting on any single creature the terrible burden of immortality.

LUBIN. I see. The old must make room for the new.

BURGE. Death is nothing but making room. Thats all there is in it or ever has been in it.

FRANKLYN. Yes; but the old must not desert their posts until the new are ripe for them. They desert them now two hundred years too soon.

SAVVY. I believe the old people are the new people reincarnated, Nunk. I suspect I am Eve. I am very fond of apples; and they always disagree with me.

CONRAD. You are Eve, in a sense. The Eternal Life persists; only It wears out Its bodies and minds and gets new ones, like new clothes. You are only a new hat and frock on Eve.

FRANKLYN. Yes. Bodies and minds ever better and better fitted to carry out Its eternal pursuit.

LUBIN [*with quiet scepticism*] What pursuit, may one ask,

Mr Barnabas?

FRANKLYN. The pursuit of omnipotence and omniscience. Greater power and greater knowledge: these are what we are all pursuing even at the risk of our lives and the sacrifice of our pleasures. Evolution is that pursuit and nothing else. It is the path to godhead. A man differs from a microbe only in being further on the path.

LUBIN. And how soon do you expect this modest end to be reached?

FRANKLYN. Never, thank God! As there is no limit to power and knowledge there can be no end. "The power and the glory, world without end": have those words meant nothing to you?

BURGE [*pulling out an old envelope*] I should like to make a note of that. [*He does so*].

CONRAD. There will always be something to live for.

BURGE [*pocketing his envelope and becoming more and more businesslike*] Right: I have got that. Now what about sin? What about the Fall? How do you work them in?

CONRAD. I dont work in the Fall. The Fall is outside Science. But I daresay Frank can work it in for you.

BURGE [*to Franklyn*] I wish you would, you know. It's important. Very important.

FRANKLYN. Well, consider it this way. It is clear that when Adam and Eve were immortal it was necessary that they should make the earth an extremely comfortable place to live in.

BURGE. True. If you take a house on a ninety-nine years lease, you spend a good deal of money on it. If you take it for three months you generally have a bill for dilapidations to pay at the end of them.

FRANKLYN. Just so. Consequently, when Adam had the Garden of Eden on a lease for ever, he took care to make it what the house agents call a highly desirable country residence. But the moment he invented death, and became a tenant for life only, the place was no longer worth the trouble. It was then that he let the thistles grow. Life was so short that it was no longer worth his while to do anything thoroughly well.

BURGE. Do you think that is enough to constitute what an average elector would consider a Fall? Is it tragic enough?

FRANKLYN. That is only the first step of the Fall. Adam did not fall down that step only: he fell down a whole flight. For instance, before he invented birth he dared not have lost his temper; for if he had killed Eve he would have been lonely and barren to all eternity. But when he invented birth, and anyone who was killed could be replaced, he could afford to let himself go. He undoubtedly invented wife-beating; and that was another step down. One of his sons invented meat-eating. The other was horrified at the innovation. With the ferocity which is still characteristic of bulls and other vegetarians, he slew his beefsteak-eating brother, and thus invented murder. That was a very steep step. It was so exciting that all the others began to kill one another for sport, and thus invented war, the steepest step of all. They even took to killing animals as a means of killing time, and then, of course, ate them to save the long and difficult labor of agriculture. I ask you to contemplate our fathers as they came crashing down all the steps of this Jacob's ladder that reached from paradise to a hell on earth in which they had multiplied the chances of death from violence, accident, and disease until they could hardly count on three score and ten years of life, much less the thousand that Adam had been ready to face! With that picture before you, will you now ask me where was the Fall? You might as well stand at the foot of Snowden and ask me where is the mountain. The very children see it so plainly that they compress its history into a two line epic:

Old Daddy Long Legs wouldnt say his prayers:
Take him by the hind legs and throw him downstairs.

LUBIN [*still immovably sceptical*] And what does Science say to this fairy tale, Doctor Barnabas? Surely Science knows nothing of Genesis, or of Adam and Eve.

CONRAD. Then it isnt Science: thats all. Science has to

account for everything; and everything includes the Bible.

FRANKLYN. The Book of Genesis is a part of nature like any other part of nature. The fact that the tale of the Garden of Eden has survived and held the imagination of men spellbound for centuries, whilst hundreds of much more plausible and amusing stories have gone out of fashion and perished like last year's popular song, is a scientific fact; and Science is bound to explain it. You tell me that Science knows nothing of it. Then Science is more ignorant than the children at any village school.

CONRAD. Of course if you think it more scientific to say that what we are discussing is not Adam and Eve and Eden, but the phylogeny of the blastoderm—

SAVVY. You neednt swear, Nunk.

CONRAD. Shut up, you: I am not swearing. [*ToLubin*] If you want the professional humbug of rewriting the Bible in words of four syllables, and pretending it's something new, I can humbug you to your heart's content. I can call Genesis Phylogenesis. Let the Creator say, if you like, "I will establish an antipathetic symbiosis between thee and the female, and between thy blastoderm and her blastoderm." Nobody will understand you; and Savvy will think you are swearing. The meaning is the same.

HASLAM. Priceless. But it's quite simple. The one version is poetry: the other is science.

FRANKLYN. The one is classroom jargon: the other is inspired human language.

LUBIN [*calmly reminiscent*] One of the few modern authors into whom I have occasionally glanced is Rousseau, who was a sort of Deist like Burge—

BURGE [*interrupting him forcibly*] Lubin: has this stupendously important communication which Professor Barnabas has just made to us: a communication for which I shall be indebted to him all my life long: has this, I say, no deeper effect on you than to set you pulling my leg by trying to make out that I am an infidel?

LUBIN. It's very interesting and amusing, Burge; and I

think I see a case in it. I think I could undertake to argue it in an ecclesiastical court. But important is hardly a word I should attach to it.

BURGE. Good God! Here is this professor: a man utterly removed from the turmoil of our political life: devoted to pure learning in its most abstract phases; and I solemnly declare he is the greatest politician, the most inspired party leader, in the kingdom. I take off my hat to him. I, Joyce Burge, give him best. And you sit there purring like an Angora cat, and can see nothing in it!

CONRAD [*opening his eyes widely*] Hallo! What have I done to deserve this tribute?

BURGE. Done! You have put the Liberal Party into power for the next thirty years, Doctor: thats what youve done.

CONRAD. God forbid!

BURGE. It's all up with the Church now. Thanks to you, we go to the country with one cry and one only: Back to the Bible! Think of the effect on the Nonconformist vote. You gather that in with one hand; and you gather in the modern scientific sceptical professional vote with the other. The village atheist and the first cornet in the local Salvation Army band meet on the village green and shake hands. You take your school children, your Bible class under the Cowper-Temple clause, into the museum. You shew the kids the Piltdown skull; and you say, "Thats Adam. Thats Eve's husband." You take the spectacled science student from the laboratory in Owens College; and when he asks you for a truly scientific history of Evolution, you put into his hand The Pilgrim's Progress. You— [*Savvy and Haslam explode into shrieks of merriment*]. What are you two laughing at?

SAVVY. Oh, go on, Mr Burge. Dont stop.

HASLAM. Priceless!

FRANKLYN. Would thirty years of office for the Liberal Party seem so important to you, Mr Burge, if you had another two and a half centuries to live?

BURGE [*decisively*] No. You will have to drop that part of

it. The constituencies wont swallow it.

LUBIN [*seriously*] I am not so sure of that, Burge. I am not sure that it may not prove the only point they *will* swallow.

BURGE. It will be no use to us even if they do. It's not a party point. It's as good for the other side as for us.

LUBIN. Not necessarily. If we get in first with it, it will be associated in the public mind with our party. Suppose I put it forward as a plank in our program that we advocate the extension of human life to three hundred years! Dunreen, as leader of the opposite party, will be bound to oppose me: to denounce me as a visionary and so forth. By doing so he will place himself in the position of wanting to rob the people of two hundred and thirty years of their natural life. The Unionists will become the party of Premature Death; and we shall become the Longevity party.

BURGE [*shaken*] You really think the electorate would swallow it?

LUBIN. My dear Burge: is there anything the electorate will not swallow if it is judiciously put to them? But we must make sure of our ground. We must have the support of the men of science. Is there serious agreement among them, Doctor, as to the possibility of such an evolution as you have described?

CONRAD. Yes. Ever since the reaction against Darwin set in at the beginning of the present century, all scientific opinion worth counting has been converging rapidly upon Creative Evolution.

FRANKLYN. Poetry has been converging on it: philosophy has been converging on it: religion has been converging on it. It is going to be the religion of the twentieth century: a religion that has its intellectual roots in philosophy and science just as medieval Christianity had its intellectual roots in Aristotle.

LUBIN. But surely any change would be so extremely gradual that—

CONRAD. Dont deceive yourself. It's only the politicians who improve the world so gradually that nobody can see the improvement. The notion that Nature does not proceed by jumps is only one of the budget of plausible lies that we call classical education. Nature always proceeds by jumps. She may spend twenty thousand years making up her mind to jump; but when she makes it up at last, the jump is big enough to take us into a new age.

LUBIN [*impressed*] Fancy my being leader of the party for the next three hundred years!

BURGE. What!!!

LUBIN. Perhaps hard on some of the younger men. I think in fairness I shall have to step aside to make room after another century or so: that is, if Mimi can be persuaded to give up Downing Street.

BURGE. This is too much. Your colossal conceit blinds you to the most obvious necessity of the political situation.

LUBIN. You mean my retirement. I really cannot see that it is a necessity. I could not see it when I was almost an old man—or at least an elderly one. Now that it appears that I am a young man, the case for it breaks down completely. [*To Conrad*] May I ask are there any alternative theories? Is there a scientific Opposition?

CONRAD. Well, some authorities hold that the human race is a failure, and that a new form of life, better adapted to high civilization, will supersede us as we have superseded the ape and the elephant.

BURGE. The superman: eh?

CONRAD. No. Some being quite different from us.

LUBIN. Is that altogether desirable?

FRANKLYN. I fear so. However that may be, we may be quite sure of one thing. We shall not be let alone. The force behind evolution, call it what you will, is determined to solve the problem of civilization; and if it cannot do it through us, it will produce some more capable agents. Man is not God's last word: God can still create. If you cannot do His work He will produce some being who can.

BURGE [*with zealous reverence*] What do we know about Him, Barnabas? What does anyone know about Him?

CONRAD. We know this about Him with absolute certainty. The power my brother calls God proceeds by the method of Trial and Error; and if we turn out to be one of the errors, we shall go the way of the mastodon and the megatherium and all the other scrapped experiments.

LUBIN [*rising and beginning to walk up and down the room with his considering cap on*] I admit that I am impressed, gentlemen. I will go so far as to say that your theory is likely to prove more interesting than ever Welsh Disestablishment was. But as a practical politician—hm! Eh, Burge?

CONRAD. We are not practical politicians. We are out to get something done. Practical politicians are people who have mastered the art of using parliament to prevent anything being done.

FRANKLYN. When we get matured statesmen and citizens—

LUBIN [*stopping short*] Citizens! Oh! Are the citizens to live three hundred years as well as the statesmen?

CONRAD. Of course.

LUBIN. I confess that had not occurred to me [*he sits down abruptly, evidently very unfavourably affected by this new light*].

Savvy and Haslam look at one another with unspeakable feelings.

BURGE. Do you think it would be wise to go quite so far at first? Surely it would be more prudent to begin with the best men.

FRANKLYN. You need not be anxious about that. It will begin with the best men.

LUBIN. I am glad to hear you say so. You see, we must put this into a practical parliamentary shape.

BURGE. We shall have to draft a Bill: that is the long and the short of it. Until you have your Bill drafted you dont know what you are really doing: that is my experience.

LUBIN. Quite so. My idea is that whilst we should interest the electorate in this as a sort of religious aspiration and personal hope, using it at the same time to remove their prejudices against those of us who are getting on in years, it would be in the last degree upsetting and even dangerous to enable everyone to live longer than usual. Take the mere question of the manufacture of the specific, whatever it may be! There are forty millions of people in the country. Let me assume for the sake of illustration that each person would have to consume, say, five ounces a day of the elixir. That would be—let me see—five times three hundred and sixty-five is—um—twenty-five—thirty-two—eighteen—eighteen hundred and twenty-five ounces a year: just two ounces over the hundredweight.

BURGE. Two million tons a year, in round numbers, of stuff that everyone would clamor for: that men would trample down women and children in the streets to get at. You couldnt produce it. There would be blue murder. It's out of the question. We must keep the actual secret to ourselves.

CONRAD [*staring at them*] The actual secret! What on earth is the man talking about?

BURGE. The stuff. The powder. The bottle. The tabloid. Whatever it is. You said it wasnt lemons.

CONRAD. My good sir: I have no powder, no bottle, no tabloid. I am not a quack: I am a biologist. This is a thing thats going to happen.

LUBIN [*completely let down*] Going to happen! Oh! Is that all? [*He looks at his watch*].

BURGE. Going to happen! What do you mean? Do you mean that you cant make it happen?

CONRAD. No more than I could have made you happen.

FRANKLYN. We can put it into men's heads that there is nothing to prevent its happening but their own will to die before their work is done, and their own ignorance of the splendid work there is for them to do.

CONRAD. Spread that knowledge and that conviction; and as surely as the sun will rise tomorrow, the thing will happen.

FRANKLYN. We dont know where or when or to whom it

will happen. It may happen first to someone in this room.

HASLAM. It wont happen to me: thats jolly sure.

CONRAD. It might happen to anyone. It might happen to the parlormaid. How do we know?

SAVVY. The parlormaid! Oh, thats nonsense, Nunk.

LUBIN [*once more quite comfortable*] I think Miss Savvy has delivered the final verdict.

BURGE. Do you mean to say that you have nothing more practical to offer than the mere wish to live longer? Why, if people could live by merely wishing to, we should all be living for ever already! Everybody would like to live for ever. Why dont they?

CONRAD. Pshaw! Everybody would like to have a million of money. Why havnt they? Because the men who would like to be millionaires wont save sixpence even with the chance of starvation staring them in the face. The men who want to live for ever wont cut off a glass of beer or a pipe of tobacco, though they believe the teetotallers and non-smokers live longer. That sort of liking is not willing. See what they do when they know they must.

FRANKLYN. Do not mistake mere idle fancies for the tremendous miracle-working force of Will nerved to creation by a conviction of Necessity. I tell you men capable of such willing, and realizing its necessity, will do it reluctantly, under inner compulsion, as all great efforts are made. They will hide what they are doing from themselves: they will take care not to know what they are doing. They will live three hundred years, not because they would like to, but because the soul deep down in them will know that they must, if the world is to be saved.

LUBIN [*turning to Franklyn and patting him almost paternally*] Well, my dear Barnabas, for the last thirty years the post has brought me at least once a week a plan from some crank or other for the establishment of the millennium. I think you are the maddest of all the cranks; but you are much the most interesting. I am conscious of a very curious mixture of relief and disappointment in finding that your plan is all moonshine, and that you have nothing practical to offer us. But what a pity! It is such a fascinating idea! I think you are too hard on us practical men; but there are men in every Government, even on the Front Bench, who deserve all you say. And now, before dropping the subject, may I put just one question to you? An idle question, since nothing can come of it; but still—

FRANKLYN. Ask your question.

LUBIN. Why do you fix three hundred years as the exact figure?

FRANKLYN. Because we must fix some figure. Less would not be enough; and more would be more than we dare as yet face.

LUBIN. Pooh! I am quite prepared to face three thousand, not to say three million.

CONRAD. Yes, because you dont believe you will be called on to make good your word.

FRANKLYN [*gently*] Also, perhaps, because you have never been troubled much by visions of the future.

BURGE [*with intense conviction*] The future does not exist for Henry Hopkins Lubin.

LUBIN. If by the future you mean the millennial delusions which you use as a bunch of carrots to lure the uneducated British donkey to the polling booth to vote for you, it certainly does not.

BURGE. I can see the future not only because, if I may say so in all humility, I have been gifted with a certain power of spiritual vision, but because I have practised as a solicitor. A solicitor has to advise families. He has to think of the future and know the past. His office is the real modern confessional. Among other things he has to make people's wills for them. He has to shew them how to provide for their daughters after their deaths. Has it occurred to you, Lubin, that if you live three hundred years, your daughters will have to wait a devilish long time for their money?

FRANKLYN. The money may not wait for them. Few investments flourish for three hundred years.

SAVVY. And what about before your death? Suppose they didnt get married! Imagine a girl living at home with her mother and on her father for three hundred years! Theyd murder her if she didnt murder them first.

LUBIN. By the way, Barnabas, is your daughter to keep her good looks all the time?

FRANKLYN. Will it matter? Can you conceive the most hardened flirt going on flirting for three centuries? At the end of half the time we shall hardly notice whether it is a woman or a man we are speaking to.

LUBIN [*not quite relishing this ascetic prospect*] Hm! [*He rises*]. Ah, well: you must come and tell my wife and my young people all about it; and you will bring your daughter with you, of course. [*He shakes hands with Savvy*]. Good-bye. [*He shakes hands with Franklyn*]. Good-bye, Doctor. [*He shakes hands with Conrad*]. Come on, Burge: you must really tell me what line you are going to take about the Church at the election?

BURGE. Havnt you heard? Havnt you taken in the revelation that has been vouchsafed to us? The line I am going to take is Back to Methuselah.

LUBIN [*decisively*] Dont be ridiculous, Burge. You dont suppose, do you, that our friends here are in earnest, or that our very pleasant conversation has had anything to do with practical politics! They have just been pulling our legs very wittily. Come along. [*He goes out, Franklyn politely going with him, but shaking his head in mute protest*].

BURGE [*shaking Conrad's hand*] It's beyond the old man, Doctor. No spiritual side to him: only a sort of classical side that goes down with his own set. Besides, he's done, gone, past, burnt out, burst up; thinks he is our leader and is only our rag and bottle department. But you may depend on me. I will work this stunt of yours in. I see its value. [*He begins moving towards the door with Conrad*]. Of course I cant put it exactly in your way; but you are quite right about our needing something fresh; and I believe an election can be fought on the death rate and on Adam and Eve as scientific facts. It will take the Opposition right out of its depth. And if we win there will be an O.M. for somebody when the first honors list comes round [*by this time he has talked himself out of the room and out of earshot, Conrad accompanying him*].

Savvy and Haslam, left alone, seize each other in an ecstasy of amusement, and jazz to the settee, where they sit down again side by side.

HASLAM [*caressing her*] Darling! What a priceless humbug old Lubin is!

SAVVY. Oh, sweet old thing! I love him. Burge is a flaming fraud if you like.

HASLAM. Did you notice one thing? It struck me as rather curious.

SAVVY. What?

HASLAM. Lubin and your father have both survived the war. But their sons were killed in it.

SAVVY [*sobered*] Yes. Jim's death killed mother.

HASLAM. And they never said a word about it!

SAVVY. Well, why should they? The subject didnt come up. *I* forgot about it too; and I was very fond of Jim.

HASLAM. *I* didnt forget it, because I'm of military age; and if I hadnt been a parson I'd have had to go out and be killed too. To me the awful thing about their political incompetence was that they had to kill their own sons. It was the war casualty lists and the starvation afterwards that finished me up with politics and the Church and everything else except you.

SAVVY. Oh, I was just as bad as any of them. I sold flags in the streets in my best clothes; and—hsh! [*she jumps up and pretends to be looking for a book on the shelves behind the settee*].

Franklyn and Conrad return, looking weary and glum.

CONRAD. Well, thats how the gospel of the brothers Barnabas is going to be received! [*He drops into Burge's chair*].

FRANKLYN [*going back to his seat at the table*] It's no use. Were you convinced, Mr Haslam?

HASLAM. About our being able to live three hundred

years? Frankly no.

CONRAD [*to Savvy*] Nor you, I suppose?

SAVVY. Oh, I dont know. I thought I was for a moment. I can believe, in a sort of way, that people might live for three hundred years. But when you came down to tin tacks, and said that the parlormaid might, then I saw how absurd it was.

FRANKLYN. Just so. We had better hold our tongues about it, Con. We should only be laughed at, and lose the little credit we earned on false pretences in the days of our ignorance.

CONRAD. I daresay. But Creative Evolution doesnt stop while people are laughing. Laughing may even lubricate its job.

SAVVY. What does that mean?

CONRAD. It means that the first man to live three hundred years maynt have the slightest notion that he is going to do it, and may be the loudest laugher of the lot.

SAVVY. Or the first woman?

CONRAD [*assenting*] Or the first woman.

HASLAM. Well, it wont be one of us, anyhow.

FRANKLYN. How do you know?

This is unanswerable. None of them have anything more to say.

PART III THE THING HAPPENS

THE THING HAPPENS

A SUMMER afternoon in the year 2170 A.D. *The official parlor of the President of the British Islands. A board table, long enough for three chairs at each side besides the presidential chair at the head and an ordinary chair at the foot, occupies the breadth of the room. On the table, opposite every chair, a small switchboard with a dial. There is no fireplace. The end wall is a silvery screen nearly as large as a pair of folding doors. The door is on your left as you face the screen; and there is a row of thick pegs, padded and covered with velvet, beside it.*

A stoutish middle-aged man, good-looking and breezily genial, dressed in a silk smock, stockings, handsomely ornamented sandals, and a gold fillet round his brows, comes in. He is like Joyce Burge, yet also like Lubin, as if Nature had made a composite photograph of the two men. He takes off the fillet and hangs it on a peg; then sits down in the presidential chair at the head of the table, which is at the end farthest from the door. He puts a peg into his switchboard; turns the pointer on the dial; puts another peg in; and presses a button. Immediately the silvery screen vanishes; and in its place appears, in reverse from right to left, another office similarly furnished, with a thin, unamiable man similarly dressed, but in duller colors, turning over some documents at the table. His gold fillet is hanging up on a similar peg beside the door. He is rather like Conrad Barnabas, but younger, and much more commonplace.

BURGE-LUBIN. Hallo, Barnabas!

BARNABAS [*without looking round*] What number?

BURGE-LUBIN. Five double x three two gamma. Burge-Lubin.

Barnabas puts a plug in number five; turns his pointer to double x; puts another plug in 32; presses a button and looks round at Burge-Lubin, who is now visible to him as well as audible.

BARNABAS [*curtly*] Oh! That you, President?

BURGE-LUBIN. Yes. They told me you wanted me to ring you up. Anything wrong?

BARNABAS [*harsh and querulous*] I wish to make a protest.

BURGE-LUBIN [*good-humored and mocking*] What! Another protest! Whats wrong now?

BARNABAS. If you only knew all the protests I havnt made, you would be surprised at my patience. It is you who are always treating me with the grossest want of consideration.

BURGH-LUBIN. What have I done now?

BARNABAS. You have put me down to go to the Record Office to-day to receive that American fellow, and do the honors of a ridiculous cinema show. That is not the business of the Accountant General: it is the business of the President. It is an outrageous waste of my time, and an unjustifiable shirking of your duty at my expense. I refuse to go. You must go.

BURGE-LUBIN. My dear boy, nothing would give me greater pleasure than to take the job off your hands—

BARNABAS. Then do it. Thats all I want [*he is about to switch off*].

BURGE-LUBIN. Dont switch off. Listen. This American has invented a method of breathing under water.

BARNABAS. What do I care? I dont want to breathe under water.

BURGE-LUBIN. You may, my dear Barnabas, at any time. You know you never look where you are going when you are immersed in your calculations. Some day you will walk into the Serpentine. This man's invention may save your life.

BARNABAS [*angrily*] Will you tell me what that has to do with your putting your ceremonial duties on to my shoulders? I will not be trifled [*he vanishes and is replaced by the blank screen*]—

BURGE-LUBIN [*indignantly holding down his button*] Dont cut us off, please: we have not finished. I am the President, speaking to the Accountant General. What are you dreaming of?

A WOMAN'S VOICE. Sorry. [*The screen shews Barnabas as*

before].

BURGE-LUBIN. Since you take it that way, I will go in your place. It's a pity, because, you see, this American thinks you are the greatest living authority on the duration of human life; and—

BARNABAS [*interrupting*] The American thinks! What do you mean? I am the the greatest living authority on the duration of human life. Who dares dispute it?

BURGE-LUBIN. Nobody, dear lad, nobody. Dont fly out at me. It is evident that you have not read the American's book.

BARNABAS. Dont tell me that you have, or that you have read any book except a novel for the last twenty years; for I wont believe you.

BURGE-LUBIN. Quite right, dear old fellow: I havnt read it. But I have read what The Times Literary Supplement says about it.

BARNABAS. I dont care two straws what it says about it. Does it say anything about me?

BURGE-LUBIN. Yes.

BARNABAS. Oh, does it? What?

BURGE-LUBIN. It points out that an extraordinary number of first-rate persons like you and me have died by drowning during the last two centuries, and that when this invention of breathing under water takes effect, your estimate of the average duration of human life will be upset.

BARNABAS [*alarmed*] Upset my estimate! Gracious Heavens! Does the fool realize what that means? Do you realize what that means?

BURGE-LUBIN. I suppose it means that we shall have to amend the Act.

BARNABAS. Amend my Act! Monstrous!

BURGE-LUBIN. But we must. We cant ask people to go on working until they are forty-three unless our figures are unchallengeable. You know what a row there was over those last three years, and how nearly the too-old-at-forty people won.

BARNABAS. They would have made the British Islands bankrupt if theyd won. But you dont care for that: you care for nothing but being popular.

BURGE-LUBIN. Oh, well: I shouldnt worry if I were you; for most people complain that there is not enough work for them, and would be only too glad to stick on instead of retiring at forty-three, if only they were asked as a favor instead of having to.

BARNABAS. Thank you: I need no consolation. [*He rises determinedly and puts on his fillet*].

BURGE-LUBIN. Are you off? Where are you going to?

BARNABAS. To that cinema tomfoolery, of course. I shall put this American impostor in his place. [*He goes out*].

BURGE-LUBIN [*calling after him*] God bless you, dear old chap! [*With a chuckle, he switches off; and the screen becomes blank. He presses a button and holds it down while he calls*] Hallo!

A WOMAN'S VOICE. Hallo!

BURGE-LUBIN [*formally*] The President respectfully solicits the privilege of an interview with the Chief Secretary, and holds himself entirely at his honor's august disposal.

A CHINESE VOICE. He is coming.

BURGE-LUBIN. Oh! That you, Confucius? So good of you. Come along [*he releases the button*].

A man in a yellow gown, presenting the general appearance of a Chinese sage, enters.

BURGE-LUBIN [*jocularly*] Well, illustrious Sage-&-Onions, how are your poor sore feet?

CONFUCIUS [*gravely*] I thank you for your kind inquiries. I am well.

BURGE-LUBIN. Thats right. Sit down and make yourself comfortable. Any business for me to-day?

CONFUCIUS [*sitting down on the first chair round the corner of the table to the President's right*] None.

BURGE-LUBIN. Have you heard the result of the bye-election?

CONFUCIUS. A walk-over. Only one candidate.

BURGE-LUBIN. Any good?

CONFUCIUS. He was released from the County Lunatic Asylum a fortnight ago. Not mad enough for the lethal chamber: not sane enough for any place but the division lobby. A very popular speaker.

BURGE-LUBIN. I wish the people would take a serious interest in politics.

CONFUCIUS. I do not agree. The Englishman is not fitted by nature to understand politics. Ever since the public services have been manned by Chinese, the country has been well and honestly governed. What more is needed?

BURGE-LUBIN. What I cant make out is that China is one of the worst governed countries on earth.

CONFUCIUS. No. It was badly governed twenty years ago; but since we forbade any Chinaman to take part in our public services, and imported natives of Scotland for that purpose, we have done well. Your information here is always twenty years out of date.

BURGE-LUBIN. People dont seem to be able to govern themselves. I cant understand it. Why should it be so?

CONFUCIUS. Justice is impartiality. Only strangers are impartial.

BURGE-LUBIN. It ends in the public services being so good that the Government has nothing to do but think.

CONFUCIUS. Were it otherwise, the Government would have too much to do to think.

BURGE-LUBIN. Is that any excuse for the English people electing a parliament of lunatics?

CONFUCIUS. The English people always did elect parliaments of lunatics. What does it matter if your permanent officials are honest and competent?

BURGE-LUBIN. You do not know the history of this country. What would my ancestors have said to the menagerie of degenerates that is still called the House of Commons? Confucius: you will not believe me; and I do not blame you for it; but England once saved the liberties of the world by inventing parliamentary government, which was her peculiar and supreme glory.

CONFUCIUS. I know the history of your country perfectly well. It proves the exact contrary.

BURGE-LUBIN. How do you make that out?

CONFUCIUS. The only power your parliament ever had was the power of withholding supplies from the king.

BURGE-LUBIN. Precisely. That great Englishman Simon de Montfort—

CONFUCIUS. He was not an Englishman: he was a Frenchman. He imported parliaments from France.

BURGE-LUBIN [*surprised*] You dont say so!

CONFUCIUS. The king and his loyal subjects killed Simon for forcing his French parliament on them. The first thing British parliaments always did was to grant supplies to the king for life with enthusiastic expressions of loyalty, lest they should have any real power, and be expected to do something.

BURGE-LUBIN. Look here, Confucius: you know more history than I do, of course; but democracy—

CONFUCIUS. An institution peculiar to China. And it was never really a success there.

BURGE-LUBIN. But the Habeas Corpus Act!

CONFUCIUS. The English always suspended it when it threatened to be of the slightest use.

BURGE-LUBIN. Well, trial by jury: you cant deny that we established that?

CONFUCIUS. All cases that were dangerous to the governing classes were tried in the Star Chamber or by Court Martial, except when the prisoner was not tried at all, but executed after calling him names enough to make him unpopular.

BURGE-LUBIN. Oh, bother! You may be right in these little details; but in the large we have managed to hold our own as a great race. Well, people who could do nothing couldnt have done that, you know.

CONFUCIUS. I did not say you could do nothing. You could fight. You could eat. You could drink. Until the twentieth century you could produce children. You could play games. You could work when you were forced to. But you could not govern yourselves.

BURGE-LUBIN. Then how did we get our reputation as the pioneers of liberty?

CONFUCIUS. By your steadfast refusal to be governed at all. A horse that kicks everyone who tries to harness and guide him may be a pioneer of liberty; but he is not a pioneer of government. In China he would be shot.

BURGE-LUBIN. Stuff! Do you imply that the administration of which I am president is no Government?

CONFUCIUS. I do. *I* am the Government.

BURGE-LUBIN. You! You!! You fat yellow lump of conceit!

CONFUCIUS. Only an Englishman could be so ignorant of the nature of government as to suppose that a capable statesman cannot be fat, yellow, and conceited. Many Englishmen are slim, red-nosed, and modest. Put them in my place, and within a year you will be back in the anarchy and chaos of the nineteenth and twentieth centuries.

BURGE-LUBIN. Oh, if you go back to the dark ages, I have nothing more to say. But we did not perish. We extricated ourselves from that chaos. We are now the best governed country in the world. How did we manage that if we are such fools as you pretend?

CONFUCIUS. You did not do it until the slaughter and ruin produced by your anarchy forced you at last to recognize two inexorable facts. First, that government is absolutely necessary to civilization, and that you could not maintain civilization by merely doing down your neighbor, as you called it, and cutting off the head of your king whenever he happened to be a logical Scot and tried to take his position seriously. Second, that government is an art of which you are congenitally incapable. Accordingly, you imported educated negresses and Chinese to govern you. Since then you have done very well.

BURGE-LUBIN. So have you, you old humbug. All the

same, I dont know how you stand the work you do. You seem to me positively to like public business. Why wont you let me take you down to the coast some week-end and teach you marine golf?

CONFUCIUS. It does not interest me. I am not a barbarian.

BURGE-LUBIN. You mean that I am?

CONFUCIUS. That is evident.

BURGE-LUBIN. How?

CONFUCIUS. People like you. They like cheerful good-natured barbarians. They have elected you President five times in succession. They will elect you five times more. *I* like you. You are better company than a dog or a horse because you can speak.

BURGE-LUBIN. Am I a barbarian because you like me?

CONFUCIUS. Surely. Nobody likes me: I am held in awe. Capable persons are never liked. I am not likeable; but I am indispensable.

BURGE-LUBIN. Oh, cheer up, old man: theres nothing so disagreeable about you as all that. I dont dislike you; and if you think I'm afraid of you, you jolly well dont know Burge-Lubin: thats all.

CONFUCIUS. You are brave: yes. It is a form of stupidity.

BURGE-LUBIN. You may not be brave: one doesnt expect it from a Chink. But you have the devil's own cheek.

CONFUCIUS. I have the assured certainty of the man who sees and knows. Your genial bluster, your cheery self-confidence, are pleasant, like the open air. But they are blind: they are vain. I seem to see a great dog wag his tail and bark joyously. But if he leaves my heel he is lost.

BURGE-LUBIN. Thank you for a handsome compliment. I have a big dog; and he is the best fellow I know. If you knew how much uglier you are than a chow, you wouldnt start those comparisons, though. [*Rising*] Well, if you have nothing for me to do, I am going to leave your heel for the rest of the day and enjoy myself. What would you recommend me to do with myself?

CONFUCIUS. Give yourself up to contemplation; and

great thoughts will come to you.

BURGE-LUBIN. Will they? If you think I am going to sit here on a fine day like this with my legs crossed waiting for great thoughts, you exaggerate my taste for them. I prefer marine golf. [*Stopping short*] Oh, by the way, I forgot something. I have a word or two to say to the Minister of Health. [*He goes back to his chair*].

CONFUCIUS. Her number is—

BURGE-LUBIN. I know it.

CONFUCIUS [*rising*] I cannot understand her attraction for you. For me a woman who is not yellow does not exist, save as an official. [*He goes out*].

Burge-Lubin operates his switchboard as before. The screen vanishes; and a dainty room with a bed, a wardrobe, and a dressing-table with a mirror and a switch on it, appears. Seated at it a handsome negress is trying on a brilliant head scarf. Her dressing-gown is thrown back from her shoulders to her chair. She is in corset, knickers, and silk stockings.

BURGE-LUBIN [*horrified*] I beg your pardon a thousand times—[*The startled negress snatches the peg out of her switchboard and vanishes*].

THE NEGRESS'S VOICE. Who is it?

BURGE-LUBIN. Me. The President. Burge-Lubin. I had no idea your bedroom switch was in. I beg your pardon.

The negress reappears. She has pulled the dressing-gown perfunctorily over her shoulders, and continues her experiments with the scarf, not at all put out, and rather amused by Burge's prudery.

THE NEGRESS. Stupid of me. I was talking to another lady this morning; and I left the peg in.

BURGE-LUBIN. But I am so sorry.

THE NEGRESS [*sunnily: still busy with the scarf*] Why? It was my fault.

BURGE-LUBIN [*embarrassed*] Well—er—er— But I suppose you were used to it in Africa.

THE NEGRESS. Your delicacy is very touching, Mr President. It would be funny if it were not so unpleasant, because, like all white delicacy, it is in the wrong place. How do you think this suits my complexion?

BURGE-LUBIN. How can any really vivid color go wrong with a black satin skin? It is our women's wretched pale faces that have to be matched and lighted. Yours is always right.

THE NEGRESS. Yes: it is a pity your white beauties have all the same ashy faces, the same colorless drab, the same age. But look at their beautiful noses and little lips! They are physically insipid: they have no beauty: you cannot love them; but how elegant!

BURGE-LUBIN. Cant you find an official pretext for coming to see me? Isnt it ridiculous that we have never met? It's so tantalizing to see you and talk to you, and to know all the time that you are two hundred miles away, and that I cant touch you?

THE NEGRESS. I cannot live on the East Coast: it is hard enough to keep my blood warm here. Besides, my friend, it would not be safe. These distant flirtations are very charming; and they teach self-control.

BURGE-LUBIN. Damn self-control! I want to hold you in my arms—to— [*the negress snatches out the peg from the switchboard and vanishes. She is still heard laughing*]. Black devil! [*He snatches out his peg furiously: her laugh is no longer heard*]. Oh, these sex episodes! Why can I not resist them? Disgraceful!

Confucius returns.

CONFUCIUS. I forgot. There is something for you to do this morning. You have to go to the Record Office to receive the American barbarian.

BURGE-LUBIN. Confucius: once for all, I object to this Chinese habit of describing white men as barbarians.

CONFUCIUS [*standing formally at the end of the table with his hands palm to palm*] I make a mental note that you do not wish the Americans to be described as barbarians.

BURGE-LUBIN. Not at all. The Americans a r e barbarians. But we are not. I suppose the particular barbarian you are speaking of is the American who has invented a means of breathing under water.

CONFUCIUS. He says he has invented such a method. For some reason which is not intelligible in China, Englishmen always believe any statement made by an American inventor, especially one who has never invented anything. Therefore you believe this person and have given him a public reception. Today the Record Office is entertaining him with a display of the cinematographic records of all the eminent Englishmen who have lost their lives by drowning since the cinema was invented. Why not go to see it if you are at a loss for something to do?

BURGE-LUBIN. What earthly interest is there in looking at a moving picture of a lot of people merely because they were drowned? If they had had any sense, they would not have been drowned, probably.

CONFUCIUS. That is not so. It has never been noticed before; but the Record Office has just made two remarkable discoveries about the public men and women who have displayed extraordinary ability during the past century. One is that they retained unusual youthfulness up to an advanced age. The other is that they all met their death by drowning.

BURGE-LUBIN. Yes: I know. Can you explain it?

CONFUCIUS. It cannot be explained. It is not reasonable. Therefore I do not believe it.

The Accountant General rushes in, looking ghastly. He staggers to the middle of the table.

BURGE-LUBIN. Whats the matter? Are you ill?

BARNABAS [*choking*] No. I— [*he collapses into the middle chair*]. I must speak to you in private.

Confucius calmly withdraws.

BURGE-LUBIN. What on earth is it? Have some oxygen.

BARNABAS. I have had some. Go to the Record Office. You will see men fainting there again and again, and being revived with oxygen, as I have been. They have seen with their own eyes as I have.

BURGE-LUBIN. Seen what?

BARNABAS. Seen the Archbishop of York.

BURGE-LUBIN. Well, why shouldnt they see the Archbishop of York? What are they fainting for? Has he been murdered?

BARNABAS. No: he has been drowned.

BURGE-LUBIN. Good God! Where? When? How? Poor fellow!

BARNABAS. Poor fellow! Poor thief! Poor swindler! Poor robber of his country's Exchequer! Poor fellow indeed! Wait til I catch him.

BURGE-LUBIN. How can you catch him when he is dead? Youre mad.

BARNABAS. Dead! Who said he was dead?

BURGE-LUBIN. You did. Drowned.

BARNABAS [*exasperated*] Will you listen to me? Was old Archbishop Haslam, the present man's last predecessor but four, drowned or not?

BURGE-LUBIN. I dont know. Look him up in the Encyclopedia Britannica.

BARNABAS. Yah! Was Archbishop Stickit, who wrote Stickit on the Psalms, drowned or not?

BURGE-LUBIN. Yes, mercifully. He deserved it.

BARNABAS. Was President Dickenson drowned? Was General Bullyboy drowned?

BURGE-LUBIN. Who is denying it?

BARNABAS. Well, weve had moving pictures of all four put on the screen today for this American; and they and the Archbishop are the same man. Now tell me I am mad.

BURGE-LUBIN. I do tell you you are mad. Stark raving mad.

BARNABAS. Am I to believe my own eyes or am I not?

BURGE-LUBIN. You can do as you please. All I can tell you is that *I* dont believe your eyes if they cant see any difference between a live archbishop and two dead ones. [*The apparatus rings, he holds the button down*]. Yes?

THE WOMAN'S VOICE. The Archbishop of York, to see the President.

BARNABAS [*hoarse with rage*] Have him in. I'll talk to the scoundrel.

BURGE-LUBIN [*releasing the button*] Not while you are in this state.

BARNABAS [*reaching furiously for his button and holding it down*] Send the Archbishop in at once.

BURGE-LUBIN. If you lose your temper, Barnabas, remember that we shall be two to one.

The Archbishop enters. He has a white band round his throat, set in a black stock. He wears a sort of kilt of black ribbons, and soft black boots that button high up on his calves. His costume does not differ otherwise from that of the President and the Accountant General; but its color scheme is black and white. He is older than the Reverend Bill Haslam was when he wooed Miss Savvy Barnabas; but he is recognizably the same man. He does not look a day over fifty, and is very well preserved even at that; but his boyishness of manner is quite gone: he now has complete authority and self-possession: in fact the President is a little afraid of him; and it seems quite natural and inevitable that he should speak first.

THE ARCHBISHOP. Good day, Mr President.

BURGE-LUBIN. Good day, Mr Archbishop. Be seated.

THE ARCHBISHOP [*sitting down between them*] Good day, Mr Accountant General.

BARNABAS [*malevolently*] Good day to you. I have a question to put to you, if you dont mind.

THE ARCHBISHOP [*looking curiously at him, jarred by his uncivil tone*] Certainly. What is it?

BARNABAS. What is your definition of a thief?

THE ARCHBISHOP. Rather an old-fashioned word, is it not?

BARNABAS. It survives officially in my department.

THE ARCHBISHOP. Our departments are full of survivals. Look at my tie! my apron! my boots! They are all mere survivals; yet it seems that without them I cannot be a proper Archbishop.

BARNABAS. Indeed! Well, in my department the word

thief survives, because in the community the thing thief survives. And a very despicable and dishonorable thing he is, too.

THE ARCHBISHOP [*coolly*] I daresay.

BARNABAS. In my department, sir, a thief is a person who lives longer than the statutory expectation of life entitles him to, and goes on drawing public money when, if he were an honest man, he would be dead.

THE ARCHBISHOP. Then let me say, sir, that your department does not understand its own business. If you have miscalculated the duration of human life, that is not the fault of the persons whose longevity you have miscalculated. And if they continue to work and produce, they pay their way, even if they live two or three centuries.

BARNABAS. I know nothing about their working and producing. That is not the business of my department. I am concerned with their expectation of life; and I say that no man has any right to go on living and drawing money when he ought to be dead.

THE ARCHBISHOP. You do not comprehend the relation between income and production.

BARNABAS. I understand my own department.

THE ARCHBISHOP. That is not enough. Your department is part of a synthesis which embraces all the departments.

BURGE-LUBIN. Synthesis! This is an intellectual difficulty. This is a job for Confucius. I heard him use that very word the other day; and I wondered what the devil he meant. [*Switching on*] Hallo! Put me through to the Chief Secretary.

CONFUCIUS'S VOICE. You are speaking to him.

BURGE-LUBIN. An intellectual difficulty, old man. Something we dont understand. Come and help us out.

THE ARCHBISHOP. May I ask how the question has arisen?

BARNABAS. Ah! You begin to smell a rat, do you? You thought yourself pretty safe. You—

BURGE-LUBIN. Steady, Barnabas. Dont be in a hurry.

Confucius enters.

THE ARCHBISHOP [*rising*] Good morning, Mr Chief Secretary.

BURGE-LUBIN [*rising in instinctive imitation of the Archbishop*] Honor us by taking a seat, O sage.

CONFUCIUS. Ceremony is needless. [*He bows to the company, and takes the chair at the foot of the table*].

The President and the Archbishop resume their seats.

BURGE-LUBIN. We wish to put a case to you, Confucius. Suppose a man, instead of conforming to the official estimate of his expectation of life, were to live for more than two centuries and a half, would the Accountant General be justified in calling him a thief?

CONFUCIUS. No. He would be justified in calling him a liar.

THE ARCHBISHOP. I think not, Mr Chief Secretary. What do you suppose my age is?

CONFUCIUS. Fifty.

BURGE-LUBIN. You dont look it. Forty-five; and young for your age.

THE ARCHBISHOP. My age is two hundred and eighty-three.

BARNABAS [*morosely triumphant*] Hmp! Mad, am I?

BURGE-LUBIN. Youre both mad. Excuse me, Archbishop; but this is getting a bit—well—

THE ARCHBISHOP [*to Confucius*] Mr Chief Secretary: will you, to oblige me, assume that I have lived nearly three centuries? As a hypothesis?

BURGE-LUBIN. What is a hypothesis?

CONFUCIUS. It does not matter. I understand. [*To the Archbishop*] Am I to assume that you have lived in your ancestors, or by metempsychosis—

BURGE-LUBIN. Met—Emp—Sy— Good Lord! What a brain, Confucius! What a brain!

THE ARCHBISHOP. Nothing of that kind. Assume in the ordinary sense that I was born in the year 1887, and that I have worked continuously in one profession or another since the year 1910. Am I a thief?

CONFUCIUS. I do not know. Was that one of your professions?

THE ARCHBISHOP. No. I have been nothing worse than an Archbishop, a President, and a General.

BARNABAS. Has he or has he not robbed the Exchequer by drawing five or six incomes when he was only entitled to one? Answer me that.

CONFUCIUS. Certainly not. The hypothesis is that he has worked continuously since 1910. We are now in the year 2170. What is the official lifetime?

BARNABAS. Seventy-eight. Of course it's an average; and we dont mind a man here and there going on to ninety, or even, as a curiosity, becoming a centenarian. But I say that a man who goes beyond that is a swindler.

CONFUCIUS. Seventy-eight into two hundred and eighty-three goes more than three and a half times. Your department owes the Archbishop two and a half educations and three and a half retiring pensions.

BARNABAS. Stuff! How can that be?

CONFUCIUS. At what age do your people begin to work for the community?

BURGE-LUBIN. Three. They do certain things every day when they are three. Just to break them in, you know. But they become self-supporting, or nearly so, at thirteen.

CONFUCIUS. And at what age do they retire?

BARNABAS. Forty-three.

CONFUCIUS. That is, they do thirty years' work; and they receive maintenance and education, without working, for thirteen years of childhood and thirty-five years of superannuation, forty-eight years in all, for each thirty years' work. The Archbishop has given you 260 years' work, and has received only one education and no superannuation. You therefore owe him over 300 years of leisure and nearly eight educations. You are thus heavily in his debt. In other words, he has effected an enormous national economy by living so long; and you, by living only seventy-eight years, are profiting at his expense. He is the benefactor: you are the thief. [*Half rising*] May I now withdraw and return to my serious business, as my own span is comparatively short?

BURGE-LUBIN. Dont be in a hurry, old chap. [*Confucius sits down again*]. This hypothecary, or whatever you call it, is put up seriously. I dont believe it; but if the Archbishop and the Accountant General are going to insist that it's true, we shall have either to lock them up or to see the thing through.

BARNABAS. It's no use trying these Chinese subtleties on me. I'm a plain man; and though I dont understand metaphysics, and dont believe in them, I understand figures; and if the Archbishop is only entitled to seventy-eight years, and he takes 283, I say he takes more than he is entitled to. Get over that if you can.

THE ARCHBISHOP. I have not taken 283 years: I have taken 23 and given 260.

CONFUCIUS. Do your accounts shew a deficiency or a surplus?

BARNABAS. A surplus. Thats what I cant make out. Thats the artfulness of these people.

BURGE-LUBIN. That settles it. Whats the use of arguing? The Chink says you are wrong; and theres an end of it.

BARNABAS. I say nothing against the Chink's arguments. But what about my facts?

CONFUCIUS. If your facts include a case of a man living 283 years, I advise you to take a few weeks at the seaside.

BARNABAS. Let there be an end of this hinting that I am out of my mind. Come and look at the cinema record. I tell you this man is Archbishop Haslam, Archbishop Stickit, President Dickenson, General Bullyboy and himself into the bargain: all five of them.

THE ARCHBISHOP. I do not deny it. I never have denied it. Nobody has ever asked me.

BURGE-LUBIN. But damn it, man—I beg your pardon, Archbishop; but really, really—

THE ARCHBISHOP. Dont mention it. What were you

going to say?

BURGE-LUBIN. Well, you were drowned four times over. You are not a cat, you know.

THE ARCHBISHOP. That is very easy to understand. Consider my situation when I first made the amazing discovery that I was destined to live three hundred years! I—

CONFUCIUS [*interrupting him*] Pardon me. Such a discovery was impossible. You have not made it yet. You may live a million years if you have already lived two hundred. There is no question of three hundred years. You have made a slip at the very beginning of your fairy tale, Mr Archbishop.

BURGE-LUBIN. Good, Confucius! [*To the Archbishop*] He has you there. I dont see how you can get over that.

THE ARCHBISHOP. Yes: it is quite a good point. But if the Accountant General will go to the British Museum library, and search the catalogue, he will find under his own name a curious and now forgotten book, dated 1924, entitled The Gospel of the Brothers Barnabas. That gospel was that men must live three hundred years if civilization is to be saved. It shewed that this extension of individual human life was possible, and how it was likely to come about. I married the daughter of one of the brothers.

BARNABAS. Do you mean to say you claim to be a connection of mine?

THE ARCHBISHOP. I claim nothing. As I have by this time perhaps three or four million cousins of one degree or another, I have ceased to call on the family.

BURGE-LUBIN. Gracious heavens! Four million relatives! Is that calculation correct, Confucius?

CONFUCIUS. In China it might be forty millions if there were no checks on population.

BURGE-LUBIN. This is a staggerer. It brings home to one —but [*recovering*] it isnt true, you know. Let us keep sane.

CONFUCIUS [*to the Archbishop*] You wish us to understand that the illustrious ancestors of the Accountant General communicated to you a secret by which you could attain the age of three hundred years.

THE ARCHBISHOP. No. Nothing of the kind. They simply believed that mankind could live any length of time it knew to be absolutely necessary to save civilization from extinction. I did not share their belief: at least I was not conscious of sharing it: I thought I was only amused by it. To me my father-in-law and his brother were a pair of clever cranks who had talked one another into a fixed idea which had become a monomania with them. It was not until I got into serious difficulties with the pension authorities after turning seventy that I began to suspect the truth.

CONFUCIUS. The truth?

THE ARCHBISHOP. Yes, Mr Chief Secretary: the truth. Like all revolutionary truths, it began as a joke. As I shewed no signs of ageing after forty-five, my wife used to make fun of me by saying that I was certainly going to live three hundred years. She was sixty-eight when she died; and the last thing she said to me, as I sat by her bedside holding her hand, was "Bill: you really dont look fifty. I wonder—" She broke off, and fell asleep wondering, and never awoke. Then I began to wonder too. That is the explanation of the three hundred years, Mr Secretary.

CONFUCIUS. It is very ingenious, Mr Archbishop. And very well told.

BURGE-LUBIN. Of course you understand that *I* dont for a moment suggest the very faintest doubt of your absolute veracity, Archbishop. You know that, dont you?

THE ARCHBISHOP. Quite, Mr President. Only you dont believe me: that is all. I do not expect you to. In your place I should not believe. You had better have a look at the films. [*Pointing to the Accountant General*] He believes.

BURGE-LUBIN. But the drowning? What about the drowning? A man might get drowned once, or even twice if he was exceptionally careless. But he couldnt be drowned four times. He would run away from water like a mad dog.

THE ARCHBISHOP. Perhaps Mr Chief Secretary can guess the explanation of that.

CONFUCIUS. To keep your secret, you had to die.

BURGE-LUBIN. But dash it all, man, he isnt dead.

CONFUCIUS. It is socially impossible not to do what everybody else does. One must die at the usual time.

BARNABAS. Of course. A simple point of honor.

CONFUCIUS. Not at all. A simple necessity.

BURGE-LUBIN. Well, I'm hanged if I see it. I should jolly well live for ever if I could.

THE ARCHBISHOP. It is not so easy as you think. You, Mr Chief Secretary, have grasped the difficulties of the position. Let me remind you, Mr President, that I was over eighty before the 1969 Act for the Redistribution of Income entitled me to a handsome retiring pension. Owing to my youthful appearance I was prosecuted for attempting to obtain public money on false pretences when I claimed it. I could prove nothing; for the register of my birth had been blown to pieces by a bomb dropped on a village church years before in the first of the big modern wars. I was ordered back to work as a man of forty, and had to work for fifteen years more, the retiring age being then fifty-five.

BURGE-LUBIN. As late as fifty-five! How did people stand it?

THE ARCHBISHOP. They made difficulties about letting me go even then, I still looked so young. For some years I was in continual trouble. The industrial police rounded me up again and again, refusing to believe that I was over age. They began to call me The Wandering Jew. You see how impossible my position was. I foresaw that in twenty years more my official record would prove me to be seventy-five; my appearance would make it impossible to believe that I was more than forty-five; and my real age would be one hundred and seventeen. What was I to do? Bleach my hair? Hobble about on two sticks? Mimic the voice of a centenarian? Better have killed myself.

BARNABAS. You *ought* to have killed yourself. As an honest man you were entitled to no more than an honest man's expectation of life.

THE ARCHBISHOP. I did kill myself. It was quite easy. I left a suit of clothes by the seashore during the bathing season, with documents in the pockets to identify me. I then turned up in a strange place, pretending that I had lost my memory, and did not know my name or my age or anything about myself. Under treatment I recovered my health, but not my memory. I have had several careers since I began this routine of life and death. I have been an archbishop three times. When I persuaded the authorities to knock down all our towns and rebuild them from the foundations, or move them, I went into the artillery, and became a general. I have been President.

BURGE-LUBIN. Dickenson?

THE ARCHBISHOP. Yes.

BURGE-LUBIN. But they found Dickenson's body: its ashes are buried in St Paul's.

THE ARCHBISHOP. They almost always found the body. During the bathing season there are plenty of bodies. I have been cremated again and again. At first I used to attend my own funeral in disguise, because I had read about a man doing that in an old romance by an author named Bennett, from whom I remember borrowing five pounds in 1912. But I got tired of that. I would not cross the street now to read my latest epitaph.

The Chief Secretary and the President look very glum. Their incredulity is vanquished at last.

BURGE-LUBIN. Look here. Do you chaps realize how awful this is? Here we are sitting calmly in the presence of a man whose death is overdue by two centuries. He may crumble into dust before our eyes at any moment.

BARNABAS. Not he. He'll go on drawing his pension until the end of the world.

THE ARCHBISHOP. Not quite that. My expectation of life is only three hundred years.

BARNABAS. You will last out my time anyhow: thats enough for me.

THE ARCHBISHOP [*coolly*] How do you know?

BARNABAS [*taken aback*] How do I know!

THE ARCHBISHOP. Yes: how do you know? I did not begin even to suspect until I was nearly seventy. I was only vain of my youthful appearance. I was not quite serious about it until I was ninety. Even now I am not sure from one moment to another, though I have given you my reason for thinking that I have quite unintentionally committed myself to a lifetime of three hundred years.

BURGE-LUBIN. But how do you do it? Is it lemons? Is it Soya beans? Is it—

THE ARCHBISHOP. I do not do it. It happens. It may happen to anyone. It may happen to you.

BURGE-LUBIN [*the full significance of this for himself dawning on him*] Then we three may be in the same boat with you, for all we know?

THE ARCHBISHOP. You may. Therefore I advise you to be very careful how you take any step that will make my position uncomfortable.

BURGE-LUBIN. Well, I'm dashed! One of my secretaries was remarking only this morning how well and young I am looking. Barnabas: I have an absolute conviction that I am one of the—the—shall I say one of the victims?—of this strange destiny.

THE ARCHBISHOP. Your great-great-great-great-great-great-grandfather formed the same conviction when he was between sixty and seventy. I knew him.

BURGE-LUBIN [*depressed*] Ah! But he died.

THE ARCHBISHOP. No.

BURGE-LUBIN [*hopefully*] Do you mean to say he is still alive?

THE ARCHBISHOP. No. He was shot. Under the influence of his belief that he was going to live three hundred years he became a changed man. He began to tell people the truth; and they disliked it so much that they took advantage of certain clauses of an Act of Parliament he had himself passed during the Four Years War, and had purposely forgotten to repeal afterwards. They took him to the Tower of

London and shot him.

The apparatus rings.

CONFUCIUS [*answering*] Yes? [*He listens*].

A WOMAN'S VOICE. The Domestic Minister has called.

BURGE-LUBIN [*not quite catching the answer*] Who does she say has called?

CONFUCIUS. The Domestic Minister.

BARNABAS. Oh, dash it! That awful woman!

BURGE-LUBIN. She certainly is a bit of a terror. I dont exactly know why; for she is not at all bad-looking.

BARNABAS [*out of patience*] For Heaven's sake, dont be frivolous.

THE ARCHBISHOP. He cannot help it, Mr Accountant General. Three of his sixteen great-great-great-grandfathers married Lubins.

BURGE-LUBIN. Tut tut! I am not frivolling. *I* did not ask the lady here. Which of you did?

CONFUCIUS. It is her official duty to report personally to the President once a quarter.

BURGE-LUBIN. Oh, that! Then I suppose it's my official duty to receive her. Theyd better send her in. You dont mind, do you? She will bring us back to real life. I dont know how you fellows feel; but I'm just going dotty.

CONFUCIUS [*into the telephone*] The President will receive the Domestic Minister at once.

They watch the door in silence for the entrance of the Domestic Minister.

BURGE-LUBIN [*suddenly, to the Archbishop*] I suppose you have been married over and over again.

THE ARCHBISHOP. Once. You do not make vows until death when death is three hundred years off.

They relapse into uneasy silence. The Domestic Minister enters. She is a handsome woman, apparently in the prime of life, with elegant, tense, well held-up figure, and the walk of a goddess. Her expression and deportment are grave, swift, decisive, awful, unanswerable. She wears a Dianesque tunic instead of a blouse, and a silver coronet instead of a gold fillet. Her dress otherwise is not markedly different from that of the men, who rise as she enters, and incline their heads with instinctive awe. She comes to the vacant chair between Barnabas and Confucius.

BURGE-LUBIN [*resolutely genial and gallant*] Delighted to see you, Mrs Lutestring.

CONFUCIUS. We are honored by your celestial presence.

BARNABAS. Good day, madam.

THE ARCHBISHOP. I have not had the pleasure of meeting you before. I am the Archbishop of York.

MRS LUTESTRING. Surely we have met, Mr Archbishop. I remember your face. We—[*she checks herself suddenly*] Ah, no: I remember now: it was someone else. [*She sits down*].

They all sit down.

THE ARCHBISHOP [*also puzzled*] Are you sure you are mistaken? I also have some association with your face, Mrs Lutestring. Something like a door opening continually and revealing you. And a smile of welcome when you recognized me. Did you ever open a door for me, I wonder?

MRS LUTESTRING. I often opened a door for the person you have just reminded me of. But he has been dead many years.

The rest, except the Archbishop, look at one another quickly.

CONFUCIUS. May I ask how many years?

MRS LUTESTRING [*struck by his tone, looks at him for a moment with some displeasure; then replies*] It does not matter. A long time.

BURGE-LUBIN. You mustnt rush to conclusions about the Archbishop, Mrs Lutestring. He is an older bird than you think. Older than you, at all events.

MRS LUTESTRING [*with a melancholy smile*] I think not, Mr President. But the subject is a delicate one. I had rather not pursue it.

CONFUCIUS. There is a question which has not been asked.

MRS LUTESTRING [*very decisively*] If it is a question about my age, Mr Chief Secretary, it had better not be asked. All that concerns you about my personal affairs can be found in the books of the Accountant General.

CONFUCIUS. The question I was thinking of will not be addressed to you. But let me say that your sensitiveness on the point is very strange, coming from a woman so superior to all common weaknesses as we know you to be.

MRS LUTESTRING. I may have reasons which have nothing to do with common weaknesses, Mr Chief Secretary. I hope you will respect them.

CONFUCIUS [*after bowing to her in assent*] I will now put my question. Have you, Mr Archbishop, any ground for assuming, as you seem to do, that what has happened to you has not happened to other people as well?

BURGE-LUBIN. Yes, by George! I never thought of that.

THE ARCHBISHOP. I have never met any case but my own.

CONFUCIUS. How do you know?

THE ARCHBISHOP. Well, no one has ever told me that they were in this extraordinary position.

CONFUCIUS. That proves nothing. Did you ever tell anybody that you were in it? You never told us. Why did you never tell us?

THE ARCHBISHOP. I am surprised at the question, coming from so astute a mind as yours, Mr Secretary. When you reach the age I reached before I discovered what was happening to me, I was old enough to know and fear the ferocious hatred with which human animals, like all other animals, turn upon any unhappy individual who has the misfortune to be unlike themselves in every respect: to be unnatural, as they call it. You will still find, among the tales of that twentieth-century classic, Wells, a story of a race of men who grew twice as big as their fellows, and another story of a man who fell into the hands of a race of blind men. The big people had to fight the little people for their lives; and the man with eyes would have had his eyes put out by the blind had he not fled to the desert, where he perished miserably. Wells's teaching, on that and other matters, was not lost on me. By the way, he lent me five pounds once which I never repaid; and it still troubles my conscience.

CONFUCIUS. And were you the only reader of Wells? If there were others like you, had they not the same reason for keeping the secret?

THE ARCHBISHOP. That is true. But I should know. You short-lived people are so childish. If I met a man of my own age I should recognize him at once. I have never done so.

MRS LUTESTRING. Would you recognize a woman of your age, do you think?

THE ARCHBISHOP. I—[*He stops and turns upon her with a searching look, startled by the suggestion and the suspicion it rouses*].

MRS LUTESTRING. What is your age, Mr Archbishop?

BURGE-LUBIN. Two hundred and eighty-three, he says. That is his little joke. Do you know, Mrs Lutestring, he had almost talked us into believing him when you came in and cleared the air with your robust common sense.

MRS LUTESTRING. Do you really feel that, Mr President? I hear the note of breezy assertion in your voice. I miss the note of conviction.

BURGE-LUBIN [*jumping up*] Look here. Let us stop talking damned nonsense. I dont wish to be disagreeable; but it's getting on my nerves. The best joke wont bear being pushed beyond a certain point. That point has been reached. I—I'm rather busy this morning. We all have our hands pretty full. Confucius here will tell you that I have a heavy day before me.

BARNABAS. Have you anything more important than this thing, if it's true?

BURGE-LUBIN. Oh, if, if, if it's true! But it isnt true.

BARNABAS. Have you anything at all to do?

BURGE-LUBIN. Anything to do! Have you forgotten Barnabas, that I happen to be President, and that the weight of the entire public business of this country is on my shoulders?

BARNABAS. Has he anything to do, Confucius?

CONFUCIUS. He has to be President.

BARNABAS. That means that he has nothing to do.

BURGE-LUBIN [*sulkily*] Very well, Barnabas. Go on making a fool of yourself. [*He sits down*]. Go on.

BARNABAS. I am not going to leave this room until we get to the bottom of this swindle.

MRS LUTESTRING [*turning with deadly gravity on the Accountant General*] This what, did you say?

CONFUCIUS. These expressions cannot be sustained. You obscure the discussion in using them.

BARNABAS [*glad to escape from her gaze by addressing Confucius*] Well, this unnatural horror. Will that satisfy you?

CONFUCIUS. That is in order. But we do not commit ourselves to the implications of the word horror.

THE ARCHBISHOP. By the word horror the Accountant General means only something unusual.

CONFUCIUS. I notice that the honorable Domestic Minister, on learning the advanced age of the venerable prelate, shews no sign of surprise or incredulity.

BURGE-LUBIN. She doesnt take it seriously. Who would? Eh, Mrs Lutestring?

MRS LUTESTRING. I take it very seriously indeed, Mr President. I see now that I was not mistaken at first. I have met the Archbishop before.

THE ARCHBISHOP. I felt sure of it. This vision of a door opening to me, and a woman's face welcoming me, must be a reminiscence of something that really happened; though I see it now as an angel opening the gate of heaven.

MRS LUTESTRING. Or a parlormaid opening the door of the house of the young woman you were in love with?

THE ARCHBISHOP [*making a wry face*] Is that the reality? How these things grow in our imagination! But may I say, Mrs Lutestring, that the transfiguration of a parlormaid to an angel is not more amazing than her transfiguration to the very dignified and able Domestic Minister I am addressing. I recognize the angel in you. Frankly, I do not recognize the parlormaid.

BURGE-LUBIN. Whats a parlormaid?

MRS LUTESTRING. An extinct species. A woman in a black

dress and white apron, who opened the house door when people knocked or rang, and was either your tyrant or your slave. I was a parlormaid in the house of one of the Accountant General's remote ancestors. [*To Confucius*] You asked me my age, Mr Chief Secretary. I am two hundred and seventy-four.

BURGE-LUBIN [*gallantly*] You dont look it. You really dont look it.

MRS LUTESTRING [*turning her face gravely towards him*] Look again, Mr President.

BURGE-LUBIN [*looking at her bravely until the smile fades from his face, and he suddenly covers his eyes with his hands*] Yes: you d o look it. I am convinced. It's true. Now call up the Lunatic Asylum, Confucius; and tell them to send an ambulance for me.

MRS LUTESTRING [*to the Archbishop*] Why have you given away your secret? our secret?

THE ARCHBISHOP. They found it out. The cinema records betrayed me. But I never dreamt that there were others. Did you?

MRS LUTESTRING. I knew one other. She was a cook. She grew tired, and killed herself.

THE ARCHBISHOP. Dear me! However, her death simplifies the situation, as I have been able to convince these gentlemen that the matter had better go no further.

MRS LUTESTRING. What! When the President knows! It will be all over the place before the end of the week.

BURGE-LUBIN [*injured*] Really, Mrs Lutestring! You speak as if I were a notoriously indiscreet person. Barnabas: have I such a reputation?

BARNABAS [*resignedly*] It cant be helped. It's constitutional.

CONFUCIUS. It is utterly unconstitutional. But, as you say, it cannot be helped.

BURGE-LUBIN [*solemnly*] I deny that a secret of State has ever passed my lips—except perhaps to the Minister of Health, who is discretion personified. People think, because she is a negress—

MRS LUTESTRING. It does not matter much now. Once, it would have mattered a great deal. But my children are all dead.

THE ARCHBISHOP. Yes: the children must have been a terrible difficulty. Fortunately for me, I had none.

MRS LUTESTRING. There was one daughter who was the child of my very heart. Some years after my first drowning I learnt that she had lost her sight. I went to her. She was an old woman of ninety-six, blind. She asked me to sit and talk with her because my voice was like the voice of her dead mother.

BURGE-LUBIN. The complications must be frightful. Really I hardly know whether I d o want to live much longer than other people.

MRS LUTESTRING. You can always kill yourself, as cook did; but that was influenza. Long life is complicated, and even terrible; but it is glorious all the same. I would no more change places with an ordinary woman than with a mayfly that lives only an hour.

THE ARCHBISHOP. What set you thinking of it first?

MRS LUTESTRING. Conrad Barnabas's book. Your wife told me it was more wonderful than Napoleon's Book of Fate and Old Moore's Almanac, which cook and I used to read. I was very ignorant: it did not seem so impossible to me as to an educated woman. Yet I forgot all about it, and married and drudged as a poor man's wife, and brought up children, and looked twenty years older than I really was, until one day, long after my husband died and my children were out in the world working for themselves, I noticed that I looked twenty years younger than I really was. The truth came to me in a flash.

BURGE-LUBIN. An amazing moment. Your feelings must have been beyond description. What was your first thought?

MRS LUTESTRING. Pure terror. I saw that the little money I had laid up would not last, and that I must go out and work again. They had things called Old Age Pensions then:

miserable pittances for worn-out old laborers to die on. I thought I should be found out if I went on drawing it too long. The horror of facing another lifetime of drudgery, of missing my hard-earned rest and losing my poor little savings, drove everything else out of my mind. You people nowadays can have no conception of the dread of poverty that hung over us then, or of the utter tiredness of forty years' unending overwork and striving to make a shilling do the work of a pound.

THE ARCHBISHOP. I wonder you did not kill yourself. I often wonder why the poor in those evil old times did not kill themselves. They did not even kill other people.

MRS LUTESTRING. You never kill yourself, because you always may as well wait until tomorrow. And you have not energy or conviction enough to kill the others. Besides, how can you blame them when you would do as they do if you were in their place?

BURGE-LUBIN. Devilish poor consolation, that.

MRS LUTESTRING. There were other consolations in those days for people like me. We drank preparations of alcohol to relieve the strain of living and give us an artificial happiness.

BURGE-LUBIN [*all together,* Alcohol!
CONFUCIUS *making* Pfff.. . .!
BARNABAS *wry faces*] Disgusting.

MRS LUTESTRING. A little alcohol would improve your temper and manners, and make you much easier to live with, Mr Accountant General.

BURGE-LUBIN [*laughing*] By George, I believe you! Try it, Barnabas.

CONFUCIUS. No. Try tea. It is the more civilized poison of the two.

MRS LUTESTRING. You, Mr President, were born intoxicated with your own well-fed natural exuberance. You cannot imagine what alcohol was to an underfed poor woman. I had carefully arranged my little savings so that I could get drunk, as we called it, once a week; and my only pleasure was looking forward to that poor little debauch. That is what saved me from suicide. I could not bear to miss my next carouse. But when I stopped working, and lived on my pension, the fatigue of my life's drudgery began to wear off, because, you see, I was not really old. I recuperated. I looked younger and younger. And at last I was rested enough to have courage and strength to begin life again. Besides, political changes were making it easier: life was a little better worth living for the nine-tenths of the people who used to be mere drudges. After that, I never turned back or faltered. My only regret now is that I shall die when I am three hundred or thereabouts. There was only one thing that made life hard; and that is gone now.

CONFUCIUS. May we ask what that was?

MRS LUTESTRING. Perhaps you will be offended if I tell you.

BURGE-LUBIN. Offended! My dear lady, do you suppose, after such a stupendous revelation, that anything short of a blow from a sledge-hammer could produce the smallest impression on any of us?

MRS LUTESTRING. Well, you see, it has been so hard on me never to meet a grown-up person. You are all such children. And I never was very fond of children, except that one girl who woke up the mother passion in me. I have been very lonely sometimes.

BURGE-LUBIN [*again gallant*] But surely, Mrs Lutestring, that has been your own fault. If I may say so, a lady of your attractions need never have been lonely.

MRS LUTESTRING. Why?

BURGE-LUBIN. Why! Well—. Well, er—. Well, er er—. Well! [*he gives it up*].

THE ARCHBISHOP. He means that you might have married. Curious, how little they understand our position.

MRS LUTESTRING. I did marry. I married again on my hundred and first birthday. But of course I had to marry an elderly man: a man over sixty. He was a great painter. On his deathbed he said to me "It has taken me fifty years to learn my trade, and to paint all the foolish pictures a man must paint and get rid of before he comes through them to the great things he ought to paint. And now that my foot is at last on the threshold of the temple I find that it is also the threshold of my tomb." That man would have been the greatest painter of all time if he could have lived as long as I. I saw him die of old age whilst he was still, as he said himself, a gentleman amateur, like all modern painters.

BURGE-LUBIN. But why had you to marry an elderly man? Why not marry a young one? or shall I say a middle-aged one? If my own affections were not already engaged; and if, to tell the truth, I were not a little afraid of you—for you are a very superior woman, as we all acknowledge—I should esteem myself happy in—er—er—

MRS LUTESTRING. Mr President: have you ever tried to take advantage of the innocence of a little child for the gratification of your senses?

BURGE-LUBIN. Good Heavens, madam, what do you take me for? What right have you to ask me such a question?

MRS LUTESTRING. I am at present in my two hundred and seventy-fifth year. You suggest that I should take advantage of the innocence of a child of thirty, and marry it.

THE ARCHBISHOP. Can you shortlived people not understand that as the confusion and immaturity and primitive animalism in which we live for the first hundred years of our life is worse in this matter of sex than in any other, you are intolerable to us in that relation?

BURGE-LUBIN. Do you mean to say, Mrs Lutestring, that you regard me as a child?

MRS LUTESTRING. Do you expect me to regard you as a completed soul? Oh, you may well be afraid of me. There are moments when your levity, your ingratitude, your shallow jollity, make my gorge rise so against you that if I could not remind myself that you are a child I should be tempted to doubt your right to live at all.

CONFUCIUS. Do you grudge us the few years we have? you who have three hundred!

BURGE-LUBIN. You accuse me of levity! Must I remind

you, madam, that I am the President, and that you are only the head of a department?

BARNABAS. Ingratitude too! You draw a pension for three hundred years when we owe you only seventy-eight; and you call us ungrateful!

MRS LUTESTRING. I do. When I think of the blessings that have been showered on you, and contrast them with the poverty! the humiliations! the anxieties! the heartbreak! the insolence and tyranny that were the daily lot of mankind when I was learning to suffer instead of learning to live! when I see how lightly you take it all! how you quarrel over the crumpled leaves in your beds of roses! how you are so dainty about your work that unless it is made either interesting or delightful to you you leave it to negresses and Chinamen, I ask myself whether even three hundred years of thought and experience can save you from being superseded by the Power that created you and put you on your trial.

BURGE-LUBIN. My dear lady: our Chinese and colored friends are perfectly happy. They are twenty times better off here than they would be in China or Liberia. They do their work admirably; and in doing it they set us free for higher employments.

THE ARCHBISHOP [*who has caught the infection of her indignation*] What higher employments are you capable of? you that are superannuated at seventy and dead at eighty!

MRS LUTESTRING. You are not really doing higher work. You are supposed to make the decisions and give the orders; but the negresses and the Chinese make up your minds for you and tell you what orders to give, just as my brother, who was a sergeant in the Guards, used to prompt his officers in the old days. When I want to get anything done at the Health Ministry I do not come to you: I go to the black lady who has been the real president during your present term of office, or to Confucius, who goes on for ever while presidents come and presidents go.

BURGE-LUBIN. This is outrageous. This is treason to the

white race. And let me tell you, madam, that I have never in my life met the Minister of Health, and that I protest against the vulgar color prejudice which disparages her great ability and her eminent services to the State. My relations with her are purely telephonic, gramophonic, photophonic, and, may I add, platonic.

THE ARCHBISHOP. There is no reason why you should be ashamed of them in any case, Mr President. But let us look at the position impersonally. Can you deny that what is happening is that the English people have become a Joint Stock Company admitting Asiatics and Africans as shareholders?

BARNABAS. Nothing like it. I know all about the old joint stock companies. The shareholders did no work.

THE ARCHBISHOP. That is true; but we, like them, get our dividends whether we work or not. We work partly because we know there would be no dividends if we did not, and partly because if we refuse we are regarded as mentally deficient and put into a lethal chamber. But what do we work at? Before the few changes we were forced to make by the revolutions that followed the Four Years War, our governing classes had been so rich, as it was called, that they had become the most intellectually lazy and fat-headed people on the face of the earth. There is a good deal of that fat still clinging to us.

BURGE-LUBIN. As President, I must not listen to unpatriotic criticisms of our national character, Mr Archbishop.

THE ARCHBISHOP. As Archbishop, Mr President, it is my official duty to criticize the national character unsparingly. At the canonization of Saint Henrik Ibsen, you yourself unveiled the monument to him which bears on its pedestal the noble inscription, "I came not to call sinners, but the righteous, to repentance." The proof of what I say is that our routine work, and what may be called our ornamental and figure-head work, is being more and more sought after by the English; whilst the thinking, organizing, calculating, directing work is done by yellow brains, brown brains, and black brains, just as it was done in my early days by Jewish brains, Scottish brains, Italian brains, German brains. The only white men who still do serious work are those who, like the Accountant General, have no capacity for enjoyment, and no social gifts to make them welcome outside their offices.

BARNABAS. Confound your impudence! I had gifts enough to find you out, anyhow.

THE ARCHBISHOP [*disregarding this outburst*] If you were to kill me as I stand here, you would have to appoint an Indian to succeed me. I take precedence today not as an Englishman, but as a man with more than a century and a half of fully adult experience. We are letting all the power slip into the hands of the colored people. In another hundred years we shall be simply their household pets.

BURGE-LUBIN [*reacting buoyantly*] Not the least danger of it. I grant you we leave the most troublesome part of the labor of the nation to them. And a good job too: why should we drudge at it? But think of the activities of our leisure! Is there a jollier place on earth to live in than England out of office hours? And to whom do we owe that? To ourselves, not to the niggers. The nigger and the Chink are all right from Tuesday to Friday; but from Friday to Tuesday they are simply nowhere; and the real life of England is from Friday to Tuesday.

THE ARCHBISHOP. That is terribly true. In devising brainless amusements; in pursuing them with enormous vigor, and taking them with eager seriousness, our English people are the wonder of the world. They always were. And it is just as well; for otherwise their sensuality would become morbid and destroy them. What appals me is that their amusements should amuse them. They are the amusements of boys and girls. They are pardonable up to the age of fifty or sixty: after that they are ridiculous. I tell you, what is wrong with us is that we are a non-adult race; and the Irish and the Scots, and the niggers and Chinks, as you call them, though their lifetime is as short as ours, or shorter, yet do somehow contrive to grow up a little before they die. We die in boyhood: the maturity that should make us the greatest of all the nations lies beyond the grave for us. Either we shall go under as greybeards with golf clubs in our hands, or we must will to live longer.

MRS LUTESTRING. Yes: that is it. I could not have expressed it in words; but you have expressed it for me. I felt, even when I was an ignorant domestic slave, that we had the possibility of becoming a great nation within us; but our faults and follies drove me to cynical hopelessness. We all ended then like that. It is the highest creatures who take the longest to mature, and are the most helpless during their immaturity. I know now that it took me a whole century to grow up. I began my serious life when I was a hundred and twenty. Asiatics cannot control me: I am not a child in their hands, as you are, Mr President. Neither, I am sure, is the Archbishop. They respect me. You are not grown up enough even for that, though you were kind enough to say that I frighten you.

BURGE-LUBIN. Honestly, you do. And will you think me very rude if I say that if I must choose between a white woman old enough to be my great-grandmother and a black woman of my own age, I shall probably find the black woman more sympathetic?

MRS LUTESTRING. And more attractive in color, perhaps?

BURGE-LUBIN. Yes. Since you ask me, more—well, not more attractive: I do not deny that you have an excellent appearance—but I will say, richer. More Venetian. Tropical. "The shadowed livery of the burnished sun."

MRS LUTESTRING. Our women, and their favorite story writers, begin already to talk about men with golden complexions.

CONFUCIUS [*expanding into a smile all across both face and body*]. A-a-a-a——h!

BURGE-LUBIN. Well, what of it, madam? Have you read a very interesting book by the librarian of the Biological Society suggesting that the future of the world lies with the

Mulatto?

MRS LUTESTRING [*rising*] Mr Archbishop: if the white race is to be saved, our destiny is apparent.

THE ARCHBISHOP. Yes: our duty is pretty clear.

MRS LUTESTRING. Have you time to come home with me and discuss the matter?

THE ARCHBISHOP [*rising*] With pleasure.

BARNABAS [*rising also and rushing past Mrs Lutestring to the door, where he turns to bar her way*] No you dont. Burge: you understand, dont you?

BURGE-LUBIN. No. What is it?

BARNABAS. These two are going to marry.

BURGE-LUBIN. Why shouldnt they, if they want to?

BARNABAS. They dont want to. They will do it in cold blood because their children will live three hundred years. It mustnt be allowed.

CONFUCIUS. You cannot prevent it. There is no law that gives you power to interfere with them.

BARNABAS. If they force me to it I will obtain legislation against marriages above the age of seventy-eight.

THE ARCHBISHOP. There is not time for that before we are married, Mr Accountant General. Be good enough to get out of the lady's way.

BARNABAS. There is time to send the lady to the lethal chamber before anything comes of your marriage. Dont forget that.

MRS LUTESTRING. What nonsense, Mr Accountant General! Good afternoon, Mr President. Good afternoon, Mr Chief Secretary. [*They rise and acknowledge her salutation with bows. She walks straight at the Accountant General, who instinctively shrinks out of her way as she leaves the room*].

THE ARCHBISHOP. I am surprised at you, Mr Barnabas. Your tone was like an echo from the Dark Ages. [*He follows the Domestic Minister*].

Confucius, shaking his head and clucking with his tongue in deprecation of this painful episode, moves to the chair just vacated by the Archbishop and stands behind it with folded palms, looking at the President. The Accountant General shakes his fist after the departed visitors, and bursts into savage abuse of them.

BARNABAS. Thieves! Cursed thieves! Vampires! What are you going to do, Burge?

BURGE-LUBIN. Do?

BARNABAS. Yes, do. There must be dozens of these people in existence. Are you going to let them do what the two who have just left us mean to do, and crowd us off the face of the earth?

BURGE-LUBIN [*sitting down*] Oh, come, Barnabas! What harm are they doing? Arnt you interested in them? Dont you like them?

BARNABAS. Like them! I hate them. They are monsters, unnatural monsters. They are poison to me.

BURGE-LUBIN. What possible objection can there be to their living as long as they can? It does not shorten our lives, does it?

BARNABAS. If I have to die when I am seventy-eight, I dont see why another man should be privileged to live to be two hundred and seventy-eight. It does shorten my life, relatively. It makes us ridiculous. If they grew to be twelve feet high they would make us all dwarfs. They talked to us as if we were children. There is no love lost between us: their hatred of us came out soon enough. You heard what the woman said, and how the Archbishop backed her up?

BURGE-LUBIN. But what can we do to them?

BARNABAS. Kill them.

BURGE-LUBIN. Nonsense!

BARNABAS. Lock them up. Sterilize them somehow, anyhow.

BURGE-LUBIN. But what reason could we give?

BARNABAS. What reason can you give for killing a snake? Nature tells you to do it.

BURGE-LUBIN. My dear Barnabas, you are out of your mind.

BARNABAS. Havnt you said that once too often already

this morning?

BURGE-LUBIN. I dont believe you will carry a single soul with you.

BARNABAS. I understand. I know you. You think you are one of them.

CONFUCIUS. Mr Accountant General: you may be one of them.

BARNABAS. How dare you accuse me of such a thing? I am an honest man, not a monster. I won my place in public life by demonstrating that the true expectation of human life is seventy-eight point six. And I will resist any attempt to alter or upset it to the last drop of my blood if need be.

BURGE-LUBIN. Oh, tut tut! Come, come! Pull yourself together. How can you, a descendant of the great Conrad Barnabas, the man who is still remembered by his masterly Biography of a Black Beetle, be so absurd?

BARNABAS. You had better go and write the autobiography of a jackass. I am going to raise the country against this horror, and against you, if you shew the slightest sign of weakness about it.

CONFUCIUS [*very impressively*] You will regret it if you do.

BARNABAS. What is to make me regret it?

CONFUCIUS. Every mortal man and woman in the community will begin to count on living for three centuries. Things will happen which you do not foresee: terrible things. The family will dissolve: parents and children will be no longer the old and the young: brothers and sisters will meet as strangers after a hundred years separation: the ties of blood will lose their innocence. The imaginations of men, let loose over the possibilities of three centuries of life, will drive them mad and wreck human society. This discovery must be kept a dead secret. [*He sits down*].

BARNABAS. And if I refuse to keep the secret?

CONFUCIUS. I shall have you safe in a lunatic asylum the day after you blab.

BARNABAS. You forget that I can produce the Archbishop to prove my statement.

CONFUCIUS. So can I. Which of us do you think he will support when I explain to him that your object in revealing his age is to get him killed?

BARNABAS [*desperate*] Burge: are you going to back up this yellow abomination against me? Are we public men and members of the Government? or are we damned blackguards?

CONFUCIUS [*unmoved*] Have you ever known a public man who was not what vituperative people called a damned blackguard when some inconsiderate person wanted to tell the public more than was good for it?

BARNABAS. Hold your tongue, you insolent heathen. Burge: I spoke to you.

BURGE-LUBIN. Well, you know, my dear Barnabas, Confucius is a very long-headed chap. I see his point.

BARNABAS. Do you? Then let me tell you that, except officially, I will never speak to you again. Do you hear?

BURGE-LUBIN [*cheerfully*] You will. You will.

BARNABAS. And dont you ever dare speak to me again. Do you hear? [*He turns to the door*].

BURGE-LUBIN. I will. I will. Goodbye, Barnabas. God bless you.

BARNABAS. May you live forever, and be the laughingstock of the whole world! [*he dashes out in a fury*].

BURGE-LUBIN [*laughing indulgently*] He will keep the secret all right. I know Barnabas. You neednt worry.

CONFUCIUS [*troubled and grave*] There are no secrets except the secrets that keep themselves. Consider. There are those films at the Record Office. We have no power to prevent the Master of the Records from publishing this discovery made in his department. We cannot silence the American—who can silence an American?—nor the people who were there today to receive him. Fortunately, a film can prove nothing but a resemblance.

BURGE-LUBIN. Thats very true. After all, the whole thing is confounded nonsense, isnt it?

CONFUCIUS [*raising his head to look at him*] You have decided not to believe it now that you realize its inconveniences. That is the English method. It may not work in this case.

BURGE-LUBIN. English be hanged! It's common sense. You know, those two people got us hypnotized: not a doubt of it. They must have been kidding us. They were, werent they?

CONFUCIUS. You looked into that woman's face; and you believed.

BURGE-LUBIN. Just so. Thats where she had me. I shouldnt have believed her a bit if she'd turned her back to me.

CONFUCIUS [*shakes his head slowly and repeatedly*]???

BURGE-LUBIN. You really think—? [*he hesitates*].

CONFUCIUS. The Archbishop has always been a puzzle to me. Ever since I learnt to distinguish between one English face and another I have noticed what the woman pointed out: that the English face is not an adult face, just as the English mind is not an adult mind.

BURGE-LUBIN. Stow it, John Chinaman. If ever there was a race divinely appointed to take charge of the non-adult races and guide them and train them and keep them out of mischief until they grow up to be capable of adopting our institutions, that race is the English race. It is the only race in the world that has that characteristic. Now!

CONFUCIUS. That is the fancy of a child nursing a doll. But it is ten times more childish of you to dispute the highest compliment ever paid you.

BURGE-LUBIN. You call it a compliment to class us as grown-up children.

CONFUCIUS. Not grown-up children, children at fifty, sixty, seventy. Your maturity is so late that you never attain to it. You have to be governed by races which are mature at forty. That means that you are potentially the most highly developed race on earth, and would be actually the greatest if you could live long enough to attain to maturity.

BURGE-LUBIN [*grasping the idea at last*] By George, Confucius, youre right! I never thought of that. That explains everything. We a r e just a lot of schoolboys: theres no denying it. Talk to an Englishman about anything serious, and he listens to you curiously for a moment just as he listens to a chap playing classical music. Then he goes back to his marine golf, or motoring, or flying, or women, just like a bit of stretched elastic when you let it go. [*Soaring to the height of his theme*] Oh, youre quite right. We are only in our infancy. I ought to be in a perambulator, with a nurse shoving me along. It's true: it's absolutely true. But some day we'll grow up; and then, by Jingo, we'll shew em.

CONFUCIUS. The Archbishop is an adult. When I was a child I was dominated and intimidated by people whom I now know to have been weaker and sillier than I, because there was some mysterious quality in their mere age that overawed me. I confess that, though I have kept up appearances, I have always been afraid of the Archbishop.

BURGE-LUBIN. Between ourselves, Confucius, so have I.

CONFUCIUS. It is this that convinced me. It was this in the woman's face that convinced you. Their new departure in the history of the race is no fraud. It does not even surprise me.

BURGE-LUBIN. Oh, come! Not surprise you! It's your pose never to be surprised at anything; but if you are not surprised at this you are not human.

CONFUCIUS. I am staggered, just as a man may be staggered by an explosion for which he has himself laid the charge and lighted the fuse. But I am not surprised, because, as a philosopher and a student of evolutionary biology, I have come to regard some such development as this as inevitable. If I had not thus prepared myself to be credulous, no mere evidence of films and well-told tales would have persuaded me to believe. As it is, I do believe.

BURGE-LUBIN. Well, that being settled, what the devil is to happen next? Whats the next move for us?

CONFUCIUS. We do not make the next move. The next move will be made by the Archbishop and the woman.

BURGE-LUBIN. Their marriage?

CONFUCIUS. More than that. They have made the momentous discovery that they are not alone in the world.

BURGE-LUBIN. You think there are others?

CONFUCIUS. There must be many others. Each of them believes that he or she is the only one to whom the miracle has happened. But the Archbishop knows better now. He will advertize in terms which only the longlived people will understand. He will bring them together and organize them. They will hasten from all parts of the earth. They will become a great Power.

BURGE-LUBIN [*a little alarmed*] I say, will they? I suppose they will. I wonder is Barnabas right after all? Ought we to allow it?

CONFUCIUS. Nothing that we can do will stop it. We cannot in our souls really want to stop it: the vital force that has produced this change would paralyse our opposition to it, if we were mad enough to oppose. But we will not oppose. You and I may be of the elect, too.

BURGE-LUBIN. Yes: thats what gets us every time. What the deuce ought we to do? Something must be done about it, you know.

CONFUCIUS. Let us sit still, and meditate in silence on the vistas before us.

BURGE-LUBIN. By George, I believe youre right. Let us.

They sit meditating, the Chinaman naturally, the President with visible effort and intensity. He is positively glaring into the future when the voice of the Negress is heard.

THE NEGRESS. Mr President.

BURGE-LUBIN [*joyfully*] Yes. [*Taking up a peg*] Are you at home?

THE NEGRESS. No. Omega, zero, x squared.

The President rapidly puts the peg in the switchboard; works the dial; and presses the button. The screen becomes transparent; and the Negress, brilliantly dressed, appears on what looks like the bridge of a steam yacht in glorious sea weather. The installation with which she is communicating is beside the binnacle.

CONFUCIUS [*looking round, and recoiling with a shriek of disgust*] Ach! Avaunt! Avaunt! [*He rushes from the room*].

BURGE-LUBIN. What part of the coast is that?

THE NEGRESS. Fishguard Bay. Why not run over and join me for the afternoon? I am disposed to be approachable at last.

BURGE-LUBIN. But Fishguard! Two hundred and seventy miles!

THE NEGRESS. There is a lightning express on the Irish Air Service at half-past sixteen. They will drop you by a parachute in the bay. The dip will do you good. I will pick you up and dry you and give you a first-rate time.

BURGE-LUBIN. Delightful. But a little risky, isnt it?

THE NEGRESS. Risky! I thought you were afraid of nothing.

BURGE-LUBIN. I am not exactly afraid; but—

THE NEGRESS [*offended*] But you think it is not good enough. Very well [*she raises her hand to take the peg out of her switchboard*].

BURGE-LUBIN [*imploringly*] No: stop: let me explain: hold the line just one moment. Oh, please.

THE NEGRESS [*waiting with her hand poised over the peg*] Well?

BURGE-LUBIN. The fact is, I have been behaving very recklessly for some time past under the impression that my life would be so short that it was not worth bothering about. But I have just learnt that I may live—well, much longer than I expected. I am sure your good sense will tell you that this alters the case. I—

THE NEGRESS [*with suppressed rage*] Oh, quite. Pray dont risk your precious life on my account. Sorry for troubling you. Goodbye. [*She snatches out her peg and vanishes*].

BURGE-LUBIN [*urgently*] No: please hold on. I can convince you—[*a loud buzz-uzz-uzz*]. Engaged! Who is she calling up now? [*He presses the button and calls*] The Chief Secretary. Say I want to see him again, just for a moment.

CONFUCIUS'S VOICE. Is the woman gone?

BURGE-LUBIN. Yes, yes: it's all right. Just a moment, if— [*Confucius returns*] Confucius: I have some important business at Fishguard. The Irish Air Service can drop me in the bay by parachute. I suppose it's quite safe, isnt it?

CONFUCIUS. Nothing is quite safe. The air service is as safe as any other travelling service. The parachute is safe. But the water is not safe.

BURGE-LUBIN. Why? They will give me an unsinkable tunic, wont they?

CONFUCIUS. You will not sink; but the sea is very cold. You may get rheumatism for life.

BURGE-LUBIN. For life! That settles it: I wont risk it.

CONFUCIUS. Good. You have at last become prudent: you are no longer what you call a sportsman: you are a sensible coward, almost a grown-up man. I congratulate you.

BURGE-LUBIN [*resolutely*] Coward or no coward, I will not face an eternity of rheumatism for any woman that ever was born. [*He rises and goes to the rack for his fillet*] I have changed my mind: I am going home. [*He cocks the fillet rakishly*] Good evening.

CONFUCIUS. So early? If the Minister of Health rings you up, what shall I tell her?

BURGE-LUBIN. Tell her to go to the devil. [*He goes out*].

CONFUCIUS [*shaking his head, shocked at the President's impoliteness*] No. No, no, no, no, no. Oh, these English! these crude young civilizations! Their manners! Hogs. Hogs.

PART IV

TRAGEDY OF AN ELDERLY GENTLEMAN

TRAGEDY OF AN ELDERLY GENTLEMAN

ACT I

BURRIN pier on the south shore of Galway Bay in Ireland, a region of stone-capped hills and granite fields. It is a fine summer day in the year 3000 A.D. *On an ancient stone stump, about three feet thick and three feet high, used for securing ships by ropes to the shore, and called a bollard or hold-fast, an elderly gentleman sits facing the land, with his head bowed and his face in his hands, sobbing. His sunburnt skin contrasts with his white whiskers and eyebrows. He wears a black frock-coat, a white waistcoat, lavender trousers, a brilliant silk cravat with a jewelled pin stuck in it, a tall hat of grey felt, and patent leather boots with white spats. His starched linen cuffs protrude from his coat sleeves; and his collar, also of starched white linen, is Gladstonian. On his right, three or four full sacks, lying side by side on the flags, suggest that the pier, unlike many remote Irish piers, is occasionally useful as well as romantic. On his left, behind him, a flight of stone steps descends out of sight to the sea level.*

A woman in a silk tunic and sandals, wearing little else except a cap with the number 2 on it in gold, comes up the steps from the sea, and stares in astonishment at the sobbing man. Her age cannot be guessed: her face is firm and chiselled like a young face; but her expression is unyouthful in its severity and determination.

THE WOMAN. What is the matter?

The elderly gentleman looks up; hastily pulls himself together; takes out a silk handkerchief and dries his tears lightly with a brave attempt to smile through them; and tries to rise gallantly, but sinks back.

THE WOMAN. Do you need assistance?

THE ELDERLY GENTLEMAN. No. Thank you very much. No. Nothing. The heat. [*He punctuates with sniffs, and dabs with his handkerchief at his eyes and nose*]. Hay fever.

THE WOMAN. You are a foreigner, are you not?

THE ELDERLY GENTLEMAN. No. You must not regard me as a foreigner. I am a Briton.

THE WOMAN. You come from some part of the British Commonwealth?

THE ELDERLY GENTLEMAN [*amiably pompous*] From its capital, madam.

THE WOMAN. From Baghdad?

THE ELDERLY GENTLEMAN. Yes. You may not be aware, madam, that these islands were once the centre of the British Commonwealth, during a period now known as The Exile. They were its headquarters a thousand years ago. Few people know this interesting circumstance now; but I assure you it is true. I have come here on a pious pilgrimage to one of the numerous lands of my fathers. We are of the same stock, you and I. Blood is thicker than water. We are cousins.

THE WOMAN. I do not understand. You say you have come here on a pious pilgrimage. Is that some new means of transport?

THE ELDERLY GENTLEMAN [*again shewing signs of distress*] I find it very difficult to make myself understood here. I was not referring to a machine, but to a—a—a sentimental journey.

THE WOMAN. I am afraid I am as much in the dark as before. You said also that blood is thicker than water. No doubt it is; but what of it?

THE ELDERLY GENTLEMAN. Its meaning is obvious.

THE WOMAN. Perfectly. But I assure you I am quite aware that blood is thicker than water.

THE ELDERLY GENTLEMAN [*sniffing: almost in tears again*] We will leave it at that, madam.

THE WOMAN [*going nearer to him and scrutinizing him with some concern*] I am afraid you are not well. Were you not warned that it is dangerous for shortlived people to come to this country? There is a deadly disease called discouragement, against which shortlived people have to take very strict precautions. Intercourse with us puts too great a strain on them.

THE ELDERLY GENTLEMAN [*pulling himself together huffily*]

It has no effect on me, madam. I fear my conversation does not interest you. If not, the remedy is in your own hands.

THE WOMAN [*looking at her hands, and then looking inquiringly at him*] Where?

THE ELDERLY GENTLEMAN [*breaking down*] Oh, this is dreadful. No understanding, no intelligence, no sympathy —[*his sobs choke him*].

THE WOMAN. You see, you are ill.

THE ELDERLY GENTLEMAN [*nerved by indignation*] I am not ill. I have never had a day's illness in my life.

THE WOMAN. May I advise you?

THE ELDERLY GENTLEMAN. I have no need of a lady doctor, thank you, madam.

THE WOMAN [*shaking her head*] I am afraid I do not understand. I said nothing about a butterfly.

THE ELDERLY GENTLEMAN. Well, *I* said nothing about a butterfly.

THE WOMAN. You spoke of a lady doctor. The word is known here only as the name of a butterfly.

THE ELDERLY GENTLEMAN [*insanely*] I give up. I can bear this no longer. It is easier to go out of my mind at once. [*He rises and dances about, singing*]

> I'd be a butterfly, born in a bower,
> Making apple dumplings without any flour.

THE WOMAN [*smiling gravely*] It must be at least a hundred and fifty years since I last laughed. But if you do that any more I shall certainly break out like a primary of sixty. Your dress is so extraordinarily ridiculous.

THE ELDERLY GENTLEMAN [*halting abruptly in his antics*] My dress ridiculous! I may not be dressed like a Foreign Office clerk; but my clothes are perfectly in fashion in my native metropolis, where yours—pardon my saying so—would be considered extremely unusual and hardly decent.

THE WOMAN. Decent? There is no such word in our language. What does it mean?

THE ELDERLY GENTLEMAN. It would not be decent for me

to explain. Decency cannot be discussed without indecency.

THE WOMAN. I cannot understand you at all. I fear you have not been observing the rules laid down for shortlived visitors.

THE ELDERLY GENTLEMAN. Surely, madam, they do not apply to persons of my age and standing. I am not a child, nor an agricultural laborer.

THE WOMAN [*severely*] They apply to you very strictly. You are expected to confine yourself to the society of children under sixty. You are absolutely forbidden to approach fully adult natives under any circumstances. You cannot converse with persons of my age for long without bringing on a dangerous attack of discouragement. Do you realize that you are already shewing grave symptoms of that very distressing and usually fatal complaint?

THE ELDERLY GENTLEMAN. Certainly not, madam. I am fortunately in no danger of contracting it. I am quite accustomed to converse intimately and at the greatest length with the most distinguished persons. If you cannot discriminate between hay fever and imbecility, I can only say that your advanced years carry with them the inevitable penalty of dotage.

THE WOMAN. I am one of the guardians of this district; and I am responsible for your welfare—

THE ELDERLY GENTLEMAN. The Guardians! Do you take me for a pauper?

THE WOMAN. I do not know what a pauper is. You must tell me who you are, if it is possible for you to express yourself intelligibly—

THE ELDERLY GENTLEMAN [*snorts indignantly*]!

THE WOMAN [*continuing*]—and why you are wandering here alone without a nurse.

THE ELDERLY GENTLEMAN [*outraged*] Nurse!

THE WOMAN. Shortlived visitors are not allowed to go about here without nurses. Do you not know that rules are meant to be kept?

THE ELDERLY GENTLEMAN. By the lower classes, no doubt.

But to persons in my position there are certain courtesies which are never denied by well-bred people; and—

THE WOMAN. There are only two human classes here: the shortlived and the normal. The rules apply to the shortlived, and are for their own protection. Now tell me at once who you are.

THE ELDERLY GENTLEMAN [*impressively*] Madam, I am a retired gentleman, formerly Chairman of the All-British Synthetic Egg and Vegetable Cheese Trust in Baghdad, and now President of the British Historical and Archæological Society, and a Vice-President of the Travellers' Club.

THE WOMAN. All that does not matter.

THE ELDERLY GENTLEMAN [*again snorting*] Hm! Indeed!

THE WOMAN. Have you been sent here to make your mind flexible?

THE ELDERLY GENTLEMAN. What an extraordinary question! Pray do you find my mind noticeably stiff?

THE WOMAN. Perhaps you do not know that you are on the west coast of Ireland, and that it is the practice among natives of the Eastern Island to spend some years here to acquire mental flexibility. The climate has that effect.

THE ELDERLY GENTLEMAN [*haughtily*] I was born, not in the Eastern Island, but, thank God, in dear old British Baghdad; and I am not in need of a mental health resort.

THE WOMAN. Then why are you here?

THE ELDERLY GENTLEMAN. Am I trespassing? I was not aware of it.

THE WOMAN. Trespassing? I do not understand the word.

THE ELDERLY GENTLEMAN. Is this land private property? If so, I make no claim. I proffer a shilling in satisfaction of damage (if any), and am ready to withdraw if you will be good enough to shew me the nearest way. [*He offers her a shilling*].

THE WOMAN [*taking it and examining it without much interest*] I do not understand a single word of what you have just said.

THE ELDERLY GENTLEMAN. I am speaking the plainest English. Are you the landlord?

THE WOMAN [*shaking her head*] There is a tradition in this part of the country of an animal with a name like that. It used to be hunted and shot in the barbarous ages. It is quite extinct now.

THE ELDERLY GENTLEMAN [*breaking down again*] It is a dreadful thing to be in a country where nobody understands civilized institutions. [*He collapses on the bollard, struggling with his rising sobs*]. Excuse me. Hay fever.

THE WOMAN [*taking a tuning-fork from her girdle and holding it to her ear; then speaking into space on one note, like a chorister intoning a psalm*] Burrin Pier Galway please send someone to take charge of a discouraged shortliver who has escaped from his nurse male harmless babbles unintelligibly with moments of sense distressed hysterical foreign dress very funny has curious fringe of white sea-weed under his chin.

THE GENTLEMAN. This is a gross impertinence. An insult.

THE WOMAN [*replacing her tuning-fork and addressing the elderly gentleman*] These words mean nothing to me. In what capacity are you here? How did you obtain permission to visit us?

THE ELDERLY GENTLEMAN [*importantly*] Our Prime Minister, Mr Badger Bluebin, has come to consult the oracle. He is my son-in-law. We are accompanied by his wife and daughter: my daughter and granddaughter. I may mention that General Aufsteig, who is one of our party, is really the Emperor of Turania travelling incognito. I understand he has a question to put to the oracle informally. I have come solely to visit the country.

THE WOMAN. Why should you come to a place where you have no business?

THE ELDERLY GENTLEMAN. Great Heavens, madam, can anything be more natural? I shall be the only member of the Travellers' Club who has set foot on these shores. Think of that! My position will be unique.

THE WOMAN. Is that an advantage? We have a person here who has lost both legs in an accident. His position is unique. But he would much rather be like everyone else.

THE ELDERLY GENTLEMAN. This is maddening. There is no analogy whatever between the two cases.

THE WOMAN. They are both unique.

THE ELDERLY GENTLEMAN. Conversation in this place seems to consist of ridiculous quibbles. I am heartily tired of them.

THE WOMAN. I conclude that your Travellers' Club is an assembly of persons who wish to be able to say that they have been in some place where nobody else has been.

THE ELDERLY GENTLEMAN. Of course if you wish to sneer at us—

THE WOMAN. What is sneer?

THE ELDERLY GENTLEMAN [*with a wild sob*] I shall drown myself.

He makes desperately for the edge of the pier, but is confronted by a man with the number one on his cap, who comes up the steps and intercepts him. He is dressed like the woman, but a slight moustache proclaims his sex.

THE MAN [*to the elderly gentleman*] Ah, here you are. I shall really have to put a collar and lead on you if you persist in giving me the slip like this.

THE WOMAN. Are you this stranger's nurse?

THE MAN. Yes. I am very tired of him. If I take my eyes off him for a moment, he runs away and talks to everybody.

THE WOMAN [*after taking out her tuning-fork and sounding it, intones as before*] Burrin Pier. Wash out. [*She puts up the fork, and addresses the man*]. I sent a call for someone to take care of him. I have been trying to talk to him; but I can understand very little of what he says. You must take better care of him: he is badly discouraged already. If I can be of any further use, Fusima, Gort, will find me. [*She goes away*].

THE ELDERLY GENTLEMAN. Any further use! She has been of no use to me. She spoke to me without any introduction, like any improper female. And she has made off with my shilling.

THE MAN. Please speak slowly: I cannot follow. What is a shilling? What is an introduction? Improper female doesnt make sense.

THE ELDERLY GENTLEMAN. Nothing seems to make sense here. All I can tell you is that she was the most impenetrably stupid woman I have ever met in the whole course of my life.

THE MAN. That cannot be. She cannot appear stupid to you. She is a secondary, and getting on for a tertiary at that.

THE ELDERLY GENTLEMAN. What is a tertiary? Everybody here keeps talking to me about primaries and secondaries and tertiaries as if people were geological strata.

THE MAN. The primaries are in their first century. The secondaries are in their second century. I am still classed as a primary [*he points to his number*]; but I may almost call myself a secondary, as I shall be ninety-five next January. The tertiaries are in their third century. Did you not see the number two on her badge? She is an advanced secondary.

THE ELDERLY GENTLEMAN. That accounts for it. She is in her second childhood.

THE MAN. Her second childhood! She is in her fifth childhood.

THE ELDERLY GENTLEMAN [*again resorting to the bollard*] Oh! I cannot bear these unnatural arrangements.

THE MAN [*impatient and helpless*] You shouldnt have come among us. This is no place for you.

THE ELDERLY GENTLEMAN [*nerved by indignation*] May I ask why? I am a Vice-President of the Travellers' Club. I have been everywhere: I hold the record in the Club for civilized countries.

THE MAN. What is a civilized country?

THE ELDERLY GENTLEMAN. It is—well, it is a civilized country. [*Desperately*] I dont know: I—I—I—I shall go mad if you keep on asking me to tell you things that everybody knows. Countries where you can travel comfortably. Where there are good hotels. Excuse me; but, though you say you are ninety-four, you are worse company than a child of five with your eternal questions. Why not call me Daddy at once?

THE MAN. I did not know your name was Daddy.

THE ELDERLY GENTLEMAN. My name is Joseph Popham Bolge Bluebin Barlow, O.M.

THE MAN. That is five men's names. Daddy is shorter. And O.M. will not do here. It is our name for certain wild creatures, descendants of the aboriginal inhabitants of this coast. They used to be called the O'Mulligans. We will stick to Daddy.

THE ELDERLY GENTLEMAN. People will think I am your father.

THE MAN [*shocked*] Sh-sh! People here never allude to such relationships. It is not quite delicate, is it? What does it matter whether you are my father or not?

THE ELDERLY GENTLEMAN. My worthy nonagenarian friend: your faculties are totally decayed. Could you not find me a guide of my own age?

THE MAN. A young person?

THE ELDERLY GENTLEMAN. Certainly not. I cannot go about with a young person.

THE MAN. Why?

THE ELDERLY GENTLEMAN. Why! Why!! Why!!! Have you no moral sense?

THE MAN. I shall have to give you up. I cannot understand you.

THE ELDERLY GENTLEMAN. But you meant a young woman, didnt you?

THE MAN. I meant simply somebody of your own age. What difference does it make whether the person is a man or a woman?

THE ELDERLY GENTLEMAN. I could not have believed in the existence of such scandalous insensibility to the elementary decencies of human intercourse.

THE MAN. What are decencies?

THE ELDERLY GENTLEMAN [*shrieking*] Everyone asks me that.

THE MAN [*taking out a tuning-fork and using it as the woman did*] Zozim on Burrin Pier to Zoo Ennistymon I have found the discouraged shortliver he has been talking to a secondary and is much worse I am too old he is asking for someone of his own age or younger come if you can. [*He puts up his fork and turns to the Elderly Gentleman*]. Zoo is a girl of fifty, and rather childish at that. So perhaps she may make you happy.

THE ELDERLY GENTLEMAN. Make me happy! A bluestocking of fifty! Thank you.

THE MAN. Bluestocking? The effort to make out your meaning is fatiguing. Besides, you are talking too much to me: I am old enough to discourage you. Let us be silent untill Zoo comes. [*He turns his back on the Elderly Gentleman, and sits down on the edge of the pier, with his legs dangling over the water*].

THE ELDERLY GENTLEMAN. Certainly. I have no wish to force my conversation on any man who does not desire it. Perhaps you would like to take a nap. If so, pray do not stand on ceremony.

THE MAN. What is a nap?

THE ELDERLY GENTLEMAN [*exasperated, going to him and speaking with great precision and distinctness*] A nap, my friend, is a brief period of sleep which overtakes superannuated persons when they endeavour to entertain unwelcome visitors or to listen to scientific lectures. Sleep. Sleep. [*Bawling into his ear*] Sleep.

THE MAN. I tell you I am nearly a secondary. I never sleep.

THE ELDERLY GENTLEMAN [*awestruck*] Good Heavens!

A young woman with the number one on her cap arrives by land. She looks no older than Savvy Barnabas, whom she somewhat resembles, looked a thousand years before. Younger, if anything.

THE YOUNG WOMAN. Is this the patient?

THE MAN [*scrambling up*] This is Zoo. [*To Zoo*] Call him Daddy.

THE ELDERLY GENTLEMAN [*vehemently*] No.

THE MAN [*ignoring the interruption*] Bless you for taking him off my hands! I have had as much of him as I can bear. [*He goes down the steps and disappears*].

THE ELDERLY GENTLEMAN [*ironically taking off his hat and making a sweeping bow from the edge of the pier in the direction of the Atlantic Ocean*] Good afternoon, sir; and thank you very much for your extraordinary politeness, your exquisite consideration for my feelings, your courtly manners. Thank you from the bottom of my heart. [*Clapping his hat on again*] Pig! Ass!

ZOO [*laughs very heartily at him*]!!!

THE ELDERLY GENTLEMAN [*turning sharply on her*] Good afternoon, madam. I am sorry to have had to put your friend in his place; but I find that here as elsewhere it is necessary to assert myself if I am to be treated with proper consideration. I had hoped that my position as a guest would protect me from insult.

ZOO. Putting my friend in his place. That is some poetic expression, is it not? What does it mean?

THE ELDERLY GENTLEMAN. Pray, is there no one in these islands who understands plain English?

ZOO. Well, nobody except the oracles. They have to make a special historical study of what we call the dead thought.

THE ELDERLY GENTLEMAN. Dead thought! I have heard of the dead languages, but never of the dead thought.

ZOO. Well, thoughts die sooner than languages. I understand your language; but I do not always understand your thought. The oracles will understand you perfectly. Have you had your consultation yet?

THE ELDERLY GENTLEMAN. I did not come to consult the oracle, madam. I am here simply as a gentleman travelling for pleasure in the company of my daughter, who is the wife of the British Prime Minister, and of General Aufsteig, who, I may tell you in confidence, is really the Emperor of Turania, the greatest military genius of the age.

ZOO. Why should you travel for pleasure! Can you not enjoy yourself at home?

THE ELDERLY GENTLEMAN. I wish to see the world.

ZOO. It is too big. You can see a bit of it anywhere.

THE ELDERLY GENTLEMAN [*out of patience*] Damn it, madam, you dont want to spend your life looking at the same bit of it! [*Checking himself*] I beg your pardon for swearing in your presence.

ZOO. Oh! That is swearing, is it? I have read about that. It sounds quite pretty. Dammitmaddam, dammitmaddam, dammitmaddam, dammitmaddam. Say it is often as you please: I like it.

THE ELDERLY GENTLEMAN [*expanding with intense relief*] Bless you for those profane but familiar words! Thank you, thank you. For the first time since I landed in this terrible country I begin to feel at home. The strain which was driving me mad relaxes: I feel almost as if I were at the club. Excuse my taking the only available seat: I am not so young as I was. [*He sits on the bollard*]. Promise me that you will not hand me over to one of these dreadful tertiaries or secondaries or whatever you call them.

ZOO. Never fear. They had no business to give you in charge to Zozim. You see he is just on the verge of becoming a secondary; and these adolescents will give themselves the airs of tertiaries. You naturally feel more at home with a flapper like me. [*She makes herself comfortable on the sacks*].

THE ELDERLY GENTLEMAN. Flapper? What does that mean?

ZOO. It is an archaic word which we still use to describe a female who is no longer a girl and is not yet quite adult.

THE ELDERLY GENTLEMAN. A very agreeable age to associate with, I find. I am recovering rapidly. I have a sense of blossoming like a flower. May I ask your name?

ZOO. Zoo.

THE ELDERLY GENTLEMAN. Miss Zoo.

ZOO. Not Miss Zoo. Zoo.

THE ELDERLY GENTLEMAN. Precisely. Er—Zoo what?

ZOO. No. Not Zoo What. Zoo. Nothing but Zoo.

THE ELDERLY GENTLEMAN [*puzzled*] Mrs Zoo, perhaps.

ZOO. No. Zoo. Cant you catch it? Zoo.

THE ELDERLY GENTLEMAN. Of course. Believe me, I did not really think you were married: you are obviously too young; but here it is so hard to feel sure—er—

ZOO [*hopelessly puzzled*] What?

THE ELDERLY GENTLEMAN. Marriage makes a difference, you know. One can say things to a married lady that would perhaps be in questionable taste to anyone without that experience.

ZOO. You are getting out of my depth: I dont understand a word you are saying. Married and questionable taste convey nothing to me. Stop, though. Is married an old form of the word mothered?

THE ELDERLY GENTLEMAN. Very likely. Let us drop the subject. Pardon me for embarrassing you. I should not have mentioned it.

ZOO. What does embarrassing mean?

THE ELDERLY GENTLEMAN. Well, really! I should have thought that so natural and common a condition would be understood as long as human nature lasted. To embarrass is to bring a blush to the cheek.

ZOO. What is a blush?

THE ELDERLY GENTLEMAN [*amazed*] Dont you blush???

ZOO. Never heard of it. We have a word flush, meaning a rush of blood to the skin. I have noticed it in my babies, but not after the age of two.

THE ELDERLY GENTLEMAN. Your babies!!! I fear I am treading on very delicate ground; but your appearance is extremely youthful; and if I may ask how many—?

ZOO. Only four as yet. It is a long business with us. I specialize in babies. My first was such a success that they made me go on. I—

THE ELDERLY GENTLEMAN [*reeling on the bollard*] Oh! dear!

ZOO. Whats the matter? Anything wrong?

THE ELDERLY GENTLEMAN. In Heaven's name, madam,

how old are you?

ZOO. Fifty-six.

THE ELDERLY GENTLEMAN. My knees are trembling. I fear I am really ill. Not so young as I was.

ZOO. I noticed that you are not strong on your legs yet. You have many of the ways and weaknesses of a baby. No doubt that is why I feel called on to mother you. You certainly are a very silly little Daddy.

THE ELDERLY GENTLEMAN [*stimulated by indignation*] My name, I repeat, is Joseph Popham Bolge Bluebin Barlow, O.M.

ZOO. What a ridiculously long name! I cant call you all that. What did your mother call you?

THE ELDERLY GENTLEMAN. You recall the bitterest struggles of my childhood. I was sensitive on the point. Children suffer greatly from absurd nicknames. My mother thoughtlessly called me Iddy Toodles. I was called Iddy until I went to school, when I made my first stand for children's rights by insisting on being called at least Joe. At fifteen I refused to answer to anything shorter than Joseph. At eighteen I discovered that the name Joseph was supposed to indicate an unmanly prudery because of some old story about a Joseph who rejected the advances of his employer's wife: very properly in my opinion. I then became Popham to my family and intimate friends, and Mister Barlow to the rest of the world. My mother slipped back into Iddy when her faculties began to fail her, poor woman; but I could not resent that, at her age.

ZOO. Do you mean to say that your mother bothered about you after you were ten?

THE ELDERLY GENTLEMAN. Naturally, madam. She was my mother. What would you have had her do?

ZOO. Go on to the next, of course. After eight or nine children become quite uninteresting, except to themselves. I shouldnt know my two eldest if I met them.

THE ELDERLY GENTLEMAN [*again drooping*] I am dying. Let me die. I wish to die.

ZOO [*going to him quickly and supporting him*] Hold up. Sit up straight. Whats the matter?

THE ELDERLY GENTLEMAN [*faintly*] My spine, I think. Shock. Concussion.

ZOO [*maternally*] Pow wow wow! What is there to shock you? [*Shaking him playfully*] There! Sit up; and be good.

THE ELDERLY GENTLEMAN [*still feebly*] Thank you. I am better now.

ZOO [*resuming her seat on the sacks*] But what was all the rest of that long name for? There was a lot more of it. Blops Booby or something.

THE ELDERLY GENTLEMAN [*impressively*] Bolge Bluebin, madam: a historical name. Let me inform you that I can trace my family back for more than a thousand years, from the Eastern Empire to its ancient seat in these islands, to a time when two of my ancestors, Joyce Bolge and Hengist Horsa Bluebin, wrestled with one another for the prime ministership of the British Empire, and occupied that position successively with a glory of which we can in these degenerate days form but a faint conception. When I think of these mighty men, lions in war, sages in peace, not babblers and charlatans like the pigmies who now occupy their places in Baghdad, but strong silent men, ruling an empire on which the sun never set, my eyes fill with tears: my heart bursts with emotion: I feel that to have lived but to the dawn of manhood in their day, and then died for them, would have been a nobler and happier lot than the ignominious ease of my present longevity.

ZOO. Longevity! [*she laughs*].

THE ELDERLY GENTLEMAN. Yes, madam, r e l a t i v e longevity. As it is, I have to be content and proud to know that I am descended from both those heroes.

ZOO. You must be descended from every Briton who was alive in their time. Dont you know that?

THE ELDERLY GENTLEMAN. Do not quibble, madam. I bear their names, Bolge and Bluebin; and I hope I have inherited something of their majestic spirit. Well, they were born in these islands. I repeat, these islands were then, incredible as it now seems, the centre of the British Empire. When that centre shifted to Baghdad, and the Englishman at last returned to the true cradle of his race in Mesopotamia, the western islands were cast off, as they had been before by the Roman Empire. But it was to the British race, and in these islands, that the greatest miracle in history occurred.

ZOO. Miracle?

THE ELDERLY GENTLEMAN. Yes: the first man to live three hundred years was an Englishman. The first, that is, since the contemporaries of Methuselah.

ZOO. Oh, *that*!

THE ELDERLY GENTLEMAN. Yes, *that*, as you call it so flippantly. Are you aware, madam, that at that immortal moment the English race had lost intellectual credit to such an extent that they habitually spoke of one another as fatheads? Yet England is now a sacred grove to which statesmen from all over the earth come to consult English sages who speak with the experience of two and a half centuries of life. The land that once exported cotton shirts and hardware now exports nothing but wisdom. You see before you, madam, a man utterly weary of the week-end riverside hotels of the Euphrates, the minstrels and pierrots on the sands of the Persian Gulf, the toboggans and funiculars of the Hindoo Koosh. Can you wonder that I turn, with a hungry heart, to the mystery and beauty of these haunted islands, thronged with spectres from a magic past, made holy by the footsteps of the wise men of the West. Consider this island on which we stand, the last foothold of man on this side of the Atlantic: this Ireland, described by the earliest bards as an emerald gem set in a silver sea! Can I, a scion of the illustrious British race, ever forget that when the Empire transferred its seat to the East, and said to the turbulent Irish race which it had oppressed but never conquered, "At last we leave you to yourselves; and much good may it do you," the Irish as one man uttered the historic shout "No: we'll be damned if you do," and emigrated to the countries where there was still a Nationalist question, to India, Persia, and Corea, to Morocco, Tunis, and Tripoli. In these countries they were ever foremost in the struggle for national independence; and the world rang continually with the story of their sufferings and wrongs. And what poem can do justice to the end, when it came at last? Hardly two hundred years had elapsed when the claims of nationality were so universally conceded that there was no longer a single country on the face of the earth with a national grievance or a national movement. Think of the position of the Irish, who had lost all their political faculties by disuse except that of nationalist agitation, and who owed their position as the most interesting race on earth solely to their sufferings! The very countries they had helped to set free boycotted them as intolerable bores. The communities which had once idolized them as the incarnation of all that is adorable in the warm heart and witty brain, fled from them as from a pestilence. To regain their lost prestige, the Irish claimed the city of Jerusalem, on the ground that they were the lost tribes of Israel; but on their approach the Jews abandoned the city and redistributed themselves throughout Europe. It was then that these devoted Irishmen, not one of whom had ever seen Ireland, were counselled by an English Archbishop, the father of the oracles, to go back to their own country. This had never once occurred to them, because there was nothing to prevent them and nobody to forbid them. They jumped at the suggestion. They landed here: here in Galway Bay, on this very ground. When they reached the shore the older men and women flung themselves down and passionately kissed the soil of Ireland, calling on the young to embrace the earth that had borne their ancestors. But the young looked gloomily on, and said "There is no earth, only stone." You will see by looking round you why they said that: the fields here are of stone: the hills are capped with granite. They all left for England next day; and no Irishman ever again confessed to being Irish, even to his own children; so that when that generation passed away the Irish race vanished from human knowledge. And the dispersed Jews did the same lest they should be sent back to Palestine. Since then the world, bereft of its Jews and its Irish, has been a tame dull place. Is there no pathos for you in this story? Can you not understand now why I am come to visit the scene of this tragic effacement of a race of heroes and poets?

ZOO. We still tell our little children stories like that, to help them to understand. But such things do not happen really. That scene of the Irish landing here and kissing the ground might have happened to a hundred people. It couldnt have happened to a hundred thousand: you know that as well as I do. And what a ridiculous thing to call people Irish because they live in Ireland! you might as well call them Airish because they live in air. They must be just the same as other people. Why do you shortlivers persist in making up silly stories about the world and trying to act as if they were true? Contact with truth hurts and frightens you: you escape from it into an imaginary vacuum in which you can indulge your desires and hopes and loves and hates without any obstruction from the solid facts of life. You love to throw dust in your own eyes.

THE ELDERLY GENTLEMAN. It is my turn now, madam, to inform you that I do not understand a single word you are saying. I should have thought that the use of a vacuum for removing dust was a mark of civilization rather than of savagery.

ZOO [*giving him up as hopeless*] Oh, Daddy, Daddy: I can hardly believe that you are human, you are so stupid. It was well said of your people in the olden days, "Dust thou art; and to dust thou shalt return."

THE ELDERLY GENTLEMAN [*nobly*] My body is dust, madam: not my soul. What does it matter what my body is made of? the dust of the ground, the particles of the air, or even the slime of the ditch? The important thing is that when my Creator took it, whatever it was, He breathed into its nostrils the breath of life; and Man became a living soul. Yes, madam, a living soul. I am not the dust of the ground: I am a living soul. That is an exalting, a magnificent thought. It is also a great scientific fact. I am not interested in the chemicals and the microbes: I leave them to the chumps and noodles, to the blockheads and the muckrakers who are incapable of their own glorious destiny, and unconscious of their own divinity. They tell me there are leucocytes in my blood, and sodium and carbon in my flesh. I thank them for the information, and tell them that there are blackbeetles in my kitchen, washing soda in my laundry, and coal in my cellar. I do not deny their existence; but I keep them in their proper place, which is not, if I may be allowed to use an antiquated form of expression, the temple of the Holy Ghost. No doubt you think me behind the times; but I rejoice in my enlightenment; and I recoil from your ignorance, your blindness, your imbecility. Humanly I pity you. Intellectually I despise you.

ZOO. Bravo, Daddy! You have the root of the matter in you. You will not die of discouragement after all.

THE ELDERLY GENTLEMAN. I have not the smallest intention of doing so, madam. I am no longer young; and I have moments of weakness; but when I approach this subject the divine spark in me kindles and glows, the corruptible becomes incorruptible, and the mortal Bolge Bluebin Barlow puts on immortality. On this ground I am your equal, even if you survive me by ten thousand years.

ZOO. Yes; but what do we know about this breath of life that puffs you up so exaltedly? Just nothing. So let us shake hands as cultivated Agnostics, and change the subject.

THE ELDERLY GENTLEMAN. Cultivated fiddlesticks, madam! You cannot change this subject until the heavens and the earth pass away. I am not an Agnostic: I am a gentleman. When I believe a thing I say I believe it: when I dont believe it I say I dont believe it. I do not shirk my responsibilities by pretending that I know nothing and therefore can believe nothing. We cannot disclaim knowledge and shirk responsibility. We must proceed on assumptions of some sort or we cannot form a human society.

ZOO. The assumptions must be scientific, Daddy. We must live by science in the long run.

THE ELDERLY GENTLEMAN. I have the utmost respect, madam, for the magnificent discoveries which we owe to science. But any fool can make a discovery. Every baby has to discover more in the first years of its life than Roger Bacon ever discovered in his laboratory. When I was seven years old I discovered the sting of the wasp. But I do not ask you to worship me on that account. I assure you, madam, the merest mediocrities can discover the most surprising facts about the physical universe as soon as they are civilized enough to have time to study these things, and to invent instruments and apparatus for research. But what is the consequence? Their discoveries discredit the simple stories of our religion. At first we had no idea of astronomical space. We believed the sky to be only the ceiling of a room as large as the earth, with another room on top of it. Death was to us a going upstairs into that room, or, if we did not obey the priests, going downstairs into the coal cellar. We founded our religion, our morality, our laws, our lessons, our poems, our prayers, on that simple belief. Well, the moment men became astronomers and made telescopes, their belief perished. When they could no longer believe in the sky, they found that they could no longer believe in their Deity, because they had always thought of him as living in the sky. When the priests themselves ceased to believe in their Deity and began to believe in astronomy, they changed their name and their dress, and called themselves doctors and men of science. They set up a new religion in which there was no Deity, but only wonders and miracles, with scientific instruments and apparatus as the wonder workers. Instead of worshipping the greatness and wisdom of the Deity, men gaped foolishly at the million billion miles of space and worshipped the astronomer as infallible and omniscient. They built temples for his telescopes. Then they looked into their own bodies with microscopes, and found there, not the soul they had formerly believed in, but millions of micro-organisms; so they gaped at these as foolishly as at the millions of miles, and built microscope temples in which horrible sacrifices were offered. They even gave their own bodies to be sacrificed by the microscope man, who was worshipped, like the astronomer, as infallible and omniscient. Thus our discoveries, instead of increasing our wisdom, only destroyed the little childish wisdom we had. All I can grant you is that they increased our knowledge.

ZOO. Nonsense! Consciousness of a fact is not knowledge of it: if it were, the fish would know more of the sea than the geographers and the naturalists.

THE ELDERLY GENTLEMAN. That is an extremely acute remark, madam. The dullest fish could not possibly know less of the majesty of the ocean than many geographers and naturalists of my acquaintance.

ZOO. Just so. And the greatest fool on earth, by merely looking at a mariners' compass, may become conscious of the fact that the needle turns always to the pole. Is he any the less a fool with that consciousness than he was without it?

THE ELDERLY GENTLEMAN. Only a more conceited one, madam, no doubt. Still, I do not quite see how you can be aware of the existence of a thing without knowing it.

ZOO. Well, you can see a man without knowing him, can you not?

THE ELDERLY GENTLEMAN [*illuminated*] Oh how true! Of course, of course. There is a member of the Travellers' Club who has questioned the veracity of an experience of mine at the South Pole. I see that man almost every day when I am at home. But I refuse to know him.

ZOO. If you could see him much more distinctly through a magnifying glass, or examine a drop of his blood through a microscope, or dissect out all his organs and analyze them chemically, would you know him then?

THE ELDERLY GENTLEMAN. Certainly not. Any such investigation could only increase the disgust with which he inspires me, and make me more determined than ever not to know him on any terms.

ZOO. Yet you would be much more conscious of him, would you not?

THE ELDERLY GENTLEMAN. I should not allow that to commit me to any familiarity with the fellow. I have been twice at the Summer Sports at the South Pole; and this man pretended he had been to the North Pole, which can hardly be said to exist, as it is in the middle of the sea. He declared he had hung his hat on it.

ZOO [*laughing*] He knew that travellers are amusing only when they are telling lies. Perhaps if you looked at that man through a microscope you would find some good in him.

THE ELDERLY GENTLEMAN. I do not want to find any good in him. Besides, madam, what you have just said encourages me to utter an opinion of mine which is so advanced! so intellectually daring! that I have never ventured to confess to it before, lest I should be imprisoned for blasphemy, or even burnt alive.

ZOO. Indeed! What opinion is that?

THE ELDERLY GENTLEMAN [*after looking cautiously round*] I do not approve of microscopes. I never have.

ZOO. You call that advanced! Oh, Daddy, that is pure obscurantism.

THE ELDERLY GENTLEMAN. Call it so if you will, madam; but I maintain that it is dangerous to shew too much to people who do not know what they are looking at. I think that a man who is sane as long as he looks at the world through his own eyes is very likely to become a dangerous madman if he takes to looking at the world through telescopes and microscopes. Even when he is telling fairy stories about giants and dwarfs, the giants had better not be too big nor the dwarfs too small and too malicious. Before the microscope came, our fairy stories only made the children's flesh creep pleasantly, and did not frighten grown-up persons at all. But the microscope men terrified themselves and everyone else out of their wits with the invisible monsters they saw: poor harmless little things that die at the touch of a ray of sunshine, and are themselves the victims of all the diseases they are supposed to produce! Whatever the scientific people may say, imagination without microscopes was kindly and often courageous, because it worked on things of which it had some real knowledge. But imagination with microscopes, working on a terrifying spectacle of millions of grotesque creatures of whose nature it had no knowledge, became a cruel, terror-stricken, persecuting delirium. Are you aware, madam, that a general massacre of men of science took place in the twenty-first century of the pesudo-Christian era, when all their laboratories were demolished, and all their apparatus destroyed?

ZOO. Yes: the shortlived are as savage in their advances as in their relapses. But when Science crept back, it had been taught its place. The mere collectors of anatomical or chemical facts were not supposed to know more about Science than the collector of used postage stamps about international trade or literature. The scientific terrorist who was afraid to use a spoon or a tumbler until he had dipt it in some poisonous acid to kill the microbes, was no longer given titles, pensions, and monstrous powers over the bodies of other people: he was sent to an asylum, and treated there until his recovery. But all that is an old story: the extension of life to three hundred years has provided the human race with capable leaders, and made short work of such childish stuff.

THE ELDERLY GENTLEMAN [*pettishly*] You seem to credit every advance in civilization to your inordinately long lives. Do you not know that this question was familiar to men who died before they had reached my own age?

ZOO. Oh yes: one or two of them hinted at it in a feeble way. An ancient writer whose name has come down to us in several forms, such as Shakespear, Shelley, Sheridan, and Shoddy, has a remarkable passage about your dispositions being horridly shaken by thoughts beyond the reaches of your souls. That does not come to much, does it?

THE ELDERLY GENTLEMAN. At all events, madam I may

remind you, if you come to capping ages, that whatever your secondaries and tertiaries may be, you are younger than I am.

ZOO. Yes, Daddy; but it is not the number of years we have behind us, but the number we have before us, that makes us careful and responsible and determined to find out the truth about everything. What does it matter to you whether anything is true or not? your flesh is as grass: you come up like a flower, and wither in your second childhood. A lie will last your time: it will not last mine. If I knew I had to die in twenty years it would not be worth my while to educate myself: I should not bother about anything but having a little pleasure while I lasted.

THE ELDERLY GENTLEMAN. Young woman: you are mistaken. Shortlived as we are, we—the best of us, I mean—regard civilization and learning, art and science, as an ever-burning torch, which passes from the hand of one generation to the hand of the next, each generation kindling it to a brighter, prouder flame. Thus each lifetime, however short, contributes a brick to a vast and growing edifice, a page to a sacred volume, a chapter to a Bible, a Bible to a literature. We may be insects; but like the coral insect we build islands which become continents: like the bee we store sustenance for future communities. The individual perishes; but the race is immortal. The acorn of today is the oak of the next millennium. I throw my stone on the cairn and die; but later comers add another stone and yet another; and lo! a mountain. I—

ZOO [*interrupts him by laughing heartily at him*] !!!!!!

THE ELDERLY GENTLEMAN [*with offended dignity*] May I ask what I have said that calls for this merriment?

ZOO. Oh, Daddy, Daddy, Daddy, you are a funny little man, with your torches, and your flames, and your bricks and edifices and pages and volumes and chapters and coral insects and bees and acorns and stones and mountains.

THE ELDERLY GENTLEMAN. Metaphors, madam. Metaphors merely.

ZOO. Images, images, images. I was talking about men, not about images.

THE ELDERLY GENTLEMAN. I was illustrating—not, I hope, quite infelicitously—the great march of Progress. I was shewing you how, shortlived as we orientals are, mankind gains in stature from generation to generation, from epoch to epoch, from barbarism to civilization, from civilization to perfection.

ZOO. I see. The father grows to be six feet high, and hands on his six feet to his son, who adds another six feet and becomes twelve feet high, and hands his twelve feet on to his son, who is full-grown at eighteen feet, and so on. In a thousand years you would all be three or four miles high. At that rate your ancestors Bilge and Bluebeard, whom you call giants, must have been about quarter of an inch high.

THE ELDERLY GENTLEMAN. I am not here to bandy quibbles and paradoxes with a girl who blunders over the greatest names in history. I am in earnest. I am treating a solemn theme seriously. I never said that the son of a man six feet high would be twelve feet high.

ZOO. You didnt mean that?

THE ELDERLY GENTLEMAN. Most certainly not.

ZOO. Then you didnt mean anything. Now listen to me, you little ephemeral thing. I knew quite well what you meant by your torch handed on from generation to generation. But every time that torch is handed on, it dies down to the tiniest spark; and the man who gets it can rekindle it only by his own light. You are no taller than Bilge or Bluebeard; and you are no wiser. Their wisdom, such as it was, perished with them: so did their strength, if their strength ever existed outside your imagination. I do not know how old your are: you look about five hundred—

THE ELDERLY GENTLEMAN. Five hundred! Really, madam—

ZOO [*continuing*]; but I know, of course, that you are an ordinary shortliver. Well, your wisdom is only such wisdom as a man can have before he has had experience enough to distinguish his wisdom from his folly, his destiny from his delusions, his—

THE ELDERLY GENTLEMAN. In short, such wisdom as your own.

ZOO. No, no, no, no. How often must I tell you that we are made wise not by the recollections of our past, but by the responsibilities of our future. I shall be more reckless when I am a tertiary than I am today. If you cannot understand that, at least you must admit that I have learnt from tertiaries. I have seen their work and lived under their institutions. Like all young things I rebelled against them; and in their hunger for new lights and new ideas they listened to me and encouraged me to rebel. But my ways did not work; and theirs did; and they were able to tell me why. They have no power over me except that power: they refuse all other power; and the consequence is that there are no limits to their power except the limits they set themselves. You are a child governed by children, who make so many mistakes and are so naughty that you are in continual rebellion against them; and as they can never convince you that they are right: they can govern you only by beating you, imprisoning you, torturing you, killing you if you disobey them without being strong enough to kill or torture them.

THE ELDERLY GENTLEMAN. That may be an unfortunate fact. I condemn it and deplore it. But our minds are greater than the facts. We know better. The greatest ancient teachers, followed by the galaxy of Christs who arose in the twentieth century, not to mention such comparatively modern spiritual leaders as Blitherinjam, Tosh, and Spiffkins, all taught that punishment and revenge, coercion and militarism, are mistakes, and that the golden rule—

ZOO [*interrupting*] Yes, yes, yes, Daddy: we longlived people know that quite well. But did any of their disciples ever succeed in governing you for a single day on their Christlike principles? It is not enough to know what is good: you must be able to do it. They couldnt do it because they did not live long enough to find out how to do it, or to outlive the childish passions that prevented them from really wanting to do it. You know very well that they could only keep order—such as it was—by the very coercion and militarism they were denouncing and deploring. They had actually to kill one another for preaching their own gospel, or be killed themselves.

THE ELDERLY GENTLEMAN. The blood of the martyrs, madam, is the seed of the Church.

ZOO. More images, Daddy! The blood of the shortlived falls on stony ground.

THE ELDERLY GENTLEMAN [*rising, very testy*] You are simply mad on the subject of longevity. I wish you would change it. It is rather personal and in bad taste. Human nature is human nature, longlived or shortlived, and always will be.

ZOO. Then you give up the idea of progress? You cry off the torch, and the brick, and the acorn, and all the rest of it?

THE ELDERLY GENTLEMAN. I do nothing of the sort. I stand for progress and for freedom broadening down from precedent to precedent.

ZOO. You are certainly a true Briton.

THE ELDERLY GENTLEMAN. I am proud of it. But in your mouth I feel that the compliment hides some insult; so I do not thank you for it.

ZOO. All I meant was that though Britons sometimes say quite clever things and deep things as well as silly and shallow things, they always forget them ten minutes after they have uttered them.

THE ELDERLY GENTLEMAN. Leave it at that, madam: leave it at that. [*He sits down again*]. Even a Pope is not expected to be continually pontificating. Our flashes of inspiration shew that our hearts are in the right place.

ZOO. Of course. You cannot keep your heart in any place but the right place.

THE ELDERLY GENTLEMAN. Tcha!

ZOO. But you can keep your hands in the wrong place. In your neighbors' pockets, for example. So, you see, it is your hands that really matter.

THE ELDERLY GENTLEMAN [*exhausted*] Well, a woman must have the last word. I will not dispute it with you.

ZOO. Good. Now let us go back to the really interesting subject of our discussion. You remember? The slavery of the shortlived to images and metaphors.

THE ELDERLY GENTLEMAN [*aghast*] Do you mean to say, madam, that after having talked my head off, and reduced me to despair and silence by your intolerable loquacity, you actually propose to begin all over again? I shall leave you at once.

ZOO. You must not. I am your nurse; and you must stay with me.

THE ELDERLY GENTLEMAN. I absolutely decline to do anything of the sort [*he rises and walks away with marked dignity*].

ZOO [*using her tuning-fork*] Zoo on Burrin Pier to Oracle Police at Ennistymon have you got me? . . . What? . . . I am picking you up now but you are flat to my pitch. . . . Just a shade sharper. . . . Thats better: still a little more. . . . Got you: right. Isolate Burrin Pier quick.

THE ELDERLY GENTLEMAN [*is heard to yell*] Oh!

ZOO [*still intoning*] Thanks. . . . Oh nothing serious I am nursing a shortliver and the silly creature has run away he has discouraged himself very badly by gadding about and talking to secondaries and I must keep him strictly to heel.

The Elderly Gentleman returns, indignant.

ZOO. Here he is you can release the Pier thanks. Goodbye. [*She puts up her tuning-fork*].

THE ELDERLY GENTLEMAN. This is outrageous. When I tried to step off the pier on to the road, I received a shock, followed by an attack of pins and needles which ceased only when I stepped back on to the stones.

ZOO. Yes: there is an electric hedge there. It is a very old and very crude method of keeping animals from straying.

THE ELDERLY GENTLEMAN. We are perfectly familiar with it in Baghdad, madam; but I little thought I should live to have it ignominiously applied to myself. You have actually

Kiplingized me.

ZOO. Kiplingized! What is that?

THE ELDERLY GENTLEMAN. About a thousand years ago there were two authors named Kipling. One was an eastern and a writer of merit: the other, being a western, was of course only an amusing barbarian. He is said to have invented the electric hedge. I consider that in using it on me you have taken a very great liberty.

ZOO. What is a liberty?

THE ELDERLY GENTLEMAN [*exasperated*] I shall not explain, madam. I believe you know as well as I do. [*He sits down on the bollard in dudgeon*].

ZOO. No: even you can tell me things I do not know. Havnt you noticed that all the time you have been here we have been asking you questions?

THE ELDERLY GENTLEMAN. Noticed it! It has almost driven me mad. Do you see my white hair? It was hardly grey when I landed: there were patches of its original auburn still distinctly discernible.

ZOO. That is one of the symptoms of discouragement. But have you noticed something much more important to yourself: that is, that you have never asked us any questions, although we know so much more than you do?

THE ELDERLY GENTLEMAN. I am not a child, madam. I believe I have had occasion to say that before. And I am an experienced traveller. I know that what the traveller observes must really exist, or he could not observe it. But what the natives tell him is invariably pure fiction.

ZOO. Not here, Daddy. With us life is too long for telling lies. They all get found out. Youd better ask me questions while you have the chance.

THE ELDERLY GENTLEMAN. If I have occasion to consult the oracle I shall address myself to a proper one: to a tertiary: not to a primary flapper playing at being an oracle. If you are a nurserymaid, attend to your duties; and do not presume to ape your elders.

ZOO [*rising ominously and reddening*] You silly—

THE ELDERLY GENTLEMAN [*thundering*] Silence! Do you hear! Hold your tongue.

ZOO. Something very disagreeable is happening to me. I feel hot all over. I have a horrible impulse to injure you. What have you done to me?

THE ELDERLY GENTLEMAN [*triumphant*] Aha! I have made you blush. Now you know what blushing means. Blushing with shame!

ZOO. Whatever you are doing, it is something so utterly evil that if you do not stop I will kill you.

THE ELDERLY GENTLEMAN [*apprehending his danger*] Doubtless you think it safe to threaten an old man—

ZOO [*fiercely*] Old! You are a child: an evil child. We kill evil children here. We do it even against our own wills by instinct. Take care.

THE ELDERLY GENTLEMAN [*rising with crestfallen courtesy*] I did not mean to hurt your feelings. I—[*swallowing the apology with an effort*] I beg your pardon. [*He takes off his hat, and bows*].

ZOO. What does that mean?

THE ELDERLY GENTLEMAN. I withdraw what I said.

ZOO. How can you withdraw what you said?

THE ELDERLY GENTLEMAN. I can say no more than that I am sorry.

ZOO. You have reason to be. That hideous sensation you gave me is subsiding; but you have had a very narrow escape. Do not attempt to kill me again; for at the first sign in your voice or face I shall strike you dead.

THE ELDERLY GENTLEMAN. *I* attempt to kill you! What a monstrous accusation!

ZOO [*frowns*]!

THE ELDERLY GENTLEMAN [*prudently correcting himself*] I mean misunderstanding. I never dreamt of such a thing. Surely you cannot believe that I am a murderer.

ZOO. I k n o w you are a murderer. It is not merely that you threw words at me as if they were stones, meaning to hurt me. It was the instinct to kill that you roused in me. I did not know it was in my nature: never before has it wakened and sprung out at me, warning me to kill or be killed. I must now reconsider my whole political position. I am no longer a Conservative.

THE ELDERLY GENTLEMAN [*dropping his hat*] Gracious Heavens! you have lost your senses. I am at the mercy of a madwoman: I might have known it from the beginning. I can bear no more of this. [*Offering his chest for the sacrifice*] Kill me at once; and much good may my death do you!

ZOO. It would be useless unless all the other shortlivers were killed at the same time. Besides, it is a measure which should be taken politically and constitutionally, not privately. However, I am prepared to discuss it with you.

THE ELDERLY GENTLEMAN. No, no, no. I had much rather discuss your intention of withdrawing from the Conservative party. How the Conservatives have tolerated your opinions so far is more than I can imagine: I can only conjecture that you have contributed very liberally to the party funds. [*He picks up his hat, and sits down again*].

ZOO. Do not babble so senselessly: our chief political controversy is the most momentous in the world for you and your like.

THE ELDERLY GENTLEMAN [*interested*] Indeed? Pray, may I ask what it is? I am a keen politician, and may perhaps be of some use. [*He puts on his hat, cocking it slightly*].

ZOO. We have two great parties: the Conservative party and the Colonization party. The Colonizers are of opinion that we should increase our numbers and colonize. The Conservatives hold that we should stay as we are, confined to these islands, a race apart, wrapped up in the majesty of our wisdom on a soil held as holy ground for us by an adoring world, with our sacred frontier traced beyond dispute by the sea. They contend that it is our destiny to rule the world, and that even when we were shortlived we did so. They say that our power and our peace depend on our remoteness, our exclusiveness, our separation, and the restriction of our numbers. Five minutes ago that was my political faith. Now

I do not think there should be any shortlived people at all. [*She throws herself again carelessly on the sacks*].

THE ELDERLY GENTLEMAN. Am I to infer that you deny my right to live because I allowed myself—perhaps injudiciously—to give you a slight scolding?

ZOO. Is it worth living for so short a time? Are you any good to yourself?

THE ELDERLY GENTLEMAN [*stupent*] Well, upon my soul!

ZOO. It is such a very little soul. You only encourage the sin of pride in us, and keep us looking down at you instead of up to something higher than ourselves.

THE ELDERLY GENTLEMAN. Is not that a selfish view, madam? Think of the good you do us by your oracular counsels!

ZOO. What good have our counsels ever done you? You come to us for advice when you know you are in difficulties. But you never know you are in difficulties until twenty years after you have made the mistakes that led to them; and then it is too late. You cannot understand our advice: you often do more mischief by trying to act on it than if you had been left to your own childish devices. If you were not childish you would not come to us at all: you would learn from experience that your consultations of the oracle are never of any real help to you. You draw wonderful imaginary pictures of us, and write fictitious tales and poems about our beneficent operations in the past, our wisdom, our justice, our mercy: stories in which we often appear as sentimental dupes of your prayers and sacrifices; but you do it only to conceal from yourselves the truth that you are incapable of being helped by us. Your Prime Minister pretends that he has come to be guided by the oracle; but we are not deceived: we know quite well that he has come here so that when he goes back he may have the authority and dignity of one who has visited the holy islands and spoken face to face with the ineffable ones. He will pretend that all the measures he wishes to take for his own purposes have been enjoined on him by the oracle.

THE ELDERLY GENTLEMAN. But you forget that the answers

of the oracle cannot be kept secret or misrepresented. They are written and promulgated. The Leader of the Opposition can obtain copies. All the nations know them. Secret diplomacy has been totally abolished.

ZOO. Yes: you publish documents; but they are garbled or forged. And even if you published our real answers it would make no difference, because the shortlived cannot interpret the plainest writings. Your scriptures command you in the plainest terms to do exactly the contrary of everything your own laws and chosen rulers command and execute. You cannot defy Nature. It is a law of Nature that there is a fixed relation between conduct and length of life.

THE ELDERLY GENTLEMAN. I have never heard of any such law, madam.

ZOO. Well, you are hearing of it now.

THE ELDERLY GENTLEMAN. Let me tell you that we shortlivers, as you call us, have lengthened our lives very considerably.

ZOO. How?

THE ELDERLY GENTLEMAN. By saving time. By enabling men to cross the ocean in an afternoon, and to see and speak to one another when they are thousands of miles apart. We hope shortly to organize their labor, and press natural forces into their service, so scientifically that the burden of labor will cease to be perceptible, leaving common men more leisure than they will know what to do with.

ZOO. Daddy: the man whose life is lengthened in this way may be busier than a savage; but the difference between such men living seventy years and those living three hundred would be all the greater; for to a shortliver increase of years is only increase of sorrow; but to a longliver every extra year is a prospect which forces him to stretch his faculties to the utmost to face it. Therefore I say that we who live three hundred years can be of no use to you who live less than a hundred, and that our true destiny is not to advise and govern you, but to supplant and supersede you. In that faith I now declare myself a Colonizer and an Exterminator.

THE ELDERLY GENTLEMAN. Oh, steady! steady! Pray! pray! Reflect, I implore you. It is possible to colonize without exterminating the natives. Would you treat us less mercifully than our barbarous forefathers treated the Redskin and the Negro? Are we not, as Britons, entitled at least to some reservations?

ZOO. What is the use of prolonging the agony? You would perish slowly in our presence, no matter what we did to preserve you. You were almost dead when I took charge of you today, merely because you had talked for a few minutes to a secondary. Besides, we have our own experience to go upon. Have you never heard that our children occasionally revert to the ancestral type, and are born short-lived?

THE ELDERLY GENTLEMAN [*eagerly*] Never. I hope you will not be offended if I say that it would be a great comfort to me if I could be placed in charge of one of those normal individuals.

ZOO. Abnormal, you mean. What you ask is impossible: we weed them all out.

THE ELDERLY GENTLEMAN. When you say that you weed them out, you send a cold shiver down my spine. I hope you dont mean that you—that you—that you assist Nature in any way?

ZOO. Why not? Have you not heard the saying of the Chinese sage Dee Ning, that a good garden needs weeding? But it is not necessary for us to interfere. We are naturally rather particular as to the conditions on which we consent to live. One does not mind the accidental loss of an arm or a leg or an eye: after all, no one with two legs is unhappy because he has not three; so why should a man with one be unhappy because he has not two? But infirmities of mind and temper are quite another matter. If one of us has no self-control, or is too weak to bear the strain of our truthful life without wincing, or is tormented by depraved appetites and superstitions, or is unable to keep free from pain and depression, he naturally becomes discouraged, and refuses to live.

THE ELDERLY GENTLEMAN. Good Lord! Cuts his throat, do you mean?

ZOO. No: why should he cut his throat? He simply dies. He wants to. He is out of countenance, as we call it.

THE ELDERLY GENTLEMAN. Well!!! But suppose he is depraved enough not to want to die, and to settle the difficulty by killing all the rest of you?

ZOO. Oh, he is one of the thoroughly degenerate shortlivers whom we occasionally produce. He emigrates.

THE ELDERLY GENTLEMAN. And what becomes of him then?

ZOO. You shortlived people always think very highly of him. You accept him as what you call a great man.

THE ELDERLY GENTLEMAN. You astonish me; and yet I must admit that what you tell me accounts for a great deal of the little I know of the private life of our great men. We must be very convenient to you as a dumping place for your failures.

ZOO. I admit that.

THE ELDERLY GENTLEMAN. Good. Then if you carry out your plan of colonization, and leave no shortlived countries in the world, what will you do with your undesirables?

ZOO. Kill them. Our tertiaries are not at all squeamish about killing.

THE ELDERLY GENTLEMAN. Gracious Powers!

ZOO [*glancing up at the sun*] Come. It is just sixteen o'clock; and you have to join your party at half-past in the temple in Galway.

THE ELDERLY GENTLEMAN [*rising*] Galway! Shall I at last be able to boast of having seen that magnificent city?

ZOO. You will be disappointed: we have no cities. There is a temple of the oracle: that is all.

THE ELDERLY GENTLEMAN. Alas! and I came her to fulfil two long-cherished dreams. One was to see Galway. It has been said, "See Galway and die." The other was to contemplate the ruins of London.

ZOO. Ruins! We do not tolerate ruins. Was London a

place of any importance?

THE ELDERLY GENTLEMAN [*amazed*] What! London! It was the mightiest city of antiquity. [*Rhetorically*] Situate just where the Dover Road crosses the Thames, it—

ZOO [*curtly interrupting*] There is nothing there now. Why should anybody pitch on such a spot to live? The nearest houses are at a place called Strand-on-the-Green: it is very old. Come. We shall go across the water. [*She goes down the steps*]. thus passes away the glory of the world.

THE ELDERLY GENTLEMAN. Sic transit gloria mundi!

ZOO [*from below*] What did you say?

THE ELDERLY GENTLEMAN [*despairingly*] Nothing. You would not understand. [*He goes down the steps*].

ACT II

A *COURTYARD before the columned portico of a temple. The temple door is in the middle of the portico. A veiled and robed woman of majestic carriage passes along behind the columns towards the entrance. From the opposite direction a man of compact figure, clean-shaven, saturnine, and self-centred: in short, very like Napoleon I., and wearing a military uniform of Napoleonic cut, marches with measured steps; places his hand in his lapel in the traditional manner; and fixes the woman with his eye. She stops, her attitude expressing haughty amazement at his audacity. He is on her right: she on his left.*

NAPOLEON [*impressively*] I am the Man of Destiny.

THE VEILED WOMAN [*unimpressed*] How did you get in here?

NAPOLEON. I walked in. I go on until I am stopped. I never am stopped. I tell you I am the Man of Destiny.

THE VEILED WOMAN. You will be a man of very short destiny if you wander about here without one of our children to guide you. I suppose you belong to the Baghdad envoy.

NAPOLEON. I came with him; but I do not belong to him. I belong to myself. Direct me to the oracle if you can. If not, do not waste my time.

THE VEILED WOMAN. Your time, poor creature, is short. I will not waste it. Your envoy and his party will be here presently. The consultation of the oracle is arranged for them, and will take place according to the prescribed ritual. You can wait here until they come [*she turns to go into the temple*].

NAPOLEON. I never wait. [*She stops*]. The prescribed ritual is, I believe, the classical one of the pythoness on her tripod, the intoxicating fumes arising from the abyss, the convulsions of the priestess as she delivers the message of the God, and so on. That sort of thing does not impose on me: I use it myself to impose on simpletons. I believe that what is, is. I know that what is not, is not. The antics of a woman sitting on a tripod and pretending to be drunk do not interest me. Her words are put into her mouth, not by a god, but by a man three hundred years old, who has had the capacity to profit by his experience. I wish to speak to that man face to face, without mummery or imposture.

THE VEILED WOMAN. You seem to be an unusually sensible person. But there is no old man. I am the oracle on duty today. I am on my way now to take my place on the tripod, and go through the usual mummery, as you rightly call it, to impress your friend the envoy. As you are superior to that kind of thing, you may consult me now. [*She leads the way into the middle of the courtyard*]. What do you want to know?

NAPOLEON [*following her*] Madam: I have not come all this way to discuss matters of State with a woman. I must ask you to direct me to one of your oldest and ablest men.

THE ORACLE. None of our oldest and ablest men or women would dream of wasting their time on you. You would die of discouragement in their presence in less than three hours.

NAPOLEON. You can keep this idle fable of discouragement for people credulous enough to be intimidated by it, madam. I do not believe in metaphysical forces.

THE ORACLE. No one asks you to. A field is something physical, is it not. Well, I have a field.

NAPOLEON. I have several million fields. I am Emperor of Turania.

THE ORACLE. You do not understand. I am not speaking of an agricultural field. Do you not know that every mass of matter in motion carries with it an invisible gravitational field, every magnet an invisible magnetic field, and every living organism a mesmeric field? Even you have a perceptible mesmeric field. Feeble as it is, it is the strongest I have yet observed in a shortliver.

NAPOLEON. By no means feeble, madam. I understand you now; and I may tell you that the strongest characters blench in my presence, and submit to my domination. But I do not call that a physical force.

THE ORACLE. What else do you call it, pray? Our physicists deal with it. Our mathematicians express its measurements in algebraic equations.

NAPOLEON. Do you mean that they could measure mine?

THE ORACLE. Yes: by a figure infinitely near to zero. Even in us the force is negligible during our first century of life. In our second century it develops quickly, and becomes dangerous to shortlivers who venture into its field. If I were not veiled and robed in insulating material you could not endure my presence; and I am still a young woman: one hundred and seventy if you wish to know exactly.

NAPOLEON [*folding his arms*] I am not intimidated: no woman alive, old or young, can put me out of countenance. Unveil, madam. Disrobe. You will move this temple as easily as shake me.

THE ORACLE. Very well [*she throws back her veil*].

NAPOLEON [*shrieking, staggering, and covering his eyes*] No. Stop. Hide your face again. [*Shutting his eyes and distractedly clutching at his throat and heart*] Let me go. Help! I am dying.

THE ORACLE. Do you still wish to consult an older person?

NAPOLEON. No, no. The veil, the veil, I beg you.

THE ORACLE [*replacing the veil*] So.

NAPOLEON. Ouf! One cannot always be at one's best. Twice before in my life I have lost my nerve and behaved like a poltroon. But I warn you not to judge my quality by these involuntary moments.

THE ORACLE. I have no occasion to judge of your quality. You want my advice. Speak quickly; or I shall go about my business.

NAPOLEON [*After a moment's hesitation, sinks respectfully on one knee*] I—

THE ORACLE. Oh, rise, rise. Are you so foolish as to offer me this mummery which even you despise?

NAPOLEON [*rising*] I knelt in spite of myself. I compliment you on your impressiveness, madam.

THE ORACLE [*impatiently*] Time! time! time! time!

NAPOLEON. You will not grudge me the necessary time, madam, when you know my case. I am a man gifted with a certain specific talent in a degree altogether extraordinary. I am not otherwise a very extraordinary person: my family is not influential; and without this talent I should cut no particular figure in the world.

THE ORACLE. Why cut a figure in the world?

NAPOLEON. Superiority will make itself felt, madam. But when I say I possess this talent I do not express myself accurately. The truth is that my talent possesses me. It is genius. It drives me to exercise it. I *must* exercise it. I am great when I exercise it. At other moments I am nobody.

THE ORACLE. Well, exercise it. Do you need an oracle to tell you that?

NAPOLEON. Wait. This talent involves the shedding of human blood.

THE ORACLE. Are you a surgeon, or a dentist?

NAPOLEON. Psha! You do not appreciate me, madam. I mean the shedding of oceans of blood, the death of millions of men.

THE ORACLE. They object, I suppose.

NAPOLEON. Not at all. They adore me.

THE ORACLE. Indeed!

NAPOLEON. I have never shed blood with my own hand. They kill each other: they die with shouts of triumph on their lips. Those who die cursing do not curse me. My talent is to organize this slaughter; to give mankind this terrible joy which they call glory; to let loose the devil in them that peace has bound in chains.

THE ORACLE. And you? Do you share their joy?

NAPOLEON. Not at all. What satisfaction is it to me to see one fool pierce the entrails of another with a bayonet? I am a man of princely character, but of simple personal tastes and habits. I have the virtues of a laborer: industry and indifference to personal comfort. But I must rule, because I am so superior to other men that it is intolerable to me to be misruled by them. Yet only as a slayer can I become a ruler. I cannot be great as a writer: I have tried and failed. I have no talent as a sculptor or painter; and as lawyer, preacher, doctor, or actor, scores of second-rate men can do as well as

I, or better. I am not even a diplomatist: I can only play my trump card of force. What I c a n do is to organize war. Look at me! I seem a man like other men, because nine-tenths of me is common humanity. But the other tenth is a faculty for seeing things as they are that no other man possesses.

THE ORACLE. You mean that you have no imagination?

NAPOLEON [*forcibly*] I mean that I have the only imagination worth having: the power of imagining things as they are, even when I cannot see them. You feel yourself my superior, I know: nay, you are my superior: have I not bowed my knee to you by instinct? Yet I challenge you to a test of our respective powers. Can you calculate what the mathematicians call vectors, without putting a single algebraic symbol on paper? Can you launch ten thousand men across a frontier and a chain of mountains and know to a mile exactly where they will be at the end of seven weeks? The rest is nothing: I got it all from the books at my military school. Now this great game of war, this playing with armies as other men play with bowls and skittles, is one which I must go on playing, partly because a man must do what he can and not what he would like to do, and partly because, if I stop, I immediately lose my power and become a beggar in the land where I now make men drunk with glory.

THE ORACLE. No doubt then you wish to know how to extricate yourself from this unfortunate position?

NAPOLEON. It is not generally considered unfortunate, madam. Supremely fortunate rather.

THE ORACLE. If you think so, go on making them drunk with glory. Why trouble me with their folly and your vectors?

NAPOLEON. Unluckily, madam, men are not only heroes: they are also cowards. They desire glory; but they dread death.

THE ORACLE. Why should they? Their lives are too short to be worth living. That is why they think your game of war worth playing.

NAPOLEON. They do not look at it quite in that way. The

most worthless soldier wants to live for ever. To make him risk being killed by the enemy I have to convince him that if he hesitates he will inevitably be shot at dawn by his own comrades for cowardice.

THE ORACLE. And if his comrades refuse to shoot him?

NAPOLEON. They will be shot too, of course.

THE ORACLE. By whom?

NAPOLEON. By their comrades.

THE ORACLE. And if t h e y refuse?

NAPOLEON. Up to a certain point they do not refuse.

THE ORACLE. But when that point is reached, you have to do the shooting yourself, eh?

NAPOLEON. Unfortunately, madam, when that point is reached, they shoot m e.

THE ORACLE. Mf! It seems to me they might as well shoot you first as last. Why dont they?

NAPOLEON. Because their love of fighting, their desire for glory, their shame of being branded as dastards, their instinct to test themselves in terrible trials, their fear of being killed or enslaved by the enemy, their belief that they are defending their hearths and homes, overcome their natural cowardice, and make them willing not only to risk their own lives but to kill everyone who refuses to take that risk. But if war continues too long, there comes a time when the soldiers, and also the taxpayers who are supporting and munitioning them, reach a condition which they describe as being fed up. The troops have proved their courage, and want to go home and enjoy in peace the glory it has earned them. Besides, the risk of death for each soldier becomes a certainty if the fighting goes on for ever: he hopes to escape for six months, but knows he cannot escape for six years. The risk of bankruptcy for the citizen becomes a certainty in the same way. Now what does this mean for me?

THE ORACLE. Does that matter in the midst of such calamity?

NAPOLEON. Psha! madam: it is the only thing that matters: the value of human life is the value of the greatest living man. Cut off that infinitesimal layer of grey matter which distinguishes my brain from that of the common man, and you cut down the stature of humanity from that of a giant to that of a nobody. I matter supremely: my soldiers do not matter at all: there are plenty more where they came from. If you kill me, or put a stop to my activity (it is the same thing), the nobler part of human life perishes. You must save the world from that catastrophe, madam. War has made me popular, powerful, famous, historically immortal. But I foresee that if I go on to the end it will leave me execrated, dethroned, imprisoned, perhaps executed. Yet if I stop fighting I commit suicide as a great man and become a common one. How am I to escape the horns of this tragic dilemma? Victory I can guarantee: I am invincible. But the cost of victory is the demoralization, the depopulation, the ruin of the victors no less than of the vanquished. How am I to satisfy my genius by fighting until I die? that is my question to you.

THE ORACLE. Were you not rash to venture into these sacred islands with such a question on your lips? Warriors are not popular here, my friend.

NAPOLEON. If a soldier were restrained by such a consideration, madam, he would no longer be a soldier. Besides, [*he produces a pistol*] I have not come unarmed.

THE ORACLE. What is that thing?

NAPOLEON. It is an instrument of my profession, madam. I raise this hammer; I point the barrel at you; I pull this trigger that is against my forefinger; and you fall dead.

THE ORACLE. Shew it to me [*she puts out her hand to take it from him*].

NAPOLEON [*retreating a step*] Pardon me, madam. I never trust my life in the hands of a person over whom I have no control.

THE ORACLE [*sternly*] Give it to me [*she raises her hand to her veil*].

NAPOLEON [*dropping the pistol and covering his eyes*] Quarter! Kamerad! Take it, madam [*he kicks it towards her*]:

I surrender.

THE ORACLE. Give me that thing. Do you expect me to stoop for it?

NAPOLEON [*taking his hands from his eyes with an effort*] A poor victory, madam [*he picks up the pistol and hands it to her*]: there was no vector strategy needed to win it. [*Making a pose of his humiliation*] But enjoy your triumph: you have made me—ME! Cain Adamson Charles Napoleon! Emperor of Turania! cry for quarter.

THE ORACLE. The way out of your difficulty, Cain Adamson, is very simple.

NAPOLEON [*eagerly*] Good. What is it?

THE ORACLE. To die before the tide of glory turns. Allow me [*she shoots him*].

He falls with a shriek. She throws the pistol away and goes haughtily into the temple.

NAPOLEON [*scrambling to his feet*] Murderess! Monster! She-devil! Unnatural, inhuman wretch! You deserve to be hanged, guillotined, broken on the wheel, burnt alive. No sense of the sacredness of human life! No thought for my wife and children! Bitch! Sow! Wanton! [*He picks up the pistol*]. And missed me at five yards! Thats a woman all over.

He is going away whence he came when Zoo arrives and confronts him at the head of a party consisting of the British Envoy, the Elderly Gentleman, the Envoy's wife, and her daughter, aged about eighteen. The Envoy, a typical politician, looks like an imperfectly reformed criminal disguised by a good tailor. The dress of the ladies is coeval with that of the Elderly Gentleman, and suitable for public official ceremonies in western capitals at the XVIII-XIX fin de siècle.

They file in under the portico. Zoo immediately comes out imperiously to Napoleon's right, whilst the Envoy's wife hurries effusively to his left. The Envoy meanwhile passes along behind the columns to the door, followed by his daughter. The Elderly Gentleman stops just where he entered, to see why Zoo has swooped so abruptly on the Emperor of Turania.

ZOO [*to Napoleon, severely*] What are you doing here by

yourself? You have no business to go about here alone. What was that noise just now? What is that in your hand?

Napoleon glares at her in speechless fury; pockets the pistol; and produces a whistle.

THE ENVOY'S WIFE. Arnt you coming with us to the oracle, sire?

NAPOLEON. To hell with the oracle, and with you too [*he turns to go*]!

THE ENVOY'S WIFE } [*together*] { Oh, sire!!
ZOO } { Where are you going?

NAPOLEON. To fetch the police [*He goes out past Zoo, almost jostling her, and blowing piercing blasts on his whistle*].

ZOO [*whipping out her tuning-fork and intoning*] Hallo Galway Central. [*The whistling continues*]. Stand by to isolate. [*To the Elderly Gentleman, who is staring after the whistling Emperor*] How far has he gone?

THE ELDERLY GENTLEMAN. To that curious statue of a fat old man.

ZOO [*quickly, intoning*] Isolate the Falstaff monument isolate hard. Paralyze—[*the whistling stops*]. Thank you. [*She puts up her tuning-fork*]. He shall not move a muscle until I come to fetch him.

THE ENVOY'S WIFE. Oh! he *will* be frightfully angry! Did you hear what he said to me?

ZOO. Much we care for his anger!

THE DAUGHTER [*coming forward between her mother and Zoo*]. Please, madam, whose statue is it? and where can I buy a picture postcard of it? It is so funny. I will take a snapshot when we are coming back; but they come out so badly sometimes.

ZOO. They will give you pictures and toys in the temple to take away with you. The story of the statue is too long. It would bore you [*she goes past them across the courtyard to get rid of them*].

THE WIFE [*gushing*] Oh no, I assure you.

THE DAUGHTER [*copying her mother*] We should be so interested.

ZOO. Nonsense! All I can tell you about it is that a thousand years ago, when the whole world was given over to you shortlived people, there was a war called the War to end War. In the war which followed it about ten years later, hardly any soldiers were killed; but seven of the capital cities of Europe were wiped out of existence. It seems to have been a great joke; for the statesmen who thought they had sent ten million common men to their deaths were themselves blown into fragments with their houses and families, while the ten million men lay snugly in the caves they had dug for themselves. Later on even the houses escaped; but their inhabitants were poisoned by gas that spared no living soul. Of course the soldiers starved and ran wild; and that was the end of pseudo-Christian civilization. The last civilized thing that happened was that the statesmen discovered that cowardice was a great patriotic virtue; and a public monument was erected to its first preacher, an ancient and very fat sage called Sir John Falstaff. Well [*pointing*], thats Falstaff.

THE ELDERLY GENTLEMAN [*coming from the portico to his granddaughter's right*] Great Heavens! And at the base of this monstrous poltroon's statue the War God of Turania is now gibbering impotently.

ZOO. Serve him right! War God indeed!

THE ENVOY [*coming between his wife and Zoo*] I dont know any history: a modern Prime Minister has something better to do than sit reading books; but—

THE ELDERLY GENTLEMAN [*interrupting him encouragingly*] You make history, Ambrose.

THE ENVOY. Well, perhaps I do; and perhaps history makes me. I hardly recognise myself in the newspapers sometimes, though I suppose leading articles are the materials of history, as you might say. But what I want to know is, how did war come back again? and how did they make those poisonous gases you speak of? We should be glad to know; for they might come in very handy if we have to fight Turania. Of course I am all for peace, and dont hold with the race of armaments in principle; still, we must keep ahead or be wiped out.

ZOO. You can make the gases for yourselves when your chemists find out how. Then you will do as you did before: poison each other until there are no chemists left, and no civilization. You will then begin all over again as half-starved ignorant savages, and fight with boomerangs and poisoned arrows until you work up to the poison gases and high explosives once more, with the same result. That is, unless we have sense enough to make an end of this ridiculous game by destroying *you*.

THE ENVOY [*aghast*] Destroying us!

THE ELDERLY GENTLEMAN. I told you, Ambrose. I warned you.

THE ENVOY. But—

ZOO [*impatiently*] I wonder what Zozim is doing. He ought to be here to receive you.

THE ELDERLY GENTLEMAN. Do you mean that rather insufferable young man whom you found boring me on the pier?

ZOO. Yes. He has to dress-up in a Druids' robe, and put on a wig and a long false beard, to impress you silly people. *I* have to put on a purple mantle. I have no patience with such mummery; but you expect it from us; so I suppose it must be kept up. Will you wait here until Zozim comes, please [*she turns to enter the temple*].

THE ENVOY. My good lady, is it worth while dressing-up and putting on false beards for us if you tell us beforehand that it is all humbug?

ZOO. One would not think so; but if you wont believe in anyone who is not dressed-up, why, we must dress-up for you. It was you who invented all this nonsense, not we.

THE ELDERLY GENTLEMAN. But do you expect us to be impressed, after this?

ZOO. I dont expect anything. I know, as a matter of experience, that you *will* be impressed. The oracle will frighten you out of your wits. [*She goes into the temple*].

THE WIFE. These people treat us as if we were dirt beneath their feet. I wonder at you putting up with it, Amby. It would serve them right if we went home at once: wouldnt it, Eth?

THE DAUGHTER. Yes, mamma. But perhaps they wouldnt mind.

THE ENVOY. No use talking like that, Molly. Ive got to see this oracle. The folks at home wont know how we have been treated: all theyll know is that Ive stood face to face with the oracle and had the straight tip from her. I hope this Zozim chap is not going to keep us waiting much longer; for I feel far from comfortable about the approaching interview; and thats the honest truth.

THE ELDERLY GENTLEMAN. I never thought I should want to see that man again; but now I wish he would take charge of us instead of Zoo. She was charming at first: quite charming; but she turned into a fiend because I had a few words with her. You would not believe: she very nearly killed me. You heard what she said just now. She belongs to a party here which wants to have us all killed.

THE WIFE [*terrified*] Us! But we have done nothing: we have been as nice to them as nice could be. Oh, Amby, come away, come away: there is something dreadful about this place and these people.

THE ENVOY. There is, and no mistake. But youre safe with me: you ought to have sense enough to know that.

THE ELDERLY GENTLEMAN. I am sorry to say, Molly, that it is not merely us four poor weak creatures they want to kill, but the entire race of Man, except themselves.

THE ENVOY. Not so poor neither, Poppa. Nor so weak, if you are going to take in all the Powers. If it comes to killing, two can play at that game, longlived or shortlived.

THE ELDERLY GENTLEMAN. No, Ambrose: we should have no chance. We are worms beside these fearful people: mere worms.

Zozim comes from the temple, robed majestically, and wearing a wreath of mistletoe in his flowing white wig. His false beard reaches almost to his waist. He carries a staff with a curiously carved top.

ZOZIM [*in the doorway, impressively*] Hail, strangers!

ALL [*reverently*] Hail!

ZOZIM. Are ye prepared?

THE ENVOY. We are.

ZOZIM [*unexpectedly becoming conversational, and strolling down carelessly to the middle of the group between the two ladies*] Well, I'm sorry to say the oracle is not. She was delayed by some member of your party who got loose; and as the show takes a bit of arranging, you will have to wait a few minutes. The ladies can go inside and look round the entrance hall and get pictures and things if they want them.

THE WIFE [*together*] Thank you.
THE DAUGHTER [*together*] I should like to, very much. [*They go into the temple*].

THE ELDERLY GENTLEMAN [*in dignified rebuke of Zozim's levity*] Taken in this spirit, sir, the show, as you call it, becomes almost an insult to our common sense.

ZOZIM. Quite, I should say. You need not keep it up with me.

THE ENVOY [*suddenly making himself very agreeable*] Just so: just so. We can wait as long as you please. And now, if I may be allowed to seize the opportunity of a few minutes' friendly chat—?

ZOZIM. By all means, if only you will talk about things I can understand.

THE ENVOY. Well, about this colonizing plan of yours. My father-in-law here has been telling me something about it; and he has just now let out that you want not only to colonize us, but to—to—to—well, shall we say to supersede us? Now why supersede us? Why not live and let live? Theres not a scrap of ill-feeling on our side. We should welcome a colony of immortals—we may almost call you that—in the British Middle East. No doubt the Turanian Empire, with its Mahometan traditions, overshadows us now. We have had to bring the Emperor with us on this expedition, though of course you know as well as I do that he has imposed himself on my party just to spy on me. I dont deny that he has the whip hand of us to some extent, because if it came to a war none of our generals could stand up against him. I give him best at that game: he is the finest soldier in the world. Besides, he is an emperor and an autocrat; and I am only an elected representative of the British democracy. Not that our British democrats wont fight: they will fight the heads off all the Turanians that ever walked; but then it takes so long to work them up to it, while he has only to say the word and march. But you people would never get on with him. Believe me, you would not be as comfortable in Turania as you would be with us. We understand you. We like you. We are easy-going people; and we are rich people. That will appeal to you. Turania is a poor place when all is said. Five-eighths of it is desert. They dont irrigate as we do. Besides—now I am sure this will appeal to you and to all right-minded men—we are Christians.

ZOZIM. The old uns prefer Mahometans.

THE ENVOY [*shocked*] What!

ZOZIM [*distinctly*] They prefer Mahometans. Whats wrong with that?

THE ENVOY. Well, of all the disgraceful—

THE ELDERLY GENTLEMAN [*diplomatically interrupting his scandalized son-in-law*] There can be no doubt, I am afraid, that by clinging too long to the obsolete features of the old pseudo-Christian Churches we allowed the Mahometans to get ahead of us at a very critical period of the development of the Eastern world. When the Mahometan Reformation took place, it left its followers with the enormous advantage of having the only established religion in the world in whose articles of faith any intelligent and educated person could believe.

THE ENVOY. But what about our Reformation? Dont give the show away, Poppa. We followed suit, didnt we?

THE ELDERLY GENTLEMAN. Unfortunately, Ambrose, we could not follow suit very rapidly. We had not only a religion to deal with, but a Church.

ZOZIM. What is a Church?

THE ENVOY. Not know what a Church is! Well!

THE ELDERLY GENTLEMAN. You must excuse me; but if I attempted to explain you would only ask me what a bishop is; and that is a question that no mortal man can answer. All I can tell you is that Mahomet was a truly wise man; for he founded a religion without a Church; consequently when the time came for a Reformation of the mosques there were no bishops and priests to obstruct it. Our bishops and priests prevented us for two hundred years from following suit; and we have never recovered the start we lost then. I can only plead that we did reform our Church at last. No doubt we had to make a few compromizes as a matter of good taste; but there is now very little in our Articles of Religion that is not accepted as at least allegorically true by our Higher Criticism.

THE ENVOY [*encouragingly*] Besides, does it matter? Why, *I* have never read the Articles in my life; and I am Prime Minister! Come! if my services in arranging for the reception of a colonizing party would be acceptable, they are at your disposal. And when I say a reception I mean a reception. Royal honors, mind you! A salute of a hundred and one guns! The streets lined with troops! The Guards turned out at the Palace! Dinner at the Guildhall!

ZOZIM. Discourage me if I know what youre talking about! I wish Zoo would come: she understands these things. All I can tell you is that the general opinion among the Colonizers is in favor of beginning in a country where the people are of a different color from us; so that we can make short work without any risk of mistakes.

THE ENVOY. What do you mean by short work? I hope—

ZOZIM [*with obviously feigned geniality*] Oh, nothing, nothing, nothing. We are thinking of trying North America: thats all. You see, the Red Men of that country used to be white. They passed through a period of sallow complexions, followed by a period of no complexions at all, into the red characteristic of their climate. Besides, several cases of long life have occurred in North America. They joined us here; and their stock soon reverted to the original white of these islands.

THE ELDERLY GENTLEMAN. But have you considered the possibility of your colony turning red?

ZOZIM. That wont matter. We are not particular about our pigmentation. The old books mention red-faced Englishmen: they appear to have been common objects at one time.

THE ELDERLY GENTLEMAN [*very persuasively*] But do you think you would be popular in North America? It seems to me, if I may say so, that on your own shewing you need a country in which society is organized in a series of highly exclusive circles, in which the privacy of private life is very jealously guarded, and in which no one presumes to speak to anyone else without an introduction following a strict examination of social credentials. It is only in such a country that persons of special tastes and attainments can form a little world of their own, and protect themselves absolutely from intrusion by common persons. I think I may claim that our British society has developed this exclusiveness to perfection. If you would pay us a visit and see the working of our caste system, our club system, our guild system, you would admit that nowhere else in the world, least of all, perhaps in North America, which has a regrettable tradition of social promiscuity, could you keep yourselves so entirely to yourselves.

ZOZIM [*good-naturedly embarrassed*] Look here. There is no good discussing this. I had rather not explain; but it wont make any difference to our Colonizers what sort of shortlivers they come across. We shall arrange all that. Never mind how. Let us join the ladies.

THE ELDERLY GENTLEMAN [*throwing off his diplomatic attitude and abandoning himself to despair*] We understand you only too well, sir. Well, kill us. End the lives you have made miserably unhappy by opening up to us the possibility that any of us may live three hundred years. I solemnly curse that possibility. To you it may be a blessing, because you do live three hundred years. To us, who live less than a hundred, whose flesh is as grass, it is the most unbearable burden our poor tortured humanity has ever groaned under.

THE ENVOY. Hullo, Poppa! Steady! How do you make that out?

ZOZIM. What is three hundred years? Short enough, if you ask me. Why, in the old days you people lived on the assumption that you were going to last out for ever and ever and ever. Immortal, you thought yourselves. Were you any happier then?

THE ELDERLY GENTLEMAN. As President of the Baghdad Historical Society I am in a position to inform you that the communities which took this monstrous pretension seriously were the most wretched of which we have any record. My Society has printed an editio princeps of the works of the father of history, Thucyderodotus Macollybuckle. Have you read his account of what was blasphemously called the Perfect City of God, and the attempt made to reproduce it in the northern part of these islands by Jonhobsnoxius, called the Leviathan? Those misguided people sacrificed the fragment of life that was granted to them to an imaginary immortality. They crucified the prophet who told them to take no thought for the morrow, and that here and now was their Australia: Australia being a term signifying paradise, or an eternity of bliss. They tried to produce a condition of death in life: to mortify the flesh, as they called it.

ZOZIM. Well, you are not suffering from that, are you? You have not a mortified air.

THE ELDERLY GENTLEMAN. Naturally we are not absolutely insane and suicidal. Nevertheless we impose on ourselves abstinences and disciplines and studies that are meant to prepare us for living three centuries. And we seldom live one. My childhood was made unnecessarily painful, my boyhood unnecessarily laborious, by ridiculous preparations for a length of days which the chances were fifty thousand to one against my ever attaining. I have been cheated out of the natural joys and freedoms of my life by this dream to which the existence of these islands and their oracles gives a delusive possibility of realization. I curse the day when long life was invented, just as the victims of Jonhobsnoxius cursed the day when eternal life was invented.

ZOZIM. Pooh! You could live three centuries if you chose.

THE ELDERLY GENTLEMAN. That is what the fortunate always say to the unfortunate. Well, I do not choose. I accept my three score and ten years. If they are filled with usefulness, with justice, with mercy, with good-will: if they are the lifetime of a soul that never loses its honor and a brain that never loses its eagerness, they are enough for me, because these things are infinite and eternal, and can make ten of my years as long as thirty of yours. I shall not conclude by saying live as long as you like and be damned to you, because I have risen for the moment far above any ill-will to you or to any fellow-creature; but I am your equal before that eternity in which the difference between your lifetime and mine is as the difference between one drop of water and three in the eyes of the Almighty Power from which we have both proceeded.

ZOZIM [*impressed*] You spoke that piece very well, Daddy. I couldnt talk like that if I tried. It sounded fine. Ah! here come the ladies.

To his relief, they have just appeared on the threshold of the temple.

THE ELDERLY GENTLEMAN [*passing from exaltation to distress*] It means nothing to him: in this land of discouragement the sublime has become the ridiculous. [*Turning on the hopelessly puzzled Zozim*] "Behold, thou hast made my days as it were a span long; and mine age is even as nothing in respect of thee."

THE WIFE [*running to him*] Poppa, Poppa: dont look like that.
THE DAUGHTER [*running to him*] Oh, granpa, whats the matter?

ZOZIM [*with a shrug*] Discouragement!

THE ELDERLY GENTLEMAN [*throwing off the women with a superb gesture*] Liar! [*Recollecting himself, he adds, with noble courtesy, raising his hat and bowing*] I beg your pardon, sir; but I am NOT discouraged.

A burst of orchestral music, through which a powerful gong sounds, is heard from the temple. Zoo, in a purple robe, appears in the doorway.

ZOO. Come. The oracle is ready.

Zozim motions them to the threshold with a wave of his staff. The Envoy and the Elderly Gentleman take off their hats and go into the temple on tiptoe, Zoo leading the way. The Wife and Daughter, frightened as they are, raise their heads uppishly and follow flatfooted, sustained by a sense of their Sunday clothes and social consequence. Zozim remains in the portico, alone.

ZOZIM [*taking off his wig, beard, and robe, and bundling them under his arm*] Ouf! [*He goes home*].

ACT III

INSIDE *the temple. A gallery overhanging an abyss. Dead silence. The gallery is brightly lighted; but beyond is a vast gloom, continually changing in intensity. A shaft of violet light shoots upward; and a very harmonious and silvery carillon chimes. When it ceases the violet ray vanishes.*

Zoo comes along the gallery, followed by the Envoy's daughter, his wife, the Envoy himself, and the Elderly Gentleman. The two men are holding their hats with the brims near their noses, as if prepared to pray into them at a moment's notice. Zoo halts: they all follow her example. They contemplate the void with awe. Organ music of the kind called sacred in the nineteenth century begins. Their awe deepens. The violet ray, now a diffused mist, rises again from the abyss.

THE WIFE [*to Zoo, in a reverent whisper*] Shall we kneel?

ZOO [*loudly*] Yes, if you want to. You can stand on your head if you like. [*She sits down carelessly on the gallery railing, with her back to the abyss*].

THE ELDERLY GENTLEMAN [*jarred by her callousness*] We desire to behave in a becoming manner.

ZOO. Very well. Behave just as you feel. It doesnt matter how you behave. But keep your wits about you when the pythoness ascends, or you will forget the questions you have come to ask her.

THE ENVOY } [*simultaneously*] [*very nervous, takes out a paper to refresh his memory*] Ahem!
THE DAUGHTER } [*simultaneously*] [*alarmed*] The pythoness? Is she a snake?

THE ELDERLY GENTLEMAN. Tch-ch! The priestess of the oracle. A sybil. A prophetess. Not a snake.

THE WIFE. How awful!

ZOO. I'm glad you think so.

THE WIFE. Oh dear! Dont you think so?

ZOO. No. This sort of thing is got up to impress *you*, not to impress me.

THE ELDERLY GENTLEMAN. I wish you would let it impress

us, then, madam. I am deeply impressed; but you are spoiling the effect.

ZOO. You just wait. All this business with coloured lights and chords on that old organ is only tomfoolery. Wait til you see the pythoness.

The Envoy's wife falls on her knees, and takes refuge in prayer.

THE DAUGHTER [*trembling*] Are we really going to see a woman who has lived three hundred years?

ZOO. Stuff! Youd drop dead if a tertiary as much as looked at you. The oracle is only a hundred and seventy; and youll find it hard enough to stand her.

THE DAUGHTER [*piteously*] Oh! [*she falls on her knees*].

THE ENVOY. Whew! Stand by me, Poppa. This is a little more than I bargained for. Are you going to kneel; or how?

THE ELDERLY GENTLEMAN. Perhaps it would be in better taste.

The two men kneel.

The vapor of the abyss thickens; and a distant roll of thunder seems to come from its depths. The pythoness, seated on her tripod, rises slowly from it. She has discarded the insulating robe and veil in which she conversed with Napoleon, and is now draped and hooded in voluminous folds of a single piece of grey-white stuff. Something supernatural about her terrifies the beholders, who throw themselves on their faces. Her outline flows and waves: she is almost distinct at moments, and again vague and shadowy: above all, she is larger than life-size, not enough to be measured by the flustered congregation, but enough to affect them with a dreadful sense of her supernaturalness.

ZOO. Get up, get up. Do pull yourselves together, you people.

The Envoy and his family, by shuddering negatively, intimate that it is impossible. The Elderly Gentleman manages to get on his hands and knees.

ZOO. Come on, Daddy: you are not afraid. Speak to her. She wont wait here all day for you, you know.

THE ELDERLY GENTLEMAN [*rising very deferentially to his*

feet] Madam: you will excuse my very natural nervousness in addressing, for the first time in my life, a—a—a—a goddess. My friend and relative the Envoy is unhinged. I throw myself upon your indulgence—

ZOO [*interrupting him intolerantly*] Dont throw yourself on anything belonging to her or you will go right through her and break your neck. She isnt solid, like you.

THE ELDERLY GENTLEMAN. I was speaking figuratively—

ZOO. You have been told not to do it. Ask her what you want to know; and be quick about it.

THE ELDERLY GENTLEMAN [*stooping and taking the prostrate Envoy by the shoulders*] Ambrose: you must make an effort. You cannot go back to Baghdad without the answers to your questions.

THE ENVOY [*rising to his knees*] I shall be only too glad to get back alive on any terms. If my legs would support me I'd just do a bunk straight for the ship.

THE ELDERLY GENTLEMAN. No, no. Remember: your dignity—

THE ENVOY. Dignity be damned! I'm terrified. Take me away, for God's sake.

THE ELDERLY GENTLEMAN [*producing a brandy flask and taking the cap off*] Try some of this. It is still nearly full, thank goodness!

THE ENVOY [*clutching it and drinking eagerly*] Ah! Thats better. [*He tries to drink again. Finding that he has emptied it, he hands it back to his father-in-law upside down*].

THE ELDERLY GENTLEMAN [*taking it*] Great heavens! He has swallowed half-a-pint of neat brandy. [*Much perturbed, he screws the cap on again, and pockets the flask*].

THE ENVOY [*staggering to his feet; pulling a paper from his pocket; and speaking with boisterous confidence*] Get up, Molly. Up with you, Eth.

The two women rise to their knees.

THE ENVOY. What I want to ask is this. [*He refers to the paper*]. Ahem! Civilization has reached a crisis. We are at the parting of the ways. We stand on the brink of the

Rubicon. Shall we take the plunge? Already a leaf has been torn out of the book of the Sybil. Shall we wait until the whole volume is consumed? On our right is the crater of the volcano: on our left the precipice. One false step, and we go down to annihilation dragging the whole human race with us. [*He pauses for breath*].

THE ELDERLY GENTLEMAN [*recovering his spirits under the familiar stimulus of political oratory*] Hear, hear!

ZOO. What are you raving about? Ask your question while you have the chance? What is it you want to know?

THE ENVOY [*patronizing her in the manner of a Premier debating with a very young member of the Opposition*] A young woman asks me a question. I am always glad to see the young taking an interest in politics. It is an impatient question; but it is a practical question, an intelligent question. She asks why we seek to lift a corner of the veil that shrouds the future from our feeble vision.

ZOO. I dont. I ask you to tell the oracle what you want, and not keep her sitting there all day.

THE ELDERLY GENTLEMAN [*warmly*] Order, order!

ZOO. What does "Order, order!" mean?

THE ENVOY. I ask the august oracle to listen to my voice—

ZOO. You people seem never to tire of listening to your voices; but it doesnt amuse us. What do you want?

THE ENVOY. I want, young woman, to be allowed to proceed without unseemly interruptions.

A low roll of thunder comes from the abyss.

THE ELDERLY GENTLEMAN. There! Even the oracle is indignant. [*To the Envoy*] Do not allow yourself to be put down by this lady's rude clamor, Ambrose. Take no notice. Proceed.

THE ENVOY'S WIFE. I cant bear this much longer, Amby. Remember: *I* havnt had any brandy.

HIS DAUGHTER [*trembling*] There are serpents curling in the vapor. I am afraid of the lightning. Finish it, Papa; or I shall die.

THE ENVOY [*sternly*] Silence. The destiny of British civilization is at stake. Trust me. I am not afraid. As I was saying—where was I?

ZOO. I dont know. Does anybody?

THE ELDERLY GENTLEMAN [*tactfully*] You were just coming to the election, I think.

THE ENVOY [*reassured*] Just so. The election. Now what we want to know is this: ought we to dissolve in August, or put it off until next spring?

ZOO. Dissolve? In what? [*Thunder*]. Oh! My fault this time. That means that the oracle understands you, and desires me to hold my tongue.

THE ENVOY [*fervently*] I thank the oracle.

THE WIFE [*to Zoo*] Serve you right!

THE ELDERLY GENTLEMAN. Before the oracle replies, I should like to be allowed to state a few of the reasons why, in my opinion, the Government should hold on until the spring. In the first—

Terrific lightning and thunder. The Elderly Gentleman is knocked flat; but as he immediately sits up again dazedly it is clear that he is none the worse for the shock. The ladies cower in terror. The Envoy's hat is blown off; but he seizes it just as it quits his temples, and holds it on with both hands. He is recklessly drunk, but quite articulate, as he seldom speaks in public without taking stimulants beforehand.

THE ENVOY [*taking one hand from his hat to make a gesture of stilling the tempest*] Thats enough. We know how to take a hint. I'll put the case in three words. I am the leader of the Potterbill party. My party is in power. I am Prime Minister. The Opposition—the Rotterjacks—have won every bye-election for the last six months. They—

THE ELDERLY GENTLEMAN [*scrambling heatedly to his feet*] Not by fair means. By bribery, by misrepresentation, by pandering to the vilest prejudices [*muttered thunder*]—I beg your pardon [*he is silent*].

THE ENVOY. Never mind the bribery and lies. The oracle knows all about that. The point is that though our five years will not expire until the year after next, our majority will be eaten away at the bye-elections by about Easter. We cant wait: we must start some question that will excite the public, and go to the country on it. But some of us say do it now. Others say wait til the spring. We cant make up our minds one way or the other. Which would you advise?

ZOO. But what is the question that is to excite your public?

THE ENVOY. That doesnt matter. I dont know yet. We will find a question all right enough. The oracle can foresee the future: we cannot. [*Thunder*]. What does that mean? What have I done now?

ZOO [*severely*] How often must you be told that we cannot foresee the future? There is no such thing as the future until it is the present.

THE ELDERLY GENTLEMAN. Allow me to point out, madam, that when the Potterbill party sent to consult the oracle fifteen years ago, the oracle prophesied that the Potterbills would be victorious at the General Election; and they were. So it is evident that the oracle c a n foresee the future, and is sometimes willing to reveal it.

THE ENVOY. Quite true. Thank you, Poppa. I appeal now, over your head, young woman, direct to the August Oracle, to repeat the signal favor conferred on my illustrious predecessor, Sir Fuller Eastwind, and to answer me exactly as he was answered.

The oracle raises her hand to command silence.

ALL. Sh-sh-sh!

Invisible trombones utter three solemn blasts in the manner of Die Zauberflöte.

THE ELDERLY GENTLEMAN. May I—

ZOO [*quickly*] Hush. The oracle is going to speak.

THE ORACLE. Go home, poor fool.

She vanishes; and the atmosphere changes to prosaic daylight. Zoo comes off the railing; throws off her robe; makes a bundle of it; and tucks it under her arm. The magic and mystery are gone. The women rise to their feet. The Envoy's party stare at one another helplessly.

zoo. The same reply, word for word, that your illustrious predecessor, as you call him, got fifteen years ago. You asked for it; and you got it. And just think of all the important questions you might have asked. She would have answered them, you know. It is always like that. I will go and arrange to have you sent home: you can wait for me in the entrance hall [*she goes out*].

THE ENVOY. What possessed me to ask for the same answer old Eastwind got?

THE ELDERLY GENTLEMAN. But it was not the same answer. The answer to Eastwind was an inspiration to our party for years. It won us the election.

THE ENVOY'S DAUGHTER. I learnt it at school, granpa. It wasnt the same at all, I can repeat it. [*She quotes*] "When Britain was cradled in the west, the east wind hardened her and made her great. Whilst the east wind prevails Britain shall prosper. The east wind shall wither Britain's enemies in the day of contest. Let the Rotterjacks look to it."

THE ENVOY. The old man invented that. I see it all. He was a doddering old ass when he came to consult the oracle. The oracle naturally said "Go home, poor fool." There was no sense in saying that to me; but as that girl said, I asked for it. What else could the poor old chap do but fake up an answer fit for publication? There were whispers about it; but nobody believed them. I believe them now.

THE ELDERLY GENTLEMAN. Oh, I cannot admit that Sir Fuller Eastwind was capable of such a fraud.

THE ENVOY. He was capable of anything: I knew his private secretary. And now what are we going to say? You dont suppose I am going back to Baghdad to tell the British Empire that the oracle called me a fool, do you?

THE ELDERLY GENTLEMAN. Surely we must tell the truth, however painful it may be to our feelings.

THE ENVOY. I am not thinking of my feelings: I am not so selfish as that, thank God. I am thinking of the country: of our party. The truth, as you call it, would put the Rotterjacks in for the next twenty years. It would be the end of me politically. Not that I care for that: I am only too willing to retire if you can find a better man. Dont hesitate on my account.

THE ELDERLY GENTLEMAN. No, Ambrose: you are indispensable. There is no one else.

THE ENVOY. Very well, then. What are you going to do?

THE ELDERLY GENTLEMAN. My dear Ambrose, you are the leader of the party, not I. What are you going to do?

THE ENVOY. I am going to tell the exact truth: thats what I'm going to do. Do you take me for a liar?

THE ELDERLY GENTLEMAN [*puzzled*] Oh. I beg your pardon. I understood you to say—

THE ENVOY [*cutting him short*] You understood me to say that I am going back to Baghdad to tell the British electorate that the oracle repeated to me, word for word, what it said to Sir Fuller Eastwind fifteen years ago. Molly and Ethel can bear me out. So must you, if you are an honest man. Come on.

He goes out, followed by his wife and daughter.

THE ELDERLY GENTLEMAN [*left alone and shrinking into an old and desolate figure*] What am I to do? I am a most perplexed and wretched man. [*He falls on his knees, and stretches his hands in entreaty over the abyss*]. I invoke the oracle. I cannot go back and connive at a blasphemous lie. I implore guidance.

The Pythoness walks in on the gallery behind him, and touches him on the shoulder. Her size is now natural. Her face is hidden by her hood. He flinches as if from an electric shock; turns to her; and cowers, covering his eyes in terror.

THE ELDERLY GENTLEMAN. No: not close to me. I'm afraid I cant bear it.

THE ORACLE [*with grave pity*] Come: look at me. I am my natural size now: what you saw there was only a foolish picture of me thrown on a cloud by a lantern. How can I help you?

THE ELDERLY GENTLEMAN. They have gone back to lie about your answer. I cannot go with them. I cannot live among people to whom nothing is real. I have become incapable of it through my stay here. I implore to be allowed to stay.

THE ORACLE. My friend: if you stay with us you will die of discouragement.

THE ELDERLY GENTLEMAN. If I go back I shall die of disgust and despair. I take the nobler risk. I beg you, do not cast me out.

He catches her robe and holds her.

THE ORACLE. Take care. I have been here one hundred and seventy years. Your death does not mean to me what it means to you.

THE ELDERLY GENTLEMAN. It is the meaning of life, not of death, that makes banishment so terrible to me.

THE ORACLE. Be it so, then. You may stay.

She offers him her hands. He grasps them and raises himself a little by clinging to her. She looks steadily into his face. He stiffens; a little convulsion shakes him; his grasp relaxes; and he falls dead.

THE ORACLE [*looking down at the body*] Poor shortlived thing! What else could I do for you?

PART V

AS FAR AS THOUGHT CAN REACH

AS FAR AS THOUGHT CAN REACH

SUMMER *afternoon in the year* 31,920 A.D. *A sunlit glade at the southern foot of a thickly wooded hill. On the west side of it, the steps and columned porch of a dainty little classic temple. Between it and the hill, a rising path to the wooded heights begins with rough steps of stones in the moss. On the opposite side, a grove. In the middle of the glade, an altar in the form of a low marble table as long as a man, set parallel to the temple steps and pointing to the hill. Curved marble benches radiate from it into the foreground; but they are not joined to it: there is plenty of space to pass between the altar and the benches.*

A dance of youths and maidens is in progress. The music is provided by a few fluteplayers seated carelessly on the steps of the temple. There are no children; and none of the dancers seems younger than eighteen. Some of the youths have beards. Their dress, like the architecture of the theatre and the design of the altar and curved seats, resembles Grecian of the fourth century B.C., *freely handled. They move with perfect balance and remarkable grace, racing through a figure like a farandole. They neither romp nor hug in our manner.*

At the first full close they clap their hands to stop the musicians, who recommence with a saraband, during which a strange figure appears on the path beyond the temple. He is deep in thought, with his eyes closed and his feet feeling automatically for the rough irregular steps as he slowly descends them. Except for a sort of linen kilt consisting mainly of a girdle carrying a sporran and a few minor pockets, he is naked. In physical hardihood and uprightness he seems to be in the prime of life; and his eyes and mouth shew no signs of age; but his face, though fully and firmly fleshed, bears a network of lines, varying from furrows to hairbreadth reticulations, as if Time had worked over every inch of it incessantly through whole geologic periods. His head is finely domed and utterly bald. Except for his eyelashes he is quite hairless. He is unconscious of his surroundings, and walks right into one of the dancing couples, separating them. He wakes up and stares about him. The couple stop indignantly. The rest stop. The music stops. The youth whom he has jostled accosts him without malice, but without anything that we should call manners.

THE YOUTH. Now, then, ancient sleepwalker, why dont you keep your eyes open and mind where you are going?

THE ANCIENT [*mild, bland, and indulgent*] I did not know there was a nursery here, or I should not have turned my face in this direction. Such accidents cannot always be avoided. Go on with your play: I will turn back.

THE YOUTH. Why not stay with us and enjoy life for once in a way? We will teach you to dance.

THE ANCIENT. No, thank you. I danced when I was a child like you. Dancing is a very crude attempt to get into the rhythm of life. It would be painful to me to go back from that rhythm to your babyish gambols: in fact I could not do it if I tried. But at your age it is pleasant; and I am sorry I disturbed you.

THE YOUTH. Come! own up: arnt you very unhappy? It's dreadful to see you ancients going about by yourselves, never noticing anything, never dancing, never laughing, never singing, never getting anything out of life. None of us are going to be like that when we grow up. It's a dog's life.

THE ANCIENT. Not at all. You repeat that old phrase without knowing that there was once a creature on earth called a dog. Those who are interested in extinct forms of life will tell you that it loved the sound of its own voice and bounded about when it was happy, just as you are doing here. It is you, my children, who are living the dog's life.

THE YOUTH. The dog must have been a good sensible creature: it set you a very wise example. You should let yourself go occasionally and have a good time.

THE ANCIENT. My children: be content to let us ancients go our ways and enjoy ourselves in our own fashion.

He turns to go.

THE MAIDEN. But wait a moment. Why will you not tell us how you enjoy yourself? You must have secret pleasures that you hide from us, and that you never get tired of. I get tired of all our dances and all our tunes. I get tired of all my partners.

THE YOUTH [*suspiciously*] Do you? I shall bear that in mind.

They all look at one another as if there were some sinister significance in what she has said.

THE MAIDEN. We all do: what is the use of pretending we dont? It is natural.

SEVERAL YOUNG PEOPLE. No, no. We dont. It is not natural.

THE ANCIENT. You are older than he is, I see. You are growing up.

THE MAIDEN. How do you know? I do not look so much older, do I?

THE ANCIENT. Oh, I was not looking at you. Your looks do not interest me.

THE MAIDEN. Thank you.

They all laugh.

THE YOUTH. You old fish! I believe you dont know the difference between a man and a woman.

THE ANCIENT. It has long ceased to interest me in the way it interests you. And when anything no longer interests us we no longer know it.

THE MAIDEN. You havnt told me how I shew my age. That is what I want to know. As a matter of fact I am older than this boy here: older than he thinks. How did you find that out?

THE ANCIENT. Easily enough. You are ceasing to pretend that these childish games—this dancing and singing and mating—do not become tiresome and unsatisfying after a while. And you no longer care to pretend that you are younger than you are. These are the signs of adolescence. And then, see these fantastic rags with which you have draped yourself. [*He takes up a piece of her draperies in his hand*]. It is rather badly worn here. Why do you not get a new one?

THE MAIDEN. Oh, I did not notice it. Besides, it is too

much trouble. Clothes are a nuisance. I think I shall do without them some day, as you ancients do.

THE ANCIENT. Signs of maturity. Soon you will give up all these toys and games and sweets.

THE YOUTH. What! And be as miserable as you?

THE ANCIENT. Infant: one moment of the ecstasy of life as we live it would strike you dead. [*He stalks gravely out through the grove*].

They stare after him, much damped.

THE YOUTH [*to the musicians*] Let us have another dance.

The musicians shake their heads; get up from their seats on the steps; and troop away into the temple. The others follow them, except the Maiden, who sits down on the altar.

A MAIDEN [*as she goes*] There! The ancient has put them out of countenance. It is your fault, Strephon, for provoking him. [*She leaves, much disappointed*].

A YOUTH. Why need you have cheeked him like that? [*He goes, grumbling*].

STREPHON [*calling after him*] I thought it was understood that we are always to cheek the ancients on principle.

ANOTHER YOUTH. Quite right too! There would be no holding them if we didnt. [*He goes*].

THE MAIDEN. Why dont you really stand up to them? *I* did.

ANOTHER YOUTH. Sheer, abject, pusillanimous, dastardly cowardice. Thats why. Face the filthy truth. [*He goes*].

ANOTHER YOUTH [*turning on the steps as he goes out*] And dont you forget, infant, that one moment of the ecstasy of life as I live it would strike you dead. Haha!

STREPHON [*now the only one left, except the Maiden*] Arnt you coming, Chloe?

THE MAIDEN [*shakes her head*]!

THE YOUTH [*hurrying back to her*] What is the matter?

THE MAIDEN [*tragically pensive*] I dont know.

THE YOUTH. Then there is something the matter. Is that what you mean?

THE MAIDEN. Yes. Something is happening to me. I dont know what.

THE YOUTH. You no longer love me. I have seen it for a month past.

THE MAIDEN. Dont you think all that is rather silly? We cannot go on as if this kind of thing, this dancing and sweet-hearting, were everything.

THE YOUTH. What is there better? What else is there worth living for?

THE MAIDEN. Oh, stuff! Dont be frivolous.

THE YOUTH. Something horrible is happening to you. You are losing all heart, all feeling. [*He sits on the altar beside her and buries his face in his hands*]. I am bitterly unhappy.

THE MAIDEN. Unhappy! Really, you must have a very empty head if there is nothing in it but a dance with one girl who is no better than any of the other girls.

THE YOUTH. You did not always think so. You used to be vexed if I as much as looked at another girl.

THE MAIDEN. What does it matter what I did when I was a baby? Nothing existed for me then except what I tasted and touched and saw; and I wanted all that for myself, just as I wanted the moon to play with. Now the world is opening out for me. More than the world: the universe. Even little things are turning out to be great things, and becoming intensely interesting. Have you ever thought about the properties of numbers?

THE YOUTH [*sitting up, markedly disenchanted*] Numbers!!! I cannot imagine anything drier or more repulsive.

THE MAIDEN. They are fascinating, just fascinating. I want to get away from our eternal dancing and music, and just sit down by myself and think about numbers.

THE YOUTH [*rising indignantly*] Oh, this is too much. I have suspected you for some time past. We have all suspected you. All the girls say that you have deceived us as to your age: that you are getting flat-chested; that you are bored with us; that you talk to the ancients when you get the chance. Tell me the truth: how old are you?

THE MAIDEN. Just twice your age, my poor boy.

THE YOUTH. Twice my age! Do you mean to say you are

four?

THE MAIDEN. Very nearly four.

THE YOUTH [*collapsing on the altar with a groan*] Oh!

THE MAIDEN. My poor Strephon: I pretended I was only two for your sake. I was two when you were born. I saw you break from your shell; and you were such a charming child! You ran round and talked to us all so prettily, and were so handsome and well grown, that I lost my heart to you at once. But now I seem to have lost it altogether: bigger things are taking possession of me. Still, we were very happy in our childish way for the first year, werent we?

STREPHON. I was happy until you began cooling towards me.

THE MAIDEN. Not towards you, but towards all the trivialities of our life here. Just think. I have hundreds of years to live: perhaps thousands. Do you suppose I can spend centuries dancing; listening to flutes ringing changes on a few tunes and a few notes; raving about the beauty of a few pillars and arches; making jingles with words; lying about with your arms round me, which is really neither comfortable nor convenient; everlastingly choosing colors for dresses, and putting them on, and washing; making a business of sitting together at fixed hours to absorb our nourishment; taking little poisons with it to make us delirious enough to imagine we are enjoying ourselves; and then having to pass the nights in shelters lying in cots and losing half our lives in a state of unconsciousness. Sleep is a shameful thing: I have not slept at all for weeks past. I have stolen out at night when you were all lying insensible—quite disgusting, I call it—and wandered about the woods, thinking, thinking, thinking; grasping the world; taking it to pieces; building it up again; devising methods; planning experiments to test the methods; and having a glorious time. Every morning I have come back here with greater and greater reluctance; and I know that the time will soon come —perhaps it has come already—when I shall not come back at all.

STREPHON. How horridly cold and uncomfortable!

THE MAIDEN. Oh, dont talk to me of comfort! Life is not worth living if you have to bother about comfort. Comfort makes winter a torture, spring an illness, summer an oppression, and autumn only a respite. The ancients could make life one long frowsty comfort if they chose. But they never lift a finger to make themselves comfortable. They will not sleep under a roof. They will not clothe themselves: a girdle with a few pockets hanging to it to carry things about in is all they wear: they will sit down on the wet moss or in a gorse bush when there is dry heather within two yards of them. Two years ago, when you were born, I did not understand this. Now I feel that I would not put myself to the trouble of walking two paces for all the comfort in the world.

STREPHON. But you dont know what this means to me. It means that you are dying to me: yes, just dying. Listen to me [*he puts his arm around her*].

THE MAIDEN [*extricating herself*] Dont. We can talk quite as well without touching one another.

STREPHON [*horrified*] Chloe! Oh, this is the worst symptom of all! The ancients never touch one another.

THE MAIDEN. Why should they?

STREPHON. Oh, I dont know. But dont you w a n t to touch me? You used to.

THE MAIDEN. Yes: that is true: I used to. We used to think it would be nice to sleep in one another's arms; but we never could go to sleep because our weight stopped our circulations just above the elbows. Then somehow my feeling began to change bit by bit. I kept a sort of interest in your head and arms long after I lost interest in your whole body. And now that has gone.

STREPHON. You no longer care for me at all, then?

THE MAIDEN. Nonsense! I care for you much more seriously than before; though perhaps not so much for you in particular. I mean I care more for everybody. But I dont want to touch you unnecessarily; and I certainly dont want you to touch me.

STREPHON [*rising decisively*] That finishes it. You dislike me.

THE MAIDEN [*impatiently*] I tell you again, I do not dislike you; but you bore me when you cannot understand; and I think I shall be happier by myself in future. You had better get a new companion. What about the girl who is to be born today?

STREPHON. I do not want the girl who is to be born today. How do I know what she will be like? I want you.

THE MAIDEN. You cannot have me. You must recognize facts and face them. It is no use running after a woman twice your age. I cannot make my childhood last to please you. The age of love is sweet; but it is short; and I must pay nature's debt. You no longer attract me; and I no longer care to attract you. Growth is too rapid at my age: I am maturing from week to week.

STREPHON. You are maturing, as you call it—I call it ageing—from minute to minute. You are going much further than you did when we began this conversation.

THE MAIDEN. It is not the ageing that is so rapid. It is the realization of it when it has actually happened. Now that I have made up my mind to the fact that I have left childhood behind me, it comes home to me in leaps and bounds with every word you say.

STREPHON. But your vow. Have you forgotten that? We all swore together in that temple: the temple of love. You were more earnest than any of us.

THE MAIDEN [*with a grim smile*] Never to let our hearts grow cold! Never to become as the ancients! Never to let the sacred lamp be extinguished! Never to change or forget! To be remembered for ever as the first company of true lovers faithful to this vow so often made and broken by past generations! Ha! ha! Oh, dear!

STREPHON. Well, you need not laugh. It is a beautiful and holy compact; and I will keep it whilst I live. Are you going to break it?

THE MAIDEN. Dear child: it has broken itself. The change has come in spite of my childish vow. [*She rises*]. Do you mind if I go into the woods for a walk by myself? This chat of ours seems to me an unbearable waste of time. I have so much to think of.

STREPHON [*again collapsing on the altar and covering his eyes with his hands*]. My heart is broken. [*He weeps*].

THE MAIDEN [*with a shrug*] I have luckily got through my childhood without that experience. It shows how wise I was to choose a lover half my age. [*She goes towards the grove, and is disappearing among the trees, when another youth, older and manlier than Strephon, with crisp hair and firm arms, comes from the temple, and calls to her from the threshold*].

THE TEMPLE YOUTH. I say, Chloe. Is there any sign of the Ancient yet? The hour of birth is overdue. The baby is kicking like mad. She will break her shell prematurely.

THE MAIDEN [*looks across to the hill path; then points up it, and says*] She is coming, Acis.

The Maiden turns away through the grove and is lost to sight among the trees.

ACIS [*coming to Strephon*] Whats the matter? Has Chloe been unkind?

STREPHON. She has grown up in spite of all her promises. She deceived us about her age. She is four.

ACIS. Four! I am sorry, Strephon. I am getting on for three myself; and I know what old age is. I hate to say "I told you so"; but she was getting a little hard set and flat-chested and thin on the top, wasnt she?

STREPHON [*breaking down*] Dont.

ACIS. You must pull yourself together. This is going to be a busy day. First the birth. Then the Festival of the Artists.

STREPHON [*rising*] What is the use of being born if we have to decay into unnatural, heartless, loveless, joyless monsters in four short years? What use are the artists if they cannot bring their beautiful creations to life? I have a great mind to die and have done with it all. [*He moves away to the corner of the curved seat farthest from the theatre, and throws himself moodily into it*].

An Ancient Woman has descended the hill path during Strephon's lament, and has heard most of it. She is like the He-Ancient, equally bald, and equally without sexual charm, but intensely interesting and rather terrifying. Her sex is discoverable only by her voice, as her breasts are manly, and her figure otherwise not very different. She wears no clothes, but has draped herself rather perfunctorily with a ceremonial robe, and carries two implements like long slender saws. She comes to the altar between the two young men.

THE SHE-ANCIENT [*to Strephon*] Infant: you are only at the beginning of it all. [*To Acis*] Is the child ready to be born?

ACIS. More than ready, Ancient. Shouting and kicking and cursing. We have called to her to be quiet and wait until you come; but of course she only half understands, and is very impatient.

THE SHE-ANCIENT. Very well. Bring her out into the sun.

ACIS [*going quickly into the temple*] All ready. Come along.

Joyous processional music strikes up in the temple.

THE SHE-ANCIENT [*going close to Strephon*] Look at me.

STREPHON [*sulkily keeping his face averted*] Thank you; but I dont want to be cured. I had rather be miserable in my own way than callous in yours.

THE SHE-ANCIENT. You like being miserable? You will soon grow out of that. [*She returns to the altar*].

The procession, headed by Acis, emerges from the temple. Six youths carry on their shoulders a burden covered with a gorgeous but light pall. Before them certain official maidens carry a new tunic, ewers of water, silver dishes pierced with holes, cloths, and immense sponges. The rest carry wands with ribbons, and strew flowers. The burden is deposited on the altar, and the pall removed. It is a huge egg.

THE SHE-ANCIENT [*freeing her arms from her robe, and placing her saws on the altar ready to her hand in a businesslike manner*] A girl, I think you said?

ACIS. Yes.

THE TUNIC BEARER. It is a shame. Why cant we have more boys?

SEVERAL YOUTHS [*protesting*] Not at all. More girls. We want new girls.

A GIRL'S VOICE FROM THE EGG. Let me out. Let me out. I want to be born. I want to be born. [*The egg rocks*].

ACIS [*snatching a wand from one of the others and whacking the egg with it*] Be quiet, I tell you. Wait. You will be born presently.

THE EGG. No, no: at once, at once. I want to be born: I want to be born. [*Violent kicking within the egg, which rocks so hard that it has to be held on the altar by the bearers*].

THE SHE-ANCIENT. Silence. [*The music stops; and the egg behaves itself*].

The She-Ancient takes her two saws, and with a couple of strokes rips the egg open. The Newly Born, a pretty girl who would have been guessed as seventeen in our day, sits up in the broken shell, exquisitely fresh and rosy, but with filaments of spare albumen clinging to her here and there.

THE NEWLY BORN [*as the world bursts on her vision*] Oh! Oh!! Oh!!! Oh!!!! [*She continues this ad libitum during the following remonstrances*].

ACIS. Hold your noise, will you?

The washing begins. The Newly Born shrieks and struggles.

A YOUTH. Lie quiet, you clammy little devil.

A MAIDEN. You must be washed, dear. Now quiet, quiet, quiet: be good.

ACIS. Shut your mouth, or I'll shove the sponge in it.

THE MAIDEN. Shut your eyes. Itll hurt if you dont.

ANOTHER MAIDEN. Dont be silly. One would think nobody had ever been born before.

THE NEWLY BORN [*yells*] !!!!!!

ACIS. Serve you right! You were told to shut your eyes.

THE YOUTH. Dry her off quick. I can hardly hold her. Shut it, will you; or I'll smack you into a pickled cabbage.

The dressing begins. The Newly Born chuckles with delight.

THE MAIDEN. Your arms go here, dear. Isnt it pretty? Youll look lovely.

THE NEWLY BORN [*rapturously*] Oh! Oh!! Oh!!! Oh!!!!

ANOTHER YOUTH. No: the other arm: youre putting it on back to front. You *are* a silly little beast.

ACIS. Here! Thats it. Now youre clean and decent. Up with you! Oopsh! [*He hauls her to her feet. She cannot walk at first, but masters it after a few steps*]. Now then: march. Here she is, Ancient: put her through the catechism.

THE SHE-ANCIENT. What name have you chosen for her?

ACIS. Amaryllis.

THE SHE-ANCIENT [*to the Newly Born*] Your name is Amaryllis.

THE NEWLY BORN. What does it mean?

A YOUTH. Love.

A MAIDEN. Mother.

ANOTHER YOUTH. Lilies.

THE NEWLY BORN. [*to Acis*] What is your name?

ACIS. Acis.

THE NEWLY BORN. I love you, Acis. I must have you all to myself. Take me in your arms.

ACIS. Steady, young one. I am three years old.

THE NEWLY BORN. What has that to do with it? I love you; and I must have you or I will go back into my shell again.

ACIS. You cant. It's broken. Look here [*pointing to Strephon, who has remained in his seat without looking round at the birth, wrapped up in his sorrow*]! Look at this poor fellow!

THE NEWLY BORN. What is the matter with him?

ACIS. When he was born he chose a girl two years old for his sweetheart. He is two years old now himself; and already his heart is broken because she is four. That means that she has grown up like this Ancient here, and has left him. If you choose me, we shall have only a year's happiness before I break your heart by growing up. Better choose the youngest you can find.

THE NEWLY BORN. I will not choose anyone but you. You must not grow up. We will love one another for ever. [*They all laugh*]. What are you laughing at?

THE SHE-ANCIENT. Listen, child—

THE NEWLY BORN. Do not come near me, you dreadful old creature. You frighten me.

ACIS. Just give her another moment. She is not quite reasonable yet. What can you expect from a child less than five minutes old?

THE NEWLY BORN. I think I feel a little more reasonable now. Of course I was rather young when I said that; but the inside of my head is changing very rapidly. I should like to have things explained to me.

ACIS [*to the She-Ancient*] Is she all right, do you think?

The She-Ancient looks at the Newly Born critically; feels her bumps like a phrenologist; grips her muscles and shakes her limbs; examines her teeth; looks into her eyes for a moment; and finally relinquishes her with an air of having finished her job.

THE SHE-ANCIENT. She will do. She may live.

They all wave their hands and shout for joy.

THE NEWLY BORN [*indignant*] I may live! Suppose there had been anything wrong with me?

THE SHE-ANCIENT. Children with anything wrong do not live here, my child. Life is not cheap with us. But you would not have felt anything.

THE NEWLY BORN. You mean that you would have murdered me!

THE SHE-ANCIENT. That is one of the funny words the newly born bring with them out of the past. You will forget it tomorrow. Now listen. You have four years of childhood before you. You will not be very happy; but you will be interested and amused by the novelty of the world; and your companions here will teach you how to keep up an imitation of happiness during your four years by what they call arts and sports and pleasures. The worst of your troubles is already over.

THE NEWLY BORN. What! In five minutes?

THE SHE-ANCIENT. No: you have been growing for two years in the egg. You began by being several sorts of creatures that no longer exist, though we have fossils of them. Then you became human; and you passed in fifteen months through a development that once cost human beings twenty years of awkward stumbling immaturity after they were born. They had to spend fifty years more in the sort of childhood you will complete in four years. And then they died of decay. But you need not die until your accident comes.

THE NEWLY BORN. What is my accident?

THE SHE-ANCIENT. Sooner or later you will fall and break your neck; or a tree will fall on you; or you will be struck by lightning. Something or other must make an end of you someday.

THE NEWLY BORN. But why should any of these things happen to me?

THE SHE-ANCIENT. There is no why. They do. Everything happens to everybody sooner or later if there is time enough. And with us there is eternity.

THE NEWLY BORN. Nothing need happen. I never heard such nonsense in all my life. I shall know how to take care of myself.

THE SHE-ANCIENT. So you think.

THE NEWLY BORN. I dont think: I know. I shall enjoy life for ever and ever.

THE SHE-ANCIENT. If you should turn out to be a person of infinite capacity, you will no doubt find life infinitely interesting. However, all you have to do now is to play with your companions. They have many pretty toys, as you see: a playhouse, pictures, images, flowers, bright fabrics, music: above all, themselves; for the most amusing child's toy is another child. At the end of four years, your mind will change: you will become wise; and then you will be entrusted with power.

THE NEWLY BORN. But I want power now.

THE SHE-ANCIENT. No doubt you do; so that you could play with the world by tearing it to pieces.

THE NEWLY BORN. Only to see how it is made. I should put it all together again much better than before.

THE SHE-ANCIENT. There was a time when children were given the world to play with because they promised to improve it. They did not improve it; and they would have wrecked it had their power been as great as that which you will yield when you are no longer a child. Until then your young companions will instruct you in whatever is necessary. You are not forbidden to speak to the ancients; but you had better not do so, as most of them have long ago exhausted all the interest there is in observing children and conversing with them. [*She turns to go*].

THE NEWLY BORN. Wait. Tell me some things that I ought to do and ought not to do. I feel the need of education.

They all laugh at her, except the She-Ancient.

THE SHE-ANCIENT. You will have grown out of that by to-morrow. Do what you please. [*She goes away up the hill path*].

The officials take their paraphernalia and the fragments of the egg back into the temple.

ACIS. Just fancy: that old girl has been going for seven hundred years and hasnt had her fatal accident yet; and she is not a bit tired of it all.

THE NEWLY BORN. How could anyone ever get tired of life?

ACIS. They do. That is, of the same life. They manage to change themselves in a wonderful way. You meet them sometimes with a lot of extra heads and arms and legs: they make you split laughing at them. Most of them have forgotten how to speak: the ones that attend to us have to brush up their knowledge of the language once a year or so. Nothing makes any difference to them that I can see. They never enjoy themselves. I dont know how they can stand it. They dont even come to our festivals of the arts. That old one who saw you out of your shell has gone off to moodle about doing nothing; though she knows that this is Festival Day.

THE NEWLY BORN. What is Festival Day?

ACIS. Two of our greatest sculptors are bringing us their latest masterpieces; and we are going to crown them with flowers and sing dithyrambs to them and dance round them.

THE NEWLY BORN. How jolly! What is a sculptor?

ACIS. Listen here, young one. You must find out things for yourself, and not ask questions. For the first day or two you must keep your eyes and ears open and your mouth shut. Children should be seen and not heard.

THE NEWLY BORN. Who are you calling a child? I am fully quarter of an hour old. [*She sits down on the curved bench near Strephon with her maturest air*].

VOICES IN THE TEMPLE [*all expressing protest, disappointment, disgust*] Oh! Oh! Scandalous. Shameful. Disgraceful. What filth! Is this a joke? Why, theyre ancients! Ss-s-s-sss! Are you mad, Arjillax? This is an outrage. An insult. Yah! etc. etc. etc. [*The malcontents appear on the steps, grumbling*].

ACIS. Hullo: whats the matter? [*He goes to the steps of the temple*].

The two sculptors issue from the temple. One has a beard two feet long: the other is beardless. Between them comes a handsome nymph with marked features, dark hair richly waved, and authoritative bearing.

THE AUTHORITATIVE NYMPH [*swooping down to the centre of the glade with the sculptors, between Acis and the Newly Born*] Do not try to browbeat me, Arjillax, merely because you are clever with your hands. Can you play the flute?

ARJILLAX [*the bearded sculptor on her right*] No, Ecrasia: I cannot. What has that to do with it? [*He is half derisive, half impatient, wholly resolved not to take her seriously in spite of her beauty and imposing tone*].

ECRASIA. Well, have you ever hesitated to criticize our best flute players, and to declare whether their music is good or bad? Pray have I not the same right to criticize your busts, though I cannot make images any more than you can play?

ARJILLAX. Any fool can play the flute, or play anything else, if he practises enough; but sculpture is a creative art, not a mere business of whistling into a pipe. The sculptor must have something of the god in him. From his hand comes a form which reflects a spirit. He does not make it to please you, nor even to please himself, but because he must. You must take what he gives you, or leave it if you are not worthy of it.

ECRASIA [*scornfully*] Not worthy of it! Ho! May I not leave it because it is not worthy of me?

ARJILLAX. Of you! Hold your silly tongue, you conceited humbug. What do you know about it?

ECRASIA. I know what every person of culture knows: that the business of the artist is to create beauty. Until today your works have been full of beauty; and I have been the first to point that out.

ARJILLAX. Thank you for nothing. People have eyes, havnt they, to see what is as plain as the sun in the heavens without your pointing it out?

ECRASIA. You were very glad to have it pointed out. You did not call me a conceited humbug then. You stifled me with caresses. You modelled me as the genius of art presiding over the infancy of your master here [*indicating the other sculptor*], Martellus.

MARTELLUS [*a silent and meditative listener, shudders and shakes his head, but says nothing*].

ARJILLAX [*quarrelsomely*] I was taken in by your talk.

ECRASIA. I discovered your genius before anyone else did. Is that true, or is it not?

ARJILLAX. Everybody knew I was an extraordinary person. When I was born my beard was three feet long.

ECRASIA. Yes; and it has shrunk from three feet to two. Your genius seems to have been in the last foot of your beard; for you have lost both.

MARTELLUS [*with a short sardonic cachinnation*] Ha! My beard was three and a half feet long when I was born; and a flash of lightning burnt it off and killed the ancient who was delivering me. Without a hair on my chin I became the greatest sculptor in ten generations.

ECRASIA. And yet you come to us today with empty hands. We shall actually have to crown Arjillax here because no other sculptor is exhibiting.

ACIS [*returning from the temple steps to behind the curved seat on the right of the three*] Whats the row, Ecrasia? Why have you fallen out with Arjillax?

ECRASIA. He has insulted us! outraged us! profaned his art! You know how much we hoped from the twelve busts he placed in the temple to be unveiled today. Well, go in and look at them. That is all I have to say. [*She sweeps to the curved seat, and sits down just where Acis is leaning over it*].

ACIS. I am no great judge of sculpture. Art is not my line. What is wrong with the busts?

ECRASIA. Wrong with them! Instead of being ideally beautiful nymphs and youths, they are horribly realistic studies of—but I really cannot bring my lips to utter it.

The Newly Born, full of curiosity, runs to the temple, and peeps in.

ACIS. Oh, stow it, Ecrasia. Your lips are not so squeamish as all that. Studies of what?

THE NEWLY BORN [*from the temple steps*] Ancients.

ACIS [*surprised but not scandalized*] Ancients!

ECRASIA. Yes, ancients. The one subject that is by the universal consent of all connoisseurs absolutely excluded from the fine arts. [*To Arjillax*] How can you defend such a proceeding?

ARJILLAX. If you come to that, what interest can you find in the statues of smirking nymphs and posturing youths you stick up all over the place?

ECRASIA. You did not ask that when your hand was still skilful enough to model them.

ARJILLAX. Skilful! You high-nosed idiot, I could turn such things out by the score with my eyes bandaged and one hand tied behind me. But what use would they be? They would bore me; and they would bore you if you had any sense. Go in and look at my busts. Look at them again and yet again until you receive the full impression of the intensity of mind that is stamped on them; and then go back to the pretty-pretty confectionery you call sculpture, and see whether you can endure its vapid emptiness. [*He mounts the altar impetuously*] Listen to me, all of you; and do you, Ecrasia, be silent if you are capable of silence.

ECRASIA. Silence is the most perfect expression of scorn. Scorn! That is what I feel for your revolting busts.

ARJILLAX. Fool: the busts are only the beginning of a mighty design. Listen.

ACIS. Go ahead, old sport. We are listening.

Martellus stretches himself on the sward beside the altar. The Newly Born sits on the temple steps with her chin on her hands, ready to devour the first oration she has ever heard. The rest sit or stand at ease.

ARJILLAX. In the records which generations of children have rescued from the stupid neglect of the ancients, there has come down to us a fable which, like many fables, is not a thing that was done in the past, but a thing that is to be done in the future. It is a legend of a supernatural being called the Archangel Michael.

THE NEWLY BORN. Is this a story? I want to hear a story. [*She runs down the steps and sits on the altar at Arjillax's feet*].

ARJILLAX. The Archangel Michael was a mighty sculptor and painter. He found in the centre of the world a temple erected to the goddess of the centre, called Mediterranea. This temple was full of silly pictures of pretty children, such as Ecrasia approves.

ACIS. Fair play, Arjillax! If she is to keep silent, let her alone.

ECRASIA. I shall not interrupt, Acis. Why should I not prefer youth and beauty to age and ugliness?

ARJILLAX. Just so. Well, the Archangel Michael was of my opinion, not yours. He began by painting on the ceiling the newly born in all their childish beauty. But when he had done this he was not satisfied; for the temple was no more impressive than it had been before, except that there was a strength and promise of greater things about his newly born ones than any other artist had attained to. So he painted all round these newly born a company of ancients, who were in those days called prophets and sybils, whose majesty was that of the mind alone at its intensest. And this painting was acknowledged through ages and ages to be the summit and masterpiece of art. Of course we cannot believe such a tale literally. It is only a legend. We do not believe in archangels; and the notion that thirty thousand years ago sculpture and painting existed, and had even reached the glorious perfection they have reached with us, is absurd. But what men cannot realize they can at least aspire to. They please themselves by pretending that it was realized in a golden age of the past. This splendid legend endured because it lived as a desire in the hearts of the greatest artists. The temple of Mediterranea never was built in the past, nor did Michael the Archangel exist. But today the temple is here [*he points to the porch*]; and the man is here [*he slaps himself on the chest*]. I, Arjillax, am the man. I will place in your theatre such images of the newly born as must satisfy even Ecrasia's appetite for beauty; and I will surround them with ancients more august than any who walk through our woods.

MARTELLUS [*as before*] Ha!

ARJILLAX [*stung*] Why do you laugh, you who have come empty-handed, and, it seems, empty-headed?

ECRASIA [*rising indignantly*] Oh, shame! You dare disparage Martellus, twenty times your master.

ACIS. Be quiet, will you [*he seizes her shoulders and thrusts her back into her seat*].

MARTELLUS. Let him disparage his fill, Ecrasia. [*Sitting up*] My poor Arjillax, I too had this dream. I too found one day that my images of loveliness had become vapid, uninteresting, tedious, a waste of time and material. I too lost my desire to model limbs, and retained only my interest in heads and faces. I, too, made busts of ancients; but I had not your courage: I made them in secret, and hid them from you all.

ARJILLAX [*jumping down from the altar behind Martellus in his surprise and excitement*] You made busts of ancients! Where are they, man? Will you be talked out of your inspiration by Ecrasia and the fools who imagine she speaks with authority? Let us have them all set up beside mine in the theatre. I have opened the way for you; and you see I am none the worse.

MARTELLUS. Impossible. They are all smashed. [*He rises, laughing*].

ALL. Smashed!

ARJILLAX. Who smashed them?

MARTELLUS. I did. That is why I laughed at you just now. You will smash yours before you have completed a dozen of them. [*He goes to the end of the altar and sits down beside the Newly Born*].

ARJILLAX. But why?

MARTELLUS. Because you cannot give them life. A live ancient is better than a dead statue. [*He takes the Newly Born on his knee: she is flattered and voluptuously responsive*]. Anything alive is better than anything that is only pretending to be alive. [*To Arjillax*] Your disillusion with your works of beauty is only the beginning of your disillusion with images of all sorts. As your hand became more skilful and your chisel cut deeper, you strove to get nearer and nearer to truth and reality, discarding the fleeting fleshly lure, and making images of the mind that fascinates to the end. But how can so noble an inspiration be satisfied with any image, even an image of the truth? In the end the intellectual conscience that tore you away from the fleeting in art to the eternal must tear you away from art altogether, because art is false and life alone is true.

THE NEWLY BORN [*flings her arms round his neck and kisses him enthusiastically*].

MARTELLUS [*rises; carries her to the curved bench on his left; deposits her beside Strephon as if she were his overcoat; and continues without the least change of tone*] Shape it as you will, marble remains marble, and the graven image an idol. As I have broken my idols, and cast away my chisel and modelling tools, so will you too break these busts of yours.

ARJILLAX. Never.

MARTELLUS. Wait, my friend. I do not come empty-handed today, as you imagined. On the contrary, I bring with me such a work of art as you have never seen, and an artist who has surpassed both you and me further than we have surpassed all our competitors.

ECRASIA. Impossible. The greatest things in art can never be surpassed.

ARJILLAX. Who is this paragon whom you declare greater than I?

MARTELLUS. I declare him greater than myself, Arjillax.

ARJILLAX [*frowning*] I understand. Sooner than not drown me, you are willing to clasp me round the waist and jump overboard with me.

ACIS. Oh, stop squabbling. That is the worst of you artists. You are always in little squabbling cliques; and the worst cliques are those which consist of one man. Who is this new fellow you are throwing in one another's teeth?

ARJILLAX. Ask Martellus: do not ask me. I know nothing of him. [*He leaves Martellus, and sits down beside Ecrasia, on her left*].

MARTELLUS. You know him quite well. Pygmalion.

ECRASIA [*indignantly*] Pygmalion! That soulless creature! A scientist! A laboratory person!

ARJILLAX. Pygmalion produce a work of art! You have lost your artistic senses. The man is utterly incapable of modelling a thumb nail, let alone a human figure.

MARTELLUS. That does not matter: I have done the modelling for him.

ARJILLAX. What on earth do you mean?

MARTELLUS [*calling*] Pygmalion: come forth.

Pygmalion, a square-fingered youth with his face laid out in horizontal blocks, and a perpetual smile of eager benevolent interest in everything, and expectation of equal interest from everybody else, comes from the temple to the centre of the group, who regard him for the most part with dismay, as dreading that he will bore them. Ecrasia is openly contemptuous.

MARTELLUS. Friends: it is unfortunate that Pygmalion is

constitutionally incapable of exhibiting anything without first giving a lecture about it to explain it; but I promise you that if you will be patient he will shew you the two most wonderful works of art in the world, and that they will contain some of my own very best workmanship. Let me add that they will inspire a loathing that will cure you of the lunacy of art for ever. [*He sits down next the Newly Born, who pouts and turns a very cold right shoulder to him, a demonstration utterly lost on him*].

Pygmalion, with the smile of a simpleton, and the eager confidence of a fanatical scientist, climbs awkwardly on to the altar. They prepare for the worst.

PYGMALION. My friends: I will omit the algebra—

ACIS. Thank God!

PYGMALION [*continuing*]—because Martellus has made me promise to do so. To come to the point, I have succeeded in making artificial human beings. Real live ones, I mean.

INCREDULOUS VOICES. Oh, come! Tell us another. Really, Pyg! Get out. You havnt. What a lie!

PYGMALION. I tell you I have. I will shew them to you. It has been done before. One of the very oldest documents we possess mentions a tradition of a biologist who extracted certain unspecified minerals from the earth and, as it quaintly expresses it, "breathed into their nostrils the breath of life." This is the only tradition from the primitive ages which we can regard as really scientific. There are later documents which specify the minerals with great precision, even to their atomic weights, but they are utterly unscientific, because they overlook the element of life which makes all the difference between a mere mixture of salts and gases and a living organism. These mixtures were made over and over again in the crude laboratories of the Silly-Clever Ages; but nothing came of them until the ingredient which the old chronicler called the breath of life was added by this very remarkable early experimenter. In my view he was the founder of biological science.

ARJILLAX. Is that all we know about him? It doesnt

amount to very much, does it?

PYGMALION. There are some fragments of pictures and documents which represent him as walking in a garden and advising people to cultivate their gardens. His name has come down to us in several forms. One of them is Jove. Another is Voltaire.

ECRASIA. You are boring us to distraction with your Voltaire. What about your human beings?

ARJILLAX. Aye: come to them.

PYGMALION. I assure you that these details are intensely interesting. [*Cries of* No! They are not! Come to the human beings! Conspuez Voltaire! Cut it short, Pyg! *interrupt him from all sides*]. You will see their bearing presently. I promise you I will not detain you long. We know, we children of science, that the universe is full of forces and powers and energies of one kind and another. The sap rising in a tree, the stone holding together in a definite crystalline structure, the thought of a philosopher holding his brain in form and operation with an inconceivably powerful grip, the urge of evolution: all these forces can be used by us. For instance, I use the force of gravitation when I put a stone on my tunic to prevent it being blown away when I am bathing. By substituting appropriate machines for the stone we have made not only gravitation our slave, but also electricity and magnetism, atomic attraction, repulsion, polarization, and so forth. But hitherto the vital force has eluded us; so it has had to create machinery for itself. It has created and developed bony structure of the requisite strength, and clothed them with cellular tissue of such amazing sensitiveness that the organs it forms will adapt their action to all the normal variations in the air they breathe, the food they digest, and the circumstances about which they have to think. Yet, as these live bodies, as we call them, are only machines after all, it must be possible to construct them mechanically.

ARJILLAX. Everything is possible. Have you done it? that is the question.

PYGMALION. Yes. But that is a mere fact. What is interesting is the explanation of the fact. Forgive my saying so: but it is such a pity that you artists have no intellect.

ECRASIA [*sententiously*] I do not admit that. The artist divines by inspiration all the truths that the so-called scientist grubs up in his laboratory slowly and stupidly long afterwards.

ARJILLAX [*to Ecrasia, quarrelsomely*] What do you know about it? You are not an artist.

ACIS. Shut your heads, both of you. Let us have the artificial men. Trot them out, Pygmalion.

PYGMALION. It is a man and a woman. But I really must explain first.

ALL [*groaning*] !!!

PYGMALION. Yes: I—

ACIS. We want results, not explanations.

PYGMALION [*hurt*] I see I am boring you. Not one of you takes the least interest in science. Good-bye. [*He descends from the altar and makes for the temple*].

SEVERAL YOUTHS AND MAIDENS [*rising and rushing to him*] No, no. Dont go. Dont be offended. We want to see the artificial pair. We will listen. We are tremendously interested. Tell us all about it.

PYGMALION [*relenting*] I shall not detain you two minutes.

ALL. Half an hour if you like. Please go on, Pygmalion. [*They rush him back to the altar, and hoist him on to it*]. Up you go.

They return to their former places.

PYGMALION. As I told you, lots of attempts were made to produce protoplasm in the laboratory. Why were these synthetic plasms, as they called them, no use?

ECRASIA. We are waiting for you to tell us.

THE NEWLY BORN [*modelling herself on Ecrasia, and trying to outdo her intellectually*] Clearly because they were dead.

PYGMALION. Not bad for a baby, my pet. But dead and alive are very loose terms. You are not half as much alive as you will be in another month or so. What was wrong with the synthetic protoplasm was that it could not fix and conduct the Life Force. It was like a wooden magnet or a lightning conductor made of silk: it would not take the current.

ACIS. Nobody but a fool would make a wooden magnet, and expect it to attract anything.

PYGMALION. He might if he were so ignorant as not to be able to distinguish between wood and soft iron. In those days they were very ignorant of the differences between things, because their methods of analysis were crude. They mixed up messes that were so like protoplasm that they could not tell the difference. But the difference was there, though their analysis was too superficial and incomplete to detect it. You must remember that these poor devils were very little better than our idiots: we should never dream of letting one of them survive the day of its birth. Why, the Newly Born there already knows by instinct many things that their greatest physicists could hardly arrive at by forty years of strenuous study. Her simple direct sense of space-time and quantity unconsciously solves problems which cost their most famous mathematicians years of prolonged and laborious calculations requiring such intense mental application that they frequently forgot to breathe when engaged in them, and almost suffocated themselves in consequence.

ECRASIA. Leave these obscure prehistoric abortions; and come back to your synthetic man and woman.

PYGMALION. When I undertook the task of making synthetic men, I did not waste my time on protoplasm. It was evident to me that if it were possible to make protoplasm in the laboratory, it must be equally possible to begin higher up and make fully evolved muscular and nervous tissues, bone, and so forth. Why make the seed when the making of the flower would be no greater miracle? I tried thousands of combinations before I succeeded in producing anything that would fix high-potential Life Force.

ARJILLAX. High what?

PYGMALION. High-po-tential. The Life Force is not so simple as you think. A high-potential current of it will turn a bit of dead tissue into a philosopher's brain. A low-potential current will reduce the same bit of tissue to a mass of corruption. Will you believe me when I tell you that, even in man himself, the Life Force used to slip suddenly down from its human level to that of a fungus, so that men found their flesh no longer growing as flesh, but proliferating horribly in a lower form which was called cancer, until the lower form of life killed the higher, and both perished together miserably?

MARTELLUS. Keep off the primitive tribes, Pygmalion. They interest you; but they bore these young things.

PYGMALION. I am only trying to make you understand. There was the Life Force raging all round me: there was I, trying to make organs that would capture it as a battery captures electricity, and tissues that would conduct it and operate it. It was easy enough to make eyes more perfect than our own, and ears with a larger range of sound; but they could neither see nor hear, because they were not susceptible to the Life Force. But it was far worse when I discovered how to make them susceptible; for the first thing that happened was that they ceased to be eyes and ears and turned into heaps of maggots.

ECRASIA. Disgusting! Please stop.

ACIS. If you dont want to hear, go away. You go ahead, Pyg.

PYGMALION. I went ahead. You see, the lower potentials of the Life Force could make maggots, but not human eyes or ears. I improved the tissue until it was susceptible to a higher potential.

ARJILLAX [*intensely interested*] Yes; and then?

PYGMALION. Then the eyes and ears turned into cancers.

ECRASIA. Oh, hideous!

PYGMALION. Not at all. That was a great advance. It encouraged me so much that I put aside the eyes and ears, and made a brain. It wouldnt take the Life Force at all until I had altered its constitution a dozen times; but when it did, it took a much higher potential, and did not dissolve; and neither did the eyes and ears when I connected them up with the brain. I was able to make a sort of monster: a thing without arms or legs; and it really and truly lived for half-an-hour.

THE NEWLY BORN. Half-an-hour! What good was that? Why did it die?

PYGMALION. Its blood went wrong. But I got that right; and then I went ahead with a complete human body: arms and legs and all. He was my first man.

ARJILLAX. Who modelled him?

PYGMALION. I did.

MARTELLUS. Do you mean to say you tried your own hand before you sent for me?

PYGMALION. Bless you, yes, several times. My first man was the ghastliest creature: a more dreadful mixture of horror and absurdity than you who have not seen him can conceive.

ARJILLAX. If you modelled him, he must indeed have been a spectacle.

PYGMALION. Oh, it was not his shape. You see I did not invent that. I took actual measurements and moulds from my own body. Sculptors do that sometimes, you know; though they pretend they dont.

MARTELLUS. Hm!

ARJILLAX. Hah!

PYGMALION. He was all right to look at, at first, or nearly so. But he behaved in the most appalling manner; and the subsequent developments were so disgusting that I really cannot describe them to you. He seized all sorts of things and swallowed them. He drank every fluid in the laboratory. I tried to explain to him that he must take nothing that he could not digest and assimilate completely; but of course he could not understand me. He assimilated a little of what he swallowed; but the process left horrible residues which he had no means of getting rid of. His blood turned to poison; and he perished in torments, howling. I then perceived that I had produced a prehistoric man; for there are certain traces in our own bodies of arrangements which enabled the earlier forms of mankind to renew their bodies by swallowing flesh and grains and vegetables and all sorts of unnatural and hideous foods, and getting rid of what they could not digest.

ECRASIA. But what a pity he died! What a glimpse of the past we have lost! He could have told us stories of the Golden Age.

PYGMALION. Not he. He was a most dangerous beast. He was afraid of me, and actually tried to kill me by snatching up things and striking at me with them. I had to give him two or three pretty severe shocks before I convinced him that he was at my mercy.

THE NEWLY BORN. Why did you not make a woman instead of a man? She would have known how to behave herself.

MARTELLUS. Why did you not make a man and a woman? Their children would have been interesting.

PYGMALION. I intended to make a woman; but after my experience with the man it was out of the question.

ECRASIA. Pray why?

PYGMALION. Well, it is difficult to explain if you have not studied prehistoric methods of reproduction. You see the only sort of men and women I could make were men and women just like us as far as their bodies were concerned. That was how I killed the poor beast of a man. I hadnt provided for his horrible prehistoric methods of feeding himself. Suppose the woman had reproduced in some prehistoric way instead of being oviparous as we are? She couldnt have done it with a modern female body. Besides, the experiment might have been painful.

ECRASIA. Then you have nothing to shew us at all?

PYGMALION. Oh yes I have. I am not so easily beaten as that. I set to work again for months to find out how to make a digestive system that would deal with waste products and a reproductive system capable of internal nourishment and incubation.

ECRASIA. Why did you not find out how to make them

like us?

STREPHON [*crying out in his grief for the first time*] Why did you not make a woman whom you could love? That was the secret you needed.

THE NEWLY BORN. Oh yes. How true! How great of you, darling Strephon! [*She kisses him impulsively*].

STREPHON [*passionately*] Let me alone.

MARTELLUS. Control your reflexes, child.

THE NEWLY BORN. My what!

MARTELLUS. Your reflexes. The things you do without thinking. Pygmalion is going to shew you a pair of human creatures who are all reflexes and nothing else. Take warning by them.

THE NEWLY BORN. But wont they be alive, like us?

PYGMALION. That is a very difficult question to answer, my dear. I confess I thought at first I had created living creatures; but Martellus declares they are only automata. But then Martellus is a mystic: *I* am a man of science. He draws a line between an automaton and a living organism. I cannot draw that line to my own satisfaction.

MARTELLUS. Your artificial men have no self-control. They only respond to stimuli from without.

PYGMALION. But they are conscious. I have taught them to talk and read; and now they tell lies. That is so very lifelike.

MARTELLUS. Not at all. If they were alive they would tell the truth. You can provoke them to tell any silly lie; and you can foresee exactly the sort of lie they will tell. Give them a clip below the knee, and they will jerk their foot forward. Give them a clip in their appetites or vanities or any of their lusts and greeds, and they will boast and lie, and affirm and deny, and hate and love without the slightest regard to the facts that are staring them in the face, or to their own obvious limitations. That proves that they are automata.

PYGMALION [*unconvinced*] I know, dear old chap; but there really is some evidence that we are descended from creatures quite as limited and absurd as these. After all, the baby there is three-quarters an automaton. Look at the way she has been going on!

THE NEWLY BORN [*indignantly*] What do you mean? How have I been going on?

ECRASIA. If they have no regard for truth, they can have no real vitality.

PYGMALION. Truth is sometimes so artificial: so relative, as we say in the scientific world, that it is very hard to feel quite sure that what is false and even ridiculous to us may not be true to them.

ECRASIA. I ask you again, why did you not make them like us? Would any true artist be content with less than the best?

PYGMALION. I couldnt. I tried. I failed. I am convinced that what I am about to shew you is the very highest living organism that can be produced in the laboratory. The best tissues we can manufacture will not take as high potentials as the natural product: that is where Nature beats us. You dont seem to understand, any of you, what an enormous triumph it was to produce consciousness at all.

ACIS. Cut the cackle; and come to the synthetic couple.

SEVERAL YOUTHS AND MAIDENS. Yes, yes. No more talking. Let us have them. Dry up, Pyg; and fetch them along. Come on: out with them! The synthetic couple: the synthetic couple.

PYGMALION [*waving his hands to appease them*] Very well, very well. Will you please whistle for them? They respond to the stimulus of a whistle.

All who can, whistle like streetboys.

ECRASIA [*makes a wry face and puts her fingers in her ears*]!

PYGMALION. Sh-sh-sh! Thats enough: thats enough: thats enough. [*Silence*]. Now let us have some music. A dance tune. Not too fast.

The flutists play a quiet dance.

MARTELLUS. Prepare yourselves for something ghastly.

Two figures, a man and woman of noble appearance, beautifully modelled and splendidly attired, emerge hand in hand from the temple. Seeing that all eyes are fixed on them, they halt on the steps, smiling with gratified vanity. The woman is on the man's left.

PYGMALION [*rubbing his hands with the purring satisfaction of a creator*] This way, please.

The Figures advance condescendingly and pose themselves centrally between the curved seats.

PYGMALION. Now if you will be so good as to oblige us with a little something. You dance so beautifully, you know. [*He sits down next Martellus, and whispers to him*] It is extraordinary how sensitive they are to the stimulus of flattery.

The Figures, with a gracious air, dance pompously, but very passably. At the close they bow to one another.

ON ALL HANDS [*clapping*] Bravo! Thank you. Wonderful! Splendid. Perfect.

The Figures acknowledge the applause in an obvious condition of swelled head.

THE NEWLY BORN. Can they make love?

PYGMALION. Yes: they can respond to every stimulus. They have all the reflexes. Put your arm round the man's neck, and he will put his arm round your body. He cannot help it.

THE FEMALE FIGURE [*frowning*] Round mine, you mean.

PYGMALION. Yours, too, of course, if the stimulus comes from you.

ECRASIA. Cannot he do anything original?

PYGMALION. No. But then, you know, I do not admit that any of us can do anything really original, though Martellus thinks we can.

ACIS. Can he answer a question?

PYGMALION. Oh yes. A question is a stimulus, you know. Ask him one.

ACIS [*to the Male Figure*] What do you think of what you see around you? Of us, for instance, and our ways and doings?

THE MALE FIGURE. I have not seen the newspaper today.

THE FEMALE FIGURE. How can you expect my husband to

know what to think of you if you give him his breakfast without his paper?

MARTELLUS. You see. He is a mere automaton.

THE NEWLY BORN. I dont think I should like him to put his arm round my neck. I dont like them. [*The Male Figure looks offended, and the Female jealous*]. Oh, I thought they couldnt understand. Have they feelings?

PYGMALION. Of course they have. I tell you they have all the reflexes.

THE NEWLY BORN. But feelings are not reflexes.

PYGMALION. They are sensations. When the rays of light enter their eyes and make a picture on their retinas, their brains become conscious of the picture and they act accordingly. When the waves of sound started by your speaking enter their ears and record a disparaging remark on their keyboards, their brains become conscious of the disparagement and resent it accordingly. If you did not disparage them they would not resent it. They are merely responding to a stimulus.

THE MALE FIGURE. We are part of a cosmic system. Free will is an illusion. We are the children of Cause and Effect. We are the Unalterable, the Irresistible, the Irresponsible, the Inevitable.

My name is Ozymandias, king of kings:
Look on my works, ye mighty, and despair.

There is a general stir of curiosity at this.

ACIS. What the dickens does he mean?

THE MALE FIGURE. Silence, base accident of Nature. This [*taking the hand of the Female Figure and introducing her*] is Cleopatra-Semiramis, consort of the king of kings, and therefore queen of queens. Ye are things hatched from eggs by the brainless sun and the blind fire; but the king of kings and queen of queens are not accidents of the egg: they are thought-out and hand-made to receive the sacred Life Force. There is one person of the king and one of the queen; but the Life Force of the king and queen is all one: the glory equal, the majesty co-eternal. Such as the king is so is the queen, the king thought-out and hand-made, the queen thought-out and hand-made. The actions of the king are caused, and therefore determined, from the beginning of the world to the end; and the actions of the queen are likewise. The king logical and predetermined and inevitable, and the queen logical and predetermined and inevitable. And yet they are not two logical and predetermined and inevitable, but one logical and predetermined and inevitable. Therefore confound not the persons, nor divide the substance; but worship us twain as one throne, two in one and one in two, lest by error ye fall into irretrievable damnation.

THE FEMALE FIGURE. And if any say unto you "Which one?" remember that though there is one person of the king and one of the queen, yet these two persons are not alike, but are woman and man, and that as woman was created after man, the skill and practice gained in making him were added to her, wherefore she is to be exalted above him in all personal respects, and—

THE MALE FIGURE. Peace, woman; for this is a damnable heresy. Both Man and Woman are what they are and must do what they must according to the eternal laws of Cause and Effect. Look to your words; for if they enter my ear and jar too repugnantly on my sensorium, who knows that the inevitable response to that stimulus may not be a message to my muscles to snatch up some heavy object and break you in pieces.

The Female Figure picks up a stone and is about to throw it at her consort.

ARJILLAX [*springing up and shouting to Pygmalion, who is fondly watching the Male Figure*] Look out, Pygmalion! Look at the woman!

Pygmalion, seeing what is happening, hurls himself on the Female Figure and wrenches the stone out of her hand.

All spring up in consternation.

ARJILLAX. She meant to kill him.

STREPHON. This is horrible.

THE FEMALE FIGURE [*wrestling with Pygmalion*] Let me

go. Let me go, will you [*she bites his hand*].

PYGMALION [*releasing her and staggering*] Oh!

A general shriek of horror echoes his exclamation. He turns deadly pale, and supports himself against the end of the curved seat.

THE FEMALE FIGURE [*to her consort*] You would stand there and let me be treated like this, you unmanly coward.

Pygmalion falls dead.

THE NEWLY BORN. Oh! Whats the matter? Why did he fall? What has happened to him?

They look on anxiously as Martellus kneels down and examines the body of Pygmalion.

MARTELLUS. She has bitten a piece out of his hand nearly as large as a finger nail: enough to kill ten men. There is no pulse, no breath.

ECRASIA. But his thumb is clinched.

MARTELLUS. No: it has just straightened out. See! He has gone. Poor Pygmalion!

THE NEWLY BORN. Oh! [*She weeps*].

STREPHON. Hush, dear: thats childish.

THE NEWLY BORN [*subsiding with a sniff*] !!

MARTELLUS [*rising*] Dead in his third year. What a loss to Science!

ARJILLAX. Who cares about Science? Serve him right for making that pair of horrors!

THE MALE FIGURE [*glaring*] Ha!

THE FEMALE FIGURE. Keep a civil tongue in your head, you.

THE NEWLY BORN. Oh, do not be so unkind, Arjillax. You will make water come out of my eyes again.

MARTELLUS [*contemplating the Figures*] Just look at these two devils. I modelled them out of the stuff Pygmalion made for them. They are masterpieces of art. And see what they have done! Does that convince you of the value of art, Arjillax?

STREPHON. They look dangerous. Keep away from them.

ECRASIA. No need to tell us that, Strephon. Pf! They

poison the air.

THE MALE FIGURE. Beware, woman. The wrath of Ozymandias strikes like the lightning.

THE FEMALE FIGURE. You just say that again if you dare, you filthy creature.

ACIS. What are you going to do with them, Martellus? You are responsible for them, now that Pygmalion has gone.

MARTELLUS. If they were marble it would be simple enough: I could smash them. As it is, how am I to kill them without making a horrible mess?

THE MALE FIGURE [*posing heroically*] Ha! [*He declaims*]

Come one: come all: this rock shall fly
From its firm base as soon as I.

THE FEMALE FIGURE [*fondly*] My man! My hero husband! I am proud of you. I love you.

MARTELLUS. We must send out a message for an ancient.

ACIS. Need we bother an ancient about such a trifle? It will take less than half a second to reduce our poor Pygmalion to a pinch of dust. Why not calcine the two along with him?

MARTELLUS. No: the two automata are trifles; but the use of our powers of destruction is never a trifle. I had rather have the case judged.

The He-Ancient emerges from the grove. The Figures are panic-stricken.

THE HE-ANCIENT [*mildly*] Am I wanted? I feel called. [*Seeing the body of Pygmalion, and immediately taking a sterner tone*] What! A child lost! A life wasted! How has this happened?

THE FEMALE FIGURE [*frantically*] I didnt do it. It was not me. May I be struck dead if I touched him! It was he [*pointing to the Male Figure*].

ALL [*amazed at the lie*] Oh!

THE MALE FIGURE. Liar. You bit him. Everyone here saw you do it.

THE HE-ANCIENT. Silence. [*Going between the Figures*] Who made these two loathsome dolls?

THE MALE FIGURE [*trying to assert himself with his knees knocking*] My name is Ozymandias, king of—

THE HE-ANCIENT [*with a contemptuous gesture*] Pooh!

THE MALE FIGURE [*falling on his knees*] Oh dont, sir. D o n t. She did it, sir: indeed she did.

THE FEMALE FIGURE [*howling lamentably*] Boohoo! oo! ooh!

THE HE-ANCIENT. Silence, I say.

He knocks the Male Automaton upright by a very light flip under the chin. The Female Automaton hardly dares to sob. The immortals contemplate them with shame and loathing. The She-Ancient comes from the trees opposite the temple.

THE SHE-ANCIENT. Somebody wants me. What is the matter? [*She comes to the left hand of the Female Figure, not seeing the body of Pygmalion.* Pf! [*Severely*] You have been making dolls. You must not: they are not only disgusting: they are dangerous.

THE FEMALE FIGURE [*snivelling piteously*] I'm not a doll, mam. I'm only poor Cleopatra-Semiramis, queen of queens. [*Covering her face with her hands*] Oh, dont look at me like that, mam. I meant no harm. He hurt me: indeed he did.

THE HE-ANCIENT. The creature has killed that poor youth.

THE SHE-ANCIENT [*seeing the body of Pygmalion*] What! This clever child, who promised so well!

THE FEMALE FIGURE. He made me. I had as much right to kill him as he had to make me. And how was I to know that a little thing like that would kill him? I shouldnt die if he cut off my arm or leg.

ECRASIA. What nonsense!

MARTELLUS. It may not be nonsense. I daresay if you cut off her leg she would grow another, like the lobsters and the little lizards.

THE HE-ANCIENT. Did this dead boy make these two things?

MARTELLUS. He made them in his laboratory. I moulded their limbs. I am sorry. I was thoughtless: I did not foresee that they would kill and pretend to be persons they were not, and declare things that were false, and wish evil. I thought they would be merely mechanical fools.

THE MALE FIGURE. Do you blame us for our human nature?

THE FEMALE FIGURE. We are flesh and blood and not angels.

THE MALE FIGURE. Have you no hearts?

ARJILLAX. They are mad as well as mischievous. May we not destroy them?

STREPHON. We abhor them.

THE NEWLY BORN. We loathe them.

ECRASIA. They are noisome.

ACIS. I dont want to be hard on the poor devils; but they are making me feel uneasy in my inside. I never had such a sensation before.

MARTELLUS. I took a lot of trouble with them. But as far as I am concerned, destroy them by all means. I loathed them from the beginning.

ALL. Yes, yes: we all loathe them. Let us calcine them.

THE FEMALE FIGURE. Oh, dont be so cruel. I'm not fit to die. I will never bite anyone again. I will tell the truth. I will do good. Is it my fault if I was not made properly? Kill him; but spare me.

THE MALE FIGURE. No! I have done no harm: she has. Kill her if you like: you have no right to kill me.

THE NEWLY BORN. Do you hear that? They want to have one another killed.

ARJILLAX. Monstrous! Kill them both.

THE HE-ANCIENT. Silence. These things are mere automata: they cannot help shrinking from death at any cost. You see that they have no self-control, and are merely shuddering through a series of reflexes. Let us see whether we cannot put a little more life into them. [*He takes the Male Figure by the hand, and places his disengaged hand on its head*]. Now listen. One of you two is to be destroyed. Which of you shall it be?

THE MALE FIGURE [*after a slight convulsion during which his eyes are fixed on the He-Ancient*] Spare her; and kill me.

STREPHON. Thats better.

THE NEWLY BORN. Much better.

THE SHE-ANCIENT [*handling the Female Automaton in the same manner*] Which of you shall we kill?

THE FEMALE FIGURE. Kill us both. How could either of us live without the other?

ECRASIA. The woman is more sensible than the man.

The Ancients release the Automata.

THE MALE FIGURE [*sinking to the ground*] I am discouraged. Life is too heavy a burden.

THE FEMALE FIGURE [*collapsing*] I am dying. I am glad. I am afraid to live.

THE NEWLY BORN. I think it would be nice to give the poor things a little music.

ARJILLAX. Why?

THE NEWLY BORN. I dont know. But it would.

The Musicians play.

THE FEMALE FIGURE. Ozymandias: do you hear that? [*She rises on her knees and looks raptly into space*]. Queen of queens! [*She dies*].

THE MALE FIGURE [*crawling feebly towards her until he reaches her hand*] I knew I was really a king of kings. [*To the others*] Illusions, farewell: we are going to our thrones. [*He dies*].

The music stops. There is dead silence for a moment.

THE NEWLY BORN. That was funny.

STREPHON. It was. Even the Ancients are smiling.

THE NEWLY BORN. Just a little.

THE SHE-ANCIENT [*quickly recovering her grave and peremptory manner*] Take these two abominations away to Pygmalion's laboratory, and destroy them with the rest of the laboratory refuse. [*Some of them move to obey*]. Take care: do not touch their flesh: it is noxious: lift them by their robes. Carry Pygmalion into the temple; and dispose of his remains in the usual way.

The three bodies are carried out as directed, Pygmalion into the temple by his bare arms and legs, and the two Figures through the grove by their clothes. Martellus superintends the removal of the Figures, Acis that of Pygmalion. Ecrasia, Arjillax, Strephon, and the Newly Born sit down as before, but on contrary benches; so that Strephon and the Newly Born now face the grove, and Ecrasia and Arjillax the temple. The Ancients remain standing at the altar.

ECRASIA [*as she sits down*] Oh for a breeze from the hills!

STREPHON. Or the wind from the sea at the turn of the tide!

THE NEWLY BORN. I want some clean air.

THE HE-ANCIENT. The air will be clean in a moment. This doll flesh that children make decomposes quickly at best; but when it is shaken by such passions as the creatures are capable of, it breaks up at once and becomes horribly tainted.

THE SHE-ANCIENT. Let it be a lesson to you all to be content with lifeless toys, and not attempt to make living ones. What would you think of us ancients if we made toys of you children?

THE NEWLY BORN [*coaxingly*] Why do you not make toys of us? Then you would play with us; and that would be very nice.

THE SHE-ANCIENT. It would not amuse us. When you play with one another you play with your bodies, and that makes you supple and strong; but if we play with you we should play with your minds, and perhaps deform them.

STREPHON. You are a ghastly lot, you ancients. I shall kill myself when I am four years old. What do you live for?

THE HE-ANCIENT. You will find out when you grow up. You will not kill yourself.

STREPHON. If you make me believe that, I shall kill myself now.

THE NEWLY BORN. Oh no. I want you. I love you.

STREPHON. I love someone else. And she has gone old, old. Lost to me for ever.

THE HE-ANCIENT. How old?

STREPHON. You saw her when you barged into us as we were dancing. She is four.

THE NEWLY BORN. How I should have hated her twenty minutes ago! But I have grown out of that now.

THE HE-ANCIENT. Good. That hatred is called jealousy, the worst of our childish complaints.

Martellus, dusting his hands and puffing, returns from the grove.

MARTELLUS. Ouf! [*He sits down next the Newly Born*] That job's finished.

ARJILLAX. Ancients: I should like to make a few studies of you. Not portraits, of course: I shall idealize you a little. I have come to the conclusion that you ancients are the most interesting subjects after all.

MARTELLUS. What! Have those two horrors, whose ashes I have just deposited with peculiar pleasure in poor Pygmalion's dustbin, not cured you of this silly image-making?

ARJILLAX. Why did you model them as young things, you fool? If Pygmalion had come to me, I should have made ancients of them for him. Not that I should have modelled them any better. I have always said that no one can beat you at your best as far as handwork is concerned. But this job required brains. That is where I should have come in.

MARTELLUS. Well, my brainy boy, you are welcome to try your hand. There are two of Pygmalion's pupils at the laboratory who helped him to manufacture the bones and tissues and all the rest of it. They can turn out a couple of new automatons; and you can model them as ancients if this venerable pair will sit for you.

ECRASIA [*decisively*] No. No more automata. They are too disgusting.

ACIS [*returning from the temple*] Well, thats done. Poor old Pyg!

ECRASIA. Only fancy, Acis! Arjillax wants to make more of those abominable things, and to destroy even their artistic character by making ancients of them.

THE NEWLY BORN. You wont sit for them, will you?

Please dont.

THE HE-ANCIENT. Children, listen.

ACIS [*striding down the steps to the bench and seating himself next Ecrasia*] What! Even the Ancient wants to make a speech! Give it mouth, O Sage.

STREPHON. For heaven's sake dont tell us that the earth was once inhabited by Ozymandiases and Cleopatras. Life is hard enough for us as it is.

THE HE-ANCIENT. Life is not meant to be easy, my child; but take courage: it can be delightful. What I wanted to tell you is that ever since men existed, children have played with dolls.

ECRASIA. You keep using that word. What are dolls, pray?

THE SHE-ANCIENT. What you call works of art. Images. We call them dolls.

ARJILLAX. Just so. You have no sense of art; and you instinctively insult it.

THE HE-ANCIENT. Children have been known to make dolls out of rags, and to caress them with the deepest fondness.

THE SHE-ANCIENT. Eight centuries ago, when I was a child, I made a rag doll. The rag doll is the dearest of all.

THE NEWLY BORN [*eagerly interested*] Oh! Have you got it still?

THE SHE-ANCIENT. I kept it a full week.

ECRASIA. Even in your childhood, then, you did not understand high art, and adored your own amateur crudities.

THE SHE-ANCIENT. How old are you?

ECRASIA. Eight months.

THE SHE-ANCIENT. When you have lived as long as I have—

ECRASIA [*interrupting rudely*] I shall worship rag dolls, perhaps. Thank heaven, I am still in my prime.

THE HE-ANCIENT. You are still capable of thanking, though you do not know what you thank. You are a thanking little animal, a blaming little animal, a—

ACIS. A gushing little animal.

ARJILLAX. And, as she thinks, an artistic little animal.

ECRASIA [*nettled*] I am an animated being with a reasonable soul and human flesh subsisting. If your Automata had been properly animated, Martellus, they would have been more successful.

THE SHE-ANCIENT. That is where you are wrong, my child. If those two loathsome things had been rag dolls, they would have been amusing and lovable. The Newly Born here would have played with them; and you would all have laughed and played with them too until you had torn them to pieces; and then you would have laughed more than ever.

THE NEWLY BORN. Of course we should. Isnt that funny?

THE HE-ANCIENT. When a thing is funny, search it for a hidden truth.

STREPHON. Yes; and take all the fun out of it.

THE SHE-ANCIENT. Do not be so embittered because your sweetheart has outgrown her love for you. The Newly Born will make amends.

THE NEWLY BORN. Oh yes: I will be more than she could ever have been.

STREPHON. Psha! Jealous!

THE NEWLY BORN. Oh no. I have grown out of that. I love her now because she loved you, and because you love her.

THE HE-ANCIENT. That is the next stage. You are getting on very nicely, my child.

MARTELLUS. Come! what is the truth that was hidden in the rag doll?

THE HE-ANCIENT. Well, consider why you are not content with the rag doll, and must have something more closely resembling a real living creature. As you grow up you make images and paint pictures. Those of you who cannot do that make stories about imaginary dolls. Or you dress yourselves up as dolls and act plays about them.

THE SHE-ANCIENT. And, to deceive yourself the more completely, you take them so very very seriously that Ecrasia here declares that the making of dolls is the holiest work of creation, and the words you put into the mouths of dolls the sacredest of scriptures and the noblest of utterances.

ECRASIA. Tush!

ARJILLAX. Tosh!

THE SHE-ANCIENT. Yet the more beautiful they become the further they retreat from you. You cannot caress them as you caress the rag doll. You cannot cry for them when they are broken or lost, or when you pretend they have been unkind to you, as you could when you played with rag dolls.

THE HE-ANCIENT. At last, like Pygmalion, you demand from your dolls the final perfection of resemblance to life. They must move and speak.

THE SHE-ANCIENT. They must love and hate.

THE HE-ANCIENT. They must think that they think.

THE SHE-ANCIENT. They must have soft flesh and warm blood.

THE HE-ANCIENT. And then, when you have achieved this as Pygmalion did; when the marble masterpiece is dethroned by the automaton and the homo by the homunculus; when the body and the brain, the reasonable soul and human flesh subsisting, as Ecrasia says, stand before you unmasked as mere machinery, and your impulses are shewn to be nothing but reflexes, you are filled with horror and loathing, and would give worlds to be young enough to play with your rag doll again, since every step away from it has been a step away from love and happiness. Is it not true?

THE SHE-ANCIENT. Speak, Martellus: you who have travelled the whole path.

MARTELLUS. It is true. With fierce joy I turned a temperature of a million degrees on those two things I had modelled, and saw them vanish in an instant into inoffensive dust.

THE SHE-ANCIENT. Speak, Arjillax: you who have advanced from imitating the lightly living child to the intensely living ancient. Is it true, so far?

ARJILLAX. It is partly true: I cannot pretend to be satisfied now with modelling pretty children.

THE HE-ANCIENT. And you, Ecrasia: you cling to your

highly artistic dolls as the noblest projections of the Life Force, do you not?

ECRASIA. Without art, the crudeness of reality would make the world unbearable.

THE NEWLY BORN [*anticipating the She-Ancient, who is evidently going to challenge her*] Now you are coming to me, because I am the latest arrival. But I dont understand your art and your dolls at all. I want to caress my darling Strephon, not to play with dolls.

ACIS. I am in my fourth year; and I have got on very well without your dolls. I had rather walk up a mountain and down again than look at all the statues Martellus and Arjillax ever made. You prefer a statue to an automaton, and a rag doll to a statue. So do I; but I prefer a man to a rag doll. Give me friends, not dolls.

THE HE-ANCIENT. Yet I have seen you walking over the mountains alone. Have you not found your best friend in yourself?

ACIS. What are you driving at, old one? What does all this lead to?

THE HE-ANCIENT. It leads, young man, to the truth that you can create nothing but yourself.

ACIS [*musing*] I can create nothing but myself. Ecrasia: you are clever. Do *you* understand it? I dont.

ECRASIA. It is as easy to understand as any other ignorant error. What artist is as great as his own works? He can create masterpieces; but he cannot improve the shape of his own nose.

ACIS. There! What have you to say to that, old one?

THE HE-ANCIENT. He can alter the shape of his own soul. He could alter the shape of his nose if the difference between a turned-up nose and a turned-down one were worth the effort. One does not face the throes of creation for trifles.

ACIS. What have you to say to that, Ecrasia?

ECRASIA. I say that if the ancients had thoroughly grasped the theory of fine art they would understand that the difference between a beautiful nose and an ugly one is of supreme importance: that it is indeed the only thing that matters.

THE SHE-ANCIENT. That is, they would understand something they could not believe, and that you do not believe.

ACIS. Just so, mam. Art is not honest: that is why I never could stand much of it. It is all make-believe. Ecrasia never really says things: she only rattles her teeth in her mouth.

ECRASIA. Acis: you are rude.

ACIS. You mean that I wont play the game of make-believe. Well, I dont ask you to play it with me; so why should you expect me to play it with you?

ECRASIA. You have no right to say that I am not sincere. I have found a happiness in art that real life has never given me. I am intensely in earnest about art. There is a magic and mystery in art that you know nothing of.

THE SHE-ANCIENT. Yes, child: art is the magic mirror you make to reflect your invisible dreams in visible pictures. You use a glass mirror to see your face: you use works of art to see your soul. But we who are older use neither glass mirrors nor works of art. We have a direct sense of life. When you gain that you will put aside your mirrors and statues, your toys and your dolls.

THE HE-ANCIENT. Yet we too have our toys and our dolls. That is the trouble of the ancients.

ARJILLAX. What! The ancients have their troubles! It is the first time I ever heard one of them confess it.

THE HE-ANCIENT. Look at us. Look at me. This is my body, my blood, my brain; but it is not me. I am the eternal life, the perpetual resurrection; but [*striking his body*] this structure, this organism, this makeshift, can be made by a boy in a laboratory, and is held back from dissolution only by my use of it. Worse still, it can be broken by a slip of the foot, drowned by a cramp in the stomach, destroyed by a flash from the clouds. Sooner or later, its destruction is certain.

THE SHE-ANCIENT. Yes: this body is the last doll to be discarded. When I was a child, Ecrasia, I, too, was an artist, like your sculptor friends there, striving to create perfection in things outside myself. I made statues: I painted pictures: I tried to worship them.

THE HE-ANCIENT. I had no such skill; but I, like Acis, sought perfection in friends, in lovers, in nature, in things outside myself. Alas! I could not create it: I could only imagine it.

THE SHE-ANCIENT. I, like Arjillax, found out that my statues of bodily beauty were no longer even beautiful to me; and I pressed on and made statues and pictures of men and women of genius, like those in the old fable of Michael Angelo. Like Martellus, I smashed them when I saw that there was no life in them: that they were so dead that they would not even dissolve as a dead body does.

THE HE-ANCIENT. And I, like Acis, ceased to walk over the mountains with my friends, and walked alone; for I found that I had creative power over myself but none over my friends. And then I ceased to walk on the mountains; for I saw that the mountains were dead.

ACIS [*protesting vehemently*] No. I grant you about the friends perhaps; but the mountains are still the mountains, each with its name, its individuality, its upstanding strength and majesty, its beauty—

ECRASIA. What! Acis among the rhapsodists!

THE HE-ANCIENT. Mere metaphor, my poor boy: the mountains are corpses.

ALL THE YOUNG [*repelled*] Oh!

THE HE-ANCIENT. Yes. In the hardpressed heart of the earth, where the inconceivable heat of the sun still glows, the stone lives in fierce atomic convulsion, as we live in our slower way. When it is cast out to the surface it dies like a deep-sea fish: what you see is only its cold dead body. We have tapped that central heat as prehistoric man tapped water springs; but nothing has come up alive from those flaming depths: your landscapes, your mountains, are only the world's cast skins and decaying teeth on which we live like microbes.

ECRASIA. Ancient: you blaspheme against Nature and

against Man.

THE SHE-ANCIENT. Child, child, how much enthusiasm will you have for man when you have endured eight centuries of him, as I have, and seen him perish by an empty mischance that is yet a certainty? When I discarded my dolls as he discarded his friends and his mountains, it was to myself I turned as to the final reality. Here, and here alone, I could shape and create. When my arm was weak and I willed it to be strong, I could create a roll of muscle on it; and when I understood that, I understood that I could without any greater miracle give myself ten arms and three heads.

THE HE-ANCIENT. I also came to understand such miracles. For fifty years I sat contemplating this power in myself and concentrating my will.

THE SHE-ANCIENT. So did I; and for five more years I made myself into all sorts of fantastic monsters. I walked upon a dozen legs: I worked with twenty hands and a hundred fingers: I looked to the four quarters of the compass with eight eyes out of four heads. Children fled in amazement from me until I had to hide myself from them; and the ancients, who had forgotten how to laugh, smiled grimly when they passed.

THE HE-ANCIENT. We have all committed these follies. You will all commit them.

THE NEWLY BORN. Oh, do grow a lot of arms and legs and heads for us. It would be so funny.

THE HE-ANCIENT. My child: I am just as well as I am. I would not lift my finger now to have a thousand heads.

THE SHE-ANCIENT. But what would I not give to have no head at all?

ALL THE YOUNG. Whats that? No head at all? Why? How?

THE HE-ANCIENT. Can you not understand?

ALL THE YOUNG [*shaking their heads*] No.

THE SHE-ANCIENT. One day, when I was tired of learning to walk forward with some of my feet and backwards with others and sideways with the rest all at once, I sat on a rock with my four chins resting on four of my palms, and four of my elbows resting on four of my knees. And suddenly it came into my mind that this monstrous machinery of heads and limbs was no more me than my statues had been me, and that it was only an automaton that I had enslaved.

MARTELLUS. Enslaved? What does that mean?

THE SHE-ANCIENT. A thing that must do what you command it is a slave; and its commander is its master. These are words you will learn when your turn comes.

THE HE-ANCIENT. You will also learn that when the master has come to do everything through the slave, the slave becomes his master, since he cannot live without him.

THE SHE-ANCIENT. And so I perceived that I had made myself the slave of a slave.

THE HE-ANCIENT. When we discovered that, we shed our superfluous heads and legs and arms until we had our old shapes again, and no longer startled the children.

THE SHE-ANCIENT. But still I am the slave of this slave, my body. How am I to be delivered from it?

THE HE-ANCIENT. That, children, is the trouble of the ancients. For whilst we are tied to this tyrannous body we are subject to its death, and our destiny is not achieved.

THE NEWLY BORN. What is your destiny?

THE HE-ANCIENT. To be immortal.

THE SHE-ANCIENT. The day will come when there will be no people, only thought.

THE HE-ANCIENT. And that will be life eternal.

ECRASIA. I trust I shall meet my fatal accident before that day dawns.

ARJILLAX. For once, Ecrasia, I agree with you. A world in which there were nothing plastic would be an utterly miserable one.

ECRASIA. No limbs, no contours, no exquisite lines and elegant shapes, no worship of beautiful bodies, no poetic embraces in which cultivated lovers pretend that their caressing hands are wandering over celestial hills and enchanted valleys, no—

ACIS [*interrupting her disgustedly*] What an inhuman mind

you have, Ecrasia!

ECRASIA. Inhuman!

ACIS. Yes: inhuman. Why dont you fall in love with someone?

ECRASIA. I! I have been in love all my life. I burned with it even in the egg.

ACIS. Not a bit of it. You and Arjillax are just as hard as two stones.

ECRASIA. You did not always think so, Acis.

ACIS. Oh, I know. I offered you my love once, and asked for yours.

ECRASIA. And did I deny it to you, Acis?

ACIS. You didnt even know what love was.

ECRASIA. Oh! I adored you, you stupid oaf, until I found that you were a mere animal.

ACIS. And I made no end of a fool of myself about you until I discovered that you were a mere artist. You appreciated my contours! I was plastic, as Arjillax says. I wasnt a man to you: I was a masterpiece appealing to your tastes and your senses. Your tastes and senses had overlaid the direct impulse of life in you. And because I cared only for our life, and went straight to it, and was bored by your calling my limbs fancy names and mapping me into mountains and valleys and all the rest of it, you called me an animal. Well, I am an animal, if you call a live man an animal.

ECRASIA. You need not explain. You refused to be refined. I did my best to lift your prehistoric impulses on to the plane of beauty, of imagination, of romance, of poetry, of art, of—

ACIS. These things are all very well in their way and in their proper places. But they are not love. They are an unnatural adulteration of love. Love is a simple thing and a deep thing: it is an act of life and not an illusion. Art is an illusion.

ARJILLAX. That is false. The statue comes to life always. The statues of today are the men and women of the next incubation. I hold up the marble figure before the mother and say, "This is the model you must copy." We produce what we see. Let no man dare to create in art a thing that he would not have exist in life.

MARTELLUS. Yes: I have been through all that. But you yourself are making statues of ancients instead of beautiful nymphs and swains. And Ecrasia is right about the ancients being inartistic. They are damnably inartistic.

ECRASIA [*triumphant*] Ah! Our greatest artist vindicates me. Thanks, Martellus.

MARTELLUS. The body always ends by being a bore. Nothing remains beautiful and interesting except thought, because the thought is the life. Which is just what this old gentleman and this old lady seem to think too.

THE SHE-ANCIENT. Quite so.

THE HE-ANCIENT. Precisely.

THE NEWLY BORN [*to the He-Ancient*] But you cant be nothing. What do you want to be?

THE HE-ANCIENT. A vortex.

THE NEWLY BORN. A what?

THE SHE-ANCIENT. A vortex. I began as a vortex: why should I not end as one?

ECRASIA. Oh! That is what you old people are. Vorticists.

ACIS. But if life is thought, can you live without a head?

THE HE-ANCIENT. Not now perhaps. But prehistoric men thought they could not live without tails. I can live without a tail. Why should I not live without a head?

THE NEWLY BORN. What is a tail?

THE HE-ANCIENT. A habit of which your ancestors managed to cure themselves.

THE SHE-ANCIENT. None of us now believe that all this machinery of flesh and blood is necessary. It dies.

THE HE-ANCIENT. It imprisons us on this petty planet and forbids us to range through the stars.

ACIS. But even a vortex is a vortex in something. You cant have a whirlpool without water; and you cant have a vortex without gas, or molecules or atoms or ions or electrons or something, not nothing.

THE HE-ANCIENT. No: the vortex is not the water nor the gas nor the atoms: it is a power over these things.

THE SHE-ANCIENT. The body was the slave of the vortex; but the slave has become the master; and we must free ourselves from that tyranny. It is this stuff [*indicating her body*], this flesh and blood and bone and all the rest of it, that is intolerable. Even prehistoric man dreamed of what he called an astral body, and asked who would deliver him from the body of this death.

ACIS [*evidently out of his depth*] I shouldnt think too much about it if I were you. You have to keep sane, you know.

The two Ancients look at one another; shrug their shoulders; and address themselves to their departure.

THE HE-ANCIENT. We are staying too long with you, children. We must go.

All the young people rise rather eagerly.

ARJILLAX. Dont mention it.

THE SHE-ANCIENT. It is tiresome for us, too. You see, children, we have to put things very crudely to you to make ourselves intelligible.

THE HE-ANCIENT. And I am afraid we do not quite succeed.

STREPHON. Very kind of you to come at all and talk to us, I'm sure.

ECRASIA. Why do the other ancients never come and give us a turn?

THE SHE-ANCIENT. It is so difficult for them. They have forgotten how to speak; how to read; even how to think in your fashion. We do not communicate with one another in that way or apprehend the world as you do.

THE HE-ANCIENT. I find it more and more difficult to keep up your language. Another century or two and it will be impossible. I shall have to be relieved by a younger shepherd.

ACIS. Of course we are always delighted to see you; but still, if it tries you very severely, we could manage pretty well by ourselves, you know.

THE SHE-ANCIENT. Tell me, Acis: do you ever think of

yourself as having to live perhaps for thousands of years?

ACIS. Oh, dont talk about it. Why, I know very well that I have only four years of what any reasonable person would call living; and three and a half of them are already gone.

ECRASIA. You must not mind our saying so; but really you cannot call being an ancient living.

THE NEWLY BORN [*almost in tears*] Oh, this dreadful shortness of our lives! I cannot bear it.

STREPHON. I made up my mind on that subject long ago. When I am three years and fifty weeks old, I shall have my fatal accident. And it will not be an accident.

THE HE-ANCIENT. We are very tired of this subject. I must leave you.

THE NEWLY BORN. What is being tired?

THE SHE-ANCIENT. The penalty of attending to children. Farewell.

The two Ancients go away severally, she into the grove, he up to the hills behind the temple.

ALL. Ouf! [*A great sigh of relief*].

ECRASIA. Dreadful people!

STREPHON. Bores!

MARTELLUS. Yet one would like to follow them; to enter into their life; to grasp their thought; to comprehend the universe as they must.

ARJILLAX. Getting old, Martellus?

MARTELLUS. Well, I have finished with the dolls; and I am no longer jealous of you. That looks like the end. Two hours sleep is enough for me. I am afraid I am beginning to find you all rather silly.

STREPHON. I know. My girl went off this morning. She hadnt slept for weeks. And she found mathematics more interesting than me.

MARTELLUS. There is a prehistoric saying that has come down to us from a famous woman teacher. She said: "Leave women; and study mathematics." It is the only remaining fragment of a lost scripture called The Confessions of St Augustin, the English Opium Eater. That primitive savage must have been a great woman, to say a thing that still lives after three hundred centuries. I too will leave women and study mathematics, which I have neglected too long. Farewell, children, my old playmates. I almost wish I could feel sentimental about parting from you; but the cold truth is that you bore me. Do not be angry with me: your turn will come. [*He passes away gravely into the grove*].

ARJILLAX. There goes a great spirit. What a sculptor he was! And now, nothing! It is as if he had cut off his hands.

THE NEWLY BORN. Oh, will you all leave me as he has left you?

ECRASIA. Never. We have sworn it.

STREPHON. What is the use of swearing? She swore. He swore. You have sworn. They have sworn.

ECRASIA. You speak like a grammar.

STREPHON. That is how one ought to speak, isnt it? We shall all be forsworn.

THE NEWLY BORN. Do not talk like that. You are saddening us; and you are chasing the light away. It is growing dark.

ACIS. Night is falling. The light will come back tomorrow.

THE NEWLY BORN. What is tomorrow?

ACIS. The day that never comes. [*He turns towards the temple*].

All begin trooping into the temple.

THE NEWLY BORN [*holding Acis back*] That is no answer. What—

ARJILLAX. Silence. Little children should be seen and not heard.

THE NEWLY BORN [*putting out her tongue at him*]!

ECRASIA. Ungraceful. You must not do that.

THE NEWLY BORN. I will do what I like. But there is something the matter with me. I want to lie down. I cannot keep my eyes open.

ECRASIA. You are falling asleep. You will wake up again.

THE NEWLY BORN [*drowsily*] What is sleep?

ACIS. Ask no questions; and you will be told no lies. [*He takes her by the ear, and leads her firmly towards the temple*].

THE NEWLY BORN. Ai! oi! ai! Dont. I want to be carried. [*She reels into the arms of Acis, who carries her into the temple*].

ECRASIA. Come, Arjillax: you at least are still an artist. I adore you.

ARJILLAX. Do you? Unfortunately for you, I am not still a child. I have grown out of cuddling. I can only appreciate your figure. Does that satisfy you?

ECRASIA. At what distance?

ARJILLAX. Arm's length or more.

ECRASIA. Thank you: not for me. [*She turns away from him*].

ARJILLAX. Ha! ha! [*He strides off into the temple*].

ECRASIA [*calling to Strephon, who is on the threshold of the temple, going in*] Strephon.

STREPHON. No. My heart is broken. [*He goes into the temple*].

ECRASIA. Must I pass the night alone? [*She looks round, seeking another partner; but they have all gone*]. After all, I can imagine a lover nobler than any of you. [*She goes into the temple*].

It is now quite dark. A vague radiance appears near the temple and shapes itself into the ghost of Adam.

A WOMAN'S VOICE [*in the grove*] Who is that?

ADAM. The ghost of Adam, the first father of mankind. Who are you?

THE VOICE. The ghost of Eve, the first mother of mankind.

ADAM. Come forth, wife; and shew yourself to me.

EVE [*appearing near the grove*] Here I am, husband. You are very old.

A VOICE [*in the hills*] Ha! ha! ha!

ADAM. Who laughs? Who dares laugh at Adam?

EVE. Who has the heart to laugh at Eve?

THE VOICE. The ghost of Cain, the first child, and the first murderer. [*He appears between them; and as he does so there is a prolonged hiss*]. Who dares hiss at Cain, the lord of death?

A VOICE. The ghost of the serpent, that lived before Adam and before Eve, and taught them how to bring forth Cain. [*She becomes visible, coiled in the trees*].

A VOICE. There is one that came before the serpent.

THE SERPENT. That is the voice of Lilith, in whom the father and mother were one. Hail, Lilith!

Lilith becomes visible between Cain and Adam.

LILITH. I suffered unspeakably; I tore myself asunder; I lost my life, to make of my one flesh these twain, man and woman. And this is what has come of it. What do you make of it, Adam, my son?

ADAM. I made the earth bring forth by my labor, and the woman bring forth by my love. And this is what has come of it. What do you make of it, Eve, my wife?

EVE. I nourished the egg in my body and fed it with my blood. And now they let it fall as the birds did, and suffer not at all. What do you make of it, Cain, my first-born?

CAIN. I invented killing and conquest and mastery and the winnowing out of the weak by the strong. And now the strong have slain one another; and the weak live for ever; and their deeds do nothing for the doer more than for another. What do you make of it, snake?

THE SERPENT. I am justified. For I chose wisdom and the knowledge of good and evil; and now there is no evil; and wisdom and good are one. It is enough. [*She vanishes*].

CAIN. There is no place for me on earth any longer. You cannot deny that mine was a splendid game while it lasted. But now! Out, out, brief candle! [*He vanishes*].

EVE. The clever ones were always my favorites. The diggers and the fighters have dug themselves in with the worms. My clever ones have inherited the earth. All's well. [*She fades away*].

ADAM. I can make nothing of it, neither head nor tail. What is it all for? Why? Whither? Whence? We were well enough in the garden. And now the fools have killed all the animals; and they are dissatisfied because they cannot be bothered with their bodies! Foolishness, I call it. [*He dis-*

appears].

LILITH. They have accepted the burden of eternal life. They have taken the agony from birth; and their life does not fail them even in the hour of their destruction. Their breasts are without milk: their bowels are gone: the very shapes of them are only ornaments for their children to admire and caress without understanding. Is this enough; or shall I labor again? Shall I bring forth something that will sweep them away and make an end of them as they have swept away the beasts of the garden, and made an end of the crawling things and the flying things and of all them that refuse to live for ever? I had patience with them for many ages: they tried me very sorely. They did terrible things: they embraced death, and said that eternal life was a fable. I stood amazed at the malice and destructiveness of the things I had made: Mars blushed as he looked down on the shame of his sister planet: cruelty and hypocrisy became so hideous that the face of the earth was pitted with the graves of little children among which living skeletons crawled in search of horrible food. The pangs of another birth were already upon me when one man repented and lived three hundred years; and I waited to see what would come of that. And so much came of it that the horrors of that time seem now but an evil dream. They have redeemed themselves from their vileness, and turned away from their sins. Best of all, they are still not satisfied: the impulse I gave them in that day when I sundered myself in twain and launched Man and Woman on the earth still urges them: after passing a million goals they press on to the goal of redemption from the flesh, to the vortex freed from matter, to the whirlpool in pure intelligence that, when the world began, was a whirlpool in pure force. And though all that they have done seems but the first hour of the infinite work of creation, yet I will not supersede them until they have forded this last stream that lies between flesh and spirit, and disentangled their life from the matter that has always mocked it. I can wait: waiting and patience mean nothing to the eternal. I gave the woman the greatest of gifts: curiosity. By that her seed has been saved from my wrath; for I also am curious; and I have waited always to see what they will do tomorrow. Let them feed that appetite well for me. I say, let them dread, of all things, stagnation; for from the moment I, Lilith, lose hope and faith in them, they are doomed. In that hope and faith I have let them live for a moment; and in that moment I have spared them many times. But mightier creatures than they have killed hope and faith, and perished from the earth; and I may not spare them for ever. I am Lilith: I brought life into the whirlpool of force, and compelled my enemy, Matter, to obey a living soul. But in enslaving Life's enemy I made him Life's master; for that is the end of all slavery; and now I shall see the slave set free and the enemy reconciled, the whirlpool become all life and no matter. And be-because these infants that call themselves ancients are reaching out towards that, I will have patience with them still; though I know well that when they attain it they shall become one with me and supersede me, and Lilith will be only a legend and a lay that has lost its meaning. Of Life only is there no end; and though of its million starry mansions many are empty and many still unbuilt, and though its vast domain is as yet unbearably desert, my seed shall one day fill it and master its matter to its uttermost confines. And for what may be beyond, the eyesight of Lilith is too short. It is enough that there is a beyond. [*She vanishes*].

SAINT JOAN

A CHRONICLE PLAY IN SIX SCENES AND AN EPILOGUE

Written in 1923

First Performed New York 1923

PREFACE TO SAINT JOAN

JOAN THE ORIGINAL AND PRESUMPTUOUS

JOAN OF ARC, a village girl from the Vosges, was born about 1412; burnt for heresy, witchcraft, and sorcery in 1431; rehabilitated after a fashion in 1456; designated venerable in 1904; declared Blessed in 1908; and finally canonized in 1920. She is the most notable Warrior Saint in the Christian calendar, and the queerest fish among the eccentric worthies of the Middle Ages. Though a professed and most pious Catholic, and the projector of a Crusade against the Husites, she was in fact one of the first Protestant martyrs. She was also one of the first apostles of Nationalism, and the first French practitioner of Napoleonic realism in warfare as distinguished from the sporting ransom gambling chivalry of her time. She was the pioneer of rational dressing for women, and, like Queen Christina of Sweden two centuries later, to say nothing of Catalina de Erauso and innumerable obscure heroines who have disguised themselves as men to serve as soldiers and sailors, she refused to accept the specific woman's lot, and dressed and fought and lived as men did.

As she contrived to assert herself in all these ways with such force that she was famous throughout western Europe before she was out of her teens (indeed she never got out of them), it is hardly surprising that she was judicially burnt, ostensibly for a number of capital crimes which we no longer punish as such, but essentially for what we call unwomanly and insufferable presumption. At eighteen Joan's pretensions were beyond those of the proudest Pope or the haughtiest emperor. She claimed to be the ambassador and plenipotentiary of God, and to be, in effect, a member of the Church Triumphant whilst still in the flesh on earth. She patronized her own king, and summoned the English king to repentance and obedience to her commands. She lectured, talked down, and overruled statesmen and prelates. She poohpoohed the plans of generals, leading their troops to victory on plans of her own. She had an unbounded and quite unconcealed contempt for official opinion, judgment, and authority, and for War Office tactics and strategy. Had she been a sage and monarch in whom the most venerable hierarchy and the most illustrious dynasty converged, her pretensions and proceedings would have been as trying to the official mind as the pretensions of Caesar were to Cassius. As her actual condition was pure upstart, there were only two opinions about her. One was that she was miraculous: the other that she was unbearable.

JOAN AND SOCRATES

If Joan had been malicious, selfish, cowardly or stupid, she would have been one of the most odious persons known to history instead of one of the most attractive. If she had been old enough to know the effect she was producing on the men whom she humiliated by being right when they were wrong, and had learned to flatter and manage them, she might have lived as long as Queen Elizabeth. But she was too young and rustical and inexperienced to have any such arts. When she was thwarted by men whom she thought fools, she made no secret of her opinion of them or her impatience with their folly; and she was naïve enough to expect them to be obliged to her for setting them right and keeping them out of mischief. Now it is always hard for superior wits to understand the fury roused by their exposures of the stupidities of comparative dullards. Even Socrates, for all his age and experience, did not defend himself at his trial like a man who understood the long accumulated fury that had burst on him, and was clamoring for his death. His accuser, if born 2300 years later, might have been picked out of any first class carriage on a suburban railway during the evening or morning rush from or to the City; for he had really nothing to say except that he and his like could not endure being shewn up as idiots every time Socrates opened his mouth. Socrates, unconscious of this, was paralyzed by his sense that somehow he was missing the point of the attack. He petered out after he had established the fact that he was an old soldier and a man of honorable life, and that his accuser was a silly snob. He had no suspicion of the extent to which his mental superiority had roused fear and hatred against him in the hearts of men towards whom he was conscious of nothing but good will and good service.

CONTRAST WITH NAPOLEON

If Socrates was as innocent as this at the age of seventy, it may be imagined how innocent Joan was at the age of seventeen. Now Socrates was a man of argument, operating slowly and peacefully on men's minds, whereas Joan was a woman of action, operating with impetuous violence on their bodies. That, no doubt, is why the contemporaries of Socrates endured him so long, and why Joan was destroyed before she was fully grown. But both of them combined terrifying ability with a frankness, personal modesty, and benevolence which made the furious dislike to which they fell victims absolutely unreasonable, and therefore inapprehensible by themselves. Napoleon, also possessed of terrifying ability, but neither frank nor disinterested, had no illusions as to the nature of his popularity. When he was asked how the world would take his death, he said it would give a gasp of relief. But it is not so easy for mental giants who neither hate nor intend to injure their fellows to realize that nevertheless their fellows hate mental giants and would like to destroy them, not only enviously because the juxtaposition of a superior wounds their vanity, but quite humbly and honestly because it frightens them. Fear will drive men to any extreme; and the fear inspired by a superior being is a mystery which cannot be reasoned away. Being immeasurable it is unbearable when there is no presumption or guarantee of its benevolence and moral responsibility: in other words, when it has no official status. The legal and conventional superiority of Herod and Pilate, and of Annas and Caiaphas, inspires fear; but the fear, being a reasonable fear of measurable and avoidable consequences which seem salutary and protective, is bearable; whilst the strange superiority of Christ and the fear it inspires elicit a shriek of

Crucify Him from all who cannot divine its benevolence. Socrates has to drink the hemlock, Christ to hang on the cross, and Joan to burn at the stake, whilst Napoleon, though he ends in St Helena, at least dies in his bed there; and many terrifying but quite comprehensible official scoundrels die natural deaths in all the glory of the kingdoms of this world, proving that it is far more dangerous to be a saint than to be a conqueror. Those who have been both, like Mahomet and Joan, have found that it is the conqueror who must save the saint, and that defeat and capture mean martyrdom. Joan was burnt without a hand lifted on her own side to save her. The comrades she had led to victory and the enemies she had disgraced and defeated, the French king she had crowned and the English king whose crown she had kicked into the Loire, were equally glad to be rid of her.

WAS JOAN INNOCENT OR GUILTY?

As this result could have been produced by a crapulous inferiority as well as by a sublime superiority, the question which of the two was operative in Joan's case has to be faced. It was decided against her by her contemporaries after a very careful and conscientious trial; and the reversal of the verdict twentyfive years later, in form a rehabilitation of Joan, was really only a confirmation of the validity of the coronation of Charles VII. It is the more impressive reversal by a unanimous Posterity, culminating in her canonization, that has quashed the original proceedings, and put her judges on their trial, which, so far, has been much more unfair than their trial of her. Nevertheless the rehabilitation of 1456, corrupt job as it was, really did produce evidence enough to satisfy all reasonable critics that Joan was not a common termagant, not a harlot, not a witch, not a blasphemer, no more an idolater than the Pope himself, and not ill conducted in any sense apart from her soldiering, her wearing of men's clothes, and her audacity, but on the contrary goodhumored, an intact virgin, very pious, very temperate (we should call her meal of bread soaked in the common wine which is the drinking water of France ascetic), very kindly, and, though a brave and hardy soldier, unable to endure loose language or licentious conduct. She went to the stake without a stain on her character except the overweening presumption, the superbity as they called it, that led her thither. It would therefore be waste of time now to prove that the Joan of the first part of the Elizabethan chronicle play of Henry VI (supposed to have been tinkered by Shakespear) grossly libels her in its concluding scenes in deference to Jingo patriotism. The mud that was thrown at her has dropped off by this time so completely that there is no need for any modern writer to wash up after it. What is far more difficult to get rid of is the mud that is being thrown at her judges, and the whitewash which disfigures her beyond recognition. When Jingo scurrility had done its worst to her, sectarian scurrility (in this case Protestant scurrility) used her stake to beat the Roman Catholic Church and the Inquisition. The easiest way to make these institutions the villains of a melodrama was to make The Maid its heroine. That melodrama may be dismissed as rubbish. Joan got a far fairer trial from the Church and the Inquisition than any prisoner of her type and in her situation gets nowadays in any official secular court; and the decision was strictly according to law. And she was not a melodramatic heroine: that is, a physically beautiful lovelorn parasite on an equally beautiful hero, but a genius and a saint, about as completely the opposite of a melodramatic heroine as it is possible for a human being to be.

Let us be clear about the meaning of the terms. A genius is a person who, seeing farther and probing deeper than other people, has a different set of ethical valuations from theirs, and has energy enough to give effect to this extra vision and its valuations in whatever manner best suits his or her specific talents. A saint is one who having practised heroic virtues, and enjoyed revelations or powers of the order which The Church classes technically as supernatural, is eligible for canonization. If a historian is an Anti-Feminist, and does not believe women to be capable of genius in the traditional masculine departments, he will never make anything of Joan, whose genius was turned to practical account mainly in soldiering and politics. If he is Rationalist enough to deny that saints exist, and to hold that new ideas cannot come otherwise than by conscious ratiocination, he will never catch Joan's likeness. Her ideal biographer must be free from nineteenth century prejudices and biases; must understand the Middle Ages, the Roman Catholic Church, and the Holy Roman Empire much more intimately than our Whig historians have ever understood them; and must be capable of throwing off sex partialities and their romance, and regarding woman as the female of the human species, and not as a different kind of animal with specific charms and specific imbecilities.

JOAN'S GOOD LOOKS

To put the last point roughly, any book about Joan which begins by describing her as a beauty may be at once classed as a romance. Not one of Joan's comrades, in village, court, or camp, even when they were straining themselves to please the king by praising her, ever claimed that she was pretty. All the men who alluded to the matter declared most emphatically that she was unattractive sexually to a degree that seemed to them miraculous, considering that she was in the bloom of youth, and neither ugly, awkward, deformed, nor unpleasant in her person. The evident truth is that like most women of her hardy managing type she seemed neutral in the conflict of sex because men were too much afraid of her to fall in love with her. She herself was not sexless: in spite of the virginity she had vowed up to a point, and preserved to her death, she never excluded the possibility of marriage for herself. But marriage, with its preliminary of the attraction, pursuit, and capture of a husband, was not her business: she had something else to do. Byron's formula, "Man's love is of man's life a thing apart: 'tis woman's whole existence" did not apply to her any more than to George Washington or any other masculine worker on the heroic scale. Had she lived in our time, picture postcards might have been sold of her as a general: they would not have been sold of her as a sultana. Nevertheless there is one reason for crediting her with a very remarkable face. A sculptor of her time in Orleans made a statue of a helmeted young woman with a face that is unique in art in point of being evidently not an ideal face but a portrait, and yet so uncommon as to be unlike any real woman one has ever seen. It is surmised that Joan served unconsciously as the sculptor's model. There is no proof of this; but those extraordinarily spaced eyes raise so powerfully the question "If this woman be not Joan, who is she?" that I dispense with further evidence, and challenge those who disagree with me to prove a negative. It is a wonderful face, but quite neutral from the point of view of the operatic beauty fancier.

Such a fancier may perhaps be finally chilled by the prosaic fact that Joan was the defendant in a suit for breach of promise of marriage, and that she conducted her own case and won it.

JOAN'S SOCIAL POSITION

By class Joan was the daughter of a working farmer who was one of the headmen of his village, and transacted its feudal business for it with the neighboring squires and their lawyers. When the castle in which the villagers were entitled to take refuge from raids became derelict, he organized a combination of half a dozen farmers to obtain possession of it so as to occupy it when there was any danger of invasion. As a child, Joan could please herself at times with being the young lady of this castle. Her mother and brothers were able to follow and share her fortune at court without making themselves notably ridiculous. These facts leave us no excuse for the popular romance that turns every heroine into either a princess or a beggarmaid. In the somewhat similar case of Shakespear a whole inverted pyramid of wasted research has been based on the assumption that he was an illiterate laborer, in the face of the plainest evidence that his father was a man of business, and at one time a very prosperous one, married to a woman of some social pretensions. There is the same tendency to drive Joan into the position of a hired shepherd girl, though a hired shepherd girl in Domrémy would have deferred to her as the young lady of the farm.

The difference between Joan's case and Shakespear's is that Shakespear was not illiterate. He had been to school, and knew as much Latin and Greek as most university passmen retain: that is, for practical purposes, none at all. Joan was absolutely illiterate. "I do not know A from B" she said. But many princesses at that time and for long after might have said the same. Marie Antoinette, for instance, at Joan's age could not spell her own name correctly. But this does not mean that Joan was an ignorant person, or that she suffered from the diffidence and sense of social disadvantage now felt by people who cannot read or write. If she could not write letters, she could and did dictate them and attach full and indeed excessive importance to them. When she was called a shepherd lass to her face she very warmly resented it, and challenged any woman to compete with her in the household arts of the mistresses of well furnished houses. She understood the political and military situation in France much better than most of our newspaper fed university women-graduates understand the corresponding situation of their own country today. Her first convert was the neighboring commandant at Vaucouleurs; and she converted him by telling him about the defeat of the Dauphin's troops at the Battle of Herrings so long before he had official news of it that he concluded she must have had a divine revelation. This knowledge of and interest in public affairs was nothing extraordinary among farmers in a warswept countryside. Politicians came to the door too often sword in hand to be disregarded: Joan's people could not afford to be ignorant of what was going on in the feudal world. They were not rich; and Joan worked on the farm as her father did, driving the sheep to pasture and so forth; but there is no evidence or suggestion of sordid poverty, and no reason to believe that Joan had to work as a hired servant works, or indeed to work at all when she preferred to go to confession, or dawdle about waiting for visions and listening to the church bells to hear voices in them. In short, much more of a young lady, and even of an intellectual, than most of the daughters of our petty bourgeoisie.

JOAN'S VOICES AND VISIONS

Joan's voices and visions have played many tricks with her reputation. They have been held to prove that she was mad, that she was a liar and impostor, that she was a sorceress (she was burned for this), and finally that she was a saint. They do not prove any of these things; but the variety of the conclusions reached shew how little our matter-of-fact historians know about other people's minds, or even about their own. There are people in the world whose imagination is so vivid that when they have an idea it comes to them as an audible voice, sometimes uttered by a visible figure. Criminal lunatic asylums are occupied largely by murderers who have obeyed voices. Thus a woman may hear voices telling her that she must cut her husband's throat and strangle her child as they lie asleep; and she may feel obliged to do what she is told. By a medico-legal superstition it is held in our courts that criminals whose temptations present themselves under these illusions are not responsible for their actions, and must be treated as insane. But the seers of visions and the hearers of revelations are not always criminals. The inspirations and intuitions and unconsciously reasoned conclusions of genius sometimes assume similar illusions. Socrates, Luther, Swedenborg, Blake saw visions and heard voices just as Saint Francis and Saint Joan did. If Newton's imagination had been of the same vividly dramatic kind he might have seen the ghost of Pythagoras walk into the orchard and explain why the apples were falling. Such an illusion would have invalidated neither the theory of gravitation nor Newton's general sanity. What is more, the visionary method of making the discovery would not be a whit more miraculous than the normal method. The test of sanity is not the normality of the method but the reasonableness of the discovery. If Newton had been informed by Pythagoras that the moon was made of green cheese, then Newton would have been locked up. Gravitation, being a reasoned hypothesis which fitted remarkably well into the Copernican version of the observed physical facts of the universe, established Newton's reputation for extraordinary intelligence, and would have done so no matter how fantastically he had arrived at it. Yet his theory of gravitation is not so impressive a mental feat as his astounding chronology, which established him as the king of mental conjurors, but a Bedlamite king whose authority no one now accepts. On the subject of the eleventh horn of the beast seen by the prophet Daniel he was more fantastic than Joan, because his imagination was not dramatic but mathematical and therefore extraordinarily susceptible to numbers: indeed if all his works were lost except his chronology we should say that he was as mad as a hatter. As it is, who dares diagnose Newton as a madman?

In the same way Joan must be judged a sane woman in spite of her voices because they never gave her any advice that might not have come to her from her mother wit exactly as gravitation came to Newton. We can all see now, especially since the late war threw so many of our women into military life, that Joan's campaigning could not have been carried on in petticoats. This was not only because she did a man's work, but because it was morally necessary that sex should be left out of the question as between her and her comrades-in-arms. She gave this reason herself when she was pressed on the subject; and the fact that this entirely reasonable necessity came to her imagination first as an order from God delivered through the mouth of Saint Catherine does not prove that she was mad. The soundness of the order proves that she was unusually sane; but its form proves that her dramatic imagination played tricks with her senses. Her policy was also quite sound: nobody disputes that the relief of Orleans, followed up by the coronation at Rheims of the Dauphin as a counterblow to the suspicions then current of his legitimacy and consequently of his title, were military and political masterstrokes that saved France. They might have been planned by Napoleon or any other illusionproof genius. They came to Joan as an instruction from her Counsel, as she called her visionary saints; but she was none the less an able leader of men for imagining her ideas in this way.

THE EVOLUTIONARY APPETITE

What then is the modern view of Joan's voices and visions and messages from God? The nineteenth century said that they were delusions, but that as she was a pretty girl, and had been abominably ill-treated and finally done to death by a superstitious rabble of medieval priests hounded on by a corrupt political bishop, it must be assumed that she was the innocent dupe of these delusions. The twentieth century finds this explanation too vapidly commonplace, and demands something more mystic. I think the twentieth century is right, because an explanation which amounts to Joan being mentally defective instead of, as she obviously was, mentally excessive, will not wash. I cannot believe, nor, if I could, could I expect all my readers to believe, as Joan did, that three ocularly visible well dressed persons, named respectively Saint Catherine, Saint Margaret, and Saint Michael, came down from heaven and gave her certain instructions with which they were charged by God for her. Not that such a belief would be more improbable or fantastic than some modern beliefs which we all swallow; but there are fashions and family habits in belief, and it happens that, my fashion being Victorian and my family habit Protestant, I find myself unable to attach any such objective validity to the form of Joan's visions.

But that there are forces at work which use individuals for purposes far transcending the purpose of keeping these individuals alive and prosperous and respectable and safe and happy in the middle station in life, which is all any good bourgeois can reasonably require, is established by the fact that men will, in the pursuit of knowledge and of social readjustments for which they will not be a penny the better, and are indeed often many pence the worse, face poverty, infamy, exile, imprisonment, dreadful hardship, and death. Even the selfish pursuit of personal power does not nerve men to the efforts and sacrifices which are eagerly made in pursuit of extensions of our power over nature, though these extensions may not touch the personal life of the seeker at any point. There is no more mystery about this appetite for knowledge and power than about the appetite for food: both are known as facts and as facts only, the difference between them being that the appetite for food is necessary to the life of the hungry man and is therefore a personal appetite, whereas the other is an appetite for evolution, and therefore a superpersonal need.

The diverse manners in which our imaginations dramatize the approach of the superpersonal forces is a problem for the psychologist, not for the historian. Only, the historian must understand that visionaries are neither impostors nor lunatics. It is one thing to say that the figure Joan recognized as St Catherine was not really St Catherine, but the dramatization by Joan's imagination of that pressure upon her of the driving force that is behind evolution which I have just called the evolutionary appetite. It is quite another to class her visions with the vision of two moons seen by a drunken person, or with Brocken spectres, echoes and the like. Saint Catherine's instructions were far too cogent for that; and the simplest French peasant who believes in apparitions of celestial personages to favored mortals is nearer to the scientific truth about Joan than the Rationalist and Materialist historians and essayists who feel obliged to set down a girl who saw saints and heard them talking to her as either crazy or mendacious. If Joan was mad, all Christendom was mad too; for people who believe devoutly in the existence of celestial personages are every whit as mad in that sense as the people who think they see them. Luther, when he threw his inkhorn at the devil, was no more mad than any other Augustinian monk: he had a more vivid imagination, and had perhaps eaten and slept less: that was all.

THE MERE ICONOGRAPHY DOES NOT MATTER

All the popular religions in the world are made apprehensible by an array of legendary personages, with an Almighty Father, and sometimes a mother and divine child, as the central figures. These are presented to the mind's eye in childhood; and the result is a hallucination which persists strongly throughout life when it has been well impressed. Thus all the thinking of the hallucinated adult about the fountain of inspiration which is continually flowing in the universe, or about the promptings of virtue and the revulsions of shame: in short, about aspiration and conscience, both of which forces are matters of fact more obvious than electro-magnetism, is thinking in terms of the celestial vision. And when in the case of exceptionally imaginative persons, especially those practising certain appropriate austerities, the hallucination extends from the mind's eye to the body's, the visionary sees Krishna or the Buddha or the Blessed Virgin or St Catherine as the case may be.

THE MODERN EDUCATION WHICH JOAN ESCAPED

It is important to everyone nowadays to understand this, because modern science is making short work of the hallucinations without regard to the vital importance of the things they symbolize. If Joan were reborn today she would be sent, first to a convent school in which she would be mildly taught to connect inspiration and conscience with St Catherine and St Michael exactly as she was in the fifteenth century, and then finished up with a very energetic training in the gospel of Saints Louis Pasteur and Paul Bert, who would tell her (possibly in visions but more probably in pamphlets) not to be a superstitious little fool, and to empty out St Catherine and the rest of the Catholic hagiology as an obsolete iconography of exploded myths. It would be rubbed into her that Galileo was a martyr, and his persecutors incorrigible ignoramuses, and that St Teresa's hormones had gone astray and left her incurably hyperpituitary or hyperadrenal or hysteroid or epileptoid or anything but asteroid. She would have been convinced by precept and experiment that baptism and receiving the body of her Lord were contemptible superstitions, and that vaccination and vivisection were enlightened practices. Behind her new Saints Louis and Paul there would be not only Science purifying Religion and being purified by it, but hypochondria, melancholia, cowardice, stupidity, cruelty, muckraking curiosity, knowledge without wisdom, and everything that the eternal soul in Nature loathes, instead of the virtues of which St Catherine was the figure head. As to the new rites, which would be the saner Joan? the one who carried little children to be baptized of water and the spirit, or the one who sent the police to force their parents to have the most villainous racial poison we know thrust into their veins? the one who told them the story of the angel and Mary, or the one who questioned them as to their experiences of the Edipus complex? the one to whom the consecrated wafer was the very body of the virtue that was her salvation, or the one who looked forward to a precise and convenient regulation of her health and her desires by a nicely calculated diet of thyroid extract, adrenalin, thymin, pituitrin, and insulin, with pick-me-ups of hormone stimulants, the blood being first carefully fortified with antibodies against all possible infections by inoculations of infected bacteria and serum from infected animals, and against old age by surgical extirpation of the reproductive ducts or weekly doses of monkey gland?

It is true that behind all these quackeries there is a certain body of genuine scientific physiology. But was there any the less a certain body of genuine psychology behind St Catherine and the Holy Ghost? And which is the healthier mind? the saintly mind or the monkey gland mind? Does not the present cry of Back to the Middle Ages, which has been incubating ever since the pre-Raphaelite movement began, mean that it is no longer our Academy pictures that are intolerable, but our credulities that have not the excuse of being superstitions, our cruelties that have not the excuse of barbarism, our persecutions that have not the excuse of religious faith, our shameless substitution of successful swindlers and scoundrels and quacks for saints as objects of worship, and our deafness and blindness to the calls and visions of the inexorable power that made us, and will destroy us if we disregard it? To Joan and her contemporaries we should appear as a drove of Gadarene swine, possessed by all the unclean spirits cast out by the faith and civilization of the Middle Ages, running violently down a steep place into a hell of high explosives. For us to set up our condition as a standard of sanity, and declare Joan mad because she never condescended to it, is to prove that we are not only lost but irredeemable. Let us then once for all drop all nonsense about Joan being cracked, and accept her as at least as sane as Florence Nightingale, who also combined a very simple iconography of religious belief with a mind so exceptionally powerful that it kept her in continual trouble with the medical and military panjandrums of her time.

FAILURES OF THE VOICES

That the voices and visions were illusory, and their wisdom all Joan's own, is shewn by the occasions on which they failed her, notably during her trial, when they assured her that she would be rescued. Here her hopes flattered her; but they were not unreasonable: her military colleague La Hire was in command of a considerable force not so very far off; and if the Armagnacs, as her party was called, had really wanted to rescue her, and had put anything like her own vigor into the enterprise, they could have attempted it with very fair chances of success. She did not understand that they were glad to be rid of her, nor that the rescue of a prisoner from the hands of the Church was a much more serious business for a medieval captain, or even a medieval king, than its mere physical difficulty as a military exploit suggested. According to her lights her expectation of a rescue was reasonable; therefore she heard Madame Saint Catherine assuring her it would happen, that being her way of finding out and making up her own mind. When it became evident that she had miscalculated: when she was led to the stake, and La Hire was not thundering at the gates of Rouen nor charging Warwick's men at arms, she threw over Saint Catherine at once, and recanted. Nothing could be more sane or practical. It was not until she discovered that she had gained nothing by her recantation but close imprisonment for life that she withdrew it, and deliberately and explicitly chose burning instead: a decision which shewed not only the extraordinary decision of her character, but also a Rationalism carried to its ultimate human test of suicide. Yet even in this the illusion persisted; and she announced her relapse as dictated to her by her voices.

JOAN A GALTONIC VISUALIZER

The most sceptical scientific reader may therefore accept as a flat fact, carrying no implication of unsoundness of mind, that Joan was what Francis Galton and other modern investigators of human faculty call a visualizer. She saw imaginary saints just as some other people see imaginary diagrams and landscapes with numbers dotted about them, and are thereby able to perform feats of memory and arithmetic impossible to non-visualizers. Visualizers will understand this at once. Non-visualizers who have never read Galton will be puzzled and incredulous. But a very little inquiry among their acquaintances will reveal to them that the mind's eye is more or less a magic lantern, and that the street is full of normally sane people who have hallucinations of all sorts which they believe to be part of the normal permanent equipment of all human beings.

JOAN'S MANLINESS AND MILITARISM

Joan's other abnormality, too common among uncommon things to be properly called a peculiarity, was her craze for soldiering and the masculine life. Her father tried to frighten her out of it by threatening to drown her if she ran away with the soldiers, and ordering her brothers to drown her if he were not on the spot. This extravagance was clearly not serious: it must have been addressed to a child young enough to imagine that he was in earnest. Joan must therefore as a child have wanted to run away and be a soldier. The awful prospect of being thrown into the Meuse and drowned by a terrible father and her big brothers kept her quiet until the father had lost his terrors and the brothers yielded to her natural leadership; and by that time she had sense enough to know that the masculine and military life was not a mere matter of running away from home. But the taste for it never left her, and was fundamental in determining her career.

If anyone doubts this, let him ask himself why a maid charged with a special mission from heaven to the Dauphin (this was how Joan saw her very able plan for retrieving the desperate situation of the uncrowned king) should not have simply gone to the court as a maid, in woman's dress, and urged her counsel upon him in a woman's way, as other women with similar missions had come to his mad father and his wise grandfather. Why did she insist on having a soldier's dress and arms and sword and horse and equipment, and on treating her escort of soldiers as comrades, sleeping side by side with them on the floor at night as if there were no difference of sex between them? It may be answered that this was the safest way of travelling through a country infested with hostile troops and bands of marauding deserters from both sides. Such an answer has no weight because it applies to all the women who travelled in France at that time, and who never dreamt of travelling otherwise than as women. But even if we accept it, how does it account for the fact that when the danger was over, and she could present herself at court in feminine attire with perfect safety and obviously with greater propriety, she presented herself in her man's dress, and instead of urging Charles, like Queen Victoria urging the War Office to send Roberts to the Transvaal, to send D'Alençon, De Rais, La Hire and the rest to the relief of Dunois at Orleans, insisted that she must go herself and lead the assault in person? Why did she give exhibitions of her dexterity in handling a lance, and of her seat as a rider? Why did she accept presents of armor and chargers and masculine surcoats, and in every action repudiate the conventional character of a woman? The simple answer to all these questions is that she was the sort of woman that wants to lead a man's life. They are to be found wherever there are armies on foot or navies on the seas, serving in male disguise, eluding detection for astonishingly long periods, and sometimes, no doubt, escaping it entirely. When they are in a position to defy public opinion they throw off all concealment. You have your Rosa Bonheur painting in male blouse and trousers, and George Sand living a man's life and almost compelling her Chopins and De Mussets to live women's lives to amuse her. Had Joan not been one of those "unwomanly women," she might have been canonized much sooner.

But it is not necessary to wear trousers and smoke big cigars to live a man's life any more than it is necessary to wear petticoats to live a woman's. There are plenty of gowned and bodiced women in ordinary civil life who manage their own affairs and other people's, including those of their menfolk, and are entirely masculine in their tastes and pursuits. There always were such women, even in the Victorian days when women had fewer legal rights than men, and our modern women magistrates, mayors, and members of Parliament were unknown. In reactionary Russia in our own century a woman soldier organized an effective regiment of amazons, which disappeared only because it was Aldershottian enough to be against the Revolution. The exemption of women from military service is founded, not on any natural inaptitude that men do not share, but on the fact that communities cannot reproduce themselves without plenty of women. Men are more largely dispensable, and are sacrificed accordingly.

WAS JOAN SUICIDAL?

These two abnormalities were the only ones that were irresistibly prepotent in Joan; and they brought her to the stake. Neither of them was peculiar to her. There was nothing peculiar about her except the vigor and scope of her mind and character, and the intensity of her vital energy. She was accused of a suicidal tendency; and it is a fact that when she attempted to escape from Beaurevoir Castle by jumping from a tower said to be sixty feet high, she took a risk beyond reason, though she recovered from the crash after a few days fasting. Her death was deliberately chosen as an alternative to life without liberty. In battle she challenged death as Wellington did at Waterloo, and as Nelson habitually did when he walked his quarter deck during his battles with all his decorations in full blaze. As neither Nelson nor Wellington nor any of those who have performed desperate feats, and preferred death to captivity, has been accused of suicidal mania, Joan need not be suspected of it. In the Beaurevoir affair there was more at stake than her freedom. She was distracted by the news that Compiègne was about to fall; and she was convinced that she could save it if only she could get free. Still, the leap was so perilous that her conscience was not quite easy about it; and she expressed this, as usual, by saying that Saint Catherine had forbidden her to do it, but forgave her afterwards for her disobedience.

JOAN SUMMED UP

We may accept and admire Joan, then, as a sane and shrewd country girl of extraordinary strength of mind and hardihood of body. Everything she did was thoroughly calculated; and though the process was so rapid that she was hardly conscious of it, and ascribed it all to her voices, she was a woman of policy and not of blind impulse. In war she was as much a realist as Napoleon: she had his eye for artillery and his knowledge of what it could do. She did not expect besieged cities to fall Jerichowise at the sound of her trumpet, but, like Wellington, adapted her methods of attack to the peculiarities of the defence; and she anticipated the Napoleonic calculation that if you only hold on long enough the other fellow will give in: for example, her final triumph at Orleans was achieved after her commander Dunois had sounded the retreat at the end of a day's fighting without a decision. She was never for a moment what so many romancers and playwrights have pretended: a romantic young lady. She was a thorough daughter of the soil in her peasantlike matter-of-factness and doggedness, and her acceptance of great lords and kings and prelates as such without idolatry or snobbery, seeing at a glance how much they were individually good for. She had the respectable countrywoman's sense of the value of public decency, and would not tolerate foul language and neglect of religious observances, nor allow disreputable women to hang about her soldiers. She had one pious ejaculation "En nom Dé!" and one meaningless oath "Par mon martin"; and this much swearing she allowed to the incorrigibly blasphemous La Hire equally with herself. The value of this prudery was so great in restoring the self-respect of the badly demoralized army that, like most of her policy, it justified itself as soundly calculated. She talked to and dealt with people of all classes, from laborers to kings, without embarrassment or affectation, and got them to do what she wanted when they were not afraid or corrupt. She could coax and she could hustle, her tongue having a soft side and a sharp edge. She was very capable: a born boss.

JOAN'S IMMATURITY AND IGNORANCE

All this, however, must be taken with one heavy qualification. She was only a girl in her teens. If we could think of her as a managing woman of fifty we should seize her type at once; for we have plenty of managing women among us of that age who illustrate perfectly the sort of person she would have become had she lived. But she, being only a lass when all is said, lacked their knowledge of men's vanities and of the weight and proportion of social forces. She knew nothing of iron hands in velvet gloves: she just used her fists. She thought political changes much easier than they are, and, like Mahomet in his innocence of any world but the tribal world, wrote letters to kings calling on them to make millennial rearrangements. Consequently it was only in the enterprises that were really simple and compassable by swift physical force, like the coronation and the Orleans campaign, that she was successful.

Her want of academic education disabled her when she had to deal with such elaborately artificial structures as the great ecclesiastical and social institutions of the Middle Ages. She had a horror of heretics without suspecting that she was herself a heresiarch, one of the precursors of a schism that rent Europe in two, and cost centuries of bloodshed that is not yet staunched. She objected to foreigners on the sensible ground that they were not in their proper place in France; but she had no notion of how this brought her into conflict with Catholicism and Feudalism, both essentially international. She worked by commonsense; and where scholarship was the only clue to institutions she was in the dark, and broke her shins against them, all the more rudely because of her enormous self-confidence, which made her the least cautious of human beings in civil affairs.

This combination of inept youth and academic ignorance with great natural capacity, push, courage, devotion, originality and oddity, fully accounts for all the facts in Joan's career, and makes her a credible historical and human phenomenon; but it clashes most discordantly both with the idolatrous romance that has grown up round her, and the belittling scepticism that reacts against that romance.

THE MAID IN LITERATURE

English readers would probably like to know how these idolizations and reactions have affected the books they are most familiar with about Joan. There is the first part of the Shakesperean, or pseudo-Shakesperean trilogy of Henry VI, in which Joan is one of the leading characters. This portrait of Joan is not more authentic than the descriptions in the London papers of George Washington in 1780, of

Napoleon in 1803, of the German Crown Prince in 1915, or of Lenin in 1917. It ends in mere scurrility. The impression left by it is that the playwright, having begun by an attempt to make Joan a beautiful and romantic figure, was told by his scandalized company that English patriotism would never stand a sympathetic representation of a French conqueror of English troops, and that unless he at once introduced all the old charges against Joan of being a sorceress and a harlot, and assumed her to be guilty of all of them, his play could not be produced. As likely as not, this is what actually happened: indeed there is only one other apparent way of accounting for the sympathetic representation of Joan as a heroine culminating in her eloquent appeal to the Duke of Burgundy, followed by the blackguardly scurrility of the concluding scenes. That other way is to assume that the original play was wholly scurrilous, and that Shakespear touched up the earlier scenes. As the work belongs to a period at which he was only beginning his practice as a tinker of old works, before his own style was fully formed and hardened, it is impossible to verify this guess. His finger is not unmistakably evident in the play, which is poor and base in its moral tone; but he may have tried to redeem it from downright infamy by shedding a momentary glamor on the figure of The Maid.

When we jump over two centuries to Schiller, we find Die Jungfrau von Orleans drowned in a witch's caldron of raging romance. Schiller's Joan has not a single point of contact with the real Joan, nor indeed with any mortal woman that ever walked this earth. There is really nothing to be said of his play but that it is not about Joan at all, and can hardly be said to pretend to be; for he makes her die on the battlefield, finding her burning unbearable. Before Schiller came Voltaire, who burlesqued Homer in a mock epic called La Pucelle. It is the fashion to dismiss this with virtuous indignation as an obscene libel; and I certainly cannot defend it against the charge of extravagant indecorum. But its purpose was not to depict Joan, but to kill with ridicule everything that Voltaire righteously hated in the institutions and fashions of his own day. He made Joan ridiculous, but not contemptible nor (comparatively) unchaste; and as he also made Homer and St Peter and St Denis and the brave Dunois ridiculous, and the other heroines of the poem very unchaste indeed, he may be said to have let Joan off very easily. But indeed the personal adventures of the characters are so outrageous, and so Homerically free from any pretence at or even possibility of historical veracity, that those who affect to take them seriously only make themselves Pecksniffian. Samuel Butler believed The Iliad to be a burlesque of Greek Jingoism and Greek religion, written by a hostage or a slave; and La Pucelle makes Butler's theory almost convincing. Voltaire represents Agnes Sorel, the Dauphin's mistress, whom Joan never met, as a woman with a consuming passion for the chastest concubinal fidelity, whose fate it was to be continually falling into the hands of licentious foes and suffering the worst extremities of rapine. The combats in which Joan rides a flying donkey, or in which, taken unaware with no clothes on, she defends Agnes with her sword, and inflicts appropriate mutilations on her assailants, can be laughed at as they are intended to be without scruple; for no sane person could mistake them for sober history; and it may be that their ribald irreverence is more wholesome than the beglamored sentimentality of Schiller. Certainly Voltaire should not have asserted that Joan's father was a priest; but when he was out to *écraser l'infâme* (the French Church) he stuck at nothing.

So far, the literary representations of The Maid were legendary. But the publication by Quicherat in 1841 of the reports of her trial and rehabilitation placed the subject on a new footing. These entirely realistic documents created a living interest in Joan which Voltaire's mock Homerics and Schiller's romantic nonsense missed. Typical products of that interest in America and England are the histories of Joan by Mark Twain and Andrew Lang. Mark Twain was converted to downright worship of Joan directly by Quicherat. Later on, another man of genius, Anatole France, reacted against the Quicheratic wave of enthusiasm, and wrote a Life of Joan in which he attributed Joan's ideas to clerical prompting and her military success to an adroit use of her by Dunois as a *mascotte*: in short, he denied that she had any serious military or political ability. At this Andrew saw red, and went for Anatole's scalp in a rival Life of her which should be read as a corrective to the other. Lang had no difficulty in shewing that Joan's ability was not an unnatural fiction to be explained away as an illusion manufactured by priests and soldiers, but a straightforward fact.

It has been lightly pleaded in explanation that Anatole France is a Parisian of the art world, into whose scheme of things the able, hardheaded, hardhanded female, though she dominates provincial France and business Paris, does not enter; whereas Lang was a Scot, and every Scot knows that the grey mare is as likely as not to be the better horse. But this explanation does not convince me. I cannot believe that Anatole France does not know what everybody knows. I wish everybody knew all that he knows. One feels antipathies at work in his book. He is not anti-Joan; but he is anti-clerical, anti-mystic, and fundamentally unable to believe that there ever was any such person as the real Joan.

Mark Twain's Joan, skirted to the ground, and with as many petticoats as Noah's wife in a toy ark, is an attempt to combine Bayard with Esther Summerson from Bleak House into an unimpeachable American school teacher in armor. Like Esther Summerson she makes her creator ridiculous, and yet, being the work of a man of genius, remains a credible human goodygoody in spite of her creator's infatuation. It is the description rather than the valuation that is wrong. Andrew Lang and Mark Twain are equally determined to make Joan a beautiful and most ladylike Victorian; but both of them recognize and insist on her capacity for leadership, though the Scots scholar is less romantic about it than the Mississippi pilot. But then Lang was, by lifelong professional habit, a critic of biographies rather than a biographer, whereas Mark Twain writes his biography frankly in the form of a romance.

PROTESTANT MISUNDERSTANDINGS OF THE MIDDLE AGES

They had, however, one disability in common. To understand Joan's history it is not enough to understand her character: you must understand her environment as well. Joan in a nineteenth-twentieth century environment is as incongruous a figure as she would appear were she to walk down Piccadilly today in her fifteenth century armor. To see her in her proper perspective you must understand Christendom and the Catholic Church, the Holy Roman Empire and the Feudal System, as they existed and were understood in the Middle Ages. If you confuse the Middle Ages with the Dark Ages, and are in the habit of ridiculing your aunt for wearing "medieval clothes," meaning those in vogue in the eighteen-nineties, and are quite convinced that the world has progressed enormously, both morally and mechanically, since Joan's time, then you will never understand why Joan was burnt, much less feel that you might have voted for burning her yourself if you had been a member of the court that tried her; and until you feel that you know nothing essential about her.

That the Mississippi pilot should have broken down on this misunderstanding is natural enough. Mark Twain, the Innocent Abroad, who saw the lovely churches of the Middle Ages without a throb of emotion, author of A Yankee at the Court of King Arthur, in which the heroes and heroines of medieval chivalry are guys seen through the eyes of a street arab, was clearly out of court from the beginning. Andrew Lang was better read; but, like Walter Scott, he enjoyed medieval history as a string of Border romances rather than as the record of a high European civilization based on a catholic faith. Both of them were baptized as Protestants, and impressed by all their schooling and most of their reading with the belief that Catholic bishops who burnt heretics were persecutors capable of any villainy; that all heretics were Albigensians or Husites or Jews or Protestants of the highest character; and that the Inquisition was a Chamber of Horrors invented expressly and exclusively for such burnings. Accordingly we find them representing Peter Cauchon, Bishop of Beauvais, the judge who sent Joan to the stake, as an unconscionable scoundrel, and all the questions put to her as "traps" to ensnare and destroy her. And they assume unhesitatingly that the two or three score of canons and doctors of law and divinity who sat with Cauchon as assessors, were exact reproductions of him on slightly less elevated chairs and with a different headdress.

COMPARATIVE FAIRNESS OF JOAN'S TRIAL

The truth is that Cauchon was threatened and insulted by the English for being too considerate to Joan. A recent French writer denies that Joan was burnt, and holds that Cauchon spirited her away and burnt somebody or something else in her place, and that the pretender who subsequently personated her at Orleans and elsewhere was not a pretender but the real authentic Joan. He is able to cite Cauchon's pro-Joan partiality in support of his view. As to the assessors, the objection to them is not that they were a row of uniform rascals, but that they were political partisans of Joan's enemies. This is a valid objection to all such trials; but in the absence of neutral tribunals they are unavoidable. A trial by Joan's French partisans would have been as unfair as the trial by her French opponents; and an equally mixed tribunal would have produced a deadlock. Such recent trials as those of Edith Cavell by a German tribunal and Roger Casement by an English one were open to the same objection; but they went forward to the death nevertheless, because neutral tribunals were not available. Edith, like Joan, was an arch heretic: in the middle of the war she declared before the world that "Patriotism is not enough." She nursed enemies back to health, and assisted their prisoners to escape, making it abundantly clear that she would help any fugitive or distressed person without asking whose side he was on, and acknowledging no distinction before Christ between Tommy and Jerry and Pitou the *poilu*. Well might Edith have wished that she could bring the Middle Ages back, and have fifty civilians, learned in the law or vowed to the service of God, to support two skilled judges in trying her case according to the Catholic law of Christendom, and to argue it out with her at sitting after sitting for many weeks. The modern military Inquisition was not so squeamish. It shot her out of hand; and her countrymen, seeing in this a good opportunity for lecturing the enemy on his intolerance, put up a statue to her, but took particular care not to inscribe on the pedestal "Patriotism is not enough," for which omission, and the lie it implies, they will need Edith's intercession when they are themselves brought to judgment, if any heavenly power thinks such moral cowards capable of pleading to an intelligible indictment.

The point need be no further labored. Joan was persecuted essentially as she would be persecuted today. The change from burning to hanging or shooting may strike us as a change for the better. The change from careful trial under ordinary law to recklessly summary military terrorism may strike us a change for the worse. But as far as toleration is concerned the trial and execution in Rouen in 1431 might have been an event of today; and we may charge our consciences accordingly. If Joan had to be dealt with by us in London she would be treated with no more toleration than Miss Sylvia Pankhurst, or the Peculiar People, or the parents who keep their children from the elementary school, or any of the others who cross the line we have to draw, rightly or wrongly, between the tolerable and the intolerable.

JOAN NOT TRIED AS A POLITICAL OFFENDER

Besides, Joan's trial was not, like Casement's, a national political trial. Ecclesiastical courts and the courts of the Inquisition (Joan was tried by a combination of the two) were Courts Christian: that is, international courts; and she was tried, not as a traitress, but as a heretic, blasphemer, sorceress and idolater. Her alleged offences were not political offences against England, nor against the Burgundian faction in France, but against God and against the common morality of Christendom. And although the idea we call Nationalism was so foreign to the medieval conception of Christian society that it might almost have been directly charged against Joan as an additional heresy, yet it was not so charged; and it is unreasonable to suppose that the political bias of a body of Frenchmen like the assessors would on this point have run strongly in favor of the English foreigners (even if they had been making themselves particularly agreeable in France instead of just the contrary) against a Frenchwoman who had vanquished them.

The tragic part of the trial was that Joan, like most prisoners tried for anything but the simplest breaches of the ten commandments, did not understand what they were accusing her of. She was much more like Mark Twain than like Peter Cauchon. Her attachment to the Church was very different from the Bishop's, and does not, in fact, bear close examination from his point of view. She delighted in the solaces the Church offers to sensitive souls: to her, confession and communion were luxuries beside which the vulgar pleasures of the senses were trash. Her prayers were wonderful conversations with her three saints. Her piety seemed superhuman to the formally dutiful people whose religion was only a task to them. But when the Church was not offering her her favorite luxuries, but calling on her to accept its interpretation of God's will, and to sacrifice her own, she flatly refused, and made it clear that her notion of a Catholic Church was one in which the Pope was Pope Joan. How could the Church tolerate that, when it had just destroyed Hus, and had watched the career of Wycliffe with a growing anger that would have brought him, too, to the stake, had he not died a natural death before the wrath fell on him in his grave? Neither Hus nor Wycliffe was as bluntly defiant as Joan: both were reformers of the Church like Luther; whilst Joan, like Mrs Eddy, was quite prepared to supersede St Peter as the rock on which the Church was built, and, like Mahomet, was always ready with a private revelation from God to settle every question and fit every occasion.

The enormity of Joan's pretension was proved by her own unconsciousness of it, which we call her innocence, and her friends called her simplicity. Her solutions of the problems presented to her seemed, and indeed mostly were, the plainest commonsense, and their revelation to her by her Voices was to her a simple matter of fact. How could plain commonsense and simple fact seem to her to be that hideous thing, heresy? When rival prophetesses came into the field, she was down on them at once for liars and humbugs; but she never thought of them as heretics. She was in a state of invincible ignorance as to the Church's view; and the Church could not tolerate her pretensions without either waiving its authority or giving her a place beside the Trinity during her lifetime and in her teens, which was unthinkable. Thus an irresistible force met an immovable obstacle, and developed the heat that consumed poor Joan.

Mark and Andrew would have shared her innocence and her fate had they been dealt with by the Inquisition: that is why their accounts of the trial are as absurd as hers might have been could she have written one. All that can be said for their assumption that Cauchon was a vulgar villain, and that the questions put to Joan were traps, is that it has the support of the inquiry which rehabilitated her twentyfive years later. But this rehabilitation was as corrupt as the contrary proceeding applied to Cromwell by our Restoration reactionaries. Cauchon had been dug up, and his body thrown into the common sewer. Nothing was easier than to accuse him of cozenage, and declare the whole trial void on that account. That was what everybody wanted, from Charles the Victorious, whose credit was bound up with The Maid's, to the patriotic Nationalist populace, who idolized Joan's memory. The English were gone; and a verdict in their favor would have been an outrage on the throne and on the patriotism which Joan had set on foot.

We have none of these overwhelming motives of political convenience and popularity to bias us. For us the first trial stands valid and the rehabilitation would be negligible but for the mass of sincere testimony it produced as to Joan's engaging personal character. The question then arises: how did The Church get over the verdict at the first trial when it canonized Joan five hundred years later?

THE CHURCH UNCOMPROMISED BY ITS AMENDS

Easily enough. In the Catholic Church, far more than in law, there is no wrong without a remedy. It does not defer to Joanesque private judgment as such, the supremacy of private judgment for the individual being the quintessence of Protestantism; nevertheless it finds a place for private judgment *in excelsis* by admitting that the highest wisdom may come as a divine revelation to an individual. On sufficient evidence it will declare that individual a saint. Thus, as revelation may come by way of an enlightenment of the private judgment no less than by the words of a celestial personage appearing in a vision, a saint may be defined as a person of heroic virtue whose private judgment is privileged. Many innovating saints, notably Francis and Clare, have been in conflict with the Church during their lives, and have thus raised the question whether they were heretics or saints. Francis might have gone to the stake had he lived longer. It is therefore by no means impossible for a person to be excommunicated as a heretic, and on further consideration canonized as a saint. Excommunication by a provincial ecclesiastical court is not one of the acts for which the Church claims infallibility. Perhaps I had better inform my Protestant readers that the famous Dogma of Papal Infallibility is by far the most modest pretension of the kind in existence. Compared with our infallible democracies, our infallible medical councils, our infallible astronomers, our infallible judges, and our infallible parliaments, the Pope is on his knees in the dust confessing his ignorance before the throne of God, asking only that as to certain historical matters on which he has clearly more sources of information open to him than anyone else his decision shall be taken as final. The Church may, and perhaps some day will, canonize Galileo without compromising such infallibility as it claims for the Pope, if not without compromising the infallibility claimed for the Book of Joshua by simple souls whose rational faith in more important things has become bound up with a quite irrational faith in the chronicle of Joshua's campaigns as a treatise on physics. Therefore the Church will probably not canonize Galileo yet awhile, though it might do worse. But it has been able to canonize Joan without any compromise at all. She never doubted that the sun went round the earth: she had seen it do so too often.

Still, there was a great wrong done to Joan and to the conscience of the world by her burning. *Tout comprendre, c'est tout pardonner*, which is the Devil's sentimentality, cannot excuse it. When we have admitted that the tribunal was not only honest and legal, but exceptionally merciful in respect of sparing Joan the torture which was customary when she was obdurate as to taking the oath, and that Cauchon was far more self-disciplined and conscientious both as priest and lawyer than any English judge ever dreams of being in a political case in which his party and class prejudices are involved, the human fact remains that the burning of Joan of Arc was a horror, and that a historian who would defend it would defend anything. The final criticism of its physical side is implied in the refusal of the Marquesas islanders to be persuaded that the English did not eat Joan. Why, they ask, should anyone take the trouble to roast a human being except with that object? They cannot conceive its being a pleasure. As we have no answer for them that is not shameful to us, let us blush for our more complicated and pretentious savagery before we proceed to unravel the business further, and see what other lessons it contains for us.

CRUELTY, MODERN AND MEDIEVAL

First, let us get rid of the notion that the mere physical cruelty of the burning has any special significance. Joan was burnt just as dozens of less interesting heretics were burnt in her time. Christ, in being crucified, only shared the fate of thousands of forgotten malefactors. They have no pre-eminence in mere physical pain: much more horrible executions than theirs are on record, to say nothing of the agonies of so-called natural death as its worst.

Joan was burnt more than five hundred years ago. More than three hundred years later: that is, only about a hundred years before I was born, a woman was burnt on Stephen's Green in my native city of Dublin for coining, which was held to be treason. In my preface to the recent volume on English Prisons under Local Government, by Sidney and Beatrice Webb, I have mentioned that when I was already a grown man I saw Richard Wagner conduct two concerts, and that when Richard Wagner was a young man he saw and avoided a crowd of people hastening to see a soldier broken on the wheel by the more cruel of the two ways of carrying out that hideous method of execution. Also that the penalty of hanging, drawing, and quartering, unmentionable in its details, was abolished so recently that there are men living who have been sentenced to it. We are still flogging criminals, and clamoring for more flogging. Not even the most sensationally frightful of these atrocities inflicted on its victim the misery, degradation, and conscious waste and loss of life suffered in our modern prisons, especially the model ones, without, as far as I can see, rousing any more compunction than the burning of heretics did in the Middle Ages. We have not even the excuse of getting some fun out of our prisons as the Middle Ages did out of their stakes and wheels and gibbets. Joan herself judged this matter when she had to choose between imprisonment and the stake, and chose the stake. And thereby she deprived The Church of the plea that it was guiltless of her death, which was the work of the secular arm. The Church should have confined itself to excommunicating her. There it was within its rights: she had refused to accept its authority or comply with its conditions; and it could say with truth "You are not one of us: go forth and find the religion that suits you, or found one for yourself." It had no right to say "You may return to us now that you have recanted; but you shall stay in a dungeon all the rest of your life." Unfortunately, The Church did not believe that there was any genuine soul saving religion outside itself; and it was deeply corrupted, as all the Churches were and still are, by primitive Calibanism (in Browning's sense), or the propitiation of a dreaded deity by suffering and sacrifice. Its method was not cruelty for cruelty's sake, but cruelty for the salvation of Joan's soul. Joan, however, believed that the saving of her soul was her own business, and not that of *les gens d'église*. By using that term as she did, mistrustfully and contemptuously, she announced herself as, in germ, an anti-Clerical as thoroughgoing as Voltaire or Anatole France. Had she said in so many words "To the dustbin with the Church Militant and its blackcoated officials: I recognize only the Church Triumphant in heaven," she would hardly have put her view more plainly.

CATHOLIC ANTI-CLERICALISM

I must not leave it to be inferred here that one cannot be an anti-Clerical and a good Catholic too. All the reforming Popes have been vehement anti-Clericals, veritable scourges of the clergy. All the great Orders arose from dissatisfaction with the priests: that of the Franciscans with priestly snobbery, that of the Dominicans with priestly laziness and Laodiceanism, that of the Jesuits with priestly apathy and ignorance and indiscipline. The most bigoted Ulster Orangeman or Leicester Low Church bourgeois (as described by Mr Henry Nevinson) is a mere Gallio compared to Machiavelli, who, though no Protestant, was a fierce anti-Clerical. Any Catholic may, and many Catholics do, denounce any priest or body of priests, as lazy, drunken, idle, dissolute, and unworthy of their great Church and their function as the pastors of their flocks of human souls. But to say that the souls of the people are no business of the Churchmen is to go a step further, a step across the Rubicon. Joan virtually took that step.

CATHOLICISM NOT YET CATHOLIC ENOUGH

And so, if we admit, as we must, that the burning of Joan was a mistake, we must broaden Catholicism sufficiently to include her in its charter. Our Churches must admit that no official organization of mortal men whose vocation does not carry with it extraordinary mental powers (and this is all that any Church Militant can in the face of fact and history pretend to be), can keep pace with the private judgment of persons of genius except when, by a very rare accident, the genius happens to be Pope, and not even then unless he is an exceedingly overbearing Pope. The Churches must learn humility as well as teach it. The Apostolic Succession cannot be secured or confined by the laying on of hands: the tongues of fire have descended on heathens and outcasts too often for that, leaving anointed Churchmen to scandalize History as worldly rascals. When the Church Militant behaves as if it were already the Church Triumphant, it makes these appalling blunders about Joan and Bruno and Galileo and the rest which make it so difficult for a Freethinker to join it; and a Church which has no place for Freethinkers: nay, which does not inculcate and encourage freethinking with a complete belief that thought, when really free, must by its own law take the path that leads to The Church's bosom, not only has no future in modern culture, but obviously has no faith in the valid science of its own tenets, and is guilty of the heresy that theology and science are two different and opposite impulses, rivals for human allegiance.

I have before me the letter of a Catholic priest. "In your play," he writes, "I see the dramatic presentation of the conflict of the Regal, sacerdotal, and Prophetical powers, in which Joan was crushed. To me it is not the victory of any one of them over the others that will bring peace and the

Reign of the Saints in the Kingdom of God, but their fruitful interaction in a costly but noble state of tension." The Pope himself could not put it better; nor can I. We must accept the tension, and maintain it nobly without letting ourselves be tempted to relieve it by burning the thread. This is Joan's lesson to The Church; and its formulation by the hand of a priest emboldens me to claim that her canonization was a magnificently Catholic gesture as the canonization of a Protestant saint by the Church of Rome. But its special value and virtue cannot be apparent until it is known and understood as such. If any simple priest for whom this is too hard a saying tells me that it was not so intended, I shall remind him that the Church is in the hands of God, and not, as simple priests imagine, God in the hands of the Church; so if he answers too confidently for God's intentions he may be asked "Hast thou entered into the springs of the sea? or hast thou walked in the recesses of the deep?" And Joan's own answer is also the answer of old: "Though He slay me, yet will I trust in Him; *but I will maintain my own ways before Him.*"

THE LAW OF CHANGE IS THE LAW OF GOD

When Joan maintained her own ways she claimed, like Job, that there was not only God and the Church to be considered, but the Word made Flesh: that is, the unaveraged individual, representing life possibly at its highest actual human evolution and possibly at its lowest, but never at its merely mathematical average. Now there is no deification of the democratic average in the theory of the Church: it is an avowed hierarchy in which the members are sifted until at the end of the process an individual stands supreme as the Vicar of Christ. But when the process is examined it appears that its successive steps of selection and election are of the superior by the inferior (the cardinal vice of democracy), with the result that great popes are as rare and accidental as great kings, and that it has sometimes been safer for an aspirant to the Chair and the Keys to pass as a moribund dotard than as an energetic saint. At best very few popes have been canonized, or could be without letting down the standard of sanctity set by the self-elected saints.

No other result could have been reasonably expected; for it is not possible that an official organization of the spiritual needs of millions of men and women, mostly poor and ignorant, should compete successfully in the selection of its principals with the direct choice of the Holy Ghost as it flashes with unerring aim upon the individual. Nor can any College of Cardinals pray effectively that its choice may be inspired. The conscious prayer of the inferior may be that his choice may light on a greater than himself; but the sub-conscious intention of his self-preserving individuality must be to find a trustworthy servant for his own purposes. The saints and prophets, though they may be accidentally in this or that official position or rank, are always really self-selected, like Joan. And since neither Church nor State, by the secular necessities of its constitution, can guarantee even the recognition of such self-chosen missions, there is nothing for us but to make it a point of honour to privilege heresy to the last bearable degree on the simple ground that all evolution in thought and conduct must at first appear as heresy and misconduct. In short, though all society is founded on intolerance, all improvement is founded on tolerance, or the recognition of the fact that the law of evolution is Ibsen's law of change. And as the law of God in any sense of the word which can now command a faith proof against science is a law of evolution, it follows that the law of God is a law of change, and that when the Churches set themselves against change as such, they are setting themselves against the law of God.

CREDULITY, MODERN AND MEDIEVAL

When Abernethy, the famous doctor, was asked why he indulged himself with all the habits he warned his patients against as unhealthy, he replied that his business was that of a direction post, which points out the way to a place, but does not go thither itself. He might have added that neither does it compel the traveller to go thither, nor prevent him from seeking some other way. Unfortunately our clerical direction posts always do coerce the traveller when they have the political power to do so. When the Church was a temporal as well as a spiritual power, and for long after to the full extent to which it could control or influence the temporal power, it enforced conformity by persecutions that were all the more ruthless because their intention was so excellent. Today, when the doctor has succeeded to the priest, and can do practically what he likes with parliament and the press through the blind faith in him which has succeeded to the far more critical faith in the parson, legal compulsion to take the doctor's prescription, however poisonous, is carried to an extent that would have horrified the Inquisition and staggered Archbishop Laud. Our credulity is grosser than that of the Middle Ages, because the priest had no such direct pecuniary interest in our sins as the doctor has in our diseases: he did not starve when all was well with his flock, nor prosper when they were perishing, as our private commercial doctors must. Also the medieval cleric believed that something extremely unpleasant would happen to him after death if he was unscrupulous, a belief now practically extinct among persons receiving a dogmatically materialist education. Our professional corporations are Trade Unions without souls to be damned; and they will soon drive us to remind them that they have bodies to be kicked. The Vatican was never soulless: at worst it was a political conspiracy to make the Church supreme temporally as well as spiritually. Therefore the question raised by Joan's burning is a burning question still, though the penalties involved are not so sensational. That is why I am probing it. If it were only an historical curiosity I would not waste my readers' time and my own on it for five minutes.

TOLERATION, MODERN AND MEDIEVAL

The more closely we grapple with it the more difficult it becomes. At first sight we are disposed to repeat that Joan should have been excommunicated and then left to go her own way, though she would have protested vehemently against so cruel a deprivation of her spiritual food; for confession, absolution, and the body of her Lord were first necessaries of life to her. Such a spirit as Joan's might have got over that difficulty as the Church of England got over the Bulls of Pope Leo, by making a Church of her own, and affirming it to be the temple of the true and original faith from which her persecutors had strayed. But as such a proceeding was, in the eyes of both Church and State at that time, a spreading of damnation and anarchy, its toleration involved a greater strain on faith in freedom than political and ecclesiastical human nature could bear. It is easy to say that the Church should have waited for the alleged evil results instead of assuming that they would occur, and what they would be. That sounds simple enough; but if a modern Public Health Authority were to leave people entirely to their own devices in the matter of sanitation, saying, "We have nothing to do with drainage or your views about drainage; but if you catch smallpox or typhus we will prosecute you and have you punished very severely like the authorities in Butler's Erewhon," it would either be removed to the County Asylum or reminded that A's neglect of sanitation may kill the child of B two miles off, or start an epidemic in which the most conscientious sanitarians may perish.

We must face the fact that society is founded on intolerance. There are glaring cases of the abuse of intolerance; but they are quite as characteristic of our own age as of the Middle Ages. The typical modern example and contrast is compulsory inoculation replacing what was virtually compulsory baptism. But compulsion to inoculate is objected to as a crudely unscientific and mischievous anti-sanitary quackery, not in the least because we think it wrong to compel people to protect their children from disease. Its opponents would make it a crime, and will probably succeed in doing so; and that will be just as intolerant as making it compulsory. Neither the Pasteurians nor their opponents the Sanitarians would leave parents free to bring up their children naked, though that course also has some plausible advocates. We may prate of toleration as we will; but society must always draw a line somewhere between allowable conduct and insanity or crime, in spite of the risk of mistaking sages for lunatics and saviors for blasphemers. We must persecute, even to the death; and all we can do to mitigate the danger of persecution is, first, to be very careful what we persecute, and second, to bear in mind that unless there is a large liberty to shock conventional people, and a well informed sense of the value of originality, individuality, and eccentricity, the result will be apparent stagnation covering a repression of evolutionary forces which will eventually explode with extravagant and probably destructive violence.

VARIABILITY OF TOLERATION

The degree of tolerance attainable at any moment depends on the strain under which society is maintaining its cohesion. In war, for instance, we suppress the gospels and put Quakers in prison, muzzle the newspapers, and make it a serious offence to shew a light at night. Under the strain of invasion the French Government in 1792 struck off 4000 heads, mostly on grounds that would not in time of settled peace have provoked any Government to chloroform a dog; and in 1920 the British Government slaughtered and burnt in Ireland to persecute the advocates of a constitutional change which it had presently to effect itself. Later on the Fascisti in Italy did everything that the Black and Tans did in Ireland, with some grotesquely ferocious variations, under the strain of an unskilled attempt at industrial revolution by Socialists who understood Socialism even less than Capitalists understand Capitalism. In the United States an incredibly savage persecution of Russians took place during the scare spread by the Russian Bolshevik revolution after 1917. These instances could easily be multiplied; but they are enough to shew that between a maximum of indulgent toleration and a ruthlessly intolerant Terrorism there is a scale through which toleration is continually rising or falling, and that there was not the smallest ground for the self-complacent conviction of the nineteenth century that it was more tolerant than the fifteenth, or that such an event as the execution of Joan could not possibly occur in what we call our own more enlightened times. Thousands of women, each of them a thousand times less dangerous and terrifying to our Governments than Joan was to the Government of her day, have within the last ten years been slaughtered, starved to death, burnt out of house and home, and what not that Persecution and Terror could do to them, in the course of Crusades far more tyrannically pretentious than the medieval Crusades which proposed nothing more hyperbolical than the rescue of the Holy Sepulchre from the Saracens. The Inquisition, with its English equivalent the Star Chamber, are gone in the sense that their names are now disused; but can any of the modern substitutes for the Inquisition, the Special Tribunals and Commissions, the punitive expeditions, the suspensions of the Habeas Corpus Act, the proclamations of martial law and of minor states of siege, and the rest of them, claim that their victims have as fair a trial, as well considered a body of law to govern their cases, or as conscientious a judge to insist on strict legality of procedure as Joan had from the Inquisition and from the spirit of the Middle Ages even when her country was under the heaviest strain of civil and foreign war? From us she would have had no trial and no law except a Defence of The Realm Act suspending all law; and for judge she would have had, at best, a bothered major, and at worst a promoted advocate in ermine and scarlet to whom the scruples of a trained ecclesiastic like Cauchon would seem ridiculous and ungentlemanly.

THE CONFLICT BETWEEN GENIUS AND DISCIPLINE

Having thus brought the matter home to ourselves, we may now consider the special feature of Joan's mental constitution which made her so unmanageable. What is to be done on the one hand with rulers who will not give any reason for their orders, and on the other with people who cannot understand the reasons when they are given? The government of the world, political, industrial, and domestic, has to be carried on mostly by the giving and obeying of orders under just these conditions. "Dont argue: do as you are told" has to be said not only to children and soldiers, but practically to everybody. Fortunately most people do not want to argue: they are only too glad to be saved the trouble of thinking for themselves. And the ablest and most independent thinkers are content to understand their own special department. In other departments they will unhesitatingly ask for and accept the instructions of a policeman or the advice of a tailor without demanding or desiring explanations.

Nevertheless, there must be some ground for attaching authority to an order. A child will obey its parents, a soldier his officer, a philosopher a railway porter, and a workman a foreman, all without question, because it is generally accepted that those who give the orders understand what they are about, and are duly authorized and even obliged to give them, and because, in the practical emergencies of daily life, there is no time for lessons and explanations, or for arguments as to their validity. Such obediences are as necessary to the continuous operation of our social system as the revolutions of the earth are to the succession of night and day. But they are not so spontaneous as they seem: they have to be very carefully arranged and maintained. A bishop will defer to and obey a king; but let a curate venture to give him an order, however necessary and sensible, and the bishop will forget his cloth and damn the curate's impudence. The more obedient a man is to accredited authority the more jealous he is of allowing any unauthorized person to order him about.

With all this in mind, consider the career of Joan. She was a village girl, in authority over sheep and pigs, dogs and chickens, and to some extent over her father's hired laborers when he hired any, but over no one else on earth. Outside the farm she had no authority, no prestige, no claim to the smallest deference. Yet she ordered everybody about, from her uncle to the king, the archbishop, and the military General Staff. Her uncle obeyed her like a sheep, and took her to the castle of the local commander, who, on being ordered about, tried to assert himself, but soon collapsed and obeyed. And so on up to the king, as we have seen. This would have been unbearably irritating even if her orders had been offered as rational solutions of the desperate difficulties in which her social superiors found themselves just then. But they were not so offered. Nor were they offered as the expression of Joan's arbitrary will. It was never "I say so," but always "God says so."

JOAN AS THEOCRAT

Leaders who take that line have no trouble with some people, and no end of trouble with others. They need never fear a lukewarm reception. Either they are messengers of God, or they are blasphemous impostors. In the Middle Ages the general belief in witchcraft greatly intensified this contrast, because when an apparent miracle happened (as in the case of the wind changing at Orleans) it proved the divine mission to the credulous, and proved a contract with the devil to the sceptical. All through, Joan had to depend on those who accepted her as an incarnate angel against those who added to an intense resentment of her presumption a bigoted abhorrence of her as a witch. To this abhorrence we must add the extreme irritation of those who did not believe in the voices, and regarded her as a liar and impostor. It is hard to conceive anything more infuriating to a statesman or a military commander, or to a court favorite, than to be overruled at every turn, or to be robbed of the ear of the reigning sovereign, by an impudent young upstart practising on the credulity of the populace and the vanity and silliness of an immature prince by exploiting a few of those lucky coincidences which pass as miracles with uncritical people. Not only were the envy, snobbery, and competitive ambition of the baser natures exacerbated by Joan's success, but among the friendly ones that were clever enough to be critical a quite reasonable scepticism and mistrust of her ability, founded on a fair observation of her obvious ignorance and temerity, were at work against her. And as she met all remonstrances and all criticisms, not with arguments or persuasion, but with a flat appeal to the authority of God and a claim to be in God's special confidence, she must have seemed, to all who were not infatuated by her, so insufferable that nothing but an unbroken chain of overwhelming successes in the military and political field could have saved her from the wrath that finally destroyed her.

UNBROKEN SUCCESS ESSENTIAL IN THEOCRACY

To forge such a chain she needed to be the King, the Archbishop of Rheims, the Bastard of Orleans, and herself into the bargain; and that was impossible. From the moment when she failed to stimulate Charles to follow up his coronation with a swoop on Paris she was lost. The fact that she insisted on this whilst the king and the rest timidly and foolishly thought they could square the Duke of Burgundy, and effect a combination with him against the English, made her a terrifying nuisance to them; and from that time onward she could do nothing but prowl about the battlefields waiting for some lucky chance to sweep the captains into a big move. But it was to the enemy that the chance came: she was taken prisoner by the Burgundians fighting before Compiègne, and at once discovered that she had not a friend in the political world. Had she escaped she would probably have fought on until the English were gone, and then had to shake the dust of the court off her feet, and retire to Domrémy as Garibaldi had to retire to Caprera.

MODERN DISTORTIONS OF JOAN'S HISTORY

This, I think, is all that we can now pretend to say about the prose of Joan's career. The romance of her rise, the tragedy of her execution, and the comedy of the attempts of posterity to make amends for that execution, belong to my play and not to my preface, which must be confined to a sober essay on the facts. That such an essay is badly needed can be ascertained by examining any of our standard works of reference. They give accurately enough the facts about the visit to Vaucouleurs, the annunciation to Charles at Chinon, the raising of the siege of Orleans and the subsequent battles, the coronation at Rheims, the capture at Compiègne, and the trial and execution at Rouen, with their dates and the names of the people concerned; but they all break down on the melodramatic legend of the wicked bishop and the entrapped maiden and the rest of it. It would be far less misleading if they were wrong as to the facts, and right in their view of the facts. As it is, they illustrate the too little considered truth that the fashion in which we think changes like the fashion of our clothes, and that it is difficult, if not impossible, for most people to think otherwise than in the fashion of their own period.

HISTORY ALWAYS OUT OF DATE

This, by the way, is why children are never taught contemporary history. Their history books deal with periods of which the thinking has passed out of fashion, and the circumstances no longer apply to active life. For example, they are taught history about Washington, and told lies about Lenin. In Washington's time they were told lies (the same lies) about Washington, and taught history about Cromwell. In the fifteenth and sixteenth centuries they were told lies about Joan, and by this time might very well be told the truth about her. Unfortunately the lies did not cease when the political circumstances became obsolete. The Reformation, which Joan had unconsciously anticipated, kept the questions which arose in her case burning up to our own day (you can see plenty of the burnt houses still in Ireland), with the result that Joan has remained the subject of anti-Clerical lies, of specifically Protestant lies, and of Roman Catholic evasions of her unconscious Protestantism. The truth sticks in our throats with all the sauces it is served with: it will never go down until we take it without any sauce at all.

THE REAL JOAN NOT MARVELLOUS ENOUGH FOR US

But even in its simplicity, the faith demanded by Joan is one which the anti-metaphysical temper of nineteenth century civilization, which remains powerful in England and America, and is tyrannical in France, contemptuously refuses her. We do not, like her contemporaries, rush to the opposite extreme in a recoil from her as from a witch self-sold to the devil, because we do not believe in the devil nor in the possibility of commercial contracts with him. Our credulity, though enormous, is not boundless; and our stock of it is quite used up by our mediums, clairvoyants, hand readers, slate writers, Christian Scientists, psycho-analysts, electronic vibration diviners, therapeutists of all schools registered and unregistered, astrologers, astronomers who tell us that the sun is nearly a hundred million miles away and that Betelgeuse is ten times as big as the whole universe, physicists who balance Betelgeuse by describing the incredible smallness of the atom, and a host of other marvel mongers whose credulity would have dissolved the Middle Ages in a roar of sceptical merriment. In the Middle Ages people believed that the earth was flat, for which they had at least the evidence of their senses: we believe it to be round, not because as many as one per cent of us could give the physical reasons for so quaint a belief, but because modern science has convinced us that nothing that is obvious is true, and that everything that is magical, improbable, extraordinary, gigantic, microscopic, heartless, or outrageous is scientific.

I must not, by the way, be taken as implying that the earth is flat, or that all or any of our amazing credulities are delusions or impostures. I am only defending my own age against the charge of being less imaginative than the Middle Ages. I affirm that the nineteenth century, and still more the twentieth, can knock the fifteenth into a cocked hat in point of susceptibility to marvels and miracles and saints and prophets and magicians and monsters and fairy tales of all kinds. The proportion of marvel to immediately credible statement in the latest edition of the Encyclopædia Britannica is enormously greater than in the Bible. The medieval doctors of divinity who did not pretend to settle how many angels could dance on the point of a needle cut a very poor figure as far as romantic credulity is concerned beside the modern physicists who have settled to the billionth of a millimetre every movement and position in the dance of the electrons. Not for worlds would I question the precise accuracy of these calculations or the existence of electrons (whatever they may be). The fate of Joan is a warning to me against such heresy. But why the men who believe in electrons should regard themselves as less credulous than the men who believed in angels is not apparent to me. If they refuse to believe, with the Rouen assessors of 1431, that Joan was a witch, it is not because that explanation is too marvellous, but because it is not marvellous enough.

THE STAGE LIMITS OF HISTORICAL REPRESENTATION

For the story of Joan I refer the reader to the play which follows. It contains all that need be known about her; but as it is for stage use I have had to condense into three and a half hours a series of events which in their historical happening were spread over four times as many months; for the theatre imposes unities of time and place from which Nature in her boundless wastefulness is free. Therefore the reader must not suppose that Joan really put Robert de Baudricourt in her pocket in fifteen minutes, nor that her excommunication, recantation, relapse, and death at the stake were a matter of half an hour or so. Neither do I claim more for my dramatizations of Joan's contemporaries than that some of them are probably slightly more like the originals than those imaginary portraits of all the Popes from Saint Peter onward through the Dark Ages which are still gravely exhibited in the Uffizi in Florence (or were when I was there last). My Dunois would do equally well for the Duc d'Alençon. Both left descriptions of Joan so similar that, as a man always describes himself unconsciously whenever he describes anyone else, I have inferred that these good-natured young men were very like one another in mind; so I have lumped the twain into a single figure, thereby saving the theatre manager a salary and a suit of armor. Dunois' face, still on record at Châteaudun, is a suggestive help. But I really know no more about these men and their circle than Shakespear knew about Falconbridge and the Duke of Austria, or about Macbeth and Macduff. In view of the things they did in history, and have to do again in the play, I can only invent appropriate characters for them in Shakespear's manner.

A VOID IN THE ELIZABETHAN DRAMA

I have, however, one advantage over the Elizabethans. I write in full view of the Middle Ages, which may be said to have been rediscovered in the middle of the nineteenth century after an eclipse of about four hundred and fifty years. The Renascence of antique literature and art in the sixteenth century, and the lusty growth of Capitalism, between them buried the Middle Ages; and their resurrection is a second Renascence. Now there is not a breath of medieval atmosphere in Shakespear's histories. His John of Gaunt is like a study of the old age of Drake. Although he was a Catholic by family tradition, his figures are all intensely Protestant, individualist, sceptical, self-centered in everything but their love affairs, and completely personal and selfish even in them. His kings are not statesmen: his cardinals have no religion: a novice can read his plays from one end to the other without learning that the world is finally governed by forces expressing themselves in religions and laws which make epochs rather than by vulgarly ambitious individuals who make rows. The divinity which shapes our ends, rough hew them how we will, is mentioned fatalistically only to be forgotten immediately like a passing vague apprehension. To Shakespear as to Mark Twain, Cauchon would have been a tyrant and a bully instead of a Catholic, and the inquisitor Lemaître would have been a Sadist instead of a lawyer. Warwick would have had no more feudal quality than his successor the King Maker has in the play of Henry VI. We should have seen them all completely satisfied that if they would only to their own selves be true they could not then be false to any man (a precept which represents the reaction against medievalism at its intensest) as if they were beings in the air, without public responsibilities of any kind. All Shakespear's characters are so: that is why they seem natural to our middle classes, who are comfortable and irresponsible at other people's expense, and are neither ashamed of that condition nor even conscious of it. Nature abhors this vacuum in Shakespear; and I have taken care to let the medieval atmosphere blow through my play freely. Those who see it performed will not mistake the startling event it records for a mere personal accident. They will have before them not only the visible and human puppets, but the Church, the Inquisition, the Feudal System, with divine inspiration always beating against their too inelastic limits: all more terrible in their dramatic force than any of the little mortal figures clanking about in plate armor or moving silently in the frocks and hoods of the order of St Dominic.

TRAGEDY, NOT MELODRAMA

There are no villains in the piece. Crime, like disease, is not interesting: it is something to be done away with by general consent, and that is all about it. It is what men do at their best, with good intentions, and what normal men and women find that they must and will do in spite of their intentions, that really concern us. The rascally bishop and the cruel inquisitor of Mark Twain and Andrew Lang are as dull as pickpockets; and they reduce Joan to the level of the even less interesting person whose pocket is picked. I have represented both of them as capable and eloquent exponents of The Church Militant and The Church Litigant, because only by doing so can I maintain my drama on the level of high tragedy and save it from becoming a mere police court sensation. A villain in a play can never be anything more than a *diabolus ex machina*, possibly a more exciting expedient than a *deus ex machina*, but both equally mechanical, and therefore interesting only as mechanism. It is, I repeat, what normally innocent people do that concerns us; and if Joan had not been burnt by normally innocent people in the energy of their righteousness her death at their hands would have no more significance than the Tokyo earthquake, which burnt a great many maidens. The tragedy of such murders is that they are not committed by murderers. They are judicial murders, pious murders; and this contradiction at once brings an element of comedy into the tragedy: the angels may weep at the murder, but the gods laugh at the murderers.

THE INEVITABLE FLATTERIES OF TRAGEDY

Here then we have a reason why my drama of Saint Joan's career, though it may give the essential truth of it, gives an inexact picture of some accidental facts. It goes almost without saying that the old Jeanne d'Arc melodramas, reducing everything to a conflict of villain and hero, or in Joan's case villain and heroine, not only miss the point entirely, but falsify the characters, making Cauchon a scoundrel, Joan a prima donna, and Dunois a lover. But the writer of high tragedy and comedy, aiming at the innermost attainable truth, must needs flatter Cauchon nearly as much as the melodramatist vilifies him. Although there is, as far as I have been able to discover, nothing against Cauchon that convicts him of bad faith or exceptional severity in his judicial relations with Joan, or of as much anti-prisoner, pro-police, class and sectarian bias as we now take for granted in our own courts, yet there is hardly more warrant for classing him as a great Catholic churchman, completely proof against the passions roused by the temporal situation. Neither does the inquisitor Lemaître, in such scanty accounts of him as are now recoverable, appear quite so able a master of his duties and of the case before him as I have given him credit for being. But it is the business of the stage to make its figures more intelligible to themselves than they would be in real life; for by no other means can they be made intelligible to the audience. And in this case Cauchon and Lemaître have to make intelligible not only themselves but the Church and the Inquisition, just as Warwick has to make the feudal system intelligible, the three between them having thus to make a twentieth-century audience conscious of an epoch fundamentally different from its own. Obviously the real Cauchon, Lemaître, and Warwick could not have done this: they were part of the Middle Ages themselves, and therefore as unconscious of its peculiarities as of the atomic formula of the air they breathed. But the play would be unintelligible if I had not endowed them with enough of this consciousness to enable them to explain their attitude to the twentieth century. All I claim is that by this inevitable sacrifice of verisimilitude I have secured in the only possible way sufficient veracity to justify me in claiming that as far as I can gather from the available documentation, and from such powers of divination as I possess, the things I represent these three exponents of the drama as saying are the things they actually would have said if they had known what they were really doing. And beyond this neither drama nor history can go in my hands.

SOME WELL-MEANT PROPOSALS FOR THE IMPROVEMENT OF THE PLAY

I have to thank several critics on both sides of the Atlantic, including some whose admiration for my play is most generously enthusiastic, for their heartfelt instructions as to how it can be improved. They point out that by the excision of the epilogue and all the references to such undramatic and tedious matters as the Church, the feudal system, the Inquisition, the theory of heresy and so forth, all of which, they point out, would be ruthlessly blue pencilled by any experienced manager, the play could be considerably shortened. I think they are mistaken. The experienced knights of the blue pencil, having saved an hour and a half by disembowelling the play, would at once proceed to waste two hours in building elaborate scenery, having real water in the river Loire and a real bridge across it, and staging an obviously sham fight for possession of it, with the victorious French led by Joan on a real horse. The coronation would eclipse all previous theatrical displays, shewing, first, the procession through the streets of Rheims, and then the service in the cathedral, with special music written for both. Joan would be burnt on the stage, as Mr Matheson Lang always is in The Wandering Jew, on the principle that it does not matter in the least why a woman is burnt provided she is burnt, and people can pay to see it done. The intervals between the acts whilst these splendors were being built up and then demolished by the stage carpenters would seem eternal, to the great profit of the refreshment bars. And the weary and demoralized audience would lose their last trains and curse me for writing such inordinately long and intolerably dreary and meaningless plays. But the applause of the press would be unanimous. Nobody who knows the stage history of Shakespear will doubt that this is what would happen if I knew my business so little as to listen to these well intentioned but disastrous counsellors: indeed it probably will happen when I am no longer in control of the performing rights. So perhaps it will be as well for the public to see the play while I am still alive.

THE EPILOGUE

As to the epilogue, I could hardly be expected to stultify myself by implying that Joan's history in the world ended unhappily with her execution, instead of beginning there. It was necessary by hook or crook to shew the canonized Joan as well as the incinerated one; for many a woman has got herself burnt by carelessly whisking a muslin skirt into the drawing room fireplace, but getting canonized is a different matter, and a more important one. So I am afraid the epilogue must stand.

TO THE CRITICS, LEST THEY SHOULD FEEL IGNORED

To a professional critic (I have been one myself) theatregoing is the curse of Adam. The play is the evil he is paid to endure in the sweat of his brow; and the sooner it is over, the better. This would seem to place him in irreconcilable opposition to the paying playgoer, from whose point of view the longer the play, the more entertainment he gets for his money. It does in fact so place him, especially in the provinces, where the playgoer goes to the theatre for the sake of the play solely, and insists so effectively on a certain number of hours' entertainment that touring managers are sometimes seriously embarrassed by the brevity of the London plays they have to deal in.

For in London the critics are reinforced by a considerable body of persons who go to the theatre as many others go to church, to display their best clothes and compare them with other people's; to be in the fashion, and have something to talk about at dinner parties; to adore a pet performer; to pass the evening anywhere rather than at home: in short, for any or every reason except interest in dramatic art as such. In fashionable centres the number of irreligious people who go to church, of unmusical people who go to concerts and operas, and of undramatic people who go to the theatre, is so prodigious that sermons have been cut down to ten minutes and plays to two hours; and, even at that, congregations sit longing for the benediction and audiences for the final curtain, so that they may get away to the lunch or supper they really crave for, after arriving as late as (or later than) the hour of beginning can possibly be made for them.

Thus from the stalls and in the Press an atmosphere of hypocrisy spreads. Nobody says straight out that genuine drama is a tedious nuisance, and that to ask people to endure more than two hours of it (with two long intervals of relief) is an intolerable imposition. Nobody says "I hate classical tragedy and comedy as I hate sermons and symphonies; but I like police news and divorce news and any kind of dancing or decoration that has an aphrodisiac effect on me or on my wife or husband. And whatever superior people may pretend, I cannot associate pleasure with any sort of intellectual activity; and I dont believe anyone else can either." Such things are not said; yet nine-tenths of what is offered as criticism of the drama in the metropolitan Press of Europe and America is nothing but a muddled paraphrase of it. If it does not mean that, it means nothing.

I do not complain of this, though it complains very unreasonably of me. But I can take no more notice of it than Einstein of the people who are incapable of mathematics. I write in the classical manner for those who pay for admission to a theatre because they like classical comedy or tragedy for its own sake, and like it so much when it is good of its kind and well done that they tear themselves away from it with reluctance to catch the very latest train or omnibus that will take them home. Far from arriving late from an eight or half-past eight o'clock dinner so as to escape at least the first half-hour of the performance, they stand in queues outside the theatre doors for hours beforehand in bitingly cold weather to secure a seat. In countries where a play lasts a week, they bring baskets of provisions and sit it out. These are the patrons on whom I depend for my bread. I do not give them performances twelve hours long, because circumstances do not at present make such entertainments feasible; though a performance beginning after breakfast and ending at sunset is as possible physically and artistically in Surrey or Middlesex as in Ober-Ammergau; and an all-night sitting in a theatre would be at least as enjoyable as an all-night sitting in the House of Commons, and much more useful. But in St Joan I have done my best by going to the well-established classical limit of three and a half hours practically continuous playing, barring the one interval imposed by considerations which have nothing to do with art. I know that this is hard on the pseudo-critics and on the fashionable people whose playgoing is a hypocrisy. I cannot help feeling some compassion for them when they assure me that my play, though a great play, must fail hopelessly, because it does not begin at a quarter to nine and end at eleven. The facts are overwhelmingly against them. They forget that all men are not as they are. Still, I am sorry for them; and though I cannot for their sakes undo my work and help the people who hate the theatre to drive out the people who love it, yet I may point out to them that they have several remedies in their own hands. They can escape the first part of the play by their usual practice of arriving late. They can escape the epilogue by not waiting for it. And if the irreducible minimum thus attained is still too painful, they can stay away altogether. But I deprecate this extreme course, because it is good neither for my pocket nor for their own souls. Already a few of them, noticing that what matters is not the absolute length of time occupied by a play, but the speed with which that times passes, are discovering that the theatre, though purgatorial in its Aristotelian moments, is not necessarily always the dull place they have so often found it. What do its discomforts matter when the play makes us forget them?

AYOT ST LAWRENCE,
May 1924.

SAINT JOAN

SCENE I

A FINE spring morning on the river Meuse, between Lorraine and Champagne, in the year 1429 A.D., *in the castle of Vaucouleurs.*

Captain Robert de Baudricourt, a military squire, handsome and physically energetic, but with no will of his own, is disguising that defect in his usual fashion by storming terribly at his steward, a trodden worm, scanty of flesh, scanty of hair, who might be any age from 18 *to* 55, *being the sort of man whom age cannot wither because he has never bloomed.*

The two are in a sunny stone chamber on the first floor of the castle. At a plain strong oak table, seated in chair to match, the captain presents his left profile. The steward stands facing him at the other side of the table, if so deprecatory a stance as his can be called standing. The mullioned thirteenth-century window is open behind him. Near it in the corner is a turret with a narrow arched doorway leading to a winding stair which descends to the courtyard. There is a stout fourlegged stool under the table, and a wooden chest under the window.

ROBERT. No eggs! No eggs!! Thousand thunders, man, what do you mean by no eggs?

STEWARD. Sir: it is not my fault. It is the act of God.

ROBERT. Blasphemy. You tell me there are no eggs; and you blame your Maker for it.

STEWARD. Sir: what can I do? I cannot lay eggs.

ROBERT [*sarcastic*] Ha! You jest about it.

STEWARD. No, sir, God knows. We all have to go without eggs just as you have, sir. The hens will not lay.

ROBERT. Indeed! [*Rising*] Now listen to me, you.

STEWARD [*humbly*] Yes, sir.

ROBERT. What am I?

STEWARD. What are you, sir?

ROBERT [*coming at him*] Yes: what am I? Am I Robert, squire of Baudricourt and captain of this castle of Vaucouleurs; or am I a cowboy?

STEWARD. Oh, sir, you know you are a greater man here

than the king himself.

ROBERT. Precisely. And now, do you know what you are?

STEWARD. I am nobody, sir, except that I have the honor to be your steward.

ROBERT [*driving him to the wall, adjective by adjective*] You have not only the honor of being my steward, but the privilege of being the worst, most incompetent, drivelling snivelling jibbering jabbering idiot of a steward in France. [*He strides back to the table*].

STEWARD [*cowering on the chest*] Yes, sir: to a great man like you I must seem like that.

ROBERT [*turning*] My fault, I suppose. Eh?

STEWARD [*coming to him deprecatingly*] Oh, sir: you always give my most innocent words such a turn!

ROBERT. I will give your neck a turn if you dare tell me, when I ask you how many eggs there are, that you cannot lay any.

STEWARD [*protesting*] Oh sir, oh sir—

ROBERT. No: not oh sir, oh sir, but no sir, no sir. My three Barbary hens and the black are the best layers in Champagne. And you come and tell me that there are no eggs! Who stole them? Tell me that, before I kick you out through the castle gate for a liar and a seller of my goods to thieves. The milk was short yesterday, too: do not forget that.

STEWARD [*desperate*] I know, sir. I know only too well. There is no milk: there are no eggs: tomorrow there will be nothing.

ROBERT. Nothing! You will steal the lot: eh?

STEWARD. No, sir: nobody will steal anything. But there is a spell on us: we are bewitched.

ROBERT. That story is not good enough for me. Robert de Baudricourt burns witches and hangs thieves. Go. Bring me four dozen eggs and two gallons of milk here in this room before noon, or Heaven have mercy on your bones! I will teach you to make a fool of me. [*He resumes his seat with an air of finality*].

STEWARD. Sir: I tell you there are no eggs. There will be

none—not if you were to kill me for it—as long as The Maid is at the door.

ROBERT. The Maid! What maid? What are you talking about?

STEWARD. The girl from Lorraine, sir. From Domrémy.

ROBERT [*rising in fearful wrath*] Thirty thousand thunders! Fifty thousand devils! Do you mean to say that that girl, who had the impudence to ask to see me two days ago, and whom I told you to send back to her father with my orders that he was to give her a good hiding, is here still?

STEWARD. I have told her to go, sir. She wont.

ROBERT. I did not tell you to tell her to go: I told you to throw her out. You have fifty men-at-arms and a dozen lumps of ablebodied servants to carry out my orders. Are they afraid of her?

STEWARD. She is so positive, sir.

ROBERT [*seizing him by the scruff of the neck*] Positive! Now see here. I am going to throw you downstairs.

STEWARD. No, sir. Please.

ROBERT. Well, stop me by being positive. It's quite easy: any slut of a girl can do it.

STEWARD [*hanging limp in his hands*] Sir, sir: you cannot get rid of h e r by throwing m e out. [*Robert has to let him drop. He squats on his knees on the floor, contemplating his master resignedly*]. You see, sir, you are much more positive than I am. But so is she.

ROBERT. I am stronger than you are, you fool.

STEWARD. No, sir: it isnt that: it's your strong character, sir. She is weaker than we are: she is only a slip of a girl; but we cannot make her go.

ROBERT. You parcel of curs: you are afraid of her.

STEWARD [*rising cautiously*] No, sir: we are afraid of you; but she puts courage into us. She really doesnt seem to be afraid of anything. Perhaps you could frighten her, sir.

ROBERT [*grimly*] Perhaps. Where is she now?

STEWARD. Down in the courtyard, sir, talking to the soldiers as usual. She is always talking to the soldiers except when she is praying.

ROBERT. Praying! Ha! You believe she prays, you idiot. I know the sort of girl that is always talking to soldiers. She shall talk to me a bit. [*He goes to the window and shouts fiercely through it*] Hallo, you there!

A GIRL'S VOICE [*bright, strong and rough*] Is it me, sir?

ROBERT. Yes, you.

THE VOICE. Be you captain?

ROBERT. Yes, damn your impudence, I be captain. Come up here. [*To the soldiers in the yard*] Shew her the way, you. And shove her along quick. [*He leaves the window, and returns to his place at the table, where he sits magisterially*].

STEWARD [*whispering*] She wants to go and be a soldier herself. She wants you to give her soldier's clothes. Armor, sir! And a sword! Actually! [*He steals behind Robert*].

Joan appears in the turret doorway. She is an ablebodied country girl of 17 *or* 18, *respectably dressed in red, with an uncommon face: eyes very wide apart and bulging as they often do in very imaginative people, a long well-shaped nose with wide nostrils, a short upper lip, resolute but full-lipped mouth, and handsome fighting chin. She comes eagerly to the table, delighted at having penetrated to Baudricourt's presence at last, and full of hope as to the result. His scowl does not check or frighten her in the least. Her voice is normally a hearty coaxing voice, very confident, very appealing, very hard to resist.*

JOAN [*bobbing a curtsey*] Good morning, captain squire. Captain: you are to give me a horse and armor and some soldiers, and send me to the Dauphin. Those are your orders from my Lord.

ROBERT [*outraged*] Orders from your lord! And who the devil may your lord be? Go back to him, and tell him that I am neither duke nor peer at his orders: I am squire of Baudricourt; and I take no orders except from the king.

JOAN [*reassuringly*] Yes, squire: that is all right. My Lord is the King of Heaven.

ROBERT. Why, the girl's mad. [*To the steward*] Why didnt you tell me so, you blockhead?

STEWARD. Sir: do not anger her: give her what she wants.

JOAN [*impatient, but friendly*] They all say I am mad until I talk to them, squire. But you see that it is the will of God that you are to do what He has put into my mind.

ROBERT. It is the will of God that I shall send you back to your father with orders to put you under lock and key and thrash the madness out of you. What have you to say to that?

JOAN. You think you will, squire; but you will find it all coming quite different. You said you would not see me; but here I am.

STEWARD [*appealing*] Yes, sir. You see, sir.

ROBERT. Hold your tongue, you.

STEWARD [*abjectly*] Yes, sir.

ROBERT [*to Joan, with a sour loss of confidence*] So you are presuming on my seeing you, are you?

JOAN [*sweetly*] Yes, squire.

ROBERT [*feeling that he has lost ground, brings down his two fists squarely on the table, and inflates his chest imposingly to cure the unwelcome and only too familiar sensation*] Now listen to me. I am going to assert myself.

JOAN [*busily*] Please do, squire. The horse will cost sixteen francs. It is a good deal of money; but I can save it on the armor. I can find a soldier's armor that will fit me well enough: I am very hardy; and I do not need beautiful armor made to my measure like you wear. I shall not want many soldiers: the Dauphin will give me all I need to raise the siege of Orleans.

ROBERT [*flabbergasted*] To raise the siege of Orleans!

JOAN [*simply*] Yes, squire: that is what God is sending me to do. Three men will be enough for you to send with me if they are good men and gentle to me. They have promised to come with me. Polly and Jack and—

ROBERT. Polly!! You impudent baggage, do you dare call squire Bertrand de Poulengey Polly to my face?

JOAN. His friends call him so, squire: I did not know he had any other name. Jack—

ROBERT. That is Monsieur John of Metz, I suppose?

JOAN. Yes, squire. Jack will come willingly: he is a very kind gentleman, and gives me money to give to the poor. I think John Godsave will come, and Dick the Archer, and their servants John of Honecourt and Julian. There will be no trouble for you, squire: I have arranged it all: you have only to give the order.

ROBERT [*contemplating her in a stupor of amazement*] Well, I am damned!

JOAN [*with unruffled sweetness*] No, squire: God is very merciful; and the blessed saints Catherine and Margaret, who speak to me every day [*he gapes*], will intercede for you. You will go to paradise; and your name will be remembered for ever as my first helper.

ROBERT [*to the steward, still much bothered, but changing his tone as he pursues a new clue*] Is this true about Monsieur de Poulengey?

STEWARD [*eagerly*] Yes, sir, and about Monsieur de Metz too. They both want to go with her.

ROBERT [*thoughtful*] Mf! [*He goes to the window, and shouts into the courtyard*] Hallo! You there: send Monsieur de Poulengey to me, will you? [*He turns to Joan*]. Get out; and wait in the yard.

JOAN [*smiling brightly at him*] Right, squire. [*She goes out*].

ROBERT [*to the steward*] Go with her, you, you dithering imbecile. Stay within call; and keep your eye on her. I shall have her up here again.

STEWARD. Do so in God's name, sir. Think of those hens, the best layers in Champagne; and—

ROBERT. Think of my boot; and take your backside out of reach of it.

The steward retreats hastily and finds himself confronted in the doorway by Bertrand de Poulengey, a lymphatic French gentleman-at-arms, aged 36 or thereabout, employed in the department of the provost-marshal, dreamily absent-minded, seldom speaking unless spoken to, and then slow and obstinate in reply: altogether in contrast to the self-assertive, loud-mouthed, super-

ficially energetic, fundamentally will-less Robert. The steward makes way for him, and vanishes.

Poulengey salutes, and stands awaiting orders.

ROBERT [*genially*] It isnt service, Polly. A friendly talk. Sit down. [*He hooks the stool from under the table with his instep*].

Poulengey relaxing, comes into the room; places the stool between the table and the window; and sits down ruminatively. Robert, half sitting on the end of the table, begins the friendly talk.

ROBERT. Now listen to me, Polly. I must talk to you like a father.

Poulengey looks up at him gravely for a moment, but says nothing.

ROBERT. It's about this girl you are interested in. Now, I have seen her. I have talked to her. First, she's mad. That doesnt matter. Second, she's not a farm wench. She's a bourgeoise. That matters a good deal. I know her class exactly. Her father came here last year to represent his village in a lawsuit: he is one of their notables. A farmer. Not a gentleman farmer: he makes money by it, and lives by it. Still, not a laborer. Not a mechanic. He might have a cousin a lawyer, or in the Church. People of this sort may be of no account socially; but they can give a lot of bother to the authorities. That is to say, to me. Now no doubt it seems to you a very simple thing to take this girl away, humbugging her into the belief that you are taking her to the Dauphin. But if you get her into trouble, you may get me into no end of a mess, as I am her father's lord, and responsible for her protection. So friends or no friends, Polly, hands off her.

POULENGEY [*with deliberate impressiveness*] I should as soon think of the Blessed Virgin herself in that way, as of this girl.

ROBERT [*coming off the table*] But she says you and Jack and Dick have offered to go with her. What for? You are not going to tell me that you take her crazy notion of going to the Dauphin seriously, are you?

POULENGEY [*slowly*] There is something about her. They

are pretty foulmouthed and foulminded down there in the guardroom, some of them. But there hasnt been a word that has anything to do with her being a woman. They have stopped swearing before her. There is something. Something. It may be worth trying.

ROBERT. Oh, come, Polly! pull yourself together. Commonsense was never your strong point; but this is a little too much. [*He retreats disgustedly*].

POULENGEY [*unmoved*] What is the good of commonsense? If we had any commonsense we should join the Duke of Burgundy and the English king. They hold half the country, right down to the Loire. They have Paris. They have this castle: you know very well that we had to surrender it to the Duke of Bedford, and that you are only holding it on parole. The Dauphin is in Chinon, like a rat in a corner, except that he wont fight. We dont even know that he is the Dauphin: his mother says he isnt; and she ought to know. Think of that! the queen denying the legitimacy of her own son!

ROBERT. Well, she married her daughter to the English king. Can you blame the woman?

POULENGEY. I blame nobody. But thanks to her, the Dauphin is down and out; and we may as well face it. The English will take Orleans: the Bastard will not be able to stop them.

ROBERT. He beat the English the year before last at Montargis. I was with him.

POULENGEY. No matter: his men are cowed now; and he cant work miracles. And I tell you that nothing can save our side now but a miracle.

ROBERT. Miracles are all right, Polly. The only difficulty about them is that they dont happen nowadays.

POULENGEY. I used to think so. I am not so sure now. [*Rising, and moving ruminatively towards the window*] At all events this is not a time to leave any stone unturned. There is something about the girl.

ROBERT. Oh! You think the girl can work miracles, do

you?

POULENGEY. I think the girl herself is a bit of a miracle. Anyhow, she is the last card left in our hand. Better play her than throw up the game. [*He wanders to the turret*].

ROBERT [*wavering*] You really think that?

POULENGEY [*turning*] Is there anything else left for us to think?

ROBERT [*going to him*] Look here, Polly. If you were in my place would you let a girl like that do you out of sixteen francs for a horse?

POULENGEY. I will pay for the horse.

ROBERT. You will!

POULENGEY. Yes: I will back my opinion.

ROBERT. You will really gamble on a forlorn hope to the tune of sixteen francs?

POULENGEY. It is not a gamble.

ROBERT. What else is it?

POULENGEY. It is a certainty. Her words and her ardent faith in God have put fire into me.

ROBERT [*giving him up*] Whew! You are as mad as she is.

POULENGEY [*obstinately*] We want a few mad people now. See where the sane ones have landed us!

ROBERT [*his irresoluteness now openly swamping his affected decisiveness*] I shall feel like a precious fool. Still, if you feel sure—?

POULENGEY. I feel sure enough to take her to Chinon—unless you stop me.

ROBERT. This is not fair. You are putting the responsibility on me.

POULENGEY. It is on you whichever way you decide.

ROBERT. Yes: thats just it. Which way am I to decide? You dont see how awkward this is for me. [*Snatching at a dilatory step with an unconscious hope that Joan will make up his mind for him*] Do you think I ought to have another talk to her?

POULENGEY [*rising*] Yes. [*He goes to the window and calls*] Joan!

JOAN'S VOICE. Will he let us go, Polly?

POULENGEY. Come up. Come in. [*Turning to Robert*] Shall I leave you with her?

ROBERT. No: stay here; and back me up.

Poulengey sits down on the chest. Robert goes back to his magisterial chair, but remains standing to inflate himself more imposingly. Joan comes in, full of good news.

JOAN. Jack will go halves for the horse.

ROBERT. Well!! [*He sits, deflated*]

POULENGEY [*Gravely*] Sit down, Joan.

JOAN [*checked a little, and looking to Robert*] May I?

ROBERT. Do what you are told.

Joan curtsies and sits down on the stool between them. Robert outfaces his perplexity with his most peremptory air.

ROBERT. What is your name?

JOAN [*chattily*] They always call me Jenny in Lorraine. Here in France I am Joan. The soldiers call me The Maid.

ROBERT. What is your surname?

JOAN. Surname? What is that? My father sometimes calls himself d'Arc; but I know nothing about it. You met my father. He—

ROBERT. Yes, yes: I remember. You come from Domrémy in Lorraine, I think.

JOAN. Yes; but what does it matter? we all speak French.

ROBERT. Dont ask questions: answer them. How old are you?

JOAN. Seventeen: so they tell me. It might be nineteen. I dont remember.

ROBERT. What did you mean when you said that St Catherine and St Margaret talked to you every day?

JOAN. They do.

ROBERT. What are they like?

JOAN [*suddenly obstinate*] I will tell you nothing about that: they have not given me leave.

ROBERT. But you actually see them; and they talk to you just as I am talking to you?

JOAN. No: it is quite different. I cannot tell you: you

must not talk to me about my voices.

ROBERT. How do you mean? voices?

JOAN. I hear voices telling me what to do. They come from God.

ROBERT. They come from your imagination.

JOAN. Of course. That is how the messages of God come to us.

POULENGEY. Checkmate.

ROBERT. No fear! [*To Joan*] So God says you are to raise the siege of Orleans?

JOAN. And to crown the Dauphin in Rheims Cathedral.

ROBERT [*gasping*] Crown the D——! Gosh!

JOAN. And to make the English leave France.

ROBERT [*sarcastic*] Anything else?

JOAN [*charming*] Not just at present, thank you, squire.

ROBERT. I suppose you think raising a siege is as easy as chasing a cow out of a meadow. You think soldiering is anybody's job?

JOAN. I do not think it can be very difficult if God is on your side, and you are willing to put your life in His hand. But many soldiers are very simple.

ROBERT [*grimly*] Simple! Did you ever see English soldiers fighting?

JOAN. They are only men. God made them just like us; but He gave them their own country and their own language; and it is not His will that they should come into our country and try to speak our language.

ROBERT. Who has been putting such nonsense into your head? Dont you know that soldiers are subject to their feudal lord, and that it is nothing to them or to you whether he is the duke of Burgundy or the king of England or the king of France? What has their language to do with it?

JOAN. I do not understand that a bit. We are all subject to the King of Heaven; and He gave us our countries and our languages, and meant us to keep to them. If it were not so it would be murder to kill an Englishman in battle; and you, squire, would be in great danger of hell fire. You must not think about your duty to your feudal lord, but about your duty to God.

POULENGEY. It's no use, Robert: she can choke you like that every time.

ROBERT. Can she, by Saint Dennis! We shall see. [*To Joan*] We are not talking about God: we are talking about practical affairs. I ask you again, girl, have you ever seen English soldiers fighting? Have you ever seen them plundering, burning, turning the countryside into a desert? Have you heard no tales of their Black Prince who was blacker than the devil himself, or of the English king's father?

JOAN. You must not be afraid, Robert—

ROBERT. Damn you, I am not afraid. And who gave you leave to call me Robert?

JOAN. You were called so in church in the name of our Lord. All the other names are your father's or your brother's or anybody's.

ROBERT. Tcha!

JOAN. Listen to me, squire. At Domrémy we had to fly to the next village to escape from the English soldiers. Three of them were left behind, wounded. I came to know these three poor goddams quite well. They had not half my strength.

ROBERT. Do you know why they are called goddams?

JOAN. No. Everyone calls them goddams.

ROBERT. It is because they are always calling on their God to condemn their souls to perdition. That is what goddam means in their language. How do you like it?

JOAN. God will be merciful to them; and they will act like His good children when they go back to the country He made for them, and made them for. I have heard the tales of the Black Prince. The moment he touched the soil of our country the devil entered into him and made him a black fiend. But at home, in the place made for him by God, he was good. It is always so. If I went into England against the will of God to conquer England, and tried to live there and speak its language, the devil would enter into me; and when I was old I should shudder to remember the wickednesses I did.

ROBERT. Perhaps. But the more devil you were the better you might fight. That is why the goddams will take Orleans. And you cannot stop them, nor ten thousand like you.

JOAN. One thousand like me can stop them. Ten like me can stop them with God on our side. [*She rises impetuously, and goes at him, unable to sit quiet any longer*]. You do not understand, squire. Our soldiers are always beaten because they are fighting only to save their skins; and the shortest way to save your skin is to run away. Our knights are thinking only of the money they will make in ransoms: it is not kill or be killed with them, but pay or be paid. But I will teach them all to fight that the will of God may be done in France; and then they will drive the poor goddams before them like sheep. You and Polly will live to see the day when there will not be an English soldier on the soil of France; and there will be but one king there: not the feudal English king, but God's French one.

ROBERT [*to Poulengey*] This may be all rot, Polly; but the troops might swallow it, though nothing that we can say seems able to put any fight into them. Even the Dauphin might swallow it. And if she can put fight into him, she can put it into anybody.

POULENGEY. I can see no harm in trying. Can you? And there is something about the girl—

ROBERT [*turning to Joan*] Now listen you to me; and [*desperately*] dont cut in before I have time to think.

JOAN [*plumping down on the stool again, like an obedient schoolgirl*] Yes, squire.

ROBERT. Your orders are, that you are to go to Chinon under the escort of this gentleman and three of his friends.

JOAN [*radiant, clasping her hands*] Oh, squire! Your head is all circled with light, like a saint's.

POULENGEY. How is she to get into the royal presence?

ROBERT [*who has looked up for his halo rather apprehensively*] I dont know: how did she get into my presence? If the Dauphin can keep her out he is a better man than I take him for. [*Rising*] I will send her to Chinon; and she can say I sent her. Then let come what may: I can do no more.

JOAN. And the dress? I may have a soldier's dress, maynt I, squire?

ROBERT. Have what you please. I wash my hands of it.

JOAN [*wildly excited by her success*] Come, Polly. [*She dashes out*].

ROBERT [*shaking Poulengey's hand*] Goodbye, old man, I am taking a big chance. Few other men would have done it. But as you say, there is something about her.

POULENGEY. Yes: there is something about her. Goodbye. [*He goes out*].

Robert, still very doubtful whether he has not been made a fool of by a crazy female, and a social inferior to boot, scratches his head and slowly comes back from the door.

The steward runs in with a basket.

STEWARD. Sir, sir—

ROBERT. What now?

STEWARD. The hens are laying like mad, sir. Five dozen eggs!

ROBERT [*stiffens convulsively; crosses himself; and forms with his pale lips the words*] Christ in heaven! [*Aloud but breathless*] She did come from God.

SCENE II

CHINON, in Touraine. An end of the throne-room in the castle, curtained off to make an antechamber. The Archbishop of Rheims, close on 50, a full-fed political prelate with nothing of the ecclesiastic about him except his imposing bearing, and the Lord Chamberlain, Monseigneur de la Trémouille, a monstrous arrogant wineskin of a man, are waiting for the Dauphin. There is a door in the wall to the right of the two men. It is late in the afternoon on the 8th of March, 1429. The Archbishop stands with dignity whilst the Chamberlain, on his left, fumes about in the worst of tempers.

LA TRÉMOUILLE. What the devil does the Dauphin mean by keeping us waiting like this? I dont know how you have the patience to stand there like a stone idol.

THE ARCHBISHOP. You see, I am an archbishop; and an archbishop is a sort of idol. At any rate he has to learn to keep still and suffer fools patiently. Besides, my dear Lord Chamberlain, it is the Dauphin's royal privilege to keep you waiting, is it not?

LA TRÉMOUILLE. Dauphin be damned! saving your reverence. Do you know how much money he owes me?

THE ARCHBISHOP. Much more than he owes me, I have no doubt, because you are a much richer man. But I take it he owes you all you could afford to lend him. That is what he owes me.

LA TRÉMOUILLE. Twentyseven thousand: that was his last haul. A cool twentyseven thousand!

THE ARCHBISHOP. What becomes of it all? He never has a suit of clothes that I would throw to a curate.

LA TRÉMOUILLE. He dines on a chicken or a scrap of mutton. He borrows my last penny; and there is nothing to shew for it. [*A page appears in the doorway*]. At last!

THE PAGE. No, my lord: it is not His Majesty. Monsieur de Rais is approaching.

LA TRÉMOUILLE. Young Bluebeard! Why announce him?

THE PAGE. Captain La Hire is with him. Something has

happened, I think.

Gilles de Rais, a young man of 25, very smart and self-possessed, and sporting the extravagance of a little curled beard dyed blue at a clean-shaven court, comes in. He is determined to make himself agreeable, but lacks natural joyousness, and is not really pleasant. In fact when he defies the Church some eleven years later he is accused of trying to extract pleasure from horrible cruelties, and hanged. So far, however, there is no shadow of the gallows on him. He advances gaily to the Archbishop. The page withdraws.

BLUEBEARD. Your faithful lamb, Archbishop. Good day, my lord. Do you know what has happened to La Hire?

LA TRÉMOUILLE. He has sworn himself into a fit, perhaps.

BLUEBEARD. No: just the opposite. Foul Mouthed Frank, the only man in Touraine who could beat him at swearing, was told by a soldier that he shouldnt use such language when he was at the point of death.

THE ARCHBISHOP. Nor at any other point. But was Foul Mouthed Frank on the point of death?

BLUEBEARD. Yes: he has just fallen into a well and been drowned. La Hire is frightened out of his wits.

Captain La Hire comes in: a war dog with no court manners and pronounced camp ones.

BLUEBEARD. I have just been telling the Chamberlain and the Archbishop. The Archbishop says you are a lost man.

LA HIRE [*striding past Bluebeard, and planting himself between the Archbishop and La Trémouille*] This is nothing to joke about. It is worse than we thought. It was not a soldier, but an angel dressed as a soldier.

THE ARCHBISHOP
THE CHAMBERLAIN
BLUEBEARD } [*exclaiming all together*] An angel!

LA HIRE. Yes, an angel. She has made her way from Champagne with half a dozen men through the thick of everything: Burgundians, Goddams, deserters, robbers, and Lord knows who; and they never met a soul except the country folk. I know one of them: de Poulengey. He says she's an angel. If ever I utter an oath again may my soul be blasted to eternal damnation!

THE ARCHBISHOP. A very pious beginning, Captain.

Bluebeard and La Trémouille laugh at him. The page returns.

THE PAGE. His Majesty.

They stand perfunctorily at court attention. The Dauphin, aged 26, really King Charles the Seventh since the death of his father, but as yet uncrowned, comes in through the curtains with a paper in his hands. He is a poor creature physically; and the current fashion of shaving closely, and hiding every scrap of hair under the head-covering or headdress, both by women and men, makes the worst of his appearance. He has little narrow eyes, near together, a long pendulous nose that droops over his thick short upper lip, and the expression of a young dog accustomed to be kicked, yet incorrigible and irrepressible. But he is neither vulgar nor stupid; and he has a cheeky humor which enables him to hold his own in conversation. Just at present he is excited, like a child with a new toy. He comes to the Archbishop's left hand. Bluebeard and La Hire retire towards the curtains.

CHARLES. Oh, Archbishop, do you know what Robert de Baudricourt is sending me from Vaucouleurs?

THE ARCHBISHOP [*contemptuously*] I am not interested in the newest toys.

CHARLES [*indignantly*] It isnt a toy. [*Sulkily*] However, I can get on very well without your interest.

THE ARCHBISHOP. Your Highness is taking offence very unnecessarily.

CHARLES. Thank you. You are always ready with a lecture, arnt you?

LA TRÉMOUILLE [*roughly*] Enough grumbling. What have you got there?

CHARLES. What is that to you?

LA TRÉMOUILLE. It is my business to know what is passing between you and the garrison at Vaucouleurs. [*He snatches the paper from the Dauphin's hand, and begins reading it with some difficulty, following the words with his finger and spelling them out syllable by syllable.*]

CHARLES [*mortified*] You all think you can treat me as you please because I owe you money, and because I am no good at fighting. But I have the blood royal in my veins.

THE ARCHBISHOP. Even that has been questioned, your Highness. One hardly recognizes in you the grandson of Charles the Wise.

CHARLES. I want to hear no more of my grandfather. He was so wise that he used up the whole family stock of wisdom for five generations, and left me the poor fool I am, bullied and insulted by all of you.

THE ARCHBISHOP. Control yourself, sir. These outbursts of petulance are not seemly.

CHARLES. Another lecture! Thank you. What a pity it is that though you are an archbishop saints and angels dont come to see you!

THE ARCHBISHOP. What do you mean?

CHARLES. Aha! Ask that bully there [*pointing to La Trémouille*].

LA TRÉMOUILLE [*furious*] Hold your tongue. Do you hear?

CHARLES. Oh, I hear. You neednt shout. The whole castle can hear. Why dont you go and shout at the English, and beat them for me?

LA TRÉMOUILLE [*raising his fist*] You young—

CHARLES [*running behind the Archbishop*] Dont you raise your hand to me. It's high treason.

LA HIRE. Steady, Duke! Steady!

THE ARCHBISHOP [*resolutely*] Come, come! this will not do. My lord Chamberlain: please! please! we must keep some sort of order. [*To the Dauphin*] And you, sir: if you cannot rule your kingdom, at least try to rule yourself.

CHARLES. Another lecture! Thank you.

LA TRÉMOUILLE [*handing the paper to the Archbishop*] Here: read the accursed thing for me. He has sent the blood boiling into my head: I cant distinguish the letters.

CHARLES [*coming back and peering round La Trémouille's left shoulder*] I will read it for you if you like. I can read, you know.

LA TRÉMOUILLE [*with intense contempt, not at all stung by the taunt*] Yes: reading is about all you are fit for. Can you make it out, Archbishop?

THE ARCHBISHOP. I should have expected more commonsense from De Baudricourt. He is sending some cracked country lass here—

CHARLES [*interrupting*] No: he is sending a saint: an angel. And she is coming to me: to me, the king, and not to you, Archbishop, holy as you are. She knows the blood royal if you dont. [*He struts up to the curtains between Bluebeard and La Hire*].

THE ARCHBISHOP. You cannot be allowed to see this crazy wench.

CHARLES [*turning*] But I am the king; and I will.

LA TRÉMOUILLE [*brutally*] Then she cannot be allowed to see you. Now!

CHARLES. I tell you I will. I am going to put my foot down—

BLUEBEARD [*laughing at him*] Naughty! What would your wise grandfather say?

CHARLES. That just shews your ignorance, Bluebeard. My grandfather had a saint who used to float in the air when she was praying, and told him everything he wanted to know. My poor father had two saints, Marie de Maillé and the Gasque of Avignon. It is in our family; and I dont care what you say: I will have my saint too.

THE ARCHBISHOP. This creature is not a saint. She is not even a respectable woman. She does not wear women's clothes. She is dressed like a soldier, and rides round the country with soldiers. Do you suppose such a person can be admitted to your Highness's court?

LA HIRE. Stop. [*Going to the Archbishop*] Did you say a girl in armor, like a soldier?

THE ARCHBISHOP. So De Baudricourt describes her.

LA HIRE. But by all the devils in hell—Oh, God forgive me, what am I saying?— by Our Lady and all the saints, this must be the angel that struck Foul Mouthed Frank dead for swearing.

CHARLES. [*triumphantly*] You see! A miracle!

LA HIRE. She may strike the lot of us dead if we cross her. For Heaven's sake, Archbishop, be careful what you are doing.

THE ARCHBISHOP [*severely*] Rubbish! Nobody has been struck dead. A drunken blackguard who has been rebuked a hundred times for swearing has fallen into a well, and been drowned. A mere coincidence.

LA HIRE. I do not know what a coincidence is. I do know that the man is dead, and that she told him he was going to die.

THE ARCHBISHOP. We are all going to die, Captain.

LA HIRE [*crossing himself*] I hope not. [*He backs out of the conversation*].

BLUEBEARD. We can easily find out whether she is an angel or not. Let us arrange when she comes that I shall be the Dauphin, and see whether she will find me out.

CHARLES. Yes: I agree to that. If she cannot find the blood royal I will have nothing to do with her.

THE ARCHBISHOP. It is for the Church to make saints: let De Baudricourt mind his own business, and not dare usurp the function of his priest. I say the girl shall not be admitted.

BLUEBEARD. But, Archbishop—

THE ARCHBISHOP [*sternly*] I speak in the Church's name. [*To the Dauphin*] Do you dare say she shall?

CHARLES [*intimidated but sulky*] Oh, if you make it an excommunication matter, I have nothing more to say, of course. But you havnt read the end of the letter. De Baudricourt says she will raise the siege of Orleans, and beat the English for us.

LA TRÉMOUILLE. Rot!

CHARLES. Well, will you save Orleans for us, with all your bullying?

LA TRÉMOUILLE [*savagely*] Do not throw that in my face again: do you hear? I have done more fighting than you ever did or ever will. But I cannot be everywhere.

THE DAUPHIN. Well, thats something.

BLUEBEARD [*coming between the Archbishop and Charles*] You have Jack Dunois at the head of your troops in Orleans: the brave Dunois, the handsome Dunois, the wonderful invincible Dunois, the darling of all the ladies, the beautiful bastard. Is it likely that the country lass can do what he cannot do?

CHARLES. Why doesnt he raise the siege, then?

LA HIRE. The wind is against him.

BLUEBEARD. How can the wind hurt him at Orleans? It is not on the Channel.

LA HIRE. It is on the river Loire; and the English hold the bridgehead. He must ship his men across the river and upstream, if he is to take them in the rear. Well, he cannot, because there is a devil of a wind blowing the other way. He is tired of paying the priests to pray for a west wind. What he needs is a miracle. You tell me that what the girl did to Foul Mouthed Frank was no miracle. No matter: it finished Frank. If she changes the wind for Dunois, that may not be a miracle either; but it may finish the English. What harm is there in trying?

THE ARCHBISHOP [*who has read the end of the letter and become more thoughtful*] It is true that De Baudricourt seems extraordinarily impressed.

LA HIRE. De Baudricourt is a blazing ass; but he is a soldier; and if he thinks she can beat the English, all the rest of the army will think so too.

LA TRÉMOUILLE [*to the Archbishop, who is hesitating*] Oh, let them have their way. Dunois' men will give up the town in spite of him if somebody does not put some fresh spunk into them.

THE ARCHBISHOP. The Church must examine the girl before anything decisive is done about her. However, since his Highness desires it, let her attend the Court.

LA HIRE. I will find her and tell her. [*He goes out*].

CHARLES. Come with me, Bluebeard; and let us arrange

so that she will not know who I am. You will pretend to be me. [*He goes out through the curtains*].

BLUEBEARD. Pretend to be that thing! Holy Michael! [*He follows the Dauphin*].

LA TRÉMOUILLE. I wonder will she pick him out!

THE ARCHBISHOP. Of course she will.

LA TRÉMOUILLE. Why? How is she to know?

THE ARCHBISHOP. She will know what everybody in Chinon knows: that the Dauphin is the meanest-looking and worst-dressed figure in the Court, and that the man with the blue beard is Gilles de Rais.

LA TRÉMOUILLE. I never thought of that.

THE ARCHBISHOP. You are not so accustomed to miracles as I am. It is part of my profession.

LA TRÉMOUILLE [*puzzled and a little scandalized*] But that would not be a miracle at all.

THE ARCHBISHOP [*calmly*] Why not?

LA TRÉMOUILLE. Well, come! what is a miracle?

THE ARCHBISHOP. A miracle, my friend, is an event which creates faith. That is the purpose and nature of miracles. They may seem very wonderful to the people who witness them, and very simple to those who perform them. That does not matter: if they confirm or create faith they are true miracles.

LA TRÉMOUILLE. Even when they are frauds, do you mean?

THE ARCHBISHOP. Frauds deceive. An event which creates faith does not deceive: therefore it is not a fraud, but a miracle.

LA TRÉMOUILLE [*scratching his neck in his perplexity*] Well, I suppose as you are an archbishop you must be right. It seems a bit fishy to me. But I am no churchman, and dont understand these matters.

THE ARCHBISHOP. You are not a churchman; but you are a diplomatist and a soldier. Could you make our citizens pay war taxes, or our soldiers sacrifice their lives, if they knew what is really happening instead of what seems to them to be happening?

LA TRÉMOUILLE. No, by Saint Dennis: the fat would be in the fire before sundown.

THE ARCHBISHOP. Would it not be quite easy to tell them the truth?

LA TRÉMOUILLE. Man alive, they wouldnt believe it.

THE ARCHBISHOP. Just so. Well, the Church has to rule men for the good of their souls as you have to rule them for the good of their bodies. To do that, the Church must do as you do: nourish their faith by poetry.

LA TRÉMOUILLE. Poetry! I should call it humbug.

THE ARCHBISHOP. You would be wrong, my friend. Parables are not lies because they describe events that have never happened. Miracles are not frauds because they are often—I do not say always—very simple and innocent contrivances by which the priest fortifies the faith of his flock. When this girl picks out the Dauphin among his courtiers, it will not be a miracle for me, because I shall know how it has been done, and my faith will not be increased. But as for the others, if they feel the thrill of the supernatural, and forget their sinful clay in a sudden sense of the glory of God, it will be a miracle and a blessed one. And you will find that the girl herself will be more affected than anyone else. She will forget how she really picked him out. So, perhaps, will you.

LA TRÉMOUILLE. Well, I wish I were clever enough to know how much of you is God's archbishop and how much the most artful fox in Touraine. Come on, or we shall be late for the fun; and I want to see it, miracle or no miracle.

THE ARCHBISHOP [*detaining him a moment*] Do not think that I am a lover of crooked ways. There is a new spirit rising in men: we are at the dawning of a wider epoch. If I were a simple monk, and had not to rule men, I should seek peace for my spirit with Aristotle and Pythagoras rather than with the saints and their miracles.

LA TRÉMOUILLE. And who the deuce was Pythagoras?

THE ARCHBISHOP. A sage who held that the earth is round, and that it moves round the sun.

LA TRÉMOUILLE. What an utter fool! Couldnt he use his eyes?

They go out together through the curtains, which are presently withdrawn, revealing the full depth of the throne-room with the Court assembled. On the right are two Chairs of State on a dais. Bluebeard is standing theatrically on the dais, playing the king, and, like the courtiers, enjoying the joke rather obviously. There is a curtained arch in the wall behind the dais; but the main door, guarded by men-at-arms, is at the other side of the room; and a clear path across is kept and lined by the courtiers. Charles is in this path in the middle of the room. La Hire is on his right. The Archbishop, on his left, has taken his place by the dais: La Trémouille at the other side of it. The Duchess de la Trémouille, pretending to be the Queen, sits in the Consort's chair, with a group of ladies in waiting close by, behind the Archbishop.

The chatter of the courtiers makes such a noise that nobody notices the appearance of the page at the door.

THE PAGE. The Duke of— [*Nobody listens*]. The Duke of—[*The chatter continues. Indignant at his failure to command a hearing, he snatches the halberd of the nearest man-at-arms, and thumps the floor with it. The chatter ceases; and everybody looks at him in silence*]. Attention! [*He restores the halberd to the man-at-arms*]. The Duke of Vendôme presents Joan the Maid to his Majesty.

CHARLES [*putting his finger on his lip*] Ssh! [*He hides behind the nearest courtier, peering out to see what happens*].

BLUEBEARD [*majestically*] Let her approach the throne.

Joan, dressed as a soldier, with her hair bobbed and hanging thickly round her face, is led in by a bashful and speechless nobleman, from whom she detaches herself to stop and look round eagerly for the Dauphin.

THE DUCHESS [*to the nearest lady in waiting*] My dear! Her hair!

All the ladies explode in uncontrollable laughter.

BLUEBEARD [*trying not to laugh, and waving his hand in deprecation of their merriment*] Ssh—ssh! Ladies! Ladies!!

JOAN [*not at all embarrassed*] I wear it like this because

I am a soldier. Where be Dauphin?

A titter runs through the Court as she walks to the dais.

BLUEBEARD [*condescendingly*] You are in the presence of the Dauphin.

Joan looks at him sceptically for a moment, scanning him hard up and down to make sure. Dead silence, all watching her. Fun dawns in her face.

JOAN. Coom, Bluebeard! Thou canst not fool me. Where be Dauphin?

A roar of laughter breaks out as Gilles, with a gesture of surrender, joins in the laugh, and jumps down from the dais beside La Trémouille. Joan, also on the broad grin, turns back, searching along the row of courtiers, and presently makes a dive, and drags out Charles by the arm.

JOAN [*releasing him and bobbing him a little curtsey*] Gentle little Dauphin, I am sent to you to drive the English away from Orleans and from France, and to crown you king in the cathedral at Rheims, where all true kings of France are crowned.

CHARLES [*triumphant, to the Court*] You see, all of you: she knew the blood royal. Who dare say now that I am not my father's son? [*To Joan*] But if you want me to be crowned at Rheims you must talk to the Archbishop, not to me. There he is [*he is standing behind her*]!

JOAN [*turning quickly, overwhelmed with emotion*] Oh, my lord! [*She falls on both knees before him, with bowed head, not daring to look up*] My lord: I am only a poor country girl; and you are filled with the blessedness and glory of God Himself; but you will touch me with your hands, and give me your blessing, wont you?

BLUEBEARD [*whispering to La Trémouille*] The old fox blushes.

LA TRÉMOUILLE. Another miracle!

THE ARCHBISHOP [*touched, putting his hand on her head*] Child: you are in love with religion.

JOAN [*startled: looking up at him*] Am I? I never thought of that. Is there any harm in it?

THE ARCHBISHOP. There is no harm in it, my child. But there is danger.

JOAN [*rising, with a sunflush of reckless happiness irradiating her face*] There is always danger, except in heaven. Oh, my lord, you have given me such strength, such courage. It must be a most wonderful thing to be Archbishop.

The Court smiles broadly: even titters a little.

THE ARCHBISHOP [*drawing himself up sensitively*] Gentlemen: your levity is rebuked by this maid's faith. I am, God help me, all unworthy; but your mirth is a deadly sin.

Their faces fall. Dead silence.

BLUEBEARD. My lord: we were laughing at her, not at you.

THE ARCHBISHOP. What? Not at my unworthiness but at her faith! Gilles de Rais: this maid prophesied that the blasphemer should be drowned in his sin—

JOAN [*distressed*] No!

THE ARCHBISHOP [*silencing her by a gesture*] I prophesy now that you will be hanged in yours if you do not learn when to laugh and when to pray.

BLUEBEARD. My lord: I stand rebuked. I am sorry: I can say no more. But if you prophesy that I shall be hanged, I shall never be able to resist temptation, because I shall always be telling myself that I may as well be hanged for a sheep as a lamb.

The courtiers take heart at this. There is more tittering.

JOAN [*scandalized*] You are an idle fellow, Bluebeard; and you have great impudence to answer the Archbishop.

LA HIRE [*with a huge chuckle*] Well said, lass! Well said!

JOAN [*impatiently to the Archbishop*] Oh, my lord, will you send all these silly folks away so that I may speak to the Dauphin alone?

LA HIRE [*goodhumoredly*] I can take a hint. [*He salutes; turns on his heel; and goes out*].

THE ARCHBISHOP. Come, gentlemen. The Maid comes with God's blessing, and must be obeyed.

The courtiers withdraw, some through the arch, others at the opposite side. The Archbishop marches across to the door, fol-

lowed by the Duchess and La Trémouille. As the Archbishop passes Joan, she falls on her knees, and kisses the hem of his robe fervently. He shakes his head in instinctive remonstrance; gathers the robe from her; and goes out. She is left kneeling directly in the Duchess's way.

THE DUCHESS [*coldly*] Will you allow me to pass, please?

JOAN [*hastily rising, and standing back*] Beg pardon, maam, I am sure.

The Duchess passes on. Joan stares after her; then whispers to the Dauphin.

JOAN. Be that Queen?

CHARLES. No. She thinks she is.

JOAN [*again staring after the Duchess*] Oo-oo-ooh! [*Her awestruck amazement at the figure cut by the magnificently dressed lady is not wholly complimentary*].

LA TRÉMOUILLE [*very surly*] I'll trouble your Highness not to gibe at my wife. [*He goes out. The others have already gone*].

JOAN [*to the Dauphin*] Who be old Gruff-and-Grum?

CHARLES. He is the Duke de la Trémouille.

JOAN. What be his job?

CHARLES. He pretends to command the army. And whenever I find a friend I can care for, he kills him.

JOAN. Why dost let him?

CHARLES [*petulantly moving to the throne side of the room to escape from her magnetic field*] How can I prevent him? He bullies me. They all bully me.

JOAN. Art afraid?

CHARLES. Yes: I am afraid. It's no use preaching to me about it. It's all very well for these big men with their armor that is too heavy for me, and their swords that I can hardly lift, and their muscle and their shouting and their bad tempers. They like fighting: most of them are making fools of themselves all the time they are not fighting; but I am quiet and sensible; and I dont want to kill people: I only want to be left alone to enjoy myself in my own way. I never asked to be a king: it was pushed on me. So if you are going to say

"Son of St Louis: gird on the sword of your ancestors, and lead us to victory" you may spare your breath to cool your porridge; for I cannot do it. I am not built that way; and there is an end of it.

JOAN [*trenchant and masterful*] Blethers! We are all like that to begin with. I shall put courage into thee.

CHARLES. But I dont want to have courage put into me. I want to sleep in a comfortable bed, and not live in continual terror of being killed or wounded. Put courage into the others, and let them have their bellyful of fighting; but let me alone.

JOAN. It's no use, Charlie: thou must face what God puts on thee. If thou fail to make thyself king, thoult be a beggar: what else art fit for? Come! Let me see thee sitting on the throne. I have looked forward to that.

CHARLES. What is the good of sitting on the throne when the other fellows give all the orders? However! [*he sits enthroned, a piteous figure*] here is the king for you! Look your fill at the poor devil.

JOAN. Thourt not king yet, lad: thourt but Dauphin. Be not led away by them around thee. Dressing up dont fill empty noddle. I know the people: the real people that make thy bread for thee; and I tell thee they count no man king of France until the holy oil has been poured on his hair, and himself consecrated and crowned in Rheims Cathedral. And thou needs new clothes, Charlie. Why does not Queen look after thee properly?

CHARLES. We're too poor. She wants all the money we can spare to put on her own back. Besides, I like to see her beautifully dressed; and I dont care what I wear myself: I should look ugly anyhow.

JOAN. There is some good in thee, Charlie; but it is not yet a king's good.

CHARLES. We shall see. I am not such a fool as I look. I have my eyes open; and I can tell you that one good treaty is worth ten good fights. These fighting fellows lose all on the treaties that they gain on the fights. If we can only have a treaty, the English are sure to have the worst of it, because they are better at fighting than at thinking.

JOAN. If the English win, it is they that will make the treaty; and then God help poor France! Thou must fight, Charlie, whether thou will or no. I will go first to hearten thee. We must take our courage in both hands: aye, and pray for it with both hands too.

CHARLES [*descending from his throne and again crossing the room to escape from her dominating urgency*] Oh do stop talking about God and praying. I cant bear people who are always praying. Isnt it bad enough to have to do it at the proper times?

JOAN [*pitying him*] Thou poor child, thou hast never prayed in thy life. I must teach thee from the beginning.

CHARLES. I am not a child: I am a grown man and a father; and I will not be taught any more.

JOAN. Aye, you have a little son. He that will be Louis the Eleventh when you die. Would you not fight for him?

CHARLES. No: a horrid boy. He hates me. He hates everybody, selfish little beast! I dont want to be bothered with children. I dont want to be a father; and I dont want to be a son: especially a son of St Louis. I dont want to be any of these fine things you all have your heads full of: I want to be just what I am. Why cant you mind your own business, and let me mind mine?

JOAN [*again contemptuous*] Minding your own business is like minding your own body: it's the shortest way to make yourself sick. What is my business? Helping mother at home. What is thine? Petting lapdogs and sucking sugar-sticks. I call that muck. I tell thee it is God's business we are here to do: not our own. I have a message to thee from God; and thou must listen to it, though thy heart break with the terror of it.

CHARLES. I dont want a message; but can you tell me any secrets? Can you do any cures? Can you turn lead into gold, or anything of that sort?

JOAN. I can turn thee into a king, in Rheims Cathedral;

and that is a miracle that will take some doing, it seems.

CHARLES. If we go to Rheims, and have a coronation, Anne will want new dresses. We cant afford them. I am all right as I am.

JOAN. As you are! And what is that? Less than my father's poorest shepherd. Thourt not lawful owner of thy own land of France till thou be consecrated.

CHARLES. But I shall not be lawful owner of my own land anyhow. Will the consecration pay off my mortgages? I have pledged my last acre to the Archbishop and that fat bully. I owe money even to Bluebeard.

JOAN [*earnestly*] Charlie: I come from the land, and have gotten my strength working on the land; and I tell thee that the land is thine to rule righteously and keep God's peace in, and not to pledge at the pawnshop as a drunken woman pledges her children's clothes. And I come from God to tell thee to kneel in the cathedral and solemnly give thy kingdom to Him for ever and ever, and become the greatest king in the world as His steward and His bailiff, His soldier and His servant. The very clay of France will become holy: her soldiers will be the soldiers of God: the rebel dukes will be rebels against God: the English will fall on their knees and beg thee let them return to their lawful homes in peace. Wilt be a poor little Judas, and betray me and Him that sent me?

CHARLES [*tempted at last*] Oh, if I only dare!

JOAN. I shall dare, dare, and dare again, in God's name! Art for or against me?

CHARLES [*excited*] I'll risk it. I warn you I shant be able to keep it up; but I'll risk it. You shall see. [*Running to the main door and shouting*] Hallo! Come back, everybody. [*To Joan, as he runs back to the arch opposite*] Mind you stand by and dont let me be bullied. [*Through the arch*] Come along, will you: the whole Court. [*He sits down in the royal chair as they all hurry in to their former places, chattering and wondering*]. Now I'm in for it; but no matter: here goes! [*To the page*] Call for silence, you little beast, will you?

THE PAGE [*snatching a halberd as before and thumping with*

it repeatedly] Silence for His Majesty the King. The King speaks. [*Peremptorily*] Will you be silent there? [*Silence*].

CHARLES [*rising*] I have given the command of the army to The Maid. The Maid is to do as she likes with it. [*He descends from the dais*].

General amazement. La Hire, delighted, slaps his steel thigh-piece with his gauntlet.

LA TRÉMOUILLE [*turning threateningly towards Charles*] What is this? *I* command the army.

Joan quickly puts her hand on Charles's shoulder as he instinctively recoils. Charles, with a grotesque effort culminating in an extravagant gesture, snaps his fingers in the Chamberlain's face.

JOAN. Thourt answered, old Gruff-and-Grum. [*Suddenly flashing out her sword as she divines that her moment has come*] Who is for God and His Maid? Who is for Orleans with me?

LA HIRE [*carried away, drawing also*] For God and His Maid! To Orleans!

ALL THE KNIGHTS [*following his lead with enthusiasm*] To Orleans!

Joan, radiant, falls on her knees in thanksgiving to God. They all kneel, except the Archbishop, who gives his benediction with a sign, and La Trémouille, who collapses, cursing.

SCENE III

ORLEANS, *May 29th, 1429. Dunois, aged 26, is pacing up and down a patch of ground on the south bank of the silver Loire, commanding a long view of the river in both directions. He has had his lance stuck up with a pennon, which streams in a strong east wind. His shield with its bend sinister lies beside it. He has his commander's baton in his hand. He is well built, carrying his armor easily. His broad brow and pointed chin give him an equilaterally triangular face, already marked by active service and responsibility, with the expression of a goodnatured and capable man who has no affectations and no foolish illusions. His page is sitting on the ground, elbows on knees, cheeks on fists, idly watching the water. It is evening; and both man and boy are affected by the loveliness of the Loire.*

DUNOIS [*halting for a moment to glance up at the streaming pennon and shake his head wearily before he resumes his pacing*] West wind, west wind, west wind. Strumpet: steadfast when you should be wanton, wanton when you should be steadfast. West wind on the silver Loire: what rhymes to Loire? [*He looks again at the pennon, and shakes his fist at it*] Change, curse you, change, English harlot of a wind, change. West, west, I tell you. [*With a growl he resumes his march in silence, but soon begins again*] West wind, wanton wind, wilful wind, womanish wind, false wind from over the water, will you never blow again?

THE PAGE [*bounding to his feet*] See! There! There she goes!

DUNOIS [*startled from his reverie: eagerly*] Where? Who? The Maid?

THE PAGE. No: the kingfisher. Like blue lightning. She went into that bush.

DUNOIS [*furiously disappointed*] Is that all? You infernal young idiot: I have a mind to pitch you into the river.

THE PAGE [*not afraid, knowing his man*] It looked frightfully jolly, that flash of blue. Look! There goes the other!

DUNOIS [*running eagerly to the river brim*] Where? Where?

THE PAGE [*pointing*] Passing the reeds.

DUNOIS [*delighted*] I see.

They follow the flight till the bird takes cover.

THE PAGE. You blew me up because you were not in time to see them yesterday.

DUNOIS. You knew I was expecting The Maid when you set up your yelping. I will give you something to yelp for next time.

THE PAGE. Arnt they lovely? I wish I could catch them.

DUNOIS. Let me catch you trying to trap them, and I will put you in the iron cage for a month to teach you what a cage feels like. You are an abominable boy.

THE PAGE [*laughs, and squats down as before*]!

DUNOIS [*pacing*] Blue bird, blue bird, since I am friend to thee, change thou the wind for me. No: it does not rhyme. He who has sinned for thee: thats better. No sense in it, though. [*He finds himself close to the page*] You abominable boy! [*He turns away from him*] Mary in the blue snood, kingfisher color: will you grudge me a west wind?

A SENTRY'S VOICE WESTWARD. Halt! Who goes there?

JOAN'S VOICE. The Maid.

DUNOIS. Let her pass. Hither, Maid! To me!

Joan, in splendid armor, rushes in in a blazing rage. The wind drops; and the pennon flaps idly down the lance; but Dunois is too much occupied with Joan to notice it.

JOAN [*bluntly*] Be you Bastard of Orleans?

DUNOIS [*cool and stern, pointing to his shield*] You see the bend sinister. Are you Joan the Maid?

JOAN. Sure.

DUNOIS. Where are your troops?

JOAN. Miles behind. They have cheated me. They have brought me to the wrong side of the river.

DUNOIS. I told them to.

JOAN. Why did you? The English are on the other side!

DUNOIS. The English are on both sides.

JOAN. But Orleans is on the other side. We must fight the English there. How can we cross the river?

DUNOIS [*grimly*] There is a bridge.

JOAN. In God's name, then, let us cross the bridge, and fall on them.

DUNOIS. It seems simple; but it cannot be done.

JOAN. Who says so?

DUNOIS. I say so; and older and wiser heads than mine are of the same opinion.

JOAN [*roundly*] Then your older and wiser heads are fatheads: they have made a fool of you; and now they want to make a fool of me too, bringing me to the wrong side of the river. Do you not know that I bring you better help than ever came to any general or any town?

DUNOIS [*smiling patiently*] Your own?

JOAN. No: the help and counsel of the King of Heaven. Which is the way to the bridge?

DUNOIS. You are impatient, Maid.

JOAN. Is this a time for patience? Our enemy is at our gates; and here we stand doing nothing. Oh, why are you not fighting? Listen to me: I will deliver you from fear. I—

DUNOIS [*laughing heartily, and waving her off*] No, no, my girl: if you delivered me from fear I should be a good knight for a story book, but a very bad commander of the army. Come! let me begin to make a soldier of you. [*He takes her to the water's edge*]. Do you see those two forts at this end of the bridge? the big ones?

JOAN. Yes. Are they ours or the goddams'?

DUNOIS. Be quiet, and listen to me. If I were in either of those forts with only ten men I could hold it against an army. The English have more than ten times ten goddams in those forts to hold them against us.

JOAN. They cannot hold them against God. God did not give them the land under those forts: they stole it from Him. He gave it to us. I will take those forts.

DUNOIS. Single-handed?

JOAN. Our men will take them. I will lead them.

DUNOIS. Not a man will follow you.

JOAN. I will not look back to see whether anyone is

following me.

DUNOIS [*recognizing her mettle, and clapping her heartily on the shoulder*] Good. You have the makings of a soldier in you. You are in love with war.

JOAN [*startled*] Oh! And the Archbishop said I was in love with religion.

DUNOIS. I, God forgive me, am a little in love with war myself, the ugly devil! I am like a man with two wives. Do you want to be like a woman with two husbands?

JOAN [*matter-of-fact*] I will never take a husband. A man in Toul took an action against me for breach of promise; but I never promised him. I am a soldier: I do not want to be thought of as a woman. I will not dress as a woman. I do not care for the things women care for. They dream of lovers, and of money. I dream of leading a charge, and of placing the big guns. You soldiers do not know how to use the big guns: you think you can win battles with a great noise and smoke.

DUNOIS [*with a shrug*] True. Half the time the artillery is more trouble than it is worth.

JOAN. Aye, lad; but you cannot fight stone walls with horses: you must have guns, and much bigger guns too.

DUNOIS [*grinning at her familiarity, and echoing it*] Aye, lass; but a good heart and a stout ladder will get over the stoniest wall.

JOAN. I will be first up the ladder when we reach the fort, Bastard. I dare you to follow me.

DUNOIS. You must not dare a staff officer, Joan: only company officers are allowed to indulge in displays of personal courage. Besides, you must know that I welcome you as a saint, not as a soldier. I have daredevils enough at my call, if they could help me.

JOAN. I am not a daredevil: I am a servant of God. My sword is sacred: I found it behind the altar in the church of St Catherine, where God hid it for me; and I may not strike a blow with it. My heart is full of courage, not of anger. I will lead; and your men will follow: that is all I can do. But I must do it: you shall not stop me.

DUNOIS. All in good time. Our men cannot take those forts by a sally across the bridge. They must come by water, and take the English in the rear on this side.

JOAN [*her military sense asserting itself*] Then make rafts and put big guns on them; and let your men cross to us.

DUNOIS. The rafts are ready; and the men are embarked. But they must wait for God.

JOAN. What do you mean? God is waiting for them.

DUNOIS. Let Him send us a wind then. My boats are downstream: they cannot come up against both wind and current. We must wait until God changes the wind. Come: let me take you to the church.

JOAN. No. I love church; but the English will not yield to prayers: they understand nothing but hard knocks and slashes. I will not go to church until we have beaten them.

DUNOIS. You must: I have business for you there.

JOAN. What business?

DUNOIS. To pray for a west wind. I have prayed; and I have given two silver candlesticks; but my prayers are not answered. Yours may be: you are young and innocent.

JOAN. Oh yes: you are right. I will pray: I will tell St Catherine: she will make God give me a west wind. Quick: shew me the way to the church.

THE PAGE [*sneezes violently*] At-cha!!!

JOAN. God bless you, child! Coom, Bastard.

They go out. The page rises to follow. He picks up the shield, and is taking the spear as well when he notices the pennon, which is now streaming eastward.

THE PAGE [*dropping the shield and calling excitedly after them*] Seigneur! Seigneur! Mademoiselle!

DUNOIS [*running back*] What is it? The kingfisher? [*He looks eagerly for it up the river*].

JOAN. [*joining them*] Oh, a kingfisher! Where?

THE PAGE. No: the wind, the wind, the wind [*pointing to the pennon*]: that is what made me sneeze.

DUNOIS [*looking at the pennon*] The wind has changed.

[*He crosses himself*] God has spoken. [*Kneeling and handing his baton to Joan*] You command the king's army. I am your soldier.

THE PAGE [*looking down the river*] The boats have put off. They are ripping upstream like anything.

DUNOIS [*rising*] Now for the forts. You dared me to follow. Dare you lead?

JOAN [*bursting into tears and flinging her arms round Dunois, kissing him on both cheeks*] Dunois, dear comrade in arms, help me. My eyes are blinded with tears. Set my foot on the ladder, and say "Up, Joan."

DUNOIS [*dragging her out*] Never mind the tears: make for the flash of the guns.

JOAN [*in a blaze of courage*] Ah!

DUNOIS [*dragging her along with him*] For God and Saint Dennis!

THE PAGE [*shrilly*] The Maid! The Maid! God and The Maid! Hurray-ay-ay! [*He snatches up the shield and lance, and capers out after them, mad with excitement*].

SCENE IV

A TENT *in the English camp. A bullnecked English chaplain of 50 is sitting on a stool at a table, hard at work writing. At the other side of the table an imposing nobleman, aged 46, is seated in a handsome chair turning over the leaves of an illuminated Book of Hours. The nobleman is enjoying himself: the chaplain is struggling with suppressed wrath. There is an unoccupied leather stool on the nobleman's left. The table is on his right.*

THE NOBLEMAN. Now this is what I call workmanship. There is nothing on earth more exquisite than a bonny book, with well-placed columns of rich black writing in beautiful borders, and illuminated pictures cunningly inset. But nowadays, instead of looking at books, people read them. A book might as well be one of those orders for bacon and bran that you are scribbling.

THE CHAPLAIN. I must say, my lord, you take our situation very coolly. Very coolly indeed.

THE NOBLEMAN [*supercilious*] What is the matter?

THE CHAPLAIN. The matter, my lord, is that we English have been defeated.

THE NOBLEMAN. That happens, you know. It is only in history books and ballads that the enemy is always defeated.

THE CHAPLAIN. But we are being defeated over and over again. First, Orleans—

THE NOBLEMAN [*poohpoohing*] Oh, Orleans!

THE CHAPLAIN. I know what you are going to say, my lord: that was a clear case of witchcraft and sorcery. But we are still being defeated. Jargeau, Meung, Beaugency, just like Orleans. And now we have been butchered at Patay, and Sir John Talbot taken prisoner. [*He throws down his pen, almost in tears*] I feel it, my lord: I feel it very deeply. I cannot bear to see my countrymen defeated by a parcel of foreigners.

THE NOBLEMAN. Oh! you are an Englishman, are you?

THE CHAPLAIN. Certainly not, my lord: I am a gentleman. Still, like your lordship, I was born in England; and it makes a difference.

THE NOBLEMAN. You are attached to the soil, eh?

THE CHAPLAIN. It pleases your lordship to be satirical at my expense: your greatness privileges you to be so with impunity. But your lordship knows very well that I am not attached to the soil in a vulgar manner, like a serf. Still, I have a feeling about it; [*with growing agitation*] and I am not ashamed of it; and [*rising wildly*] by God, if this goes on any longer I will fling my cassock to the devil, and take arms myself, and strangle the accursed witch with my own hands.

THE NOBLEMAN [*laughing at him goodnaturedly*] So you shall, chaplain: so you shall, if we can do nothing better. But not yet, not quite yet.

The Chaplain resumes his seat very sulkily.

THE NOBLEMAN [*airily*] I should not care very much about the witch—you see, I have made my pilgrimage to the Holy Land; and the Heavenly Powers, for their own credit, can hardly allow me to be worsted by a village sorceress—but the Bastard of Orleans is a harder nut to crack; and as he has been to the Holy Land too, honors are easy between us as far as that goes.

THE CHAPLAIN. He is only a Frenchman, my lord.

THE NOBLEMAN. A Frenchman! Where did you pick up that expression? Are these Burgundians and Bretons and Picards and Gascons beginning to call themselves Frenchmen, just as our fellows are beginning to call themselves Englishmen? They actually talk of France and England as their countries. Theirs, if you please! What is to become of me and you if that way of thinking comes into fashion?

THE CHAPLAIN. Why, my lord? Can it hurt us?

THE NOBLEMAN. Men cannot serve two masters. If this cant of serving their country once takes hold of them, goodbye to the authority of their feudal lords, and goodbye to the authority of the Church. That is, goodbye to you and me.

THE CHAPLAIN. I hope I am a faithful servant of the Church; and there are only six cousins between me and the barony of Stogumber, which was created by the Conqueror.

But is that any reason why I should stand by and see Englishmen beaten by a French bastard and a witch from Lousy Champagne?

THE NOBLEMAN. Easy, man, easy: we shall burn the witch and beat the bastard all in good time. Indeed I am waiting at present for the Bishop of Beauvais, to arrange the burning with him. He has been turned out of his diocese by her faction.

THE CHAPLAIN. You have first to catch her, my lord.

THE NOBLEMAN. Or buy her. I will offer a king's ransom.

THE CHAPLAIN. A king's ransom! For that slut!

THE NOBLEMAN. One has to leave a margin. Some of Charles's people will sell her to the Burgundians; the Burgundians will sell her to us; and there will probably be three or four middlemen who will expect their little commissions.

THE CHAPLAIN. Monstrous. It is all those scoundrels of Jews: they get in every time money changes hands. I would not leave a Jew alive in Christendom if I had my way.

THE NOBLEMAN. Why not? The Jews generally give value. They make you pay; but they deliver the goods. In my experience the men who want something for nothing are invariably Christians.

A page appears.

THE PAGE. The Right Reverend the Bishop of Beauvais: Monseigneur Cauchon.

Cauchon, aged about 60, *comes in. The page withdraws. The two Englishmen rise.*

THE NOBLEMAN [*with effusive courtesy*] My dear Bishop, how good of you to come! Allow me to introduce myself: Richard de Beauchamp, Earl of Warwick, at your service.

CAUCHON. Your lordship's fame is well known to me.

WARWICK. This reverend cleric is Master John de Stogumber.

THE CHAPLAIN [*glibly*] John Bowyer Spenser Neville de Stogumber, at your service, my lord: Bachelor of Theology, and Keeper of the Private Seal to His Eminence the Cardinal of Winchester.

WARWICK [*to Cauchon*] You call him the Cardinal of England, I believe. Our king's uncle.

CAUCHON. Messire John de Stogumber: I am always the very good friend of His Eminence. [*He extends his hand to the chaplain, who kisses his ring.*]

WARWICK. Do me the honor to be seated. [*He gives Cauchon his chair, placing it at the head of the table*].

Cauchon accepts the place of honor with a grave inclination. Warwick fetches the leather stool carelessly, and sits in his former place. The chaplain goes back to his chair.

Though Warwick has taken second place in calculated deference to the Bishop, he assumes the lead in opening the proceedings as a matter of course. He is still cordial and expansive; but there is a new note in his voice which means that he is coming to business.

WARWICK. Well, my Lord Bishop, you find us in one of our unlucky moments. Charles is to be crowned at Rheims, practically by the young woman from Lorraine; and—I must not deceive you, nor flatter your hopes—we cannot prevent it. I suppose it will make a great difference to Charles's position.

CAUCHON. Undoubtedly. It is a masterstroke of The Maid's.

THE CHAPLAIN [*again agitated*] We were not fairly beaten, my lord. No Englishman is ever fairly beaten.

Cauchon raises his eyebrow slightly, then quickly composes his face.

WARWICK. Our friend here takes the view that the young woman is a sorceress. It would, I presume, be the duty of your reverend lordship to denounce her to the Inquisition, and have her burnt for that offence.

CAUCHON. If she were captured in my diocese: yes.

WARWICK [*feeling that they are getting on capitally*] Just so. Now I suppose there can be no reasonable doubt that she is a sorceress.

THE CHAPLAIN. Not the least. An arrant witch.

WARWICK [*gently reproving the interruption*] We are asking

for the Bishop's opinion, Messire John.

CAUCHON. We shall have to consider not merely our own opinions here, but the opinions—the prejudices, if you like—of a French court.

WARWICK [*correcting*] A Catholic court, my lord.

CAUCHON. Catholic courts are composed of mortal men, like other courts, however sacred their function and inspiration may be. And if the men are Frenchmen, as the modern fashion calls them, I am afraid the bare fact that an English army has been defeated by a French one will not convince them that there is any sorcery in the matter.

THE CHAPLAIN. What! Not when the famous Sir John Talbot himself has been defeated and actually taken prisoner by a drab from the ditches of Lorraine!

CAUCHON. Sir John Talbot, we all know, is a fierce and formidable soldier, Messire; but I have yet to learn that he is an able general. And though it pleases you to say that he has been defeated by this girl, some of us may be disposed to give a little of the credit to Dunois.

THE CHAPLAIN [*contemptuously*] The Bastard of Orleans!

CAUCHON. Let me remind—

WARWICK [*interposing*] I know what you are going to say, my lord. Dunois defeated me at Montargis.

CAUCHON [*bowing*] I take that as evidence that the Seigneur Dunois is a very able commander indeed.

WARWICK. Your lordship is the flower of courtesy. I admit, on our side, that Talbot is a mere fighting animal, and that it probably served him right to be taken at Patay.

THE CHAPLAIN [*chafing*] My lord: at Orleans this woman had her throat pierced by an English arrow, and was seen to cry like a child from the pain of it. It was a death wound; yet she fought all day; and when our men had repulsed all her attacks like true Englishmen, she walked alone to the wall of our fort with a white banner in her hand; and our men were paralyzed, and could neither shoot nor strike whilst the French fell on them and drove them on to the bridge, which immediately burst into flames and crumbled under

them, letting them down into the river, where they were drowned in heaps. Was this your bastard's generalship? or were those flames the flames of hell, conjured up by witchcraft?

WARWICK. You will forgive Messire John's vehemence, my lord; but he has put our case. Dunois is a great captain, we admit; but why could he do nothing until the witch came?

CAUCHON. I do not say that there were no supernatural powers on her side. But the names on that white banner were not the names of Satan and Beelzebub, but the blessed names of our Lord and His holy mother. And your commander who was drowned—Clahz-da I think you call him—

WARWICK. Glasdale. Sir William Glasdale.

CAUCHON. Glass-dell, thank you. He was no saint; and many of our people think that he was drowned for his blasphemies against The Maid.

WARWICK [*beginning to look very dubious*] Well, what are we to infer from all this, my lord? Has The Maid converted you?

CAUCHON. If she had, my lord, I should have known better than to have trusted myself here within your grasp.

WARWICK [*blandly deprecating*] Oh! oh! My lord!

CAUCHON. If the devil is making use of this girl—and I believe he is—

WARWICK [*reassured*] Ah! You hear, Messire John? I knew your lordship would not fail us. Pardon my interruption. Proceed.

CAUCHON. If it be so, the devil has longer views than you give him credit for.

WARWICK. Indeed? In what way? Listen to this, Messire John.

CAUCHON. If the devil wanted to damn a country girl, do you think so easy a task would cost him the winning of half a dozen battles? No, my lord: any trumpery imp could do that much if the girl could be damned at all. The Prince of Darkness does not condescend to such cheap drudgery. When he strikes, he strikes at the Catholic Church, whose realm is the whole spiritual world. When he damns, he damns the souls of the entire human race. Against that dreadful design The Church stands ever on guard. And it is as one of the instruments of that design that I see this girl. She is inspired, but diabolically inspired.

THE CHAPLAIN. I told you she was a witch.

CAUCHON [*fiercely*] She is not a witch. She is a heretic.

THE CHAPLAIN. What difference does that make?

CAUCHON. You, a priest, ask me that! You English are strangely blunt in the mind. All these things that you call witchcraft are capable of a natural explanation. The woman's miracles would not impose on a rabbit: she does not claim them as miracles herself. What do her victories prove but that she has a better head on her shoulders than your swearing Glass-dells and mad bull Talbots, and that the courage of faith, even though it be a false faith, will always outstay the courage of wrath?

THE CHAPLAIN [*hardly able to believe his ears*] Does your lordship compare Sir John Talbot, three times Governor of Ireland, to a mad bull? ! ! !

WARWICK. It would not be seemly for you to do so, Messire John, as you are still six removes from a barony. But as I am an earl, and Talbot is only a knight, I may make bold to accept the comparison. [*To the Bishop*] My lord: I wipe the slate as far as the witchcraft goes. None the less, we must burn the woman.

CAUCHON. I cannot burn her. The Church cannot take life. And my first duty is to seek this girl's salvation.

WARWICK. No doubt. But you do burn people occasionally.

CAUCHON. No. When The Church cuts off an obstinate heretic as a dead branch from the tree of life, the heretic is handed over to the secular arm. The Church has no part in what the secular arm may see fit to do.

WARWICK. Precisely. And I shall be the secular arm in

this case. Well, my lord, hand over your dead branch; and I will see that the fire is ready for it. If you will answer for The Church's part, I will answer for the secular part.

CAUCHON [*with smouldering anger*] I can answer for nothing. You great lords are too prone to treat The Church as a mere political convenience.

WARWICK [*smiling and propitiatory*] Not in England, I assure you.

CAUCHON. In England more than anywhere else. No, my lord: the soul of this village girl is of equal value with yours or your king's before the throne of God; and my first duty is to save it. I will not suffer your lordship to smile at me as if I were repeating a meaningless form of words, and it were well understood between us that I should betray the girl to you. I am no mere political bishop: my faith is to me what your honor is to you; and if there be a loophole through which this baptized child of God can creep to her salvation, I shall guide her to it.

THE CHAPLAIN [*rising in a fury*] You are a traitor.

CAUCHON [*springing up*] You lie, priest. [*Trembling with rage*] If you dare do what this woman has done—set your country above the holy Catholic Church—you shall go to the fire with her.

THE CHAPLAIN. My lord: I—I went too far. I— [*he sits down with a submissive gesture*].

WARWICK [*who has risen apprehensively*] My lord: I apologize to you for the word used by Messire John de Stogumber. It does not mean in England what it does in France. In your language traitor means betrayer: one who is perfidious, treacherous, unfaithful, disloyal. In our country it means simply one who is not wholly devoted to our English interests.

CAUCHON. I am sorry: I did not understand. [*He subsides into his chair with dignity*].

WARWICK [*resuming his seat, much relieved*] I must apologize on my own account if I have seemed to take the burning of this poor girl too lightly. When one has seen whole countrysides burnt over and over again as mere items in military routine, one has to grow a very thick skin. Otherwise one might go mad: at all events, I should. May I venture to assume that your lordship also, having to see so many heretics burned from time to time, is compelled to take—shall I say a professional view of what would otherwise be a very horrible incident?

CAUCHON. Yes: it is a painful duty: even, as you say, a horrible one. But in comparison with the horror of heresy it is less than nothing. I am not thinking of this girl's body, which will suffer for a few moments only, and which must in any event die in some more or less painful manner, but of her soul, which may suffer to all eternity.

WARWICK. Just so; and God grant that her soul may be saved! But the practical problem would seem to be how to save her soul without saving her body. For we must face it, my lord: if this cult of The Maid goes on, our cause is lost.

THE CHAPLAIN [*his voice broken like that of a man who has been crying*] May I speak, my lord?

WARWICK. Really, Messire John, I had rather you did not, unless you can keep your temper.

THE CHAPLAIN. It is only this. I speak under correction; but The Maid is full of deceit: she pretends to be devout. Her prayers and confessions are endless. How can she be accused of heresy when she neglects no observance of a faithful daughter of The Church?

CAUCHON [*flaming up*] A faithful daughter of The Church! The Pope himself at his proudest dare not presume as this woman presumes. She acts as if she herself were The Church. She brings the message of God to Charles; and The Church must stand aside. She will crown him in the cathedral of Rheims: she, not The Church! She sends letters to the king of England giving him God's command through her to return to his island on pain of God's vengeance, which she will execute. Let me tell you that the writing of such letters was the practice of the accursed Mahomet, the anti-Christ. Has she ever in all her utterances said one word of The Church? Never. It is always God and herself.

WARWICK. What can you expect? A beggar on horseback! Her head is turned.

CAUCHON. Who has turned it? The devil. And for a mighty purpose. He is spreading this heresy everywhere. The man Hus, burnt only thirteen years ago at Constance, infected all Bohemia with it. A man named WcLeef, himself an anointed priest, spread the pestilence in England; and to your shame you let him die in his bed. We have such people here in France too: I know the breed. It is cancerous: if it be not cut out, stamped out, burnt out, it will not stop until it has brought the whole body of human society into sin and corruption, into waste and ruin. By it an Arab camel driver drove Christ and His Church out of Jerusalem, and ravaged his way west like a wild beast until at last there stood only the Pyrenees and God's mercy between France and damnation. Yet what did the camel driver do at the beginning more than this shepherd girl is doing? He had his voices from the angel Gabriel: she has her voices from St Catherine and St Margaret and the Blessed Michael. He declared himself the messenger of God, and wrote in God's name to the kings of the earth. Her letters to them are going forth daily. It is not the Mother of God now to whom we must look for intercession, but to Joan the Maid. What will the world be like when The Church's accumulated wisdom and knowledge and experience, its councils of learned, venerable pious men, are thrust into the kennel by every ignorant laborer or dairymaid whom the devil can puff up with the monstrous self-conceit of being directly inspired from heaven? It will be a world of blood, of fury, of devastation, of each man striving for his own hand: in the end a world wrecked back into barbarism. For now you have only Mahomet and his dupes, and the Maid and her dupes; but what will it be when every girl thinks herself a Joan and every man a Mahomet? I shudder to the very marrow of my bones when I think of it. I have fought it all my life; and I will fight it to the end. Let all this woman's sins be forgiven her except only this sin; for it is the sin against the Holy Ghost; and if she does not recant in the dust before the world, and submit herself to the last inch of her soul to her Church, to the fire she shall go if she once falls into my hand.

WARWICK [*unimpressed*] You feel strongly about it, naturally.

CAUCHON. Do not you?

WARWICK. I am a soldier, not a churchman. As a pilgrim I saw something of the Mahometans. They were not so ill-bred as I had been led to believe. In some respects their conduct compared favorably with ours.

CAUCHON [*displeased*] I have noticed this before. Men go to the East to convert the infidels. And the infidels pervert them. The Crusader comes back more than half a Saracen. Not to mention that all Englishmen are born heretics.

THE CHAPLAIN. Englishmen heretics!!! [*Appealing to Warwick*] My lord: must we endure this? His lordship is beside himself. How can what an Englishman believes be heresy? It is a contradiction in terms.

CAUCHON. I absolve you, Messire de Stogumber, on the ground of invincible ignorance. The thick air of your country does not breed theologians.

WARWICK. You would not say so if you heard us quarrelling about religion, my lord! I am sorry you think I must be either a heretic or a blockhead because, as a travelled man, I know that the followers of Mahomet profess great respect for our Lord, and are more ready to forgive St Peter for being a fisherman than your lordship is to forgive Mahomet for being a camel driver. But at least we can proceed in this matter without bigotry.

CAUCHON. When men call the zeal of the Christian Church bigotry I know what to think.

WARWICK. They are only east and west views of the same thing.

CAUCHON [*bitterly ironical*] Only east and west! Cnly!!

WARWICK. Oh, my Lord Bishop, I am not gainsaying you. You will carry The Church with you; but you have to carry the nobles also. To my mind there is a stronger case against The Maid than the one you have so forcibly put. Frankly, I am not afraid of this girl becoming another Mahomet, and superseding The Church by a great heresy. I think you exaggerate that risk. But have you noticed that in these letters of hers, she proposes to all the kings of Europe, as she has already pressed on Charles, a transaction which would wreck the whole social structure of Christendom?

CAUCHON. Wreck The Church. I tell you so.

WARWICK [*whose patience is wearing out*] My lord: pray get The Church out of your head for a moment; and remember that there are temporal institutions in the world as well as spiritual ones. I and my peers represent the feudal aristocracy as you represent The Church. We are the temporal power. Well, do you not see how this girl's idea strikes at us?

CAUCHON. How does her idea strike at you, except as it strikes at all of us, through The Church?

WARWICK. Her idea is that the kings should give their realms to God, and then reign as God's bailiffs.

CAUCHON [*not interested*] Quite sound theologically, my lord. But the king will hardly care, provided he reign. It is an abstract idea: a mere form of words.

WARWICK. By no means. It is a cunning device to supersede the aristocracy, and make the king sole and absolute autocrat. Instead of the king being merely the first among his peers, he becomes their master. That we cannot suffer: we call no man master. Nominally we hold our lands and dignities from the king, because there must be a keystone to the arch of human society; but we hold our lands in our own hands, and defend them with our own swords and those of our own tenants. Now by The Maid's doctrine the king will take our lands—our lands!—and make them a present to God; and God will then vest them wholly in the king.

CAUCHON. Need you fear that? You are the makers of kings after all. York or Lancaster in England, Lancaster or Valois in France: they reign according to your pleasure.

WARWICK. Yes; but only as long as the people follow their feudal lords, and know the king only as a travelling show, owning nothing but the highway that belongs to everybody. If the people's thoughts and hearts were turned to the king, and their lords became only the king's servants in their eyes, the king could break us across his knee one by one; and then what should we be but liveried courtiers in his halls?

CAUCHON. Still you need not fear, my lord. Some men are born kings; and some are born statesmen. The two are seldom the same. Where would the king find counsellors to plan and carry out such a policy for him?

WARWICK [*with a not too friendly smile*] Perhaps in the Church, my lord.

Cauchon, with an equally sour smile, shrugs his shoulders, and does not contradict him.

WARWICK. Strike down the barons; and the cardinals will have it all their own way.

CAUCHON [*conciliatory, dropping his polemical tone*] My lord: we shall not defeat The Maid if we strive against one another. I know well that there is a Will to Power in the world. I know that while it lasts there will be a struggle between the Emperor and the Pope, between the dukes and the political cardinals, between the barons and the kings. The devil divides us and governs. I see you are no friend to The Church: you are an earl first and last, as I am a churchman first and last. But can we not sink our differences in the face of a common enemy? I see now that what is in your mind is not that this girl has never once mentioned The Church, and thinks only of God and herself, but that she has never once mentioned the peerage, and thinks only of the king and herself.

WARWICK. Quite so. These two ideas of hers are the same idea at bottom. It goes deep, my lord. It is the protest of the individual soul against the interference of priest or peer between the private man and his God. I should call it Protestantism if I had to find a name for it.

CAUCHON [*looking hard at him*] You understand it wonderfully well, my lord. Scratch an Englishman, and find a Protestant.

WARWICK [*playing the pink of courtesy*] I think you are not entirely void of sympathy with The Maid's secular heresy, my lord. I leave you to find a name for it.

CAUCHON. You mistake me, my lord. I have no sympathy with her political presumptions. But as a priest I have gained a knowledge of the minds of the common people; and there you will find yet another most dangerous idea. I can express it only by such phrases as France for the French, England for the English, Italy for the Italians, Spain for the Spanish, and so forth. It is sometimes so narrow and bitter in country folk that it surprises me that this country girl can rise above the idea of her village for its villagers. But she can. She does. When she threatens to drive the English from the soil of France she is undoubtedly thinking of the whole extent of country in which French is spoken. To her the French-speaking people are what the Holy Scriptures describe as a nation. Call this side of her heresy Nationalism if you will: I can find you no better name for it. I can only tell you that it is essentially anti-Catholic and anti-Christian; for the Catholic Church knows only one realm, and that is the realm of Christ's kingdom. Divide that kingdom into nations, and you dethrone Christ. Dethrone Christ, and who will stand between our throats and the sword? The world will perish in a welter of war.

WARWICK. Well, if you will burn the Protestant, I will burn the Nationalist, though perhaps I shall not carry Messire John with me there. England for the English will appeal to him.

THE CHAPLAIN. Certainly England for the English goes without saying: it is the simple law of nature. But this woman denies to England her legitimate conquests, given her by God because of her peculiar fitness to rule over less civilized races for their own good. I do not understand what your lordships mean by Protestant and Nationalist: you are too learned and subtle for a poor clerk like myself. But I know as a matter of plain commonsense that the woman is a rebel; and that is enough for me. She rebels against Nature by wearing man's clothes, and fighting. She rebels against The Church by usurping the divine authority of the Pope. She rebels against God by her damnable league with Satan and his evil spirits against our army. And all these rebellions are only excuses for her great rebellion against England. That is not to be endured. Let her perish. Let her burn. Let her not infect the whole flock. It is expedient that one woman die for the people.

WARWICK [*rising*] My lord: we seem to be agreed.

CAUCHON [*rising also, but in protest*] I will not imperil my soul. I will uphold the justice of The Church. I will strive to the utmost for this woman's salvation.

WARWICK. I am sorry for the poor girl. I hate these severities. I will spare her if I can.

THE CHAPLAIN [*implacably*] I would burn her with my own hands.

CAUCHON [*blessing him*] Sancta simplicitas!

SCENE V

THE ambulatory in the cathedral of Rheims, near the door of the vestry. A pillar bears one of the stations of the cross. The organ is playing the people out of the nave after the coronation. Joan is kneeling in prayer before the station. She is beautifully dressed, but still in male attire. The organ ceases as Dunois, also splendidly arrayed, comes into the ambulatory from the vestry.

DUNOIS. Come, Joan! you have had enough praying. After that fit of crying you will catch a chill if you stay here any longer. It is all over: the cathedral is empty; and the streets are full. They are calling for The Maid. We have told them you are staying here alone to pray; but they want to see you again.

JOAN. No: let the king have all the glory.

DUNOIS. He only spoils the show, poor devil. No, Joan: you have crowned him; and you must go through with it.

JOAN [*shakes her head reluctantly*].

DUNOIS [*raising her*] Come come! it will be over in a couple of hours. It's better than the bridge at Orleans: eh?

JOAN. Oh, dear Dunois, how I wish it were the bridge at Orleans again! We l i v e d at that bridge.

DUNOIS. Yes, faith, and died too: some of us.

JOAN. Isnt it strange, Jack? I am such a coward: I am frightened beyond words before a battle; but it is so dull afterwards when there is no danger: oh, so dull! dull! dull!

DUNOIS. You must learn to be abstemious in war, just as you are in your food and drink, my little saint.

JOAN. Dear Jack: I think you like me as a soldier likes his comrade.

DUNOIS. You need it, poor innocent child of God. You have not many friends at court.

JOAN. Why do all these courtiers and knights and churchmen hate me? What have I done to them? I have asked nothing for myself except that my village shall not be taxed; for we cannot afford war taxes. I have brought them luck and victory: I have set them right when they were doing all sorts of stupid things: I have crowned Charles and made him a real king; and all the honors he is handing out have gone to them. Then why do they not love me?

DUNOIS [*rallying her*] Sim-ple-ton! Do you expect stupid people to love you for shewing them up? Do blundering old military dug-outs love the successful young captains who supersede them? Do ambitious politicians love the climbers who take the front seats from them? Do archbishops enjoy being played off their own altars, even by saints? Why, I should be jealous of you myself if I were ambitious enough.

JOAN. You are the pick of the basket here, Jack: the only friend I have among all these nobles. I'll wager your mother was from the country. I will go back to the farm when I have taken Paris.

DUNOIS. I am not so sure that they will let you take Paris.

JOAN [*startled*] What!

DUNOIS. I should have taken it myself before this if they had all been sound about it. Some of them would rather Paris took you, I think. So take care.

JOAN. Jack: the world is too wicked for me. If the goddams and the Burgundians do not make an end of me, the French will. Only for my voices I should lose all heart. That is why I had to steal away to pray here alone after the coronation. I'll tell you something, Jack. It is in the bells I hear my voices. Not to-day, when they all rang: that was nothing but jangling. But here in this corner, where the bells come down from heaven, and the echoes linger, or in the fields, where they come from a distance through the quiet of the countryside, my voices are in them. [*The cathedral clock chimes the quarter*] Hark! [*She becomes rapt*] Do you hear? "Dear-child-of-God": just what you said. At the half-hour they will say "Be-brave-go-on." At the three-quarters they will say "I-am-thy-Help." But it is at the hour, when the great bell goes after "God-will-save-France": it is then that St Margaret and St Catherine and sometimes even the blessed Michael will say things that I cannot tell beforehand. Then, oh then—

DUNOIS [*interrupting her kindly but not sympathetically*] Then, Joan, we shall hear whatever we fancy in the booming of the bell. You make me uneasy when you talk about your voices: I should think you were a bit cracked if I hadnt noticed that you give me very sensible reasons for what you do, though I hear you telling others you are only obeying Madame Saint Catherine.

JOAN [*crossly*] Well, I have to find reasons for you, because you do not believe in my voices. But the voices come first; and I find the reasons after: whatever you may choose to believe.

DUNOIS. Are you angry, Joan?

JOAN. Yes. [*Smiling*] No: not with you. I wish you were one of the village babies.

DUNOIS. Why?

JOAN. I could nurse you for awhile.

DUNOIS. You are a bit of a woman after all.

JOAN. No: not a bit: I am a soldier and nothing else. Soldiers always nurse children when they get a chance.

DUNOIS. That is true. [*He laughs*].

King Charles, with Bluebeard on his left and La Hire on his right, comes from the vestry, where he has been disrobing. Joan shrinks away behind the pillar. Dunois is left between Charles and La Hire.

DUNOIS. Well, your Majesty is an anointed king at last. How do you like it?

CHARLES. I would not go through it again to be emperor of the sun and moon. The weight of those robes! I thought I should have dropped when they loaded that crown on to me. And the famous holy oil they talked so much about was rancid: phew! The Archbishop must be nearly dead: his robes must have weighed a ton: they are stripping him still in the vestry.

DUNOIS [*drily*] Your majesty should wear armor oftener. That would accustom you to heavy dressing.

CHARLES. Yes: the old jibe! Well, I am not going to wear armor: fighting is not my job. Where is The Maid?

JOAN [*coming forward between Charles and Bluebeard, and falling on her knee*] Sire: I have made you king: my work is done. I am going back to my father's farm.

CHARLES [*surprised, but relieved*] Oh, are you? Well, that will be very nice.

Joan rises, deeply discouraged.

CHARLES [*continuing heedlessly*] A healthy life, you know.

DUNOIS. But a dull one.

BLUEBEARD. You will find the petticoats tripping you up after leaving them off for so long.

LA HIRE. You will miss the fighting. It's a bad habit, but a grand one, and the hardest of all to break yourself of.

CHARLES [*anxiously*] Still, we dont want you to stay if you would really rather go home.

JOAN [*bitterly*] I know well that none of you will be sorry to see me go. [*She turns her shoulder to Charles and walks past him to the more congenial neighborhood of Dunois and La Hire*].

LA HIRE. Well, I shall be able to swear when I want to. But I shall miss you at times.

JOAN. La Hire: in spite of all your sins and swears we shall meet in heaven; for I love you as I love Pitou, my old sheep dog. Pitou could kill a wolf. You will kill the English wolves until they go back to their country and become good dogs of God, will you not?

LA HIRE. You and I together: yes.

JOAN. No: I shall last only a year from the beginning.

ALL THE OTHERS. What!

JOAN. I know it somehow.

DUNOIS. Nonsense!

JOAN. Jack: do you think you will be able to drive them out?

DUNOIS [*with quiet conviction*] Yes: I shall drive them out. They beat us because we thought battles were tournaments and ransom markets. We played the fool while the goddams took war seriously. But I have learnt my lesson, and taken their measure. They have no roots here. I have beaten them before; and I shall beat them again.

JOAN. You will not be cruel to them, Jack?

DUNOIS. The goddams will not yield to tender handling. We did not begin it.

JOAN [*suddenly*] Jack: before I go home, let us take Paris.

CHARLES [*terrified*] Oh no no. We shall lose everything we have gained. Oh dont let us have any more fighting. We can make a very good treaty with the Duke of Burgundy.

JOAN. Treaty! [*She stamps with impatience*].

CHARLES. Well, why not, now that I am crowned and anointed? Oh, that oil!

The Archbishop comes from the vestry, and joins the group between Charles and Bluebeard.

CHARLES. Archbishop: The Maid wants to start fighting again.

THE ARCHBISHOP. Have we ceased fighting, then? Are we at peace?

CHARLES. No: I suppose not; but let us be content with what we have done. Let us make a treaty. Our luck is too good to last; and now is our chance to stop before it turns.

JOAN. Luck! God has fought for us; and you call it luck! And you would stop while there are still Englishmen on this holy earth of dear France!

THE ARCHBISHOP [*sternly*] Maid: the king addressed himself to me, not to you. You forget yourself. You very often forget yourself.

JOAN [*unabashed, and rather roughly*] Then speak, you; and tell him that it is not God's will that he should take his hand from the plough.

THE ARCHBISHOP. If I am not so glib with the name of God as you are, it is because I interpret His will with the authority of The Church and of my sacred office. When you first came you respected it, and would not have dared to speak as you are now speaking. You came clothed with the virtue of humility; and because God blessed your enterprises accordingly, you have stained yourself with the sin of pride. The old Greek tragedy is rising among us. It is the chastisement of hubris.

CHARLES. Yes: she thinks she knows better than everyone else.

JOAN [*distressed, but naïvely incapable of seeing the effect she is producing*] But I do know better than any of you seem to. And I am not proud: I never speak unless I know I am right.

BLUEBEARD } [*exclaiming together*] { Ha ha!
CHARLES } { Just so.

THE ARCHBISHOP. How do you know you are right?

JOAN. I always know. My voices—

CHARLES. Oh, your voices, your voices. Why dont the voices come to me? I am king, not you.

JOAN. They do come to you; but you do not hear them. You have not sat in the field in the evening listening for them. When the angelus rings you cross yourself and have done with it; but if you prayed from your heart, and listened to the thrilling of the bells in the air after they stop ringing, you would hear the voices as well as I do. [*Turning brusquely from him*] But what voices do you need to tell you what the blacksmith can tell you: that you must strike while the iron is hot? I tell you we must make a dash at Compiégne and relieve it as we relieved Orleans. Then Paris will open its gates; or if not, we will break through them. What is your crown worth without your capital?

LA HIRE. That is what I say too. We shall go through them like a red hot shot through a pound of butter. What do you say, Bastard?

DUNOIS. If our cannon balls were all as hot as your head, and we had enough of them, we should conquer the earth, no doubt. Pluck and impetuosity are good servants in war, but bad masters: they have delivered us into the hands of the English every time we have trusted to them. We never know when we are beaten: that is our great fault.

JOAN. You never know when you are victorious: that is a worse fault. I shall have to make you carry looking-glasses in battle to convince you that the English have not cut off all your noses. You would have been besieged in Orleans still, you and your councils of war, if I had not made you attack. You should always attack; and if you only hold on long enough the enemy will stop first. You dont know how to begin a battle; and you dont know how to use your cannons. And I do.

She squats down on the flags with crossed ankles, pouting.

DUNOIS. I know what you think of us, General Joan.

JOAN. Never mind that, Jack. Tell them what you think of me.

DUNOIS. I think that God was on your side; for I have not forgotten how the wind changed, and how our hearts changed when you came; and by my faith I shall never deny that it was in your sign that we conquered. But I tell you as a soldier that God is no man's daily drudge, and no maid's either. If you are worthy of it he will sometimes snatch you out of the jaws of death and set you on your feet again; but that is all: once on your feet you must fight with all your might and all your craft. For he has to be fair to your enemy too: dont forget that. Well, he set us on our feet through you at Orleans; and the glory of it has carried us through a few good battles here to the coronation. But if we presume on it further, and trust to God to do the work we should do ourselves, we shall be defeated; and serve us right!

JOAN. But—

DUNOIS. Sh! I have not finished. Do not think, any of you, that these victories of ours were won without generalship. King Charles: you have said no word in your proclamations of my part in this campaign; and I make no complaint of that; for the people will run after The Maid and her miracles and not after the Bastard's hard work finding troops for her and feeding them. But I know exactly how much God did for us through The Maid, and how much He left me to do by my own wits; and I tell you that your little hour of miracles is over, and that from this time on he who plays the war game best will win—if the luck is on his side.

JOAN. Ah! if, if, if, if! If ifs and ans were pots and pans there'd be no need of tinkers. [*Rising impetuously*] I tell you, Bastard, your art of war is no use, because your knights are no good for real fighting. War is only a game to them, like tennis and all their other games: they make rules as to what is fair and what is not fair, and heap armor on themselves and on their poor horses to keep out the arrows; and when they fall they cant get up, and have to wait for their squires to come and lift them to arrange about the ransom with the man that has poked them off their horse. Cant you see that all the like of that is gone by and done with? What use is armor against gunpowder? And if it was, do you think men that are fighting for France and for God will stop to bargain about ransoms, as half your knights live by doing? No: they will fight to win; and they will give up their lives out of their own hand into the hand of God when they go into battle, as I do. Common folks understand this. They cannot afford armor and cannot pay ransoms; but they follow me half naked into the moat and up the ladder and over the wall. With them it is my life or thine, and God defend the right! You may shake your head, Jack; and Bluebeard may twirl his billygoat's beard and cock his nose at me; but remember the day your knights and captains refused to follow me to attack the English at Orleans! You locked the gates to keep me in; and it was the townsfolk and the common people that followed me, and forced the gate, and shewed you the way to fight in earnest.

BLUEBEARD [*offended*] Not content with being Pope Joan, you must be Caesar and Alexander as well.

THE ARCHBISHOP. Pride will have a fall, Joan.

JOAN. Oh, never mind whether it is pride or not: is it true? is it commonsense?

LA HIRE. It is true. Half of us are afraid of having our handsome noses broken; and the other half are out for paying off their mortgages. Let her have her way, Dunois: she does not know everything; but she has got hold of the right end of the stick. Fighting is not what it was; and those who know least about it often make the best job of it.

DUNOIS. I know all that. I do not fight in the old way: I have learnt the lesson of Agincourt, of Poitiers and Crecy. I know how many lives any move of mine will cost; and if the move is worth the cost I make it and pay the cost. But Joan never counts the cost at all: she goes ahead and trusts to God: she thinks she has God in her pocket. Up to now she has had the numbers on her side; and she has won. But I know Joan; and I see that some day she will go ahead when she has only ten men to do the work of a hundred. And then she will find that God is on the side of the big battalions. She will be taken by the enemy. And the lucky man that makes the capture will receive sixteen thousand pounds from the Earl of Ouareek.

JOAN [*flattered*] Sixteen thousand pounds! Eh, laddie, have they offered that for me? There cannot be so much money in the world.

DUNOIS. There is, in England. And now tell me, all of you, which of you will lift a finger to save Joan once the English have got her? I speak first, for the army. The day after she has been dragged from her horse by a goddam or a Burgundian, and he is not struck dead: the day after she is locked in a dungeon, and the bars and bolts do not fly open at the touch of St Peter's angel: the day when the enemy finds out that she is as vulnerable as I am and not a bit more invincible, she will not be worth the life of a single soldier to us; and I will not risk that life, much as I cherish her as a companion-in-arms.

JOAN. I dont blame you, Jack: you are right. I am not worth one soldier's life if God lets me be beaten; but France may think me worth my ransom after what God has done for her through me.

CHARLES. I tell you I have no money; and this coronation, which is all your fault, has cost me the last farthing I can borrow.

JOAN. The Church is richer than you. I put my trust in

The Church.

THE ARCHBISHOP. Woman: they will drag you through the streets, and burn you as a witch.

JOAN [*running to him*] Oh, my lord, do not say that. It is impossible. I a witch!

THE ARCHBISHOP. Peter Cauchon knows his business. The University of Paris has burnt a woman for saying that what you have done was well done, and according to God.

JOAN [*bewildered*] But why? What sense is there in it? What I have done is according to God. They could not burn a woman for speaking the truth.

THE ARCHBISHOP. They did.

JOAN. But you know that she was speaking the truth. You would not let them burn me.

THE ARCHBISHOP. How could I prevent them?

JOAN. You would speak in the name of The Church. You are a great prince of The Church. I would go anywhere with your blessing to protect me.

THE ARCHBISHOP. I have no blessing for you while you are proud and disobedient.

JOAN. Oh, why will you go on saying things like that? I am not proud and disobedient. I am a poor girl, and so ignorant that I do not know A from B. How could I be proud? And how can you say that I am disobedient when I always obey my voices, because they come from God.

THE ARCHBISHOP. The voice of God on earth is the voice of the Church Militant; and all the voices that come to you are the echoes of your own wilfulness.

JOAN. It is not true.

THE ARCHBISHOP [*flushing angrily*] You tell the Archbishop in his cathedral that he lies; and yet you say you are not proud and disobedient.

JOAN. I never said you lied. It was you that as good as said my voices lied. When have they ever lied? If you will not believe in them: even if they are only the echoes of my own commonsense, are they not always right? and are not your earthly counsels always wrong?

THE ARCHBISHOP [*indignantly*] It is waste of time admonishing you.

CHARLES. It always comes back to the same thing. She is right; and everyone else is wrong.

THE ARCHBISHOP. Take this as your last warning. If you perish through setting your private judgment above the instructions of your spiritual directors, The Church disowns you, and leaves you to whatever fate your presumption may bring upon you. The Bastard has told you that if you persist in setting up your military conceit above the counsels of your commanders—

DUNOIS [*interposing*] To put it quite exactly, if you attempt to relieve the garrison in Compiègne without the same superiority in numbers you had at Orleans—

THE ARCHBISHOP. The army will disown you, and will not rescue you. And His Majesty the King has told you that the throne has not the means of ransoming you.

CHARLES. Not a penny.

THE ARCHBISHOP. You stand alone: absolutely alone, trusting to your own conceit, your own ignorance, your own headstrong presumption, your own impiety in hiding all these sins under the cloak of a trust in God. When you pass through these doors into the sunlight, the crowd will cheer you. They will bring you their little children and their invalids to heal: they will kiss your hands and feet, and do what they can, poor simple souls, to turn your head, and madden you with the self-confidence that is leading you to your destruction. But you will be none the less alone: they cannot save you. We and we only can stand between you and the stake at which our enemies have burnt that wretched woman in Paris.

JOAN [*her eyes skyward*] I have better friends and better counsel than yours.

THE ARCHBISHOP. I see that I am speaking in vain to a hardened heart. You reject our protection, and are determined to turn us all against you. In future, then, fend for yourself; and if you fail, God have mercy on your soul.

DUNOIS. That is the truth, Joan. Heed it.

JOAN. Where would you all have been now if I had heeded that sort of truth? There is no help, no counsel, in any of you. Yes: I am alone on earth: I have always been alone. My father told my brothers to drown me if I would not stay to mind his sheep while France was bleeding to death: France might perish if only our lambs were safe. I thought France would have friends at the court of the king of France; and I find only wolves fighting for pieces of her poor torn body. I thought God would have friends everywhere, because He is the friend of everyone; and in my innocence I believed that you who now cast me out would be like strong towers to keep harm from me. But I am wiser now; and nobody is any the worse for being wiser. Do not think you can frighten me by telling me that I am alone. France is alone; and God is alone; and what is my loneliness before the loneliness of my country and my God? I see now that the loneliness of God is His strength: what would He be if He listened to your jealous little counsels? Well, my loneliness shall be my strength too: it is better to be alone with God: His friendship will not fail me, nor His counsel, nor His love. In His strength I will dare, and dare, and dare, until I die. I will go out now to the common people, and let the love in their eyes comfort me for the hate in yours. You will all be glad to see me burnt; but if I go through the fire I shall go through it to their hearts for ever and ever. And so, God be with me!

She goes from them. They stare after her in glum silence for a moment. Then Gilles de Rais twirls his beard.

BLUEBEARD. You know, the woman is quite impossible. I dont dislike her, really; but what are you to do with such a character?

DUNOIS. As God is my judge, if she fell into the Loire I would jump in in full armor to fish her out. But if she plays the fool at Compiègne, and gets caught, I must leave her to her doom.

LA HIRE. Then you had better chain me up; for I could

follow her to hell when the spirit rises in her like that.

THE ARCHBISHOP. She disturbs my judgment too: there is a dangerous power in her outbursts. But the pit is open at her feet; and for good or evil we cannot turn her from it.

CHARLES. If only she would keep quiet, or go home!

They follow her dispiritedly.

SCENE VI

ROUEN, *30th May* 1431. *A great stone hall in the castle, arranged for a trial-at-law, but not a trial-by-jury, the court being the Bishop's court with the Inquisition participating: hence there are two raised chairs side by side for the Bishop and the Inquisitor as judges. Rows of chairs radiating from them at an obtuse angle are for the canons, the doctors of law and theology, and the Dominican monks, who act as assessors. In the angle is a table for the scribes, with stools. There is also a heavy rough wooden stool for the prisoner. All these are at the inner end of the hall. The further end is open to the courtyard through a row of arches. The court is shielded from the weather by screens and curtains.*

Looking down the great hall from the middle of the inner end, the judicial chairs and scribes' table are to the right. The prisoner's stool is to the left. There are arched doors right and left. It is a fine sunshiny May morning.

Warwick comes in through the arched doorway on the judges' side, followed by his page.

THE PAGE [*pertly*] I suppose your lordship is aware that we have no business here. This is an ecclesiastical court; and we are only the secular arm.

WARWICK. I am aware of that fact. Will it please your impudence to find the Bishop of Beauvais for me, and give him a hint that he can have a word with me here before the trial, if he wishes?

THE PAGE [*going*] Yes, my lord.

WARWICK. And mind you behave yourself. Do not address him as Pious Peter.

THE PAGE. No, my lord. I shall be kind to him, because, when The Maid is brought in, Pious Peter will have to pick a peck of pickled pepper.

Cauchon enters through the same door with a Dominican monk and a canon, the latter carrying a brief.

THE PAGE. The Right Reverend his lordship the Bishop of Beauvais. And two other reverend gentlemen.

WARWICK. Get out; and see that we are not interrupted.

THE PAGE. Right, my lord [*he vanishes airily*].

CAUCHON. I wish your lordship good-morrow.

WARWICK. Good-morrow to your lordship. Have I had the pleasure of meeting your friends before? I think not.

CAUCHON [*introducing the monk, who is on his right*] This, my lord, is Brother John Lemaître, of the order of St Dominic. He is acting as deputy for the Chief Inquisitor into the evil of heresy in France. Brother John: the Earl of Warwick.

WARWICK. Your Reverence is most welcome. We have no Inquisitor in England, unfortunately; though we miss him greatly, especially on occasions like the present.

The Inquisitor smiles patiently, and bows. He is a mild elderly gentleman, but has evident reserves of authority and firmness.

CAUCHON [*introducing the Canon, who is on his left*] This gentleman is Canon John D'Estivet, of the Chapter of Bayeux. He is acting as Promoter.

WARWICK. Promoter?

CAUCHON. Prosecutor, you would call him in civil law.

WARWICK. Ah! prosecutor. Quite, quite. I am very glad to make your acquaintance, Canon D'Estivet.

D'Estivet bows. [*He is on the young side of middle age, well mannered, but vulpine beneath his veneer*].

WARWICK. May I ask what stage the proceedings have reached? It is now more than nine months since The Maid was captured at Compiègne by the Burgundians. It is fully four months since I bought her from the Burgundians for a very handsome sum, solely that she might be brought to justice. It is very nearly three months since I delivered her up to you, my Lord Bishop, as a person suspected of heresy. May I suggest that you are taking a rather unconscionable time to make up your minds about a very plain case? Is this trial never going to end?

THE INQUISITOR [*smiling*] It has not yet begun, my lord.

WARWICK. Not yet begun! Why, you have been at it eleven weeks!

CAUCHON. We have not been idle, my lord. We have held fifteen examinations of The Maid: six public and nine private.

THE INQUISITOR [*always patiently smiling*] You see, my lord, I have been present at only two of these examinations. They were proceedings of the Bishop's court solely, and not of the Holy Office. I have only just decided to associate myself—that is, to associate the Holy Inquisition—with the Bishop's court. I did not at first think that this was a case of heresy at all. I regarded it as a political case, and The Maid as a prisoner of war. But having now been present at two of the examinations, I must admit that this seems to be one of the gravest cases of heresy within my experience. Therefore everything is now in order; and we proceed to trial this morning. [*He moves towards the judicial chairs*].

CAUCHON. This moment, if your lordship's convenience allows.

WARWICK [*graciously*] Well, that is good news, gentlemen. I will not attempt to conceal from you that our patience was becoming strained.

CAUCHON. So I gathered from the threats of your soldiers to drown those of our people who favor The Maid.

WARWICK. Dear me! At all events their intentions were friendly to you, my lord.

CAUCHON [*sternly*] I hope not. I am determined that the woman shall have a fair hearing. The justice of The Church is not a mockery, my lord.

THE INQUISITOR [*returning*] Never has there been a fairer examination within my experience, my lord. The Maid needs no lawyers to take her part: she will be tried by her most faithful friends, all ardently desirous to save her soul from perdition.

D'ESTIVET. Sir: I am the Promoter; and it has been my painful duty to present the case against the girl; but believe me, I would throw up my case today and hasten to her I did not know that men far my superiors in d piety, in eloquence and persuasiveness, have been sent to reason with her, to explain to her the danger she is running, and the ease with which she may avoid it. [*Suddenly bursting into forensic eloquence, to the disgust of Cauchon and the Inquisitor, who have listened to him so far with patronizing approval*] Men have dared to say that we are acting from hate; but God is our witness that they lie. Have we tortured her? No. Have we ceased to exhort her; to implore her to have pity on herself; to come to the bosom of her Church as an erring but beloved child? Have we—

CAUCHON [*interrupting drily*] Take care, Canon. All that you say is true; but if you make his lordship believe it I will not answer for your life, and hardly for my own.

WARWICK [*deprecating, but by no means denying*] Oh, my lord, you are very hard on us poor English. But we certainly do not share your pious desire to save The Maid: in fact I tell you now plainly that her death is a political necessity which I regret but cannot help. If The Church lets her go—

CAUCHON [*with fierce and menacing pride*] If The Church lets her go, woe to the man, were he the Emperor himself, who dares lay a finger on her! The Church is not subject to political necessity, my lord.

THE INQUISITOR [*interposing smoothly*] You need have no anxiety about the result, my lord. You have an invincible ally in the matter: one who is far more determined than you that she shall burn.

WARWICK. And who is this very convenient partisan, may I ask?

THE INQUISITOR. The Maid herself. Unless you put a gag in her mouth you cannot prevent her from convicting herself ten times over every time she opens it.

D'ESTIVET. That is perfectly true, my lord. My hair bristles on my head when I hear so young a creature utter such blasphemies.

WARWICK. Well, by all means do your best for her if you are quite sure it will be of no avail. [*Looking hard at Cauchon*] I should be sorry to have to act without the blessing of The Church.

CAUCHON [*with a mixture of cynical admiration and contempt*] And yet they say Englishmen are hypocrites! You play for your side, my lord, even at the peril of your soul. I cannot but admire such devotion; but I dare not go so far myself. I fear damnation.

WARWICK. If we feared anything we could never govern England, my lord. Shall I send your people in to you?

CAUCHON. Yes: it will be very good of your lordship to withdraw and allow the court to assemble.

Warwick turns on his heel, and goes out through the courtyard. Cauchon takes one of the judicial seats; and D'Estivet sits at the scribes' table, studying his brief.

CAUCHON [*casually, as he makes himself comfortable*] What scoundrels these English nobles are!

THE INQUISITOR [*taking the other judicial chair on Cauchon's left*] All secular power makes men scoundrels. They are not trained for the work; and they have not the Apostolic Succession. Our own nobles are just as bad.

The Bishop's assessors hurry into the hall, headed by Chaplain de Stogumber and Canon de Courcelles, a young priest of 30. The scribes sit at the table, leaving a chair vacant opposite D'Estivet. Some of the assessors take their seats: others stand chatting, waiting for the proceedings to begin formally. De Stogumber, aggrieved and obstinate, will not take his seat: neither will the Canon, who stands on his right.

CAUCHON. Good morning, Master de Stogumber. [*To the Inquisitor*] Chaplain to the Cardinal of England.

THE CHAPLAIN [*correcting him*] Of Winchester, my lord. I have to make a protest, my lord.

CAUCHON. You make a great many.

THE CHAPLAIN. I am not without support, my lord. Here is Master de Courcelles, Canon of Paris, who associates himself with me in my protest.

CAUCHON. Well, what is the matter?

THE CHAPLAIN [*sulkily*] Speak you, Master de Courcelles, since I do not seem to enjoy his lordship's confidence. [*He sits down in dudgeon next to Cauchon, on his right*].

COURCELLES. My lord: we have been at great pains to draw up an indictment of The Maid on sixtyfour counts. We are now told that they have been reduced, without consulting us.

THE INQUISITOR. Master de Courcelles: I am the culprit. I am overwhelmed with admiration for the zeal displayed in your sixtyfour counts; but in accusing a heretic, as in other things, enough is enough. Also you must remember that all the members of the court are not so subtle and profound as you, and that some of your very great learning might appear to them to be very great nonsense. Therefore I have thought it well to have your sixtyfour articles cut down to twelve—

COURCELLES [*thunderstruck*] Twelve!!!

THE INQUISITOR. Twelve will, believe me, be quite enough for your purpose.

THE CHAPLAIN. But some of the most important points have been reduced almost to nothing. For instance, The Maid has actually declared that the blessed saints Margaret and Catherine, and the holy Archangel Michael, spoke to her in French. That is a vital point.

THE INQUISITOR. You think, doubtless, that they should have spoken in Latin?

CAUCHON. No: he thinks they should have spoken in English.

THE CHAPLAIN. Naturally, my lord.

THE INQUISITOR. Well, as we are all here agreed, I think, that these voices of The Maid are the voices of evil spirits tempting her to her damnation, it would not be very courteous to you, Master de Stogumber, or to the King of England, to assume that English is the devil's native language. So let it pass. The matter is not wholly omitted from the twelve articles. Pray take your places, gentlemen; and let us proceed to business.

All who have not taken their seats, do so.

THE CHAPLAIN. Well, I protest. That is all.

COURCELLES. I think it hard that all our work should go for nothing. It is only another example of the diabolical influence which this woman exercises over the court. [*He takes his chair, which is on the Chaplain's right*].

CAUCHON. Do you suggest that I am under diabolical influence?

COURCELLES. I suggest nothing, my lord. But it seems to me that there is a conspiracy here to hush up the fact that The Maid stole the Bishop of Senlis's horse.

CAUCHON [*keeping his temper with difficulty*] This is not a police court. Are we to waste our time on such rubbish?

COURCELLES [*rising, shocked*] My lord: do you call the Bishop's horse rubbish?

THE INQUISITOR [*blandly*] Master de Courcelles: The Maid alleges that she paid handsomely for the Bishop's horse, and that if he did not get the money the fault was not hers. As that may be true, the point is one on which The Maid may well be acquitted.

COURCELLES. Yes, if it were an ordinary horse. But the Bishop's horse! how can she be acquitted for that? [*He sits down again, bewildered and discouraged*].

THE INQUISITOR. I submit to you, with great respect, that if we persist in trying The Maid on trumpery issues on which we may have to declare her innocent, she may escape us on the great main issue of heresy, on which she seems so far to insist on her own guilt. I will ask you, therefore, to say nothing, when The Maid is brought before us, of these stealings of horses, and dancings round fairy trees with the village children, and prayings at haunted wells, and a dozen other things which you were diligently inquiring into until my arrival. There is not a village girl in France against whom you could not prove such things: they all dance round haunted trees, and pray at magic wells. Some of them would steal the Pope's horse if they got the chance. Heresy, gentlemen, heresy is the charge we have to try. The detection and suppression of heresy is my peculiar business: I am here as an inquisitor, not as an ordinary magistrate. Stick to the heresy, gentlemen; and leave the other matters alone.

CAUCHON. I may say that we have sent to the girl's village

to make inquiries about her; and there is practically nothing serious against her.

THE CHAPLAIN COURCELLES.	[*rising and clamoring together*]	Nothing serious, my lord— What! The fairy tree not—

CAUCHON [*out of patience*] Be silent, gentlemen; or speak one at a time.

Courcelles collapses into his chair, intimidated.

THE CHAPLAIN [*sulkily resuming his seat*] That is what The Maid said to us last Friday.

CAUCHON. I wish you had followed her counsel, sir. When I say nothing serious, I mean nothing that men of sufficiently large mind to conduct an inquiry like this would consider serious. I agree with my colleague the Inquisitor that it is on the count of heresy that we must proceed.

LADVENU [*a young but ascetically fine-drawn Dominican who is sitting next Courcelles, on his right*] But is there any great harm in the girl's heresy? Is it not merely her simplicity? Many saints have said as much as Joan.

THE INQUISITOR [*dropping his blandness and speaking very gravely*] Brother Martin: if you had seen what I have seen of heresy, you would not think it a light thing even in its most apparently harmless and even lovable and pious origins. Heresy begins with people who are to all appearance better than their neighbours. A gentle and pious girl, or a young man who has obeyed the command of our Lord by giving all his riches to the poor, and putting on the garb of poverty, the life of austerity, and the rule of humility and charity, may be the founder of a heresy that will wreck both Church and Empire if not ruthlessly stamped out in time. The records of the holy Inquisition are full of histories we dare not give to the world, because they are beyond the belief of honest men and innocent women; yet they all began with saintly simpletons. I have seen this again and again. Mark what I say: the woman who quarrels with her clothes, and puts on the dress of a man, is like the man who throws off his fur gown and dresses like John the Baptist: they are followed, as surely as the night follows the day, by bands of wild women and men who refuse to wear any clothes at all. When maids will neither marry nor take regular vows, and men reject marriage and exalt their lusts into divine inspirations, then, as surely as the summer follows the spring, they begin with polygamy, and end by incest. Heresy at first seems innocent and even laudable; but it ends in such a monstrous horror of unnatural wickedness that the most tender-hearted among you, if you saw it at work as I have seen it, would clamor against the mercy of The Church in dealing with it. For two hundred years the Holy Office has striven with these diabolical madnesses; and it knows that they begin always by vain and ignorant persons setting up their own judgment against The Church, and taking it upon themselves to be the interpreters of God's will. You must not fall into the common error of mistaking these simpletons for liars and hypocrites. They believe honestly and sincerely that their diabolical inspiration is divine. Therefore you must be on your guard against your natural compassion. You are all, I hope, merciful men: how else could you have devoted your lives to the service of our gentle Savior? You are going to see before you a young girl, pious and chaste; for I must tell you, gentlemen, that the things said of her by our English friends are supported by no evidence, whilst there is abundant testimony that her excesses have been excesses of religion and charity and not of worldliness and wantonness. This girl is not one of those whose hard features are the sign of hard hearts, and whose brazen looks and lewd demeanor condemn them before they are accused. The devilish pride that has led her into her present peril has left no mark on her countenance. Strange as it may seem to you, it has even left no mark on her character outside those special matters in which she is proud; so that you will see a diabolical pride and a natural humility seated side by side in the selfsame soul. Therefore be on your guard. God forbid that I should tell you to harden your hearts; for her punishment if we condemn her will be so cruel that we should forfeit our own hope of divine mercy were there one grain of malice against her in our hearts. But if you hate cruelty—and if any man here does not hate it I command him on his soul's salvation to quit this holy court —I say, if you hate cruelty, remember that nothing is so cruel in its consequences as the toleration of heresy. Remember also that no court of law can be so cruel as the common people are to those whom they suspect of heresy. The heretic in the hands of the Holy Office is safe from violence, is assured of a fair trial, and cannot suffer death, even when guilty, if repentance follows sin. Innumerable lives of heretics have been saved because the Holy Office has taken them out of the hands of the people, and because the people have yielded them up, knowing that the Holy Office would deal with them. Before the Holy Inquisition existed, and even now when its officers are not within reach, the unfortunate wretch suspected of heresy, perhaps quite ignorantly and unjustly, is stoned, torn in pieces, drowned, burned in his house with all his innocent children, without a trial, unshriven, unburied save as a dog is buried: all of them deeds hateful to God and most cruel to man. Gentlemen: I am compassionate by nature as well as by my profession; and though the work I have to do may seem cruel to those who do not know how much more cruel it would be to leave it undone, I would go to the stake myself sooner than do it if I did not know its righteousness, its necessity, its essential mercy. I ask you to address yourself to this trial in that conviction. Anger is a bad counsellor: cast out anger. Pity is sometimes worse: cast out pity. But do not cast out mercy. Remember only that justice comes first. Have you anything to say, my lord, before we proceed to trial?

CAUCHON. You have spoken for me, and spoken better than I could. I do not see how any sane man could disagree with a word that has fallen from you. But this I will add. The crude heresies of which you have told us are horrible; but their horror is like that of the black death: they rage for a while and then die out, because sound and sensible men will not under any incitement be reconciled to nakedness and incest and polygamy and the like. But we are confronted today throughout Europe with a heresy that is spreading among men not weak in mind nor diseased in brain: nay, the stronger the mind, the more obstinate the heretic. It is neither discredited by fantastic extremes nor corrupted by the common lusts of the flesh; but it, too, sets up the private judgment of the single erring mortal against the considered wisdom and experience of The Church. The mighty structure of Catholic Christendom will never be shaken by naked madmen or by the sins of Moab and Ammon. But it may be betrayed from within, and brought to barbarous ruin and desolation, by this arch heresy which the English Commander calls Protestantism.

THE ASSESSORS [*whispering*] Protestantism! What was that? What does the Bishop mean? Is it a new heresy? The English Commander, he said. Did you ever hear of Protestantism? etc., etc.

CAUCHON [*continuing*] And that reminds me. What provision has the Earl of Warwick made for the defence of the secular arm should The Maid prove obdurate, and the people be moved to pity her?

THE CHAPLAIN. Have no fear on that score, my lord. The noble earl has eight hundred men-at-arms at the gates. She will not slip through our English fingers even if the whole city be on her side.

CAUCHON [*revolted*] Will you not add, God grant that she repent and purge her sin?

THE CHAPLAIN. That does not seem to me to be consistent; but of course I agree with your lordship.

CAUCHON [*giving him up with a shrug of contempt*] The court sits.

THE INQUISITOR. Let the accused be brought in.

LADVENU [*calling*] The accused. Let her be brought in.

Joan, chained by the ankles, is brought in through the arched door behind the prisoner's stool by a guard of English soldiers. With them is the Executioner and his assistants. They lead her to the prisoner's stool, and place themselves behind it after taking off her chain. She wears a page's black suit. Her long imprisonment and the strain of the examinations which have preceded the trial have left their mark on her; but her vitality still holds: she confronts the court unabashed, without a trace of the awe which their formal solemnity seems to require for the complete success of its impressiveness.

THE INQUISITOR [*kindly*] Sit down, Joan. [*She sits on the prisoner's stool*]. You look very pale today. Are you not well?

JOAN. Thank you kindly: I am well enough. But the Bishop sent me some carp; and it made me ill.

CAUCHON. I am sorry. I told them to see that it was fresh.

JOAN. You meant to be good to me, I know; but it is a fish that does not agree with me. The English thought you were trying to poison me—

CAUCHON } [*together*] { What!
THE CHAPLAIN } { No, my lord.

JOAN [*continuing*] They are determined that I shall be burnt as a witch; and they sent their doctor to cure me; but he was forbidden to bleed me because the silly people believe that a witch's witchery leaves her if she is bled; so he only called me filthy names. Why do you leave me in the hands of the English? I should be in the hands of The Church. And why must I be chained by the feet to a log of wood? Are you afraid I will fly away?

D'ESTIVET [*harshly*] Woman: it is not for you to question the court: it is for us to question you.

COURCELLES. When you were left unchained, did you not try to escape by jumping from a tower sixty feet high? If you cannot fly like a witch, how is it that you are still alive?

JOAN. I suppose because the tower was not so high then. It has grown higher every day since you began asking me questions about it.

D'ESTIVET. Why did you jump from the tower?

JOAN. How do you know that I jumped?

D'ESTIVET. You were found lying in the moat. Why did you leave the tower?

JOAN. Why would anybody leave a prison if they could get out?

D'ESTIVET. You tried to escape?

JOAN. Of course I did; and not for the first time either. If you leave the door of the cage open the bird will fly out.

D'ESTIVET [*rising*] That is a confession of heresy. I call the attention of the court to it.

JOAN. Heresy, he calls it! Am I a heretic because I try to escape from prison?

D'ESTIVET. Assuredly, if you are in the hands of The Church, and you wilfully take yourself out of its hands, you are deserting The Church; and that is heresy.

JOAN. It is great nonsense. Nobody could be such a fool as to think that.

D'ESTIVET. You hear, my lord, how I am reviled in the execution of my duty by this woman. [*He sits down indignantly*].

CAUCHON. I have warned you before, Joan, that you are doing yourself no good by these pert answers.

JOAN. But you will not talk sense to me. I am reasonable if you will be reasonable.

THE INQUISITOR [*interposing*] This is not yet in order. You forget, Master Promoter, that the proceedings have not been formally opened. The time for questions is after she has sworn on the Gospels to tell us the whole truth.

JOAN. You say this to me every time. I have said again and again that I will tell you all that concerns this trial. But I cannot tell you the whole truth: God does not allow the whole truth to be told. You do not understand it when I tell it. It is an old saying that he who tells too much truth is sure to be hanged. I am weary of this argument: we have been over it nine times already. I have sworn as much as I will swear; and I will swear no more.

COURCELLES. My lord: she should be put to the torture.

THE INQUISITOR. You hear, Joan? That is what happens to the obdurate. Think before you answer. Has she been shewn the instruments?

THE EXECUTIONER. They are ready, my lord. She has seen them.

JOAN. If you tear me limb from limb until you separate my soul from my body you will get nothing out of me beyond what I have told you. What more is there to tell that you could understand? Besides, I cannot bear to be hurt; and if you hurt me I will say anything you like to stop the pain. But I will take it all back afterwards; so what is the use of it?

LADVENU. There is much in that. We should proceed mercifully.

COURCELLES. But the torture is customary.

THE INQUISITOR. It must not be applied wantonly. If the accused will confess voluntarily, then its use cannot be justified.

COURCELLES. But this is unusual and irregular. She refuses to take the oath.

LADVENU [*disgusted*] Do you want to torture the girl for the mere pleasure of it?

COURCELLES [*bewildered*] But it is not a pleasure. It is the law. It is customary. It is always done.

THE INQUISITOR. That is not so, Master, except when the inquiries are carried on by people who do not know their legal business.

COURCELLES. But the woman is a heretic. I assure you it is always done.

CAUCHON [*decisively*] It will not be done today if it is not necessary. Let there be an end of this. I will not have it said that we proceeded on forced confessions. We have sent our best preachers and doctors to this woman to exhort and implore her to save her soul and body from the fire: we shall not now send the executioner to thrust her into it.

COURCELLES. Your lordship is merciful, of course. But it is a great responsibility to depart from the usual practice.

JOAN. Thou art a rare noodle, Master. Do what was done last time is thy rule, eh?

COURCELLES [*rising*] Thou wanton: dost thou dare call

me noodle?

THE INQUISITOR. Patience, Master, patience: I fear you will soon be only too terribly avenged.

COURCELLES [*mutters*] Noodle indeed! [*He sits down, much discontented*].

THE INQUISITOR. Meanwhile, let us not be moved by the rough side of a shepherd lass's tongue.

JOAN. Nay: I am no shepherd lass, though I have helped with the sheep like anyone else. I will do a lady's work in the house—spin or weave—against any woman in Rouen.

THE INQUISITOR. This is not a time for vanity, Joan. You stand in great peril.

JOAN. I know it: have I not been punished for my vanity? If I had not worn my cloth of gold surcoat in battle like a fool, that Burgundian soldier would never have pulled me backwards off my horse; and I should not have been here.

THE CHAPLAIN. If you are so clever at woman's work why do you not stay at home and do it?

JOAN. There are plenty of other women to do it; but there is nobody to do my work.

CAUCHON. Come! we are wasting time on trifles. Joan: I am going to put a most solemn question to you. Take care how you answer; for your life and salvation are at stake on it. Will you for all you have said and done, be it good or bad, accept the judgment of God's Church on earth? More especially as to the acts and words that are imputed to you in this trial by the Promoter here, will you submit your case to the inspired interpretation of the Church Militant?

JOAN. I am a faithful child of The Church. I will obey The Church—

CAUCHON [*hopefully leaning forward*] You will?

JOAN. —provided it does not command anything impossible.

Cauchon sinks back in his chair with a heavy sigh. The Inquisitor purses his lips and frowns. Ladvenu shakes his head pitifully.

D'ESTIVET. She imputes to The Church the error and folly of commanding the impossible.

JOAN. If you command me to declare that all that I have done and said, and all the visions and revelations I have had, were not from God, then that is impossible: I will not declare it for anything in the world. What God made me do I will never go back on; and what He has commanded or shall command I will not fail to do in spite of any man alive. That is what I mean by impossible. And in case The Church should bid me do anything contrary to the command I have from God, I will not consent to it, no matter what it may be.

THE ASSESSORS [*shocked and indignant*] Oh! The Church contrary to God! What do you say now? Flat heresy. This is beyond everything, etc., etc.

D'ESTIVET [*throwing down his brief*] My lord: do you need anything more than this?

CAUCHON. Woman: you have said enough to burn ten heretics. Will you not be warned? Will you not understand?

THE INQUISITOR. If the Church Militant tells you that your revelations and visions are sent by the devil to tempt you to your damnation, will you not believe that The Church is wiser than you?

JOAN. I believe that God is wiser than I; and it is His commands that I will do. All the things that you call my crimes have come to me by the command of God. I say that I have done them by the order of God: it is impossible for me to say anything else. If any Churchman says the contrary I shall not mind him: I shall mind God alone, whose command I always follow.

LADVENU [*pleading with her urgently*] You do not know what you are saying, child. Do you want to kill yourself? Listen. Do you not believe that you are subject to the Church of God on earth?

JOAN. Yes. When have I ever denied it?

LADVENU. Good. That means, does it not, that you are subject to our Lord the Pope, to the cardinals, the archbishops, and the bishops for whom his lordship stands here today?

JOAN. God must be served first.

D'ESTIVET. Then your voices command you not to submit yourself to the Church Militant?

JOAN. My voices do not tell me to disobey The Church; but God must be served first.

CAUCHON. And you, and not The Church, are to be the judge?

JOAN. What other judgment can I judge by but my own?

THE ASSESSORS [*scandalized*] Oh! [*They cannot find words*].

CAUCHON. Out of your own mouth you have condemned yourself. We have striven for your salvation to the verge of sinning ourselves: we have opened the door to you again and again; and you have shut it in our faces and in the face of God. Dare you pretend, after what you have said, that you are in a state of grace?

JOAN. If I am not, may God bring me to it: if I am, may God keep me in it!

LADVENU. That is a very good reply, my lord.

COURCELLES. Were you in a state of grace when you stole the Bishop's horse?

CAUCHON [*rising in a fury*] Oh, devil take the Bishop's horse and you too! We are here to try a case of heresy; and no sooner do we come to the root of the matter than we are thrown back by idiots who understand nothing but horses. [*Trembling with rage, he forces himself to sit down*].

THE INQUISITOR. Gentlemen, gentlemen: in clinging to these small issues you are The Maid's best advocates. I am not surprised that his lordship has lost patience with you. What does the Promoter say? Does he press these trumpery matters?

D'ESTIVET. I am bound by my office to press everything; but when the woman confesses a heresy that must bring upon her the doom of excommunication, of what consequence is it that she has been guilty also of offences which expose her to minor penances? I share the impatience of his lordship as to these minor charges. Only, with great respect, I must emphasize the gravity of two very horrible and blasphemous crimes which she does not deny. First, she has intercourse with evil spirits, and is therefore a sorceress. Second, she wears men's clothes, which is indecent, unnatural, and abominable; and in spite of our most earnest remonstrances and entreaties, she will not change them even to receive the sacrament.

JOAN. Is the blessed St Catherine an evil spirit? Is St Margaret? Is Michael the Archangel?

COURCELLES. How do you know that the spirit which appears to you is an archangel? Does he not appear to you as a naked man?

JOAN. Do you think God cannot afford clothes for him?

The assessors cannot help smiling, especially as the joke is against Courcelles.

LADVENU. Well answered, Joan.

THE INQUISITOR. It is, in effect, well answered. But no evil spirit would be so simple as to appear to a young girl in a guise that would scandalize her when he meant her to take him for a messenger from the Most High. Joan: The Church instructs you that these apparitions are demons seeking your soul's perdition. Do you accept the instruction of The Church?

JOAN. I accept the messenger of God. How could any faithful believer in The Church refuse him?

CAUCHON. Wretched woman: again I ask you, do you know what you are saying?

THE INQUISITOR. You wrestle in vain with the devil for her soul, my lord: she will not be saved. Now as to this matter of the man's dress. For the last time, will you put off that impudent attire, and dress as becomes your sex?

JOAN. I will not.

D'ESTIVET [*pouncing*] The sin of disobedience, my lord.

JOAN [*distressed*] But my voices tell me I must dress as a soldier.

LADVENU. Joan, Joan: does not that prove to you that the voices are the voices of evil spirits? Can you suggest to us one good reason why an angel of God should give you such shameless advice?

JOAN. Why, yes: what can be plainer commonsense? I was a soldier living among soldiers. I am a prisoner guarded by soldiers. If I were to dress as a woman they would think of me as a woman; and then what would become of me? If I dress as a soldier they think of me as a soldier, and I can live with them as I do at home with my brothers. That is why St Catherine tells me I must not dress as a woman until she gives me leave.

COURCELLES. When will she give you leave?

JOAN. When you take me out of the hands of the English soldiers. I have told you that I should be in the hands of The Church, and not left night and day with four soldiers of the Earl of Warwick. Do you want me to live with them in petticoats?

LADVENU. My lord: what she says is, God knows, very wrong and shocking; but there is a grain of worldly sense in it such as might impose on a simple village maiden.

JOAN. If we were as simple in the village as you are in your courts and palaces, there would soon be no wheat to make bread for you.

CAUCHON. That is the thanks you get for trying to save her, Brother Martin.

LADVENU. Joan: we are all trying to save you. His lordship is trying to save you. The Inquisitor could not be more just to you if you were his own daughter. But you are blinded by a terrible pride and self-sufficiency.

JOAN. Why do you say that? I have said nothing wrong. I cannot understand.

THE INQUISITOR. The blessed St Athanasius has laid it down in his creed that those who cannot understand are damned. It is not enough to be simple. It is not enough even to be what simple people call good. The simplicity of a darkened mind is no better than the simplicity of a beast.

JOAN. There is great wisdom in the simplicity of a beast, let me tell you; and sometimes great foolishness in the wisdom of scholars.

LADVENU. We know that, Joan: we are not so foolish as you think us. Try to resist the temptation to make pert replies to us. Do you see that man who stands behind you [*he indicates the Executioner*]?

JOAN [*turning and looking at the man*] Your torturer? But the Bishop said I was not to be tortured.

LADVENU. You are not to be tortured because you have confessed everything that is necessary to your condemnation. That man is not only the torturer: he is also the Executioner. Executioner: let The Maid hear your answers to my questions. Are you prepared for the burning of a heretic this day?

THE EXECUTIONER. Yes, Master.

LADVENU. Is the stake ready?

THE EXECUTIONER. It is. In the market-place. The English have built it too high for me to get near her and make the death easier. It will be a cruel death.

JOAN [*horrified*] But you are not going to burn me now?

THE INQUISITOR. You realize it at last.

LADVENU. There are eight hundred English soldiers waiting to take you to the market-place the moment the sentence of excommunication has passed the lips of your judges. You are within a few short moments of that doom.

JOAN [*looking round desperately for rescue*] Oh God!

LADVENU. Do not despair, Joan. The Church is merciful. You can save yourself.

JOAN [*hopefully*] Yes: my voices promised me I should not be burnt. St Catherine bade me be bold.

CAUCHON. Woman: are you quite mad? Do you not yet see that your voices have deceived you?

JOAN. Oh no: that is impossible.

CAUCHON. Impossible! They have led you straight to your excommunication, and to the stake which is there waiting for you.

LADVENU [*pressing the point hard*] Have they kept a single promise to you since you were taken at Compiègne? The devil has betrayed you. The Church holds out its arms to you.

JOAN [*despairing*] Oh, it is true: it is true: my voices have deceived me. I have been mocked by devils: my faith is broken. I have dared and dared; but only a fool will walk into a fire: God, who gave me my commonsense, cannot will me to do that.

LADVENU. Now God be praised that He has saved you at the eleventh hour! [*He hurries to the vacant seat at the scribes' table, and snatches a sheet of paper, on which he sets to work writing eagerly*].

CAUCHON. Amen!

JOAN. What must I do?

CAUCHON. You must sign a solemn recantation of your heresy.

JOAN. Sign? That means to write my name. I cannot write.

CAUCHON. You have signed many letters before.

JOAN. Yes; but someone held my hand and guided the pen. I can make my mark.

THE CHAPLAIN [*who has been listening with growing alarm and indignation*] My lord: do you mean that you are going to allow this woman to escape us?

THE INQUISITOR. The law must take its course, Master de Stogumber. And you know the law.

THE CHAPLAIN [*rising, purple with fury*] I know that there is no faith in a Frenchman. [*Tumult, which he shouts down*]. I know what my lord the Cardinal of Winchester will say when he hears of this. I know what the Earl of Warwick will do when he learns that you intend to betray him. There are eight hundred men at the gate who will see that this abominable witch is burnt in spite of your teeth.

THE ASSESSORS [*meanwhile*] What is this? What did he say? He accuses us of treachery! This is past bearing. No faith in a Frenchman! Did you hear that? This is an intolerable fellow. Who is he? Is this what English Churchmen are like? he must be mad or drunk, etc., etc.

THE INQUISITOR [*rising*] Silence, pray! Gentlemen: pray silence! Master Chaplain: bethink you a moment of your holy office: of what you are, and where you are. I direct you to sit down.

THE CHAPLAIN [*folding his arms doggedly, his face working convulsively*] I will NOT sit down.

CAUCHON. Master Inquisitor: this man has called me a traitor to my face before now.

THE CHAPLAIN. So you are a traitor. You are all traitors. You have been doing nothing but begging this damnable witch on your knees to recant all through this trial.

THE INQUISITOR [*placidly resuming his seat*] If you will not sit, you must stand: that is all.

THE CHAPLAIN. I will NOT stand [*he flings himself back into his chair*].

LADVENU [*rising with the paper in his hand*] My lord: here is the form of recantation for The Maid to sign.

CAUCHON. Read it to her.

JOAN. Do not trouble. I will sign it.

THE INQUISITOR. Woman: you must know what you are putting your hand to. Read it to her, Brother Martin. And let all be silent.

LADVENU [*reading quietly*] "I, Joan, commonly called The Maid, a miserable sinner, do confess that I have most grievously sinned in the following articles. I have pretended to have revelations from God and the angels and the blessed saints, and perversely rejected The Church's warnings that these were temptations by demons. I have blasphemed abominably by wearing an immodest dress, contrary to the Holy Scripture and the canons of The Church. Also I have clipped my hair in the style of a man, and, against all the duties which have made my sex specially acceptable in heaven, have taken up the sword, even to the shedding of human blood, inciting men to slay each other, invoking evil spirits to delude them, and stubbornly and most blasphemously imputing these sins to Almighty God. I confess to the sin of sedition, to the sin of idolatry, to the sin of disobedience, to the sin of pride, and to the sin of heresy. All of which sins I now renounce and abjure and depart from, humbly thanking you Doctors and Masters who have brought me back to the truth and into the grace of our Lord. And I will never return to my errors, but will remain in communion with our Holy Church and in obedience to our Holy Father the Pope of Rome. All this I swear by God Almighty and the Holy Gospels, in witness whereto I sign my name to this recantation."

THE INQUISITOR. You understand this, Joan?

JOAN [*listless*] It is plain enough, sir.

THE INQUISITOR. And it is true?

JOAN. It may be true. If it were not true, the fire would not be ready for me in the market-place.

LADVENU [*taking up his pen and a book, and going to her quickly lest she should compromise herself again*] Come, child: let me guide your hand. Take the pen. [*She does so; and they begin to write, using the book as a desk*] J.E.H.A.N.E. So. Now make your mark by yourself.

JOAN [*makes her mark, and gives him back the pen, tormented by the rebellion of her soul against her mind and body*] There!

LADVENU [*replacing the pen on the table, and handing the recantation to Cauchon with a reverence*] Praise be to God, my brothers, the lamb has returned to the flock; and the shepherd rejoices in her more than in ninety and nine just persons. [*He returns to his seat*].

THE INQUISITOR [*taking the paper from Cauchon*] We declare thee by this act set free from the danger of excommunication in which thou stoodest. [*He throws the paper down to the table*].

JOAN. I thank you.

THE INQUISITOR. But because thou hast sinned most presumptuously against God and the Holy Church, and that thou mayst repent thy errors in solitary contemplation, and be shielded from all temptation to return to them, we, for the good of thy soul, and for a penance that may wipe out thy sins and bring thee finally unspotted to the throne of grace, do condemn thee to eat the bread of sorrow and drink the water of affliction to the end of thy earthly days in perpetual imprisonment.

JOAN [*rising in consternation and terrible anger*] Perpetual imprisonment! Am I not then to be set free?

LADVENU [*mildly shocked*] Set free, child, after such wickedness as yours! What are you dreaming of?

JOAN. Give me that writing. [*She rushes to the table; snatches up the paper; and tears it into fragments*] Light your fire: do you think I dread it as much as the life of a rat in a hole? My voices were right.

LADVENU. Joan! Joan!

JOAN. Yes: they told me you were fools [*the word gives great offence*], and that I was not to listen to your fine words nor trust to your charity. You promised me my life; but you lied [*indignant exclamations*]. You think that life is nothing but not being stone dead. It is not the bread and water I fear: I can live on bread: when have I asked for more? It is no hardship to drink water if the water be clean. Bread has no sorrow for me, and water no affliction. But to shut me from the light of the sky and the sight of the fields and flowers; to chain my feet so that I can never again ride with the soldiers nor climb the hills; to make me breathe foul damp darkness, and keep from me everything that brings me back to the love of God when your wickedness and foolishness tempt me to hate Him: all this is worse than the furnace in the Bible that was heated seven times. I could do without my warhorse; I could drag about in a skirt; I could let the banners and the trumpets and the knights and soldiers pass me and leave me behind as they leave the other women, if only I could still hear the wind in the trees, the larks in the sunshine, the young lambs crying through the healthy frost, and the blessed blessed church bells that send my angel voices floating to me on the wind. But without these things I cannot live; and by your wanting to take them away from me, or from any human creature, I know that your counsel is of the devil, and that mine is of God.

THE ASSESSORS [*in great commotion*] Blasphemy! blasphemy! She is possessed. She said our counsel was of the devil. And hers of God. Monstrous! The devil is in our midst, etc., etc.

D'ESTIVET [*shouting above the din*] She is a relapsed heretic, obstinate, incorrigible, and altogether unworthy of the mercy we have shewn her. I call for her excommunication.

THE CHAPLAIN [*to the Executioner*] Light your fire, man. To the stake with her.

The Executioner and his assistants hurry out through the courtyard.

LADVENU. You wicked girl: if your counsel were of God would He not deliver you?

JOAN. His ways are not your ways. He wills that I go through the fire to His bosom; for I am His child, and you are not fit that I should live among you. That is my last word to you.

The soldiers seize her.

CAUCHON [*rising*] Not yet.

They wait. There is a dead silence. Cauchon turns to the Inquisitor with an inquiring look. The Inquisitor nods affirmatively. They rise solemnly, and intone the sentence antiphonally.

CAUCHON. We decree that thou art a relapsed heretic.

THE INQUISITOR. Cast out from the unity of the Church.

CAUCHON. Sundered from her body.

THE INQUISITOR. Infected with the leprosy of heresy.

CAUCHON. A member of Satan.

THE INQUISITOR. We declare that thou must be excommunicate.

CAUCHON. And now we do cast thee out, segregate thee, and abandon thee to the secular power.

THE INQUISITOR. Admonishing the same secular power that it moderate its judgment of thee in respect of death and division of the limbs. [*He resumes his seat*].

CAUCHON. And if any true sign of penitence appear in thee, to permit out Brother Martin to administer to thee the sacrament of penance.

THE CHAPLAIN. Into the fire with the witch [*he rushes at her, and helps the soldiers to push her out*].

Joan is taken away through the courtyard. The assessors rise in disorder, and follow the soldiers, except Ladvenu, who has hidden his face in his hands.

CAUCHON [*rising again in the act of sitting down*] No, no: this is irregular. The representative of the secular arm should be here to receive her from us.

THE INQUISITOR [*also on his feet again*] That man is an incorrigible fool.

CAUCHON. Brother Martin: see that everything is done in order.

LADVENU. My place is at her side, my lord. You must exercise your own authority. [*He hurries out*].

CAUCHON. These English are impossible: they will thrust her straight into the fire. Look!

He points to the courtyard, in which the glow and flicker of fire can now be seen reddening the May daylight. Only the Bishop and the Inquisitor are left in the court.

CAUCHON [*turning to go*] We must stop that.

THE INQUISITOR [*calmly*] Yes; but not too fast, my lord.

CAUCHON [*halting*] But there is not a moment to lose.

THE INQUISITOR. We have proceeded in perfect order. If the English choose to put themselves in the wrong, it is not our business to put them in the right. A flaw in the procedure may be useful later on: one never knows. And the sooner it is over, the better for that poor girl.

CAUCHON [*relaxing*] That is true. But I suppose we must see this dreadful thing through.

THE INQUISITOR. One gets used to it. Habit is everything. I am accustomed to the fire: it is soon over. But it is a terrible thing to see a young and innocent creature crushed between these mighty forces, The Church and the Law.

CAUCHON. You call her innocent!

THE INQUISITOR. Oh, quite innocent. What does she know of The Church and the Law? She did not understand a word we were saying. It is the ignorant who suffer. Come, or we shall be late for the end.

CAUCHON [*going with him*] I shall not be sorry if we are: I am not so accustomed as you.

They are going out when Warwick comes in, meeting them.

WARWICK. Oh, I am intruding. I thought it was all over. [*He makes a feint of retiring*].

CAUCHON. Do not go, my lord. It is all over.

THE INQUISITOR. The execution is not in our hands, my lord; but it is desirable that we should witness the end. So by your leave—[*He bows, and goes out through the courtyard*].

CAUCHON. There is some doubt whether your people have observed the forms of law, my lord.

WARWICK. I am told that there is some doubt whether your authority runs in this city, my lord. It is not in your diocese. However, if you will answer for that I will answer for the rest.

CAUCHON. It is to God that we both must answer. Good morning, my lord.

WARWICK. My lord: good morning.

They look at one another for a moment with unconcealed hostility. Then Cauchon follows the Inquisitor out. Warwick looks round. Finding himself alone, he calls for attendance.

WARWICK. Hallo: some attendance here! [*Silence*]. Hallo, there! [*Silence*]. Hallo! Brian, you young blackguard, where are you? [*Silence*]. Guard! [*Silence*]. They have all gone to see the burning: even that child.

The silence is broken by someone frantically howling and sobbing.

WARWICK. What in the devil's name—?

The Chaplain staggers in from the courtyard like a demented creature, his face streaming with tears, making the piteous sounds that Warwick has heard. He stumbles to the prisoner's stool, and throws himself upon it with heartrending sobs.

WARWICK [*going to him and patting him on the shoulder*] What is it, Master John? What is the matter?

THE CHAPLAIN [*clutching at his hands*] My lord, my lord: for Christ's sake pray for my wretched guilty soul.

WARWICK [*soothing him*] Yes, yes: of course I will. Calmly, gently—

THE CHAPLAIN [*blubbering miserably*] I am not a bad man, my lord.

WARWICK. No, no: not at all.

THE CHAPLAIN. I meant no harm. I did not know what it would be like.

WARWICK [*hardening*] Oh! You saw it, then?

THE CHAPLAIN. I did not know what I was doing. I am a hotheaded fool; and I shall be damned to all eternity for it.

WARWICK. Nonsense! Very distressing, no doubt; but it was not your doing.

THE CHAPLAIN [*lamentably*] I let them do it. If I had known, I would have torn her from their hands. You dont know: you havnt seen: it is so easy to talk when you dont know. You madden yourself with words: you damn yourself because it feels grand to throw oil on the flaming hell of your own temper. But when it is brought home to you; when you see the thing you have done; when it is blinding your eyes, stifling your nostrils, tearing your heart, then—then— [*Falling on his knees*] O God, take away this sight from me! O Christ, deliver me from this fire that is consuming me! She cried to Thee in the midst of it: Jesus! Jesus! Jesus! She is in Thy bosom; and I am in hell for evermore.

WARWICK [*summarily hauling him to his feet*] Come come, man! you must pull yourself together. We shall have the whole town talking of this. [*He throws him not too gently into a chair at the table*] If you have not the nerve to see these things, why do you not do as I do, and stay away?

THE CHAPLAIN [*bewildered and submissive*] She asked for a cross. A soldier gave her two sticks tied together. Thank God he was an Englishman! I might have done it; but I did not: I am a coward, a mad dog, a fool. But he was an Englishman too.

WARWICK. The fool! they will burn him too if the priests get hold of him.

THE CHAPLAIN [*shaken with a convulsion*] Some of the

people laughed at her. They would have laughed at Christ. They were French people, my lord: I know they were French.

WARWICK. Hush? someone is coming. Control yourself.

Ladvenu comes back through the courtyard to Warwick's right hand, carrying a bishop's cross which he has taken from a church. He is very grave and composed.

WARWICK. I am informed that it is all over, Brother Martin.

LADVENU [*enigmatically*] We do not know, my lord. It may have only just begun.

WARWICK. What does that mean, exactly?

LADVENU. I took this cross from the church for her that she might see it to the last: she had only two sticks that she put into her bosom. When the fire crept round us, and she saw that if I held the cross before her I should be burnt myself, she warned me to get down and save myself. My lord: a girl who could think of another's danger in such a moment was not inspired by the devil. When I had to snatch the cross from her sight, she looked up to heaven. And I do not believe that the heavens were empty. I firmly believe that her Savior appeared to her then in His tenderest glory. She called to Him and died. This is not the end for her, but the beginning.

WARWICK. I am afraid it will have a bad effect on the people.

LADVENU. It had, my lord, on some of them. I heard laughter. Forgive me for saying that I hope and believe it was English laughter.

THE CHAPLAIN [*rising frantically*] No: it was not. There was only one Englishman there that disgraced his country; and that was the mad dog, de Stogumber. [*He rushes wildly out, shrieking*] Let them torture him. Let them burn him. I will go pray among her ashes. I am no better than Judas: I will hang myself.

WARWICK. Quick, Brother Martin: follow him: he will do himself some mischief. After him, quick.

Ladvenu hurries out, Warwick urging him. The Executioner comes in by the door behind the judges' chairs; and Warwick, returning, finds himself face to face with him.

WARWICK. Well, fellow: who are you?

THE EXECUTIONER [*with dignity*] I am not addressed as fellow, my lord. I am the Master Executioner of Rouen: it is a highly skilled mystery. I am come to tell your lordship that your orders have been obeyed.

WARWICK. I crave your pardon, Master Executioner; and I will see that you lose nothing by having no relics to sell. I have your word, have I, that nothing remains, not a bone, not a nail, not a hair?

THE EXECUTIONER. Her heart would not burn, my lord; but everything that was left is at the bottom of the river. You have heard the last of her.

WARWICK [*with a wry smile, thinking of what Ladvenu said*] The last of her? Hm! I wonder!

EPILOGUE

A RESTLESS fitfully windy night in June 1456, *full of summer lightning after many days of heat. King Charles the Seventh of France, formerly Joan's Dauphin, now Charles the Victorious, aged* 51, *is in bed in one of his royal chateaux. The bed, raised on a dais of two steps, is towards the side of the room so as to avoid blocking a tall lancet window in the middle. Its canopy bears the royal arms in embroidery. Except for the canopy and the huge down pillows there is nothing to distinguish it from a broad settee with bed-clothes and a valance. Thus its occupant is in full view from the foot.*

Charles is not asleep: he is reading in bed, or rather looking at the pictures in Fouquet's Boccaccio with his knees doubled up to make a reading desk. Beside the bed on his left is a little table with a picture of the Virgin, lighted by candles of painted wax. The walls are hung from ceiling to floor with painted curtains which stir at times in the draughts. At first glance the prevailing yellow and red in these hanging pictures is somewhat flamelike when the folds breathe in the wind.

The door is on Charles's left, but in front of him close to the corner farthest from him. A large watchman's rattle, handsomely designed and gaily painted, is in the bed under his hand.

Charles turns a leaf. A distant clock strikes the half-hour softly. Charles shuts the book with a clap; throws it aside; snatches up the rattle; and whirls it energetically, making a deafening clatter. Ladvenu enters, 25 *years older, strange and stark in bearing, and still carrying the cross from Rouen. Charles evidently does not expect him; for he springs out of bed on the farther side from the door.*

CHARLES. Who are you? Where is my gentleman of the bedchamber? What do you want?

LADVENU [*solemnly*] I bring you glad tidings of great joy. Rejoice, O king; for the taint is removed from your blood, and the stain from your crown. Justice, long delayed, is at last triumphant.

CHARLES. What are you talking about? Who are you?

LADVENU. I am Brother Martin.

CHARLES. And who, saving your reverence, may Brother Martin be?

LADVENU. I held this cross when The Maid perished in the fire. Twenty-five years have passed since then: nearly ten thousand days. And on every one of those days I have prayed God to justify His daughter on earth as she is justified in heaven.

CHARLES [*reassured, sitting down on the foot of the bed*] Oh, I remember now. I have heard of you. You have a bee in your bonnet about The Maid. Have you been at the inquiry?

LADVENU. I have given my testimony.

CHARLES. Is it over?

LADVENU. It is over.

CHARLES. Satisfactorily?

LADVENU. The ways of God are very strange.

CHARLES. How so?

LADVENU. At the trial which sent a saint to the stake as a heretic and a sorceress, the truth was told; the law was upheld; mercy was shewn beyond all custom; no wrong was done but the final and dreadful wrong of the lying sentence and the pitiless fire. At this inquiry from which I have just come, there was shameless perjury, courtly corruption, calumny of the dead who did their duty according to their lights, cowardly evasion of the issue, testimony made of idle tales that could not impose on a ploughboy. Yet out of this insult to justice, this defamation of The Church, this orgy of lying and foolishness, the truth is set in the noonday sun on the hilltop; the white robe of innocence is cleansed from the smirch of the burning faggots; the holy life is sanctified; the true heart that lived through the flame is consecrated; a great lie is silenced for ever; and a great wrong is set right before all men.

CHARLES. My friend: provided they can no longer say that I was crowned by a witch and a heretic, I shall not fuss about how the trick has been done. Joan would not have fussed about it if it came all right in the end: she was not that sort: I knew her. Is her rehabilitation complete? I made it pretty clear that there was to be no nonsense about it.

LADVENU. It is solemnly declared that her judges were full of corruption, cozenage, fraud, and malice. Four falsehoods.

CHARLES. Never mind the falsehoods: her judges are dead.

LADVENU. The sentence on her is broken, annulled, annihilated, set aside as non-existent, without value or effect.

CHARLES. Good. Nobody can challenge my consecration now, can they?

LADVENU. Not Charlemagne nor King David himself was more sacredly crowned.

CHARLES [*rising*] Excellent. Think of what that means to me!

LADVENU. I think of what it means to her!

CHARLES. You cannot. None of us ever knew what anything meant to her. She was like nobody else; and she must take care of herself wherever she is; for *I* cannot take care of her; and neither can you, whatever you may think: you are not big enough. But I will tell you this about her. If you could bring her back to life, they would burn her again within six months, for all their present adoration of her. And you would hold up the cross, too, just the same. So [*crossing himself*] let her rest; and let you and I mind our own business, and not meddle with hers.

LADVENU. God forbid that I should have no share in her, nor she in me! [*He turns and strides out as he came, saying*] Henceforth my path will not lie through palaces, nor my conversation be with kings.

CHARLES [*following him towards the door, and shouting after him*] Much good may it do you, holy man! [*He returns to the middle of the chamber, where he halts, and says quizzically to himself*] That was a funny chap. How did he get in? Where are my people? [*He goes impatiently to the bed, and swings the rattle. A rush of wind through the open door sets the walls sway-*

ing agitatedly. The candles go out. He calls in the darkness] Hallo! Someone come and shut the windows: everything is being blown all over the place. [*A flash of summer lightning shews up the lancet window. A figure is seen in silhouette against it*] Who is there? Who is that? Help! Murder! [*Thunder. He jumps into bed, and hides under the clothes*].

JOAN'S VOICE. Easy, Charlie, easy. What art making all that noise for? No one can hear thee. Thourt asleep. [*She is dimly seen in a pallid greenish light by the bedside*].

CHARLES [*peeping out*] Joan! Are you a ghost, Joan?

JOAN. Hardly even that, lad. Can a poor burnt-up lass have a ghost? I am but a dream that thourt dreaming. [*The light increases: they become plainly visible as he sits up*] Thou looks older, lad.

CHARLES. I am older. Am I really asleep?

JOAN. Fallen asleep over thy silly book.

CHARLES. That's funny.

JOAN. Not so funny as that I am dead, is it?

CHARLES. Are you really dead?

JOAN. As dead as anybody ever is, laddie. I am out of the body.

CHARLES. Just fancy! Did it hurt much?

JOAN. Did what hurt much?

CHARLES. Being burnt.

JOAN. Oh, that! I cannot remember very well. I think it did at first; but then it all got mixed up; and I was not in my right mind until I was free of the body. But do not thou go handling fire and thinking it will not hurt thee. How hast been ever since?

CHARLES. Oh, not so bad. Do you know, I actually lead my army out and win battles? Down into the moat up to my waist in mud and blood. Up the ladders with the stones and hot pitch raining down. Like you.

JOAN. No! Did I make a man of thee after all, Charlie?

CHARLES. I am Charles the Victorious now. I had to be brave because you were. Agnes put a little pluck into me too.

JOAN. Agnes! Who was Agnes?

CHARLES. Agnes Sorel. A woman I fell in love with. I dream of her often. I never dreamed of you before.

JOAN. Is she dead, like me?

CHARLES. Yes. But she was not like you. She was very beautiful.

JOAN [*laughing heartily*] Ha ha! I was no beauty: I was always a rough one: a regular soldier. I might almost as well have been a man. Pity I wasnt: I should not have bothered you all so much then. But my head was in the skies; and the glory of God was upon me; and, man or woman, I should have bothered you as long as your noses were in the mud. Now tell me what has happened since you wise men knew no better than to make a heap of cinders of me?

CHARLES. Your mother and brothers have sued the courts to have your case tried over again. And the courts have declared that your judges were full of corruption and cozenage, fraud and malice.

JOAN. Not they. They were as honest a lot of poor fools as ever burned their betters.

CHARLES. The sentence on you is broken, annihilated, annulled: null, non-existent, without value or effect.

JOAN. I was burned, all the same. Can they unburn me?

CHARLES. If they could, they would think twice before they did it. But they have decreed that a beautiful cross be placed where the stake stood, for your perpetual memory and for your salvation.

JOAN. It is the memory and the salvation that sanctify the cross, not the cross that sanctifies the memory and the salvation. [*She turns away, forgetting him*] I shall outlast that cross. I shall be remembered when men will have forgotten where Rouen stood.

CHARLES. There you go with your self-conceit, the same as ever! I think you might say a word of thanks to me for having had justice done at last.

CAUCHON [*appearing at the window between them*] Liar!

CHARLES. Thank you.

JOAN. Why, if it isnt Peter Cauchon! How are you,

Peter? What luck have you had since you burned me?

CAUCHON. None. I arraign the justice of Man. It is not the justice of God.

JOAN. Still dreaming of justice, Peter? See what justice came to with me! But what has happened to thee? Art dead or alive?

CAUCHON. Dead. Dishonored. They pursued me beyond the grave. They excommunicated my dead body: they dug it up and flung it into the common sewer.

JOAN. Your dead body did not feel the spade and the sewer as my live body felt the fire.

CAUCHON. But this thing that they have done against me hurts justice; destroys faith; saps the foundation of the Church. The solid earth sways like the treacherous sea beneath the feet of men and spirits alike when the innocent are slain in the name of law, and their wrongs are undone by slandering the pure of heart.

JOAN. Well, well, Peter, I hope men will be the better for remembering me; and they would not remember me so well if you had not burned me.

CAUCHON. They will be the worse for remembering me: they will see in me evil triumphing over good, falsehood over truth, cruelty over mercy, hell over heaven. Their courage will rise as they think of you, only to faint as they think of me. Yet God is my witness I was just: I was merciful: I was faithful to my light: I could do no other than I did.

CHARLES [*scrambling out of the sheets and enthroning himself on the side of the bed*] Yes: it is always you good men that do the big mischiefs. Look at me! I am not Charles the Good, nor Charles the Wise, nor Charles the Bold. Joan's worshippers may even call me Charles the Coward because I did not pull her out of the fire. But I have done less harm than any of you. You people with your heads in the sky spend all your time trying to turn the world upside down; but I take the world as it is, and say that top-side-up is right-side-up; and I keep my nose pretty close to the ground. And I ask you, what king of France has done better, or been a better fellow in his little way?

JOAN. Art really king of France, Charlie? Be the English gone?

DUNOIS [*coming through the tapestry on Joan's left, the candles relighting themselves at the same moment, and illuminating his armour and surcoat cheerfully*] I have kept my word: the English are gone.

JOAN. Praised be God! now is fair France a province in heaven. Tell me all about the fighting, Jack. Was it thou that led them? Wert thou God's captain to thy death?

DUNOIS. I am not dead. My body is very comfortably asleep in my bed at Chateaudun; but my spirit is called here by yours.

JOAN. And you fought them my way, Jack: eh? Not the old way, chaffering for ransoms; but The Maid's way: staking life against death, with the heart high and humble and void of malice, and nothing counting under God but France free and French. Was it my way, Jack?

DUNOIS. Faith, it was any way that would win. But the way that won was always your way. I give you best, lassie. I wrote a fine letter to set you right at the new trial. Perhaps I should never have let the priests burn you; but I was busy fighting; and it was The Church's business, not mine. There was no use in both of us being burned, was there?

CAUCHON. Ay! put the blame on the priests. But I, who am beyond praise and blame, tell you that the world is saved neither by its priests nor its soldiers, but by God and His Saints. The Church Militant sent this woman to the fire; but even as she burned, the flames whitened into the radiance of the Church Triumphant.

The clock strikes the third quarter. A rough male voice is heard trolling an improvised tune.

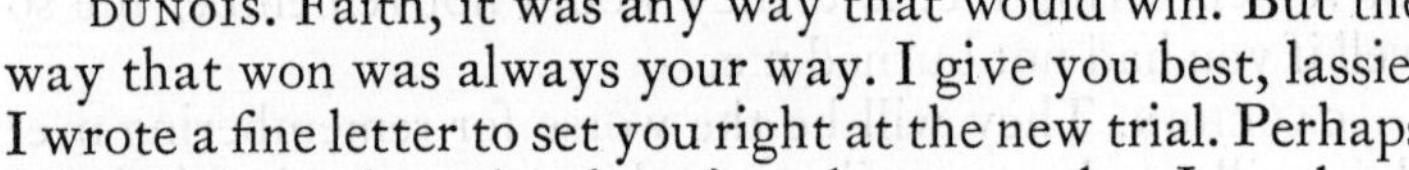

Rum tum trumpledum,
Bacon fat and rumpledum,

Old Saint mumpledum,
Pull his tail and stumpledum
O my Ma—ry Ann!

A ruffianly English soldier comes through the curtains and marches between Dunois and Joan.

DUNOIS. What villainous troubadour taught you that doggrel?

THE SOLDIER. No troubadour. We made it up ourselves as we marched. We were not gentlefolks and troubadours. Music straight out of the heart of the people, as you might say. Rum tum trumpledum, Bacon fat and rumpledum, Old Saint mumpledum, Pull his tail and stumpledum: that dont mean anything, you know; but it keeps you marching. Your servant, ladies and gentlemen. Who asked for a saint?

JOAN. Be you a saint?

THE SOLDIER. Yes, lady, straight from hell.

DUNOIS. A saint, and from hell!

THE SOLDIER. Yes, noble captain: I have a day off. Every year, you know. Thats my allowance for my one good action.

CAUCHON. Wretch! In all the years of your life did you do only one good action?

THE SOLDIER. I never thought about it: it came natural like. But they scored it up for me.

CHARLES. What was it?

THE SOLDIER. Why, the silliest thing you ever heard of. I—

JOAN [*interrupting him by strolling across to the bed, where she sits beside Charles*] He tied two sticks together, and gave them to a poor lass that was going to be burned.

THE SOLDIER. Right. Who told you that?

JOAN. Never mind. Would you know her if you saw her again?

THE SOLDIER. Not I. There are so many girls! and they all expect you to remember them as if there was only one in the world. This one must have been a prime sort; for I have a day off every year for her; and so, until twelve o'clock punctually, I am a saint, at your service, noble lords and lovely ladies.

CHARLES. And after twelve?

THE SOLDIER. After twelve, back to the only place fit for the likes of me.

JOAN [*rising*] Back there! You! that gave the lass the cross!

THE SOLDIER [*excusing his unsoldierly conduct*] Well, she asked for it; and they were going to burn her. She had as good a right to a cross as they had; and they had dozens of them. It was her funeral, not theirs. Where was the harm in it?

JOAN. Man: I am not reproaching you. But I cannot bear to think of you in torment.

THE SOLDIER [*cheerfully*] No great torment, lady. You see I was used to worse.

CHARLES. What! worse than hell?

THE SOLDIER. Fifteen years' service in the French wars. Hell was a treat after that.

Joan throws up her arms, and takes refuge from despair of humanity before the picture of the Virgin.

THE SOLDIER [*continuing*]—Suits me somehow. The day off was dull at first, like a wet Sunday. I dont mind it so much now. They tell me I can have as many as I like as soon as I want them.

CHARLES. What is hell like?

THE SOLDIER. You wont find it so bad, sir. Jolly. Like as if you were always drunk without the trouble and expense of drinking. Tip top company too: emperors and popes and kings and all sorts. They chip me about giving that young judy the cross; but I dont care: I stand up to them proper, and tell them that if she hadnt a better right to it than they, she'd be where they are. That dumbfounds them, that does. All they can do is gnash their teeth, hell fashion; and I just laugh, and go off singing the old chanty: Rum tum trumple —Hullo! Who's that knocking at the door?

They listen. A long gentle knocking is heard.

CHARLES. Come in.

The door opens; and an old priest, white-haired, bent, with a silly but benevolent smile, comes in and trots over to Joan.

THE NEWCOMER. Excuse me, gentle lords and ladies. Do not let me disturb you. Only a poor old harmless English rector. Formerly chaplain to the cardinal: to my lord of Winchester. John de Stogumber, at your service. [*He looks at them inquiringly*] Did you say anything? I am a little deaf, unfortunately. Also a little—well, not always in my right mind, perhaps; but still, it is a small village with a few simple people. I suffice: I suffice: they love me there; and I am able to do a little good. I am well connected, you see; and they indulge me.

JOAN. Poor old John! What brought thee to this state?

DE STOGUMBER. I tell my folks they must be very careful. I say to them, "If you only saw what you think about you would think quite differently about it. It would give you a great shock. Oh, a great shock." And they all say "Yes, parson: we all know you are a kind man, and would not harm a fly." That is a great comfort to me. For I am not cruel by nature, you know.

THE SOLDIER. Who said you were?

DE STOGUMBER. Well, you see, I did a very cruel thing once because I did not know what cruelty was like. I had not seen it, you know. That is the great thing: you must see it. And then you are redeemed and saved.

CAUCHON. Were not the sufferings of our Lord Christ enough for you?

DE STOGUMBER. No. Oh no: not at all. I had seen them in pictures, and read of them in books, and been greatly moved by them, as I thought. But it was no use: it was not our Lord that redeemed me, but a young woman whom I saw actually burned to death. It was dreadful: oh, most dreadful. But it saved me. I have been a different man ever since, though a little astray in my wits sometimes.

CAUCHON. Must then a Christ perish in torment in every age to save those that have no imagination?

JOAN. Well, if I saved all those he would have been cruel to if he had not been cruel to me, I was not burnt for nothing, was I?

DE STOGUMBER. Oh no; it was not you. My sight is bad: I cannot distinguish your features: but you are not she: oh no: she was burned to a cinder: dead and gone, dead and gone.

THE EXECUTIONER [*stepping from behind the bed curtains on Charles's right, the bed being between them*] She is more alive than you, old man. Her heart would not burn; and it would not drown. I was a master at my craft: better than the master of Paris, better than the master of Toulouse; but I could not kill The Maid. She is up and alive everywhere.

THE EARL OF WARWICK [*sallying from the bed curtains on the other side, and coming to Joan's left hand*] Madam: my congratulations on your rehabilitation. I feel that I owe you an apology.

JOAN. Oh, please dont mention it.

WARWICK [*pleasantly*] The burning was purely political. There was no personal feeling against you, I assure you.

JOAN. I bear no malice, my lord.

WARWICK. Just so. Very kind of you to meet me in that way: a touch of true breeding. But I must insist on apologizing very amply. The truth is, these political necessities sometimes turn out to be political mistakes; and this one was a veritable howler; for your spirit conquered us, madam, in spite of our faggots. History will remember me for your sake, though the incidents of the connection were perhaps a little unfortunate.

JOAN. Ay, perhaps just a little, you funny man.

WARWICK. Still, when they make you a saint, you will owe your halo to me, just as this lucky monarch owes his crown to you.

JOAN [*turning from him*] I shall owe nothing to any man: I owe everything to the spirit of God that was within me. But fancy me a saint! What would St Catherine and St Margaret say if the farm girl was cocked up beside them!

A clerical-looking gentleman in black frockcoat and trousers, and tall hat, in the fashion of the year 1920, *suddenly appears before them in the corner on their right. They all stare at him. Then they burst into uncontrollable laughter.*

THE GENTLEMAN. Why this mirth, gentlemen?

WARWICK. I congratulate you on having invented a most extraordinarily comic dress.

THE GENTLEMAN. I do not understand. You are all in fancy dress: I am properly dressed.

DUNOIS. All dress is fancy dress, is it not, except our natural skins?

THE GENTLEMAN. Pardon me: I am here on serious business, and cannot engage in frivolous discussions. [*He takes out a paper, and assumes a dry official manner*]. I am sent to announce to you that Joan of Arc, formerly known as The Maid, having been the subject of an inquiry instituted by the Bishop of Orleans—

JOAN [*interrupting*] Ah! They remember me still in Orleans.

THE GENTLEMAN [*emphatically, to mark his indignation at the interruption*]—by the Bishop of Orleans into the claim of the said Joan of Arc to be canonized as a saint—

JOAN [*again interrupting*] But I never made any such claim.

THE GENTLEMAN [*as before*]—The Church has examined the claim exhaustively in the usual course, and, having admitted the said Joan successively to the ranks of Venerable and Blessed,—

JOAN [*chuckling*] Me venerable!

THE GENTLEMAN. —has finally declared her to have been endowed with heroic virtues and favored with private revelations, and calls the said Venerable and Blessed Joan to the communion of the Church Triumphant as Saint Joan.

JOAN [*rapt*] Saint Joan!

THE GENTLEMAN. On every thirtieth day of May, being the anniversary of the death of the said most blessed daughter of God, there shall in every Catholic church to the end of time be celebrated a special office in commemoration of her; and it shall be lawful to dedicate a special chapel to her, and to place her image on its altar in every such church. And it shall be lawful and laudable for the faithful to kneel and address their prayers through her to the Mercy Seat.

JOAN. Oh no. It is for the saint to kneel. [*She falls on her knees, still rapt*].

THE GENTLEMAN [*putting up his paper, and retiring beside the Executioner*] In Basilica Vaticana, the sixteenth day of May, nineteen hundred and twenty.

DUNOIS [*raising Joan*] Half an hour to burn you, dear Saint; and four centuries to find out the truth about you!

DE STOGUMBER. Sir: I was chaplain to the Cardinal of Winchester once. They always would call him the Cardinal of England. It would be a great comfort to me and to my master to see a fair statue to The Maid in Winchester Cathedral. Will they put one there, do you think?

THE GENTLEMAN. As the building is temporarily in the hands of the Anglican heresy, I cannot answer for that.

A vision of the statue in Winchester Cathedral is seen through the window.

DE STOGUMBER. Oh look! look! that is Winchester.

JOAN. Is that meant to be me? I was stiffer on my feet.

The vision fades.

THE GENTLEMAN. I have been requested by the temporal authorities of France to mention that the multiplication of public statues to The Maid threatens to become an obstruction to traffic. I do so as a matter of courtesy to the said authorities, but must point out on behalf of The Church that The Maid's horse is no greater obstruction to traffic than any other horse.

JOAN. Eh! I am glad they have not forgotten my horse.

A vision of the statue before Rheims Cathedral appears.

JOAN. Is that funny little thing me too?

CHARLES. That is Rheims Cathedral where you had me crowned. It must be you.

JOAN. Who has broken my sword? My sword was never

broken. It is the sword of France.

DUNOIS. Never mind. Swords can be mended. Your soul is unbroken; and you are the soul of France.

The vision fades. The Archbishop and the Inquisitor are now seen on the right and left of Cauchon.

JOAN. My sword shall conquer yet: the sword that never struck a blow. Though men destroyed my body, yet in my soul I have seen God.

CAUCHON [*kneeling to her*] The girls in the field praise thee; for thou hast raised their eyes; and they see that there is nothing between them and heaven.

DUNOIS [*kneeling to her*] The dying soldiers praise thee, because thou art a shield of glory between them and the judgment.

THE ARCHBISHOP [*kneeling to her*] The princes of The Church praise thee, because thou hast redeemed the faith their worldlinesses have dragged through the mire.

WARWICK [*kneeling to her*] The cunning counsellors praise thee, because thou hast cut the knots in which they have tied their own souls.

DE STOGUMBER [*kneeling to her*] The foolish old men on their deathbeds praise thee, because their sins against thee are turned into blessings.

THE INQUISITOR [*kneeling to her*] The judges in the blindness and bondage of the law praise thee, because thou hast vindicated the vision and the freedom of the living soul.

THE SOLDIER [*kneeling to her*] The wicked out of hell praise thee, because thou hast shewn them that the fire that is not quenched is a holy fire.

THE EXECUTIONER [*kneeling to her*] The tormentors and executioners praise thee, because thou hast shewn that their hands are guiltless of the death of the soul.

CHARLES [*kneeling to her*] The unpretending praise thee, because thou hast taken upon thyself the heroic burdens that are too heavy for them.

JOAN. Woe unto me when all men praise me! I bid you remember that I am a saint, and that saints can work miracles. And now tell me: shall I rise from the dead, and come back to you a living woman?

A sudden darkness blots out the walls of the room as they all spring to their feet in consternation. Only the figures and the bed remain visible.

JOAN. What! Must I burn again? Are none of you ready to receive me?

CAUCHON. The heretic is always better dead. And mortal eyes cannot distinguish the saint from the heretic. Spare them. [*He goes out as he came*].

DUNOIS. Forgive us, Joan: we are not yet good enough for you. I shall go back to my bed. [*He also goes*].

WARWICK. We sincerely regret our little mistake; but political necessities, though occasionally erroneous, are still imperative; so if you will be good enough to excuse me— [*He steals discreetly away*].

THE ARCHBISHOP. Your return would not make me the man you once thought me. The utmost I can say is that though I dare not bless you, I hope I may one day enter into your blessedness. Meanwhile, however— [*He goes*].

THE INQUISITOR. I who am of the dead, testified that day that you were innocent. But I do not see how The Inquisition could possibly be dispensed with under existing circumstances. Therefore— [*He goes*].

DE STOGUMBER. Oh, do not come back: you must not come back. I must die in peace. Give us peace in our time, O Lord! [*He goes*].

THE GENTLEMAN. The possibility of your resurrection was not contemplated in the recent proceedings for your canonization. I must return to Rome for fresh instructions. [*He bows formally, and withdraws*].

THE EXECUTIONER. As a master in my profession I have to consider its interests. And, after all, my first duty is to my wife and children. I must have time to think over this. [*He goes*].

CHARLES. Poor old Joan! They have all run away from you except this blackguard who has to go back to hell at twelve o'clock. And what can I do but follow Jack Dunois' example, and go back to bed too? [*He does so*].

JOAN [*sadly*] Goodnight, Charlie.

CHARLES [*mumbling in his pillows*] Goo ni. [*He sleeps. The darkness envelops the bed*].

JOAN [*to the soldier*] And you, my one faithful? What comfort have you for Saint Joan?

THE SOLDIER. Well, what do they all amount to, these kings and captains and bishops and lawyers and such like? They just leave you in the ditch to bleed to death; and the next thing is, you meet them down there, for all the airs they give themselves. What I say is, you have as good a right to your notions as they have to theirs, and perhaps better. [*Settling himself for a lecture on the subject*] You see, it's like this. If— [*the first stroke of midnight is heard softly from a distant bell*]. Excuse me: a pressing appointment— [*He goes on tiptoe*].

The last remaining rays of light gather into a white radiance descending on Joan. The hour continues to strike.

JOAN. O God that madest this beautiful earth, when will it be ready to receive Thy saints? How long, O Lord, how long?

PROGRAM NOTE

The following note was included in the program on the first London production of the play:

For the convenience of professional critics, and the satisfaction of the general interest in Saint Joan, I had better point out how far the play this evening will depart from historical facts. It does not depart from ascertainable historical truth in any essential particular; but historical facts cannot be put on the stage exactly as they occurred, because they will not fit into its limits of time and space.

The visit of Joan to the castle of Vaucouleurs, and her conquest of its captain, occupy about twenty minutes on the stage. Actually she made three visits before she carried her point with him. The apparent miracle which impressed him was the news of the Battle of Herrings. Joan learnt this from the mouth-to-mouth wireless of the peasantry. She was therefore able to tell him what had happened several days before the news reached him by the official routine of mounted messenger. This seemed to him miraculous. A much simpler form of miracle has been substituted in the play to save tedious and unnecessary explanations.

Joan's second adventure: the visit to Chinon and the conquest of the Dauphin, has been compressed in the same way. Actually, Joan was received after days of hesitation, and sent to Poitiers to be examined by a body of Churchmen there before she was sent with reinforcements to Orleans. The miracles of the drowned blasphemer and the change of wind on the Loire are historical.

Joan's unconscious confessions of heresy at her trial, her recantation, her relapse, and her execution, occupied several days. On the stage they occupy forty minutes; but nothing essential is misrepresented; and nothing is omitted except the adjournments and matters irrelevant to the final issue.

The Epilogue is obviously not a representation of an actual scene, or even of a recorded dream; but it is none the less historical. Without it the play would be only a sensational tale of a girl who was burnt, leaving the spectators plunged in horror, despairing of humanity. The true tale of Saint Joan is a tale with a glorious ending; and any play that did not make this clear would be an insult to her memory.

But this play is more likely to puzzle by its conflict with current fictions about Saint Joan than by its adaptation of facts to the stage. In any generally accessible work of reference, and in such well known books as those by Mark Twain and Andrew Lang it is stated that Joan's trial was corrupt, her judges scoundrels, and the questions put to her devised to trap her into fatal admissions. For these slanders of the Church and the Inquisition there is not a shred of evidence in the records of the trial. Joan's judges were as straightforward as Joan herself; and the law took its regular course. She was burnt for heresy because she was guided by her inner light to the position taken two hundred years later by the Society of Friends, for which women were judicially flogged mercilessly at the instance of the Church of England, and would have been burnt had they been Joan's contemporaries. Her insistence on wearing male attire is still a punishable offence. The opinion of the court that her visions were temptations of the devil was quite sincere. Like all prisoners of war, Joan was tried by her political enemies instead of by an impartial international tribunal; but a medieval Catholic court was far more impartial than a modern national one. How violently the English were prejudiced against her may be seen in the scurrilous popular representation of her in the XVI century play of Henry VI (supposed to have been touched up by Shakespear); but it was not an English court that excommunicated her; and she would have been burnt equally if the Hundred Years War in France had been a purely civil one. Not until the Church privileged her private judgment and classed her visions and her inner light as celestial by canonizing her in 1904–1920 was the verdict of 1431 really reversed. Thus it cannot be too clearly understood that there were no villains in the tragedy of Joan's death. She was entirely innocent; but her excommunication was a genuine act of faith and piety; and her execution followed inevitably.

All the characters in the play are historical to the extent that they bear the names of persons who actually existed in Joan's time and were concerned with her as represented. But the information we have about them varies from such comparatively documented lives as those of Charles, Dunois, and Warwick, to that of Chaplain de Stogumber, who is known only by his having lost his temper and called Cauchon a traitor for accepting Joan's recantation. His Devonshire name is borrowed for the occasion. The English soldier represents a cherished tradition if not an authentic fact.

Several of the speeches and sallies in the play, especially those of Joan, are historical; and some of them may possibly sound like modern jokes: for instance, her use of the word *godons* (God damns) to denote English soldiers. One or two speeches have been transposed for stage purposes; and it has been assumed that the military conversation of Dunois may safely be founded on that of his colleague the Duc d'Alençon, who does not appear in the play.

To the more romantic spectators, I must break the news that though Joan inspired strong likes and dislikes, and was not at all bad looking, she had no love affairs. There is overwhelming testimony that her complete neutrality in this respect was accepted as evidence of her divine mission by her soldier comrades.

No portrait of Joan was made to her knowledge; but a head sculptured at Orleans by an artist who presumably saw her is so extraordinary, being obviously a portrait and yet stranger in its impressiveness and the spacing of its features than any ideal head, that it can be accounted for only as an image of a very singular woman; and no other such woman than Joan is discoverable.

JOHN BULL'S OTHER ISLAND

Written in 1904

First Performed London 1904

PREFACE TO THE HOME RULE EDITION OF 1912

[*I reprint this interim preface after much hesitation. It is based on two confident political assumptions that have since been not merely disproved but catastrophically shattered.*

The first was that Parliament in 1912 *was still what it had been in the heyday of Gladstonian Liberalism, when it was utterly inconceivable that an Act of constitutional reform which had been duly passed and assented-to by the Crown could be dropped into the waste paper basket because a handful of ladies and gentlemen objected to it, and the army officers' messes blustered mutinously against it.*

The second assumption was that Ireland was politically one and indivisible, and, consequently, that when Home Rule came, as it was evident it must come, the Protestants of Ireland must stand together and make the best of it. The possibility of a Partition by which Belfast Protestantism should accept Home Rule for itself in a concentration camp and thus abandon its co-religionists outside the camp to what must then inevitably become a Roman Catholic Home Rule Government of the rest of Ireland, was undreamt of.

How both these things nevertheless happened I have described in a postscript to the original preface which will be found on a later page. Readers who skip to that preface will lose nothing by missing this one except a possibly instructive example of how our eternal march into the future must always be a blindfold march. I guessed ahead, and guessed wrongly, whilst stupider and more ignorant fellow-pilgrims guessed rightly].

JOHN BULL'S OTHER ISLAND was written when a Unionist Government was in power, and had been in power with one brief interval for twenty years. The reason for this apparent eclipse of Home Rule was that the Liberal Party had during that period persisted in assuring the English people anxiously that it had no intention of doing anything for England (its object being to shew its abhorrence of Socialism) and that it cared for nothing but Home Rule in Ireland. Now as the English electors, being mostly worse off than the Irish, were anxious to have something done to alleviate their own wretched condition, they steadily voted for the Unionist Party (not because it was Unionist, but because it cared more for England than for Ireland), except on one occasion in 1893, when the Liberals put all their Home Rule tracts in the fire, and fought on a program of English Social Reform, known as the Newcastle Program, drawn up by my friend and Fabian colleague, Mr. Sidney Webb, and ingeniously foisted on the Liberals by myself and other Fabians disguised as artless Gladstonian members of certain little local caucuses which called themselves Liberal and Radical Associations, and were open to any passer-by who might astonish them by seeming to take an interest in their routine of bleeding candidates for registration expenses and local subscriptions. The program won the election for the Home Rulers. It was a close thing; but it won it. The Liberals then dropped it; and Lord Rosebery made his famous discovery that programs are a mistake, a view which, though supported with deep conviction by his Party, which still had no desire to do or mean or understand anything that could conceivably benefit anyone in England, had the immediate effect of extinguishing its noble author politically, and sending his party back into opposition for another ten years, at the end of which the Unionists, quite as ignorant of what the people of England were thinking about as Lord Rosebery, entered upon an impassioned defence of the employment of Chinese labor in South Africa without considering the fact that every one of their arguments was equally valid for the introduction of Chinese labor into Lancashire. And as the people of Lancashire were concerned about Lancashire and not at all about South Africa, the Unionist Party followed Lord Rosebery into the shades.

One consequence of this political swing of the pendulum was that John Bull's Other Island, which had up to that moment been a topical play, immediately became a historical one. Broadbent is no longer up-to-date. His *bête noir*, Mr. Joseph Chamberlain, has retired from public life. The controversies about Tariff Reform, the Education and Licensing Bills, and the South African war, have given way to the far more vital questions raised by Mr. Lloyd George's first unskilful essays in Collectivism, and to the agitation for Votes for Women. Broadbent is still strong on the question of Persia: stronger than he was on that of Armenia (probably because Persia is further off); but there is little left of the subjects that excited him in 1904 except Home Rule. And Home Rule is to be disposed of this year.

The Government will no doubt be glad to be rid of it. The English people, with prices up and wages down, care less, if possible, than they ever did about it. Even the governing classes are feeling the pressure of the Home Rule agitations in Egypt and India more than in Ireland; for the Irish, now confident that their battle is won, are keeping comparatively quiet, whilst in the East the question is in the acute stage in which the Government has to explain that really very few people have had confessions extorted by torture in the police stations, and that if the natives would only be reasonable and recognize the advantages of British rule, and their own utter unfitness for self-government, there would be no need to imprison nationalists either in India or Egypt; so that, in effect, the natives have themselves to thank for whatever unpleasantness may happen to them.

The only considerable body of Englishmen really concerned about Home Rule except as a Party question, are those members of the Free Churches, vulgarly called Dissenters or Nonconformists, who believe that the effect of Home Rule would be to deliver Ireland into the hands of the Roman Catholic Church, which they regard as The Scarlet Woman. It is clearly not a very deeply considered apprehension, because there is not a country in the world, not even Spain, where the people are so completely in the hands of the Roman Catholic Church as they are in Ireland under English rule and because of English rule. In the non-Protestant

Christian countries which are politically independent, the clericals are struggling, not to regain their lost supremacy (that survives only in Ireland), but for their houses, their property, their right to live in the country they were born in, and to have the political weight due to their merits; for they have merits: the priest is not so black as he is painted in all free countries nowadays. But our Free Churchmen are too much afraid of the Pope, and of the confessional, and of the priest in the house, to see how weak these forces are in the face of democracy. Also, they are not all well off enough to buy plays in six-shilling, or even in eighteenpenny volumes. Therefore, I think it opportune to issue this cheap edition of John Bull's Other Island this Home Rule Year, because its preface was written by an Irishman of Protestant family and Protestant prejudices, and shews that the one way in which the power of the priest can be kept within its proper limits in Ireland is by setting the Irish people free to take it in hand themselves without seeming to be treacherously taking the side of England against their own country.

Still more needed is this cheap edition in Ireland, where nobody can well afford to pay more than sixpence for anything, since, if I may put it elliptically, the only people in Ireland who can afford more than sixpence are those who live in England. I should like to call the attention of my nervous fellow Protestants in Ireland to the fact that in Italy, the centre of Roman Catholicism, the Pope is in a position closely resembling what that of Louis XVI. would have been during the first years of the French Revolution if he, like the Pope, had had no wife to bring him to the scaffold by tempting him to betray his country to a foreign foe. Also that in France, in spite of the revocation of the Edict of Nantes by the Roman Catholic Church at the height of its power, the Huguenots have always wielded, and still wield to-day, a power that is out of all proportion to their comparative numbers, and even, I am afraid I must add, to their merits. The Huguenot of Ulster is a coward only when he breaks his own backbone by taking the part of a foreign country against his own. Shut him up in Derry with an English King besieging him, and he does not shriek for the Germans to come and help him as if the thumbscrews of the Spanish Armada were already on his hands: he chalks up No Surrender merrily, and puts up one of the famous fights of history. After all, what is the use of protesting that you will not be governed from Rome if the alternative is to be governed from London? The great Protestant Irishmen have been all the more powerful because they loved Ireland better, not only than Rome, but than England. Why was it that the priests had no power to impose a Roman Catholic Leader on the Home Rule movement instead of Parnell? Simply because Parnell was so proud of his Irish birthright that he would rather have been one of even a persecuted minority in an Irish parliament than the Premier of an English Cabinet. He was not afraid of his countrymen: he knew that Protestantism could hold its own only too well in a free Ireland; and even if he had not known it he would have taken his chance rather than sell his birthright and his country. It is the essential dishonor of acting as a foreign garrison in a land where they are not foreigners that makes the position of the Orangemen so impossible, and breaks in them the spirit that animates every man in Europe who is fighting for a minority; and what man of any dignity to-day is not one of a minority that cries in the wilderness against one or other of the manifold iniquities and falsehoods of our civilization? I think if I as a Home Ruler (and many other less orthodox things) can live in England and hold my own in a minority which on some very sensitive points reaches the odds of about 1 to 48,000,000, an Ulster Orangeman should be able to face Home Rule without his knees knocking shamefully in the face of a contemptuous England which despises him none the less because his cowardice seems to serve her own turn.

There are, I know, men and women who are political perverts by nature. The supreme misfortune of being born with one's natural instincts turned against nature by a freak of nature is a phenomenon that occurs politically as well as physiologically. There are Poles who are devoted with all their soul to Russia and the maintenance of Russian rule in Poland, Persians who are risking their lives to introduce it in Persia, Indians and Egyptians who are ready to sacrifice all they possess for England and English rule. And it is not to be denied that among these are persons of high character and remarkable ability, comparing very favorably with the dregs of the nationalist movements, which, just because they are national and normal, are made up of all sorts, and consequently have dregs: pretty nasty ones too. For that matter, if ever a Book of Spies be written, it will include examples of courage, conviction, perseverance, and ability, that will almost persuade shallow people that spies are the real heroes of military history. Even in more personal relations, natural passion cannot pretend to inspire more intense devotion than perverted passion. But when all is said, the pervert, however magnificently he may conduct his campaign against nature, remains abhorrent. When Napoleon, though he boasted of having made peers and marshals of peasants and ostlers, drew the line at promoting a spy, he followed a universal instinct and a sound one. When the Irish Catholic who, feeling bitterly that the domination of the priest is making his own lot hopeless, nevertheless stands shoulder to shoulder with the priest for Home Rule against Dublin Castle, he is behaving naturally and rightly. When the Orangeman sacrifices his nationality to his hatred of the priest, and fights against his own country for its conqueror, he is doing something for which, no matter how bravely he fights, history and humanity will never forgive him: English history and humanity, to their credit be it said, least of all.

Please do not suppose for a moment that I propose that the Irish Protestant should submit to the Irish Roman Catholic. I reproach the Irish Roman Catholic for his submission to Rome exactly as I reproach the Orangeman for his submission to England. If Catholicism is to be limited in Ireland by any geographical expression (in which case it ceases to be Catholic) let it be Irish Catholicism, not Italian Catholicism. Let us maintain our partnership with Rome as carefully as our partnership with England; but let it be, in the one case as in the other, a free partnership. But the Irish Catholics are not Italian in their politics. They do not oppose Home Rule; and that gives them the right to the support of every Irish Protestant until Home Rule is achieved. After that, let us by all means begin a civil war next day if we are fools enough. A war for an idea may be a folly; but it is not a dishonor. Both parties would be fighting for Ireland; and though the slaying of an Irishman by an Irishman for Ireland may be a tragedy—may be even a crime to those who think that all war is crime—at least it is not unnatural crime, like the slaying of an Irishman by an Irishman for England's sake. There will, of course, be no war of religion: I have shewn in this book that the Protestant under Home Rule will be far safer and stronger than he is today; but even if there were, that is the way to look at it.

The question is still more important for England than for Ireland, in spite of England's indifference to it. In Ireland we are still sane: we do not sneer at our country as "Little Ireland," and cheer for a doubtful commercial speculation called The Empire which we could not point out accurately on the map, and which is populated by such an overwhelming majority of what an Irish peasant would call "black heathens," that they force us to punish our own missionaries for asking them to buy and read The Bible, and compel the Protestant Passive Resisters, who will be sold up rather than pay a rate to maintain a Church school, to pay without a murmur for the establishment of the Roman Catholic Church in Malta. Formerly "Little England," the "right little, tight little Island," despised Spain for her imperial policy, and saw her lose her place, not only among the empires, but even among the nations, with self-satisfied superiority. Today England is letting herself be dragged into the path of Spain. She dreams of nothing but the old beginning: an Invincible Armada. Spain reckoned without the Lord of Hosts, who scattered that Invincible Armada for Little England. The modern Imperialist does not believe in the Lord of Hosts; but the Armada was defeated for all that, though England's fleet was far more inferior to it than the German fleet will ever again be to the English fleet. The Lord of Hosts may not be quite the sort of power that Philip of Spain conceived it to be: many of us are dropping the personal pronoun, as I have just dropped it lest I should be prosecuted for superstition by the Society for the Encouragement of Cruelty to Animals; but it can still send bigger fleets to the bottom than England can build, and exalt smaller nations than England ever was above drifting congeries of derelict regions held desperately together by terrified soldiers trying to wave half a dozen flags all at once in the name of Empire: a name that every man who has ever felt the sacredness of his own native soil to him, and thus learnt to regard that feeling in other men as something holy and inviolable, spits out of his mouth with enormous contempt.

Not that I have any delusions about Drake and his Elizabethan comrades: they were pirates and slave-traders, not a whit better than the Algerine corsairs who shared with them what modern idiots call "the command of the sea" (much the sea cares about their command!); but it is better to be a pirate trading in slaves out of sheer natural wickedness than a bankrupt in a cocked hat, doing the same things, and worse, against your own conscience, because you are paid for it and are afraid to do anything else. Drake thought nothing of burning a Spanish city; but he was not such a fool as to suppose that if he told off some of his crew to stay and govern that Spanish city by force when it was rebuilt, all the reasonable inhabitants of that town would recognize the arrangement as an enormous improvement, and be very much obliged to him, which is the modern Imperial idea. To singe the King of Spain's beard; pick his pocket; and run away, was, in the absence of any international police, a profitable bit of sport, if a rascally one; but if Drake had put a chain round the King's neck and led him round a prisoner for the rest of his life, he would have suffered as much by such a folly as the King, and probably died sooner of worry, anxiety, expense, and loss through the neglect of his own proper affairs, than the King would have died of captivity. Bermondsey goes to the dogs whilst those whose business it is to govern it are sitting on Bengal; and the more Bengal kicks, the more Bermondsey is neglected, except by the tax collector. The notion that the way to prosper is to insist on managing everybody else's affairs is, on the face of it, a fool's notion. It is at bottom the folly of the ignorant simpletons who long to be kings and chiefs because they imagine that a king or a chief is an idle voluptuary with lots of money, leisure, and power over others, to use irresponsibly for his own amusement.

In short, then, the future is not to the empires, but to federations of self-governing nations, exactly as, within these nations, the future is not to Capitalist Oligarchies, but to Collectivist organizations of free and equal citizens. In short, to Commonwealths.

In expressing this irresistible sentiment of nationality with all the rhetoric to which it lends itself, I am not forgetting that there are international rights as well as national ones. We are not only natives within our own frontiers but inheritors of the earth. England has rights in Ireland as Ireland has rights in England. I demand of every nation right of ingress and egress, roads, police, an efficient post office, and, in reason, freedom of conscience. I am prepared to steam-roller Tibet if Tibet persist in refusing me my international rights. If the Moors and Arabs cannot or will not secure these common human conditions for me in North Africa, I am quite prepared to co-operate with the French, the Italians, and the Spaniards in Morocco, Algeria, Tunisia, and Tripoli, with the Russians in Siberia, with all three and the English and Germans as well in Africa, or with the Americans in the hunting grounds of the red man, to civilize these places; though I know as well as anyone that there are many detestable features in our civilization, many virtues in village and tribal communities, and a very large alloy indeed of brigandage in our explorations and colonizations.

I know also that what compels us to push our frontiers farther and farther into regions we call barbarous is the necessity of policing, not the barbarians, but the European dregs and riffraff who set up little hells of anarchy and infamy just beyond the border, and thus compel us to advance and rope them in, step by step, no matter how much we are adding to that "white man's burden," which is none the less a real thing because it is not specially a white man's burden any more than it is specially an Englishman's burden, as most of Mr. Kipling's readers seem to interpret it. Tribes must make themselves into nations before they can claim the rights of nations; and this they can do only by civilization.

Also I cannot deny that the exclusion of the Chinese from America and Australia is a violation of international right which the Chinese will be perfectly justified in resisting by arms as soon as they feel strong enough. If nations are to limit immigration, inter-marriage with foreigners, and even international trade by tariffs, it had better be done by international law than by arbitrary national force as at present. It will be seen that I am under no delusion as to the freedom of Nationalism from abuse. I know that there are abuses in England which would not exist if she were governed by Germany, and that there will no doubt be abuses in Ireland under Home Rule which do not exist under English rule, just as things have been done under the Irish Local Government Act that the old oligarchical grand juries would not have tolerated. There are, indeed, a hundred horses on which I could ride off if I wished to shirk the main issue. But when all is said, it is so certain that in the long run all civilized nations must at the same time become more dependent one on another and do their own governing work themselves, that if Ireland refused Home Rule now, it would sooner or later be forced on her by England because England will need all her time and political energy for her own affairs when once she realizes that the day for letting them slide and muddling through is past.

LONDON,
19th January 1912.

PREFACE FOR POLITICIANS
(TO THE FIRST EDITION IN 1906)

JOHN BULL'S OTHER ISLAND was written in 1904 at the request of Mr William Butler Yeats, as a patriotic contribution to the repertory of the Irish Literary Theatre. Like most people who have asked me to write plays, Mr Yeats got rather more than he bargained for. The play was at that time beyond the resources of the new Abbey Theatre, which the Irish enterprise owed to the public spirit of Miss A. E. F. Horniman (an Englishwoman, of course), who, twelve years ago, played an important part in the history of the modern English stage as well as in my own personal destiny by providing the necessary capital for that memorable season at the Avenue Theatre which forced my Arms and The Man and Mr Yeats's Land of Heart's Desire on the recalcitrant London playgoer, and gave a third Irish playwright, Dr John Todhunter, an opportunity which the commercial theatres could not have afforded him.

There was another reason for changing the destination of John Bull's Other Island. It was uncongenial to the whole spirit of the neo-Gaelic movement, which is bent on creating a new Ireland after its own ideal, whereas my play is a very uncompromising presentment of the real old Ireland. The next thing that happened was the production of the play in London at the Court Theatre by Messrs Vedrenne and Barker, and its immediate and enormous popularity with delighted and flattered English audiences. This constituted it a successful commercial play, and made it unnecessary to resort to the special machinery or tax the special resources of the Irish Literary Theatre for its production.

HOW TOM BROADBENT TOOK IT

Now I have a good deal more to say about the relations between the Irish and the English than will be found in my play. Writing the play for an Irish audience, I thought it would be good for them to be shewn very clearly that the loudest laugh they could raise at the expense of the absurdest Englishman was not really a laugh on their side; that he would succeed where they would fail; that he could inspire strong affection and loyalty in an Irishman who knew the world and was moved only to dislike, mistrust, impatience and even exasperation by his own countrymen; that his power of taking himself seriously, and his insensibility to anything funny in danger and destruction, was the first condition of economy and concentration of force, sustained purpose, and rational conduct. But the need for this lesson in Ireland is the measure of its demoralizing superfluousness in England. English audiences very naturally swallowed it eagerly and smacked their lips over it, laughing all the more heartily because they felt that they were taking a caricature of themselves with the most tolerant and large-minded goodhumor. They were perfectly willing to allow me to represent Tom Broadbent as infatuated in politics, hypnotized by his newspaper leader-writers and parliamentary orators into an utter paralysis of his common sense, without moral delicacy or social tact, provided I made him cheerful, robust, goodnatured, free from envy, and above all, a successful muddler-through in business and love. Not only did no English critic allow that the success in business of Messrs English Broadbent and Irish Doyle might possibly have been due to some extent to Doyle, but one writer actually dwelt with much feeling on the pathos of Doyle's failure as an engineer (a circumstance not mentioned nor suggested in my play) in contrast with Broadbent's solid success. No doubt, when the play is performed in Ireland, the Dublin critics will regard it as self-evident that without Doyle Broadbent would have become bankrupt in six months. I should say, myself, that the combination was probably much more effective than either of the partners would have been alone. I am persuaded further—without pretending to know more about it than anyone else—that Broadbent's special contribution was simply the strength, self-satisfaction, social confidence and cheerful bumptiousness that money, comfort, and good feeding bring to all healthy people; and that Doyle's special contribution was the freedom from illusion, the power of facing facts, the nervous industry, the sharpened wits, the sensitive pride of the imaginative man who has fought his way up through social persecution and poverty. I do not say that the confidence of the Englishman in Broadbent is not for the moment justified. The virtues of the English soil are not less real because they consist of coal and iron, not of metaphysical sources of character. The virtues of Broadbent are not less real because they are the virtues of the money that coal and iron have produced. But as the mineral virtues are being discovered and developed in other soils, their derivative virtues are appearing so rapidly in other nations that Broadbent's relative advantage is vanishing. In truth I am afraid (the misgiving is natural to a by-this-time slightly elderly playwright) that Broadbent is out of date. The successful Englishman of today, when he is not a transplanted Scotchman or Irishman, often turns out on investigation to be, if not an American, an Italian, or a Jew, at least to be depending on the brains, the nervous energy, and the freedom from romantic illusions (often called cynicism) of such foreigners for the management of his sources of income. At all events I am persuaded that a modern nation that is satisfied with Broadbent is in a dream. Much as I like him, I object to be governed by him, or entangled in his political destiny. I therefore propose to give him a piece of my mind here, as an Irishman, full of an instinctive pity for those of my fellow-creatures who are only English.

WHAT IS AN IRISHMAN?

When I say that I am an Irishman I mean that I was born in Ireland, and that my native language is the English of Swift and not the unspeakable jargon of the mid-XIX century London newspapers. My extraction is the extraction of most Englishmen: that is, I have no trace in me of the commercially imported North Spanish strain which passes for aboriginal Irish: I am a genuine typical Irishman of the Danish, Norman, Cromwellian, and (of course) Scotch invasions. I am violently and arrogantly Protestant by family tradition; but let no English Government therefore count on my allegiance: I am English enough to be an inveterate Republican and Home Ruler. It is true that one of my grandfathers was an Orangeman; but then his sister was an abbess; and his uncle, I am proud to say, was hanged as a rebel. When I look round me on the hybrid cosmopolitans, slum poisoned or square pampered, who call themselves Englishmen today, and see them bullied by the Irish Protestant garrison as no Bengalee now lets himself be bullied by an Englishman; when I see the Irishman everywhere standing clearheaded, sane, hardily callous to the boyish sentimentalities, susceptibilities, and credulities that make the Englishman the dupe of every charlatan and the idolater of every numskull, I perceive that Ireland is the only spot on earth which still produces the ideal Englishman of history. Blackguard, bully, drunkard, liar, foulmouth, flatterer, beggar, backbiter, venal functionary, corrupt judge, envious friend, vindictive opponent, unparalleled political traitor: all these your Irishman may easily be, just as he may be a gentleman (a species extinct in England, and nobody a penny the worse); but he is never quite the hysterical, nonsense-crammed, fact-proof, truth-terrified, unballasted sport of all the bogey panics and all the silly enthusiasms that now calls itself "God's Englishman." England cannot do without its Irish and its Scots today, because it cannot do without at least a little sanity.

THE PROTESTANT GARRISON

The more Protestant an Irishman is—the more English he is, if it flatters you to have it put that way, the more intolerable he finds it to be ruled by English instead of Irish folly. A "loyal" Irishman is an abhorrent phenomenon, because it is an unnatural one. No doubt English rule is vigorously exploited in the interests of the property, power, and promotion of the Irish classes as against the Irish masses. Our delicacy is part of a keen sense of reality which makes us a very practical, and even, on occasion, a very coarse people. The Irish soldier takes the King's shilling and drinks the King's health; and the Irish squire takes the title deeds of the English settlement and rises uncovered to the strains of the English national anthem. But do not mistake this cupboard loyalty for anything deeper. It gains a broad base from the normal attachment of every reasonable man to the established government as long as it is bearable; for we all, after a certain age, prefer peace to revolution and order to chaos, other things being equal. Such considerations produce loyal Irishmen as they produce loyal Poles and Fins, loyal Hindoos, loyal Filipinos, and faithful slaves. But there is nothing more in it than that. If there is an entire lack of gall in the feeling of the Irish gentry towards the English, it is because the Englishman is always gaping admiringly at the Irishman as at some clever child prodigy. He overrates him with a generosity born of a traditional conviction of his own superiority in the deeper aspects of human character. As the Irish gentleman, tracing his pedigree to the conquest or one of the invasions, is equally convinced that if this superiority really exists, he is the genuine true blue heir to it, and as he is easily able to hold his own in all the superficial social accomplishments, he finds English society agreeable, and English houses very comfortable, Irish establishments being generally straitened by an attempt to keep a park and a stable on an income which would not justify an Englishman in venturing upon a wholly detached villa.

OUR TEMPERAMENTS CONTRASTED

But however pleasant the relations between the Protestant garrison and the English gentry may be, they are always essentially of the nature of an *entente cordiale* between foreigners. Personally I like Englishmen much better than Irishmen (no doubt because they make more of me) just as many Englishmen like Frenchmen better than Englishmen, and never go on board a Peninsular and Oriental steamer when one of the ships of the Messageries Maritimes is available. But I never think of an Englishman as my countryman. I should as soon think of applying that term to a German. And the Englishman has the same feeling. When a Frenchman fails to make the distinction, we both feel a certain disparagement involved in the misapprehension. Macaulay, seeing that the Irish had in Swift an author worth stealing, tried to annex him by contending that he must be classed as an Englishman because he was not an aboriginal Celt. He might as well have refused the name of Briton to Addison because he did not stain himself blue and attach scythes to the poles of his sedan chair. In spite of all such trifling with facts, the actual distinction between the idolatrous Englishman and the fact-facing Irishman, of the same extraction though they be, remains to explode those two hollowest of fictions, the Irish and English "races." There is no Irish race any more than there is an English race or a Yankee race. There *is* an Irish climate, which will stamp an immigrant more deeply and durably in two years, apparently, than the English climate will in two hundred. It is reinforced by an artificial economic climate which does some of the work attributed to the natural geographic one; but the geographic climate is eternal and irresistible, making a mankind and a womankind that Kent, Middlesex, and East Anglia cannot produce and do not want to imitate.

How can I sketch the broad lines of the contrast as they strike me? Roughly I should say that the Englishman is wholly at the mercy of his imagination, having no sense of reality to check it. The Irishman, with a far subtler and more fastidious imagination, has one eye always on things as they are. If you compare Moore's visionary Minstrel Boy with Mr Rudyard Kipling's quasi-realistic Soldiers Three, you may yawn over Moore or gush over him, but you will not suspect him of having had any illusions about the contemporary British private; whilst as to Mr Kipling, you will see that he has not, and unless he settles in Ireland for a few years will always remain constitutionally and congenitally incapable of having, the faintest inkling of the reality which he idolizes as Tommy Atkins. Perhaps you have never thought of illustrating the contrast between English and Irish by Moore and Mr Kipling, or even by Parnell and Gladstone. Sir Boyle Roche and Shakespear may seem more to your point. Let me find you a more dramatic instance. Think of the famous meeting between the Duke of Wellington, that intensely Irish Irishman, and Nelson, that intensely English Englishman. Wellington's contemptuous disgust at Nelson's theatricality as a professed hero, patriot, and rhapsode, a theatricality which in an Irishman would have been an insufferably vulgar affectation, was quite natural and inevitable. Wellington's formula for that kind of thing was a well-known Irish one: "Sir: dont be a damned fool." It is the formula of all Irishmen for all Englishmen to this day. It is the formula of Larry Doyle for Tom Broadbent in my play, in spite of Doyle's affection for Tom. Nelson's genius, instead of producing intellectual keenness and scrupulousness, produced mere delirium. He was drunk with glory, exalted by his fervent faith in the sound British patriotism of the Almighty, nerved by the vulgarest anti-foreign prejudice, and apparently unchastened by any reflections on the fact that he had never had to fight a technically capable and properly equipped enemy except on land, where he had never been successful. Compare Wellington, who had to fight Napoleon's armies, Napoleon's marshals, and finally Napoleon himself, without one moment of illusion as to the human material he had to command, without one gush of the "Kiss me, Hardy" emotion which enabled Nelson to idolize his crews and his staff, without forgetting even in his dreams that the normal British officer of that time was an incapable amateur (as he still is) and the normal British soldier a never-do-well (he is now a depressed and respectable young man). No wonder Wellington became an accomplished comedian in the art of anti-climax, scandalizing the unfortunate Croker, responding to the demand for glorious sentiments by the most disenchanting touches of realism, and, generally, pricking the English windbag at its most explosive crises of distention. Nelson, intensely nervous and theatrical, made an enormous fuss about victories so cheap that he would have deserved shooting if he had lost them, and, not content with lavishing splendid fighting on helpless adversaries like the heroic De Brueys or Villeneuve (who had not even the illusion of heroism when he went like a lamb to the slaughter), got himself killed by his passion for exposing himself to death in that sublime defiance of it which was perhaps the supreme tribute of the exquisite coward to the King of Terrors (for, believe me, you cannot be a hero without being a coward: supersense cuts both ways), the result being a tremendous effect on the gallery. Wellington, most capable of captains, was neither a hero nor a patriot: perhaps not even a coward; and had it not been for the Nelsonic anecdotes invented for him—"Up guards, and at em" and so forth—and the fact that the antagonist with whom he finally closed was such a master of theatrical effect that Wellington could not fight him without getting into his limelight, nor overthrow him (most unfortunately for us all) without drawing the eyes of the whole world to the catastrophe, the Iron Duke would have been almost forgotten by this time. Now that contrast is English against Irish all over, and is the more delicious because the real Irishman in it is the Englishman of tradition, whilst the real Englishman is the traditional theatrical foreigner.

The value of the illustration lies in the fact that Nelson and Wellington were both in the highest degree efficient, and both in the highest degree incompatible with one another on any other footing than one of independence. The government of Nelson by Wellington or of Wellington by Nelson is felt at once to be a dishonorable outrage to the governed and a finally impossible task for the governor.

I daresay some Englishman will now try to steal Wellington as Macaulay tried to steal Swift. And he may plead with some truth that though it seems impossible that any other country than England could produce a hero so utterly devoid of common sense, intellectual delicacy, and international chivalry as Nelson, it may be contended that Wellington was rather an eighteenth century aristocratic type, than a specifically Irish type. George IV and Byron, contrasted with Gladstone, seem Irish in respect of a certain humorous blackguardism, and a power of appreciating art and sentiment without being duped by them into mistaking romantic figments for realities. But faithlessness and the need for carrying off the worthlessness and impotence that accompany it, produce in all nations a gay, sceptical, amusing, blaspheming, witty fashion which suits the flexibility of the Irish mind very well; and the contrast between this fashion and the energetic infatuations that have enabled intellectually ridiculous men, without wit or humor, to go on crusades and make successful revolutions, must not be confused with the contrast between the English and Irish idiosyncrasies. The Irishman makes a distinction which the Englishman is too lazy intellectually (the intellectual laziness and slovenliness of the English is almost beyond belief) to make. The Englishman, impressed with the dissoluteness of the faithless wits of the Restoration and the Regency, and with the victories of the wilful zealots of the patriotic, religious, and revolutionary wars, jumps to the conclusion that wilfulness is the main thing. In this he is right. But he overdoes his jump so far as to conclude also that stupidity and wrong-headedness are better guarantees of efficiency and trustworthiness than intellectual vivacity, which he mistrusts as a common symptom of worthlessness, vice, and instability. Now in this he is most dangerously wrong. Whether the Irishman grasps the truth as firmly as the Englishman may be open to question; but he is certainly comparatively free from the error. That affectionate and admiring love of sentimental stupidity for its own sake, both in men and women, which shines so steadily through the novels of Thackeray, would hardly be possible in the works of an Irish novelist. Even Dickens, though too vital a genius and too severely educated in the school of shabby-genteel poverty to have any doubt of the national danger of fatheadedness in high places, evidently assumes rather too hastily the superiority of Mr Meagles to Sir John Chester and Harold Skimpole. On the other hand, it takes an Irishman years of residence in England to learn to respect and like a blockhead. An Englishman will not respect nor like anyone else. Every English statesman has to maintain his popularity by pretending to be ruder, more ignorant, more sentimental, more superstitious, more stupid than any man who has lived behind the scenes of public life for ten minutes can possibly be. Nobody dares to publish really intimate memoirs of him or really private letters of his until his whole generation has passed away, and his party can no longer be compromised by the discovery that the platitudinizing twaddler and hypocritical opportunist was really a man of some perception as well as of strong constitution, peg-away industry, personal ambition, and party keenness.

ENGLISH STUPIDITY EXCUSED

I do not claim it as a natural superiority in the Irish nation that it dislikes and mistrusts fools, and expects its political leaders to be clever and humbug-proof. It may be that if our resources included the armed force and virtually unlimited money which push the political and military figureheads of England through bungled enterprises to a muddled success, and create an illusion of some miraculous and divine innate English quality that enables a general to become a conqueror with abilities that would not suffice to save a cabman from having his license marked, and a member of parliament to become Prime Minister with the outlook on life of a sporting country solicitor educated by a private governess, we should lapse into gross intellectual sottishness, and prefer leaders who encouraged our vulgarities by sharing them, and flattered us by associating them with purchased successes, to our betters. But as it is, we cannot afford that sort of encouragement and flattery in Ireland. The odds against which our leaders have to fight would be too heavy for the fourth-rate Englishmen whose leadership consists for the most part in marking time ostentatiously until they are violently shoved, and then stumbling blindly forward (or backward) wherever the shove sends them. We cannot crush England as a Pickford's van might crush a perambulator. We are the perambulator and England the Pickford. We must study her and our real weaknesses and real strength; we must practise upon her slow conscience and her quick terrors; we must deal in ideas and political principles since we cannot deal in bayonets; we must outwit, outwork, outstay her; we must embarrass, bully, even conspire and assassinate when nothing else will move her, if we are not all to be driven deeper and deeper into the shame and misery of our servitude. Our leaders must be not only determined enough, but clever enough to do this. We have no illusions as to the existence of any mysterious Irish pluck, Irish honesty, Irish bias on the part of Providence, or sterling Irish solidity of character, that will enable an Irish blockhead to hold his own against England. Blockheads are of no use to us: we were compelled to follow a supercilious, unpopular, tongue-tied, aristocratic Protestant Parnell, although there was no lack among us of fluent imbeciles, with majestic presences and oceans of dignity and sentiment, to promote into his place could they have done his work for us. It is obviously convenient that Mr Redmond should be a better speaker and rhetorician than Parnell; but if he began to use his powers to make himself agreeable instead of making himself reckoned with by the enemy; if he set to work to manufacture and support English shams and hypocrisies instead of exposing and denouncing them; if he constituted himself the permanent apologist of doing nothing, and, when the people insisted on his doing something, only roused himself to discover how to pretend to do it without really changing anything, he would lose his leadership as certainly as an English politician would, by the same course, attain a permanent place on the front bench. In short, our circumstances place a premium on political ability whilst the circumstances of England discount it; and the quality of the supply naturally follows the demand. If you miss in my writings that hero-worship of dotards and duffers which is planting England with statues of disastrous statesmen and absurd generals, the explanation is simply that I am an Irishman and you an Englishman.

IRISH PROTESTANTISM REALLY PROTESTANT

When I repeat that I am an Irish Protestant, I come to a part of the relation between England and Ireland that you will never understand unless I insist on explaining it to you with that Irish insistence on intellectual clarity to which my English critics are so intensely recalcitrant.

First, let me tell you that in Ireland Protestantism is really Protestant. It is true that there is an Irish Protestant Church (disestablished some 35 years ago) in spite of the fact that a Protestant Church is, fundamentally, a contradiction in terms. But this means only that the Protestants use the word Church to denote their secular organization, without troubling themselves about the metaphysical sense of Christ's famous pun, "Upon this rock I will build my church." The Church of England, which is a reformed Anglican Catholic Anti-Protestant Church, is quite another affair. An Anglican is acutely conscious that he is not a Wesleyan; and many Anglican clergymen do not hesitate to teach that all Methodists incur damnation. In Ireland all that the member of the Irish Protestant Church knows is that he is not a Roman Catholic. The decorations of even the "lowest" English Church seem to him to be extravagantly Ritualistic and Popish. I myself entered the Irish Church by baptism, a ceremony performed by my uncle in "his own church." But I was sent, with many boys of my own denomination, to a Wesleyan school where the Wesleyan catechism was taught without the least protest on the part of the parents, although there was so little presumption in favor of any boy there being a Wesleyan that if all the Church boys had been withdrawn at any moment, the school would have become bankrupt. And this was by no means analogous to the case of those working class members of the Church of England in London, who send their daughters to Roman Catholic schools rather than to the public elementary schools. They do so for the definite reason that the nuns teach girls good manners and sweetness of speech, which have no place in the County Council curriculum. But in Ireland the Church parent sends his son to a Wesleyan school (if it is convenient and socially eligible) because he is indifferent to the form of Protestantism, provided it is Protestantism. There is also in Ireland a characteristically Protestant refusal to take ceremonies and even sacraments very seriously except by way of strenuous objection to them when they are conducted with candles or incense. For example, I was never confirmed, although the ceremony was specially needed in my case as the failure of my appointed godfather to appear at my baptism had led to his responsibilities being assumed on the spot, at my uncle's order, by the sexton. And my case was a very common one, even among people quite untouched by modern scepticisms. Apart from the weekly churchgoing, which holds its own as a respectable habit, the initiations are perfunctory, the omissions regarded as negligible. The distinction between churchman and dissenter, which in England is a class distinction, a political distinction, and even occasionally a religious distinction, does not exist. Nobody is surprised in Ireland to find that the squire who is the local pillar of the formerly established Church is also a Plymouth Brother, and, except on certain special or fashionable occasions, attends the Methodist meeting-house. The parson has no priestly character and no priestly influence: the High Church curate of course exists and has his vogue among religious epicures of the other sex; but the general attitude of his congregation towards him is that of Dr Clifford. The clause in the Apostles' creed professing belief in a Catholic Church is a standing puzzle to Protestant children; and when they grow up they dismiss it from their minds more often than they solve it, because they really are not Catholics but Protestants to the extremest practicable degree of individualism. It is true that they talk of church and chapel with all the Anglican contempt for chapel; but in Ireland the chapel means the Roman Catholic church, for which the Irish Protestant reserves all the class rancor, the political hostility, the religious bigotry, and the bad blood generally that in England separates the Establishment from the nonconforming Protestant organizations. When a vulgar Irish Protestant speaks of a "Papist" he feels exactly as a vulgar Anglican vicar does when he speaks of a Dissenter. And when the vicar is Anglican enough to call himself a Catholic priest, wear a cassock, and bless his flock with two fingers, he becomes horrifically incomprehensible to the Irish Protestant Churchman, who, on his part, puzzles the Anglican by regarding a Methodist as tolerantly as an Irishman who likes grog regards an Irishman who prefers punch.

A FUNDAMENTAL ANOMALY

Now nothing can be more anomalous, and at bottom impossible, than a Conservative Protestant party standing for the established order against a revolutionary Catholic party. The Protestant is theoretically an anarchist as far as anarchism is practicable in human society: that is, he is an individualist, a freethinker, a self-helper, a Whig, a Liberal, a mistruster and vilifier of the State, a rebel. The Catholic is theoretically a Collectivist, a self-abnegator, a Tory, a Conservative, a supporter of Church and State one and undivisible, an obeyer. This would be a statement of fact as well as of theory if men were Protestants and Catholics by temperament and adult choice instead of by family tradition. The peasant who supposed that Wordsworth's son would carry on the business now the old gentleman was gone was not a whit more foolish than we who laugh at his ignorance of the nature of poetry whilst we take it as a matter of course that a son should "carry on" his father's religion. Hence, owing to our family system, the Catholic Churches are recruited daily at the font by temperamental Protestants, and the Protestant organizations by temperamental Catholics, with consequences most disconcerting to those who expect history to be deducible from the religious professions of the men who make it.

Still, though the Roman Catholic Church may occasionally catch such Tartars as Luther and Voltaire, or the Protestant organizations as Newman and Manning, the general run of mankind takes its impress from the atmosphere in which it is brought up. In Ireland the Roman Catholic peasant cannot escape the religious atmosphere of his Church. Except when he breaks out like a naughty child he is docile; he is reverent; he is content to regard knowledge as something not his business; he is a child before his Church, and accepts it as the highest authority in science and philosophy. He speaks of himself as a son of the Church, calling his priest father instead of brother or Mister. To rebel politically, he must break away from parish tutelage and follow a Protestant leader on national questions. His Church naturally fosters his submissiveness. The British Government and the Vatican may differ very vehemently as to whose subject the Irishman is to be; but they are quite agreed as to the propriety of his being a subject. Of the two, the British Government allows him more liberty, giving him as complete a democratic control of local government as his means will enable him to use, and a voice in the election of a formidable minority in the House of Commons, besides allowing him to read and learn what he likes—except when it makes a tufthunting onslaught on a seditious newspaper. But if he dared to claim a voice in the selection of his parish priest, or a representative at the Vatican, he would be denounced from the altar as an almost inconceivable blasphemer; and his educational opportunities are so restricted by his Church that he is heavily handicapped in every walk of life that requires any literacy. It is the aim of his priest to make him and keep him a submissive Conservative; and nothing but gross economic oppression and religious persecution could have produced the strange phenomenon of a revolutionary movement not only tolerated by the Clericals, but, up to a certain point, even encouraged by them. If there is such a thing as political science, with natural laws like any other science, it is certain that only the most violent external force could effect and maintain this unnatural combination of political revolution with Papal reaction, and of hardy individualism and independence with despotism and subjugation.

That violent external force is the clumsy thumb of English rule. If you would be good enough, ladies and gentlemen of England, to take your thumb away and leave us free to do something else than bite it, the unnaturally combined elements in Irish politics would fly asunder and recombine according to their proper nature with results entirely satisfactory to real Protestantism.

THE NATURE OF POLITICAL HATRED

Just reconsider the Home Rule question in the light of that very English characteristic of the Irish people, their political hatred of priests. Do not be distracted by the shriek of indignant denial from the Catholic papers and from those who have witnessed the charming relations between the Irish peasantry and their spiritual fathers. I am perfectly aware that the Irish love their priests as devotedly as the French loved them before the Revolution or as the Italians loved them before they imprisoned the Pope in the Vatican. They love their landlords too: many an Irish gentleman has found in his nurse a foster-mother more interested in him than his actual mother. They love the English, as every Englishman who travels in Ireland can testify. Please do not suppose that I speak satirically: the world is full of authentic examples of the concurrence of human kindliness with political rancor. Slaves and schoolboys often love their masters; Napoleon and his soldiers made desperate efforts to save from drowning the Russian soldiers under whom they had broken the ice with their cannon; even the relations between nonconformist peasants and country parsons in England are not invariably unkindly; in the southern States of America planters are often traditionally fond of negroes and kind to them, with substantial returns in humble affection; soldiers and sailors often admire and cheer their officers sincerely and heartily; nowhere is actual personal intercourse found compatible for long with the intolerable friction of hatred and malice. But people who persist in pleading these amiabilities as political factors must be summarily bundled out of the room when questions of State are to be discussed. Just as an Irishman may have English friends whom he may prefer to any Irishman of his acquaintance, and be kind, hospitable, and serviceable in his intercourse with Englishmen, whilst being perfectly prepared to make the Shannon run red with English blood if Irish freedom could be obtained at that price; so an Irish Catholic may like his priest as a man and revere him as a confessor and spiritual pastor whilst being implacably determined to seize the first opportunity of throwing off his yoke. This is political hatred: the only hatred that civilization allows to be mortal hatred.

THE REVOLT AGAINST THE PRIEST

Realize, then, that the popular party in Ireland is seething with rebellion against the tyranny of the Church. Imagine the feelings of an English farmer if the parson refused to marry him for less than £20, and if he had virtually no other way of getting married! Imagine the Church Rates revived in the form of an unofficial Income Tax scientifically adjusted to your taxable capacity by an intimate knowledge of your affairs verified in the confessional! Imagine being one of a peasantry reputed the poorest in the world, under the thumb of a priesthood reputed the richest in the world! Imagine a Catholic middle class continually defeated in the struggle of professional, official, and fashionable life by the superior education of its Protestant competitors, and yet forbidden by its priests to resort to the only efficient universities in the country! Imagine trying to get a modern education in a seminary of priests, where every modern book worth reading is on the index, and the earth is still regarded, not perhaps as absolutely flat, yet as being far from so spherical as Protestants allege! Imagine being forbidden to read this preface because it proclaims your own grievance! And imagine being bound to submit to all this because the popular side must hold together at all costs in the face of the Protestant enemy! That is, roughly, the predicament of Roman Catholic Ireland.

PROTESTANT LOYALTY: A FORECAST

Now let us have a look at Protestant Ireland. I have already said that a "loyal" Irishman is an abhorrent phenomenon, because he is an unnatural one. In Ireland it is not "loyalty" to drink the English king's health and stand uncovered to the English national anthem: it is simply exploitation of English rule in the interests of the property, power, and promotion of the Irish classes as against the Irish masses. From any other point of view it is cowardice and dishonor. I have known a Protestant go to Dublin Castle to be sworn in as a special constable, quite resolved to take the baton and break the heads of a patriotic faction just then upsetting the peace of the town, yet back out at the last moment because he could not bring himself to swallow the oath of allegiance tendered with the baton. There is no such thing as genuine loyalty in Ireland. There is a separation of the Irish people into two hostile camps: one Protestant, gentlemanly, and oligarchical; the other Roman Catholic, popular, and democratic. The oligarchy governs Ireland as a bureaucracy deriving authority from the king of England. It cannot cast him off without casting off its own ascendancy. Therefore it naturally exploits him sedulously, drinking his health, waving his flag, playing his anthem, and using the foolish word "traitor" freely in its cups. But let the English Government make a step towards the democratic party, and the Protestant garrison revolts at once, not with tears and prayers and anguish of soul and years of trembling reluctance, as the parliamentarians of the XVII century revolted against Charles I, but with acrid promptitude and strident threatenings. When England finally abandons the garrison by yielding to the demand for Home Rule, the Protestants will not go under, nor will they waste much time in sulking over their betrayal, and comparing their fate with that of Gordon left by Gladstone to perish on the spears of heathen fanatics. They cannot afford to retire into an Irish Faubourg St Germain. They will take an energetic part in the national government, which will be sorely in need of parliamentary and official forces independent of Rome. They will get not only the Protestant votes, but the votes of Catholics in that spirit of toleration which is everywhere extended to heresies that happen to be politically serviceable to the orthodox. They will not relax their determination to hold every inch of the government of Ireland that they can grasp; but as that government will then be a national Irish government instead of as now an English government, their determination will make them the vanguard of Irish Nationalism and Democracy as against Romanism and Sacerdotalism, leaving English Unionists grieved and shocked at their discovery of the true value of an Irish Protestant's loyalty.

But there will be no open break in the tradition of the party. The Protestants will still be the party of Union, which will then mean, not the Repeal of Home Rule, but the maintenance of the Federal Union of English-speaking commonwealths, now theatrically called the Empire. They will pull down the Union Jack without the smallest scruple; but they know the value of the Channel Fleet, and will cling closer than brothers to that and any other Imperial asset that can be exploited for the protection of Ireland against foreign aggression or the sharing of expenses with the British taxpayer. They know that the Irish coast is for the English invasion-scaremonger the heel of Achilles, and that they can use this to make him pay for the boot.

PROTESTANT PUGNACITY

If any Englishman feels incredulous as to this view of Protestantism as an essentially Nationalist force in Ireland, let him ask himself which leader he, if he were an Irishman, would rather have back from the grave to fight England: the Catholic Daniel O'Connell or the Protestant Parnell.

O'Connell organized the Nationalist movement only to draw its teeth, to break its determination, and to declare that Repeal of the Union was not worth the shedding of a drop of blood. He died in the bosom of his Church, not in the bosom of his country. The Protestant leaders, from Lord Edward Fitzgerald to Parnell, have never divided their devotion. If any Englishman thinks that they would have been more sparing of blood than the English themselves are, if only so cheap a fluid could have purchased the honor of Ireland, he greatly mistakes the Irish Protestant temper. The notion that Ireland is the only country in the world not worth shedding a drop of blood for is not a Protestant one, and certainly not countenanced by English practice. It was hardly reasonable to ask Parnell to shed blood *quant. suff.* in Egypt to put an end to the misgovernment of the Khedive and replace him by Lord Cromer for the sake of the English bondholders, and then to expect him to become a Tolstoyan or an O'Connellite in regard to his own country. With a wholly Protestant Ireland at his back he might have bullied England into conceding Home Rule; for the insensibility of the English governing classes to philosophical, moral, social considerations—in short, to any considerations which require a little intellectual exertion and sympathetic alertness—is tempered, as we Irish well know, by an absurd susceptibility to intimidation.

For let me halt a moment here to impress on you, O English reader, that no fact has been more deeply stamped into us than that we can do nothing with an English Government unless we frighten it, any more than you can yourself. When power and riches are thrown haphazard into children's cradles as they are in England, you get a governing class without industry, character, courage, or real experience; and under such circumstances reforms are produced only by catastrophes followed by panics in which "something must be done." Thus it costs a cholera epidemic to achieve a Public Health Act, a Crimean War to reform the Civil Service, and a gunpowder plot to disestablish the Irish Church. It was by the light, not of reason, but of the moon, that the need for paying serious attention to the Irish land question was seen in England. It cost the American War of Independence and the Irish Volunteer movement to obtain the Irish parliament of 1782, the constitution of which far overshot the nationalist mark of today in the matter of independence.

It is vain to plead that this is human nature and not class weakness. The Japanese have proved that it is possible to conduct social and political changes intelligently and providentially instead of drifting along helplessly until public disasters compel a terrified and inconsiderate rearrangement. Innumerable experiments in local government have shewn that when men are neither too poor to be honest nor too rich to understand and share the needs of the people—as in New Zealand, for example—they can govern much more providently than our little circle of aristocrats and plutocrats.

THE JUST ENGLISHMAN

English Unionists, when asked what they have to say in defence of their rule of subject peoples, often reply that the Englishman is just, leaving us divided between our derision of so monstrously inhuman a pretension, and our impatience with so gross a confusion of the mutually exclusive functions of judge and legislator. For there is only one condition on which a man can do justice between two litigants, and that is that he shall have no interest in common with either of them, whereas it is only by having every interest in common with both of them that he can govern them tolerably. The indispensable preliminary to Democracy is the representation of every interest: the indispensable preliminary to justice is the elimination of every interest. When we want an arbitrator or an umpire, we turn to a stranger: when we want a government, a stranger is the one person we will not endure. The Englishman in India, for example, stands, a very statue of justice, between two natives. He says, in effect, "I am impartial in your religious disputes because I believe in neither of your religions. I am impartial in your conflicts of custom and sentiment because your customs and sentiments are different from, and abysmally inferior to, my own. Finally, I am impartial as to your interests because they are both equally opposed to mine, which is to keep you both equally powerless against me in order that I may extract money from you to pay salaries and pensions to myself and my fellow Englishmen as judges and rulers over you. In return for which you get the inestimable benefit of a government that does absolute justice as between Indian and Indian, being wholly preoccupied with the maintenance of absolute injustice as between India and England."

It will be observed that no Englishman, without making himself ridiculous, could pretend to be perfectly just or disinterested in English affairs, or would tolerate a proposal to establish the Indian or Irish system in Great Britain. Yet if the justice of the Englishman is sufficient to ensure the welfare of India or Ireland, it ought to suffice equally for England. But the English are wise enough to refuse to trust to English justice themselves, preferring democracy. They can hardly blame the Irish for taking the same view.

In short, dear English reader, the Irish Protestant stands outside that English Mutual Admiration Society which you call the Union or the Empire. You may buy a common and not ineffective variety of Irish Protestant by delegating your powers to him, and in effect making him the oppressor and you his sorely bullied and bothered catspaw and military maintainer; but if you offer him nothing for his loyalty except the natural superiority of the English character, you will—well, try the experiment, and see what will happen! You would have a ten-times better chance with the Roman Catholic; for he has been saturated from his youth up with the Imperial idea of foreign rule by a spiritually superior international power, and is trained to submission and abnegation of his private judgment. A Roman Catholic garrison would take its orders from England and let her rule Ireland if England were Roman Catholic. The Protestant garrison simply seizes on the English power; uses it for its own purposes; and occasionally orders the English Government to remove an Irish secretary who has dared to apply English ideas to the affairs of the garrison. Whereupon the English Government abjectly removes him, and implores him, as a gentleman and a loyal Englishman, not to reproach it in the face of the Nationalist enemy.

Such incidents naturally do not shake the sturdy conviction of the Irish Protestant that he is more than a match for any English Government in determination and intelligence. Here, no doubt, he flatters himself; for his advantage is not really an advantage of character, but of comparative directness of interest, concentration of force on one narrow issue, simplicity of aim, with freedom from the scruples and responsibilities of world-politics. The business is Irish business, not English; and he is Irish. And his object, which is simply to secure the dominance of his own caste and creed behind the power of England, is simpler and clearer than the confused aims of English Cabinets struggling ineptly with the burdens of empire, and biassed by the pressure of capital anywhere rather than in Ireland. He has no responsibility, no interest, no status outside his own country and his own movement, which means that he has no conscience in dealing with England; whereas England, having a very uneasy conscience, and many hindering and hampering responsibilities and interests in dealing with him, gets bullied and driven by him, and finally learns sympathy with Nationalist aims by her experience of the tyranny of the Orange party.

IRISH CATHOLICISM FORECAST

Let us suppose that the establishment of a national government were to annihilate the oligarchic party by absorbing the Protestant garrison and making it a Protestant National Guard. The Roman Catholic laity, now a cipher, would organize itself; and a revolt against Rome and against the priesthood would ensue. The Roman Catholic Church would become the official Irish Church. The Irish parliament would insist on a voice in the promotion of churchmen; fees and contributions would be regulated; blackmail would be resisted; sweating in conventual factories and workshops would be stopped; and the ban would be taken off the universities. In a word, the Roman Catholic Church, against which Dublin Castle is powerless, would meet the one force on earth that can cope with it victoriously. That force is Democracy, a thing far more Catholic than itself. Until that force is let loose against it, the Protestant garrison can do nothing to the priesthood except consolidate it and drive the people to rally round it in defence of their altars against the foreigner and the heretic. When it *is* let loose, the Catholic laity will make as short work of sacerdotal tyranny in Ireland as it has done in France and Italy. And in doing so it will be forced to face the old problem of the relations of Church and State. A Roman Catholic party must submit to Rome: an anti-clerical Catholic party must of necessity become an Irish Catholic party. The Holy Roman Empire, like the other Empires, has no future except as a Federation of national Catholic Churches; for Christianity can no more escape Democracy than Democracy can escape Socialism. It is noteworthy in this connection that the Anglican Catholics have played and are playing a notable part in the Socialist movement in England in opposition to the individualist Secularists of the urban proletariat; but they are quit of the preliminary dead lift that awaits the Irish Catholic. Their Church has thrown off the yoke of Rome, and is safely and permanently Anglicized. But the Catholic Church in Ireland is still Roman. Home Rule will herald the day when the Vatican will go the way of Dublin Castle, and the island of the saints assume the headship of her own Church. It may seem incredible that long after the last Orangeman shall lay down his chalk for ever, the familiar scrawl on every blank wall in the north of Ireland "To hell with the Pope!" may reappear in the south, traced by the hands of Catholics who shall have forgotten the traditional counter legend, "To hell with King

William!" (of glorious, pious, and immortal memory); but it may happen so. "The island of the saints" is no idle phrase. Religious genius is one of our national products; and Ireland is no bad rock to build a Church on. Holy and beautiful is the soul of Catholic Ireland: her prayers are lovelier than the teeth and claws of Protestantism, but not so effective in dealing with the English.

ENGLISH VOLTAIREANISM

Let me familiarize the situation by shewing how closely it reproduces the English situation in its essentials. In England, as in France, the struggle between the priesthood and the laity has produced a vast body of Voltaireans. But the essential identity of the French and English movements has been obscured by the ignorance of the ordinary Englishman, who, instead of knowing the distinctive tenets of his church or sect, vaguely believes them to be the eternal truth as opposed to the damnable error of all the other denominations. He thinks of Voltaire as a French "infidel," instead of as the champion of the laity against the official theocracy of the State Church. The Nonconformist leaders of our Free Churches are all Voltaireans. The warcry of the Passive Resisters is Voltaire's warcry, "Ecrasez l'infâme." No account need be taken of the technical difference between Voltaire's "infâme" and Dr Clifford's. One was the unreformed Roman Church of France: the other is the reformed Anglican Church; but in both cases the attack has been on a priestly tyranny and a professional monopoly. Voltaire convinced the Genevan ministers that he was the philosophic champion of their Protestant, Individualistic, Democratic Deism against the State Church of Roman Catholic France; and his heroic energy and beneficence as a philanthropist, which now only makes the list of achievements on his monument at Ferney the most impressive epitaph in Europe, then made the most earnest of the Lutheran ministers glad to claim a common inspiration with him. Unfortunately Voltaire had an irrepressible sense of humor. He joked about Habakkuk; and jokes about Habakkuk smelt too strongly of brimstone to be tolerated by Protestants to whom the Bible was not a literature but a fetish and a talisman. And so Voltaire, in spite of the church he "erected to God," became in England the bogey-atheist of three generations of English ignoramuses, instead of the legitimate successor of Martin Luther and John Knox.

Nowadays, however, Voltaire's jokes are either forgotten or else fall flat on a world which no longer venerates Habakkuk; and his true position is becoming apparent. The fact that Voltaire was a Roman Catholic layman, educated at a Jesuit college, is the conclusive reply to the shallow people who imagine that Ireland delivered up to the Irish democracy—that is, to the Catholic laity—would be delivered up to the tyranny of the priesthood.

SUPPOSE!

Suppose, now, that the conquest of France by Henry V of England had endured, and that France in the XVIII century had been governed by an English viceroy through a Huguenot bureaucracy and a judicial bench appointed on the understanding that loyalty for them meant loyalty to England, and patriotism a willingness to die in defence of the English conquest and of the English Church, would not Voltaire in that case have been the meanest of traitors and self-seekers if he had played the game of England by joining in its campaign against his own and his country's Church? The energy he threw into the defence of Calas and Sirven would have been thrown into the defence of the Frenchmen whom the English would have called "rebels"; and he would have been forced to identify the cause of freedom and democracy with the cause of "l'infâme." The French revolution would have been a revolution against England and English rule instead of against aristocracy and ecclesiasticism; and all the intellectual and spiritual forces in France, from Turgot to De Tocqueville, would have been burnt up in mere anti-Anglicism and nationalist dithyrambs instead of contributing to political science and broadening the thought of the world.

What would have happened in France is what has happened in Ireland; and that is why it is only the small-minded Irish, incapable of conceiving what religious freedom means to a country, who do not loathe the English rule. For in Ireland England is nothing but the Pope's policeman. She imagines she is holding the Vatican cardinals at bay when she is really strangling the Voltaires, the Foxes and Penns, the Cliffords, Hortons, Campbells, Walters, and Silvester Hornes, who are to be found among the Roman Catholic laity as plentifully as among the Anglican Catholic laity in England. She gets nothing out of Ireland but infinite trouble, infinite confusion and hindrance in her own legislation, a hatred that circulates through the whole world and poisons it against her, a reproach that makes her professions of sympathy with Finland and Macedonia ridiculous and hypocritical, whilst the priest takes all the spoils, in money, in power, in pride, and in popularity.

IRELAND'S REAL GRIEVANCE

But it is not the spoils that matter. It is the waste, the sterilization, the perversion of fruitful brain power into flatulent protest against unnecessary evil, the use of our very entrails to tie our own hands and seal our own lips in the name of our honor and patriotism. As far as money or comfort is concerned, the average Irishman has a more tolerable life—especially now that the population is so scanty—than the average Englishman. It is true that in Ireland the poor man is robbed and starved and oppressed under judicial forms which confer the imposing title of justice on a crude system of bludgeoning and perjury. But so is the Englishman. The Englishman, more docile, less dangerous, too lazy intellectually to use such political and legal power as lies within his reach, suffers more and makes less fuss about it than the Irishman. But at least he has nobody to blame but himself and his fellow countrymen. He does not doubt that if an effective majority of the English people made up their minds to alter the Constitution, as the majority of the Irish people have made up their minds to obtain Home Rule, they could alter it without having to fight an overwhelmingly powerful and rich neighboring nation, and fight, too, with ropes round their necks. He can attack any institution in his country without betraying it to foreign vengeance and foreign oppression. True, his landlord may turn him out of his cottage if he goes to a Methodist chapel instead of to the parish church. His customers may stop their orders if he votes Liberal instead of Conservative. English ladies and gentlemen who would perish sooner than shoot a fox do these things without the smallest sense of indecency and dishonor. But they cannot muzzle his intellectual leaders. The English philosopher, the English author, the English orator can attack every abuse and expose every superstition without strengthening the hands of any common enemy. In Ireland every such attack, every such exposure, is a service to England and a stab to Ireland. If you expose the tyranny and rapacity of the Church, it is an argument in favor of Protestant ascendency. If you denounce the nepotism and jobbery of the new local authorities, you are demonstrating the unfitness of the Irish to govern themselves, and the superiority of the old oligarchical grand juries.

And there is the same pressure on the other side. The Protestant must stand by the garrison at all costs: the Unionist must wink at every bureaucratic abuse, connive at every tyranny, magnify every official blockhead, because their exposure would be a victory for the Nationalist enemy. Every Irishman is in Lancelot's position: his honor rooted in dishonor stands; and faith unfaithful keeps him falsely true.

THE CURSE OF NATIONALISM

It is hardly possible for an Englishman to understand all that this implies. A conquered nation is like a man with cancer: he can think of nothing else, and is forced to place himself, to the exclusion of all better company, in the hands of quacks who profess to treat or cure cancer. The windbags of the two rival platforms are the most insufferable of all windbags. It requires neither knowledge, character, conscience, diligence in public affairs, nor any virtue, private or communal, to thump the Nationalist or Orange tub: nay, it puts a premium on the rancor or callousness that has given rise to the proverb that if you put an Irishman on a spit you can always get another Irishman to baste him. Jingo oratory in England is sickening enough to serious people: indeed one evening's mafficking in London produced a determined call for the police. Well, in Ireland all political oratory is Jingo oratory; and all political demonstrations are maffickings. English rule is such an intolerable abomination that no other subject can reach the people. Nationalism stands between Ireland and the light of the world. Nobody in Ireland of any intelligence likes Nationalism any more than a man with a broken arm likes having it set. A healthy nation is as unconscious of its nationality as a healthy man of his bones. But if you break a nation's nationality it will think of nothing else but getting it set again. It will listen to no reformer, to no philosopher, to no preacher, until the demand of the Nationalist is granted. It will attend to no business, however vital, except the business of unification and liberation.

That is why everything is in abeyance in Ireland pending the achievement of Home Rule. The great movements of the human spirit which sweep in waves over Europe are stopped on the Irish coast by the English guns of the Pigeon House Fort. Only a quaint little offshoot of English pre-Raphaelitism called the Gaelic movement has got a footing by using Nationalism as a stalking-horse, and popularizing itself as an attack on the native language of the Irish people, which is most fortunately also the native language of half the world, including England. Every election is fought on nationalist grounds; every appointment is made on nationalist grounds; every judge is a partisan in the nationalist conflict; every speech is a dreary recapitulation of nationalist twaddle; every lecture is a corruption of history to flatter nationalism or defame it; every school is a recruiting station; every church is a barrack; and every Irishman is unspeakably tired of the whole miserable business, which nevertheless is and perforce must remain his first business until Home Rule makes an end of it, and sweeps the nationalist and the garrison back together into the dustbin.

There is indeed no greater curse to a nation than a nationalist movement, which is only the agonizing symptom of a suppressed natural function. Conquered nations lose their place in the world's march because they can do nothing but strive to get rid of their nationalist movements by recovering their national liberty. All demonstrations of the virtues of a foreign government, though often conclusive, are as useless as demonstrations of the superiority of artificial teeth, glass eyes, silver windpipes, and patent wooden legs to the natural products. Like Democracy, national self-government is not for the good of the people: it is for the satisfaction of the people. One Antonine emperor, one St Louis, one Richelieu, may be worth ten democracies in point of what is called good government; but there is no satisfaction for the people in them. To deprive a dyspeptic of his dinner and hand it over to a man who can digest it better is a highly logical proceeding; but it is not a sensible one. To take the government of Ireland away from the Irish and hand it over to the English on the ground that they can govern better would be a precisely parallel case if the English had managed their own affairs so well as to place their superior faculty for governing beyond question. But as the English are avowed muddlers—rather proud of it, in fact—even the logic of that case against Home Rule is not complete. Read Mr Charles Booth's account of London, Mr Rowntree's account of York, and the latest official report on Dundee; and then pretend, if you can, that Englishmen and Scotchmen have not more cause to hand over their affairs to an Irish parliament than to clamor for another nation's cities to devastate and another people's business to mismanage.

A NATURAL RIGHT

The question is not one of logic at all, but of natural

right. English universities have for some time past encouraged an extremely foolish academic exercise which consists in disproving the existence of natural rights on the ground that they cannot be deduced from the principles of any known political system. If they could, they would not be natural rights but acquired ones. Acquired rights are deduced from political constitutions; but political constitutions are deduced from natural rights. When a man insists on certain liberties without the slightest regard to demonstrations that they are not for his own good, nor for the public good, nor moral, nor reasonable, nor decent, nor compatible with the existing constitution of society, then he is said to claim a natural right to that liberty. When, for instance, he insists on living, in spite of the irrefutable demonstrations of many able pessimists, from the author of the book of Ecclesiastes to Schopenhauer, that life is an evil, he is asserting a natural right to live. When he insists on a vote in order that his country may be governed according to his ignorance instead of the wisdom of the Privy Council, he is asserting a natural right to self-government. When he insists on guiding himself at 21 by his own inexperience and folly and immaturity instead of by the experience and sagacity of his father, or the well-stored mind of his grandmother, he is asserting a natural right to independence. Even if Home Rule were as unhealthy as an Englishman's eating, as intemperate as his drinking, as filthy as his smoking, as licentious as his domesticity, as corrupt as his elections, as murderously greedy as his commerce, as cruel as his prisons, and as merciless as his streets, Ireland's claim to self-government would still be as good as England's. King James the First proved so cleverly and conclusively that the satisfaction of natural rights was incompatible with good government that his courtiers called him Solomon. We, more enlightened, call him Fool, solely because we have learnt that nations insist on being governed by their own consent—or, as they put it, by themselves and for themselves—and that they will finally upset a good government which denies them this even if the alternative be a bad government which at least creates and maintains an illusion of democracy. America, as far as one can ascertain, is much worse governed, and has a much more disgraceful political history than England under Charles I; but the American Republic is the stabler government because it starts from a formal concession of natural rights, and keeps up an illusion of safeguarding them by an elaborate machinery of democratic election. And the final reason why Ireland must have Home Rule is that she has a natural right to it.

A WARNING

Finally, some words of warning to both nations. Ireland has been deliberately ruined again and again by England. Unable to compete with us industrially, she has destroyed our industries by the brute force of prohibitive taxation. She was perfectly right. That brute force was a more honorable weapon than the poverty which we used to undersell her. We lived with and as our pigs, and let loose our wares in the Englishman's market at prices which he could compete with only by living like a pig himself. Having the alternative of stopping our industry altogether, he very naturally and properly availed himself of it. We should have done the same in his place. To bear malice against him on that score is to poison our blood and weaken our constitutions with unintelligent rancor. In wrecking all the industries that were based on the poverty of our people England did us an enormous service. In omitting to do the same on her own soil, she did herself a wrong that has rotted her almost to the marrow. I hope that when Home Rule is at last achieved, one of our first legislative acts will be to fortify the subsistence of our people behind the bulwark of a standard wage, and to impose crushing import duties on every English trade that flourishes in the slum and fattens on the starvation of our unfortunate English neighbors.

DOWN WITH THE SOLDIER!

Now for England's share of warning. Let her look to her Empire; for unless she makes it such a Federation for civil strength and defence that all free peoples will cling to it voluntarily, it will inevitably become a military tyranny to prevent them from abandoning it; and such a tyranny will drain the English taxpayer of his money more effectually than its worst cruelties can ever drain its victims of their liberty. A political scheme that cannot be carried out except by soldiers will not be a permanent one. The soldier is an anachronism of which we must get rid. Among people who are proof against the suggestions of romantic fiction there can no longer be any question of the fact that military service produces moral imbecility, ferocity, and cowardice, and that the defence of nations must be undertaken by the civil enterprise of men enjoying all the rights and liberties of citizenship, and trained by the exacting discipline of democratic freedom and responsibility. For permanent work the soldier is worse than useless: such efficiency as he has is the result of dehumanization and disablement. His whole training tends to make him a weakling. He has the easiest of lives: he has no freedom and no responsibility. He is politically and socially a child, with rations instead of rights, treated like a child, punished like a child, dressed prettily and washed and combed like a child, excused for outbreaks of naughtiness like a child, forbidden to marry like a child, and called Tommy like a child. He has no real work to keep him from going mad except housemaid's work: all the rest is forced exercise, in the form of endless rehearsals for a destructive and terrifying performance which may never come off, and which, when it does come off, is not like the rehearsals. His officer has not even housekeeper's work to keep him sane. The work of organizing and commanding bodies of men, which builds up the character and resource of the large class of civilians who live by it, only demoralizes the military officer, because his orders, however disastrous or offensive, must be obeyed without regard to consequences: for instance, if he calls his men dogs, and perverts a musketry drill order to make them kneel to him as an act of personal humiliation, and thereby provokes a mutiny among men not yet thoroughly broken in to the abjectness of the military condition, he is not, as might be expected, shot, but, at worst, reprimanded, whilst the leader of the mutiny, instead of getting the Victoria Cross and a public testimonial, is condemned to five years' penal servitude by Lynch Law (technically called martial law) administered by a trade union of officers. Compare with this the position of, for instance, our railway managers or our heads of explosives factories. They have to handle large bodies of men whose carelessness or insubordination may cause wholesale destruction of life and property; yet any of these men may insult them, defy them, or assault them without special penalties of any sort. The military commander dares not face these conditions: he lives in perpetual terror of his men, and will undertake their command only when they are stripped of all their civil rights, gagged, and bound hand and foot by a barbarous slave code. Thus the officer learns to punish, but never to rule; and when an emergency like the Indian Mutiny comes, he breaks down; and the situation has to be saved by a few untypical officers with character enough to have retained their civilian qualities in spite of the messroom. This, unfortunately, is learnt by the public, not on the spot, but from Lord Roberts fifty years later.

Besides the Mutiny we have had the Crimean and South African wars, the Dreyfus affair in France, the incidents of the anti-militarist campaign by the Social-Democrats in Germany, and now the Denshawai affair in the Nile delta, all heaping on us sensational demonstrations of the fact that soldiers pay the penalty of their slavery and outlawry by becoming, relatively to free civilians, destructive, cruel, dishonest, tyrannical, hysterical, mendacious, alarmists at home and terrorists abroad, politically reactionary, and professionally incapable. If it were humanly possible to militarize all the humanity out of a man, there would be absolutely no defence to this indictment. But the military system is so idiotically academic and impossible, and renders its victims so incapable of carrying it out with any thoroughness except when, in an occasional hysterical outburst of terror and violence, that hackneyed comedy of civil life, the weak man putting his foot down, becomes the military tragedy of the armed man burning, flogging, and murdering in a panic, that a body of soldiers and officers is in the main, and under normal circumstances, much like any other body of laborers and gentlemen. Many of us count among our personal friends and relatives officers whose amiable and honorable character seems to contradict everything I have just said about the military character. You have only to describe Lynch courts and acts of terrorism to them as the work of Ribbonmen, Dacoits, Moonlighters, Boxers, or—to use the general term most familiar to them—"natives," and their honest and generous indignation knows no bounds: they feel about them like men, not like soldiers. But the moment you bring the professional side of them uppermost by describing precisely the same proceedings to them as the work of regular armies, they defend them, applaud them, and are ready to take part in them as if their humanity had been blown out like a candle. You find that there is a blind spot on their moral retina, and that this blind spot is the military spot.

The excuse, when any excuse is made, is that discipline is supremely important in war. Now most soldiers have no experience of war; and to assume that those who have are therefore qualified to legislate for it, is as absurd as to assume that a man who has been run over by an omnibus is thereby qualified to draw up wise regulations for the traffic of London. Neither our military novices nor our veterans are clever enough to see that in the field, discipline either keeps itself or goes to pieces; for humanity under fire is a quite different thing from humanity in barracks: when there is danger the difficulty is never to find men who will obey, but men who can command. It is in time of peace, when an army is either a police force (in which case its work can be better done by a civilian constabulary) or an absurdity, that discipline is difficult, because the wasted life of the soldier is unnatural, except to a lazy man, and his servitude galling and senseless, except to a docile one. Still, the soldier is a man, and the officer sometimes a gentleman in the literal sense of the word; and so, what with humanity, laziness, and docility combined, they manage to rub along with only occasional outbursts of mutiny on the one side and class rancor and class cowardice on the other.

They are not even discontented; for the military and naval codes simplify life for them just as it is simplified for children. No soldier is asked to think for himself, to judge for himself, to consult his own honor and manhood, to dread any consequence except the consequence of punishment to his own person. The rules are plain and simple; the ceremonies of respect and submission are as easy and mechanical as a prayer wheel; the orders are always to be obeyed thoughtlessly, however inept or dishonorable they may be. As the late Laureate said in the two stinging lines in which he branded the British soldier with the dishonor of Esau, "theirs not to reason why, theirs but to do and die." To the moral imbecile and political sluggard these conditions are as congenial and attractive as they are abhorrent and intolerable to the William Tell temperament. Just as the most incorrigible criminal is always, we are told, the best behaved convict, so the man with least conscience and initiative makes the best behaved soldier, and that not wholly through mere fear of punishment, but through a genuine fitness for and consequent happiness in the childlike military life. Such men dread freedom and responsibility as a weak man dreads a risk or a heavy burden; and the objection to the military system is that it tends to produce such men by a weakening disuse of the moral muscles. No doubt this weakness is just what the military system aims at, its ideal soldier being, not a complete man, but a docile unit of cannon-fodder which can be trusted to respond promptly and certainly to the external stimulus of a shouted order, and is intimidated to the pitch of being afraid to run away from a battle. It may be doubted whether even in the Prussian heyday of the system, when floggings of hundreds and even thousands of lashes were matters of ordinary routine, this detestable ideal was ever realized; but your courts-martial are not practical enough to take that into account: it is characteristic of the military mind continually to ignore human nature and cry for the moon instead of facing modern social facts and accepting modern democratic conditions. And when I say the military mind, I repeat that I am not forgetting the patent fact that the military mind and the humane mind can exist in the same person; so that an officer who will take all the civilian risks, from city traffic to fox-hunting, without uneasiness, and who will manage all the civil employees on his estate and in his house and stables without the aid of a Mutiny Act, will also, in his military capacity, frantically declare that he dare not walk about in a foreign country unless every crime of violence against an Englishman in uniform is punished by the bombardment and destruction of a whole village, or the wholesale flogging and execution of every native in the neighborhood, and also that unless he and his fellow-officers have power, without the intervention of a jury, to punish the slightest self-assertion or hesitation to obey orders, however grossly insulting or disastrous those orders may be, with sentences which are reserved in civil life for the worst crimes, he cannot secure the obedience and respect of his men, and the country will accordingly lose all its colonies and dependencies, and be helplessly conquered in the German invasion which he confidently expects to occur in the course of a fortnight or so. That is to say, in so far as he is an ordinary gentleman he behaves sensibly and courageously; and in so far as he is a military man he gives way without shame to the grossest folly, cruelty and poltroonery. If any other profession in the world had been stained by these vices, and by false witness, forgery, swindling, torture, compulsion of men's families to attend their executions, digging up and mutilation of dead enemies, all wantonly added to the devastation proper to its own business, as the military profession has been within recent memory in England, France, and the United States of America (to mention no other countries), it would be very difficult to induce men of capacity and character to enter it. And in England it is, in fact, largely dependent for its recruits on the refuse of industrial life, and for its officers on the aristocratic and plutocratic refuse of political and diplomatic life, who join the army and pay for their positions in the more or less fashionable clubs which the regimental messes provide them with—clubs which, by the way, occasionally figure in ragging scandals as circles of extremely coarse moral character.

Now in countries which are denied Home Rule: that is, in which the government does not rest on the consent of the people, it must rest on military coercion; and the bureaucracy, however civil and legal it may be in form and even in the character of its best officials, must connive at all the atrocities of military rule, and become infected in the end with the chronic panic characteristic of militarism. In recent witness whereof, let me shift the scene from Ireland to Egypt, and tell the story of the Denshawai affair of June 1906 by way of object-lesson.

THE DENSHAWAI HORROR

Denshawai is a little Egyptian village in the Nile delta. Besides the dilapidated huts among the reeds by the roadside, and the palm trees, there are towers of unbaked brick, as unaccountable to an English villager as a Kentish oast-house to an Egyptian. These towers are pigeon-houses; for the villagers keep pigeons just as an English farmer keeps poultry.

Try to imagine the feelings of an English village if a party of Chinese officers suddenly appeared and began shooting the ducks, the geese, the hens, and the turkeys, and carried them off, asserting that they were wild birds, as everybody in China knew, and that the pretended indignation of the farmers was a cloak for hatred of the Chinese, and perhaps for a plot to overthrow the religion of Confucius and establish the Church of England in its place! Well, that is the British equivalent of what happened at Denshawai when a party of English officers went pigeon-shooting there the year before last. The inhabitants complained and memorialized; but they obtained no redress: the law failed them in their hour of need. So one leading family of pigeon farmers, Mahfouz by name, despaired of the law; and its head, Hassan Mahfouz, aged 60, made up his mind not to submit tamely to a repetition of the outrage. Also, British officers were ordered not to shoot pigeons in the villages without the consent of the Omdeh, or headman, though nothing was settled as to what might happen to the Omdeh if he ventured to refuse.

Fancy the feelings of Denshawai when on the 13th of June last there drove to the village four khaki-clad British officers with guns, one of them being a shooter of the year before, accompanied by one other officer on horseback, and also by a dragoman and an Ombashi, or police official! The oriental blood of Hassan Mahfouz boiled; and he warned them that they would not be allowed to shoot pigeons; but as they did not understand his language, the warning had no effect. They sent their dragoman to ask the Omdeh's permission to shoot; but the Omdeh was away; and all the interpreter could get from the Omdeh's deputy, who knew better than to dare an absolute refusal, was the pretty obvious reply that they might shoot if they went far enough away from the village. On the strength of this welcome, they went from 100 to 300 yards away from the houses (these distances were afterwards officially averaged at 500 yards), and began shooting the villagers' pigeons. The villagers remonstrated and finally seized the gun of the youngest officer. It went off in the struggle, and wounded three men and the wife of one Abd-el-Nebi, a young man of 25. Now the lady, though, as it turned out, only temporarily disabled by a charge of pigeon shot in the softest part of her person, gave herself up for dead; and the feeling in the village was much as if our imaginary Chinese officers, on being interfered with in their slaughter of turkeys, had killed an English farmer's wife. Abd-el-Nebi, her husband, took the matter to heart, not altogether without reason, we may admit. His threshing-floor also caught fire somehow (the official English theory is that he set it on fire as a signal for revolt to the entire Moslem world); and all the lads and loafers in the place were presently on the spot. The other officers, seeing their friend in trouble, joined him. Abd-el-Nebi hit the supposed murderer of his wife with a stick; Hassan Mahfouz used a stick also; and the lads and loafers began to throw stones and bricks. Five London policemen would have seen that there was nothing to be done but fight their way out, as there is no use arguing with an irritated mob, especially if you do not know its language. Had the shooting party been in the charge of a capable noncommissioned officer, he would perhaps have got it safely off. As it was, the officers tried propitiation, making their overtures in pantomime. They gave up their guns; they offered watches and money to the crowd, crying Baksheesh; and the senior officer actually collared the junior and pretended to arrest him for the murder of the woman. Naturally they were mobbed worse than before; and what they did not give to the crowd was taken from them, whether as payment for the pigeons, blood money, or simple plunder was not gone into. The officers, two Irishmen and three Englishmen, having made a hopeless mess of it, and being now in serious danger, made for their carriages, but were dragged out of them again, one of the coachmen being knocked senseless. They then "agreed to run," the arrangement being that the Englishmen, being the juniors, should run away to camp and bring help to the Irishmen. They bolted accordingly; but the third, the youngest, seeing the two Irishmen hard put to it, went back and stood by them. Of the two fugitives, one, after a long race in the Egyptian afternoon sun, got to the next village and there dropped, smitten by sunstroke, of which he died. The other ran on and met a patrol, which started to the rescue.

Meanwhile, the other three officers had been taken out

of the hands of the lads and the loafers, of Abd-el-Nebi and Hassan Mahfouz, by the elders and watchmen, and saved from further injury, but not before they had been severely knocked about, one of them having one of the bones of his left arm broken near the wrist—simple fracture of the thin end of the ulna. They were also brought to the threshing-floor; shewn the wounded woman; informed by gestures that they deserved to have their throats cut for murdering her; and kicked (with naked feet, fortunately); but at this point the elders and constables stopped the mobbing. Finally the three were sent off to camp in their carriages; and the incident ended for that day.

No English mob, under similar provocation, would have behaved any better; and few would have done as little mischief. It is not many months since an old man—not a foreigner and not an unbeliever—was kicked to death in the streets of London because the action of a park constable in turning him out of a public park exposed him to suspicion of misconduct. At Denshawai, the officers were not on duty. In their private capacity as sportsmen, they committed a serious depredation on a very poor village by slaughtering its stock. In an English village they would have been tolerated because the farmers would have expected compensation for damage, and the villagers coals and blankets and employment in country house, garden and stable, or as beaters, huntsmen and the like, from them. But Denshawai had no such inducements to submit to their thoughtless and selfish aggression. One of them had apparently killed a woman and wounded three men with his gun: in fact his own comrade virtually convicted him of it before the crowd by collaring him as a prisoner. In short, the officers had given outrageous provocation; and they had shewn an amiable but disastrous want of determination and judgment in dealing with the riot they provoked. They should have been severely reprimanded and informed that they had themselves to thank for what happened to them; and the villagers who assaulted them should have been treated with leniency, and assured that pigeon-shooting would not be allowed in future.

That is what should have ensued. Now for what actually did ensue.

Abd-el-Nebi, in consideration of the injury to his wife, was only sentenced to penal servitude for life. And our clemency did not stop there. His wife was not punished at all—not even charged with stealing the shot which was found in her person. And lest Abd-el-Nebi should feel lonely at 25 in beginning penal servitude for the rest of his days, another young man, of 20, was sent to penal servitude for life with him.

No such sentimentality was shewn to Hassan Mahfouz. An Egyptian pigeon farmer who objects to British sport; threatens British officers and gentlemen when they shoot his pigeons; and actually hits those officers with a substantial stick, is clearly a ruffian to be made an example of. Penal servitude was not enough for a man of 60 who looked 70, and might not have lived to suffer five years of it. So Hassan was hanged; but as a special mark of consideration for his family, he was hanged in full view of his own house, with his wives and children and grandchildren enjoying the spectacle from the roof. And lest this privilege should excite jealousy in other households, three other Denshavians were hanged with him. They went through the ceremony with dignity, professing their faith ("Mahometan, I regret to say," Mr Pecksniff would have said). Hassan, however, "in a loud voice invoked ruin upon the houses of those who had given evidence against him"; and Darweesh was impatient and presumed to tell the hangman to be quick. But then Darweesh was a bit of a brigand: he had been imprisoned for bearing false witness; and his resistance to the British invasion is the only officially recorded incident of his life which is entirely to his credit. He and Abd-el-Nebi (who had been imprisoned for theft) were the only disreputable characters among the punished. Ages of the four hanged men respectively, 60, 50, 22 and 20.

Hanging, however, is the least sensational form of public

execution: it lacks those elements of blood and torture for which the military and bureaucratic imagination lusts. So, as they had room for only one man on the gallows, and had to leave him hanging half an hour to make sure work and give his family plenty of time to watch him swinging ("slowly turning round and round on himself," as the local papers described it), thus having two hours to kill as well as four men, they kept the entertainment going by flogging eight men with fifty lashes each: eleven more than the utmost permitted by the law of Moses in times which our Army of Occupation no doubt considers barbarous. But then Moses conceived his law as being what he called the law of God, and not simply an instrument for the gratification of his own cruelty and terror. It is unspeakably reassuring to learn from the British official reports laid before parliament that "due dignity was observed in carrying out the executions," that "all possible humanity was shewn in carrying them out," and that "the arrangements were admirable, and reflect great credit on all concerned." As this last testimonial apparently does not refer to the victims, they are evidently officially considered not to have been concerned in the proceedings at all. Finally, Lord Cromer certifies that the Englishman in charge of the proceedings is "a singularly humane man, and is very popular amongst the natives of Egypt by reason of the great sympathy he has always shewn for them." It will be seen that Parliamentary Papers, Nos. 3 and 4, Egypt, 1906, are not lacking in unconscious humor. The official walrus pledges himself in every case for the kindliness of the official carpenter.

One man was actually let off, to the great danger of the British Empire perhaps. Still, as he was an epileptic, and had already had several fits in the court of Judge Lynch, the doctor said Better not; and he escaped. This was very inconvenient; for the number of floggees had been made up solely to fill the time occupied by the hangings at the rate of two floggings per hanging; and the breakdown of the arrangement through Said Suleiman Kheirallah's inconsiderate indisposition made the execution of Darweesh tedious, as he was hanging for fully quarter of an hour without any flogging to amuse his fellow villagers and the officers and men of the Inniskilling Dragoons, the military mounted police, and the mounted infantry. A few spare sentences of floggings should have been kept in hand to provide against accidents.

In any case there was not time to flog everybody, nor to flog three of the floggees enough; so these three had a year's hard labor apiece in addition to their floggings. Six others were not flogged at all, but were sent to penal servitude for seven years each. One man got fifteen years. Total for the morning's work: four hanged, two to penal servitude for life, one to fifteen years penal servitude, six to seven years penal servitude, three to imprisonment for a year with hard labor and fifty lashes, and five to fifty lashes.

Lord Cromer certifies that these proceedings were "just and necessary." He also gives his reasons. It appears that the boasted justice introduced into Egypt by the English in 1882 was imaginary, and that the real work of coping with Egyptian disorder was done by Brigandage Commissions, composed of Egyptians. These Commissions, when an offence was reported, descended on the inculpated village; seized everybody concerned; and plied them with tortures, mentionable and unmentionable, until they accused everybody they were expected to accuse. The accused were in turn tortured until they confessed anything and everything they were accused of. They were then killed, flogged, or sent to penal servitude. This was the reality behind the illusion that soothed us after bombarding Alexandria. The bloodless, white-gloved native courts set up to flatter our sense of imperial justice had, apparently, about as much to do with the actual government of the fellaheen as the annual court which awards the Dunmow flitch of bacon has to do with our divorce court. Eventually a Belgian judge, who was appointed Procureur-Général, exposed the true state of affairs.

Then the situation had to be faced. Order had to be maintained somehow; but the regular native courts which saved the face of the British Occupation were useless for the purpose; and the Brigandage Commissions were so abominable and demoralizing that they made more mischief than they prevented. Besides, there was Mr Wilfrid Scawen Blunt on the warpath against tyranny and torture, threatening to get questions asked in parliament. A new sort of tribunal in the nature of a court-martial had therefore to be invented to replace the Brigandage Commissions; but simple British military courts-martial, though probably the best available form of official Lynch Law, were made impossible by the jealousy of the "loyal" (to England) Egyptians, who, it seems, rule the Occupation and bully England exactly as the "loyal" Irish rule the Garrison and bully the Unionists nearer home. That kind of loyalty, not being a natural product, has to be purchased; and the price is an official job of some sort with a position and a salary attached. Hence we got, in 1895, a tribunal constituted in which three English officials sat with two Egyptian officials, exercising practically unlimited powers of punishment without a jury and without appeal. They represent the best of our judicial and military officialism. And what that best is may be judged by the sentences on the Denshawai villagers.

Lord Cromer's justification of the tribunal is practically that, bad as it is, the Brigandage Commissions were worse. Also (lest we should propose to carry our moral superiority any further) that the Egyptians are so accustomed to associate law and order with floggings, executions, torture and Lynch Law, that they will not respect any tribunal which does not continue these practices. This is a far-reaching argument; for instance, it suggests that Church of England missionaries might do well to adopt the rite of human sacrifice when evangelizing tribes in whose imagination that practice is inseparably bound up with religion. It suggests that the sole reason why the Denshawai tribunal did not resort to torture for the purpose of extorting confessions and evidence was that parliament might not stand it—though really a parliament which stood the executions would, one would think, stand anything. The tribunal had certainly no intention of allowing witnesses to testify against British officers; for, as it happened, the Ombashi who accompanied them on the two shooting expeditions, one Ahmed Hassan Zakzouk, aged 26, was rash enough to insist that after the shot that struck the woman, the officers fired on the mob twice. This appears in the parliamentary paper; but the French newspaper *L'Égypte* is quoted by Mr Wilfrid Scawen Blunt as reporting that Zakzouk, on being asked by one of the English judges whether he was not afraid to say such a thing, replied "Nobody in the world is able to frighten me: the truth is the truth," and was promptly told to stand down. Mr Blunt adds that Zakzouk was then tried for his conduct in connection with the affair before a Court of Discipline, which awarded him two years imprisonment and fifty lashes. Without rudely calling this a use of torture to intimidate anti-British witnesses, I may count on the assent of most reasonable people when I say that Zakzouk probably regards himself as having received a rather strong hint to make his evidence agreeable to the Occupation in future.

Not only was there of course no jury at the trial, but considerably less than no defence. Barristers of sufficient standing to make it very undesirable for them to offend the Occupation were instructed to "defend" the prisoners. Far from defending them, they paid high compliments to the Occupation as one of the choicest benefits rained by Heaven on their country, and appealed for mercy for their miserable clients, whose conduct has "caused the unanimous indignation of all Egyptians." "Clemency," they said, "was above equity." The tribunal in delivering judgment remarked that "the counsel for the defence had a full hearing: nevertheless the defence broke down completely, and all that their counsel could say on behalf of the prisoners practically amounted to an appeal to the mercy of the Court."

Now the proper defence, if put forward, would probably have convinced Lord Cromer that nothing but the burning of the village and the crucifixion of all its inhabitants could preserve the British Empire. That defence was obvious enough: the village was invaded by five armed foreigners who attempted for the second time to slaughter the villagers' farming stock and carry it off; in resisting an attempt to disarm them four villagers had been wounded; the villagers had lost their tempers and knocked the invaders about; and the older men and watchmen had finally rescued the aggressors and sent them back with no worse handling than they would have got anywhere for the like misconduct.

One can imagine what would have happened to the man, prisoner or advocate, who should have dared to tell the truth in this fashion. The prisoners knew better than to attempt it. On the scaffold, Darweesh turned to his house as he stood on the trap, and exclaimed "May God compensate us well for this world of meanness, for this world of injustice, for this world of cruelty." If he had dared in court thus to compare God with the tribunal to the disadvantage of the latter, he would no doubt have had fifty lashes before his hanging, to teach him the greatness of the Empire. As it was, he kept his views to himself until it was too late to do anything worse to him than hang him. In court, he did as all the rest did. They lied; they denied; they set up desperate alibis; they protested they had been in the next village, or tending cattle a mile off, or threshing, or what not. One of them, when identified, said "All men are alike." He had only one eye. Darweesh, who had secured one of the officers' guns, declared that his enemies had come in the night and buried it in his house, where his mother sat on it, like Rachel on Laban's stolen teraphim, until she was dragged off. A pitiable business, yet not so pitiable as the virtuous indignation with which Judge Lynch, himself provable by his own judgment to be a prevaricator, hypocrite, tyrant, and coward of the first water, preened himself at its expense. When Lord Cromer, in his official apology for Judge Lynch, says that "the prisoners had a perfectly fair trial"—not, observe, a trial as little unfair as human frailty could make it, which is the most that can be said for any trial on earth, but "a *perfectly* fair trial"—he no doubt believes what he says; but his opinion is interesting mainly as an example of the state of his mind, and of the extent to which, after thirty years of official life in Egypt, one loses the plain sense of English words.

Lord Cromer recalls how, in the eighties, a man threatened with the courbash by a Moudir in the presence of Sir Claude MacDonald, said "You dare not flog me now that the British are here." "So bold an answer," says Lord Cromer, "was probably due to the presence of a British officer." What would that man say now? What does Lord Cromer say now? He deprecates "premature endeavours to thrust Western ideas on an Eastern people," by which he means that when you are in Egypt you must do as the Egyptians do: terrorize by the lash and the scaffold. Thus does the East conquer its conquerors. In 1883 Lord Dufferin was abolishing the bastinado as "a horrible and infamous punishment." In 1906 Lord Cromer guarantees ferocious sentences of flogging as "just and necessary," and can see "nothing reprehensible in the manner in which they were carried out." "I have," he adds, "passed nearly thirty years of my life in an earnest endeavour to raise the moral and material condition of the people of Egypt. I have been assisted by a number of very capable officials, all of whom, I may say, have been animated by the same spirit as myself." Egypt may well shudder as she reads those words. If the first thirty years have been crowned by the Denshawai incident, what will Egypt be like at the end of another thirty years of moral elevation "animated by the same spirit"?

It is pleasanter to return to Lord Cromer's first letter on Denshawai, written to Sir Edward Grey the day after the shooting party. It says that "orders will shortly be issued by the General prohibiting officers in the army from shooting pigeons in the future under any circumstances whatever." But pray why this prohibition, if, as the tribunal declared, the officers were "guests [actually *guests!*] who had done nothing to deserve blame"?

Mr Findlay is another interesting official correspondent of Sir Edward. Even after the trial, at which it had been impossible to push the medical evidence further than to say that the officer who died of sunstroke had been predisposed to it by the knocking about he had suffered and by his flight under the Egyptian sun, whilst the officers who had remained defenceless in the hands of the villagers were in court, alive and well, Mr Findlay writes that the four hanged men were "convicted of a brutal and premeditated murder," and complains that "the native press disregards the fact" and "is being conducted with such an absolute disregard for truth as to make it evident that large sums of money have been expended." Mr Findlay is also a bit of a philosopher. "The Egyptian, being a fatalist," he says, "does not greatly fear death, and there is therefore much to be said for flogging as a judicial punishment in Egypt." Logically, then, the four hanged men ought to have been flogged instead. But Mr Findlay does not draw that conclusion. Logic is not his strong point: he is a man of feeling, and a very nervous one at that. "I do not believe that this brutal attack on British officers had anything directly to do with political animosity. It is, however, due to the insubordinate spirit which has been sedulously fostered during the last year by unscrupulous and interested agitators." Again, "it is my duty to warn you of the deplorable effect which is being produced in Egypt by the fact that Members of Parliament have seriously called in question the unanimous sentence passed by a legally constituted Court, of which the best English and the best native Judge were members. This fact will, moreover, supply the lever which has, up to the present, been lacking to the venal agitators who are at the head of the so-called patriotic party." I find Mr Findlay irresistible, so exquisitely does he give us the measure and flavor of officialism. "A few days after the Denshawai affray some natives stoned and severely injured an irrigation inspector. Two days ago three natives knocked a soldier off his donkey and kicked him in the stomach: his injuries are serious. In the latter case theft appears to have been the motive. My object in mentioning these instances is to shew the results to be expected if once respect for the law is shaken. Should the present state of things continue, and, still more, should the agitation in this country find support at home, the date is not far distant when the necessity will arise for bringing in a press law and for considerably increasing the army of occupation." Just think of it! In a population of nearly ten millions, one irrigation inspector is stoned. The Denshawai executions are then carried out to make the law respected. The result is that three natives knock a soldier off his donkey and rob him. Thereupon Mr Findlay, appalled at the bankruptcy of civilization, sees nothing for it now but suppression of the native newspapers and a considerable increase in the army of occupation! And Lord Cromer writes "All I need say is that I concur generally in Mr Findlay's remarks, and that, had I remained in Egypt, I should in every respect have adopted the same course as that which he pursued."

But I must resolutely shut this rich parliamentary paper. I have extracted enough to paint the picture, and enforce my warning to England that if her Empire means ruling the world as Denshawai has been ruled in 1906—and that, I am afraid, is what the Empire does mean to the main body of our aristocratic-military caste and to our Jingo plutocrats—then there can be no more sacred and urgent political duty on earth than the disruption, defeat, and suppression of the Empire, and, incidentally, the humanization of its supporters by the sternest lessons of that adversity which comes finally to institutions which make themselves abhorred by the aspiring will of humanity towards divinity. As for the Egyptians, any man cradled by the Nile who, after the Denshawai incident, will ever voluntarily submit to British rule, or accept any bond with us except the bond of a Federation of free and equal states, will deserve the worst that Lord Cromer can consider "just and necessary" for him. That is what you get by attempting to prove your supremacy by the excesses of frightened soldiers and denaturalized officials instead of by courageous helpfulness and moral superiority.

In any case let no Englishman who is content to leave Abd-el-Nebi and his twenty-year-old neighbor in penal servitude for life, and to plume himself on the power to do it, pretend to be fit to govern either my country or his own. The responsibility cannot be confined to the tribunal and to the demoralized officials of the Occupation. The House of Commons had twenty-four hours clear notice, with the telegraph under the hand of Sir Edward Grey, to enable it to declare that England was a civilized Power and would not stand these barbarous lashings and vindictive hangings. Yet Mr Dillon, representing the Irish party, which well knows what British Occupations and Findlay "loyalism" mean, protested in vain. Sir Edward, on behalf of the new Liberal Government (still simmering with virtuous indignation at the flogging of Chinamen and the military executions in South Africa in the forced presence of the victims' families under the late Imperialist Government), not only permitted and defended the Denshawai executions, but appealed to the House almost passionately not to criticize or repudiate them, on the ground—how incredible it now appears!—that Abd-el-Nebi and Hassan Mahfouz and Darweesh and the rest were the fuglemen of a gigantic Moslem plot to rise against Christendom in the name of the Prophet and sweep Christendom out of Africa and Asia by a colossal second edition of the Indian Mutiny. That this idiotic romance, gross and ridiculous as the lies of Falstaff, should have imposed on any intelligent and politically experienced human being, is strange enough—though the secret shame of revolted humanity will make cabinet ministers snatch at fantastic excuses—but what humanity will not forgive our foreign secretary for is his failure to see that even if such a conspiracy really existed, England should have faced it and fought it bravely by honorable means, instead of wildly lashing and strangling a handful of poor peasants to scare Islam into terrified submission. Were I abject enough to grant to Sir Edward Grey as valid that main asset of "thinking Imperially," the conviction that we are all going to be murdered, I should still suggest to him that we can at least die like gentlemen? Might I even be so personal as to say that the reason for giving him a social position and political opportunities that are denied to his tradesmen is that he is supposed to understand better than they that honor is worth its danger and its cost, and that life is worthless without honor? It is true that Sir John Falstaff did not think so; but Sir John is hardly a model for Sir Edward. Yet even Sir John would have had enough gumption to see that the Denshawai panic was more dangerous to the Empire than the loss of ten pitched battles.

As cowardice is highly infectious, would it not be desirable to supersede officials who, after years of oriental service, have lost the familiar art of concealing their terrors? I am myself a sedentary literary civilian, constitutionally timid; but I find it possible to keep up appearances, and can even face the risk of being run over, or garotted, or burnt out in London without shrieking for martial law, suppression of the newspapers, exemplary flogging and hanging of motorbus drivers, and compulsory police service. Why are soldiers and officials on foreign service so much more cowardly than citizens? Is it not clearly because the whole Imperial military system of coercion and terrorism is unnatural, and that the truth formulated by William Morris that "no man is good enough to be another man's master" is true also of nations, and very specially true of those plutocrat-ridden Powers which have of late stumbled into an enormous increase of material wealth without having made any intelligent provision for its proper distribution and administration?

However, the economic reform of the Empire is a long business, whereas the release of Abd-el-Nebi and his neighbors is a matter of the stroke of a pen, once public opinion is shamed into activity. I fear I have stated their case very unfairly and inadequately, because I am hampered, as an Irishman, by my implacable hostility to English domination.

Mistrusting my own prejudices, I have taken the story from the two parliamentary papers in which our officials have done their utmost to whitewash the tribunals and the pigeon-shooting party, and to blackwash the villagers. Those who wish to have it told to them by an Englishman of unquestionable personal and social credentials, and an intimate knowledge of Egypt and the Egyptians, can find it in Mr Wilfrid Scawen Blunt's pamphlet entitled "Atrocities of British Rule in Egypt." When they have read it they will appreciate my forbearance; and when I add that English rule in Ireland has been "animated by the same spirit" (I thank Lord Cromer for the phrase) as English rule in Egypt, and that this is the inevitable spirit of all coercive military rule, they will perhaps begin to understand why Home Rule is a necessity not only for Ireland, but for all constituents of those Federations of Commonwealths which are now the only permanently practicable form of Empire.

POSTSCRIPT. These sheets had passed through the press when the news came of Lord Cromer's resignation. As he accuses himself of failing health, he will perhaps forgive me for accusing him of failing judgment, and for suggesting that his retirement from office might well be celebrated in Egypt by the retirement, at his intercession, of Abd-el-Nebi and the rest from penal servitude.

A YEAR LATER. It may be a relief to some of my readers to learn that very shortly after the publication of the above account of the Denshawai atrocity, I received a private assurance that Abd-el-Nebi and his fellow-prisoners would be released on the following New Year's Day, which is the customary occasion in Egypt for such acts of grace and clemency as the Occupation may allow the Khedive to perform, and that in the meantime their detention would not be rigorous. As the hanged men could not be unhanged nor the flogged men unflogged, this was all that could be done. I am bound to add, in justice to the Government, that this was, as far as I could ascertain, an act of pure conscience on the part of the Cabinet; for there was no sign of any serious pressure of public opinion. One or two newspapers seemed to be amused at my calling the Denshawai villagers Denshavians; but they shewed no other interest in the matter: another illustration of how hopeless it is to induce one modern nation, preoccupied as it necessarily is with its own affairs, to take any real interest in the welfare of another, even when it professes to govern that other in a superior manner for its good. Sir Edward Grey's reputation as a great Minister for Foreign Affairs was not shaken in the least: the eulogies which were heaped on him by both parties increased in volume; and an attempt which I made to call attention to the real character of the Anglo-Russian agreement as to Persia, which was held up as a masterpiece of his diplomacy (I was apparently the only person who had taken the trouble to read it) had no effect. Not until Sir Edward ventured to threaten a really formidable European Power in 1911, and threatened it successfully from his point of view, did a sudden and violent agitation against him spring up. Until then, men of both parties idolized him without knowing why, just as they had formerly idolized Lord Cromer and Lord Milner without knowing why. They will now very possibly turn on him and rend him, also without knowing why. The one thing they will not do is to blame themselves, which is the only blaming that can be of any profit to them.

TWENTYFOUR YEARS LATER. The sequel to these events confirmed my unheeded warning with a sanguinary completeness of which I had no prevision. At Easter 1916 a handful of Irishmen seized the Dublin Post Office and proclaimed an Irish Republic, with one of their number, a schoolmaster named Pearse, as President. If all Ireland had risen at this gesture it would have been a serious matter for England, then up to her neck in the war against the Central Empires. But there was no response: the gesture was a complete failure. All that was necessary was to blockade the Post

Office until its microcosmic republic was starved out and made ridiculous. What actually happened would be incredible if there were not so many living witnesses of it. From a battery planted at Trinity College (the Irish equivalent of Oxford University), and from a warship in the river Liffey, a bombardment was poured on the centre of the city which reduced more than a square mile of it to such a condition that when, in the following year, I was taken through Arras and Ypres to shew me what the German artillery had done to these cities in two and a half years, I laughed and said, "You should see what the British artillery did to my native city in a week." It would not be true to say that not one stone was left upon another; for the marksmanship was so bad that the Post Office itself was left standing amid a waste of rubbish heaps; and enough scraps of wall were left for the British Army, which needed recruits, to cover with appeals to the Irish to remember Belgium lest the fate of Louvain should befall their own hearths and homes.

Having thus worked up a harebrained romantic adventure into a heroic episode in the struggle for Irish freedom, the victorious artillerists proceeded to kill their prisoners of war in a drawn-out string of executions. Those who were executed accordingly became not only national heroes, but the martyrs whose blood was the seed of the present Irish Free State. Among those who escaped was its first President. Nothing more blindly savage, stupid, and terror-mad could have been devised by England's worst enemies. It was a very characteristic example of the mentality produced by the conventional gentleman-militarist education at Marlborough and Sandhurst and the conventional gentleman-diplomatist education at Eton and Oxford, Harrow and Cambridge. Is it surprising that the Russian Soviet Government, though fanatically credulous as to the need for popular education, absolutely refused to employ as teachers anyone who had been touched by the equivalent public school and university routine in Russia, and stuck to its resolution even at the cost of carrying on for some years with teachers who were hardly a day ahead of their pupils?

But the Post Office episode was eclipsed by an event which was much more than an episode, as it shattered the whole case for parliamentary government throughout the world. The Irish Nationalists, after thirty years of constitutional procedure in the British Parliament, had carried an Act to establish Irish Home Rule, as it was then called, which duly received the royal assent and became a statute of the realm. Immediately the British officers on service in Ireland mutinied, refusing to enforce the Act or operate against the northern Orangemen who were openly arming themselves to resist it. They were assured of support by their fellow-officers at home. The Act was suspended after prominent English statesmen had taken part in the military manœuvres of the Orangemen. The Prime Minister publicly pledged himself that Belfast, the Orange capital, would not in any case be coerced. In short, the Act was shelved under a threat of civil war; and the Clan na Gael, which in America had steadfastly maintained that the constitutional movement was useless, as England would in the last resort repudiate the constitution and hold Ireland against the Irish by physical force, and had been rebuked, lectured, and repudiated by the parliamentary Home Rulers for a whole generation for saying so, was justified. The Catholic Irish accordingly armed themselves and drilled as Volunteers in spite of the hostility of the Government, which meanwhile gave every possible assistance to the parallel preparations of the Orangemen. An Irish parliament (or Dail) sat in Dublin and claimed to be the national government. Irish courts were set up for the administration of Irish justice; Irish order was kept by Irish police; Irish taxes were collected by Irish officials; and British courts were boycotted. Upon this interesting but hopeless attempt to ignore British rule the Government let loose a specially recruited force (known to history as the Black and Tans) with *carte blanche* to kill, burn, and destroy, save only that they must stop short of rapine. They wrecked the Irish courts and produced a state of anarchy. They struck at the Irish through the popular co-operative stores and creameries, which they burnt. The people found a civil leader in Arthur Griffiths and a military one in Michael Collins. The Black and Tans had the British Government at their back: Collins had the people at his back. He threatened that for every creamery or co-operative store or cabin or cottage burnt by the Black and Tans he would burn two country houses of the Protestant gentry. The country houses that were not burnt were raided at night and laid under contribution for needed supplies. If the occupants reported the raid, the house was burnt. The Black and Tans and the ordinary constabulary were treated as enemies in uniform: that is, they were shot at sight and their stations burnt; or they were ambushed and killed in petty battles. Those who gave warnings or information of any helpful kind to them were mercilessly executed without privilege of sex or benefit of clergy. Collins, with allies in every street and hamlet, proved able to carry out his threat. He won the crown of the Reign of Terror; and the position of the Protestant gentry became unbearable.

Thus by fire and bullet, murder and torture and devastation, a situation was produced in which the British Government had either to capitulate at the cost of a far more complete concession of self-government to Ireland than that decreed by the repudiated Home Rule Act, or to let loose the military strength of England in a Cromwellian reconquest, massacre, and replantation which it knew that public opinion in England and America would not tolerate; for some of the most conspicuous English champions of Ulster warned the Government that they could stand no more of the Black and Tan terrorism. And so we settled the Irish Question, not as civilized and reasonable men should have settled it, but as dogs settle a dispute over a bone.

Future historians will probably see in these catastrophes a ritual of human sacrifice without which the savages of the twentieth century could not effect any redistribution of political power or wealth. Nothing was learnt from Denshawai or the Black and Tan terror. In India, which is still struggling for self-government, and obviously must finally have it, a military panic led to the cannonading of a forbidden public meeting at Amritsar, the crowd being dealt with precisely as if it were a body of German shocktroops rushing the British trenches in Flanders. In London the police would have broken a score or two of heads and dragged a handful of ringleaders to the police courts. And there was the usual combination of mean spite with hyperbolical violence. Indians were forced to crawl past official buildings on their hands and knees. The effect was to make British imperial rule ridiculous in Europe, and implacably resented in India.

In Egypt the British domination died of Denshawai; but at its deathbed the British Sirdar was assassinated, whereupon the British Government, just then rather drunk after a sweeping election victory secured by an anti-Russian scare, announced to an amazed world that it was going to cut off the Nile at its source and destroy Egypt by stopping its water supply. Of course nothing happened but an ignominious climb down; but the incident illustrates my contention that our authority, when it is too far flung (as our patriotic rhapsodists put it), goes stark mad at the periphery if a pin drops. As to what further panics and atrocities will ensue before India is left to govern itself as much as Ireland and Egypt now are I am in the dark until the event enlightens me. But on the folly of allowing military counsels to prevail in political settlements I may point to the frontiers established by the victors after the war of 1914–18. Almost every one of these frontiers has a new war implicit in it, because the soldier recognizes no ethnographical, linguistic, or moral boundaries: he demands a line that he can defend, or rather that Napoleon or Wellington could have defended; for he has not yet learnt to think of offence and defence in terms of airplanes which ignore his Waterloo ridges. And the inevitable nationalist rebellions against these military frontiers, and the atrocities by which they are countered, are in full swing as I write.

Meanwhile, John Bull's Other Island, though its freedom has destroyed all the romantic interest that used to attach to it, has become at last highly interesting to the student of political science as an experiment in political structure. Protestant Ulster, which armed against the rest of Ireland and defied the British Parliament to the cry of "We wont have it," meaning that they would die in the last ditch singing "O God, our help in ages past" rather than suffer or tolerate Home Rule, is now suffering and indeed hugging Home Rule on a much more homely scale than the Home Rulers ever demanded or dreamt of; for it has a Belfast Home Rule Parliament instead of an Irish one. And it has allowed Catholic Ireland to secure the Irish parliament. Thus, of the two regional parliaments which have been established on a sectarian basis, Protestant Ulster has been left with the smaller. Now it happens that Protestant Ulster is industrial Ireland and Catholic Ireland agricultural Ireland. And throughout the world for a century past the farmer, the peasant, and the Catholic have been the bulwark of the industrial capitalists against the growing political power of the industrial proletariat organized in trade unions, Labor parties, and the ubiquitous sodalities of that new ultra-Catholic Church called Socialism.

From this defensive alliance the Ulster employers, blinded by an obsolete bigotry and snobbery, have deliberately cut themselves off. In my preface of 1906, and again in my 1912 preface to a sixpenny edition of this play called the Home Rule edition, I exhorted the Protestants to take their chance, trust their grit, and play their part in a single parliament ruling an undivided Ireland. They did not take my advice. Probably they did not even read it, being too deeply absorbed in the History of Maria Monk, or the latest demonstration that all the evil in the world is the work of an underground conspiracy entitled by them "the Jesuits." It is a pity they did not begin their political education, as I began mine, by reading Karl Marx. It is true that I had occasion to point out that Marx was not infallible; but he left me with a very strong disposition to back the economic situation to control all the other situations, religious, nationalist, or romantic, in the long run. And so I do not despair of seeing Protestant Ulster seeking the alliance it repudiated. The Northern Parliament will not merge into the Oireachtas; for until both of them are superseded by a completely modernized central government, made for action and not for obstruction, they will remain more effective as regional parliaments than they would be as national ones; but they will soon have to take counsel together through conferences which will recur until they become a permanent institution and finally develop into what the Americans call Congress, or Federal Government of the whole island. No doubt this will be received in Belfast (if noticed at all) with shouts of "We wont have it." But I have heard that cry before, and regard it as a very hopeful sign that they will have it gladly enough when they have the luck to get it.

AYOT ST LAWRENCE,
November 1929.

JOHN BULL'S OTHER ISLAND

ACT I

GREAT George Street, Westminster, is the address of Doyle and Broadbent, civil engineers. On the threshold one reads that the firm consists of Mr Laurence Doyle and Mr Thomas Broadbent, and that their rooms are on the first floor. Most of these rooms are private; for the partners, being bachelors and bosom friends, live there; and the door marked Private, next the clerks' office, is their domestic sitting room as well as their reception room for clients. Let me describe it briefly from the point of view of a sparrow on the window sill. The outer door is in the opposite wall, close to the right hand corner. Between this door and the left hand corner is a hatstand and a table consisting of large drawing boards on trestles, with plans, rolls of tracing paper, mathematical instruments, and other draughtsman's accessories on it. In the left hand wall is the fireplace, and the door of an inner room between the fireplace and our observant sparrow. Against the right hand wall is a filing cabinet, with a cupboard on it, and, nearer, a tall office desk and stool for one person. In the middle of the room a large double writing table is set across, with a chair at each end for the two partners. It is a room which no woman would tolerate, smelling of tobacco, and much in need of repapering, repainting, and recarpeting; but this is the effect of bachelor untidiness and indifference, not want of means; for nothing that Doyle and Broadbent themselves have purchased is cheap; nor is anything they want lacking. On the walls hang a large map of South America, a pictorial advertisement of a steamship company, an impressive portrait of Gladstone, and several caricatures of Mr Balfour as a rabbit and Mr Chamberlain as a fox by Francis Carruthers Gould.

At twenty minutes to five o'clock on a summer afternoon in 1904, *the room is empty. Presently the outer door is opened, and a valet comes in laden with a large Gladstone bag and a strap of rugs. He carries them into the inner room. He is a respectable valet, old enough to have lost all alacrity and acquired an air of putting up patiently with a great deal of trouble and indifferent health. The luggage belongs to Broadbent, who enters after the valet. He pulls off his overcoat and hangs it with his hat on the stand. Then he comes to the writing table and looks through the letters waiting there for him. He is a robust, full-blooded, energetic man in the prime of life, sometimes eager and credulous, sometimes shrewd and roguish, sometimes portentously solemn, sometimes jolly and impetuous, always buoyant and irresistible, mostly likeable, and enormously absurd in his most earnest moments. He bursts open his letters with his thumb, and glances through them, flinging the envelopes about the floor with reckless untidiness whilst he talks to the valet.*

BROADBENT [*calling*] Hodson.

HODSON [*in the bedroom*] Yes sir.

BROADBENT. Dont unpack. Just take out the things Ive worn; and put in clean things.

HODSON [*appearing at the bedroom door*] Yes sir. [*He turns to go back into the bedroom*].

BROADBENT. And look here! [*Hodson turns again*]. Do you remember where I put my revolver?

HODSON. Revolver, sir! Yes sir. Mr Doyle uses it as a paper-weight, sir, when he's drawing.

BROADBENT. Well, I want it packed. Theres a packet of cartridges somewhere, I think. Find it and pack it as well.

HODSON. Yes sir.

BROADBENT. By the way, pack your own traps too. I shall take you with me this time.

HODSON [*hesitant*] Is it a dangerous part youre going to, sir? Should I be expected to carry a revolver, sir?

BROADBENT. Perhaps it might be as well. I'm going to Ireland.

HODSON [*reassured*] Yes sir.

BROADBENT. You dont feel nervous about it, I suppose?

HODSON. Not at all, sir. I'll risk it, sir.

BROADBENT. Ever been in Ireland?

HODSON. No sir. I understand it's a very wet climate, sir. I'd better pack your india-rubber overalls.

BROADBENT. Do. Wheres Mr Doyle?

HODSON. I'm expecting him at five, sir. He went out after

lunch.

BROADBENT. Anybody been looking for me?

HODSON. A person giving the name of Haffigan has called twice today, sir.

BROADBENT. Oh, I'm sorry. Why didnt he wait? I told him to wait if I wasnt in.

HODSON. Well sir, I didnt know you expected him; so I thought it best to—to—not to encourage him, sir.

BROADBENT. Oh, he's all right. He's an Irishman, and not very particular about his appearance.

HODSON. Yes sir: I noticed that he was rather Irish.

BROADBENT. If he calls again let him come up.

HODSON. I think I saw him waiting about, sir, when you drove up. Shall I fetch him, sir?

BROADBENT. Do, Hodson.

HODSON. Yes sir. [*He makes for the outer door*].

BROADBENT. He'll want tea. Let us have some.

HODSON [*stopping*] I shouldnt think he drank tea, sir.

BROADBENT. Well, bring whatever you think he'd like.

HODSON. Yes sir. [*An electric bell rings*]. Here he is, sir. Saw you arrive, sir.

BROADBENT. Right. Shew him in. [*Hodson goes out. Broadbent gets through the rest of his letters before Hodson returns with the visitor*].

HODSON. Mr Affigan.

Haffigan is a stunted, shortnecked, smallheaded man of about 30, *with a small bullet head, a red nose, and furtive eyes. He is dressed in seedy black, almost clerically, and might be a tenth-rate schoolmaster ruined by drink. He hastens to shake Broadbent's hand with a show of reckless geniality and high spirits, helped out by a rollicking stage brogue. This is perhaps a comfort to himself, as he is secretly pursued by the horrors of incipient delirium tremens.*

HAFFIGAN. Tim Haffigan, sir, at your service. The top o the mornin to you, Misther Broadbent.

BROADBENT [*delighted with his Irish visitor*] Good afternoon, Mr Haffigan.

TIM. An is it the afthernoon it is already? Begorra, what I

call the mornin is all the time a man fasts afther breakfast.

BROADBENT. Havnt you lunched?

TIM. Divil a lunch!

BROADBENT. I'm sorry I couldnt get back from Brighton in time to offer you some; but—

TIM. Not a word, sir, not a word. Sure itll do tomorrow. Besides, I'm Irish, sir: a poor aither, but a powerful dhrinker.

BROADBENT. I was just about to ring for tea when you came. Sit down, Mr Haffigan.

TIM. Tay is a good dhrink if your nerves can stand it. Mine cant.

Haffigan sits down at the writing table, with his back to the filing cabinet. Broadbent sits opposite him. Hodson enters empty-handed; takes two glasses, a siphon, and a tantalus from the cupboard; places them before Broadbent on the writing table; looks ruthlessly at Haffigan, who cannot meet his eye; and retires.

BROADBENT. Try a whisky and soda.

TIM [*sobered*] There you touch the national wakeness, sir. [*Piously*] Not that I share it meself. Ive seen too much of the mischief of it.

BROADBENT [*pouring the whisky*] Say when.

TIM. Not too sthrong. [*Broadbent stops and looks inquiringly at him*]. Say half-an-half. [*Broadbent, somewhat startled by this demand, pours a little more, and again stops and looks*]. Just a dhrain more: the lower half o the tumbler doesnt hold a fair half. Thankya.

BROADBENT [*laughing*] You Irishmen certainly do know how to drink. [*Pouring some whisky for himself*] Now thats my poor English idea of a whisky and soda.

TIM. An a very good idea it is too. Dhrink is the curse o me unhappy counthry. I take it meself because Ive a wake heart and a poor digestion; but in principle I'm a teetoatler.

BROADBENT [*suddenly solemn and strenuous*] So am I, of course. I'm a Local Optionist to the backbone. You have no idea, Mr Haffigan, of the ruin that is wrought in this country by the unholy alliance of the publicans, the bishops, the

Tories, and The Times. We must close the public-houses at all costs [*he drinks*].

TIM. Sure I know. It's awful [*he drinks*]. I see youre a good Liberal like meself, sir.

BROADBENT. I am a lover of liberty, like every true Englishman, Mr Haffigan. My name is Broadbent. If my name were Breitstein, and I had a hooked nose and a house in Park Lane, I should carry a Union Jack handkerchief and a penny trumpet, and tax the food of the people to support the Navy League, and clamor for the destruction of the last remnants of national liberty—

TIM. Not another word. Shake hands.

BROADBENT. But I should like to explain—

TIM. Sure I know every word youre goin to say before ye said it. *I* know the sort o man yar. An so youre thinkin o comin to Ireland for a bit?

BROADBENT. Where else can I go? I am an Englishman and a Liberal; and now that South Africa has been enslaved and destroyed, there is no country left to me to take an interest in but Ireland. Mind: I dont say that an Englishman has not other duties. He has a duty to Finland and a duty to Macedonia. But what sane man can deny that an Englishman's first duty is his duty to Ireland? Unfortunately, we have politicians here more unscrupulous than Bobrikoff, more bloodthirsty than Abdul the Damned; and it is under their heel that Ireland is now writhing.

TIM. Faith, theyve reckoned up with poor oul Bobrikoff anyhow.

BROADBENT. Not that I defend assassination: God forbid! However strongly we may feel that the unfortunate and patriotic young man who avenged the wrongs of Finland on the Russian tyrant was perfectly right from his own point of view, yet every civilized man must regard murder with abhorrence. Not even in defence of Free Trade would I lift my hand against a political opponent, however richly he might deserve it.

TIM. I'm sure you wouldnt; and I honor you for it. Youre

goin to Ireland, then, out o sympithy: is it?

BROADBENT. I'm going to develop an estate there for the Land Development Syndicate, in which I am interested. I am convinced that all it needs to make it pay is to handle it properly, as estates are handled in England. You know the English plan, Mr Haffigan, dont you?

TIM. Bedad I do, sir. Take all you can out of Ireland and spend it in England: thats it.

BROADBENT [*not quite liking this*] My plan, sir, will be to take a little money out of England and spend it in Ireland.

TIM. More power to your elbow! an may your shadda never be less! for youre the broth of a boy intirely. An how can I help you? Command me to the last dhrop o me blood.

BROADBENT. Have you ever heard of Garden City?

TIM [*doubtfully*] D'ye mane Heavn?

BROADBENT. Heaven! No: it's near Hitchin. If you can spare half an hour I'll go into it with you.

TIM. I tell you hwat. Gimme a prospectus. Lemmy take it home and reflect on it.

BROADBENT. Youre quite right: I will. [*He gives him a copy of Ebenezer Howard's book, and several pamphlets*]. You understand that the map of the city—the circular construction—is only a suggestion.

TIM. I'll make a careful note o that [*looking dazedly at the map*].

BROADBENT. What I say is, why not start a Garden City in Ireland?

TIM [*with enthusiasm*] Thats just what was on the tip o me tongue to ask you. Why not? [*Defiantly*] Tell me why not.

BROADBENT. There are difficulties. I shall overcome them; but there are difficulties. When I first arrive in Ireland I shall be hated as an Englishman. As a Protestant, I shall be denounced from every altar. My life may be in danger. Well, I am prepared to face that.

TIM. Never fear, sir. We know how to respict a brave innimy.

BROADBENT. What I really dread is misunderstanding. I

think you could help me to avoid that. When I heard you speak the other evening in Bermondsey at the meeting of the National League, I saw at once that you were—You wont mind my speaking frankly?

TIM. Tell me all me faults as man to man. I can stand anything but flatthery.

BROADBENT. May I put it in this way? that I saw at once that you are a thorough Irishman, with all the faults and all the qualities of your race; rash and improvident but brave and goodnatured; not likely to succeed in business on your own account perhaps, but eloquent, humorous, a lover of freedom, and a true follower of that great Englishman Gladstone.

TIM. Spare me blushes. I mustnt sit here to be praised to me face. But I confess to the goodnature: it's an Irish wakeness. I'd share me last shillin with a friend.

BROADBENT. I feel sure you would, Mr Haffigan.

TIM [*impulsively*] Damn it! call me Tim. A man that talks about Ireland as you do may call me anything. Gimmy a howlt o that whisky bottle [*he replenishes*].

BROADBENT [*smiling indulgently*] Well, Tim, will you come with me and help to break the ice between me and your warmhearted, impulsive countrymen?

TIM. Will I come to Madagascar or Cochin China wid you? Bedad I'll come to the North Pole wid you if yll pay me fare; for the divil a shillin I have to buy a third class ticket.

BROADBENT. Ive not forgotten that, Tim. We must put that little matter on a solid English footing, though the rest can be as Irish as you please. You must come as my—my—well, I hardly know what to call it. If we call you my agent, theyll shoot you. If we call you a bailiff, theyll duck you in the horsepond. I have a secretary already; and—

TIM. Then we'll call him the Home Secretary and me the Irish Secretary. Eh?

BROADBENT [*laughing industriously*] Capital. Your Irish wit has settled the first difficulty. Now about your salary—

TIM. A salary, is it? Sure I'd do it for nothin, only me cloes ud disgrace you; and I'd be dhriven to borra money from your friends: a thing thats agin me nacher. But I wont take a penny more than a hundherd a year. [*He looks with restless cunning at Broadbent, trying to guess how far he may go*].

BROADBENT. If that will satisfy you—

TIM [*more than reassured*] Why shouldnt it satisfy me? A hundherd a year is twelve pound a month, isnt it?

BROADBENT. No. Eight pound six and eightpence.

TIM. Oh murdher! An I'll have to send five timmy poor oul mother in Ireland. But no matther: I said a hundherd; and what I said I'll stick to, if I have to starve for it.

BROADBENT [*with business caution*]Well, let us say twelve pounds for the first month. Afterwards, we shall see how we get on.

TIM. Youre a gentleman, sir. Whin me mother turns up her toes, you shall take the five pounds off; for your expinses must be kep down wid a sthrong hand; an—[*He is interrupted by the arrival of Broadbent's partner*].

Mr Laurence Doyle is a man of 36, with cold grey eyes, strained nose, fine fastidious lips, critical brows, clever head, rather refined and goodlooking on the whole, but with a suggestion of thinskinnedness and dissatisfaction that contrasts strongly with Broadbent's eupeptic jollity.

He comes in as a man at home there, but on seeing the stranger shrinks at once, and is about to withdraw when Broadbent reassures him. He then comes forward to the table, between the two others.

DOYLE [*retreating*] Youre engaged.

BROADBENT. Not at all, not at all. Come in. [*To Tim*] This gentleman is a friend who lives with me here: my partner, Mr Doyle. [*To Doyle*] This is a new Irish friend of mine, Mr Tim Haffigan.

TIM (*rising with effusion*] Sure it's meself thats proud to meet any friend o Misther Broadbent's. The top o the mornin to you, sir! Me heart goes out teeye both. It's not often I meet two such splendid speciments iv the Anglo-Saxon race.

BROADBENT [*chuckling*] Wrong for once, Tim. My friend

Mr Doyle is a countryman of yours.

Tim is noticeably dashed by this announcement. He draws in his horns at once, and scowls suspiciously at Doyle under a vanishing mask of goodfellowship: cringing a little, too, in mere nerveless fear of him.

DOYLE [*with cool disgust*] Good evening. [*He retires to the fireplace, and says to Broadbent in a tone which conveys the strongest possible hint to Haffigan that he is unwelcome*] Will you soon be disengaged?

TIM [*his brogue decaying into a common would-be genteel accent with an unexpected strain of Glasgow in it*] I must be going. Avnmpoartnt engeegement in the west end.

BROADBENT [*rising*] It's settled then, that you come with me.

TIM. Ashll be verra pleased to accompany ye, sir.

BROADBENT. But how soon? Can you start tonight? from Paddington? We go by Milford Haven.

TIM [*hesitating*] Well—A'm afraid—A [*Doyle goes abruptly into the bedroom, slamming the door and shattering the last remnant of Tim's nerve. The poor wretch saves himself from bursting into tears by plunging again into his role of daredevil Irishman. He rushes to Broadbent; plucks his sleeve with trembling fingers; and pours forth his entreaty with all the brogue he can muster, subduing his voice lest Doyle should hear and return*]. Misther Broadbent: dont humiliate me before a fella counthryman. Look here: me cloes is up the spout. Gimmy a fypounnote—I'll pay ya nex Choosda whin me ship comes home—or you can stop it out o me month's sallery. I'll be on the platform at Paddnton punctial an ready. Gimmy it quick, before he comes back. You wont mind me axin, will ye?

BROADBENT. Not at all. I was about to offer you an advance for travelling expenses. [*He gives him a bank note*].

TIM [*pocketing it*] Thank you. I'll be there half an hour before the thrain starts. [*Larry is heard at the bedroom door, returning*]. Whisht: he's comin back. Goodbye an God bless ye. [*He hurries out almost crying, the £5 note and all the drink it means to him being too much for his empty stomach and over-*

strained nerves].

DOYLE [*returning*] Where the devil did you pick up that seedy swindler? What was he doing here? [*He goes up to the table where the plans are, and makes a note on one of them, referring to his pocket book as he does so*].

BROADBENT. There you go! Why are you so down on every Irishman you meet, especially if he's a bit shabby? poor devil! Surely a fellow-countryman may pass you the top of the morning without offence, even if his coat is a bit shiny at the seams.

DOYLE [*contemptuously*] The top of the morning! Did he call you the broth of a boy? [*He comes to the writing table*].

BROADBENT [*triumphantly*] Yes.

DOYLE. And wished you more power to your elbow?

BROADBENT. He did.

DOYLE. And that your shadow might never be less?

BROADBENT. Certainly.

DOYLE [*taking up the depleted whisky bottle and shaking his head at it*] And he got about half a pint of whisky out of you.

BROADBENT. It did him no harm. He never turned a hair.

DOYLE. How much money did he borrow?

BROADBENT. It was not borrowing exactly. He shewed a very honorable spirit about money. I believe he would share his last shilling with a friend.

DOYLE. No doubt he would share his friend's last shilling if his friend was fool enough to let him. How much did he touch you for?

BROADBENT. Oh, nothing. An advance on his salary—for travelling expenses.

DOYLE. Salary! In Heaven's name, what for?

BROADBENT. For being my Home Secretary, as he very wittily called it.

DOYLE. I dont see the joke.

BROADBENT. You can spoil any joke by being cold blooded about it. I saw it all right when he said it. It was something—something really very amusing—about the Home Secretary and the Irish Secretary. At all events, he's evidently the very man to take with me to Ireland to break the ice for me. He can gain the confidence of the people there, and make them friendly to me. Eh? [*He seats himself on the office stool, and tilts it back so that the edge of the standing desk supports his back and prevents his toppling over*].

DOYLE. A nice introduction, by George! Do you suppose the whole population of Ireland consists of drunken begging letter writers, or that even if it did, they would accept one another as references?

BROADBENT. Pooh! nonsense! he's only an Irishman. Besides, you dont seriously suppose that Haffigan can humbug me, do you?

DOYLE. No: he's too lazy to take the trouble. All he has to do is to sit there and drink your whisky while you humbug yourself. However, we neednt argue about Haffigan, for two reasons. First, with your money in his pocket he will never reach Paddington: there are too many public houses on the way. Second, he's not an Irishman at all.

BROADBENT. Not an Irishman! [*He is so amazed by the statement that he straightens himself and brings the stool bolt upright*].

DOYLE. Born in Glasgow. Never was in Ireland in his life. I know all about him.

BROADBENT. But he spoke—he behaved just like an Irishman.

DOYLE. Like an Irishman!! Man alive, dont you know that all this top-o-the-morning and broth-of-a-boy and more-power-to-your-elbow business is got up in England to fool you, like the Albert Hall concerts of Irish music? No Irishman ever talks like that in Ireland, or ever did, or ever will. But when a thoroughly worthless Irishman comes to England, and finds the whole place full of romantic duffers like you, who will let him loaf and drink and sponge and brag as long as he flatters your sense of moral superiority by playing the fool and degrading himself and his country, he soon learns the antics that take you in. He picks them up at the theatre or the music hall. Haffigan learnt the rudiments from his father, who came from my part of Ireland. I knew his uncles, Matt and Andy Haffigan of Rosscullen.

BROADBENT [*still incredulous*] But his brogue?

DOYLE. His brogue! A fat lot you know about brogues! Ive heard you call a Dublin accent that you could hang your hat on, a brogue. Heaven help you! you dont know the difference between Connemara and Rathmines. [*With violent irritation*] Oh, damn Tim Haffigan! lets drop the subject: he's not worth wrangling about.

BROADBENT. Whats wrong with you today, Larry? Why are you so bitter?

Doyle looks at him perplexedly; comes slowly to the writing table; and sits down at the end next the fireplace before replying.

DOYLE. Well: your letter completely upset me, for one thing.

BROADBENT. Why?

DOYLE. Your foreclosing this Rosscullen mortgage and turning poor Nick Lestrange out of house and home has rather taken me aback; for I liked the old rascal when I was a boy and had the run of his park to play in. I was brought up on the property.

BROADBENT. But he wouldnt pay the interest. I had to foreclose on behalf of the Syndicate. So now I'm off to Rosscullen to look after the property myself. [*He sits down at the writing table opposite Larry, and adds, casually, but with an anxious glance at his partner*] Youre coming with me, of course?

DOYLE [*rising nervously and recommencing his restless movements*] Thats it. Thats what I dread. Thats what has upset me.

BROADBENT. But dont you want to see your country again after 18 years absence? to see your people? to be in the old home again? to—

DOYLE [*interrupting him very impatiently*] Yes, yes: I know all that as well as you do.

BROADBENT. Oh well, of course [*with a shrug*] if you take it in that way, I'm sorry.

DOYLE. Never mind my temper: it's not meant for you, as you ought to know by this time. [*He sits down again, a little ashamed of his petulance; reflects a moment bitterly; then bursts out*] I have an instinct against going back to Ireland: an instinct so strong that I'd rather go with you to the South Pole than to Rosscullen.

BROADBENT. What! Here you are, belonging to a nation with the strongest patriotism! the most inveterate homing instinct in the world! and you pretend youd rather go anywhere than back to Ireland. You dont suppose I believe you, do you? In your heart—

DOYLE. Never mind my heart: an Irishman's heart is nothing but his imagination. How many of all those millions that have left Ireland have ever come back or wanted to come back? But whats the use of talking to you? Three verses of twaddle about the Irish emigrant "sitting on the stile, Mary," or three hours of Irish patriotism in Bermondsey or the Scotland Division of Liverpool, go further with you than all the facts that stare you in the face. Why, man alive, look at me! You know the way I nag, and worry, and carp, and cavil, and disparage, and am never satisfied and never quiet, and try the patience of my best friends.

BROADBENT. Oh, come, Larry! do yourself justice. Youre very amusing and agreeable to strangers.

DOYLE. Yes, to strangers. Perhaps if I was a bit stiffer to strangers, and a bit easier at home, like an Englishman, I'd be better company for you.

BROADBENT. We get on well enough. Of course you have the melancholy of the Keltic race—

DOYLE [*bounding out of his chair*] Good God!!!

BROADBENT [*slyly*]—and also its habit of using strong language when theres nothing the matter.

DOYLE. Nothing the matter! When people talk about the Celtic race, I feel as if I could burn down London. That sort of rot does more harm than ten Coercion Acts. Do you suppose a man need be a Celt to feel melancholy in Rosscullen? Why, man, Ireland was peopled just as England was; and its breed was crossed by just the same invaders.

BROADBENT. True. All the capable people in Ireland are of English extraction. It has often struck me as a most remarkable circumstance that the only party in parliament which shews the genuine old English character and spirit is the Irish party. Look at its independence, its determination, its defiance of bad Governments, its sympathy with oppressed nationalities all the world over! How English!

DOYLE. Not to mention the solemnity with which it talks old-fashioned nonsense which it knows perfectly well to be a century behind the times. Thats English, if you like.

BROADBENT. No, Larry, no. You are thinking of the modern hybrids that now monopolize England. Hypocrites, humbugs, Germans, Jews, Yankees, foreigners, Park Laners, cosmopolitan riffraff. Dont call them English. They dont belong to the dear old island, but to their confounded new empire; and by George! theyre worthy of it; and I wish them joy of it.

DOYLE [*unmoved by this outburst*] There! You feel better now, dont you?

BROADBENT [*defiantly*] I do. Much better.

DOYLE. My dear Tom, you only need a touch of the Irish climate to be as big a fool as I am myself. If all my Irish blood were poured into your veins, you wouldnt turn a hair of your constitution and character. Go and marry the most English Englishwoman you can find, and then bring up your son in Rosscullen; and that son's character will be so like mine and so unlike yours that everybody will accuse me of being his father. [*With sudden anguish*] Rosscullen! oh, good Lord, Rosscullen! The dullness! the hopelessness! the ignorance! the bigotry!

BROADBENT [*matter-of-factly*] The usual thing in the country, Larry. Just the same here.

DOYLE [*hastily*] No, no: the climate is different. Here, if the life is dull, you can be dull too, and no great harm done. [*Going off into a passionate dream*] But your wits cant thicken in that soft moist air, on those white springy roads, in those misty rushes and brown bogs, on those hillsides of granite rocks and magenta heather. Youve no such colors in the sky, no such lure in the distances, no such sadness in the evenings. Oh, the dreaming! the dreaming! the torturing, heart-scalding, never satisfying dreaming, dreaming, dreaming, dreaming! [*Savagely*] No debauchery that ever coarsened and brutalized an Englishman can take the worth and usefulness out of him like that dreaming. An Irishman's imagination never lets him alone, never convinces him, never satisfies him; but it makes him that he cant face reality nor deal with it nor handle it nor conquer it: he can only sneer at them that do, and [*bitterly, at Broadbent*] be "agreeable to strangers," like a good-for-nothing woman on the streets. [*Gabbling at Broadbent across the table*] It's all dreaming, all imagination. He cant be religious. The inspired Churchman that teaches him the sanctity of life and the importance of conduct is sent away empty; while the poor village priest that gives him a miracle or a sentimental story of a saint, has cathedrals built for him out of the pennies of the poor. He cant be intelligently political: he dreams of what the Shan Van Vocht said in ninetyeight. If you want to interest him in Ireland youve got to call the unfortunate island Kathleen ni Hollihan and pretend she's a little old woman. It saves thinking. It saves working. It saves everything except imagination, imagination, imagination; and imagination's such a torture that you cant bear it without whisky. [*With fierce shivering self-contempt*] At last you get that you can bear nothing real at all: youd rather starve than cook a meal; youd rather go shabby and dirty than set your mind to take care of your clothes and wash yourself; you nag and squabble at home because your wife isnt an angel, and she despises you because youre not a hero; and you hate the whole lot round you because theyre only poor slovenly useless devils like yourself. [*Dropping his voice like a man making some shameful confidence*] And all the while there goes on a horrible, senseless, mischievous laughter. When youre young, you exchange drinks with other young men; and you exchange vile stories with them; and as youre too futile to be able to help or cheer them, you chaff and sneer and taunt them for not doing the things you darent do yourself. And all the time you laugh! laugh! laugh! eternal derision, eternal envy, eternal folly, eternal fouling and staining and degrading, until, when you come at last to a country where men take a question seriously and give a serious answer to it, you deride them for having no sense of humor, and plume yourself on your own worthlessness as if it made you better than them.

BROADBENT [*roused to intense earnestness by Doyle's eloquence*] Never despair, Larry. There are great possibilities for Ireland. Home Rule will work wonders under English guidance.

DOYLE [*pulled up short, his face twitching with a reluctant smile*] Tom: why do you select my most tragic moments for your most irresistible strokes of humor?

BROADBENT. Humor! I was perfectly serious. What do you mean? Do you doubt my seriousness about Home Rule?

DOYLE. I am sure you are serious, Tom, about the English guidance.

BROADBENT [*quite reassured*] Of course I am. Our guidance is the important thing. We English must place our capacity for government without stint at the service of nations who are less fortunately endowed in that respect; so as to allow them to develop in perfect freedom to the English level of self-government, you know. You understand me?

DOYLE. Perfectly. And Rosscullen will understand you too.

BROADBENT [*cheerfully*] Of course it will. So thats all right. [*He pulls up his chair and settles himself comfortably to lecture Doyle*]. Now, Larry, Ive listened carefully to all youve said about Ireland; and I can see nothing whatever to prevent your coming with me. What does it all come to? Simply that you were only a young fellow when you were in Ireland. Youll find all that chaffing and drinking and not knowing what to be at in Peckham just the same as in Donnybrook.

You looked at Ireland with a boy's eyes and saw only boyish things. Come back with me and look at it with a man's; and get a better opinion of your country.

DOYLE. I daresay youre partly right in that; at all events I know very well that if I had been the son of a laborer instead of the son of a country landagent, I should have struck more grit than I did. Unfortunately I'm not going back to visit the Irish nation, but to visit my father and Aunt Judy and Nora Reilly and Father Dempsey and the rest of them.

BROADBENT. Well, why not? Theyll be delighted to see you, now that England has made a man of you.

DOYLE [*struck by this*] Ah! you hit the mark there, Tom, with true British inspiration.

BROADBENT. Common sense, you mean.

DOYLE [*quickly*] No I dont: youve no more common sense than a gander. No Englishman has any common sense, or ever had, or ever will have. Youre going on a sentimental expedition for perfectly ridiculous reasons, with your head full of political nonsense that would not take in any ordinarily intelligent donkey; but you can hit me in the eye with the simple truth about myself and my father.

BROADBENT [*amazed*] I never mentioned your father.

DOYLE [*not heeding the interruption*] There he is in Rosscullen, a landagent who's always been in a small way because he's a Catholic, and the landlords are mostly Protestants. What with land courts reducing rents and Land Purchase Acts turning big estates into little holdings, he'd be a beggar if he hadnt taken to collecting the new purchase instalments instead of the old rents. I doubt if he's been further from home than Athenmullet for twenty years. And here am I, made a man of, as you say, by England.

BROADBENT [*apologetically*] I assure you I never meant—

DOYLE. Oh, dont apologize: it's quite true. I daresay Ive learnt something in America and a few other remote and inferior spots; but in the main it is by living with you and working in double harness with you that I have learnt to live in a real world and not in an imaginary one. I owe more to you than to any Irishman.

BROADBENT [*shaking his head with a twinkle in his eye*] Very friendly of you, Larry, old man, but all blarney. I like blarney; but it's rot, all the same.

DOYLE. No it's not. I should never have done anything without you; though I never stop wondering at that blessed old head of yours with all its ideas in watertight compartments, and all the compartments warranted impervious to anything it doesnt suit you to understand.

BROADBENT [*invincible*] Unmitigated rot, Larry, I assure you.

DOYLE. Well, at any rate you will admit that all my friends are either Englishmen or men of the big world that belongs to the big Powers. All the serious part of my life has been lived in that atmosphere: all the serious part of my work has been done with men of that sort. Just think of me as I am now going back to Rosscullen! to that hell of littleness and monotony! How am I to get on with a little country land-agent that ekes out his 5 per cent with a little farming and a scrap of house property in the nearest country town? What am I to say to him? What is he to say to me?

BROADBENT [*scandalized*] But youre father and son, man!

DOYLE. What difference does that make? What would you say if I proposed a visit to your father?

BROADBENT [*with filial rectitude*] I always made a point of going to see my father regularly until his mind gave way.

DOYLE [*concerned*] Has he gone mad? You never told me.

BROADBENT. He has joined the Tariff Reform League. He would never have done that if his mind had not been weakened. [*Beginning to declaim*] He has fallen a victim to the arts of a political charlatan who—

DOYLE [*interrupting him*] You mean that you keep clear of your father because he differs from you about Free Trade, and you dont want to quarrel with him. Well, think of me and my father! He's a Nationalist and a Separatist. I'm a metallurgical chemist turned civil engineer. Now whatever else metallurgical chemistry may be, it's not national. It's international. And my business and yours as civil engineers is to join countries, not to separate them. The one real political conviction that our business has rubbed into us is that frontiers are hindrances and flags confounded nuisances.

BROADBENT [*still smarting under Mr Chamberlain's economic heresy*] Only when there is a protective tariff—

DOYLE [*firmly*] Now look here, Tom: you want to get in a speech on Free Trade; and youre not going to do it: I wont stand it. My father wants to make St George's Channel a frontier and hoist a green flag on College Green; and I want to bring Galway within 3 hours of Colchester and 24 of New York. I want Ireland to be the brains and imagination of a big Commonwealth, not a Robinson Crusoe island. Then theres the religious difficulty. My Catholicism is the Catholicism of Charlemagne or Dante, qualified by a great deal of modern science and folklore which Father Dempsey would call the ravings of an Atheist. Well, my father's Catholicism is the Catholicism of Father Dempsey.

BROADBENT [*shrewdly*] I dont want to interrupt you, Larry; but you know this is all gammon. These differences exist in all families; but the members rub on together all right. [*Suddenly relapsing into portentousness*] Of course there are some questions which touch the very foundations of morals; and on these I grant you even the closest relationships cannot excuse any compromise or laxity. For instance—

DOYLE [*impatiently springing up and walking about*] For instance, Home Rule, South Africa, Free Trade, and putting the Church schools on the Education Rate. Well, I should differ from my father on every one of them, probably, just as I differ from you about them.

BROADBENT. Yes; but you are an Irishman; and these things are not serious to you as they are to an Englishman.

DOYLE. What! not even Home Rule!

BROADBENT [*steadfastly*] Not even Home Rule. We owe Home Rule not to the Irish, but to our English Gladstone. No, Larry: I cant help thinking that theres something behind all this.

DOYLE [*hotly*] What is there behind it? Do you think I'm humbugging you?

BROADBENT. Dont fly out, old chap. I only thought—

DOYLE. What did you think?

BROADBENT. Well, a moment ago I caught a name which is new to me: a Miss Nora Reilly, I think. [*Doyle stops dead and stares at him with something like awe*]. I dont wish to be impertinent, as you know, Larry; but are you sure she has nothing to do with your reluctance to come to Ireland with me?

DOYLE [*sitting down again, vanquished*] Thomas Broadbent: I surrender. The poor silly-clever Irishman takes off his hat to God's Englishman. The man who could in all seriousness make that recent remark of yours about Home Rule and Gladstone must be simply the champion idiot of all the world. Yet the man who could in the very next sentence sweep away all my special pleading and go straight to the heart of my motives must be a man of genius. But that the idiot and the genius should be the same man! how is that possible? [*Springing to his feet*] By Jove, I see it all now. I'll write an article about it, and send it to Nature.

BROADBENT [*staring at him*] What on earth—

DOYLE. It's quite simple. You know that a caterpillar—

BROADBENT. A caterpillar!!!

DOYLE. Yes, a caterpillar. Now give your mind to what I am going to say; for it's a new and important scientific theory of the English national character. A caterpillar—

BROADBENT. Look here, Larry: dont be an ass.

DOYLE [*insisting*] I say a caterpillar and I mean a caterpillar. Youll understand presently. A caterpillar [*Broadbent mutters a slight protest, but does not press it*] when it gets into a tree, instinctively makes itself look exactly like a leaf; so that both its enemies and its prey may mistake it for one and think it not worth bothering about.

BROADBENT. Whats that got to do with our English national character?

DOYLE. I'll tell you. The world is as full of fools as a tree is full of leaves. Well, the Englishman does what the caterpillar does. He instinctively makes himself look like a fool, and eats up all the real fools at his ease while his enemies let him alone and laugh at him for being a fool like the rest. Oh, nature is cunning! cunning! [*He sits down, lost in contemplation of his word-picture*].

BROADBENT [*with hearty admiration*] Now you know, Larry, that would never have occurred to me. You Irish people are amazingly clever. Of course it's all tommy rot; but it's so brilliant, you know! How the dickens do you think of such things! You really must write an article about it: theyll pay you something for it. If Nature wont have it, I can get it into Engineering for you: I know the editor.

DOYLE. Lets get back to business. I'd better tell you about Nora Reilly.

BROADBENT. No: never mind. I shouldnt have alluded to her.

DOYLE. I'd rather. Nora has a fortune.

BROADBENT [*keenly interested*] Eh? How much?

DOYLE. Forty per annum.

BROADBENT. Forty thousand?

DOYLE. No, forty. Forty pounds.

BROADBENT [*much dashed*] Thats what you call a fortune in Rosscullen, is it?

DOYLE. A girl with a dowry of five pounds calls it a fortune in Rosscullen. Whats more, £40 a year is a fortune there; and Nora Reilly enjoys a good deal of social consideration as an heiress on the strength of it. It has helped my father's household through many a tight place. My father was her father's agent. She came on a visit to us when he died, and has lived with us ever since.

BROADBENT [*attentively, beginning to suspect Larry of misconduct with Nora, and resolving to get to the bottom of it*] Since when? I mean how old were you when she came?

DOYLE. I was seventeen. So was she: if she'd been older she'd have had more sense than to stay with us. We were together for 18 months before I went up to Dublin to study. When I went home for Christmas and Easter, she was there. I suppose it used to be something of an event for her; though of course I never thought of that then.

BROADBENT. Were you at all hard hit?

DOYLE. Not really. I had only two ideas at that time: first, to learn to do something; and then to get out of Ireland and have a chance of doing it. She didnt count. I was romantic about her, just as I was romantic about Byron's heroines or the old Round Tower of Rosscullen; but she didnt count any more than they did. Ive never crossed St George's Channel since for her sake—never even landed at Queenstown and come back to London through Ireland.

BROADBENT. But did you ever say anything that would justify her in waiting for you?

DOYLE. No, never. But she is waiting for me.

BROADBENT. How do you know?

DOYLE. She writes to me—on her birthday. She used to write on mine, and send me little things as presents; but I stopped that by pretending that it was no use when I was travelling, as they got lost in the foreign post-offices. [*He pronounces post-offices with the stress on offices, instead of on post*].

BROADBENT. You answer the letters?

DOYLE. Not very punctually. But they get acknowledged at one time or another.

BROADBENT. How do you feel when you see her handwriting?

DOYLE. Uneasy. I'd give £50 to escape a letter.

BROADBENT [*looking grave, and throwing himself back in his chair to intimate that the cross-examination is over, and the result very damaging to the witness*] Hm!

DOYLE. What d'ye mean by Hm!

BROADBENT. Of course I know that the moral code is different in Ireland. But in England it's not considered fair to trifle with a woman's affections.

DOYLE. You mean that an Englishman would get engaged to another woman and return Nora her letters and presents with a letter to say he was unworthy of her and wished her every happiness?

BROADBENT. Well, even that would set the poor girl's mind at rest.

DOYLE. Would it? I wonder! One thing I can tell you; and that is that Nora would wait until she died of old age sooner than ask my intentions or condescend to hint at the possibility of my having any. You dont know what Irish pride is. England may have knocked a good deal of it out of me; but she's never been in England; and if I had to choose between wounding that delicacy in her and hitting her in the face, I'd hit her in the face without a moment's hesitation.

BROADBENT [*who has been nursing his knee and reflecting, apparently rather agreeably*] You know, all this sounds rather interesting. Theres the Irish charm about it. Thats the worst of you: the Irish charm doesnt exist for you.

DOYLE. Oh yes it does. But it's the charm of a dream. Live in contact with dreams and you will get something of their charm: live in contact with facts and you will get something of their brutality. I wish I could find a country to live in where the facts were not brutal and the dreams not unreal.

BROADBENT [*changing his attitude and responding to Doyle's earnestness with deep conviction: his elbows on the table and his hands clenched*] Dont despair, Larry, old boy: things may look black; but there will be a great change after the next election.

DOYLE [*jumping up*] Oh, get out, you idiot!

BROADBENT [*rising also, not a bit snubbed*] Ha! ha! you may laugh; but we shall see. However, dont let us argue about that. Come now! you ask my advice about Miss Reilly?

DOYLE [*reddening*] No I dont. Damn your advice! [*Softening*] Lets have it, all the same.

BROADBENT. Well, everything you tell me about her impresses me favorably. She seems to have the feelings of a lady; and though we must face the fact that in England her income would hardly maintain her in the lower middle class—

DOYLE [*interrupting*] Now look here, Tom. That reminds me. When you go to Ireland, just drop talking about the middle class and bragging of belonging to it. In Ireland youre either a gentleman or youre not. If you want to be particularly offensive to Nora, you can call her a Papist; but if you call her a middle-class woman, Heaven help you!

BROADBENT [*irrepressible*] Never fear. Youre all descended from the ancient kings: I know that. [*Complacently*] I'm not so tactless as you think, my boy. [*Earnest again*] I expect to find Miss Reilly a perfect lady; and I strongly advise you to come and have another look at her before you make up your mind about her. By the way, have you a photograph of her?

DOYLE. Her photographs stopped at twenty-five.

BROADBENT [*saddened*] Ah yes, I suppose so. [*With feeling, severely*] Larry: youve treated that poor girl disgracefully.

DOYLE. By George, if she only knew that two men were talking about her like this—!

BROADBENT. She wouldnt like it, would she? Of course not. We ought to be ashamed of ourselves, Larry. [*More and more carried away by his new fancy*]. You know, I have a sort of presentiment that Miss Reilly is a very superior woman.

DOYLE [*staring hard at him*] Oh! you have, have you?

BROADBENT. Yes I have. There is something very touching about the history of this beautiful girl.

DOYLE. Beau—! Oho! Heres a chance for Nora! and for me! [*Calling*] Hodson.

HODSON [*appearing at the bedroom door*] Did you call, sir?

DOYLE. Pack for me too. I'm going to Ireland with Mr Broadbent.

HODSON. Right, sir. [*He retires into the bedroom*].

BROADBENT [*clapping Doyle on the shoulder*] Thank you, old chap. Thank you.

ACT II

ROSSCULLEN. *Westward a hillside of granite rock and heather slopes upward across the prospect from south to north. A huge stone stands on it in a naturally impossible place, as if it had been tossed up there by a giant. Over the brow, in the desolate valley beyond, is a round tower. A lonely white high road trending away westward past the tower loses itself at the foot of the far mountains. It is evening; and there are great breadths of silken green in the Irish sky. The sun is setting.*

A man with the face of a young saint, yet with white hair and perhaps 50 years on his back, is standing near the stone in a trance of intense melancholy, looking over the hills as if by mere intensity of gaze he could pierce the glories of the sunset and see into the streets of heaven. He is dressed in black, and is rather more clerical in appearance than most English curates are nowadays; but he does not wear the collar and waistcoat of a parish priest. He is roused from his trance by the chirp of an insect from a tuft of grass in a crevice of the stone. His face relaxes: he turns quietly, and gravely takes off his hat to the tuft, addressing the insect in a brogue which is the jocular assumption of a gentleman and not the natural speech of a peasant.

THE MAN. An is that yourself, Misther Grasshopper? I hope I see you well this fine evenin.

THE GRASSHOPPER [*prompt and shrill in answer*] X.X.

THE MAN [*encouragingly*] Thats right. I suppose now youve come out to make yourself miserable be admyerin the sunset?

THE GRASSHOPPER [*sadly*] X.X.

THE MAN. Aye, youre a thrue Irish grasshopper.

THE GRASSHOPPER [*loudly*] X.X.X.

THE MAN. Three cheers for ould Ireland, is it? That helps you to face out the misery and the poverty and the torment, doesnt it?

THE GRASSHOPPER [*plaintively*] X.X.

THE MAN. Ah, it's no use, me poor little friend. If you could jump as far as a kangaroo you couldnt jump away from your own heart an its punishment. You can only look at Heaven from here: you cant reach it. There! [*pointing with his stick to the sunset*] thats the gate o glory, isnt it?

THE GRASSHOPPER [*assenting*] X.X.

THE MAN. Sure it's the wise grasshopper yar to know that. But tell me this, Misther Unworldly Wiseman: why does the sight of Heaven wring your heart an mine as the sight of holy wather wrings the heart o the divil? What wickedness have you done to bring that curse on you? Here! where are you jumpin to? Wheres your manners to go skyrocketin like that out o the box in the middle o your confession [*he threatens it with his stick*]?

THE GRASSHOPPER [*penitently*] X.

THE MAN [*lowering the stick*] I accept your apology; but dont do it again. And now tell me one thing before I let you go home to bed. Which would you say this counthry was: hell or purgatory?

THE GRASSHOPPER. X.

THE MAN. Hell! Faith I'm afraid youre right. I wondher what you and me did when we were alive to get sent here.

THE GRASSHOPPER [*shrilly*] X.X.

THE MAN [*nodding*] Well, as you say, it's a delicate subject; and I wont press it on you. Now off widja.

THE GRASSHOPPER. X.X. [*It springs away*].

THE MAN [*waving his stick*] God speed you! [*He walks away past the stone towards the brow of the hill. Immediately a young laborer, his face distorted with terror, slips round from behind the stone.*

THE LABORER [*crossing himself repeatedly*] Oh glory be to God! glory be to God! Oh Holy Mother an all the saints! Oh murdher! murdher! [*Beside himself, calling*] Fadher Keegan! Fadher Keegan!

THE MAN [*turning*] Who's there? Whats that? [*He comes back and finds the laborer, who clasps his knees*] Patsy Farrell! What are you doing here?

PATSY. Oh for the love o God dont lave me here wi dhe grasshopper. I hard it spakin to you. Dont let it do me any harm, Fadher darlint.

KEEGAN. Get up, you foolish man, get up. Are you afraid of a poor insect because I pretended it was talking to me?

PATSY. Oh, it was no pretendin, Fadher dear. Didnt it give three cheers n say it was a divil out o hell? Oh say youll see me safe home, Fadher; n put a blessin on me or somethin [*he moans with terror*].

KEEGAN. What were you doin there, Patsy, listnin? Were you spyin on me?

PATSY. No, Fadher: on me oath an soul I wasnt: I was waitn to meet Masther Larry n carry his luggage from the car; n I fell asleep on the grass; n you woke me talkin to the grasshopper; n I hard its wicked little voice. Oh, d'ye think I'll die before the year's out, Fadher?

KEEGAN. For shame, Patsy! Is that your religion, to be afraid of a little deeshy grasshopper? Suppose it w a s a divil, what call have you to fear it? If I could ketch it, I'd make you take it home widja in your hat for a penance.

PATSY. Sure, if you wont let it harm me, I'm not afraid, your riverence. [*He gets up, a little reassured. He is a callow, flaxen polled, smoothfaced, downy chinned lad, fully grown but not yet fully filled out, with blue eyes and an instinctively acquired air of helplessness and silliness, indicating, not his real character, but a cunning developed by his constant dread of a hostile dominance, which he habitually tries to disarm and tempt into unmasking by pretending to be a much greater fool than he really is. Englishmen think him half-witted, which is exactly what he intends them to think. He is clad in corduroy trousers, unbuttoned waistcoat, and coarse blue striped shirt*].

KEEGAN [*admonitorily*] Patsy: what did I tell you about callin me Father Keegan an your reverence? What did Father Dempsey tell you about it?

PATSY. Yis, Fadher.

KEEGAN. Father!

PATSY [*desperately*] Arra, hwat am I to call you? Fadher Dempsey sez youre not a priest; n we all know youre not a man; n how do we know what ud happen to us if we shewed any disrespect to you? N sure they say wanse a priest always a priest.

KEEGAN [*sternly*] It's not for the like of you, Patsy, to go behind the instruction of your parish priest and set yourself up to judge whether your Church is right or wrong.

PATSY. Sure I know that, sir.

KEEGAN. The Church let me be its priest as long as it thought me fit for its work. When it took away my papers it meant you to know that I was only a poor madman, unfit and unworthy to take charge of the souls of the people.

PATSY. But wasnt it only because you knew more Latn than Father Dempsey that he was jealous of you?

KEEGAN [*scolding him to keep himself from smiling*] How dar you, Patsy Farrell, put your own wicked little spites and foolishnesses into the heart of your priest? For two pins I'd tell him what you just said.

PATSY [*coaxing*] Sure you wouldnt—

KEEGAN. Wouldnt I? God forgive you! youre little better than a heathen.

PATSY. Deedn I am, Fadher: it's me bruddher the tinsmith in Dublin youre thinkin of. Sure he had to be a freethinker when he larnt a thrade and went to live in the town.

KEEGAN. Well, he'll get to Heaven before you if youre not careful, Patsy. And now you listen to me, once and for all. Youll talk to me and pray for me by the name of Pether Keegan, so you will. And when youre angry and tempted to lift your hand agen the donkey or stamp your foot on the little grasshopper, remember that the donkey's Pether Keegan's brother, and the grasshopper Pether Keegan's friend. And when youre tempted to throw a stone at a sinner or a curse at a beggar, remember that Pether Keegan is a worse sinner and a worse beggar, and keep the stone and the curse for him the next time you meet him. Now say God bless you, Pether, to me before I go, just to practise you a bit.

PATSY. Sure it wouldnt be right, Fadher. I cant—

KEEGAN. Yes you can. Now out with it; or I'll put this stick into your hand an make you hit me with it.

PATSY [*throwing himself on his knees in an ecstasy of adoration*] Sure it's your blessin I want, Fadher Keegan. I'll have no luck widhout it.

KEEGAN [*shocked*] Get up out o that, man. Dont kneel to me: I'm not a saint.

PATSY [*with intense conviction*] Oh in throth yar, sir. [*The grasshopper chirps. Patsy, terrified, clutches at Keegan's hands*] Dont set it on me, Fadher: I'll do anythin you bid me.

KFEGAN [*pulling him up*] You bosthoon, you! Dont you see that it only whistled to tell me Miss Reilly's comin? There! Look at her and pull yourself together for shame. Off widja to the road: youll be late for the car if you dont make haste [*bustling him down the hill*]. I can see the dust of it in the gap already.

PATSY. The Lord save us! [*He goes down the hill towards the road like a haunted man*].

Nora Reilly comes down the hill. A slight weak woman in a pretty muslin print gown (her best), she is a figure commonplace enough to Irish eyes; but on the inhabitants of fatter-fed, crowded, hustling and bustling modern countries she makes a very different impression. The absence of any symptoms of coarseness or hardness or appetite in her, her comparative delicacy of manner and sensibility of apprehension, her fine hands and frail figure, her novel accent, with the caressing plaintive Irish melody of her speech, give her a charm which is all the more effective because, being untravelled, she is unconscious of it, and never dreams of deliberately dramatizing and exploiting it, as the Irishwomen in England do. For Tom Broadbent therefore, an attractive woman, whom he would even call ethereal. To Larry Doyle, an everyday woman fit only for the eighteenth century, helpless, useless, almost sexless, an invalid without the excuse of disease, an incarnation of everything in Ireland that drove him out of it. These judgments have little value and no finality; but they are the judgments on which her fate hangs just at present. Keegan touches his hat to her: he does not take it off.

NORA. Mr. Keegan: I want to speak to you a minute if you dont mind.

KEEGAN [*dropping the broad Irish vernacular of his speech to Patsy*] An hour if you like, Miss Reilly: youre always welcome. Shall we sit down?

NORA. Thank you. [*They sit on the heather. She is shy and anxious; but she comes to the point promptly because she can think of nothing else*]. They say you did a gradle o travelling at one time.

KEEGAN. Well, you see I'm not a Mnooth man [*he means that he was not a student at Maynooth College*]. When I was young I admired the older generation of priests that had been educated in Salamanca. So when I felt sure of my vocation I went to Salamanca. Then I walked from Salamanca to Rome, an sted in a monastery there for a year. My pilgrimage to Rome taught me that walking is a better way of travelling than the train; so I walked from Rome to the Sorbonne in Paris; and I wish I could have walked from Paris to Oxford; for I was very sick on the sea. After a year of Oxford I had to walk to Jerusalem to walk the Oxford feeling off me. From Jerusalem I came back to Patmos, and spent six months at the monastery of Mount Athos. From that I came to Ireland and settled down as a parish priest until I went mad.

NORA [*startled*] Oh dont say that.

KEEGAN. Why not? Dont you know the story? how I confessed a black man and gave him absolution? and how he put a spell on me and drove me mad?

NORA. How can you talk such nonsense about yourself? For shame!

KEEGAN. It's not nonsense at all: it's true—in a way. But never mind the black man. Now that you know what a travelled man I am, what can I do for you? [*She hesitates and plucks nervously at the heather. He stays her hand gently*]. Dear Miss Nora: dont pluck the little flower. If it was a pretty baby you wouldnt want to pull its head off and stick it in a vawse o water to look at. [*The grasshopper chirps: Keegan turns his head and addresses it in the vernacular*]. Be aisy, me son: she wont spoil the swing-swong in your little three. [*To*

Nora, resuming his urbane style] You see I'm quite cracked; but never mind: I'm harmless. Now what is it?

NORA [*embarrassed*] Oh, only idle curiosity. I wanted to know whether you found Ireland—I mean the country part of Ireland, of course—very small and backwardlike when you came back to it from Rome and Oxford and all the great cities.

KEEGAN. When I went to those great cities I saw wonders I had never seen in Ireland. But when I came back to Ireland I found all the wonders there waiting for me. You see they had been there all the time; but my eyes had never been opened to them. I did not know what my own house was like, because I had never been outside it.

NORA. D'ye think thats the same with everybody?

KEEGAN. With everybody who has eyes in his soul as well as in his head.

NORA. But really and truly now, werent the people rather disappointing? I should think the girls must have seemed rather coarse and dowdy after the foreign princesses and people? But I suppose a priest wouldnt notice that.

KEEGAN. It's a priest's business to notice everything. I wont tell you all I noticed about women; but I'll tell you this. The more a man knows, and the farther he travels, the more likely he is to marry a country girl afterwards.

NORA [*blushing with delight*] Youre joking, Mr Keegan: I'm sure yar.

KEEGAN. My way of joking is to tell the truth. It's the funniest joke in the world.

NORA [*incredulous*] Galong with you!

KEEGAN [*springing up actively*] Shall we go down to the road and meet the car? [*She gives him her hand and he helps her up*]. Patsy Farrell told me you were expecting young Doyle.

NORA [*tossing her chin up at once*] Oh, I'm not expecting him particularly. It's a wonder he's come back at all. After staying away eighteen years he can harly expect us to be very anxious to see him: can he now?

KEEGAN. Well, not anxious perhaps; but you will be curious to see how much he's changed in all these years.

NORA [*with a sudden bitter flush*] I suppose thats all that brings him back to look at us, just to see how much weve changed. Well, he can wait and see me be candlelight: I didnt come out to meet him: I'm going to walk to the Round Tower [*going west across the hill*].

KEEGAN. You couldnt do better this fine evening. [*Gravely*] I'll tell him where youve gone. [*She turns as if to forbid him; but the deep understanding in his eyes makes that impossible; and she only looks at him earnestly and goes. He watches her disappear on the other side of the hill; then says*] Aye, he's come to torment you; and youre driven already to torment him. [*He shakes his head, and goes slowly away across the hill in the opposite direction, lost in thought*].

By this time the car has arrived, and dropped three of its passengers on the high road at the foot of the hill. It is a monster jaunting car, black and dilapidated, one of the last survivors of the public vehicles known to earlier generations as Beeyankiny cars, the Irish having laid violent tongues on the name of their projector, one Bianconi, an enterprising Italian. The three passengers are the parish priest, Father Dempsey; Cornelius Doyle, Larry's father; and Broadbent, all in overcoats and as stiff as only an Irish car could make them.

The priest, stout and fatherly, falls far short of that finest type of countryside pastor which represents the genius of priesthood; but he is equally far above the base type in which a strongminded unscrupulous peasant uses the Church to extort money, power, and privilege. He is a priest neither by vocation nor ambition, but because the life suits him. He has boundless authority over his flock, and taxes them stiffly enough to be a rich man. The old Protestant ascendency is now too broken to gall him. On the whole, an easygoing, amiable, even modest man as long as his dues are paid and his authority and dignity fully admitted.

Cornelius Doyle is an elder of the small wiry type, with a hardskinned, rather worried face, clean shaven except for sandy whiskers blanching into a lustreless pale yellow and quite white at the roots. His dress is that of a country-town man of business: that is, an oldish shooting suit, with elastic sided boots quite unconnected with shooting. Feeling shy with Broadbent, he is hasty, which is his way of trying to appear genial.

Broadbent, for reasons which will appear later, has no luggage except a field glass and a guide book. The other two have left theirs to the unfortunate Patsy Farrell, who struggles up the hill after them, loaded with a sack of potatoes, a hamper, a fat goose, a colossal salmon, and several paper parcels.

Cornelius leads the way up the hill, with Broadbent at his heels. The priest follows. Patsy lags laboriously behind.

CORNELIUS. This is a bit of a climb, Mr Broadbent; but it's shorter than goin round be the road.

BROADBENT [*stopping to examine the great stone*] Just a moment, Mr Doyle: I want to look at this stone. It must be Finian's die-cast.

CORNELIUS [*in blank bewilderment*] Hwat?

BROADBENT. Murray describes it. One of your great national heroes—I cant pronounce the name—Finian Somebody, I think.

FATHER DEMPSEY [*also perplexed, and rather scandalized*] Is it Fin McCool you mean?

BROADBENT. I daresay it is. [*Referring to the guide book*] Murray says that a huge stone, probably of Druidic origin, is still pointed out as the die cast by Fin in his celebrated match with the devil.

CORNELIUS [*dubiously*] Jeuce a word I ever heard of it!

FATHER DEMPSEY [*very seriously indeed, and even a little severely*] Dont believe any such nonsense, sir. There never was any such thing. When people talk to you about Fin McCool and the like, take no notice of them. It's all idle stories and superstition.

BROADBENT [*somewhat indignantly; for to be rebuked by an Irish priest for superstition is more than he can stand*] You dont suppose I believe it, do you?

FATHER DEMPSEY. Oh, I thought you did. D'ye see the top o the Roun Tower there? thats an antiquity worth lookin at.

BROADBENT [*deeply interested*] Have you any theory as to what the Round Towers were for?

FATHER DEMPSEY [*a little offended*] A theory? Me! [*Theories are connected in his mind with the late Professor Tyndall, and with scientific scepticism generally: also perhaps with the view that the Round Towers are phallic symbols*].

CORNELIUS [*remonstrating*] Father Dempsey is the priest of the parish, Mr Broadbent. What would he be doing with a theory?

FATHER DEMPSEY [*with gentle emphasis*] I have a knowledge of what the Roun Towers were, if thats what you mean. They are the forefingers of the early Church, pointing us all to God.

Patsy, intolerably overburdened, loses his balance, and sits down involuntarily. His burdens are scattered over the hillside. Cornelius and Father Dempsey turn furiously on him, leaving Broadbent beaming at the stone and the tower with fatuous interest.

CORNELIUS. Oh, be the hokey, the sammin's broke in two! You schoopid ass, what d'ye mean?

FATHER DEMPSEY. Are you drunk, Patsy Farrell? Did I tell you to carry that hamper carefully or did I not?

PATSY [*rubbing the back of his head, which has almost dinted a slab of granite*] Sure me fut slipt. Howkn I carry three men's luggage at wanst?

FATHER DEMPSEY. You were told to leave behind what you couldnt carry, an go back for it.

PATSY. An whose things was I to lave behind? Hwat would your reverence think if I left your hamper behind in the wet grass; n hwat would the masther say if I left the sammin and the goose be the side o the road for annywan to pick up?

CORNELIUS. Oh, youve a dale to say for yourself, you butther-fingered omadhaun. Waitll Ant Judy sees the state o that sammin: she'll talk to you. Here! gimmy that birdn that fish there; an take Father Dempsey's hamper to his house for him; n them come back for the rest.

FATHER DEMPSEY. Do, Patsy. And mind you dont fall down again.

PATSY. Sure I—

CORNELIUS [*bustling him up the hill*] Whisht! heres Ant Judy. [*Patsy goes grumbling in disgrace, with Father Dempsey's hamper*].

Aunt Judy comes down the hill, a woman of 50, in no way remarkable, lively and busy without energy or grip, placid without tranquillity, kindly without concern for others indeed without much concern for herself: a contented product of a narrow, strainless life. She wears her hair parted in the middle and quite smooth, with a flattened bun at the back. Her dress is a plain brown frock, with a woollen pelerine of black and aniline mauve over her shoulders, all very trim in honor of the occasion. She looks round for Larry; is puzzled; then stares incredulously at Broadbent.

AUNT JUDY. Surely to goodness thats not you, Larry!

CORNELIUS. Arra how could he be Larry, woman alive? Larry's in no hurry home, it seems. I havnt set eyes on him. This is his friend, Mr Broadbent. Mr Broadbent: me sister Judy.

AUNT JUDY [*hospitably: going to Broadbent and shaking hands heartily*] Mr Broadbent! Fancy me takin you for Larry! Sure we havnt seen a sight of him for eighteen years, n he ony a lad when he left us.

BROADBENT. It's not Larry's fault: he was to have been here before me. He started in our motor an hour before Mr Doyle arrived, to meet us at Athenmullet, intending to get here long before me.

AUNT JUDY. Lord save us! do you think he's had n axidnt?

BROADBENT. No: he's wired to say he's had a breakdown and will come on as soon as he can. He expects to be here at about ten.

AUNT JUDY. There now! Fancy him trustn himself in a motor and we all expectn him! Just like him! he'd never do anything like anybody else. Well, what cant be cured must be injoored. Come on in, all of you. You must be dyin for your tea, Mr Broadbent.

BROADBENT [*with a slight start*] Oh, I'm afraid it's too late for tea [*he looks at his watch*].

AUNT JUDY. Not a bit: we never have it airlier than this. I hope they gave you a good dinner at Athenmullet.

BROADBENT [*trying to conceal his consternation as he realizes that he is not going to get any dinner after his drive*] Oh—er—excellent, excellent. By the way, hadnt I better see about a room at the hotel? [*They stare at him*].

CORNELIUS. The hotel!

FATHER DEMPSEY. Hwat hotel?

AUNT JUDY. Indeed youre not goin to a hotel. Youll stay with us. I'd have put you into Larry's room, ony the boy's pallyass is too short for you; but we'll make a comfortable bed for you on the sofa in the parlor.

BROADBENT. Youre very kind, Miss Doyle; but really I'm ashamed to give you so much trouble unnecessarily. I shant mind the hotel in the least.

FATHER DEMPSEY. Man alive! theres no hotel in Rosscullen.

BROADBENT. No hotel! Why, the driver told me there was the finest hotel in Ireland here. [*They regard him joylessly*].

AUNT JUDY. Arra would you mind what the like of him would tell you? Sure he'd say hwatever was the least trouble to himself and the pleasantest to you, thinkin you might give him a thruppeny bit for himself or the like.

BROADBENT. Perhaps theres a public house.

FATHER DEMPSEY [*grimly*] Theres seventeen.

AUNT JUDY. Ah then, how could you stay at a public house? theyd have no place to put you even if it was a right place for you to go. Come! is it the sofa youre afraid of? If it is, you can have me own bed. I can sleep with Nora.

BROADBENT. Not at all, not at all: I should be only too delighted. But to upset your arrangements in this way—

CORNELIUS [*anxious to cut short the discussion, which makes him ashamed of his house; for he guesses Broadbent's standard of comfort a little more accurately than his sister does*] Thats all right: itll be no trouble at all. Hweres Nora?

AUNT JUDY. Oh, how do I know? She slipped out a little while ago: I thought she was goin to meet the car.

CORNELIUS [*dissatisfied*] It's a queer thing of her to run out o the way at such a time.

AUNT JUDY. Sure she's a queer girl altogether. Come. Come in: come in.

FATHER DEMPSEY. I'll say good-night, Mr Broadbent. If there anything I can do for you in this parish, let me know. [*He shakes hands with Broadbent*].

BROADBENT [*effusively cordial*] Thank you, Father Dempsey. Delighted to have met you, sir.

FATHER DEMPSEY [*passing on to Aunt Judy*] Good-night, Miss Doyle.

AUNT JUDY. Wont you stay to tea?

FATHER DEMPSEY. Not to-night, thank you kindly: I have business to do at home. [*He turns to go, and meets Patsy Farrell returning unloaded*]. Have you left that hamper for me?

PATSY. Yis, your reverence.

FATHER DEMPSEY. Thats a good lad [*going*].

PATSY [*to Aunt Judy*] Fadher Keegan sez—

FATHER DEMPSEY [*turning sharply on him*] Whats that you say?

PATSY [*frightened*] Fadher Keegan—

FATHER DEMPSEY. How often have you heard me bid you call Mister Keegan in his proper name, the same as I do? Father Keegan indeed! Cant you tell the difference between your priest and any ole madman in a black coat?

PATSY. Sure I'm afraid he might put a spell on me.

FATHER DEMPSEY [*wrathfully*] You mind what I tell you or I'll put a spell on you thatll make you lep. D'ye mind that now? [*He goes home*].

Patsy goes down the hill to retrieve the fish, the bird, and the sack.

AUNT JUDY. Ah, hwy cant you hold your tongue, Patsy, before Father Dempsey?

PATSY. Well, hwat was I to do? Father Keegan bid me

tell you Miss Nora was gone to the Roun Tower.

AUNT JUDY. An hwy couldnt you wait to tell us until Father Dempsey was gone?

PATSY. I was afeerd o forgetn it; and then may be he'd a sent the grasshopper or the little dark looker into me at night to remind me of it. [*The dark looker is the common grey lizard, which is supposed to walk down the throats of incautious sleepers and cause them to perish in a slow decline*].

CORNELIUS. Yah, you great gaum, you! Widjer grasshoppers and dark lookers! Here: take up them things and let me hear no more o your foolish lip. [*Patsy obeys*]. You can take the sammin under your oxther. [*He wedges the salmon into Patsy's axilla*].

PATSY. I can take the goose too, sir. Put it on me back n gimmy the neck of it in me mouth. [*Cornelius is about to comply thoughtlessly*].

AUNT JUDY [*feeling that Broadbent's presence demands special punctiliousness*] For shame, Patsy! to offer to take the goose in your mouth that we have to eat after you! The masterll bring it in for you.

PATSY. Arra what would a dead goose care for me mouth? [*He takes his load up the hill*].

CORNELIUS. Hwats Nora doin at the Roun Tower?

AUNT JUDY. Oh, the Lord knows! Romancin, I suppose. Praps she thinks Larry would go there to look for her and see her safe home.

BROADBENT. Miss Reilly must not be left to wait and walk home alone at night. Shall I go for her?

AUNT JUDY [*contemptuously*] Arra hwat ud happen to her? Hurry in now, Corny. Come, Mr Broadbent: I left the tea on the hob to draw; and itll be black if we dont go in an drink it.

They go up the hill. It is dusk by this time.

Broadbent does not fare so badly after all at Aunt Judy's board. He gets not only tea and bread-and-butter, but more mutton chops than he has ever conceived it possible to eat at one sitting. There is also a most filling substance called potato cake. Hardly have his fears of being starved been replaced by his first misgiving that he is eating too much and will be sorry for it tomorrow, when his appetite is revived by the production of a bottle of illicitly distilled whisky, called potcheen, which he has read and dreamed of (he calls it pottine) and is now at last to taste. His goodhumor rises almost to excitement before Cornelius shews signs of sleepiness. The contrast between Aunt Judy's table service and that of the south and east coast hotels at which he spends his Fridays-to-Tuesdays when he is in London, seems to him delightfully Irish. The almost total atrophy of any sense of enjoyment in Cornelius, or even any desire for it or toleration of the possibility of life being something better than a round of sordid worries, relieved by tobacco, punch, fine mornings, and petty successes in buying and selling, passes with his guest as the whimsical affectation of a shrewd Irish humorist and incorrigible spendthrift. Aunt Judy seems to him an incarnate joke. The likelihood that the joke will pall after a month or so, and is probably not apparent at any time to born Rossculleners, or that he himself unconsciously entertains Aunt Judy by his fantastic English personality and English mispronunciations, does not occur to him for a moment. In the end he is so charmed, and so loth to go to bed and perhaps dream of prosaic England, that he insists on going out to smoke a cigar and look for Nora Reilly at the Round Tower. Not that any special insistence is needed; for the English inhibitive instinct does not seem to exist in Rosscullen. Just as Nora's liking to miss a meal and stay out at the Round Tower is accepted as a sufficient reason for her doing it, and for the family going to bed and leaving the door open for her, so Broadbent's whim to go out for a late stroll provokes neither hospitable remonstrance nor surprise. Indeed Aunt Judy wants to get rid if him whilst she makes a bed for him on the sofa. So off he goes, full fed, happy and enthusiastic, to explore the valley by moonlight.

The Round Tower stands about half an Irish mile from Rosscullen, some fifty yards south of the road on a knoll with a circle of wild greensward on it. The road once ran over this knoll; but modern engineering has tempered the level to the Beeyankiny car by carrying the road partly round the knoll and partly through a cutting; so that the way from the road to the tower is a footpath up the embankment through furze and brambles.

On the edge of this slope, at the top of the path, Nora is straining her eyes in the moonlight, watching for Larry. At last she gives it up with a sob of impatience, and retreats to the hoary foot of the tower, where she sits down discouraged and cries a little. Then she settles herself resignedly to wait, and hums a song—not an Irish melody, but a hackneyed English drawingroom ballad of the season before last—until some slight noise suggests a footstep, when she springs up eagerly and runs to the edge of the slope again. Some moments of silence and suspense follow, broken by unmistakable footsteps. She gives a little gasp as she sees a man approaching.

NORA. Is that you, Larry? [*Frightened a little*] Who's that?

BROADBENT'S *voice from below on the path.* Dont be alarmed.

NORA. Oh, what an English accent youve got!

BROADBENT [*rising into view*] I must introduce myself—

NORA [*violently startled, retreating*] It's not you! Who are you? What do you want?

BROADBENT [*advancing*] I'm really so sorry to have alarmed you, Miss Reilly. My name is Broadbent. Larry's friend, you know.

NORA [*chilled*] And has Mr Doyle not come with you?

BROADBENT. No. Ive come instead. I hope I am not unwelcome.

NORA [*deeply mortified*] I'm sorry Mr Doyle should have given you the trouble, I'm sure.

BROADBENT. You see, as a stranger and an Englishman, I thought it would be interesting to see the Round Tower by moonlight.

NORA. Oh, you came to see the tower. I thought—[*confused, trying to recover her manners*] Oh, of course. I was so startled. It's a beautiful night, isnt it?

BROADBENT. Lovely. I must explain why Larry has not come himself.

NORA. Why should he come? He's seen the tower often

enough: it's no attraction to h i m. [*Genteelly*] An what do you think of Ireland, Mr Broadbent? Have you ever been here before?

BROADBENT. Never.

NORA. An how do you like it?

BROADBENT [*suddenly betraying a condition of extreme sentimentality*) I can hardly trust myself to say how much I like it. The magic of this Irish scene, and—I really dont want to be personal, Miss Reilly; but the charm of your Irish voice—

NORA [*quite accustomed to gallantry, and attaching no seriousness whatever to it*] Oh, get along with you, Mr Broadbent! Youre breaking your heart about me already, I daresay, after seeing me for two minutes in the dark.

BROADBENT. The voice is just as beautiful in the dark, you know. Besides, Ive heard a great deal about you from Larry.

NORA [*with bitter indifference*] Have you now? Well, thats a great honor, I'm sure.

BROADBENT. I have looked forward to meeting you more than to anything else in Ireland.

NORA [*ironically*] Dear me! did you now?

BROADBENT. I did really. I wish you had taken half as much interest in me.

NORA. Oh, I was dying to see you, of course. I daresay you can imagine the sensation an Englishman like you would make among us poor Irish people.

BROADBENT. Ah, now youre chaffing me, Miss Reilly: you know you are. You mustnt chaff me. I'm very much in earnest about Ireland and everything Irish. I'm very much in earnest about you and about Larry.

NORA. Larry has nothing to do with me, Mr Broadbent.

BROADBENT. If I really thought that, Miss Reilly, I should—well, I should let myself feel that charm of which I spoke just now more deeply than I—than I—

NORA. Is it making love to me you are?

BROADBENT [*scared and much upset*] On my word I believe I am, Miss Reilly. If you say that to me again I shant answer for myself: all the harps of Ireland are in your voice. [*She laughs at him. He suddenly loses his head and seizes her arms, to her great indignation*]. Stop laughing: do you hear? I am in earnest: in English earnest. When I say a thing like that to a woman, I mean it. [*Releasing her and trying to recover his ordinary manner in spite of his bewildering emotion*] I beg your pardon.

NORA. How dare you touch me?

BROADBENT. There are not many things I would not dare for you. That does not sound right perhaps; but I really— [*he stops and passes his hand over his forehead, rather lost*].

NORA. I think you ought to be ashamed. I think if you were a gentleman, and me alone with you in this place at night, you would die rather than do such a thing.

BROADBENT. You mean that it's an act of treachery to Larry?

NORA. Deed I dont. What has Larry to do with it? It's an act of disrespect and rudeness to me: it shews what you take me for. You can go your way now; and I'll go mine. Goodnight, Mr Broadbent.

BROADBENT. No, please, Miss Reilly. One moment. Listen to me. I'm serious: I'm desperately serious. Tell me that I'm interfering with Larry; and I'll go straight from this spot back to London and never see you again. Thats on my honor: I will. Am I interfering with him?

NORA [*answering in spite of herself in a sudden spring of bitterness*] I should think you ought to know better than me whether youre interfering with him. Youve seen him oftener than I have. You know him better than I do, by this time. Youve come to me quicker than he has, havnt you?

BROADBENT. I'm bound to tell you, Miss Reilly, that Larry has not arrived in Rosscullen yet. He meant to get here before me; but his car broke down; and he may not arrive until to-morrow.

NORA [*her face lighting up*] Is that the truth?

BROADBENT. Yes: thats the truth. [*She gives a sigh of relief*]. Youre glad of that?

NORA [*up in arms at once*] Glad indeed! Why should I be glad? As weve waited eighteen years for him we can afford to wait a day longer, I should think.

BROADBENT. If you really feel like that about him, there may be a chance for another man yet. Eh?

NORA [*deeply offended*] I suppose people are different in England, Mr Broadbent; so perhaps you dont mean any harm. In Ireland nobody'd mind what a man'd say in fun, nor take advantage of what a woman might say in answer to it. If a woman couldnt talk to a man for two minutes at their first meeting without being treated the way youre treating me, no decent woman would ever talk to a man at all.

BROADBENT. I dont understand that. I dont admit that. I am sincere; and my intentions are perfectly honorable. I think you will accept the fact that I'm an Englishman as a guarantee that I am not a man to act hastily or romantically; though I confess that your voice had such an extraordinary effect on me just now when you asked me so quaintly whether I was making love to you—

NORA [*flushing*] I never thought—

BROADBENT [*quickly*] Of course you didnt: I'm not so stupid as that. But I couldnt bear your laughing at the feeling it gave me. You— [*again struggling with a surge of emotion*] you dont know what I—[*he chokes for a moment and then blurts out with unnatural steadiness*] Will you be my wife?

NORA [*promptly*] Deed I wont. The idea! [*Looking at him more carefully*] Arra, come home, Mr Broadbent; and get your senses back again. I think youre not accustomed to potcheen punch in the evening after your tea.

BROADBENT [*horrified*] Do you mean to say that I—I—I—my God! that I appear d r u n k to you, Miss Reilly?

NORA [*compassionately*] How many tumblers had you?

BROADBENT [*helplessly*] Two.

NORA. The flavor of the turf prevented you noticing the strength of it. Youd better come home to bed.

BROADBENT [*fearfully agitated*] But this is such a horrible doubt to put into my mind—to—to— For Heaven's sake,

Miss Reilly, am I really drunk?

NORA [*soothingly*] Youll be able to judge better in the morning. Come on now back with me, an think no more about it. [*She takes his arm with motherly solicitude and urges him gently towards the path*].

BROADBENT [*yielding in despair*] I must be drunk: frightfully drunk; for your voice drove me out of my senses—[*he stumbles over a stone*]. No: on my word, on my most sacred word of honor, Miss Reilly, I tripped over that stone. It was an accident: it was indeed.

NORA. Yes, of course it was. Just take my arm, Mr Broadbent, while we're goin down the path to the road. Youll be all right then.

BROADBENT [*submissively taking it*] I cant sufficiently apologize, Miss Reilly, or express my sense of your kindness when I am in such a disgusting state. How could I be such a bea— [*he trips again*] damn the heather! my foot caught in it.

NORA. Steady now, steady. Come along: come. [*He is led down to the road in the character of a convicted drunkard. To him there is something divine in the sympathetic indulgence she substitutes for the angry disgust with which one of his own countrywomen would resent his supposed condition. And he has no suspicion of the fact, or of her ignorance of it, that when an Englishman is sentimental he behaves very much as an Irishman does when he is drunk*].

ACT III

NEXT morning Broadbent and Larry are sitting at the ends of a breakfast table in the middle of a small grass plot before Cornelius Doyle's house. They have finished their meal, and are buried in newspapers. Most of the crockery is crowded upon a large square black tray of japanned metal. The teapot is of brown delft ware. There is no silver; and the butter on a dinner plate, is en bloc. The background to this breakfast is the house, a small white slated building, accessible by a half-glazed door. A person coming out into the garden by this door would find the table straight in front of him, and a gate leading to the road half way down the garden on his right; or, if he turned sharp to his left, he could pass round the end of the house through an unkempt shrubbery. The mutilated remnant of a huge plaster statue, nearly dissolved by the rains of a century, and vaguely resembling a majestic female in Roman draperies, with a wreath in her hand, stands neglected amid the laurels. Such statues, though apparently works of art, grow naturally in Irish gardens. Their germination is a mystery to the oldest inhabitants, to whose means and tastes they are totally foreign.

There is a rustic bench, much soiled by the birds, and decorticated and split by the weather, near the little gate. At the opposite side, a basket lies unmolested because it might as well be there as anywhere else. An empty chair at the table was lately occupied by Cornelius, who has finished his breakfast and gone in to the room in which he receives rents and keeps his books and cash, known in the household as "the office." This chair, like the two occupied by Larry and Broadbent, has a mahogany frame and is upholstered in black horsehair.

Larry rises and goes off through the shrubbery with his newspaper. Hodson comes in through the garden gate, disconsolate. Broadbent, who sits facing the gate, augurs the worst from his expression.

BROADBENT. Have you been to the village?

HODSON. No use, sir. We'll have to get everything from London by parcel post.

BROADBENT. I hope they made you comfortable last

night.

HODSON. I was no worse than you were on that sofa, sir. One expects to rough it here, sir.

BROADBENT. We shall have to look out for some other arrangement. [*Cheering up irrepressibly*] Still, it's no end of a joke. How do you like the Irish, Hodson?

HODSON. Well, sir, theyre all right anywhere but in their own country. Ive known lots of em in England, and generally liked em. But here, sir, I seem simply to hate em. The feeling come over me the moment we landed at Cork, sir. It's no use pretendin, sir: I cant bear em. My mind rises up agin their ways, somehow: they rub me the wrong way all over.

BROADBENT. Oh, their faults are on the surface: at heart they are one of the finest races on earth. [*Hodson turns away, without affecting to respond to his enthusiasm*]. By the way, Hodson—

HODSON [*turning*] Yes, sir.

BROADBENT. Did you notice anything about me last night when I came in with that lady?

HODSON [*surprised*] No, sir.

BROADBENT. Not any—er—? You may speak frankly.

HODSON. I didnt notice nothing, sir. What sort of thing did you mean, sir?

BROADBENT. Well—er—er—well, to put it plainly, was I drunk?

HODSON [*amazed*] No, sir.

BROADBENT. Quite sure?

HODSON. Well, I should a said rather the opposite, sir. Usually when youve been enjoying yourself, youre a bit hearty like. Last night you seemed rather low, if anything.

BROADBENT. I certainly have no headache. Did you try the pottine, Hodson?

HODSON. I just took a mouthful, sir. It tasted of peat: oh! something horrid, sir. The people here call peat turf. Potcheen and strong porter is what they like, sir. I'm sure I dont know how they can stand it. Give me beer, I say.

BROADBENT. By the way, you told me I couldnt have porridge for breakfast; but Mr Doyle had some.

HODSON. Yes, sir. Very sorry, sir. They call it stirabout, sir: thats how it was. They know no better, sir.

BROADBENT. All right: I'll have some tomorrow.

Hodson goes to the house. When he opens the door he finds Nora and Aunt Judy on the threshold. He stands aside to let them pass, with the air of a well trained servant oppressed by heavy trials. Then he goes in. Broadbent rises. Aunt Judy goes to the table and collects the plates and cups on the tray. Nora goes to the back of the rustic seat and looks out at the gate with the air of a woman accustomed to have nothing to do. Larry returns from the shrubbery.

BROADBENT. Good morning, Miss Doyle.

AUNT JUDY [*thinking it absurdly late in the day for such a salutation*] Oh, good morning. [*Before moving his plate*] Have you done?

BROADBENT. Quite, thank you. You must excuse us for not waiting for you. The country air tempted us to get up early.

AUNT JUDY. N d'ye call this airly, God help you?

LARRY. Aunt Judy probably breakfasted about half past six.

AUNT JUDY. Whisht, you! draggin the parlor chairs out into the gardn n givin Mr Broadbent his death over his meals out here in the cold air. [*To Broadbent*] Why d'ye put up with his foolishness, Mr Broadbent?

BROADBENT. I assure you I like the open air.

AUNT JUDY. Ah galong! How can you like whats not natural? I hope you slept well.

NORA. Did anything wake yup with a thump at three o'clock? I thought the house was falling. But then I'm a very light sleeper.

LARRY. I seem to recollect that one of the legs of the sofa in the parlor had a way of coming out unexpectedly eighteen years ago. Was that it, Tom?

BROADBENT [*hastily*] Oh, it doesnt matter: I was not hurt —at least—er—

AUNT JUDY. Oh now what a shame! An I told Patsy Farrll to put a nail in it.

BROADBENT. He did, Miss Dolye. There was a nail, certainly.

AUNT JUDY. Dear oh dear!

An oldish peasant farmer, small, leathery, peat-faced, with a deep voice and a surliness that is meant to be aggressive, and is in effect pathetic—the voice of a man of hard life and many sorrows —comes in at the gate. He is old enough to have perhaps worn a long tailed frieze coat and knee breeches in his time; but now he is dressed respectably in a black frock coat, tall hat, and pollard colored trousers; and his face is as clean as washing can make it, though that is not saying much, as the habit is recently acquired and not yet congenial.

THE NEW-COMER [*at the gate*] God save all here! [*He comes a little way into the garden*].

LARRY [*patronizingly, speaking across the garden to him*] Is that yourself, Matt Haffigan? Do you remember me?

MATTHEW [*intentionally rude and blunt*] No. Who are you?

NORA. Oh, I'm sure you remember him, Mr Haffigan.

MATTHEW [*grudgingly admitting it*] I suppose he'll be young Larry Doyle that was.

LARRY. Yes.

MATTHEW [*to Larry*] I hear you done well in America.

LARRY. Fairly well.

MATTHEW. I suppose you saw me brother Andy out dhere.

LARRY. No. It's such a big place that looking for a man there is like looking for a needle in a bundle of hay. They tell me he's a great man out there.

MATTHEW. So he is, God be praised. Wheres your father?

AUNT JUDY. He's inside, in the office, Mr Haffigan, with Barney Doarn n Father Dempsey.

Matthew, without wasting further words on the company, goes curtly into the house.

LARRY [*staring after him*] Is anything wrong with old Matt?

NORA. No. He's the same as ever. Why?

LARRY. He's not the same to me. He used to be very civil to Masther Larry: a deal too civil, I used to think. Now he's as surly and stand-off as a bear.

AUNT JUDY. Oh sure he's bought his farm in the Land Purchase. He's independent now.

NORA. It's made a great change, Larry. Youd harly know the old tenants now. Youd think it was a liberty to speak t'dhem—some o dhem. [*She goes to the table, and helps to take off the cloth, which she and Aunt Judy fold up between them*].

AUNT JUDY. I wonder what he wants to see Corny for. He hasnt been here since he paid the last of his old rent; and then he as good as threw it in Corny's face, I thought.

LARRY. No wonder! Of course they all hated us like the devil. Ugh! [*Moodily*] Ive seen them in that office, telling my father what a fine boy I was, amd plastering him with compliments, with your honor here and your honor there, when all the time their fingers were itching to be at his throat.

AUNT JUDY. Deedn why should they want to hurt poor Corny? It was he that got Matt the lease of his farm, and stood up for him as an industrious decent man.

BROADBENT. Was he industrious? Thats remarkable, you know, in an Irishman.

LARRY. Industrious! That man's industry used to make me sick, even as a boy. I tell you, an Irish peasant's industry is not human: it's worse than the industry of a coral insect. An Englishman has some sense about working: he never does more than he can help—and hard enough to get him to do that without scamping it; but an Irishman will work as if he'd die the moment he stopped. That man Matthew Haffigan and his brother Andy made a farm out of a patch of stones on the hillside: cleared it and dug it with their own naked hands and bought their first spade out of their first crop of potatoes. Talk of making two blades of wheat grow where one grew before! those two men made a whole field of wheat grow where not even a furze bush had ever got its head up between the stones.

BROADBENT. That was magnificent, you know. Only a great race is capable of producing such men.

LARRY. Such fools, you mean! What good was it to them? The moment theyd done it, the landlord put a rent of £5 a year on them, and turned them out because they couldnt pay it.

AUNT JUDY. Why couldnt they pay as well as Billy Byrne that took it after them?

LARRY [*angrily*] You know very well that Billy Byrne never paid it. He only offered it to get possession. He never paid it.

AUNT JUDY. That was because Andy Haffigan hurt him with a brick so that he was never the same again. Andy had to run away to America for it.

BROADBENT [*glowing with indignation*] Who can blame him, Miss Doyle? Who can blame him?

LARRY [*impatiently*] Oh, rubbish! whats the good of the man thats starved out of a farm murdering the man thats starved into it? Would you have done such a thing?

BROADBENT. Yes. I—I—I—I—[*stammering with fury*] I should have shot the confounded landlord, and wrung the neck of the damned agent, and blown the farm up with dynamite, and Dublin Castle along with it.

LARRY. Oh yes: youd have done great things; and a fat lot of good youd have got out of it, too! Thats an Englishman all over! make bad laws and give away all the land, and then, when your economic incompetence produces its natural and inevitable results, get virtuously indignant and kill the people that carry out your laws.

AUNT JUDY. Sure never mind him, Mr Broadbent. It doesnt matter, anyhow, because theres harly any landlords left; and therll soon be none at all.

LARRY. On the contrary, therll soon be nothing else; and the Lord help Ireland then!

AUNT JUDY. Ah, youre never satisfied, Larry. [*To Nora*] Come on, alanna, an make the paste for the pie. We can leave them to their talk. They dont want us [*she takes up the tray and goes into the house*].

BROADBENT [*rising and gallantly protesting*] Oh, Miss Doyle! Really, really—

Nora, following Aunt Judy with the rolled up cloth in her hands, looks at him and strikes him dumb. He watches her until she disappears; then comes to Larry and addresses him with sudden intensity.

BROADBENT. Larry.

LARRY. What is it?

BROADBENT. I got drunk last night, and proposed to Miss Reilly.

LARRY. You hwat??? [*He screams with laughter in the falsetto Irish register unused for that purpose in England*].

BROADBENT. What are you laughing at?

LARRY [*stopping dead*] I dont know. Thats the sort of thing an Irishman laughs at. Has she accepted you?

BROADBENT. I shall never forget that with the chivalry of her nation, though I was utterly at her mercy, she refused me.

LARRY. That was extremely improvident of her. [*Beginning to reflect*] But look here: when were you drunk? You were sober enough when you came back from the Round Tower with her.

BROADBENT. No, Larry, I was drunk, I am sorry to say. I had two tumblers of punch. She had to lead me home. You must have noticed it.

LARRY. I did not.

BROADBENT. She did.

LARRY. May I ask how long it took you to come to business? You can hardly have known her for more than a couple of hours.

BROADBENT. I am afraid it was hardly a couple of minutes. She was not here when I arrived; and I saw her for the first time at the tower.

LARRY. Well, you are a nice infant to be let loose in this country! Fancy the potcheen going to your head like that!

BROADBENT. Not to my head, I think. I have no headache; and I could speak distinctly. No: potcheen goes to the heart, not to the head. What ought I to do?

LARRY. Nothing. What need you do?

BROADBENT. There is rather a delicate moral question involved. The point is, was I drunk enough not to be morally responsible for my proposal? Or was I sober enough to be bound to repeat it now that I am undoubtedly sober?

LARRY. I should see a little more of her before deciding.

BROADBENT. No, no. That would not be right. That would not be fair. I am either under a moral obligation or I am not. I wish I knew how drunk I was.

LARRY. Well, you were evidently in a state of blithering sentimentality, anyhow.

BROADBENT. That is true, Larry: I admit it. Her voice has a most extraordinary effect on me. That Irish voice!

LARRY [*sympathetically*] Yes, I know. When I first went to London I very nearly proposed to walk out with a waitress in an Aerated Bread shop because her Whitechapel accent was so distinguished, so quaintly touching, so pretty—

BROADBENT [*angrily*] Miss Reilly is not a waitress, is she?

LARRY. Oh, come! The waitress was a very nice girl.

BROADBENT. You think every Englishwoman an angel. You really have coarse tastes in that way, Larry. Miss Reilly is one of the finer types: a type rare in England, except perhaps in the best of the aristocracy.

LARRY. Aristocracy be blowed! Do you know what Nora eats?

BROADBENT. Eats! what do you mean?

LARRY. Breakfast: tea and bread-and-butter, with an occasional rasher, and an egg on special occasions: say on her birthday. Dinner in the middle of the day, one course and nothing else. In the evening, tea and bread-and-butter again. You compare her with your Englishwomen who wolf down from three to five meat meals a day; and naturally you find her a sylph. The difference is not a difference of type: it's the difference between the woman who eats not wisely but too well, and the woman who eats not wisely but too little.

BROADBENT [*furious*] Larry: you—you—you disgust me. You are a damned fool. [*He sits down angrily on the rustic seat, which sustains the shock with difficulty*].

LARRY. Steady! stead-eee! [*He laughs and seats himself on the table*].

Cornelius Doyle, Father Dempsey, Barney Doran, and Matthew Haffigan come from the house. Doran is a stoutbodied, short armed, roundheaded, red haired man on the verge of middle age, of sanguine temperament, with an enormous capacity for derisive, obscene, blasphemous, or merely cruel and senseless fun, and a violent and impetuous intolerance of other temperaments and other opinions, all this representing energy and capacity wasted and demoralized by want of sufficient training and social pressure to force it into beneficent activity and build a character with it; for Barney is by no means either stupid or weak. He is recklessly untidy as to his person; but the worst effects of his neglect are mitigated by a powdering of flour and mill dust; and his unbrushed clothes, made of a fashionable tailor's sackcloth, were evidently chosen regardless of expense for the sake of their appearance.

Matthew Haffigan, ill at ease, coasts the garden shyly on the shrubbery side until he anchors near the basket, where he feels least in the way. The priest comes to the table and slaps Larry on the shoulder. Larry, turning quickly, and recognizing Father Dempsey, alights from the table and shakes the priest's hand warmly. Doran comes down the garden between Father Dempsey and Matt; and Cornelius, on the other side of the table, turns to Broadbent, who rises genially.

CORNELIUS. I think we all met las night.

DORAN. I hadnt that pleasure.

CORNELIUS. To be sure, Barney: I forgot. [*To Broadbent, introducing Barney*] Mr Doran. He owns that fine mill you noticed from the car.

BROADBENT [*delighted with them all*] Most happy, Mr Doran. Very pleased indeed.

Doran, not quite sure whether he is being courted or patronized, nods independently.

DORAN. Hows yourself, Larry?

LARRY. Finely, thank you. No need to ask you. [*Doran grins; and they shake hands*].

CORNELIUS. Give Father Dempsey a chair, Larry.

Matthew Haffigan runs to the nearest end of the table and takes the chair from it, placing it near the basket; but Larry has already taken the chair from the other end and placed it in front of the table. Father Dempsey accepts that more central position.

CORNELIUS. Sit down, Barney, will you; and you, Matt.

Doran takes the chair Matt is still offering to the priest; and poor Matthew, outfaced by the miller, humbly turns the basket upside down and sits on it. Cornelius brings his own breakfast chair from the table and sits down on Father Dempsey's right. Broadbent resumes his seat on the rustic bench. Larry crosses to the bench and is about to sit down beside him when Broadbent holds him off nervously.

BROADBENT. Do you think it will bear two, Larry?

LARRY. Perhaps not. Dont move. I'll stand. [*He posts himself behind the bench*].

They are all now seated, except Larry; and the session assumes a portentous air, as if something important were coming.

CORNELIUS. Praps youll explain, Father Dempsey.

FATHER DEMPSEY. No, no: go on, you: the Church has no politics.

CORNELIUS. Were yever thinkin o goin into parliament at all, Larry?

LARRY. Me!

FATHER DEMPSEY [*encouragingly*] Yes, you. Hwy not?

LARRY. I'm afraid my ideas would not be popular enough.

CORNELIUS. I dont know that. Do you, Barney?

DORAN. Theres too much blatherumskite in Irish politics: a dale too much.

LARRY. But what about your present member? Is he going to retire?

CORNELIUS. No: I dont know that he is.

LARRY [*interrogatively*] Well? then?

MATTHEW [*breaking out with surly bitterness*] Weve had enough of his foolish talk agen lanlords. Hwat call has he to talk about the lan, that never was outside of a city office in his life?

CORNELIUS. We're tired of him. He doesnt know where to stop. Every man cant own land; and some men must own it to employ them. It was all very well when solid men like Doran an Matt were kep from ownin land. But hwat man in his senses ever wanted to give land to Patsy Farrll an dhe like o him?

BROADBENT. But surely Irish landlordism was accountable for what Mr Haffigan suffered.

MATTHEW. Never mind hwat I suffered. I know what I suffered adhout you tellin me. But did I ever ask for more dhan the farm I made wid me own hans? tell me that, Corny Doyle, and you that knows. Was I fit for the responsibility or was I not? [*Snarling angrily at Cornelius*] Am I to be compared to Patsy Farrll, that doesnt harly know his right hand from his left? What did he ever suffer, I'd like to know?

CORNELIUS. Thats just what I say. I wasnt comparin you to your disadvantage.

MATTHEW [*implacable*] Then hwat did you mane be talkin about givin him lan?

DORAN. Aisy, Matt, aisy. Youre like a bear with a sore back.

MATTHEW [*trembling with rage*] An who are you, to offer to taitch me manners?

FATHER DEMPSEY [*admonitorily*] Now, now, now, Matt! none o dhat. How often have I told you youre too ready to take offence where none is meant? You dont understand: Corny Doyle is saying just what you want to have said. [*To Cornelius*] Go on, Mr Doyle; and never mind him.

MATTHEW [*rising*] Well, if me lan is to be given to Patsy and his like, I'm goin oura dhis. I—

DORAN [*with violent impatience*] Arra who's goin to give your lan to Patsy, yowl fool ye?

FATHER DEMPSEY. Aisy, Barney, aisy. [*Sternly, to Matt*]

I told you, Matthew Haffigan, that Corny Doyle was sayin nothin against you. I'm sorry your priest's word is not good enough for you. I'll go, sooner than stay to make you commit a sin against the Church. Good morning, gentlemen. [*He rises. They all rise, except Broadbent*].

DORAN [*to Matt*] There! Sarve you dam well right, you cantankerous oul noodle.

MATTHEW [*appalled*] Dont say dhat, Fadher Dempsey. I never had a thought agen you or the Holy Church. I know I'm a bit hasty when I think about the lan. I ax your pardon for it.

FATHER DEMPSEY [*resuming his seat with dignified reserve*] Very well: I'll overlook it this time. [*He sits down. The others sit down, except Matthew. Father Dempsey, about to ask Corny to proceed, remembers Matthew and turns to him, giving him just a crumb of graciousness*]. Sit down, Matt [*Matthew, crushed, sits down in disgrace, and is silent, his eyes shifting piteously from one speaker to another in an intensely mistrustful effort to understand them*]. Go on, Mr Doyle. We can make allowances. Go on.

CORNELIUS. Well, you see how it is, Larry. Round about here, weve got the land at last; and we want no more Goverment meddlin. We want a new class o man in parliament: one dhat knows dhat the farmer's the real backbone o the country, n doesnt care a snap of his fingers for the shoutn o the riff-raff in the towns, or for the foolishness of the laborers.

DORAN. Aye; an dhat can afford to live in London and pay his own way until Home Rule comes, instead o wantin subscriptions and the like.

FATHER DEMPSEY. Yes: thats a good point, Barney. When too much money goes to politics, it's the Church that has to starve for it. A member of parliament ought to be a help to the Church instead of a burden on it.

LARRY. Heres a chance for you, Tom. What do you say?

BROADBENT [*deprecatory, but important and smiling*] Oh, I have no claim whatever to the seat. Besides, I'm a Saxon.

DORAN. A hwat?

BROADBENT. A Saxon. An Englishman.

DORAN. An Englishman. Bedad I never heard it called dhat before.

MATTHEW [*cunningly*] If I might make so bould, Fadher, I wouldnt say but an English Prodestn mightnt have a more indepindent mind about the lan, an be less afeerd to spake out about it, dhan an Irish Catholic.

CORNELIUS. But sure Larry's as good as English: arnt you, Larry?

LARRY. You may put me out of your head, father, once for all.

CORNELIUS. Arra why?

LARRY. I have strong opinions which wouldnt suit you.

DORAN [*rallying him blatantly*] Is it still Larry the bould Fenian?

LARRY. No: the bold Fenian is now an older and possibly foolisher man.

CORNELIUS. Hwat does it matter to us hwat your opinions are? You know that your father's bought his place here, just the same as Matt's farm n Barney's mill. All we ask now is to be let alone. Youve nothin against that, have you?

LARRY. Certainly I have. I dont believe in letting anybody or anything alone.

CORNELIUS [*losing his temper*] Arra what d'ye mean, you young fool? Here Ive got you the offer of a good seat in parliament; n you think yourself mighty smart to stand there and talk foolishness to me. Will you take it or leave it?

LARRY. Very well: I'll take it with pleasure if youll give it to me.

CORNELIUS [*subsiding sulkily*] Well, why couldnt you say so at once? It's a good job youve made up your mind at last.

DORAN [*suspiciously*] Stop a bit: stop a bit.

MATTHEW [*writhing between his dissatisfaction and his fear of the priest*] It's not because he's your son that he's to get the sate. Fadher Dempsey: wouldnt you think well to ask him what he manes about the lan?

LARRY [*coming down on Matt promptly*] I'll tell you, Matt. I always thought it was a stupid, lazy, good-for-nothing sort of thing to leave the land in the hands of the old landlords without calling them to a strict account for the use they made of it, and the condition of the people on it. I could see for myself that they thought of nothing but what they could get out of it to spend in England; and that they mortgaged and mortgaged until hardly one of them owned his own property or could have afforded to keep it up decently if he'd wanted to. But I tell you plump and plain, Matt, that if anybody thinks things will be any better now that the land is handed over to a lot of little men like you, without calling you to account either, theyre mistaken.

MATTHEW [*sullenly*] What call have you to look down on me? I suppose you think youre everybody because your father was a land agent.

LARRY. What call have you to look down on Patsy Farrell? I suppose you think youre everybody because you own a few fields.

MATTHEW. Was Patsy Farrll ever ill used as I was ill used? tell me dhat.

LARRY. He will be, if ever he gets into your power as you were in the power of your old landlord. Do you think, because youre poor and ignorant and half-crazy with toiling and moiling morning noon and night, that youll be any less greedy and oppressive to them that have no land at all than old Nick Lestrange, who was an educated travelled gentleman that would not have been tempted as hard by a hundred pounds as youd be by five shillings? Nick was too high above Patsy Farrell to be jealous of him; but you, that are only one little step above him, would die sooner than let him come up that step; and well you know it.

MATTHEW [*black with rage, in a low growl*] Lemmy oura dhis. [*He tries to rise; but Doran catches his coat and drags him down again*] I'm goin, I say. [*Raising his voice*] Leggo me coat, Barney Doran.

DORAN. Sit down, yowl omadhaun, you. [*Whispering*]

Dont you want to stay an vote agen him?

FATHER DEMPSEY [*holding up his finger*] Matt! [*Matt subsides*]. Now, now, now! come, come! Hwats all dhis about Patsy Farrll? Hwy need you fall out about him?

LARRY. Because it was by using Patsy's poverty to undersell England in the markets of the world that we drove England to ruin Ireland. And she'll ruin us again the moment we lift our heads from the dust if we trade in cheap labor; and serve us right too! If I get into parliament, I'll try to get an Act to prevent any of you from giving Patsy less than a pound a week [*they all start, hardly able to believe their ears*] or working him harder than youd work a horse that cost you fifty guineas.

DORAN. Hwat!!!

CORNELIUS [*aghast*] A pound a—God save us! the boy's mad.

Matthew, feeling that here is something quite beyond his powers, turns openmouthed to the priest, as if looking for nothing less than the summary excommunication of Larry.

LARRY. How is the man to marry and live a decent life on less?

FATHER DEMPSEY. Man alive, hwere have you been living all these years? and hwat have you been dreaming of? Why, some o dhese honest men here cant make that much out o the land for dhemselves, much less give it to a laborer.

LARRY [*now thoroughly roused*] Then let them make room for those who can. Is Ireland never to have a chance? First she was given to the rich; and now that they have gorged on her flesh, her bones are to be flung to the poor, that can do nothing but suck the marrow out of her. If we cant have men of honor own the land, lets have men of ability. If we cant have men with ability, let us at least have men with capital. Anybody's better than Matt, who has neither honor, nor ability, nor capital, nor anything but mere brute labor and greed in him, Heaven help him!

DORAN. Well, we're not all foostherin oul doddherers like Matt. [*Pleasantly, to the subject of this description*] Are we,

Matt?

LARRY. For modern industrial purposes you might just as well be, Barney. Youre all children: the big world that I belong to has gone past you and left you. Anyhow, we Irishmen were never made to be farmers; and we'll never do any good at it. We're like the Jews: the Almighty gave us brains, and bid us farm them, and leave the clay and the worms alone.

FATHER DEMPSEY [*with gentle irony*] Oh! is it Jews you want to make of us? I must catechize you a bit meself, I think. The next thing youll be proposing is to repeal the disestablishment of the so-called Irish Church.

LARRY. Yes: why not? [*Sensation*].

MATTHEW [*rancorously*] He's a turncoat.

LARRY. St Peter, the rock on which our Church was built, was crucified head downwards for being a turncoat.

FATHER DEMPSEY [*with a quiet authoritative dignity which checks Doran, who is on the point of breaking out*] Thats true. You hold your tongue as befits your ignorance, Matthew Haffigan; and trust your priest to deal with this young man. Now, Larry Doyle, whatever the blessed St Peter was crucified for, it was not for being a Prodestan. Are you one?

LARRY. No. I am a Catholic intelligent enough to see that the Protestants are never more dangerous to us than when they are free from all alliances with the State. The so-called Irish Church is stronger today than ever it was.

MATTHEW. Fadher Dempsey: will you tell him dhat me mother's ant was shot and kilt dead in the sthreet o Rosscullen be a soljer in the tithe war? [*Frantically*] He wants to put the tithes on us again. He—

LARRY [*interrupting him with overbearing contempt*] Put the tithes on you again! Did the tithes ever come off you? Was your land any dearer when you paid the tithe to the parson than it was when you paid the same money to Nick Lestrange as rent, and he handed it over to the Church Sustentation Fund? Will you always be duped by Acts of Parliament that change nothing but the necktie of the man that picks your pocket? I'll tell you what I'd do with you, Matt Haffigan: I'd make you pay tithes to your own Church. I want the Catholic Church established in Ireland: thats what I want. Do you think that I, brought up to regard myself as the son of a great and holy Church, can bear to see her begging her bread from the ignorance and superstition of men like you? I would have her as high above worldly want as I would have her above worldly pride or ambition. Aye; and I would have Ireland compete with Rome itself for the chair of St Peter and the citadel of the Church; for Rome, in spite of all the blood of the martyrs, is pagan at heart to this day, while in Ireland the people is the Church and the Church the people.

FATHER DEMPSEY [*startled, but not at all displeased*] Whisht, man! youre worse than mad Pether Keegan himself.

BROADBENT [*who has listened in the greatest astonishment*] You amaze me, Larry. Who would have thought of your coming out like this! [*Solemnly*] But much as I appreciate your really brilliant eloquence, I implore you not to desert the great Liberal principle of Disestablishment.

LARRY. I am not a Liberal: Heaven forbid! A disestablished Church is the worst tyranny a nation can groan under.

BROADBENT [*making a wry face*] Dont be paradoxical, Larry. It really gives me a pain in my stomach.

LARRY. Youll soon find out the truth of it here. Look at Father Dempsey! he is disestablished: he has nothing to hope or fear from the State; and the result is that he's the most powerful man in Rosscullen. The member for Rosscullen would shake in his shoes if Father Dempsey looked crooked at him. [*Father Dempsey smiles, by no means averse to this acknowledgment of his authority*]. Look at yourself! you would defy the established Archbishop of Canterbury ten times a day; but catch you daring to say a word that would shock a Nonconformist! not you. The Conservative party today is the only one thats not priestridden—excuse the expression, Father [*Father Dempsey nods tolerantly*]—because it's the only one that has established its Church and can prevent a clergyman becoming a bishop if he's not a Statesman as well as a Churchman.

He stops. They stare at him dumbfounded, and leave it to the priest to answer him.

FATHER DEMPSEY [*judicially*] Young man: youll not be the member for Rosscullen; but dheres more in your head than the comb will take out.

LARRY. I'm sorry to disappoint you, father; but I told you it would be no use. And now I think the candidate had better retire and leave you to discuss his successor. [*He takes a newspaper from the table and goes away through the shrubbery amid dead silence, all turning to watch him until he passes out of sight round the corner of the house*].

DORAN [*dazed*] Hwat sort of a fella is he at all at all?

FATHER DEMPSEY. He's a clever lad: dheres the making of a man in him yet.

MATTHEW [*in consternation*] D'ye mane to say dhat yll put him into parliament to bring back Nick Lesthrange on me, and to put tithes on me, and to rob me for the like o Patsy Farrll, because he's Corny Doyle's son?

DORAN [*brutally*] Arra hould your whisht: who's goin to send him into parliament? Maybe youd like us to send you dhere to thrate dhem to a little o your anxiety about dhat dirty little podato patch o yours.

MATTHEW [*plaintively*] Am I to be towld dhis afther all me sufferins?

DORAN. Och, I'm tired o your sufferins. Weve been hearin nothin else ever since we was childher but sufferins. Hwen it wasnt yours it was somebody else's; and hwen it was nobody else's it was ould Irelan's. How the divil are we to live on wan anodher's sufferins?

FATHER DEMPSEY. Thats a thrue word, Barney Doarn; only your tongue's a little too familiar wi dhe divil. [*To Matt*] If youd think a little more o the sufferins of the blessed saints, Matt, an a little less o your own, youd find the way shorter from your farm to heaven [*Matt is about to reply*]

Dhere now! dhats enough! we know you mean well; an I'm not angry with you.

BROADBENT. Surely, Mr Haffigan, you can see the simple explanation of all this. My friend Larry Doyle is a most brilliant speaker; but he's a Tory: an ingrained old-fashioned Tory.

CORNELIUS. N how d'ye make dhat out, if I might ask you, Mr Broadbent?

BROADBENT [*collecting himself for a political deliverance*] Well, you know, Mr Doyle, theres a strong dash of Toryism in the Irish character. Larry himself says that the great Duke of Wellington was the most typical Irishman that ever lived. Of course thats an absurd paradox; but still theres a great deal of truth in it. Now I am a Liberal. You know the great principles of the Liberal Party. Peace—

FATHER DEMPSEY [*piously*] Hear! hear!

BROADBENT [*encouraged*] Thank you. Retrenchment— [*he waits for further applause*].

MATTHEW [*timidly*] What might rethrenchment mane now?

BROADBENT. It means an immense reduction in the burden of the rates and taxes.

MATTHEW [*respectfully approving*] Dhats right. Dhats right, sir.

BROADBENT [*perfunctorily*] And, of course, Reform.

CORNELIUS, FATHER DEMPSEY, DORAN [*conventionally*] Of course.

MATTHEW [*still suspicious*] Hwat does Reform mane, sir? Does it mane altherin annythin dhats as it is now?

BROADBENT [*impressively*] It means, Mr Haffigan, maintaining those reforms which have already been conferred on humanity by the Liberal Party, and trusting for future developments to the free activity of a free people on the basis of those reforms.

DORAN. Dhats right. No more meddlin. We're all right now: all we want is to be let alone.

CORNELIUS. Hwat about Home Rule?

BROADBENT [*rising so as to address them more imposingly*] I really cannot tell you what I feel about Home Rule without using the language of hyperbole.

DORAN. Savin Fadher Dempsey's presence, eh?

BROADBENT [*not understanding him*] Quite so—er—oh yes. All I can say is that as an Englishman I blush for the Union. It is the blackest stain on our national history. I look forward to the time—and it cannot be far distant, gentlemen, because Humanity is looking forward to it too, and insisting on it with no uncertain voice—I look forward to the time when an Irish legislature shall arise once more on the emerald pasture of College Green, and the Union Jack—that detestable symbol of a decadent Imperialism—be replaced by a flag as green as the island over which it waves: a flag on which we shall ask for England only a modest quartering in memory of our great party and of the immortal name of our grand old leader.

DORAN [*enthusiastically*] Dhats the style, begob! [*He smites his knee, and winks at Matt*].

MATTHEW. More power to you, sir!

BROADBENT. I shall leave you now, gentlemen, to your deliberations. I should like to have enlarged on the services rendered by the Liberal Party to the religious faith of the great majority of the people of Ireland; but I shall content myself with saying that in my opinion you should choose no representative who—no matter what his personal creed may be—is not an ardent supporter of freedom of conscience, and is not prepared to prove it by contributions, as lavish as his means will allow, to the great and beneficent work which you, Father Dempsey [*Father Dempsey bows*], are doing for the people of Rosscullen. Nor should the lighter, but still most important question of the sports of the people be forgotten. The local cricket club—

CORNELIUS. The hwat!

DORAN. Nobody plays bat n ball here, if dhats what you mane.

BROADBENT. Well, let us say quoits. I saw two men, I think, last night—but after all, these are questions of detail. The main thing is that your candidate, whoever he may be, shall be a man of some means, able to help the locality instead of burdening it. And if he were a countryman of my own, the moral effect on the House of Commons would be immense! tremendous! Pardon my saying these few words: nobody feels their impertinence more than I do. Good morning, gentlemen.

He turns impressively to the gate, and trots away, congratulating himself, with a little twist of his head and cock of his eye on having done a good stroke of political business.

HAFFIGAN [*awestruck*] Good morning, sir.

THE REST. Good morning. [*They watch him vacantly until he is out of earshot*].

CORNELIUS. Hwat d'ye think, Father Dempsey?

FATHER DEMPSEY [*indulgently*] Well, he hasnt much sense, God help him; but for the matter o that, neether has our present member.

DORAN. Arra musha he's good enough for parliament: what is there to do there but gas a bit, an chivy the Goverment, an vote wi dh Irish party?

CORNELIUS [*ruminatively*] He's the queerest Englishman *I* ever met. When he opened the paper dhis mornin the first thing he saw was that an English expedition had been bet in a battle in Inja somewhere; an he was as pleased as Punch! Larry told him that if he'd been alive when the news o Waterloo came, he'd a died o grief over it. Bedad I dont think he's quite right in his head.

DORAN. Divil a matther if he has plenty o money. He'll do for us right enough.

MATTHEW [*deeply impressed by Broadbent, and unable to understand their levity concerning him*] Did you mind what he said about rethrenchment? That was very good, I thought.

FATHER DEMPSEY. You might find out from Larry, Corny, what his means are. God forgive us all! it's poor work spoiling the Egyptians, though we have good warrant for it; so

I'd like to know how much spoil there is before I commit meself. [*He rises. They all rise respectfully*].

CORNELIUS [*ruefully*] I'd set me mind on Larry himself for the seat; but I suppose it cant be helped.

FATHER DEMPSEY [*consoling him*] Well, the boy's young yet; an he has a head on him. Goodbye, all. [*He goes out through the gate*].

DORAN. I must be goin, too. [*He directs Cornelius's attention to what is passing in the road*]. Look at me bould Englishman shakin hans wid Fadher Dempsey for all the world like a candidate on election day. And look at Fadher Dempsey givin him a squeeze an a wink as much as to say It's all right, me boy. You watch him shakin hans with me too: he's waitn for me. I'll tell him he's as good as elected. [*He goes, chuckling mischievously*].

CORNELIUS. Come in with me, Matt. I think I'll sell you the pig after all. Come in an wet the bargain.

MATTHEW [*instantly dropping into the old whine of the tenant*] I'm afeerd I cant afford the price, sir. [*He follows Cornelius into the house*].

Larry, newspaper still in hand, comes back through the shrubbery. Broadbent returns through the gate.

LARRY. Well? What has happened?

BROADBENT [*hugely self-satisfied*] I think Ive done the trick this time. I just gave them a bit of straight talk; and it went home. They were greatly impressed: everyone of those men believes in me and will vote for me when the question of selecting a candidate comes up. After all, whatever you say, Larry, they like an Englishman. They feel they can trust him, I suppose.

LARRY. Oh! theyve transferred the honor to you, have they?

BROADBENT [*complacently*] Well, it was a pretty obvious move, I should think. You know, these fellows have plenty of shrewdness in spite of their Irish oddity. [*Hodson comes from the house. Larry sits in Doran's chair and reads.*] Oh, by the way, Hodson—

HODSON [*coming between Broadbent and Larry*] Yes, sir?

BROADBENT. I want you to be rather particular as to how you treat the people here.

HODSON. I havnt treated any of em yet, sir. If I was to accept all the treats they offer me I shouldnt be able to stand at this present moment, sir.

BROADBENT. Oh well, dont be too stand-offish, you know, Hodson. I should like you to be popular. If it costs anything I'll make it up to you. It doesnt matter if you get a bit upset at first: theyll like you all the better for it.

HODSON. I'm sure youre very kind, sir; but it dont seem to matter to me whether they like me or not. I'm not going to stand for parliament here, sir.

BROADBENT. Well, I am. Now do you understand?

HODSON [*waking up at once*] Oh, I beg your pardon, sir, I'm sure. I understand, sir.

CORNELIUS [*appearing at the house door with Matt*] Patsy'll drive the pig over this evenin, Matt. Goodbye. [*He goes back into the house. Matt makes for the gate. Broadbent stops him. Hodson, pained by the derelict basket, picks it up and carries it away behind the house*].

BROADBENT [*beaming candidatorially*] I must thank you very particularly, Mr Haffigan, for your support this morning. I value it because I know that the real heart of a nation is the class you represent, the yeomanry.

MATTHEW [*aghast*] The yeomanry!!!

LARRY [*looking up from his paper*] Take care, Tom! In Rosscullen a yeoman means a sort of Orange Bashi-Bazouk. In England, Matt, they call a freehold farmer a yeoman.

MATTHEW [*huffily*] I dont need to be insthructed be you, Larry Doyle. Some people think no one knows anythin but dhemselves. [*To Broadbent, deferentially*] Of course I know a gentleman like you would not compare me to the yeomanry. Me own granfather was flogged in the sthreets of Athenmullet be them when they put a gun in the thatch of his house an then went and found it there, bad cess to them!

BROADBENT [*with sympathetic interest*] Then you are not

the first martyr of your family, Mr Haffigan?

MATTHEW. They turned me out o the farm I made out of the stones o Little Rosscullen hill wid me own hans.

BROADBENT. I have heard about it; and my blood still boils at the thought. [*Calling*] Hodson—

HODSON [*behind the corner of the house*] Yes, sir. [*He hurries forward*].

BROADBENT. Hodson: this gentleman's sufferings should make every Englishman think. It is want of thought rather than want of heart that allows such iniquities to disgrace society.

HODSON [*prosaically*] Yes, sir.

MATTHEW. Well, I'll be goin. Good mornin to you kindly, sir.

BROADBENT. You have some distance to go, Mr Haffigan: will you allow me to drive you home?

MATTHEW. Oh sure it'd be throublin your honor.

BROADBENT. I insist: it will give me the greatest pleasure, I assure you. My car is in the stable: I can get it round in five minutes.

MATTHEW. Well, sir, if you wouldnt mind, we could bring the pig Ive just bought from Corny—

BROADBENT [*with enthusiasm*] Certainly, Mr Haffigan: it will be quite delightful to drive with a pig in the car: I shall feel quite like an Irishman. Hodson: stay with Mr Haffigan; and give him a hand with the pig if necessary. Come, Larry; and help me. [*He rushes away through the shrubbery*].

LARRY [*throwing the paper ill-humoredly on the chair*] Look here, Tom! here, I say! confound it!—[*he runs after him*].

MATTHEW [*glowering disdainfully at Hodson, and sitting down on Cornelius's chair as an act of social self-assertion*] N are you the valley?

HODSON. The valley? Oh, I follow you: yes: I'm Mr Broadbent's valet.

MATTHEW. Ye have an aisy time of it: you look purty sleek. [*With suppressed ferocity*] Look at me! Do *I* look sleek?

HODSON [*sadly*] I wish I ad your ealth: you look as ard as nails. I suffer from an excess of uric acid.

MATTHEW. Musha what sort o disease is zhouragassid? Didjever suffer from injustice and starvation? Dhats the Irish disease. It's aisy for you to talk o sufferin, an you livin on the fat o the land wid money wrung from us.

HODSON [*suddenly dropping the well-spoken valet, and breaking out in his native cockney*] Wots wrong with you, aold chep? Ez ennybody been doin ennythink to you?

MATTHEW. Anythin timmy! Didnt your English masther say that the blood biled in him to hear the way they put a rint on me for the farm I made wid me own hans, and turned me out of it to give it to Billy Byrne?

HODSON. Ow, Tom Broadbent's blad boils pretty easy over ennything that eppens aht of his aown cantry. Downt you be tiken in by my aowl men, Peddy.

MATTHEW [*indignantly*] Paddy yourself! How dar you call me Paddy?

HODSON [*unmoved*] You jast keep your air on and listen to me. You Awrish people are too well off: thets wots the metter with you. [*With sudden passion*] You talk of your rotten little fawm cause you mide it by chackin a few stowns dahn a ill! Well, wot prawce maw grenfawther, Oi should lawk to knaow, that fitted ap a fust clawss shop and built ap a fust clawss dripery business in Landon by sixty years work, and then was chacked aht of it on is ed at the end of is lease withaht a penny for his goodwill. You talk of evictions! you that cawnt be moved until youve ran ap ighteen months rent. Oi once ran ap four weeks in Lembeth wen Oi was aht of a job in winter. They took the door off its inges and the winder aht of its seshes on me, an gev maw wawf pnoomownia. Oi'm a widower nah. [*Between his teeth*] Gawd! when Oi think of the things we Englishmen as to pat ap with, and eah you Awrish ahlin abaht your silly little grievances, and see the wy you mike it worse for haz by the rotten wiges youll cam over and tike and the rotten plices youll sleep in, I jast feel that I could tike the aowl bloomin

British awland and mike you a present of it, jast to let you fawnd aht wot reel awdship's lawk.

MATTHEW [*starting up, more in scandalized incredulity than in anger*] D'ye have the face to set up England agen Ireland for injustices an wrongs an disthress an sufferin?

HODSON [*with intense disgust and contempt*] Ow, chack it, Paddy. Cheese it. You danno wot awdship is owver eah: all you knaow is ah to ahl abaht it. You tike the biscuit at thet, you do. Oi'm a Owm Ruler, Oi em. Do you knaow woy?

MATTHEW [*equally contemptuous*] D'ye know, yourself?

HODSON. Yus Oi do. It's because Oi want a little attention pide to my aown cantry; and thetll never be as long as your cheps are ollerin at Wesminister as if nowbody mettered but your own bloomin selves. Send em beck to ell or C'naught, as good aowld English Cramwell said. I'm jast sick of Awrland. Let it gow. Cat the caible. Mike it a present to Germany to keep the aowl Kyzer busy for a wawl; and give poor aowld England a chawnce: thets wot Oi sy.

MATTHEW [*full of scorn for a man so ignorant as to be unable to pronounce the word Connaught, which practically rhymes with bonnet in Ireland, though in Hodson's dialect it rhymes with untaught*] Take care we dont cut the cable ourselves some day, bad scran to you! An tell me dhis: have yanny Coercion Acs in England? Have yanny Removable magisthruts? Have you Dublin Castle to suppress every newspaper dhat takes the part o your own counthry?

HODSON. We can beyive ahrselves withaht sich things.

MATTHEW. Bedad youre right. It'd ony be waste o time to muzzle a sheep. Here! wheres me pig? God forgimmy for talkin to a poor ignorant craycher like you!

HODSON [*grinning with good-humored malice, too convinced of his own superiority to feel his withers wrung*] Your pig'll ev a rare doin in that car, Peddy. Forty mawl an ahr dahn that rocky line will strawk it pretty pink, you bet.

MATTHEW [*scornfully*] Hwy cant you tell a raisonable lie when youre about it? What horse can go forty mile an hour?

HODSON. Orse! Wy, you silly aowl rotter, it's not a orse:

it's a mowtor. Do you spowse Tom Broadbent ud gow himself to fetch a orse?

MATTHEW [*in consternation*] Holy Moses! dont tell me it's the ingine he wants to take me on.

HODSON. Wot else?

MATTHEW. Your sowl to Morris Kelly! why didnt you tell me that before? The divil an ingine he'll get me on this day. [*His ear catches an approaching teuf-teuf*] Oh murdher! it's comin afther me: I hear the puff-puff of it. [*He runs away through the gate, much to Hodson's amusement. The noise of the motor ceases; and Hodson, anticipating Broadbent's return, throws off the cockney and recomposes himself as a valet. Broadbent and Larry come through the shrubbery. Hodson moves aside to the gate*].

BROADBENT. Where is Mr Haffigan? Has he gone for the pig?

HODSON. Bolted, sir? Afraid of the motor, sir.

BROADBENT [*much disappointed*] Oh, thats very tiresome. Did he leave any message?

HODSON. He was in too great a hurry, sir. Started to run home, sir, and left his pig behind him.

BROADBENT [*eagerly*] Left the pig! Then it's all right. The pig's the thing: the pig will win over every Irish heart to me. We'll take the pig home to Haffigan's farm in the motor: it will have a tremendous effect. Hodson!

HODSON. Yes, sir?

BROADBENT. Do you think you could collect a crowd to see the motor?

HODSON. Well, I'll try, sir.

BROADBENT. Thank you, Hodson: do.

Hodson goes out through the gate.

LARRY [*desperately*] Once more, Tom, will you listen to me?

BROADBENT. Rubbish! I tell you it will be all right.

LARRY. Only this morning you confessed how surprised you were to find that the people here shewed no sense of humor.

BROADBENT [*suddenly very solemn*] Yes: their sense of humor is in abeyance: I noticed it the moment we landed. Think of that in a country where every man is a born humorist! Think of what it means! [*Impressively*] Larry: we are in the presence of a great national grief.

LARRY. Whats to grieve them?

BROADBENT. I divined it, Larry: I saw it in their faces. Ireland has never smiled since her hopes were buried in the grave of Gladstone.

LARRY. Oh, whats the use of talking to such a man? Now look here, Tom. Be serious for a moment if you can.

BROADBENT [*stupent*] Serious! I!!!

LARRY. Yes, you. You say the Irish sense of humor is in abeyance. Well, if you drive through Rosscullen in a motor car with Haffigan's pig, it wont stay in abeyance. Now I warn you.

BROADBENT [*breezily*] Why, so much the better! I shall enjoy the joke myself more than any of them. [*Shouting*] Hallo, Patsy Farrell, where are you?

PATSY [*appearing in the shrubbery*] Here I am, your honor.

BROADBENT. Go and catch the pig and put in into the car: we're going to take it to Mr Haffigan's. [*He gives Larry a slap on the shoulders that sends him staggering off through the gate, and follows him buoyantly, exclaiming*] Come on, you old croaker! I'll shew you how to win an Irish seat.

PATSY [*meditatively*] Bedad, if dhat pig gets a howlt o the handle o the machine— [*He shakes his head ominously and drifts away to the pigsty*].

ACT IV

THE *parlor in Cornelius Doyle's house. It communicates with the garden by a half glazed door. The fireplace is at the other side of the room, opposite the door and windows, the architect not having been sensitive to draughts. The table, rescued from the garden, is in the middle; and at it sits Keegan, the central figure in a rather crowded apartment. Nora, sitting with her back to the fire at the end of the table, is playing backgammon across its corner with him, on his left hand. Aunt Judy, a little further back, sits facing the fire knitting, with her feet on the fender. A little to Keegan's right, in front of the table, and almost sitting on it, is Barney Doran. Half a dozen friends of his, all men, are between him and the open door, supported by others outside. In the corner behind them is the sofa, of mahogany and horsehair, made up as a bed for Broadbent. Against the wall behind Keegan stands a mahogany sideboard. A door leading to the interior of the house is near the fireplace, behind Aunt Judy. There are chairs against the wall, one at each end of the sideboard. Keegan's hat is on the one nearest the inner door; and his stick is leaning against it. A third chair, also against the wall, is near the garden door.*

There is a strong contrast of emotional atmosphere between the two sides of the room. Keegan is extraordinarily stern: no game of backgammon could possibly make a man's face so grim. Aunt Judy is quietly busy. Nora is trying to ignore Doran and attend to her game.

On the other hand Doran is reeling in an ecstasy of mischievous mirth which has infected all his friends. They are screaming with laughter, doubled up, leaning on the furniture and against the walls, shouting, screeching, crying.

AUNT JUDY [*as the noise lulls for a moment*] Arra hold your noise, Barney. What is there to laugh at?

DORAN. It got its fut into the little hweel—[*he is overcome afresh; and the rest collapse again*].

AUNT JUDY. Ah, have some sense: youre like a parcel o childher. Nora: hit him a thump on the back: he'll have a fit.

DORAN [*with squeezed eyes, exsufflicate with cachinnation*] Frens, he sez to dhem outside Doolan's: I'm takin the gintleman that pays the rint for a dhrive.

AUNT JUDY. Who did he mean be that?

DORAN. They call a pig that in England. Thats their notion of a joke.

AUNT JUDY. Musha God help them if they can joke no better than that!

DORAN [*with renewed symptoms*] Thin—

AUNT JUDY. Ah now dont be tellin it all over and settin yourself off again, Barney.

NORA. Youve told us three times, Mr Doran.

DORAN. Well but whin I think of it—!

AUNT JUDY. Then dont think of it, alanna.

DORAN. Dhere was Patsy Farrll in the back sate wi dhe pig between his knees, n me bould English boyoh in front at the machinery, n Larry Doyle in the road startin the injine wid a bed winch. At the first puff of it the pig lep out of its skin and bled Patsy's nose wi dhe ring in its snout. [*Roars of laughter: Keegan glares at them*]. Before Broadbint knew hwere he was, the pig was up his back and over into his lap; and bedad the poor baste did credit to Corny's thrainin of it; for it put in the fourth speed wid its right crubeen as if it was enthered for the Gordn Bennett.

NORA [*reproachfully*] And Larry in front of it and all! It's nothin to laugh at, Mr Doran.

DORAN. Bedad, Miss Reilly, Larry cleared six yards sideways at wan jump if he cleared an inch; and he'd a cleared seven if Doolan's granmother hadnt cotch him in her apern widhout intindin to. [*Immense merriment*].

AUNT JUDY. Ah, for shame, Barney! the poor old woman! An she was hurt before, too, when she slipped on the stairs.

DORAN. Bedad, maam, she's hurt behind now; for Larry bouled her over like a skittle. [*General delight at this typical stroke of Irish Rabelaisianism*].

NORA. It's well Mr Doyle wasnt killed.

DORAN. Faith it wasnt o Larry we were thinkin jus dhen,

wi dhe pig takin the main sthreet o Rosscullen on market day at a mile a minnit. Dh ony thing Broadbint could get at wi dhe pig in front of him was a fut brake; n the pig's tail was undher dhat; so that whin he thought he was putn non the brake he was ony squeezin the life out o the pig's tail. The more he put the brake on the more the pig squealed n the fasther he dhruv.

AUNT JUDY. Why couldnt he throw the pig out into the road?

DORAN. Sure he couldnt stand up to it, because he was spanchelled-like between his seat and dhat thing like a wheel on top of a stick between his knees.

AUNT JUDY. Lord have mercy on us!

NORA. I dont know how you can laugh. Do you, Mr Keegan?

KEEGAN [*grimly*] Why not? There is danger, destruction, torment! What more do we need to make us merry? Go on, Barney: the last drops of joy are not squeezed from the story yet. Tell us again how our brother was torn asunder.

DORAN [*puzzled*] Whose bruddher?

KEEGAN. Mine.

NORA. He means the pig, Mr Doran. You know his way.

DORAN [*rising gallantly to the occasion*] Bedad I'm sorry for your poor bruddher, Misther Keegan; but I recommend you to thry him wid a couple o fried eggs for your breakfast tomorrow. It was a case of Excelsior wi dhat ambitious baste; for not content wid jumping from the back seat into the front wan, he jumped from the front wan into the road in front of the car. And—

KEEGAN. And everybody laughed!

NORA. Dont go over that again, please, Mr. Doran.

DORAN. Faith be the time the car went over the poor pig dhere was little left for me or anywan else to go over except wid a knife an fork.

AUNT JUDY. Why didnt Mr Broadbent stop the car when the pig was gone?

DORAN. Stop the car! He might as well ha thried to stop a

mad bull. First it went wan way an made fireworks o Molly Ryan's crockery stall; an dhen it slewed round an ripped ten fut o wall out o the corner o the pound. [*With enormous enjoyment*] Begob, it just tore the town in two and sent the whole dam market to blazes. [*Nora offended, rises*].

KEEGAN [*indignantly*] Sir!

DORAN [*quickly*] Savin your presence, Miss Reilly, and Misther Keegan's. Dhere! I wont say anuddher word.

NORA. I'm surprised at you, Mr Doran. [*She sits down again*].

DORAN [*reflectively*] He has the divil's own luck, that Englishman, annyway; for hwen they picked him up he hadnt a scratch on him, barrn hwat the pig did to his cloes. Patsy had two fingers out o jynt; but the smith pulled them sthraight for him. Oh, you never heard such a hullaballoo as there was. There was Molly cryin Me chaney, me beautyful chaney! n oul Matt shoutin Me pig, me pig! n the polus takin the number o the car, n not a man in the town able to speak for laughin—

KEEGAN [*with intense emphasis*] It is hell: it is hell. Nowhere else could such a scene be a burst of happiness for the people.

Cornelius comes in hastily from the garden, pushing his way through the little crowd.

CORNELIUS. Whisht your laughin, boys! Here he is. [*He puts his hat on the sideboard, and goes to the fireplace, where he posts himself with his back to the chimneypiece*].

AUNT JUDY. Remember your behavior, now.

Everybody becomes silent, solemn, concerned, sympathetic. Broadbent enters, soiled and disordered as to his motoring coat: immensely important and serious as to himself. He makes his way to the end of the table nearest the garden door, whilst Larry, who accompanies him, throws his motoring coat on the sofa bed, and sits down, watching the proceedings.

BROADBENT [*taking off his leather cap with dignity and placing it on the table*] I hope you have not been anxious about me.

AUNT JUDY. Deedn we have, Mr Broadbent. It's a mercy you werent killed.

DORAN. Kilt! It's a mercy dheres two bones of you left houldin together. How dijjescape at all at all? Well, I never thought I'd be so glad to see you safe and sound again. Not a man in the town would say less [*murmurs of kindly assent*]. Wont you come down to Doolan's and have a dhrop o brandy to take the shock off?

BROADBENT. Youre all really too kind; but the shock has quite passed off.

DORAN [*jovially*] Never mind. Come along all the same and tell us about it over a frenly glass.

BROADBENT. May I say how deeply I feel the kindness with which I have been overwhelmed since my accident? I can truthfully declare that I am glad it happened, because it has brought out the kindness and sympathy of the Irish character to an extent I had no conception of.

SEVERAL PRESENT. {Oh, sure youre welcome!
Sure it's only natural.
Sure you might have been kilt.

A young man, feeling that he must laugh or burst, hurries out. Barney puts an iron constraint on his features.

BROADBENT. All I can say is that I wish I could drink the health of everyone of you.

DORAN. Dhen come an do it.

BROADBENT [*very solemnly*] No: I am a teetotaller.

AUNT JUDY [*incredulously*] Arra since when?

BROADBENT. Since this morning, Miss Doyle. I have had a lesson [*he looks at Nora significantly*] that I shall not forget. It may be that total abstinence has already saved my life; for I was astonished at the steadiness of my nerves when death stared me in the face today. So I will ask you to excuse me. [*He collects himself for a speech*] Gentlemen: I hope the gravity of the peril through which we have all passed—for I know that the danger to the bystanders was as great as to the occupants of the car—will prove an earnest of closer and more serious relations between us in the future. We have had a somewhat agitating day: a valuable and innocent animal has lost its life: a public building has been wrecked: an aged and infirm lady has suffered an impact for which I feel personally responsible, though my old friend Mr Laurence Doyle unfortunately incurred the first effects of her very natural resentment. I greatly regret the damage to Mr Patrick Farrell's fingers; and I have of course taken care that he shall not suffer pecuniarily by his mishap. [*Murmurs of admiration at his magnanimity, and A Voice* "Youre a gentleman, sir"]. I am glad to say that Patsy took it like an Irishman, and, far from expressing any vindictive feeling, declared his willingness to break all his fingers and toes for me on the same terms [*subdued applause, and* "More power to Patsy!"]. Gentlemen: I felt at home in Ireland from the first [*rising excitement among his hearers*]. In every Irish breast I have found that spirit of liberty [*A cheery voice* "Hear Hear"], that instinctive mistrust of the Government [*A small pious voice, with intense expression*, "God bless you, sir!"], that love of independence [*A defiant voice*, "Thats it! Independence!"], that indignant sympathy with the cause of oppressed nationalities abroad [*A threatening growl from all: the ground-swell of patriotic passion*] and with the resolute assertion of personal rights at home, which is all but extinct in my own country. If it were legally possible I should become a naturalized Irishman; and if ever it be my good fortune to represent an Irish constituency in parliament, it shall be my first care to introduce a Bill legalizing such an operation. I believe a large section of the Liberal party would avail themselves of it. [*Momentary scepticism*]. I do. [*Convulsive cheering*]. Gentlemen: I have said enough. [*Cries of* "Go on"]. No: I have as yet no right to address you at all on political subjects; and we must not abuse the warm-hearted Irish hospitality of Miss Doyle by turning her sitting room into a public meeting.

DORAN [*energetically*] Three cheers for Tom Broadbent, the future member for Rosscullen!

AUNT JUDY [*waving a half knitted sock*] Hip hip hurray!

The cheers are given with great heartiness, as it is by this time, for the more humorous spirits present, a question of vociferation or internal rupture.

BROADBENT. Thank you from the bottom of my heart, friends.

NORA [*whispering to Doran*] Take them away, Mr Doran [*Doran nods*].

DORAN. Well, good evenin, Mr Broadbent; an may you never regret the day you wint dhrivin wid Haffigan's pig! [*They shake hands*]. Good evenin, Miss Doyle.

General handshaking, Broadbent shaking hands with everybody effusively. He accompanies them to the garden and can be heard outside saying Goodnight in every inflexion known to parliamentary candidates. Nora, Aunt Judy, Keegan, Larry, and Cornelius are left in the parlor. Larry goes to the threshold and watches the scene in the garden.

NORA. It's a shame to make game of him like that. He's a gradle more good in him than Barney Doran.

CORNELIUS. It's all up with his candidature. He'll be laughed out o the town.

LARRY [*turning quickly from the doorway*] Oh no he wont: he's not an Irishman. He'll never know theyre laughing at him; and while theyre laughing he'll win the seat.

CORNELIUS. But he cant prevent the story getting about.

LARRY. He wont want to. He'll tell it himself as one of the most providential episodes in the history of England and Ireland.

AUNT JUDY. Sure he wouldnt make a fool of himself like that.

LARRY. Are you sure he's such a fool after all, Aunt Judy? Suppose you had a vote! which would you rather give it to? the man that told the story of Haffigan's pig Barney Doran's way or Broadbent's way?

AUNT JUDY. Faith I wouldnt give it to a man at all. It's a few women they want in parliament to stop their foolish blather.

BROADBENT [*bustling into the room, and taking off his dam-*

aged motoring overcoat, which he puts down on the sofa] Well, thats over. I must apologize for making a speech, Miss Doyle; but they like it, you know. Everything helps in electioneering.

Larry takes the chair near the door; draws it near the table; and sits astride it, with his elbows folded on the back.

AUNT JUDY. I'd no notion you were such an orator, Mr Broadbent.

BROADBENT. Oh, it's only a knack. One picks it up on the platform. It stokes up their enthusiasm.

AUNT JUDY. Oh, I forgot. Youve not met Mr Keegan. Let me introjoosha.

BROADBENT [*shaking hands effusively*] Most happy to meet you, Mr Keegan. I have heard of you, though I have not had the pleasure of shaking your hand before. And now may I ask you—for I value no man's opinion more—what you think of my chances here.

KEEGAN [*coldly*] Your chances, sir, are excellent. You will get into parliament.

BROADBENT [*delighted*] I hope so. I think so. [*Fluctuating*] You really think so? You are sure you are not allowing your enthusiasm for our principles to get the better of your judgment?

KEEGAN. I have no enthusiasm for your principles, sir. You will get into parliament because you w a n t to get into it enough to be prepared to take the necessary steps to induce the people to vote for you. That is how people usually get into that fantastic assembly.

BROADBENT [*puzzled*] Of course. [*Pause*]. Quite so. [*pause*]. Er—yes. [*Buoyant again*] I think they will vote for me. Eh? Yes?

AUNT JUDY. Arra why shouldnt they? Look at the people they do vote for!

BROADBENT [*encouraged*] Thats true: thats very true. When I see the windbags, the carpet-baggers, the charlatans, the—the—the fools and ignoramuses who corrupt the multitude by their wealth, or seduce them by spouting balderdash to them, I cannot help thinking that an Englishman with no humbug about him, who will talk straight common sense and take his stand on the solid ground of principle and public duty, *must* win his way with men of all classes.

KEEGAN [*quietly*] Sir: there was a time, in my ignorant youth, when I should have called you a hypocrite.

BROADBENT [*reddening*] A hypocrite!

NORA [*hastily*] Oh I'm sure you dont think anything of the sort, Mr Keegan.

BROADBENT [*emphatically*] Thank you, Miss Reilly: thank you.

CORNELIUS [*gloomily*] We all have to stretch it a bit in politics: hwats the use o pretendin we dont?

BROADBENT [*stiffly*] I hope I have said or done nothing that calls for any such observation, Mr Doyle. If there is a vice I detest—or against which my whole public life has been a protest—it is the vice of hypocrisy. I would almost rather be inconsistent than insincere.

KEEGAN. Do not be offended, sir: I know that you are quite sincere. There is a saying in the Scripture which runs—so far as the memory of an oldish man can carry the words—Let not the right side of your brain know what the left side doeth. I learnt at Oxford that this is the secret of the Englishman's strange power of making the best of both worlds.

BROADBENT. Surely the text refers to our right and left hands. I am somewhat surprised to hear a member of your Church quote so essentially Protestant a document as the Bible; but at least you might quote it accurately.

LARRY. Tom: with the best intentions youre making an ass of yourself. You dont understand Mr Keegan's peculiar vein of humor.

BROADBENT [*instantly recovering his confidence*] Ah! it was only your delightful Irish humor, Mr Keegan. Of course, of course. How stupid of me! I'm so sorry. [*He pats Keegan consolingly on the back*]. John Bull's wits are still slow, you see. Besides, calling me a hypocrite was too big a joke to swallow all at once, you know.

KEEGAN. You must also allow for the fact that I am mad.

NORA. Ah, dont talk like that, Mr Keegan.

BROADBENT [*encouragingly*] Not at all, not at all. Only a whimsical Irishman, eh?

LARRY. Are you really mad, Mr Keegan?

AUNT JUDY [*shocked*] Oh, Larry, how could you ask him such a thing?

LARRY. I dont think Mr Keegan minds. [*To Keegan*] Whats the true version of the story of that black man you confessed on his deathbed?

KEEGAN. What story have you heard about that?

LARRY. I am informed that when the devil came for the black heathen, he took off your head and turned it three times round before putting it on again; and that your head's been turned ever since.

NORA [*reproachfully*] Larry!

KEEGAN [*blandly*] That is not quite what occurred. [*He collects himself for a serious utterance: they attend involuntarily*]. I heard that a black man was dying, and that the people were afraid to go near him. When I went to the place I found an elderly Hindoo, who told me one of those tales of unmerited misfortune, of cruel ill luck, of relentless persecution by destiny, which sometimes wither the commonplaces of consolation on the lips of a priest. But this man did not complain of his misfortunes. They were brought upon him, he said, by sins committed in a former existence. Then, without a word of comfort from me, he died with a clear-eyed resignation that my most earnest exhortations have rarely produced in a Christian, and left me sitting there by his bedside with the mystery of this world suddenly revealed to me.

BROADBENT. That is a remarkable tribute to the liberty of conscience enjoyed by the subjects of our Indian Empire.

LARRY. No doubt; but may we venture to ask what is the mystery of this world?

KEEGAN. This world, sir, is very clearly a place of torment and penance, a place where the fool flourishes and the good and wise are hated and persecuted, a place where men and women torture one another in the name of love; where children are scourged and enslaved in the name of parental duty and education; where the weak in body are poisoned and mutilated in the name of healing, and the weak in character are put to the horrible torture of imprisonment, not for hours but for years, in the name of justice. It is a place where the hardest toil is a welcome refuge from the horror and tedium of pleasure, and where charity and good works are done only for hire to ransom the souls of the spoiler and the sybarite. Now, sir, there is only one place of horror and torment known to my religion; and that place is hell. Therefore it is plain to me that this earth of ours must be hell, and that we are all here, as the Indian revealed to me—perhaps he was sent to reveal it to me—to expiate crimes committed by us in a former existence.

AUNT JUDY [*awestruck*] Heaven save us, what a thing to say!

CORNELIUS [*sighing*] It's a queer world: thats certain.

BROADBENT. Your idea is a very clever one, Mr Keegan: really most brilliant: *I* should never have thought of it. But it seems to me—if I may say so—that you are overlooking the fact that, of the evils you describe, some are absolutely necessary for the preservation of society, and others are encouraged only when the Tories are in office.

LARRY. I expect you were a Tory in a former existence; and that is why you are here.

BROADBENT [*with conviction*] Never, Larry, never. But leaving politics out of the question, I find the world quite good enough for me: rather a jolly place, in fact.

KEEGAN [*looking at him with quiet wonder*] You are satisfied?

BROADBENT. As a reasonable man, yes. I see no evils in the world—except, of course, natural evils—that cannot be remedied by freedom, self-government, and English institutions. I think so, not because I am an Englishman, but as a matter of common sense.

KEEGAN. You feel at home in the world, then?

BROADBENT. Of course. Dont you?

KEEGAN [*from the very depths of his nature*] No.

BROADBENT [*breezily*] Try phosphorus pills. I always take them when my brain is overworked. I'll give you the address in Oxford Street.

KEEGAN [*enigmatically: rising*] Miss Doyle: my wandering fit has come on me: will you excuse me?

AUNT JUDY. To be sure: you know you can come in n nout as you like.

KEEGAN. We can finish the game some other time, Miss Reilly. [*He goes for his hat and stick*].

NORA. No: I'm out with you [*she disarranges the pieces and rises*]. I was too wicked in a former existence to play backgammon with a good man like you.

AUNT JUDY [*whispering to her*] Whisht, whisht, child! Dont set him back on that again.

KEEGAN [*to Nora*] When I look at you, I think that perhaps Ireland is only purgatory, after all. [*He passes on to the garden door*].

NORA. Galong with you!

BROADBENT [*whispering to Cornelius*] Has he a vote?

CORNELIUS [*nodding*] Yes. An theres lotsle vote the way he tells them.

KEEGAN [*at the garden door, with gentle gravity*] Good evening, Mr Broadbent. You have set me thinking. Thank you.

BROADBENT [*delighted, hurrying across to him to shake hands*] No, really? You find that contact with English ideas is stimulating, eh?

KEEGAN. I am never tired of hearing you talk, Mr Broadbent.

BROADBENT [*modestly remonstrating*] Oh come! come!

KEEGAN. Yes, I assure you. You are an extremely interesting man. [*He goes out*].

BROADBENT [*enthusiastically*] What a nice chap! What an intelligent, broadminded character, considering his cloth! By the way, I'd better have a wash. [*He takes up his coat and cap, and leaves the room through the inner door*].

Nora returns to her chair and shuts up the backgammon board.

AUNT JUDY. Keegan's very queer today. He has his mad fit on him.

CORNELIUS [*worried and bitter*] I wouldnt say but he's right after all. It's a contrairy world. [*To Larry*] Why would you be such a fool as to let Broadbent take the seat in parliament from you?

LARRY [*glancing at Nora*] He will take more than that from me before he's done here.

CORNELIUS. I wish he'd never set foot in my house, bad luck to his fat face! D'ye think he'd lend me £300 on the farm, Larry? When I'm so hard up, it seems a waste o money not to mortgage it now it's me own.

LARRY. *I* can lend you £300 on it.

CORNELIUS. No, no; I wasnt putn in for that. When I die and leave you the farm I should like to be able to feel that it was all me own, and not half yours to start with. Now I'll take me oath Barney Doarn's going to ask Broadbent to lend him £500 on the mill to put in a new hweel; for the old one'll harly hol together. An Haffigan cant sleep with covetn that corner o land at the foot of his medda that belongs to Doolan. He'll have to mortgage to buy it. I may as well be first as last. D'ye think Broadbent'd len me a little?

LARRY. I'm quite sure he will.

CORNELIUS. Is he as ready as that? Would he len me five hunderd, d'ye think?

LARRY. He'll lend you more than the landll ever be worth to you; so for Heaven's sake be prudent.

CORNELIUS [*judicially*] All right, all right, me son: I'll be careful. I'm goin into the office for a bit. [*He withdraws through the inner door, obviously to prepare his application to Broadbent*].

AUNT JUDY [*indignantly*] As if he hadnt seen enough o borryin when he was an agent without beginnin borryin himself! [*She rises*]. I'll borry him, so I will. [*She puts her knitting on the table and follows him out, with a resolute air that bodes trouble for Cornelius*].

Larry and Nora are left together for the first time since his arrival. She looks at him with a smile that perishes as she sees him aimlessly rocking his chair, and reflecting, evidently not about her, with his lips pursed as if he were whistling. With a catch in her throat she takes up Aunt Judy's knitting, and makes a pretence of going on with it.

NORA. I suppose it didnt seem very long to you.

LARRY [*starting*] Eh? What didnt?

NORA. The eighteen years youve been away.

LARRY. Oh, that! No: it seems hardly more than a week. I've been so busy—had so little time to think.

NORA. Ive had nothin else to do but think.

LARRY. That was very bad for you. Why didnt you give it up? Why did you stay here?

NORA. Because nobody sent for me to go anywhere else, I suppose. Thats why.

LARRY. Yes: one does stick frightfully in the same place, unless some external force comes and routs one out. [*He yawns slightly; but as she looks up quickly at him, he pulls himself together and rises with an air of waking up and setting to work cheerfully to make himself agreeable*]. And how have you been all this time?

NORA. Quite well, thank you.

LARRY. Thats right. [*Suddenly finding that he has nothing else to say, and being ill at ease in consequence, he strolls about the room humming distractedly*].

NORA [*struggling with her tears*] Is that all you have to say to me, Larry?

LARRY. Well, what is there to say? You see, we know each other so well.

NORA [*a little consoled*] Yes: of course we do. [*He does not reply*]. I wonder you came back at all.

LARRY. I couldnt help it. [*She looks up affectionately*]. Tom made me. [*She looks down again quickly to conceal the effect of this blow. He whistles another stave; then resumes*] I had a sort of dread of returning to Ireland. I felt somehow that my luck would turn if I came back. And now here I am, none the worse.

NORA. Praps it's a little dull for you.

LARRY. No: I havnt exhausted the interest of strolling about the old places and remembering and romancing about them.

NORA [*hopefully*] Oh! You do remember the places, then?

LARRY. Of course. They have associations.

NORA [*not doubting that the associations are with her*] I suppose so.

LARRY. M'yes. I can remember particular spots where I had long fits of thinking about the countries I meant to get to when I escaped from Ireland. America and London, and sometimes Rome and the east.

NORA [*deeply mortified*] Was that all you used to be thinking about?

LARRY. Well, there was precious little else to think about here, my dear Nora, except sometimes at sunset, when one got maudlin and called Ireland Erin, and imagined one was remembering the days of old, and so forth. [*He whistles Let Erin Remember*].

NORA. Did jever get a letter I wrote you last February?

LARRY. Oh yes; and I really intended to answer it. But I havnt had a moment; and I knew you wouldnt mind. You see, I am so afraid of boring you by writing about affairs you dont understand and people you dont know! And yet what else have I to write about? I begin a letter; and then I tear it up again. The fact is, fond as we are of one another, Nora, we have so little in common—I mean of course the things one can put in a letter—that correspondence is apt to become the hardest of hard work.

NORA. Yes: it's hard for me to know anything about you if you never tell me anything.

LARRY [*pettishly*] Nora: a man cant sit down and write his life day by day when he's tired enough with having lived it.

NORA. I'm not blaming you.

LARRY [*looking at her with some concern*] You seem rather out of spirits. [*Going closer to her, anxiously and tenderly*] You havnt got neuralgia, have you?

NORA. No.

LARRY [*reassured*] I get a touch of it sometimes when I am below par. [*Absently, again strolling about*] Yes, yes. [*He gazes through the doorway at the Irish landscape, and sings, almost unconsciously, but very expressively, an air from Offenbach's Whittington*].

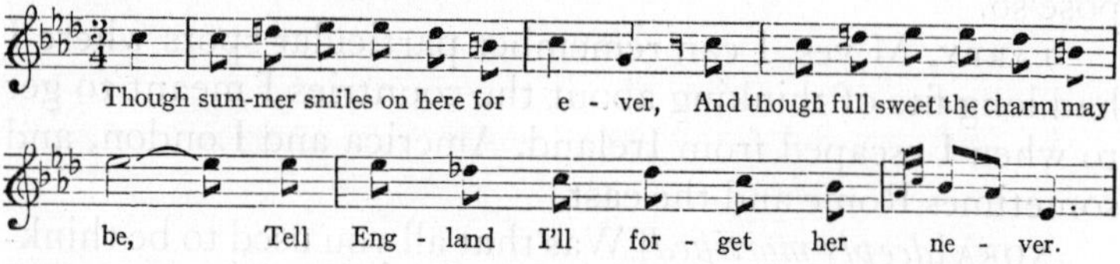

[*Nora, who has been at first touched by the tenderness of his singing, puts down her knitting at this very unexpected sentiment, and stares at him. He continues until the melody soars out of his range, when he trails off into whistling Let Erin Remember*].

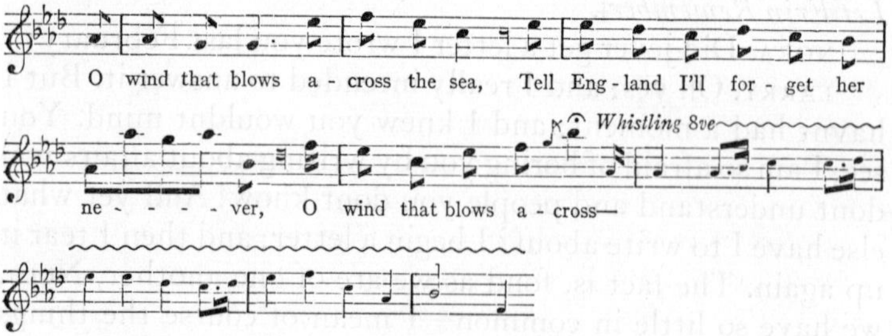

I'm afraid I'm boring you, Nora, though youre too kind to say so.

NORA. Are you wanting to get back to England already?

LARRY. Not at all. Not at all.

NORA. Thats a queer song to sing to me if youre not.

LARRY. The song! Oh, it doesnt mean anything: it's by a German Jew, like most English patriotic sentiment. Never mind me, my dear: go on with your work; and dont let me bore you.

NORA [*bitterly*] Rosscullen isnt such a lively place that I am likely to be bored by you at our first talk together after eighteen years, though you dont seem to have much to say to me after all.

LARRY. Eighteen years is a devilish long time, Nora. Now if it had been eighteen minutes, or even eighteen months, we should be able to pick up the interrupted thread, and chatter like two magpies. But as it is, I have simply nothing to say; and you seem to have less.

NORA. I—[*her tears choke her; but she keeps up appearances desperately*].

LARRY [*quite unconscious of his cruelty*] In a week or so we shall be quite old friends again. Meanwhile, as I feel that I am not making myself particularly entertaining, I'll take myself off. Tell Tom Ive gone for a stroll over the hill.

NORA. You seem very fond of Tom, as you call him.

LARRY [*the triviality going suddenly out of his voice*] Yes: I'm fond of Tom.

NORA. Oh, well, dont let me keep you from him.

LARRY. I know quite well that my departure will be a relief. Rather a failure, this first meeting after eighteen years, eh? Well, never mind: these great sentimental events always are failures; and now the worst of it's over anyhow. [*He goes out through the garden door*].

Nora, left alone, struggles wildly to save herself from breaking down, and then drops her face on the table and gives way to a convulsion of crying. Her sobs shake her so that she can hear nothing; and she has no suspicion that she is no longer alone until her head and breast are raised by Broadbent, who, returning newly washed and combed through the inner door, has seen her condition, first with surprise and concern, and then with an emotional disturbance that quite upsets him.

BROADBENT. Miss Reilly. Miss Reilly. Whats the matter? Dont cry: I cant stand it: you musnt cry. [*She makes a choked effort to speak, so painful that he continues with impulsive sympathy*] No: dont try to speak: it's all right now. Have your cry out: never mind me: trust me. [*Gathering her to him, and babbling consolatorily*] Cry on my chest: the only really comfortable place for a woman to cry is a man's chest: a real man, a real friend. A good broad chest, eh? not less than forty-two inches—no: dont fuss: never mind the conventions: we're two friends, arnt we? Come now, come, come! It's all right and comfortable and happy now, isnt it?

NORA [*through her tears*] Let me go. I want me handkerchief.

BROADBENT [*holding her with one arm and producing a large silk handkerchief from his breast pocket*] Heres a handkerchief. Let me [*he dabs her tears dry with it*]. Never mind your own: it's too small: it's one of those wretched little cambric handkerchiefs—

NORA [*sobbing*] Indeed it's a common cotton one.

BROADBENT. Of course it's a common cotton one—silly little cotton one—not good enough for the dear eyes of Nora Cryna—

NORA [*spluttering into a hysterical laugh and clutching him convulsively with her fingers while she tries to stifle her laughter against his collar bone*] Oh dont make me laugh: please dont make me laugh.

BROADBENT [*terrified*] I didnt mean to, on my soul. What is it? What is it?

NORA. Nora Creena, Nora Creena.

BROADBENT [*patting her*] Yes, yes, of course, Nora Creena, Nora acushla [*he makes cush rhyme to plush*]—

NORA. Acushla [*she makes cush rhyme to bush*].

BROADBENT. Oh, confound the language! Nora darling—my Nora—the Nora I love—

NORA [*shocked into propriety*] You musnt talk like that to me.

BROADBENT [*suddenly becoming prodigiously solemn and*

letting her go] No, of course not. I dont mean it. At least I do mean it; but I know it's premature. I had no right to take advantage of your being a little upset; but I lost my self-control for a moment.

NORA [*wondering at him*] I think youre a very kind-hearted man, Mr Broadbent; but you seem to me to have no self-control at all [*she turns her face away with a keen pang of shame and adds*] no more than myself.

BROADBENT [*resolutely*] Oh yes, I have: you should see me when I am really roused: then I have T R E M E N D O U S self-control. Remember: we have been alone together only once before; and then, I regret to say, I was in a disgusting state.

NORA. Ah no, Mr Broadbent: you wernt disgusting.

BROADBENT [*mercilessly*] Yes I was: nothing can excuse it: perfectly beastly. It must have made a most unfavorable impression on you.

NORA. Oh, sure it's all right. Say no more about that.

BROADBENT. I must, Miss Reilly: it is my duty. I shall not detain you long. May I ask you to sit down. [*He indicates her chair with oppressive solemnity. She sits down wondering. He then, with the same portentous gravity, places a chair for himself near her; sits down; and proceeds to explain*]. First, Miss Reilly, may I say that I have tasted nothing of an alcoholic nature today.

NORA. It doesnt seem to make as much difference in you as it would in an Irishman, somehow.

BROADBENT. Perhaps not. Perhaps not. I never quite lose myself.

NORA [*consolingly*] Well, anyhow, youre all right now.

BROADBENT [*fervently*] Thank you, Miss Reilly: I am. Now we shall get along. [*Tenderly, lowering his voice*] Nora: I was in earnest last night. [*Nora moves as if to rise*]. No: one moment. You must not think I am going to press you for an answer before you have known me for 24 hours. I am a reasonable man, I hope; and I am prepared to wait as long as you like, provided you will give me some small assurance that the answer will not be unfavorable.

NORA. How could I go back from it if I did? I sometimes think youre not quite right in your head, Mr Broadbent, you say such funny things.

BROADBENT. Yes: I know I have a strong sense of humor which sometimes makes people doubt whether I am quite serious. That is why I have always thought I should like to marry an Irishwoman. She would always understand my jokes. For instance, you would understand them, eh?

NORA [*uneasily*] Mr Broadbent: I couldnt.

BROADBENT [*soothingly*] Wait: let me break this to you gently, Miss Reilly: hear me out. I daresay you have noticed that in speaking to you I have been putting a very strong constraint on myself, so as to avoid wounding your delicacy by too abrupt an avowal of my feelings. Well, I feel now that the time has come to be open, to be frank, to be explicit. Miss Reilly: you have inspired in me a very strong attachment. Perhaps, with a woman's intuition, you have already guessed that.

NORA [*rising distractedly*] Why do you talk to me in that unfeeling nonsensical way?

BROADBENT [*rising also, much astonished*] Unfeeling! Nonsensical!

NORA. Dont you know that you have said things to me that no man ought to say unless—unless— [*she suddenly breaks down again and hides her face on the table as before*] Oh, go away from me: I wont get married at all: what is it but heartbreak and disappointment?

BROADBENT [*developing the most formidable symptoms of rage and grief*] Do you mean to say that you are going to refuse me? that you dont care for me?

NORA [*looking at him in consternation*] Oh, dont take it to heart, Mr Br—

BROADBENT [*flushed and almost choking*] I dont want to be petted and blarneyed. [*With childish rage*] I love you. I want you for my wife. [*In despair*] I cant help your refusing. I'm helpless: I can do nothing. You have no right to ruin my whole life. You— [*a hysterical convulsion stops him*].

NORA [*almost awestruck*] Youre not going to cry, are you? I never thought a man could cry. Dont.

BROADBENT. I'm not crying. I—I—I leave that sort of thing to your damned sentimental Irishmen. You think I have no feeling because I am a plain unemotional Englishman, with no powers of expression.

NORA. I dont think you know the sort of man you are at all. Whatever may be the matter with you, it's not want of feeling.

BROADBENT [*hurt and petulant*] It's you who have no feeling. Youre as heartless as Larry.

NORA. What do you expect me to do? Is it to throw meself at your head the minute the word is out o your mouth?

BROADBENT [*striking his silly head with his fists*] Oh, what a fool! what a brute I am! It's only your Irish delicacy: of course, of course. You mean Yes. Eh? What? Yes? yes? yes?

NORA. I think you might understand that though I might choose to be an old maid, I could never marry anybody but you now.

BROADBENT [*clasping her violently to his breast, with a crow of immense relief and triumph*] Ah, thats right, thats right: thats magnificent. I knew you would see what a first-rate thing this will be for both of us.

NORA [*incommoded and not at all enraptured by his ardor*] Youre dreadfully strong, an a gradle too free with your strength. An I never thought o whether it'd be a good thing for us or not. But when you found me here that time, I let you be kind to me, and cried in your arms, because I was too wretched to think of anything but the comfort of it. An how could I let any other man touch me after that?

BROADBENT [*moved*] Now thats very nice of you, Nora: thats really most delicately womanly [*he kisses her hand chivalrously*].

NORA [*looking earnestly and a little doubtfully at him*] Surely if you let one woman cry on you like that youd never let another touch you.

BROADBENT [*conscientiously*] One should not. One ought

not, my dear girl. But the honest truth is, if a chap is at all a pleasant sort of chap, his chest becomes a fortification that has to stand many assaults: at least it is so in England.

NORA [*curtly, much disgusted*] Then youd better marry an Englishwoman.

BROADBENT [*making a wry face*] No, no: the Englishwoman is too prosaic for my taste, too material, too much of the animated beefsteak about her. The ideal is what I like. Now Larry's taste is just the opposite: he likes em solid and bouncing and rather keen about him. It's a very convenient difference; for weve never been in love with the same woman.

NORA. An d'ye mean to tell me to me face that youve ever been in love before?

BROADBENT. Lord! yes.

NORA. I'm not your first love!

BROADBENT. First love is only a little foolishness and a lot of curiosity: no really self-respecting woman would take advantage of it. No, my dear Nora: Ive done with all that long ago. Love affairs always end in rows. We're not going to have any rows: we're going to have a solid four-square home: man and wife: comfort and common sense. And plenty of affection, eh [*he puts his arm round her with confident proprietorship*]?

NORA [*coldly, trying to get away*] I dont want any other woman's leavings.

BROADBENT [*holding her*] Nobody asked you to, maam. I never asked any woman to marry me before.

NORA [*severely*] Then why didnt you if youre an honorable man?

BROADBENT. Well, to tell you the truth, they were mostly married already. But never mind! there was nothing wrong. Come! dont take a mean advantage of me. After all, you must have had a fancy or two yourself, eh?

NORA [*conscience-stricken*] Yes. I suppose Ive no right to be particular.

BROADBENT [*humbly*] I know I'm not good enough for

you, Nora. But no man is, you know, when the woman is a really nice woman.

NORA. Oh, I'm no better than yourself. I may as well tell you about it.

BROADBENT. No, no: lets have no telling: much better not. *I* shant tell you anything: dont you tell me anything. Perfect confidence in one another and no tellings: thats the way to avoid rows.

NORA. Dont think it was anything I need be ashamed of.

BROADBENT. I dont.

NORA. It was only that I'd never known anybody else that I could care for; and I was foolish enough once to think that Larry—

BROADBENT [*disposing of the idea at once*] Larry! Oh, that wouldnt have done at all, not at all. You dont know Larry as I do, my dear. He has absolutely no capacity for enjoyment: he couldnt make any woman happy. He's as clever as be-blowed; but life's too earthly for him: he doesnt really care for anything or anybody.

NORA. Ive found that out.

BROADBENT. Of course you have. No, my dear: take my word for it, youre jolly well out of that. There! [*swinging her round against his breast*] thats much more comfortable for you.

NORA [*with Irish peevishness*] Ah, you mustnt go on like that. I dont like it.

BROADBENT [*unabashed*] Youll acquire the taste by degrees. You mustnt mind me: it's an absolute necessity of my nature that I should have somebody to hug occasionally. Besides, it's good for you: it'll plump out your muscles and make em elastic and set up your figure.

NORA. Well, I'm sure! if this is English manners! Arnt you ashamed to talk about such things?

BROADBENT [*in the highest feather*] Not a bit. By George, Nora, it's a tremendous thing to be able to enjoy oneself. Lets go off for a walk out of this stuffy little room. I want the open air to expand in, Come along. Co-o-ome along. [*He puts her arm into his and sweeps her out into the garden as an equinoctial gale might sweep a dry leaf*].

Later in the evening, the grasshopper is again enjoying the sunset by the great stone on the hill; but this time he enjoys neither the stimulus of Keegan's conversation nor the pleasure of terrifying Patsy Farrell. He is alone until Nora and Broadbent come up the hill arm in arm. Broadbent is still breezy and confident; but she has her head averted from him and is almost in tears.

BROADBENT [*stopping to snuff up the hillside air*] Ah! I like this spot. I like this view. This would be a jolly good place for a hotel and a golf links. Friday to Tuesday, railway ticket and hotel all inclusive. I tell you, Nora, I'm going to develop this place. [*Looking at her*] Hallo! Whats the matter? Tired?

NORA [*unable to restrain her tears*] I'm ashamed out o me life.

BROADBENT [*astonished*] Ashamed! What of?

NORA. Oh, how could you drag me all round the place like that, telling everybody that we're going to be married, and introjoocing me to the lowest of the low, and letting them shake hans with me, and encouraging them to make free with us? I little thought I should live to shaken hans with be Doolan in broad daylight in the public street of Rosscullen.

BROADBENT. But, my dear, Doolan's a publican: a most influential man. By the way, I asked him if his wife would be at home tomorrow. He said she would; so you must take the motor car round and call on her.

NORA [*aghast*] Is it me call on Doolan's wife!

BROADBENT. Yes, of course: call on all their wives. We must get a copy of the register and a supply of canvassing cards. No use calling on people who havent votes. Youll be a great success as a canvasser, Nora: they call you the heiress; and theyll be flattered no end by your calling, especially as youve never cheapened yourself by speaking to them before —have you?

NORA [*indignantly*] Not likely, indeed.

BROADBENT. Well, we mustnt be stiff and stand-off, you know. We must be thoroughly democratic, and patronize everybody without distinction of class. I tell you I'm a jolly lucky man, Nora Cryna. I get engaged to the most delightful woman in Ireland; and it turns out that I couldnt have done a smarter stroke of electioneering.

NORA. An would you let me demean meself like that, just to get yourself into parliament?

BROADBENT [*buoyantly*] Aha! Wait til you find out what an exciting game electioneering is: youll be mad to get me in. Besides, youd like people to say that Tom Broadbent's wife had been the making of him? that she got him into parliament? into the Cabinet, perhaps, eh?

NORA. God knows I dont grudge you me money! But to lower meself to the level of common people—

BROADBENT. To a member's wife, Nora, nobody is common provided he's on the register. Come, my dear! it's all right: do you think I'd let you do it if it wasnt? The best people do it. Everybody does it.

NORA [*who has been biting her lip and looking over the hill, disconsolate and unconvinced*] Well, praps you know best what they do in England. They must have very little respect for themselves. I think I'll go in now. I see Larry and Mr Keegan coming up the hill; and I'm not fit to talk to them.

BROADBENT. Just wait and say something nice to Keegan. They tell me he controls nearly as many votes as Father Dempsey himself.

NORA. You little know Peter Keegan. He'd see through me as if I was a pane o glass.

BROADBENT. Oh, he wont like it any the less for that. What really flatters a man is that you think him worth flattering. Not that I would flatter any man: dont think that. I'll just go and meet him. [*He goes down the hill with the eager forward look of a man about to greet a valued acquaintance. Nora dries her eyes, and turns to go as Larry strolls up the hill to her*].

LARRY. Nora. [*She turns and looks at him hardly, without*

a word. He continues anxiously, in his most conciliatory tone] When I left you that time, I was just as wretched as you. I didnt rightly know what I wanted to say; and my tongue kept clacking to cover the loss I was at. Well, Ive been thinking ever since; and now I know what I ought to have said. Ive come back to say it.

NORA. Youve come too late, then. You thought eighteen years was not long enough, and that you might keep me waiting a day longer. Well, you were mistaken. I'm engaged to your friend Mr Broadbent; and I'm done with you.

LARRY [*naïvely*] But that was the very thing I was going to advise you to do.

NORA [*involuntarily*] Oh you brute! to tell me that to me face!

LARRY [*nervously relapsing into his most Irish manner*] Nora, dear, dont you understand that I'm an Irishman, and he's an Englishman. He wants you; and he grabs you. *I* want you; and I quarrel with you and have to go on wanting you.

NORA. So you may. Youd better go back to England to the animated beefsteaks youre so fond of.

LARRY [*amazed*] Nora! [*Guessing where she got the metaphor*] He's been talking about me, I see. Well, never mind: we must be friends, you and I. I dont want his marriage to you to be his divorce from me.

NORA. You care more for him than you ever did for me.

LARRY [*with curt sincerity*] Yes of course I do: why should I tell you lies about it? Nora Reilly was a person of very little consequence to me or anyone else outside this miserable little hole. But Mrs Tom Broadbent will be a person of very considerable consequence indeed. Play your new part well, and there will be no more neglect, no more loneliness, no more idle regrettings and vain-hopings in the evenings by the Round Tower, but real life and real work and real cares and real joys among real people: solid English life in London, the very centre of the world. You will find your work cut out for you keeping Tom's house and entertaining

Tom's friends and getting Tom into parliament; but it will be worth the effort.

NORA. You talk as if I was under an obligation to him for marrying me.

LARRY. I talk as I think. Youve made a very good match, let me tell you.

NORA. Indeed! Well, some people might say he's not done so badly himself.

LARRY. If you mean that you will be a treasure to him, he thinks so now; and you can keep him thinking so if you like.

NORA. I wasnt thinking o meself at all.

LARRY. Were you thinking of your money, Nora?

NORA. I didnt say so.

LARRY. Your money will not pay your cook's wages in London.

NORA [*flaming up*] If thats true—and the more shame for you to throw it in me face if it *is* true—at all events itll make us independent; for if the worst comes to the worst, we can always come back here an live on it. An if I have to keep his house for him, at all events I can keep *you* out of it; for Ive done with you; and I wish I'd never seen you. So goodbye to you, Mister Larry Doyle. [*She turns her back on him and goes home*].

LARRY [*watching her as she goes*] Goodbye. Goodbye. Oh, thats so Irish! Irish both of us to the backbone: Irish! Irish! Iri—

Broadbent arrives, conversing energetically with Keegan.

BROADBENT. Nothing pays like a golfing hotel, if you hold the land instead of the shares, and if the furniture people stand in with you, and if you are a good man of business.

LARRY. Nora's gone home.

BROADBENT [*with conviction*] You were right this morning, Larry. I must feed up Nora. She's weak; and it makes her fanciful. Oh, by the way, did I tell you that we're engaged?

LARRY. She told me herself.

BROADBENT [*complacently*] She's rather full of it, as you may imagine. Poor Nora! Well, Mr Keegan, as I said, I begin to see my way here. I begin to see my way.

KEEGAN [*with a courteous inclination*] The conquering Englishman, sir. Within 24 hours of your arrival you have carried off our only heiress, and practically secured the parliamentary seat. And you have promised me that when I come here in the evenings to meditate on my madness; to watch the shadow of the Round Tower lengthening in the sunset; to break my heart uselessly in the curtained gloaming over the dead heart and blinded soul of the island of the saints, you will comfort me with the bustle of a great hotel, and the sight of the little children carrying the golf clubs of your tourists as a preparation for the life to come.

BROADBENT [*quite touched, mutely offering him a cigar to console him, at which he smiles and shakes his head*] Yes, Mr Keegan: youre quite right. Theres poetry in everything, even [*looking absently into the cigar case*] in the most modern prosaic things, if you know how to extract it [*he extracts a cigar for himself and offers one to Larry, who takes it*]. If I was to be shot for it I couldnt extract it myself; but thats where you come in, you see. [*Roguishly, waking up from his reverie and bustling Keegan goodhumoredly*] And then *I* shall wake y o u up a bit. Thats where *I* come in: eh? d'ye see? Eh? eh? [*He pats him very pleasantly on the shoulder, half admiringly, half pityingly*]. Just so, just so. [*Coming back to business*] By the way, I believe I can do better than a light railway here. There seems to be no question now that the motor boat has come to stay. Well, look at your magnificent river there, going to waste.

KEEGAN [*closing his eyes*]

"Silent, O Moyle, be the roar of thy waters."

BROADBENT. You know, the roar of a motor boat is quite pretty.

KEEGAN. Provided it does not drown the Angelus.

BROADBENT [*reassuringly*] Oh no: it wont do that: not the least danger. You know, a church bell can make a devil of a noise when it likes.

KEEGAN. You have an answer for everything, sir. But your plans leave one question still unanswered: how to get butter out of a dog's throat.

BROADBENT. Eh?

KEEGAN. You cannot build your golf links and hotels in the air. For that you must own our land. And how will you drag our acres from the ferret's grip of Matthew Haffigan? How will you persuade Cornelius Doyle to forego the pride of being a small landowner? How will Barney Doran's mill-race agree with your motor boats? Will Doolan help you to get a license for your hotel?

BROADBENT. My dear sir: to all intents and purposes the syndicate I represent already owns half Rosscullen. Doolan's is a tied house; and the brewers are in the syndicate. As to Haffigan's farm and Doran's mill and Mr Doyle's place and half a dozen others, they will be mortgaged to me before a month is out.

KEEGAN. But pardon me, you will not lend them more on their land than the land is worth; so they will be able to pay you the interest.

BROADBENT. Ah, you are a poet, Mr Keegan, not a man of business.

LARRY. We will lend everyone of these men half as much again on their land as it is worth, or ever can be worth, to them.

BROADBENT. You forget, sir, that we, with our capital, our knowledge, our organization, and may I say our English business habits, can make or lose ten pounds out of land that Haffigan, with all his industry, could not make or lose ten shillings out of. Doran's mill is a superannuated folly: I shall want it for electric lighting.

LARRY. What is the use of giving land to such men? they are too small, too poor, too ignorant, too simpleminded to hold it against us: you might as well give a dukedom to a crossing sweeper.

BROADBENT. Yes, Mr Keegan: this place may have an

industrial future, or it may have a residential future: I cant tell yet; but it's not going to be a future in the hands of your Dorans and Haffigans, poor devils!

KEEGAN. It may have no future at all. Have you thought of that?

BROADBENT. Oh, I'm not afraid of that. I have faith in Ireland. Great faith, Mr Keegan.

KEEGAN. And we have none: only empty enthusiasms and patriotisms, and emptier memories and regrets. Ah yes: you have some excuse for believing that if there be any future, it will be yours; for our faith seems dead, and our hearts cold and cowed. An island of dreamers who wake up in your jails, of critics and cowards whom you buy and tame for your own service, of bold rogues who help you to plunder us that they may plunder you afterwards.

BROADBENT [*a little impatient of this unbusinesslike view*] Yes, yes; but you know you might say that of any country. The fact is, there are only two qualities in the world: efficiency and inefficiency, and only two sorts of people: the efficient and the inefficient. It dont matter whether theyre English or Irish. I shall collar this place, not because I'm an Englishman and Haffigan and Co are Irishmen, but because theyre duffers, and I know my way about.

KEEGAN. Have you considered what is to become of Haffigan?

LARRY. Oh, we'll employ him in some capacity or other, and probably pay him more than he makes for himself now.

BROADBENT [*dubiously*] Do you think so? No no: Haffigan's too old. It really doesnt pay now to take on men over forty even for unskilled labor, which I suppose is all Haffigan would be good for. No: Haffigan had better go to America, or into the Union, poor old chap! He's worked out, you know: you can see it.

KEEGAN. Poor lost soul, so cunningly fenced in with invisible bars!

LARRY. Haffigan doesnt matter much. He'll die presently.

BROADBENT [*shocked*] Oh come, Larry! Don't be unfeeling. It's hard on Haffigan. It's always hard on the inefficient.

LARRY. Pah! what does it matter where an old and broken man spends his last days, or whether he has a million at the bank or only the workhouse dole? It's the young men, the able men, that matter. The real tragedy of Haffigan is the tragedy of his wasted youth, his stunted mind, his drudging over his clods and pigs until he has become a clod and a pig himself—until the soul within him has smouldered into nothing but a dull temper that hurts himself and all around him. I say let him die, and let us have no more of his like. And let young Ireland take care that it doesnt share his fate, instead of making another empty grievance of it. Let your syndicate come—

BROADBENT. Your syndicate too, old chap. You have your bit of the stock.

LARRY. Yes: mine if you like. Well, our syndicate has no conscience: it has no more regard for your Haffigans and Doolans and Dorans than it has for a gang of Chinese coolies. It will use your patriotic blatherskite and balderdash to get parliamentary powers over you as cynically as it would bait a mousetrap with toasted cheese. It will plan, and organize, and find capital while you slave like bees for it and revenge yourselves by paying politicians and penny newspapers out of your small wages to write articles and report speeches against its wickedness and tyranny, and to crack up your own Irish heroism, just as Haffigan once paid a witch a penny to put a spell on Billy Byrne's cow. In the end it will grind the nonsense out of you, and grind strength and sense into you.

BROADBENT [*out of patience*] Why cant you say a simple thing simply, Larry, without all that Irish exaggeration and talky-talky? The syndicate is a perfectly respectable body of responsible men of good position. We'll take Ireland in hand, and by straightforward business habits teach it efficiency and self-help on sound Liberal principles. You agree with me, Mr Keegan, dont you?

KEEGAN. Sir: I may even vote for you.

BROADBENT [*sincerely moved, shaking his hand warmly*] You shall never regret it, Mr Keegan: I give you my word for that. I shall bring money here: I shall raise wages: I shall found public institutions: a library, a Polytechnic (undenominational, of course), a gymnasium, a cricket club, perhaps an art school. I shall make a Garden city of Rosscullen: the round tower shall be thoroughly repaired and restored.

KEEGAN. And our place of torment shall be as clean and orderly as the cleanest and most orderly place I know in Ireland, which is our poetically named Mountjoy prison. Well, perhaps I had better vote for an efficient devil that knows his own mind and his own business than for a foolish patriot who has no mind and no business.

BROADBENT [*stiffly*] Devil is rather a strong expression in that connexion, Mr Keegan.

KEEGAN. Not from a man who knows that this world is hell. But since the word offends you, let me soften it, and compare you simply to an ass. [*Larry whitens with anger*].

BROADBENT [*reddening*] An ass!

KEEGAN [*gently*] You may take it without offence from a madman who calls the ass his brother—and a very honest, useful and faithful brother too. The ass, sir, is the most efficient of beasts, matter-of-fact, hardy, friendly when you treat him as a fellow-creature, stubborn when you abuse him, ridiculous only in love, which sets him braying, and in politics, which move him to roll about in the public road and raise a dust about nothing. Can you deny these qualities and habits in yourself, sir?

BROADBENT [*goodhumoredly*] Well, yes, I'm afraid I do, you know.

KEEGAN. Then perhaps you will confess to the ass's one fault.

BROADBENT. Perhaps so: what is it?

KEEGAN. That he wastes all his virtues—his efficiency, as you call it—in doing the will of his greedy masters instead of doing the will of Heaven that is in himself. He is efficient in the service of Mammon, mighty in mischief, skilful in ruin, heroic in destruction. But he comes to browse here without knowing that the soil his hoof touches is holy ground. Ireland, sir, for good or evil, is like no other place under heaven; and no man can touch its sod or breathe its air without becoming better or worse. It produces two kinds of men in strange perfection: saints and traitors. It is called the island of the saints; but indeed in these later years it might be more fitly called the island of the traitors; for our harvest of these is the fine flower of the world's crop of infamy. But the day may come when these islands shall live by the quality of their men rather than by the abundance of their minerals; and then we shall see.

LARRY. Mr Keegan: if you are going to be sentimental about Ireland, I shall bid you good evening. We have had enough of that, and more than enough of cleverly proving that everybody who is not an Irishman is an ass. It is neither good sense nor good manners. It will not stop the syndicate; and it will not interest young Ireland so much as my friend's gospel of efficiency.

BROADBENT. Ah, yes, yes: efficiency is the thing. I dont in the least mind your chaff, Mr Keegan; but Larry's right on the main point. The world belongs to the efficient.

KEEGAN [*with polished irony*] I stand rebuked, gentlemen. But believe me, I do every justice to the efficiency of you and your syndicate. You are both, I am told, thoroughly efficient civil engineers; and I have no doubt the golf links will be a triumph of your art. Mr Broadbent will get into parliament most efficiently, which is more than St Patrick could do if he were alive now. You may even build the hotel efficiently if you can find enough efficient masons, carpenters, and plumbers, which I rather doubt. [*Dropping his irony, and beginning to fall into the attitude of the priest rebuking sin*] When the hotel becomes insolvent [*Broadbent takes his cigar out of his mouth, a little taken aback*] your English business habits will secure the thorough efficiency of the liquidation. You will reorganize the scheme efficiently; you will liquidate its second bankruptcy efficiently [*Broadbent and Larry look quickly at one another; for this, unless the priest is an old financial hand, must be inspiration*]; you will get rid of its original shareholders efficiently after efficiently ruining them; and you will finally profit very efficiently by getting that hotel for a few shillings in the pound. [*More and more sternly*] Besides these efficient operations, you will foreclose your mortgages most efficiently [*his rebuking forefinger goes up in spite of himself*]; you will drive Haffigan to America very efficiently; you will find a use for Barney Doran's foul mouth and bullying temper by employing him to slave-drive your laborers very efficiently; and [*low and bitter*] when at last this poor desolate countryside becomes a busy mint in which we shall all slave to make money for you, with our Polytechnic to teach us how to do it efficiently, and our library to fuddle the few imaginations your distilleries will spare, and our repaired Round Tower with admission sixpence, and refreshments and penny-in-the-slot mutoscopes to make it interesting, then no doubt your English and American shareholders will spend all the money we make for them very efficiently in shooting and hunting, in operations for cancer and appendicitis, in gluttony and gambling; and you will devote what they save to fresh land development schemes. For four wicked centuries the world has dreamed this foolish dream of efficiency; and the end is not yet. But the end will come.

BROADBENT [*seriously*] Too true, Mr Keegan, only too true. And most eloquently put. It reminds me of poor Ruskin: a great man, you know. I sympathize. Believe me, I'm on your side. Dont sneer, Larry: I used to read a lot of Shelley years ago. Let us be faithful to the dreams of our youth [*he wafts a wreath of cigar smoke at large across the hill*].

KEEGAN. Come, Mr Doyle! is this English sentiment so much more efficient than our Irish sentiment, after all? Mr Broadbent spends his life inefficiently admiring the thoughts of great men, and efficiently serving the cupidity of base money hunters. We spend our lives efficiently sneering at him and doing nothing. Which of us has any right to reproach the other?

BROADBENT [*coming down the hill again to Keegan's right hand*] But you know, something m u s t be done.

KEEGAN. Yes: when we cease to do, we cease to live. Well, what shall we do?

BROADBENT. Why, what lies to our hand.

KEEGAN. Which is the making of golf links and hotels to bring idlers to a country which workers have left in millions because it is a hungry land, a naked land, an ignorant and oppressed land.

BROADBENT. But, hang it all, the idlers will bring money from England to Ireland!

KEEGAN. Just as o u r idlers have for so many generations taken money from Ireland to England. Has that saved England from poverty and degradation more horrible than we have ever dreamed of? When I went to England, sir, I hated England. Now I pity it. [*Broadbent can hardly conceive an Irishman pitying England; but as Larry intervenes angrily, he gives up and takes to the hill and his cigar again*].

LARRY. Much good your pity will do it!

KEEGAN. In the accounts kept in heaven, Mr Doyle, a heart purified of hatred may be worth more than even a Land Development Syndicate of Anglicized Irishmen and Gladstonized Englishmen.

LARRY. Oh, in heaven, no doubt. I have never been there. Can you tell me where it is?

KEEGAN. Could you have told me this morning where hell is? Yet you know now that it is here. Do not despair of finding heaven: it may be no farther off.

LARRY [*ironically*] On this holy ground, as you call it, eh?

KEEGAN [*with fierce intensity*] Yes, perhaps, even on this holy ground which such Irishmen as you have turned into a Land of Derision.

BROADBENT [*coming between them*] Take care! you will be quarrelling presently. Oh, you Irishmen, you Irishmen! Toujours Ballyhooly, eh? [*Larry, with a shrug, half comic, half impatient, turns away up the hill, but presently strolls back on Keegan's right. Broadbent adds, confidentially to Keegan*] Stick to the Englishman, Mr Keegan: he has a bad name here; but at least he can forgive you for being an Irishman.

KEEGAN. Sir: when you speak to me of English and Irish you forget that I am a Catholic. My country is not Ireland nor England, but the whole mighty realm of my Church. For me there are but two countries: heaven and hell; but two conditions of men: salvation and damnation. Standing here between you the Englishman, so clever in your foolishness, and this Irishman, so foolish in his cleverness, I cannot in my ignorance be sure which of you is the more deeply damned; but I should be unfaithful to my calling if I opened the gates of my heart less widely to one than to the other.

LARRY. In either case it would be an impertinence, Mr Keegan, as your approval is not of the slightest consequence to us. What use do you suppose all this drivel is to men with serious practical business in hand?

BROADBENT. I dont agree with that, Larry. I think these things cannot be said too often: they keep up the moral tone of the community. As you know, I claim the right to think for myself in religious matters: in fact, I am ready to avow myself a bit of a—of a—well, I dont care who knows it—a bit of a Unitarian; but if the Church of England contained a few men like Mr Keegan, I should certainly join it.

KEEGAN. You do me too much honor, sir. [*With priestly humility to Larry*] Mr Doyle: I am to blame for having unintentionally set your mind somewhat on edge against me. I beg your pardon.

LARRY [*unimpressed and hostile*] I didnt stand on ceremony with you: you neednt stand on it with me. Fine manners and fine words are cheap in Ireland: you can keep both for my friend here, who is still imposed on by them. *I* know their value.

KEEGAN. You mean you dont know their value.

LARRY [*angrily*] I mean what I say.

KEEGAN [*turning quietly to the Englishman*] You see, Mr

Broadbent, I only make the hearts of my countrymen harder when I preach to them: the gates of hell still prevail against me. I shall wish you good evening. I am better alone, at the Round Tower, dreaming of heaven. [*He goes up the hill*].

LARRY. Aye, thats it! there you are! dreaming! dreaming! dreaming! dreaming!

KEEGAN [*halting and turning to them for the last time*] Every dream is a prophecy: every jest is an earnest in the womb of Time.

BROADBENT [*reflectively*] Once, when I was a small kid, I dreamt I was in heaven. [*They both stare at him*]. It was a sort of pale blue satin place, with all the pious old ladies in our congregation sitting as if they were at a service; and there was some awful person in the study at the other side of the hall. I didnt enjoy it, you know. What is it like in your dreams?

KEEGAN. In my dreams it is a country where the State is the Church and the Church the people: three in one and one in three. It is a commonwealth in which work is play and play is life: three in one and one in three. It is a temple in which the priest is the worshipper and the worshipper the worshipped: three in one and one in three. It is a godhead in which all life is human and all humanity divine: three in one and one in three. It is, in short, the dream of a madman. [*He goes away across the hill*].

BROADBENT [*looking after him affectionately*] What a regular old Church and State Tory he is! He's a character: he'll be an attraction here. Really almost equal to Ruskin and Carlyle.

LARRY. Yes; and much good they did with all their talk!

BROADBENT. Oh tut, tut, Larry! They improved my mind: they raised my tone enormously. I feel sincerely obliged to Keegan: he has made me feel a better man: distinctly better. [*With sincere elevation*] I feel now as I never did before that I am right in devoting my life to the cause of Ireland. Come along and help me to choose the site for the hotel.

PROGRAM NOTE

DEAR SIR OR MADAM,

It is your custom to receive my plays with the most generous and unrestrained applause. You sometimes compel the performers to pause at the end of every line until your laughter has quieted down. I am not ungrateful; but may I ask you a few questions?

Are you aware that you would get out of the Theatre half an hour earlier if you listened to the play in silence and did not applaud until the fall of the curtain?

Do you really consider that a performance is improved by continual interruptions, however complimentary they may be to the actors and the author?

Do you not think that the naturalness of the representation must be destroyed, and therefore your own pleasure greatly diminished, when the audience insists on taking part in it by shouts of applause and laughter, and the actors have repeatedly to stop acting until the noise is over.

Have you considered that in all good plays tears and laughter lie very close together, and that it must be very distressing to an actress who is trying to keep her imagination fixed on pathetic emotions to hear bursts of laughter breaking out at something she is supposed to be unconscious of?

Do you know that even when there is no such conflict of comic and tragic on the stage, the strain of performing is greatly increased if the performers have to attend to the audience as well as to their parts at the same time?

Can you not imagine how a play which has been rehearsed to perfection in dead silence without an audience must be upset, disjointed, and spun out to a wearisome length by an audience which refuses to enjoy it silently?

Have you noticed that if you laugh loudly and repeatedly for two hours, you get tired and cross, and are sorry next morning that you did not stay at home?

Will you think me very ungrateful and unkind if I tell you that though you cannot possibly applaud my plays too much at each fall of the curtain to please me, yet the more applause there is during the performance the angrier I feel with you for spoiling your enjoyment and my own?

Would you dream of stopping the performance of a piece of music to applaud every bar that happened to please you? and do you not know that an act of a play is intended, just like a piece of music, to be heard without interruption from beginning to end?

Have you ever told your sons and daughters that little children should be seen and not heard? And have you ever thought how nice theatrical performances would be, and how much sooner you would get away to supper, if parents in the theatre would follow the precepts they give to their children at home?

Have you noticed that people look very nice when they smile or look pleased, but look shockingly ugly when they roar with laughter or shout excitedly or sob loudly? Smiles make no noise.

Do you know that what pleases actors and authors most is not your applauding them but your coming to see the play again and again, and that if you tire yourselves out and spoil the play with interruptions you are very unlikely to come again?

Do you know that my plays, as rehearsed, are just the right length: that is, quite as long as you can bear; and that if you delay the performances by loud laughter you will make them half an hour too long?

Can I persuade you to let the performance proceed in perfect silence just this once to see how you like it. The intervals will give you no less than five opportunities of expressing your approval or disapproval, as the case may be.

And finally, will you believe me to be acting sincerely in your own interests in this matter as

your faithful servant,

THE AUTHOR.

New Year,
1913.

THE DARK LADY OF THE SONNETS

AN INTERLUDE

Written in 1910

First Performed London 1910

PREFACE TO THE DARK LADY OF THE SONNETS

HOW THE PLAY CAME TO BE WRITTEN

I HAD better explain why, in this little *pièce d'occasion*, written for a performance in aid of the funds of the project for establishing a National Theatre as a memorial to Shakespear, I have identified the Dark Lady with Mistress Mary Fitton. First, let me say that I do not contend that the Dark Lady was Mary Fitton, because when the case in Mary's favor (or against her, if you please to consider that the Dark Lady was no better than she ought to have been) was complete, a portrait of Mary came to light and turned out to be that of a fair lady, not of a dark one. That settles the question, if the portrait is authentic, which I see no reason to doubt, and the lady's hair undyed, which is perhaps less certain. Shakespear rubbed in the lady's complexion in his sonnets mercilessly; for in his day black hair was as unpopular as red hair was in the early days of Queen Victoria. Any tinge lighter than raven black must be held fatal to the strongest claim to be the Dark Lady. And so, unless it can be shewn that Shakespear's sonnets exasperated Mary Fitton into dyeing her hair and getting painted in false colors, I must give up all pretence that my play is historical. The later suggestion of Mr Acheson that the Dark Lady, far from being a maid of honor, kept a tavern in Oxford and was the mother of Davenant the poet, is the one I should have adopted had I wished to be up to date. Why, then, did I introduce the Dark Lady as Mistress Fitton?

Well, I had two reasons. The play was not to have been written by me at all, but by Dame Edith Lyttelton; and it was she who suggested a scene of jealousy between Queen Elizabeth and the Dark Lady at the expense of the unfortunate Bard. Now this, if the Dark Lady was a maid of honor, was quite easy. If she were a tavern landlady, it would have strained all probability. So I stuck to Mary Fitton. But I had another and more personal reason. I was, in a manner, present at the birth of the Fitton theory. Its parent and I had become acquainted; and he used to consult me on obscure passages in the sonnets, on which, as far as I can remember, I never succeeded in throwing the faintest light, at a time when nobody else thought my opinion, on that or any other subject, of the slightest importance. I thought it would be friendly to immortalize him, as the silly literary saying is, much as Shakespear immortalized Mr W. H., as he said he would, simply by writing about him.

Let me tell the story formally.

THOMAS TYLER

Throughout the eighties at least, and probably for some years before, the British Museum reading room was used daily by a gentleman of such astonishing and crushing ugliness that no one who had once seen him could ever thereafter forget him. He was of fair complexion, rather golden red than sandy; aged between forty-five and sixty; and dressed in frock coat and tall hat of presentable but never new appearance. His figure was rectangular, waistless, neckless, ankleless, of middle height, looking shortish because, though he was not particularly stout, there was nothing slender about him. His ugliness was not unamiable: it was accidental, external, excrescential. Attached to his face from the left ear to the point of his chin was a monstrous goitre, which hung down to his collar bone, and was very inadequately balanced by a smaller one on his right eyelid. Nature's malice was so overdone in his case that it somehow failed to produce the effect of repulsion it seemed to have aimed at. When you first met Thomas Tyler you could think of nothing else but whether surgery could really do nothing for him. But after a very brief acquaintance you never thought of his disfigurements at all, and talked to him as you might to Romeo or Lovelace; only, so many people, especially women, would not risk the preliminary ordeal, that he remained a man apart and a bachelor all his days. I am not to be frightened or prejudiced by a tumor; and I struck up a cordial acquaintance with him, in the course of which he kept me pretty closely on the track of his work at the Museum, in which I was then, like himself, a daily reader.

He was by profession a man of letters of an uncommercial kind. He was a specialist in pessimism; had made a translation of Ecclesiastes of which eight copies a year were sold; and followed up the pessimism of Shakespear and Swift with keen interest. He delighted in a hideous conception which he called the theory of the cycles, according to which the history of mankind and the universe keeps eternally repeating itself without the slightest variation throughout all eternity; so that he had lived and died and had his goitre before and would live and die and have it again and again and again. He liked to believe that nothing that happened to him was completely novel: he was persuaded that he often had some recollection of its previous occurrence in the last cycle. He hunted out allusions to this favorite theory in his three favorite pessimists. He tried his hand occasionally at deciphering ancient inscriptions, reading them as people seem to read the stars, by discovering bears and bulls and swords and goats where, as it seems to me, no sane human being can see anything but stars higgledy-piggledy. Next to the translation of Ecclesiastes, his *magnum opus* was his work on Shakespear's Sonnets, in which he accepted a previous identification of Mr W. H., the "onlie begetter" of the sonnets, with the Earl of Pembroke (William Herbert), and promulgated his own identification of Mistress Mary Fitton with the Dark Lady. Whether he was right or wrong about the Dark Lady did not matter urgently to me: she might have been Maria Tompkins for all I cared. But Tyler would have it that she was Mary Fitton; and he tracked Mary down from the first of her marriages in her teens to her tomb in Cheshire, whither he made a pilgrimage and whence returned in triumph with a picture of her statue, and the news that he was convinced she was a dark lady by traces of paint still discernible.

In due course he published his edition of the Sonnets, with the evidence he had collected. He lent me a copy of the book, which I never returned. But I reviewed it in the Pall Mall Gazette on the 7th of January 1886, and thereby let loose the Fitton theory in a wider circle of readers than the book could reach. Then Tyler died, sinking unnoted like a stone in the sea. I observe that Mr Acheson, Mrs Davenant's champion, calls him Reverend. It may very well be that he got his knowledge of Hebrew in reading for the Church; and there was always something of the clergyman or the schoolmaster in his dress and air. Possibly he may actually have been ordained. But he never told me that or anything else about his affairs; and his black pessimism would have shot him violently out of any church at present established in the West. We never talked about affairs: we talked about Shakespear, and the Dark Lady, and Swift, and Koheleth, and the cycles, and the mysterious moments when a feeling came over us that this had happened to us before, and about the forgeries of the Pentateuch which were offered for sale to the British Museum, and about literature and things of the spirit generally. He always came to my desk at the Museum and spoke to me about something or other, no doubt finding that people who were keen on this sort of conversation were rather scarce. He remains a vivid spot of memory in the void of my forgetfulness, a quite considerable and dignified soul in a grotesquely disfigured body.

FRANK HARRIS

To the review in the Pall Mall Gazette I attribute, rightly or wrongly, the introduction of Mary Fitton to Mr Frank Harris. My reason for this is that Mr Harris wrote a play about Shakespear and Mary Fitton; and when I, as a pious duty to Tyler's ghost, reminded the world that it was to Tyler we owed the Fitton theory, Frank Harris, who clearly had not a notion of what had first put Mary into his head, believed, I think, that I had invented Tyler expressly for his discomfiture; for the stress I laid on Tyler's claims must have seemed unaccountable and perhaps malicious on the assumption that he was to me a mere name among the thousands of names in the British Museum catalogue. Therefore I make it clear that I had and have personal reasons for remembering Tyler, and for regarding myself as in some sort charged with the duty of reminding the world of his work. I am sorry for his sake that Mary's portrait is fair, and that Mr W. H. has veered round again from Pembroke to Southampton; but even so his work was not wasted: it is by exhausting all the hypotheses that we reach the verifiable one; and after all, the wrong road always leads somewhere.

Frank Harris's play was written long before mine. I read it in manuscript before the Shakespear Memorial National Theatre was mooted; and if there is anything except the Fitton theory (which is Tyler's property) in my play which is also in Mr Harris's it was I who annexed it from him and not he from me. It does not matter anyhow, because this play of mine is a brief trifle, and full of manifest impossibilities at that; whilst Mr Harris's play is serious both in size, intention, and quality. But there could not in the nature of things be much resemblance, because Frank conceives Shakespear to have been a broken-hearted, melancholy, enormously sentimental person, whereas I am convinced that he was very like myself: in fact, if I had been born in 1556 instead of in 1856, I should have taken to blank verse and given Shakespear a harder run for his money than all the other Elizabethans put together. Yet the success of Frank Harris's book on Shakespear gave me great delight.

To those who know the literary world of London there was a sharp stroke of ironic comedy in the irresistible verdict in its favor. In critical literature there is one prize that is always open to competition, one blue ribbon that always carries the highest critical rank with it. To win, you must write the best book of your generation on Shakespear. It is felt on all sides that to do this a certain fastidious refinement, a delicacy of taste, a correctness of manner and tone, and high academic distinction in addition to the indispensable scholarship and literary reputation, are needed; and men who pretend to these qualifications are constantly looked to with a gentle expectation that presently they will achieve the great feat. Now if there is a man on earth who is the utter contrary of everything that this description implies; whose very existence is an insult to the ideal it realizes; whose eye disparages, whose resonant voice denounces, whose cold shoulder jostles every decency, every delicacy, every amenity, every dignity, every sweet usage of that quiet life of mutual admiration in which perfect Shakespearian appreciation is expected to arise, that man is Frank Harris. Here is one who is extraordinarily qualified, by a range of sympathy and understanding that extends from the ribaldry of a buccaneer to the shyest tendernesses of the most sensitive poetry, to be all things to all men, yet whose proud humor it is to be to every man, provided the man is eminent and pretentious, the champion of his enemies. To the Archbishop he is an atheist, to the atheist a Catholic mystic, to the Bismarckian Imperialist an Anacharsis Klootz, to Anacharsis Klootz a Washington, to Mrs Proudie a Don Juan, to Aspasia a John Knox: in short, to everyone his complement rather than his counterpart, his antagonist rather than his fellow-creature. Always provided, however, that the persons thus affronted are respectable persons. Sophie Perovskaia, who perished on the scaffold for blowing Alexander II to fragments, may perhaps have echoed Hamlet's

Oh God, Horatio, what a wounded name—
Things standing thus unknown—I leave behind!

but Frank Harris, in his Sonia, has rescued her from that injustice, and enshrined her among the saints. He has lifted the Chicago anarchists out of their infamy, and shewn that, compared with the Capitalism that killed them, they were heroes and martyrs. He has done this with the most unusual power of conviction. The story, as he tells it, inevitably and irresistibly displaces all the vulgar, mean, purblind, spiteful versions. There is a precise realism and an unsmiling, measured, determined sincerity which gives a strange dignity to the work of one whose fixed practice and ungovernable impulse it is to kick conventional dignity whenever he sees it.

HARRIS "DURCH MITLEID WISSEND"

Frank Harris is everything except a humorist, not, apparently, from stupidity, but because scorn overcomes humor in him. Nobody ever dreamt of reproaching Milton's Lucifer for not seeing the comic side of his fall; and nobody who has read Mr Harris's stories desires to have them lightened by chapters from the hand of Artemus Ward. Yet he knows the taste and the value of humor. He was one of the few men of letters who really appreciated Oscar Wilde, though he did not rally fiercely to Wilde's side until the world deserted Oscar in his ruin. I myself was present at a curious meeting between the two, when Harris, on the eve of the Queensberry trial, prophesied to Wilde with miraculous precision exactly what immediately afterwards happened to him, and warned him to leave the country. It was the first time within my knowledge that such a forecast proved true. Wilde, though under no illusion as to the folly of the quite unselfish suit-at-law he had been persuaded to begin, nevertheless so miscalculated the force of the social vengeance he was unloosing on himself that he fancied it could be stayed by putting up the editor of The Saturday Review (as Mr Harris then was) to declare that he considered Dorian Grey a highly moral book, which it certainly is. When Harris foretold him the truth, Wilde denounced him as a fainthearted friend who was failing him in his hour of need, and left the room in anger. Harris's idiosyncratic power of pity saved him from feeling or shewing the smallest resentment; and events presently proved to Wilde how insanely he had been advised in taking the action, and how accurately Harris had gauged the situation.

The same capacity for pity governs Harris's study of Shakespear, whom, as I have said, he pities too much; but that he is not insensible to humor is shewn not only by his appreciation of Wilde, but by the fact that the group of contributors who made his editorship of The Saturday Review so remarkable, and of whom I speak none the less highly because I happened to be one of them myself, were all, in their various ways, humorists.

"SIDNEY'S SISTER: PEMBROKE'S MOTHER"

And now to return to Shakespear. Though Mr Harris

followed Tyler in identifying Mary Fitton as the Dark Lady, and the Earl of Pembroke as the addressee of the other sonnets and the man who made love successfully to Shakespear's mistress, he very characteristically refuses to follow Tyler on one point, though for the life of me I cannot remember whether it was one of the surmises which Tyler published, or only one which he submitted to me to see what I would say about it, just as he used to submit difficult lines from the sonnets.

This surmise was that "Sidney's sister: Pembroke's mother" set Shakespear on to persuade Pembroke to marry, and that this was the explanation of those earlier sonnets which so persistently and unnaturally urged matrimony on Mr W. H. I take this to be one of the brightest of Tyler's ideas, because the persuasions in the sonnets are unaccountable and out of character unless they were offered to please somebody whom Shakespear desired to please, and who took a motherly interest in Pembroke. There is a further temptation in the theory for me. The most charming of all Shakespear's old women, indeed the most charming of all his women, young or old, is the Countess of Rousillon in All's Well That Ends Well. It has a certain individuality among them which suggests a portrait. Mr Harris will have it that all Shakespear's nice old women are drawn from his beloved mother; but I see no evidence whatever that Shakespear's mother was a particularly nice woman or that he was particularly fond of her. That she was a simple incarnation of extravagant maternal pride like the mother of Coriolanus in Plutarch, as Mr Harris asserts, I cannot believe: she is quite as likely to have borne her son a grudge for becoming "one of these harlotry players" and disgracing the Ardens. Anyhow, as a conjectural model for the Countess of Rousillon, I prefer that one of whom Jonson wrote

> Sidney's sister: Pembroke's mother:
> Death ere thou has slain another,
> Learnd and fair and good as she,
> Time shall throw a dart at thee.

But Frank will not have her at any price, because his ideal Shakespear is rather like a sailor in a melodrama; and a sailor in a melodrama must adore his mother. I do not at all belittle such sailors. They are the emblems of human generosity; but Shakespear was not an emblem: he was a man and the author of Hamlet, who had no illusions about his mother. In weak moments one almost wishes he had.

SHAKESPEAR'S SOCIAL STANDING

On the vexed question of Shakespear's social standing Mr Harris says that Shakespear "had not had the advantage of a middle-class training." I suggest that Shakespear missed this questionable advantage, not because he was socially too low to have attained to it, but because he conceived himself as belonging to the upper class from which our public school boys are now drawn. Let Mr Harris survey for a moment the field of contemporary journalism. He will see there some men who have the very characteristics from which he infers that Shakespear was at a social disadvantage through his lack of middle-class training. They are rowdy, ill-mannered, abusive, mischievous, fond of quoting obscene schoolboy anecdotes, adepts in that sort of blackmail which consists in mercilessly libelling and insulting every writer whose opinions are sufficiently heterodox to make it almost impossible for him to risk perhaps five years of a slender income by an appeal to a prejudiced orthodox jury; and they see nothing in all this cruel blackguardism but an uproariously jolly rag, although they are by no means without genuine literary ability, a love of letters, and even some artistic conscience. But he will find not one of the models of this type (I say nothing of mere imitators of it) below the rank that looks at the middle class, not humbly and enviously from below, but insolently from above. Mr Harris himself notes Shakespear's contempt for the tradesman and mechanic, and his incorrigible addiction to smutty jokes. He does us the public service of sweeping away the familiar plea of the Bardolatrous ignoramus, that Shakespear's coarseness was part of the manners of his time, putting his pen with precision on the one name, Spenser, that is necessary to expose such a libel on Elizabethan decency. There was nothing whatever to prevent Shakespear from being as decent as More was before him, or Bunyan after him, and as self-respecting as Raleigh or Sidney, except the tradition of his class, in which education or statesmanship may no doubt be acquired by those who have a turn for them, but in which insolence, derision, profligacy, obscene jesting, debt contracting, and rowdy mischievousness, give continual scandal to the pious, serious, industrious, solvent bourgeois. No other class is infatuated enough to believe that gentlemen are born and not made by a very elaborate process of culture. Even kings are taught and coached and drilled from their earliest boyhood to play their part. But the man of family (I am convinced that Shakespear took that view of himself) will plunge into society without a lesson in table manners, into politics without a lesson in history, into the city without a lesson in business, and into the army without a lesson in honor.

It has been said, with the object of proving Shakespear a laborer, that he could hardly write his name. Why? Because he "had not the advantage of a middle-class training." Shakespear himself tells us, through Hamlet, that gentlemen purposely wrote badly lest they should be mistaken for scriveners; but most of them, then as now, wrote badly because they could not write any better. In short, the whole range of Shakespear's foibles: the snobbishness, the naughtiness, the contempt for tradesmen and mechanics, the assumption that witty conversation can only mean smutty conversation, the flunkeyism towards social superiors and insolence towards social inferiors, the easy ways with servants which is seen not only between The Two Gentlemen of Verona and their valets, but in the affection and respect inspired by a great servant like Adam: all these are the characteristics of Eton and Harrow, not of the public elementary or private adventure school. They prove, as everything we know about Shakespear suggests, that he thought of the Shakespears and Ardens as families of consequence, and regarded himself as a gentleman under a cloud through his father's ill luck in business, and never for a moment as a man of the people. This is at once the explanation of and excuse for his snobbery. He was not a parvenu trying to cover his humble origin with a purchased coat of arms: he was a gentleman resuming what he conceived to be his natural position as soon as he gained the means to keep it up.

THIS SIDE IDOLATRY

There is another matter which I think Mr Harris should ponder. He says that Shakespear was but "little esteemed by his own generation." He even describes Jonson's description of his "little Latin and less Greek" as a sneer, whereas it occurs in an unmistakeably sincere eulogy of Shakespear, written after his death, and is clearly meant to heighten the impression of Shakespear's prodigious natural endowments by pointing out that they were not due to scholastic acquirements. Now there is a sense in which it is true enough that Shakespear was too little esteemed by his own generation, or, for the matter of that, by any subsequent generation. The bargees on the Regent's Canal do not chant Shakespear's verses as the gondoliers in Venice are said to chant the verses of Tasso (a practice which was suspended for some reason during my stay in Venice: at least no gondolier ever did it in my hearing). Shakespear is no more a popular author than Rodin is a popular sculptor or Richard Strauss a popular composer. But Shakespear was certainly not such a fool as to expect the Toms, Dicks, and Harrys of his time to be any more interested in dramatic poetry than Newton, later on, expected them to be interested in fluxions. And when we come to the question whether Shakespear missed that assurance which all great men have had from the more capable and susceptible members of their generation that they were great men, Ben Jonson's evidence disposes of so improbable a notion at once and for ever. "I loved the man," says Ben, "this side idolatry, as well as any." Now why in the name of common sense should he have made that qualification unless there had been, not only idolatry, but idolatry fulsome enough to irritate Jonson into an express disavowal of it? Jonson, the bricklayer, must have felt sore sometimes when Shakespear spoke and wrote of bricklayers as his inferiors. He must have felt it a little hard that being a better scholar, and perhaps a braver and tougher man physically than Shakespear, he was not so successful or so well liked. But in spite of this he praised Shakespear to the utmost stretch of his powers of eulogy: in fact, notwithstanding his disclaimer, he did not stop "this side idolatry." If, therefore, even Jonson felt himself forced to clear himself of extravagance and absurdity in his appreciation of Shakespear, there must have been many people about who idolized Shakespear as American ladies idolize Paderewski, and who carried Bardolatry, even in the Bard's own time, to an extent that threatened to make his reasonable admirers ridiculous.

SHAKESPEAR'S PESSIMISM

I submit to Mr Harris that by ruling out this idolatry, and its possible effect in making Shakespear think that his public would stand anything from him, he has ruled out a far more plausible explanation of the faults of such a play as Timon of Athens than his theory that Shakespear's passion for the Dark Lady "cankered and took on proud flesh in him, and tortured him to nervous breakdown and madness." In Timon the intellectual bankruptcy is obvious enough: Shakespear tried once too often to make a play out of the cheap pessimism which is thrown into despair by a comparison of actual human nature with theoretical morality, actual law and administration with abstract justice, and so forth. But Shakespear's perception of the fact that all men, judged by the moral standard which they apply to others and by which they justify their punishment of others, are fools and scoundrels, does not date from the Dark Lady complication: he seems to have been born with it. If in The Comedy of Errors and A Midsummer Night's Dream the persons of the drama are not quite so ready for treachery and murder as Laertes and even Hamlet himself (not to mention the procession of ruffians who pass through the latest plays) it is certainly not because they have any more regard for law or religion. There is only one place in Shakespear's plays where the sense of shame is used as a human attribute; and that is where Hamlet is ashamed, not of anything he himself has done, but of his mother's relations with his uncle. This scene is an unnatural one: the son's reproaches to his mother, even the fact of his being able to discuss the subject with her, is more repulsive than her relations with her deceased husband's brother.

Here, too, Shakespear betrays for once his religious sense by making Hamlet, in his agony of shame, declare that his mother's conduct makes "sweet religion a rhapsody of words." But for that passage we might almost suppose that the feeling of Sunday morning in the country which Orlando describes so perfectly in As You Like It was the beginning and end of Shakespear's notion of religion. I say almost, because Isabella in Measure for Measure has religious charm, in spite of the conventional theatrical assumption that female religion means an inhumanly ferocious chastity. But for the most part Shakespear differentiates his heroes from his villains much more by what they do than by what they are. Don Juan in Much Ado is a true villain: a man with a malicious will; but he is too dull a duffer to be of any use in a leading part; and when we come to the great villains like Macbeth, we find, as Mr Harris points out, that they are precisely identical with the heroes: Macbeth is only Hamlet incongruously committing murders and engaging in hand-to-hand combats. And Hamlet, who does not dream of apologizing for the three murders he commits, is always apologizing because he has not yet committed a fourth, and finds, to his great bewilderment, that he does not want to commit it. "It cannot be," he says, "but I am pigeon-livered, and lack gall to make oppression bitter; else, ere this, I should have fatted all the region kites with this slave's offal." Really one is tempted to suspect that when Shylock asks "Hates any man the thing he would not kill?" he is expressing the natural and proper sentiments of the human race as

Shakespear understood them, and not the vindictiveness of a stage Jew.

GAIETY OF GENIUS

In view of these facts, it is dangerous to cite Shakespear's pessimism as evidence of the despair of a heart broken by the Dark Lady. There is an irrepressible gaiety of genius which enables it to bear the whole weight of the world's misery without blenching. There is a laugh always ready to avenge its tears of discouragement. In the lines which Mr Harris quotes only to declare that he can make nothing of them, and to condemn them as out of character, Richard III, immediately after pitying himself because

> There is no creature loves me
> And if I die no soul will pity me,

adds, with a grin,

> Nay, wherefore should they, since that I myself
> Find in myself no pity for myself?

Let me again remind Mr Harris of Oscar Wilde. We all dreaded to read De Profundis: our instinct was to stop our ears, or run away from the wail of a broken, though by no means contrite, heart. But we were throwing away our pity. De Profundis was de profundis indeed: Wilde was too good a dramatist to throw away so powerful an effect; but none the less it was de profundis in excelsis. There was more laughter between the lines of that book than in a thousand farces by men of no genius. Wilde, like Richard and Shakespear, found in himself no pity for himself. There is nothing that marks the born dramatist more unmistakeably than this discovery of comedy in his own misfortunes almost in proportion to the pathos with which the ordinary man announces their tragedy. I cannot for the life of me see the broken heart in Shakespear's latest works. "Hark, hark! the lark at heaven's gate sings" is not the lyric of a broken man; nor is Cloten's comment that if Imogen does not appreciate it, "it is a vice in her ears which horse hairs, and cats' guts, and the voice of unpaved eunuch to boot, can never amend," the sally of a saddened one. Is it not clear that to the last there was in Shakespear an incorrigible divine levity, an inexhaustible joy that derided sorrow? Think of the poor Dark Lady having to stand up to this unbearable power of extracting a grim fun from everything. Mr Harris writes as if Shakespear did all the suffering and the Dark Lady all the cruelty. But why does he not put himself in the Dark Lady's place for a moment as he has put himself so successfully in Shakespear's? Imagine her reading the hundred and thirtieth sonnet!

My mistress' eyes are nothing like the sun;
Coral is far more red than her lips' red;
If snow be white, why then her breasts are dun;
If hairs be wire, black wires grow on her head;
I have seen roses damasked, red and white,
But no such roses see I in her cheeks;
And in some perfumes is there more delight
Than in the breath that from my mistress reeks.
I love to hear her speak; yet well I know
That music hath a far more pleasing sound.
I grant I never saw a goddess go:
My mistress, when she walks, treads on the ground.
    And yet, by heaven, I think my love as rare
    As any she belied with false compare.

Take this as a sample of the sort of compliment from which she was never for a moment safe with Shakespear. Bear in mind that she was not a comedian; that the Elizabethan fashion of treating brunettes as ugly women must have made her rather sore on the subject of her complexion; that no human being, male or female, can conceivably enjoy being chaffed on that point in the fourth couplet about the perfumes; that Shakespear's revulsions, as the sonnet immediately preceding shews, were as violent as his ardors, and were expressed with the realistic power and horror that makes Hamlet say that the heavens got sick when they saw the queen's conduct; and then ask Mr Harris whether any woman could have stood it for long, or have thought the "sugred" compliment worth the cruel wounds, the cleaving of the heart in twain, that seemed to Shakespear as natural and amusing a reaction as the burlesquing of his heroics by Pistol, his sermons by Falstaff, and his poems by Cloten and Touchstone.

JUPITER AND SEMELE

This does not mean that Shakespear was cruel: evidently he was not; but it was not cruelty that made Jupiter reduce Semele to ashes: it was the fact that he could not help being a god nor she help being a mortal. The one thing Shakespear's passion for the Dark Lady was not, was what Mr Harris in one passage calls it: idolatrous. If it had been, she might have been able to stand it. The man who "dotes yet doubts; suspects, yet strongly loves," is tolerable even by a spoilt and tyrannical mistress; but what woman could possibly endure a man who dotes without doubting; who *knows* and who is hugely amused at the absurdity of his infatuation for a woman of whose mortal imperfections not one escapes him: a man always exchanging grins with Yorick's skull, and inviting "my lady" to laugh at the sepulchral humor of the fact that though she paint an inch thick (which the Dark Lady may have done), to Yorick's favor she must come at last. To the Dark Lady he must sometimes have seemed cruel beyond description: an intellectual Caliban. True, a Caliban who could say

Be not afeard: the isle is full of noises,
Sounds and sweet airs that give delight and hurt not.
Sometimes a thousand twangling instruments
Will hum about mine ears; and sometimes voices,
That, if I then had waked after long sleep,
Will make me sleep again; and then, in dreaming,
The clouds, methought, would open and shew riches
Ready to drop on me: that when I wak'd
I cried to dream again.

which is very lovely; but the Dark Lady may have had that vice in her ears which Cloten dreaded: she may not have seen the beauty of it, whereas there can be no doubt at all that of "My mistress' eyes are nothing like the sun," &c.,

not a word was lost on her.

And is it to be supposed that Shakespear was too stupid or too modest not to see at last that it was a case of Jupiter and Semele? Shakespear was most certainly not modest in that sense. The timid cough of the minor poet was never heard from him.

Not marble, nor the gilded monuments
Of princes, shall outlive this powerful rhyme

is only one out of a dozen passages in which he (possibly with a keen sense of the fun of scandalizing the modest coughers) proclaimed his place and his power in "the wide world dreaming of things to come." The Dark Lady most likely thought this side of him insufferably conceited; for there is no reason to suppose that she liked his plays any better than Minna Wagner liked Richard's music dramas: as likely as not, she thought The Spanish Tragedy worth six Hamlets. He was not stupid either: if his class limitations and a profession that cut him off from actual participation in great affairs of State had not confined his opportunities of intellectual and political training to private conversation and to the Mermaid Tavern, he would probably have become one of the ablest men of his time instead of being merely its ablest playwright. One might surmise that Shakespear found out that the Dark Lady's brains could no more keep pace with his than Anne Hathaway's, if there were any evidence that their friendship ceased when he stopped writing sonnets to her. As a matter of fact the consolidation of a passion into an enduring intimacy generally puts an end to sonnets.

That the Dark Lady broke Shakespear's heart, as Mr Harris will have it she did, is an extremely unShakespearian hypothesis. "Men have died from time to time, and worms have eaten them; but not for love," says Rosalind. Richard of Gloster, into whom Shakespear put all his own impish superiority to vulgar sentiment, exclaims

And this word "love," which greybeards call divine,
Be resident in men like one another
And not in me: I am myself alone.

Hamlet has not a tear for Ophelia: her death moves him to fierce disgust for the sentimentality of Laertes by her grave; and when he discusses the scene with Horatio immediately after, he utterly forgets her, though he is sorry he forgot himself, and jumps at the proposal of a fencing match to finish the day with. As against this view Mr Harris pleads Romeo, Orsino, and even Antonio; and he does it so penetratingly that he convinces you that Shakespear did betray himself again and again in these characters; but self-betrayal is one thing; and self-portrayal, as in Hamlet and Mercutio, is another. Shakespear never "saw himself," as actors say, in Romeo or Orsino or Antonio. In Mr Harris's own play Shakespear is presented with the most pathetic tenderness. He is tragic, bitter, pitiable, wretched and broken among a robust crowd of Jonsons and Elizabeths; but to me he is not Shakespear because I miss the Shakespearian irony and the Shakespearian gaiety. Take these away and Shakespear is no longer Shakespear: all the bite, the impetus, the strength, the grim delight in his own power of looking terrible facts in the face with a chuckle, is gone; and you have nothing left but that most depressing of all things: a victim. Now who can think of Shakespear as a man with a grievance? Even in that most thoroughgoing and inspired of all Shakespear's loves: his love of music (which Mr Harris has been the first to appreciate at anything like its value), there is a dash of mockery. "Spit in the hole, man; and tune again." "Divine air! Now is his soul ravished. Is it not strange that sheep's guts should hale the souls out of men's bodies?" "An he had been a dog that should have howled thus, they would have hanged him." There is just as much Shakespear here as in the inevitable quotation about the sweet south and the bank of violets.

I lay stress on this irony of Shakespear's, this impish rejoicing in pessimism, this exultation in what breaks the hearts of common men, not only because it is diagnostic of that immense energy of life which we call genius, but because its omission is the one glaring defect in Mr Harris's otherwise extraordinarily penetrating book. Fortunately, it is an omission that does not disable the book as (in my judgment) it disabled the hero of the play, because Mr Harris left himself out of his play, whereas he pervades his book, mordant, deep-voiced, and with an unconquerable style which is the man.

THE IDOL OF THE BARDOLATERS

There is even an advantage in having a book on Shakespear with the Shakespearian irony left out of account. I do not say that the missing chapter should not be added in the next edition: the hiatus is too great: it leaves the reader too uneasy before this touching picture of a writhing worm substituted for the invulnerable giant. But it is none the less probable that in no other way could Mr Harris have got at his man as he has. For, after all, what is the secret of the hopeless failure of the academic Bardolaters to give us a credible or even interesting Shakespear, and the easy triumph of Mr Harris in giving us both? Simply that Mr Harris has assumed that he was dealing with a man, whilst the others have assumed that they were writing about a god, and have therefore rejected every consideration of fact, tradition, or interpretation, that pointed to any human imperfection in their hero. They thus leave themselves with so little material that they are forced to begin by saying that we know very little about Shakespear. As a matter of fact, with the plays and sonnets in our hands, we know much more about Shakespear than we know about Dickens or Thackeray: the only difficulty is that we deliberately suppress it because it proves that Shakespear was not only very unlike the conception of a god current in Clapham, but was not, according to the same reckoning, even a respectable man. The academic view starts with a Shakespear who was not scurrilous; therefore the verses about "lousy Lucy" cannot have been written by him, and the cognate passages in the plays are either strokes of character-drawing or gags interpolated by the actors. This ideal Shakespear was too well behaved to get drunk; therefore the tradition that his death was hastened by a drinking bout with Jonson and Drayton must be rejected, and the remorse of Cassio treated as a thing observed, not experienced: nay, the disgust of Hamlet at the drinking customs of Denmark is taken to establish Shakespear as the superior of Alexander in self-control and the greatest of teetotalers.

Now this system of inventing your great man to start with, and then rejecting all the materials that do not fit him, with the ridiculous result that you have to declare that there are no materials at all (with your waste-paper basket full of them), ends in leaving Shakespear with a much worse character than he deserves. For though it does not greatly matter whether he wrote the lousy Lucy lines or not, and does not really matter at all whether he got drunk when he made a night of it with Jonson and Drayton, the sonnets raise an unpleasant question which does matter a good deal; and the refusal of the academic Bardolaters to discuss or even mention this question has had the effect of producing a silent verdict against Shakespear. Mr Harris tackles the question openly, and has no difficulty whatever in convincing us that Shakespear was a man of normal constitution sexually, and was not the victim of that most cruel and pitiable of all the freaks of nature: the freak which transposes the normal aim of the affections. Silence on this point means condemnation; and the condemnation has been general throughout the present generation, though it only needed Mr Harris's fearless handling of the matter to sweep away what is nothing but a morbid and very disagreeable modern fashion. There is always some stock accusation brought against eminent persons. When I was a boy every well-known man was accused of beating his wife. Later on, for some unexplained reason, he was accused of psychopathic derangement. And this fashion is retrospective. The cases of Shakespear and Michel Angelo are cited as proving that every genius of the first magnitude was a sufferer; and both here and in Germany there are circles in which such derangement is grotesquely reverenced as part of the stigmata of heroic powers.

All of which is gross nonsense. Unfortunately, in Shakespear's case, prudery, which cannot prevent the accusation from being whispered, does prevent the refutation from being shouted. Mr Harris, the deep-voiced, refuses to be silenced. He dismisses with proper contempt the stupidity which places an outrageous construction on Shakespear's apologies in the sonnets for neglecting that "perfect ceremony" of love which consists in returning calls and making protestations and giving presents and paying the trumpery attentions which men of genius always refuse to bother about, and to which touchy people who have no genius attach so much importance. No reader who had not been tampered with by the psychopathic monomaniacs could ever put any construction but the obvious and innocent one on these passages. But the general vocabulary of the sonnets to Pembroke (or whoever "Mr W. H." really was) is so overcharged according to modern ideas that a reply on the general case is necessary.

SHAKESPEAR'S ALLEGED SYCOPHANCY AND PERVERSION

That reply, which Mr Harris does not hesitate to give, is twofold: first, that Shakespear was, in his attitude towards earls, a sycophant; and, second, that the normality of Shakespear's sexual constitution is only too well attested by the excessive susceptibility to the normal impulse shewn in the whole mass of his writings. This latter is the really conclusive reply. In the case of Michel Angelo, for instance, one must admit that if his works are set beside those of Titian or Paul Veronese, it is impossible not to be struck by the absence in the Florentine of that susceptibility to feminine charm which pervades the pictures of the Venetians. But, as Mr Harris points out (though he does not use this particular illustration) Paul Veronese is an anchorite compared to Shakespear. The language of the sonnets addressed to Pembroke, extravagant as it now seems, is the language of compliment and fashion, transfigured no doubt by Shakespear's verbal magic, and hyperbolical, as Shakespear always seems to people who cannot conceive so vividly as he, but still unmistakeable for anything else than the expression of a friendship delicate enough to be wounded, and a manly loyalty deep enough to be outraged. But the language of the sonnets to the Dark Lady is the language of passion: their cruelty shews it. There is no evidence that Shakespear was capable of being unkind in cold blood. But in his revulsions from love, he was bitter, wounding, even ferocious; sparing neither himself nor the unfortunate woman whose only offence was that she had reduced the great man to the common human denominator.

In seizing on these two points Mr Harris has made so sure a stroke, and placed his evidence so featly that there is nothing left for me to do but to plead that the second is sounder than the first, which is, I think, marked by the prevalent mistake as to Shakespear's social position, or, if you prefer it, the confusion between his actual social position as a penniless tradesman's son taking to the theatre for a livelihood, and his own conception of himself as a gentleman of good family. I am prepared to contend that though Shakespear was undoubtedly sentimental in his expressions of devotion to Mr W. H. even to a point which nowadays makes both ridiculous, he was not sycophantic if Mr W. H. was really attractive and promising, and Shakespear deeply attached to him. A sycophant does not tell his patron that his fame will survive, not in the renown of his own actions, but in the sonnets of his sycophant. A sycophant, when his patron cuts him out in a love affair, does not tell his patron exactly what he thinks of him. Above all, a sycophant does not write to his patron precisely as he feels on all occasions; and this rare kind of sincerity is all over the sonnets. Shakespear, we are told, was "a very civil gentleman." This must mean that his desire to please people and be liked by them, and his reluctance to hurt their feelings, led him into amiable flattery even when his feelings were not strongly stirred. If this be taken into account along with the fact that Shakespear conceived and expressed all his emotions with a vehemence that sometimes carried him into ludicrous extravagance, making Richard offer his kingdom for a horse and Othello declare of Cassio that

> Had all his hairs been lives, my great revenge
> Had stomach for them all,

we shall see more civility and hyperbole than sycophancy even in the earlier and more coldblooded sonnets.

SHAKESPEAR AND DEMOCRACY

Now take the general case pled against Shakespear as an enemy of democracy by Tolstoy, the late Ernest Crosbie and others, and endorsed by Mr Harris. Will it really stand fire? Mr Harris emphasizes the passages in which Shakespear spoke of mechanics and even of small master tradesmen as base persons whose clothes were greasy, whose breath was rank, and whose political imbecility and caprice moved Coriolanus to say to the Roman Radical who demanded at least "good words" from him

> He that will give good words to thee will flatter
> Beneath abhorring.

But let us be honest. As political sentiments these lines are an abomination to every democrat. But suppose they are not political sentiments! Suppose they are merely a record of observed fact. John Stuart Mill told our British workmen that they were mostly liars. Carlyle told us all that we are mostly fools. Matthew Arnold and Ruskin were more circumstantial and more abusive. Everybody, including the workers themselves, know that they are dirty, drunken, foulmouthed, ignorant, gluttonous, prejudiced: in short, heirs to the peculiar ills of poverty and slavery, as well as co-heirs with the plutocracy to all the failings of human nature. Even Shelley admitted, 200 years after Shakespear wrote Coriolanus, that universal suffrage was out of the question. Surely the real test, not of Democracy, which was not a live political issue in Shakespear's time, but of impartiality in judging classes, which is what one demands from a great human poet, is not that he should flatter the poor and denounce the rich, but that he should weigh them both in the same balance. Now whoever will read Lear and Measure for Measure will find stamped on his mind such an appalled sense of the danger of dressing man in a little brief authority, such a merciless stripping of the purple from the "poor, bare, forked animal" that calls itself a king and fancies itself a god, that one wonders what was the real nature of the mysterious restraint that kept "Eliza and our James" from teaching Shakespear to be civil to crowned heads, just as one wonders why Tolstoy was allowed to go free when so many less terrible levellers went to the galleys or Siberia. From the mature Shakespear we get no such scenes of village snobbery as that between the stage country gentleman Alexander Iden and the stage Radical Jack Cade. We get the shepherd in As You Like It, and many honest, brave, human, and loyal servants, beside the inevitable comic ones. Even in the Jingo play, Henry V, we get Bates and Williams drawn with all respect and honor as normal rank and file men. In Julius Caesar, Shakespear went to work with a will when he took his cue from Plutarch in glorifying regicide and transfiguring the republicans. Indeed hero-worshippers have never forgiven him for belittling Caesar and failing to see that side of his assassination which made Goethe denounce it as the most senseless of crimes. Put the play beside the Charles I of Wills, in which Cromwell is written down to a point at which the Jack Cade of Henry VI becomes a hero in comparison; and then believe, if you can, that Shakespear was one of them that "crook the pregnant hinges of the knee where thrift may follow fawning." Think of Rosencrantz, Guildenstern, Osric, the fop who annoyed Hotspur, and a dozen passages concerning such people! If such evidence can prove anything (and Mr Harris relies throughout on such evidence) Shakespear loathed courtiers.

If, on the other hand, Shakespear's characters are mostly members of the leisured classes, the same thing is true of Mr Harris's own plays and mine. Industrial slavery is not compatible with that freedom of adventure, that personal refinement and intellectual culture, that scope of action, which the higher and subtler drama demands. Even Cervantes had finally to drop Don Quixote's troubles with innkeepers demanding to be paid for his food and lodging, and make him as free of economic difficulties as Amadis de Gaul. Hamlet's experiences simply could not have happened to a plumber. A poor man is useful on the stage only as a blind man is: to excite sympathy. The poverty of the apothecary in Romeo and Juliet produces a great effect, and even points the sound moral that a poor man cannot afford to have a conscience; but if all the characters of the play had been as poor as he, it would have been nothing but a melodrama of the sort that the Sicilian players gave us here; and that was not the best that lay in Shakespear's power. When poverty is abolished, and leisure and grace of life become general, the only plays surviving from our epoch which will have any relation to life as it will be lived then will be those in which none of the persons represented are troubled with want of money or wretched drudgery. Our plays of poverty and squalor, now the only ones that are true to the life of the majority of living men, will then be classed with the records of misers and monsters, and read only by historical students of social pathology.

Then consider Shakespear's kings and lords and gentlemen! Would even John Ball or Jeremiah complain that they are flattered? Surely a more mercilessly exposed string of scoundrels never crossed the stage. The very monarch who paralyzes a rebel by appealing to the divinity that hedges a king, is a drunken and sensual assassin, and is presently killed contemptuously before our eyes in spite of his hedge of divinity. I could write as convincing a chapter on Shakespear's Dickensian prejudice against the throne and the nobility and gentry in general as Mr Harris or Ernest Crosbie on the other side. I could even go so far as to contend that one of Shakespear's defects is his lack of an intelligent comprehension of feudalism. He had of course no prevision of democratic Collectivism. He was, except in the commonplaces of war and patriotism, a privateer through and through.

Nobody in his plays, whether king or citizen, has any civil public business or conception of such a thing, except in the method of appointing constables, to the abuses in which he called attention quite in the vein of the Fabian Society. He was concerned about drunkenness and about the idolatry and hypocrisy of our judicial system; but his implied remedy was personal sobriety and freedom from idolatrous illusion in so far as he had any remedy at all, and did not merely despair of human nature. His first and last word on parliament was "Get thee glass eyes, and, like a scurvy politician, seem to see the thing thou dost not." He had no notion of the feeling with which the land nationalizers of today regard the fact that he was a party to the enclosure of common lands at Wellcome. The explanation is, not a general deficiency in his mind, but the simple fact that in his day what English land needed was individual appropriation and cultivation, and what the English Constitution needed was the incorporation of Whig principles of individual liberty.

SHAKESPEAR AND THE BRITISH PUBLIC

I have rejected Mr Harris's view that Shakespear died broken-hearted of "the pangs of love despised." I have given my reasons for believing that Shakespear died game, and indeed in a state of levity which would have been considered unbecoming in a bishop. But Mr Harris's evidence does prove that Shakespear had a grievance and a very serious one. He might have been jilted by ten dark ladies and been none the worse for it; but his treatment by the British Public was another matter. The idolatry which exasperated Ben Jonson was by no means a popular movement; and, like all such idolatries, it was excited by the magic of Shakespear's art rather than by his views. He was launched on his career as a successful playwright by the Henry VI trilogy, a work of no originality, depth, or subtlety except the originality, depth, and subtlety of the feelings and fancies of the common people. But Shakespear was not satisfied with this. What is the use of being Shakespear if you are not allowed to express any notions but those of Autolycus? Shakespear did not see the world as Autolycus did: he saw it, if not exactly as Ibsen did (for it was not quite the same world), at least with much of Ibsen's power of penetrating its illusions and idolatries, and with all Swift's horror of its cruelty and uncleanliness.

Now it happens to some men with these powers that they are forced to impose their fullest exercise on the world because they cannot produce popular work. Take Wagner and Ibsen for instance! Their earlier works are no doubt much cheaper than their later ones; still, they were not popular when they were written. The alternative of doing popular work was never really open to them: had they stooped they would have picked up less than they snatched from above the people's heads. But Handel and Shakespear were not held to their best in this way. They could turn out anything they were asked for, and even heap up the measure. They reviled the British Public, and never forgave it for ignoring their best work and admiring their splendid commonplaces; but they produced the commonplaces all the same, and made them sound magnificent by mere brute faculty for their art. When Shakespear was forced to write popular plays to save his theatre from ruin, he did it mutinously, calling the plays As *You* Like It, and Much Ado About Nothing. All the same, he did it so well that to this day these two genial vulgarities are the main Shakespearian stock-in-trade of our theatres. Later on Burbage's power and popularity as an actor enabled Shakespear to free himself from the tyranny of the box office, and to express himself more freely in plays consisting largely of monologue to be spoken by a great actor from whom the public would stand a good deal. The history of Shakespear's tragedies has thus been the history of a long line of famous actors, from Burbage and Betterton to Forbes Robertson; and the man of whom we are told that "when he would have said that Richard died, and cried A horse! A horse! he Burbage cried" was the father of nine generations of Shakespearian playgoers, all speaking of Garrick's Richard, and Kean's Othello, and Irving's Shylock, and Forbes

Robertson's Hamlet without knowing or caring how much these had to do with Shakespear's Richard and Othello and so forth. And the plays which were written without great and predominant parts, such as Troilus and Cressida, All's Well That Ends Well, and Measure for Measure, have dropped on our stage as dead as the second part of Goethe's Faust or Ibsen's Emperor or Galilean.

Here, then, Shakespear had a real grievance; and though it is a sentimental exaggeration to describe him as a broken-hearted man in the face of the passages of reckless jollity and serenely happy poetry in his latest plays, yet the discovery that his most serious work could reach success only when carried on the back of a very fascinating actor who was enormously overcharging his part, and that the serious plays which did not contain parts big enough to hold the overcharge were left on the shelf, amply accounts for the evident fact that Shakespear did not end his life in a glow of enthusiastic satisfaction with mankind and with the theatre, which is all that Mr Harris can allege in support of his broken-heart theory. But even if Shakespear had had no failures, it was not possible for a man of his powers to observe the political and moral conduct of his contemporaries without perceiving that they were incapable of dealing with the problems raised by their own civilization, and that their attempts to carry out the codes of law and to practise the religions offered to them by great prophets and law-givers were and still are so foolish that we now call for The Superman, virtually a new species, to rescue the world from mismanagement. This is the real sorrow of great men; and in the face of it the notion that when a great man speaks bitterly or looks melancholy he must be troubled by a disappointment in love seems to me sentimental trifling.

If I have carried the reader with me thus far, he will find that trivial as this little play of mine is, its sketch of Shakespear is more complete than its levity suggests. Alas! its appeal for a National Theatre as a monument to Shakespear failed to touch the very stupid people who cannot see that a

National Theatre is worth having for the sake of the National Soul. I had unfortunately represented Shakespear as treasuring and using (as I do myself) the jewels of unconsciously musical speech which common people utter and throw away every day; and this was taken as a disparagement of Shakespear's "originality." Why was I born with such contemporaries? Why is Shakespear made ridiculous by such a posterity?

NEW PROLOGUE, 1938
ON THE OCCASION OF THE BROADCAST OF THIS PLAY ON APRIL 22ND, 1938, MR SHAW READ THE FOLLOWING PROLOGUE:—

THIS play which you are going to hear is all about Shakespear and Queen Elizabeth; but it is really only an appeal for the Shakespear Memorial National Theatre which we have been trying to make the English nation establish for thirty years past. Dame Edith Lyttelton invented the play in 1910; I wrote the dialogue; and we had a grand performance at the Haymarket Theatre with Mr Granville-Barker in the part of Shakespear. But I am not going to talk to you about the National Theatre. Shakespear does this so eloquently in the play, and Queen Elizabeth is so up-to-date with her reply to him, that if I anticipate them I shall spoil their speeches for you. So let me tell you how far the play is historical. It takes place in the old royal palace of Whitehall, where Shakespear often acted for the amusement of King James. We have Ben Jonson's word for it. He says it was "on banks of Thames" that Shakespear "did oft delight Eliza and our James."

Now I have my doubts about Eliza. She was a bit of a scholar; but she was a great out-of-doors woman; and when she was not taken up with her queen business she liked riding, hunting, staying in country-houses, dancing, flirting, and ordering the most magnificent dresses ever worn by mortal woman. There is no evidence that she took any interest in the theatre. A stage player was to her at best a nobleman's servant of much less importance to her than his cook, and at worst a rogue and a vagabond. Still, a playwright whose works got printed, had to be able to put his stage directions into good Latin; for in Eliza's time playwrights were not so illiterate as they are today. Chapman and Ben Jonson would have died rather than write "he exits" "she exits" "they exit" instead of the good Latin *exit* and *exeunt*. Even Shakespear, who, according to Ben Jonson, had "little Latin and less Greek," knew better than that, and so Queen Elizabeth, if she had ever heard of Shakespear, would have allowed him a disreputable sort of middle class professional rank. But my own belief is that she never did hear of him, and that the name Will Shakespear meant absolutely nothing to her. When Dame Edith planned this play, we both thought it was high time to introduce them to one another.

And now, as there is nothing about either Will or Eliza in the title of the play, you may be wondering who on earth the dark lady was. Well, nobody knows; but there *was* a dark lady all the same. Shakespear, in addition to his plays, wrote a batch of 154 sonnets, most of them addressed to a certain young man known as Mr W. H., who was one of those very attractive people whom we call world's sweethearts. They are mostly film stars nowadays. They are adored equally by men and women because their attraction is one of beauty and charm, and has nothing to do with sex. Shakespear's sonnets to this young gentleman are far more affectionate and admiring than any that he would have addressed to a woman. And the proof of this is that the sonnets to Mr W. H. are interrupted by some that were addressed to a woman with whom Shakespear had fallen in love. He was furious about it; for Shakespear did not like being captured in this way, especially by a lady for whose character he had no respect, and whose personal appearance was by no means satisfactory; for it happened that she was a black haired beauty; and as Queen Elizabeth had red hair, black hair was very unfashionable. And so the lady is known to us only as Shakespear's dark lady. He was fascinated by her; but he revenged himself by writing savage sonnets, one of which is the most terrible denunciation of that sort of love in existence; and another points out all the lady's defects so mercilessly that she can hardly have been consoled by the concluding lines "And yet, by Heaven, I think my love as rare as any she belied by false compare." It may gratify a woman to be told "I love you." But to be told "*and yet* I love you" after a whole string of insults, is quite another pair of shoes. No wonder the dark lady preferred Mr W. H. and thereby provoked a first class quarrel between him and Shakespear.

In the play I have assumed that the dark lady was a maid of honor at Elizabeth's court. A friend of mine, the late Thomas Tyler, discovered that one of Elizabeth's maids of honor named Mary Fytton got into scrapes at court by her gallantries. Well, I had to get the dark lady into Whitehall Palace somehow; so let us pretend that she was Mary Fytton.

Whitehall Palace was burnt long before I arrived in London 62 years ago; but it still exists in my imagination; and the place where it stood is now right under my bedroom window. It ought to bear Shakespear's name; but they call it Horseguards Avenue because all the tourists and the country folk and the provincial football fans congregate at the end of it to stare at the two mounted guardsmen in their sentry boxes and cuirasses. Not one of them ever turns round to look at the spot where the sweet swan of Avon upon banks of Thames did oft delight Eliza and our James. I wanted the National Theatre to be there; and when the Government announced their intention of pulling down the old houses which are now all Government offices, with their old-fashioned grates which make more smoke every morning when the charladies arrive than the whole city of Edinburgh, I claimed a place for Shakespear's National Theatre there. But the Government had never heard of Shakespear; and my dream of seeing the National Theatre from my window was shattered by an assurance that when the site was filled up with new offices I should not be able to see anything at all. So we have had to buy a magnificent site in Kensington, which Shakespear knew only as a far-off village.

And now I ask you to imagine the old palace still

standing. You may find it hard to imagine it by daylight; but if you imagine it at 11 o'clock at night with everybody gone to bed except the warders on duty it will be as easy as any other dream. As I see it the place is a terrace overlooking the river, with the Queen's apartments on one side, and a gateway on the other. Have you got it? Right; then up goes the curtain.

THE DARK LADY OF THE SONNETS

F*IN de siècle* 15-1600. *Midsummer night on the terrace of the Palace at Whitehall, overlooking the Thames. The Palace clock chimes four quarters and strikes eleven.*

A Beefeater on guard. A Cloaked Man approaches.

THE BEEFEATER. Stand. Who goes there? Give the word.

THE MAN. Marry! I cannot. I have clean forgotten it.

THE BEEFEATER. Then cannot you pass here. What is your business? Who are you? Are you a true man?

THE MAN. Far from it, Master Warder. I am not the same man two days together: sometimes Adam, sometimes Benvolio, and anon the Ghost.

THE BEEFEATER [*recoiling*] A ghost! Angels and ministers of grace defend us!

THE MAN. Well said, Master Warder. With your leave I will set that down in writing; for I have a very poor and unhappy brain for remembrance. [*He takes out his tablets and writes*]. Methinks this is a good scene, with you on your lonely watch, and I approaching like a ghost in the moonlight. Stare not so amazedly at me; but mark what I say. I keep tryst here tonight with a dark lady. She promised to bribe the warder. I gave her the wherewithal: four tickets for the Globe Theatre.

THE BEEFEATER. Plague on her! She gave me two only.

THE MAN [*detaching a tablet*] My friend: present this tablet, and you will be welcomed at any time when the plays of Will Shakespear are in hand. Bring your wife. Bring your friends. Bring the whole garrison. There is ever plenty of room.

THE BEEFEATER. I care not for these new-fangled plays. No man can understand a word of them. They are all talk. Will you not give me a pass for The Spanish Tragedy?

THE MAN. To see The Spanish Tragedy one pays, my friend. Here are the means. [*He gives him a piece of gold*].

THE BEEFEATER [*overwhelmed*] Gold! Oh, sir, you are a better paymaster than your dark lady.

THE MAN. Women are thrifty, my friend.

THE BEEFEATER. Tisso, sir. And you have to consider that the most open handed of us must een cheapen that which we buy every day. This lady has to make a present to a warder nigh every night of her life.

THE MAN [*turning pale*] I'll not believe it.

THE BEEFEATER. Now you, sir, I dare be sworn, do not have an adventure like this twice in the year.

THE MAN. Villian: wouldst tell me that my dark lady hath ever done thus before? that she maketh occasions to meet other men?

THE BEEFEATER. Now the Lord bless your innocence, sir, do you think you are the only pretty man in the world? A merry lady, sir: a warm bit of stuff. Go to: I'll not see her pass a deceit on a gentleman that hath given me the first piece of gold I ever handled.

THE MAN. Master Warder: is it not a strange thing that we, knowing that all women are false, should be amazed to find our own particular drab no better than the rest?

THE BEEFEATER. Not all, sir. Decent bodies, many of them.

THE MAN [*intolerantly*] No. All false. All. If thou deny it, thou liest.

THE BEEFEATER. You judge too much by the Court, sir. There, indeed, you many say of frailty that its name is woman.

THE MAN [*pulling out his tablets again*] Prithee say that again: that about frailty: the strain of music.

THE BEEFEATER. What strain of music, sir? I'm no musician, God knows.

THE MAN. There is music in your soul: many of your degree have it very notably. [*Writing*] "Frailty: thy name is woman!" [*Repeating it affectionately*] "Thy name is woman."

THE BEEFEATER. Well, sir, it is but four words. Are you a snapper-up of such unconsidered trifles?

THE MAN [*eagerly*] Snapper-up of — [*he gasps*] Oh! Immortal phrase! [*He writes it down*]. This man is a greater than I.

THE BEEFEATER. You have my lord Pembroke's trick, sir.

THE MAN. Like enough: he is my near friend. But what

call you his trick?

THE BEEFEATER. Making sonnets by moonlight. And to the same lady too.

THE MAN. No!

THE BEEFEATER. Last night he stood here on your errand, and in your shoes.

THE MAN. Thou, too, Brutus! And I called him friend!

THE BEEFEATER. Tis ever so, sir.

THE MAN. Tis ever so. Twas ever so. [*He turns away, overcome*]. Two Gentlemen of Verona! Judas! Judas!!

THE BEEFEATER. Is he so bad as that, sir?

THE MAN [*recovering his charity and self-possession*] Bad? O no. Human, Master Warder, human. We call one another names when we are offended, as children do. That is all.

THE BEEFEATER. Ay, sir: words, words, words. Mere wind, sir. We fill our bellies with the east wind, sir, as the Scripture hath it. You cannot feed capon so.

THE MAN. A good cadence. By your leave [*He makes a note of it*].

THE BEEFEATER. What manner of thing is a cadence, sir? I have not heard of it.

THE MAN. A thing to rule the world with, friend.

THE BEEFEATER. You speak strangely, sir: no offence. But, an't like you, you are a very civil gentleman, and a poor man feels drawn to you, you being, as twere, willing to share your thought with him.

THE MAN. Tis my trade. But alas! the world for the most part will none of my thoughts.

Lamplight streams from the palace door as it opens from within.

THE BEEFEATER. Here comes your lady, sir. I'll to t'other end of my ward. You may een take your time about your business: I shall not return too suddenly unless my sergeant comes prowling round. Tis a fell sergeant, sir: strict in his arrest. Good een, sir; and good luck! [*He goes*].

THE MAN. "Strict in his arrest"! "Fell sergeant"! [*As if tasting a ripe plum*] O-o-o-h! [*He makes a note of them*].

A Cloaked Lady gropes her way from the palace and wanders

along the terrace, walking in her sleep.

THE LADY [*rubbing her hands as if washing them*] Out, damned spot. You will mar all with these cosmetics. God made you one face; and you make yourself another. Think of your grave, woman, not ever of being beautified. All the perfumes of Arabia will not whiten this Tudor hand.

THE MAN. "All the perfumes of Arabia"! "Beautified"! "Beautified"! a poem in a single word. Can this be my Mary? [*To the Lady*] Why do you speak in a strange voice, and utter poetry for the first time? Are you ailing? You walk like the dead. Mary! Mary!

THE LADY [*echoing him*] Mary! Mary! Who would have thought that woman to have had so much blood in her! Is it my fault that my counsellors put deeds of blood on me? Fie! If you were women you would have more wit than to stain the floor so foully. Hold not up her head so: the hair is false. I tell you yet again, Mary's buried: she cannot come out of her grave. I fear her not: these cats that dare jump into thrones though they be fit only for men's laps must be put away. Whats done cannot be undone. Out, I say. Fie! a queen, and freckled!

THE MAN [*shaking her arm*]Mary, I say: art asleep?

The Lady wakes; starts; and nearly faints. He catches her on his arm.

THE LADY. Where am I? What art thou?

THE MAN. I cry your mercy. I have mistook your person all this while. Methought you were my Mary: my mistress.

THE LADY [*outraged*] Profane fellow: how do you dare?

THE MAN. Be not wroth with me, lady. My mistress is a marvellous proper woman. But she does not speak so well as you. "All the perfumes of Arabia"! That was well said: spoken with good accent and excellent discretion.

THE LADY. Have I been in speech with you here?

THE MAN. Why, yes, fair lady. Have you forgot it?

THE LADY. I have walked in my sleep.

THE MAN. Walk ever in your sleep, fair one; for then your words drop like honey.

THE LADY [*with cold majesty*] Know you to whom you speak, sir, that you dare express yourself so saucily?

THE MAN [*unabashed*] Not I, not care neither. You are some lady of the Court, belike. To me there are but two sorts of women: those with excellent voices, sweet and low, and cackling hens that cannot make me dream. Your voice has all manner of loveliness in it. Grudge me not a short hour of its music.

THE LADY. Sir: you are overbold. Season your admiration for a while with—

THE MAN [*holding up his hand to stop her*] "Season your admiration for a while—"

THE LADY. Fellow: do you dare mimic me to my face?

THE MAN. Tis music. Can you not hear? When a good musician sings a song, do you not sing it and sing it again till you have caught and fixed its perfect melody? "Season your admiration for a while": God! the history of man's heart is in that one word admiration. Admiration! [*Taking up his tablets*] What was it? "Suspend your admiration for a space—"

THE LADY. A very vile jingle of esses. I said "Season your—

THE MAN [*hastily*] Season: ay, season, season, season. Plague on my memory, my wretched memory! I must een write it down. [*He begins to write, but stops, his memory failing him*]. Yet tell me which was the vile jingle? You said very justly: mine own ear caught it even as my false tongue said it.

THE LADY. You said "for a space." I said "for a while."

THE MAN. "For a while" [*he corrects it*]. Good! [*Ardently*] And now be mine neither for a space nor a while, but for ever.

THE LADY. Odds my life! Are you by chance making love to me, knave?

THE MAN. Nay: tis you who have made the love: I but pour it out at your feet. I cannot but love a lass that sets such store by an apt word. Therefore vouchsafe, divine perfection of a woman—no: I have said that before somewhere; and the wordy garment of my love for you must be fire-new—

THE LADY. You talk too much, sir. Let me warn you: I am more accustomed to be listened to than preached at.

THE MAN. The most are like that that do talk well. But though you spake with the tongues of angels, as indeed you do, yet know that I am the king of words—

THE LADY. A king, ha!

THE MAN. No less. We are poor things, we men and women—

THE LADY. Dare you call me woman?

THE MAN. What nobler name can I tender you? How else can I love you? Yet you may well shrink from the name: have I not said we are but poor things? Yet there is a power that can redeem us.

THE LADY. Gramercy for your sermon, sir. I hope I know my duty.

THE MAN. This is no sermon, but the living truth. The power I speak of is the power of immortal poesy. For know that vile as this world is, and worms as we are, you have but to invest all this vileness with a magical garment of words to transfigure us and uplift our souls til earth flowers into a million heavens.

THE LADY. You spoil your heaven with your million. You are extravagant. Observe some measure in your speech.

THE MAN. You speak now as Ben does.

THE LADY. And who, pray, is Ben?

THE MAN. A learned bricklayer who thinks that the sky is at the top of his ladder, and so takes it on him to rebuke me for flying. I tell you there is no word yet coined and no melody yet sung that is extravagant and majestical enough for the glory that lovely words can reveal. It is heresy to deny it: have you not been taught that in the beginning was the Word? that the Word was with God? nay, that the Word was God?

THE LADY. Beware, fellow, how you presume to speak of holy things. The Queen is the head of the Church.

THE MAN. You are the head of my Church when you speak as you did at first. "All the perfumes of Arabia"! Can the Queen speak thus? They say she playeth well upon the virginals. Let her play so to me; and I'll kiss her hands. But until then, you are my Queen; and I'll kiss those lips that have dropt music on my heart. [*He puts his arms about her*].

THE LADY. Unmeasured impudence! On your life, take your hands from me.

The Dark Lady comes stooping along the terrace behind them like a running thrush. When she sees how they are employed, she rises angrily to her full height, and listens jealously.

THE MAN [*unaware of the Dark Lady*] Then cease to make my hands tremble with the streams of life you pour through them. You hold me as the lodestar holds the iron: I cannot but cling to you. We are lost, you and I: nothing can separate us now.

THE DARK LADY. We shall see that, false lying hound, you and your filthy trull. [*With two vigorous cuffs, she knocks the pair asunder, sending the man, who is unlucky enough to receive a righthanded blow, sprawling on the flags*]. Take that, both of you!

THE CLOAKED LADY [*in towering wrath, throwing off her cloak and turning in outraged majesty on her assailant*] High treason!

THE DARK LADY [*recognizing her and falling on her knees in abject terror*] Will: I am lost: I have struck the Queen.

THE MAN [*sitting up as majestically as his ignominious posture allows*] Woman: you have struck WILLIAM SHAKESPEAR!!!!!!

QUEEN ELIZABETH [*stupent*] Marry, come up!!! Struck William Shakespear quotha! And who in the name of all the sluts and jades and light-o'-loves and fly-by-nights that infest this palace of mine, may William Shakespear be?

THE DARK LADY. Madam: he is but a player. Oh, I could have my hand cut off—

QUEEN ELIZABETH. Belike you will, mistress. Have you bethought you that I am like to have your head cut off as well?

THE DARK LADY. Will: save me. Oh, save me.

ELIZABETH. Save you! A likely savior, on my royal word! I had thought this fellow at least an esquire; for I had hoped that even the vilest of my ladies would not have dishonored my Court by wantoning with a baseborn servant.

SHAKESPEAR [*indignantly scrambling to his feet*] Baseborn! I, a Shakespear of Stratford! I, whose mother was an Arden! baseborn! You forget yourself, madam.

ELIZABETH [*furious*] S'blood! do I so? I will teach you—

THE DARK LADY [*rising from her knees and throwing herself between them*] Will: in God's name anger her no further. It is death. Madam: do not listen to him.

SHAKESPEAR. Not were it een to save your life, Mary, not to mention mine own, will I flatter a monarch who forgets what is due to my family. I deny not that my father was brought down to be a poor bankrupt; but twas his gentle blood that was ever too generous for trade. Never did he disown his debts. Tis true he paid them not; but it is an attested truth that he gave bills for them; and twas those bills, in the hands of base hucksters, that were his undoing.

ELIZABETH [*grimly*] The son of your father shall learn his place in the presence of the daughter of Harry the Eighth.

SHAKESPEAR [*swelling with intolerant importance*] Name not that inordinate man in the same breath with Stratford's worthiest alderman. John Shakespear wedded but once: Harry Tudor was married six times. You should blush to utter his name.

THE DARK LADY } *crying out together* { Will: for pity's sake—
ELIZABETH } *crying out together* { Insolent dog—

SHAKESPEAR [*cutting them short*] How know you that King Harry was indeed your father?

ELIZABETH { Zounds! Now by— [*she stops to grind her teeth with rage*].
THE DARK LADY { She will have me whipped through the streets. Oh God! Oh God!

SHAKESPEAR. Learn to know yourself better, madam. I am an honest gentleman of unquestioned parentage, and have already sent in my demand for the coat-of-arms that is lawfully mine. Can you say as much for yourself?

ELIZABETH [*almost beside herself*] Another word; and I begin with mine own hands the work the hangman shall finish.

SHAKESPEAR. You are no true Tudor: this baggage here has as good a right to your royal seat as you. What maintains you on the throne of England? Is it your renownéd wit? your wisdom that sets at nought the craftiest statesmen of the Christian world? No. Tis the mere chance that might have happened to any milkmaid, the caprice of Nature that made you the most wondrous piece of beauty the age hath seen. [*Elizabeth's raised fists, on the point of striking him, fall to her side*]. That is what hath brought all men to your feet, and founded your throne on the impregnable rock of your proud heart, a stony island in a sea of desire. There, madam, is some wholesome blunt honest speaking for you. Now do your worst.

ELIZABETH [*with dignity*] Master Shakespear: it is well for you that I am a merciful prince. I make allowance for your rustic ignorance. But remember that there are things which be true, and yet not seemly to be said (I will not say to a queen; for you will have it that I am none) but to a virgin.

SHAKESPEAR [*bluntly*] It is no fault of mine that you are a virgin, madam, albeit tis my misfortune.

THE DARK LADY [*terrified again*] In mercy, madam, hold no further discourse with him. He hath ever some lewd jest on his tongue. You hear how he useth me! calling me baggage and the like to your Majesty's face.

ELIZABETH. As for you, mistress, I have yet to demand what your business is at this hour in this place, and how you come to be so concerned with a player that you strike blindly at your sovereign in your jealousy of him.

THE DARK LADY. Madam: as I live and hope for salvation—

SHAKESPEAR [*sardonically*] Ha!

THE DARK LADY [*angrily*]—ay, I'm as like to be saved as thou that believest naught save some black magic of words and verses—I say, madam, as I am a living woman I came here to break with him for ever. Oh, madam, if you would know what misery is, listen to this man that is more than man and less at the same time. He will tie you down to anatomize your very soul: he will wring tears of blood from your humiliation; and then he will heal the wound with flatteries that no woman can resist.

SHAKESPEAR. Flatteries! [*Kneeling*] Oh, madam, I put my case at your royal feet. I confess to much. I have a rude tongue: I am unmannerly: I blaspheme against the holiness of anointed royalty; but oh, my royal mistress, AM I a flatterer?

ELIZABETH. I absolve you as to that. You are far too plain a dealer to please me. [*He rises gratefully*].

THE DARK LADY. Madam: he is flattering you even as he speaks.

ELIZABETH [*a terrible flash in her eye*] Ha! Is it so?

SHAKESPEAR. Madam: she is jealous; and, heaven help me! not without reason. Oh, you say you are a merciful prince; but that was cruel of you, that hiding of your royal dignity when you found me here. For how can I ever be content with this black-haired, black-eyed, black-avised devil again now that I have looked upon real beauty and real majesty?

THE DARK LADY [*wounded and desperate*] He hath swore to me ten times over that the day shall come in England when black women, for all their foulness, shall be more thought on than fair ones. [*To Shakespear, scolding at him*] Deny it if thou canst. Oh, he is compact of lies and scorns. I am tired of being tossed up to heaven and dragged down to hell at every whim that takes him. I am ashamed to my very soul that I have abased myself to love one that my father would not have deemed fit to hold my stirrup—one that will talk to all the world about me—that will put my love and my shame into his plays and make me blush for myself there—that will write sonnets about me that no man of gentle strain would put his hand to. I am all disordered: I know not what I am saying to your Majesty: I am of all ladies most deject and wretched—

SHAKESPEAR. Ha! At last sorrow hath struck a note of music out of thee. "Of all ladies most deject and wretched." [*He makes a note of it*].

THE DARK LADY. Madam: I implore you give me leave to go. I am distracted with grief and shame. I—

ELIZABETH. Go [*The Dark Lady tries to kiss her hand*]. No more. Go. [*The Dark Lady goes, convulsed*]. You have been cruel to that poor fond wretch, Master Shakespear.

SHAKESPEAR. I am not cruel, madam; but you know the fable of Jupiter and Semele. I could not help my lightnings scorching her.

ELIZABETH. You have an overweening conceit of yourself, sir, that displeases your Queen.

SHAKESPEAR. Oh, madam, can I go about with the modest cough of a minor poet, belittling my inspiration and making the mightiest wonder of your reign a thing of nought? I have said that "not marble nor the gilded monuments of princes shall outlive" the words with which I make the world glorious or foolish at my will. Besides, I would have you think me great enough to grant me a boon.

ELIZABETH. I hope it is a boon that may be asked of a virgin Queen without offence, sir. I mistrust your forwardness; and I bid you remember that I do not suffer persons of your degree (if I may say so without offence to your father the alderman) to presume too far.

SHAKESPEAR. Oh, madam, I shall not forget myself again; though by my life, could I make you a serving wench, neither a queen nor a virgin should you be for so much longer as a flash of lightning might take to cross the river to the Bankside. But since you are a queen and will none of me, nor of Philip of Spain, nor of any other mortal man, I must een contain myself as best I may, and ask you only for a boon of State.

ELIZABETH. A boon of State already! You are becoming a courtier like the rest of them. You lack advancement.

SHAKESPEAR. "Lack advancement." By your Majesty's leave: a queenly phrase. [*He is about to write it down*].

ELIZABETH [*striking the tablets from his hand*] Your tables begin to anger me, sir. I am not here to write your plays for you.

SHAKESPEAR. You are here to inspire them, madam. For

this, among the rest, were you ordained. But the boon I crave is that you do endow a great playhouse, or, if I may make bold to coin a scholarly name for it, a National Theatre, for the better instruction and gracing of your Majesty's subjects.

ELIZABETH. Why, sir, are there not theatres enow on the Bankside and in Blackfriars?

SHAKESPEAR. Madam: these are the adventures of needy and desperate men that must, to save themselves from perishing of want, give the sillier sort of people what they best like; and what they best like, God knows, is not their own betterment and instruction, as we well see by the example of the churches, which must needs compel men to frequent them, though they be open to all without charge. Only when there is a matter of a murder, or a plot, or a pretty youth in petticoats, or some naughty tale of wantonness, will your subjects pay the great cost of good players and their finery, with a little profit to boot. To prove this I will tell you that I have written two noble and excellent plays setting forth the advancement of women of high nature and fruitful industry even as your Majesty is: the one a skilful physician, the other a sister devoted to good works. I have also stole from a book of idle wanton tales two of the most damnable foolishnesses in the world, in the one of which a woman goeth in man's attire and maketh impudent love to her swain, who pleaseth the groundlings by overthrowing a wrestler; whilst, in the other, one of the same kidney sheweth her wit by saying endless naughtinesses to a gentleman as lewd as herself. I have writ these to save my friends from penury, yet shewing my scorn for such follies and for them that praise them by calling the one As You Like It, meaning that it is not as *I* like it, and the other Much Ado About Nothing, as it truly is. And now these two filthy pieces drive their nobler fellows from the stage, where indeed I cannot have my lady physician presented at all, she being too honest a woman for the taste of the town. Wherefore I humbly beg your Majesty to give order that a theatre be endowed out of the public revenue for the playing of those pieces of mine which no merchant will touch, seeing that his gain is so much greater with the worse than with the better. Thereby you shall also encourage other men to undertake the writing of plays who do now despise it and leave it wholly to those whose counsels will work little good to your realm. For this writing of plays is a great matter, forming as it does the minds and affections of men in such sort that whatsoever they see done in show on the stage, they will presently be doing in earnest in the world, which is but a larger stage. Of late, as you know, the Church taught the people by means of plays; but the people flocked only to such as were full of superstitious miracles and bloody martyrdoms; and so the Church, which also was just then brought into straits by the policy of your royal father, did abandon and discountenance the art of playing; and thus it fell into the hands of poor players and greedy merchants that had their pockets to look to and not the greatness of this your kingdom. Therefore now must your Majesty take up that good work that your Church hath abandoned, and restore the art of playing to its former use and dignity.

ELIZABETH. Master Shakespear: I will speak of this matter to the Lord Treasurer.

SHAKESPEAR. Then am I undone, madam; for there was never yet a Lord Treasurer that could find a penny for anything over and above the necessary expenses of your government, save for a war or a salary for his own nephew.

ELIZABETH. Master Shakespear: you speak sooth; yet cannot I in any wise mend it. I dare not offend my unruly Puritans by making so lewd a place as the playhouse a public charge; and there be a thousand things to be done in this London of mine before your poetry can have its penny from the general purse. I tell thee, Master Will, it will be three hundred years and more before my subjects learn that man cannot live by bread alone, but by every word that cometh from the mouth of those whom God inspires. By that time you and I will be dust beneath the feet of the horses, if indeed there be any horses then, and men be still riding instead of flying. Now it may be that by then your works will be dust also.

SHAKESPEAR. They will stand, madam: fear not for that.

ELIZABETH. It may prove so. But of this I am certain (for I know my countrymen) that until every other country in the Christian world, even to barbarian Muscovy and the hamlets of the boorish Germans, have its playhouse at the public charge, England will never adventure. And she will adventure then only because it is her desire to be ever in the fashion, and to do humbly and dutifully whatso she seeth everybody else doing. In the meantime you must content yourself as best you can by the playing of those two pieces which you give out as the most damnable ever writ, but which your countrymen, I warn you, will swear are the best you have ever done. But this I will say, that if I could speak across the ages to our descendants, I should heartily recommend them to fulfil your wish; for the Scottish minstrel hath well said that he that maketh the songs of a nation is mightier than he that maketh its laws; and the same may well be true of plays and interludes. [*The clock chimes the first quarter. The warder returns on his round*]. And now, sir, we are upon the hour when it better beseems a virgin queen to be abed than to converse alone with the naughtiest of her subjects. Ho there! Who keeps ward on the queen's lodgings tonight?

THE WARDER. I do, an't please your majesty.

ELIZABETH. See that you keep it better in future. You have let pass a most dangerous gallant even to the very door of our royal chamber. Lead him forth; and bring me word when he is safely locked out; for I shall scarce dare disrobe until the palace gates are between us.

SHAKESPEAR [*kissing her hand*] My body goes through the gate into the darkness, madam; but my thoughts follow you.

ELIZABETH. How! to my bed!

SHAKESPEAR. No, madam, to your prayers, in which I beg you to remember my theatre.

ELIZABETH. That is my prayer to posterity. Forget not your own to God; and so goodnight, Master Will.

SHAKESPEAR. Goodnight, great Elizabeth. God save the

Queen!

ELIZABETH. Amen.

Exeunt severally: she to her chamber: he, in custody of the warder, to the gate nearest Blackfriars.

Ayot St Lawrence,
20th June 1910.

BEAUTY'S DUTY

Written in 1913

First Performance not recorded

BEAUTY'S DUTY

In a solicitor's private office. A client is stamping up and down. Both are youngish men.

CLIENT. No, Arthur: a separation. I'll put up with it no longer.

SOLICITOR. Listen to me, Horace.

CLIENT. I wont listen to you. I wont listen to anybody. My wife and I have come to the parting of the ways.

SOLICITOR. But, my dear Horace, you have nothing against her.

CLIENT. Nothing against her. Nothing ag—

SOLICITOR. I tell you, nothing. You dont complain of her temper: you dont complain of her housekeeping: you dont complain of anything except that she makes you jealous.

CLIENT. I'm not jealous. But if I could stoop to such a feeling, I should have cause for it.

SOLICITOR. Look here, Horace. If you have cause for a separation on that ground, you have cause for a divorce.

CLIENT. I am perfectly willing to be divorced—I mean to divorce her. But you keep telling me I cant.

SOLICITOR. Neither can you. You dont allege misconduct: but allege talk. Talk isnt good enough.

CLIENT. You mean it isnt bad enough. That shews how little you know about it.

SOLICITOR (*out of patience*) O well then, have it your own way. What do you complain of?

CLIENT. Whats that to you?

SOLICITOR. To me! Why, man, Ive got to tackle your wife here in this room this very morning, and explain to her that you are determined to separate from her. Do you suppose I am going to do that without giving her a reason?

CLIENT. I dont mind telling you this. No other man would have stood—

SOLICITOR. Thats no good. What did you stand? You neednt have any delicacy about telling me. Thats what I'm for. You pay a solicitor for the privilege of telling him all your most private affairs. Just forget that we're old friends, and remember only that I'm your solicitor. Besides, you will tell me nothing that I havnt been told fifty times by husbands sitting in that chair. Dont suppose youre the only man in the world that doesnt get on with his wife.

CLIENT. I bet you what you like youve never heard of a case like mine before.

SOLICITOR. I shall be able to judge of that when you tell me what your case is.

CLIENT. Well, look here. Did you ever hear of a woman coming to her husband and saying that Nature had gifted her with such an extraordinary talent for making people fall in love with her that she considered it a sin not to exercise it?

SOLICITOR. But she has you to make fall in love with her.

CLIENT. Yes: but she's done that; and she says it's so nice, and has improved me so much that she wants to do it again and improve somebody else. She says it's like a genius for bringing up children. The women who have that, she says, keep schools. They are so good at it that they have to be unfaithful to their own children and run after other people's, she says. And in just the same way, she maintains, a woman with a genius for improving men by love ought to improve them by the dozen. What do you think of that?

SOLICITOR (*rather taken with the idea*) Theres something in that, you know.

CLIENT. What!

SOLICITOR. I mean of course, logically. It's improper; but it makes good sense. I wonder whats the proper answer to it?

CLIENT. Thats what she says.

SOLICITOR. Oh. And what do you say to her?

CLIENT. I tell her that the proper answer to it is that she ought to be ashamed of herself.

SOLICITOR. Does that do any good?

CLIENT. No.

SOLICITOR. Has she ceased to care for you?

CLIENT. No. She says she will practise on me to keep her hand in; but that she is getting tired of me and must have some new interest in life. Now what do you say to your paragon?

SOLICITOR. My paragon! Have I said a word in her defence?

CLIENT. Have you said a word in mine?

SOLICITOR. But dont you see what the consequences will be if you separate? You will lose all control over her; and then there will be a divorce.

CLIENT. I havnt any control over her at present.

The Junior Clerk enters.

JUNIOR CLERK. A lady to see you, sir. (*With emotion*) She is a very beautiful lady. Oh, sir, if she is in any trouble, will you help her. If she is accused, do not believe a word against her. I'll stake my life on her innocence.

SOLICITOR (*almost speechless*) Well—! Really, Mr Guppy! (*Recovering himself a little*) What name?

JUNIOR CLERK. I forgot to ascertain her name, sir.

SOLICITOR. Perhaps you will be so kind as to repair that omission.

JUNIOR CLERK. I hardly dare ask her, sir. It will seem a profanation. But I think—I hope—she will forgive me. (*He goes out.*)

CLIENT. It's my wife. She's been trying it on that young lunatic.